Gender in Organizations

Gender in Organizations

Are Men Allies or Adversaries to Women's Career Advancement?

Edited by

Ronald J. Burke

Emeritus Professor of Organizational Studies, Schulich School of Business, York University, Toronto, Ontario, Canada

Debra A. Major

Professor of Psychology and Associate Chair for Research, Old Dominion University, Norfolk, Virginia, USA

Edward Elgar
Cheltenham, UK • Northampton, MA, USA

Published by
Edward Elgar Publishing Limited
The Lypiatts
15 Lansdown Road
Cheltenham
Glos GL50 2JA
UK

Edward Elgar Publishing, Inc.
William Pratt House
9 Dewey Court
Northampton
Massachusetts 01060
USA

A catalogue record for this book
is available from the British Library

Library of Congress Control Number: 2013946810

This book is available electronically in the ElgarOnline.com
Business Subject Collection, E-ISBN 978 1 78195 570 3

MIX
Paper from
responsible sources
FSC® C013056

ISBN 978 1 78195 569 7

Typeset by Servis Filmsetting Ltd, Stockport, Cheshire
Printed and bound in Great Britain by T.J. International Ltd, Padstow

Contents

v

PART III   GENDERED ORGANIZATIONAL CULTURES AND MALE PRIVILEGE

PART IV   MEN AS ALLIES: SIGNS OF PROGRESS

Figures and tables

FIGURES

TABLES

Contributors

Shahnaz Aziz, East Carolina University, USA

Ronald J. Burke, York University, Canada

Suzette Caleo, New York University, USA

Susan Schick Case, Case Western Reserve University, USA

David L. Collinson, University of Lancaster, UK

Michael Flood, University of Woolongong, Australia

Jeff Hearn, Hanken School of Economics, Finland

Madeline E. Heilman, New York University, USA

Elisabeth Kelan, King's College London, UK

Ronald F. Levant, University of Akron, USA

Michael L. Litano, Old Dominion University, USA

Mark Maier, Chapman University, USA

Debra A. Major, Old Dominion University, USA

Corinne A. Moss-Racusin, Skidmore College, USA

Dante P. Myers, Old Dominion University, USA

Hannah-Hanh D. Nguyen, University of Hawai'i at Mānoa, USA

Mike Otterman, Catalyst, New York, USA

Jeanine Prime, Catalyst, New York, USA

Thomas J. Rankin, University of Akron, USA

Bonnie A. Richley, Case Western Reserve University, USA

Sarah Rutherford, Rutherford Associates, UK

Elizabeth R. Salib, Catalyst, New York, USA

Ruth Simpson, Brunel University, UK

Valerie N. Streets, Old Dominion University, USA

Benjamin Uhrich, University of North Carolina, Charlotte, USA

Acknowledgements

I have been interested in supporting women's career development and advancement for over 25 years. My thinking has been influenced by several female colleagues: Tamara Weir, Carol McKeen, Lyn Davidson, Mary Mattis, Susan Vinnicombe and Debra Nelson. I appreciated and benefitted from their support, encouragement and wisdom.

This is my second undertaking with Debra Major. Her suggestions greatly improved the collection. Preparation of this collection was supported in part by York University. I thank Carla D'Agostino for her assistance in linking with our contributors, Edward Elgar Publishing, and managing my chapters. A special acknowledgement to Fran O'Sullivan at Elgar for her continuing interest and support of our work.

I am proud that my son Jeff supports Leanne without reservation, and Brendan does the same for Sharon.

Ronald J. Burke
Toronto

I feel fortunate that men have been allies in my career progress. As a first generation college student pursuing her undergraduate degree, Steve Kozlowski introduced me to the field of industrial/organizational (I/O) psychology and the possibility of graduate study. As a doctoral student, opportunities that I was afforded by Dan Ilgen and John Hollenbeck positioned me well for career success. As a new assistant professor, I was hired by a male department chair and welcomed into the I/O program by a group of male colleagues. Now 21 years into my career, I benefit from a male dean who supports my career goals. Of course, this is not to take anything away from the numerous women who have also supported my career as leaders, colleagues and mentors. Having spent time in male-dominated work environments, I know first hand that the support of men can be essential to women's career advancement. I also know that not every woman shares my positive experiences. I hope this volume contributes to positive change for all women.

I'm grateful to Ron Burke for inviting me to explore this topic with him and to my son Brian for always supporting my career. My work on this volume was supported by Old Dominion University.

Debra A. Major
Norfolk, VA

Introduction – an overview of the book

Ronald J. Burke and Debra A. Major

Part I of this book sets the stage for this collection. In Chapter 1, Ronald Burke and Debra Major begin by positioning the chapters that follow. Talented women continue to have difficulty advancing their careers world-wide. Organizations are gendered; they were created by men for men. Women feel uncomfortable in them, are disadvantaged, and face barriers to advancement. They argue that examining men, masculinity, and gendered organizations adds to our understanding of why women have made so little progress over the past two decades, how men can be allies in changing organizations, and that there are benefits to men, women, families, and organizations if more men get on board. Male privilege has yielded both benefits and costs. Men with daughters and men seeing the value of using the best talent available to achieve business results, are more likely to 'get it'. Other factors such as having had a working mother, more working partners, women now earning more than their partners, more women in professional schools, more women in the workplace, and more men interested in fatherhood also play a role. Potential benefits to men, women, families, and workplaces are likely to occur when men become allies instead of observers or adversaries.

The second part of the book considers the downside of masculinity. Ronald Levant and Thomas Rankin review in Chapter 2 the literature on the gender role socialization of boys into men. Gender roles are psychologically and socially constructed and they have both advantages and disadvantages. Men thus score higher on variables associated with men and masculinity. Building on the gender role strain paradigm, violating gender roles results in negative consequences, particularly for men, and some of the prescribed masculine gender role traits are dysfunctional (e.g., restricted emotions). Through social interactions associated with rewards and punishments, boys and men behave in line with male norms by exhibiting masculine behaviors. Boys and men come to believe that they should behave in these ways. The gender role strain paradigm, however, is associated with three types of strains: discrepancy, dysfunction, and trauma. The authors go on to show how gender role socialization particularly emphasizes emotional restrictions for boys and men.

In Chapter 3, David Collinson and Jeff Hearn take a critical look at the gendered dynamics of leadership. Men and specific masculinities predominate and are validated in senior management jobs, while women's identities are excluded. All forms of leadership approaches contain dominant masculinity/ies. Men are also in 'control' at home, reinforcing their control at work. Yet men and masculinity/ies are ignored in almost all leadership writing. They begin by reviewing key writings on men and masculinities before examining the gendered dynamics of leadership. They consider gender and leadership, gender and power, role of 'subordinates' in reinforcing gendered power relationships, changing masculinities (e.g., heroic to post-heroic), and why horizontal leadership dynamics are likely to be more effective than hierarchical power leadership dynamics.

Mark Maier considers in Chapter 4 the question of why men should work to change a system that seems to benefit them. He begins by describing 'corporate masculinity'. Corporate masculinity places a high value on the work role, hierarchical relations, competition, control, striving for power, and men's dominance over women. Corporate masculinity limits life possibilities and leadership performance as well as reducing ethical decision-making in organizations and organizational performance. He then contrasts the dominant leadership paradigm based on corporate masculinity with the newly emerging servant-leadership paradigm, a more feminist approach to leadership. Vivid examples of masculine managerial dysfunction are highlighted, including the NASA *Challenger* and *Columbia* disasters, the 2008 financial crisis, and the 2011 *Deepwater Horizon*/BP Macondo Well oil spill. He makes the case for leadership from a feminine perspective, servant-leadership being a useful prototype. He offers two personal reflection exercises that examine corporate masculinity and why it may have limitations.

Jobs are sex-typed but more men and women are moving into gender-atypical ones, with more women moving into men's jobs than men moving into women's jobs. There seemed to be few advantages of men moving into women's jobs, other than the possibility of their more rapid promotion. What are men's experiences in women's jobs? In Chapter 5, Ruth Simpson considers the experiences of men performing 'caring' roles. In these roles, performing 'feminine' services such as emotional labor can collide with views of masculinity. Men are then in a double bind: if they exhibit masculinity their caring skills may fall short; if they exhibit femininity their masculinity is questioned. She examines how male nurses and primary school teachers manage in these gender-atypical roles. She found that male nurses and primary school teachers drew 'emotional labor' into the masculine domain. The chapter draws on literature on men working in non-traditional occupations as well as some findings from Ruth Simpson's own research to 'explore how men in these contexts "re-gender" emotional labor by drawing it into the masculine domain as well as how they draw on and activate sameness (e.g., to higher-status men) and difference (e.g., from women) to manage tensions between gender and their "feminine" occupation'.

In Chapter 6, Ronald Burke examines men, masculinity, well-being, and health. Although men have always been 'privileged', the rise of feminism in the 1960s and 1970s has raised, for many men, questions about their roles. Men are now having more difficulties fulfilling the provider role and masculine behavior is increasingly becoming an issue in both the workplace and in families. Traditional masculinity has become an unreachable goal for most men. Men must avoid anything feminine, be strong, powerful and competitive, show no emotion, and take risks. But there are also real costs to men's masculinity: costs include physical health problems, life dissatisfaction, and feelings of falling short. It is hard to satisfy most definitions of masculinity today. Burke focuses specifically on coronary-prone behavior, work addiction, the effects of long work hours, and career success and person failure as important costs of masculinity. He concludes with suggestions for ways that men and organizations might change to benefit men, women, families, and organizations.

In Chapter 7, Shahnaz Aziz and Benjamin Uhrich examine causes and consequences of workaholism. Men generally spend more hours at work than women; men make heavier work investments than women, reflecting their presence at higher organizational levels. Workaholism is a progressive and compulsive disorder. It has both positive (that is, is rewarded) and negative connotations. Most researchers today see workaholism negatively. They begin by reviewing definitions of workaholism, concluding that workaholism is an addiction. Personal and environmental factors both contribute to the development of workaholism. The former include personality traits (Type A behavior, perfectionism, obsessive-compulsive traits) and the latter include family and organizational factors (coming from a dysfunctional family, and job characteristics such as time pressure). The authors then examine consequences of workaholism such as less life satisfaction, more ill health and burnout, negative effects on others, and negative effects on workplace performance. Both men and women who score higher on workaholism also report more negative consequences. It is difficult to conclude that men are more likely to be workaholic than women since so few studies have examined this. One would expect men to score higher on workaholism, however, since they score higher on some of the antecedents (e.g., Type A behavior) and heavy work investments.

Part III examines the ways that organizations are gendered and the advantages this gives to men. Sarah Rutherford in Chapter 8, using her own observations, consulting experiences, research, and the work of others, shows how most organizational cultures build on the interests of men and marginalize/exclude women. Organizational cultures are gendered and masculinized. Masculinity is taken for granted, thus remains invisible and unable to be confronted. Practices and structures that seem to be gender neutral aren't. She considers the following aspects of gendered organizational cultures: buildings and artifacts, gender awareness, the meaning of work, the separation of the private and the public, management style, time management and the long work hours culture, informal socializing, and sexuality. Cultures are dynamic processes that can be changed. But change is always uncomfortable and certainly means that men will have to give up some of their power. Although progress has been slow and mixed, more men are now supporting women, becoming allies in the quest for more effective organizations and fairness.

Suzette Caleo and Madeline Heilman examine in Chapter 9 the role of gender stereotypes as barriers to women in traditionally male managerial and executive jobs. These jobs 'require' characteristics consistent with stereotypes of men but not women. They first illustrate how stereotypes can be both descriptive (negative expectations of women) and prescriptive (how women should behave). Descriptive stereotypes (men are agentic, women are communal) have negative consequences for women working in male-typed contexts. These stereotyped expectations play a stronger role in ambiguous contexts, with much ambiguity existing in many organizational situations. Prescriptive stereotypes, focusing on ways women should behave, result in women being 'punished' for exhibiting stereotypically male behaviors. Women are 'punished' for pursuing male-typed careers, self-promotion, negotiating on their own behalf, communicating and influencing like men, being assertive, and merely being successful in male-typed jobs. These stereotypes, and negative outcomes (punishments) cause women to limit the expression of these behaviors. The authors conclude with suggestions for limiting these negative effects.

In Chapter 10, Elisabeth Kelan believes that business schools are a key place to alter the male domination of business. She advocates a focus on the practices in business schools that support gender inequalities. Masculinity pervades business schools; not surprisingly, business schools reflect the world of business. She addresses the question of how we can begin speaking about masculine practices in business schools. She reviews writing on women and men in business schools and how discussion of gender is silenced. She then offers interview data from business students that highlight masculinity practices (e.g., individualism, competition). She concludes with suggestions on how doing and undoing masculinity can be carried out.

In Chapter 11, Corinne Moss-Racusin first outlines how hyper-masculinity stereotypes spell out men's acceptable behavior. She notes that pressures to conform to masculine stereotypes can harm organizations and suggests that removing penalties for men who perform counter to expectations can have positive results. She begins by examining the effects of men's conforming to the hyper-masculine stereotypes on their health, relationships, aggressive behavior, and egalitarianism. Gender stereotypes spell out how people should behave as well as how they should not behave. She then reviews research findings on negative reactions to both women and men who violate gender stereotypes. Men should not behave in 'feminine' ways, should be 'winners', show no weaknesses, and fit in with male peers by conforming to masculine stereotypes. Yet she convincingly shows that fulfilling masculine stereotypes has costs such as engaging in risky health behaviors. Men face a 'catch-22' backlash for violating harmful masculine stereotypes, for supporting and mentoring women, and for expressing gender-egalitarian beliefs.

Valerie Streets and Hannah-Hanh Nguyen in Chapter 12 consider impacts of 'stereotype threat' in women's experiences and performance in work and career. Stereotype threat occurs when a common negative stereotype exists against a group, the stereotype indicating behaviors and attitudes characteristic of the group. For women, stereotype threat represents an obstacle to entering the workforce, choosing an occupation or career, and advancing in their career. Stereotype threat effects on women are influenced by their awareness of the stereotypes, their identification with the stereotype, and their levels of empowerment. They examine the effects of stereotype threat when a challenging task is at odds with female gender stereotypes, when women are aware of their low status in a stereotypical career, and when the environment reinforces female gender stereotypes. They offer intervention tactics to address stereotype threat in the chapter.

In Chapter 13, Susan Schick Case and Bonnie Richley examine perceptions of women post-doctoral bench scientists working within the science environments of 14 major US research institutions, and how both individual and institutional experiences impact their desired futures. Findings reveal three distinct career paths (research, teaching, and industry). Of significance is the shared ambition to contribute to the field of science based on traditional notions of success regardless of career choice, with none giving up being a scientist in some form. Findings provide insight into individual career decision processes, involving how gender is experienced in male-centric cultures, how experiences of barriers are reframed, and how hurdles and barriers impact their path as contributing scientists and human beings. These women emphasized a strong desire to develop as scientists, to collaborate with others, a relational aspect missing in their environments, and to have a life as well as a career. Findings suggest an environment laden with gender and family biases, contributing to difficulties in being a woman with multi-arenas of responsibility as a scientist. Bias experienced included subtle discrimination, challenges working in a male-dominated culture, and a negative impact of the environment on their lives. A strong correlation between experiences of gender and family biases, including struggles and barriers to women with families or for those hoping to have children, suggests additional burdens placed on women's career paths and their evolving identity. The post-doctoral stage is a unique transition zone marked by a period of psychological squeezing and internal sense-making, suggesting an environment laden with institutional gender bias and forced family struggles, juxtaposed by feelings of powerlessness and vulnerability. It involves a process of adaption and selection as they experience their environment, make sense of their experience, and decide how best to achieve success and fulfillment. The relational identities of many of the participants found them making contributions to science by expanding norms of achievement, including guiding and developing future generations of scientists.

In Chapter 14, Ronald Burke considers backlash against women's progress at three levels: individual, organizational, and societal. Women get 'attacked' by some men for championing women's issues. Women who violate stereotypes and stereotyped expectations get punished in subtle and not so subtle ways. Why should talented women in the workplace face double binds and a need to monitor their agency? In addition, gendered organizations make it more difficult for women to get line jobs necessary for advancement, international experience required for visibility and promotion, and access to high-level male sponsors, while being more likely offered jobs classified as 'glass cliffs'. Finally men's groups have emerged in some countries in response to women's advancement linked to the rise in feminism in the 1960s and 1970s. Some of these men's groups were a reaction to women's progress and increasing challenges that men were facing and still are facing. Some men believed that women were increasingly being advantaged while men were increasingly being disadvantaged (e.g., affirmative action, women being given child custody following divorce). They longed for a return to the 'good old days'. Interest in such groups has waned in the past decade. Another men's movement has emerged, increasing in strength but still small, and advocating for equality of women, the reduction of violence against women, a stronger commitment to engaged fatherhood, and a better quality of life for men. Finally, there are some societies in which men hate women. Men who shoot a young girl in the head because she wanted to go to school reflect this.

Part IV outlines the benefits to men, women, families, and workplaces when men become allies and offers examples of where this is taking place. In Chapter 15, Michael Litano, Dante Myers, and Debra Major focus on ways men and women can be allies in achieving work–family balance. This becomes increasingly important as more dual-earner couples become the norm. For men and women to become allies here their ways of managing work–family conflict must be aligned. They argue that men and women need to use coping strategies that foster each other's well-being. They begin by examining work–family conflict and work–family facilitation, the building blocks of work–family balance. They then examine ways that men and women can be allies or adversaries depending on crossover effects from work-to-family, family-to-work enrichment and from partners to each other. Conflict results from negative crossover while facilitation follows from positive crossover. They suggest that men and women can become allies here by engaging in work–family coping strategies that support positive crossover. They describe various effective ways of coping that support work–family facilitation and balance.

In Chapter 16, Jeanine Prime, Mike Otterman, and Elizabeth Salib make the case that organizations in the twenty-first century need to use the full pool of available talent. Since men are typically in positions of power and influence they need to spearhead efforts to attract, retain, and advance qualified women. But men are too frequently overlooked. They begin by reviewing challenges women face in business organizations. They then suggest ways of engaging men in creating more equal workplaces: tackling outdated notions about leadership, addressing male barriers to more inclusive leadership (e.g., punishment for power sharing), a lack of awareness of gender issues, apathy, and fear. They use a case study of Rockwell Automation to show how one organization successfully overcame male barriers and engaged men in efforts to address gender gaps, concluding with 'lessons learned'.

In Chapter 17, Michael Flood examines the importance of involving men in efforts to end violence against women. Men's violence against women reflects men's power over women and widespread gender inequalities. Men's violence against women takes several forms. In addition, most women who experience violence in their family and relationships are working, as are most men who commit violence against women. The author documents the widespread occurrence of violence against women. Three broad clusters of factors 'cause' men's violence against women: gender roles and relations, social norms and practices, and limited resources and support. Violence in the workplace limits productivity and fosters inequalities. Workplaces can also be critical sites for prevention of workplace violence. He lists benefits to organizations in preventing or reducing men's violence against women, and offers actions to respond to and prevent violence in terms of primary, secondary, and tertiary prevention. He also describes some organizational efforts to involve men in workplace-based violence prevention.

PART I

Men supporting women – setting the stage

1. Advancing women's careers: why men matter

Ronald J. Burke and Debra A. Major[*]

INTRODUCTION

We have been interested in supporting the advancement of qualified women into executive and CEO roles for some time. Unfortunately, progress has been both slow and uneven. We have come to realize that if more men became allies of these women instead of adversaries, significant benefits would fall to women, men, families, organizations, and societies at large.

This chapter summarizes our thinking and sets the stage for the chapters that follow. Here is a summary of what we have come to believe. Organizations are gendered and masculinized. This gives men an unacknowledged and unearned advantage. As a result, women face additional challenges in the workplace. Masculinity has potential dysfunctional consequences for men and their health, for families, for organizations and for society. Both the workforce and organizations are changing in ways that are beginning to challenge the gendered nature of organizations. As more men begin, and continue, to support capable, ambitious, and bright women in the workplace, it will enhance both women's and men's well-being, family enrichment, and organizational performance. For example, men with daughters and working partners are more likely to 'get it'.

Talented women continue to have difficulty advancing their careers in organizations worldwide. Organizations and their cultures were created by men for men and reflect the wider patriarchal society (Acker, 1990; Connell, 2012). As a consequence, women feel uncomfortable in them, are disadvantaged, and face barriers to advancement. An examination of men, masculinity, and gendered organizational cultures seems necessary to get a better understanding of why women have made such slow progress, ways in which men can become potential allies in organizational changes, and benefits to men, women, families, and organizations from getting men on board. While men have benefited from gendered cultures they have also endured some costs as well.

11

Consider the following observations relating to either women or men:

- While women have made progress in entering professional and managerial positions, their career progress has been slow and uneven (Barreto et al., 2009).
- There are now more women than men graduating from universities with undergraduate degrees, almost equal numbers of women and men graduating with advanced degrees in law and medicine, and at least one-third of MBA graduates are women – men are falling behind (Pollack, 1998; Sax, 2007; Kimmel, 2008; Hymowitz, 2011; Rosin, 2012).
- There is an increasing percentage of women now in the workforce and a decreasing percentage of men (Collins, 2009).
- There is an increasing number and percentage of female employees (Collins, 2009).
- There will be a labor shortage in all developed countries over the next two decades as the population ages and the low birth rate in these countries fails to provide enough new workforce entrants. This will add to the current war for talent (Michaels et al., 2001; Hewlett and Rashid, 2012). Organizations will no longer be able to afford to ignore half the available population.
- Eisler et al. (1995), using data from 89 nations, compared information on the status of women, with several indicators of quality of life. Women's status predicted quality of life better than GDP. Eisler (2013) cites other writing showing a relationship between the status of women and economic development and economic success.
- More women at work gives them more income and greater purchasing power. Women professionals and managers may be better able to understand the needs of these newly empowered women consumers (Wittenberg-Cox and Maitland, 2008).
- There is some evidence that companies having more women in top management positions are more financially successful. Nothing that an organization does is delivered without its employees being on board. Wilson et al. (2013) found that recently incorporated companies with female directors had a 27 percent lower risk of failing (becoming insolvent) than similar firms with all male boards. Others (e.g., Kalleberg and Leicht, 1991; Barber and Odean, 2001; Adams and Ferreira, 2009; Brammer et al., 2009; Huse et al., 2009) reported similar benefits from having more women on boards.
- There is some evidence that companies with more women in senior-level positions make less risky decisions, which protects them in times of economic challenges.

- There is some evidence that women are less greedy than men, less likely to engage in theft, fraud and corruption, are less narcissistic and show less hubris, again protecting the organization from failure and a poor reputation. Kennedy and Kray (2013) have found that women are less likely than men to sacrifice their ethical values for money and social status.
- Women continue to face discrimination in pay, promotion, and types of assignments.
- In some countries young girls are denied schooling, women are not allowed to drive, women are not allowed to leave their countries without their husband's permission, women are forced to marry men that their families chose for them, and women get murdered for dating/marrying someone that their family did not agree to (Kristoff and WuDunn, 2009).
- A few women have reached the top of their organizations and in elected offices. Consider the President of Brazil (Dilma Rousseff), the former CEO of Yahoo (Carol Bartz), Ellen Kullman at DuPont, Marissa Mayer at Yahoo, and Marin Alsop, the first female conductor at the BBC 'Last Night of the Proms' concert held in Royal Albert Hall in London in September 2013. The fact that these 'firsts' get our attention reflects the magnitude of the problem. There is still considerable work to be done to achieve full 'equal opportunity'.

The reality for women is the presence of a 'representation gap' – when women reach the top levels of organizations (CEOs) they are not at the largest, most prestigious firms (Fortune 500) but more likely to be at the top of lower-status small firms, and a pay gap – women in the same or similar jobs get paid less than men. This reflects a significant lifetime earnings loss. However, this gap is slowly closing (Blau and Kahn, 2006).

Organizations have been interested in supporting the advancement of women for some time, with some undertaking initiatives with this goal in mind. Some have been successful, but on the whole, relatively little progress has been made, as reflected in the above observations and in country analyses (Davidson and Burke, 2011). An interesting question then becomes, why?

Several barriers to women's advancement have been identified (Morrison, 1992; Catalyst, 1998; Burke and Mattis, 2005; Rutherford, 2011). These include negative assumptions about women, their abilities and their commitment to careers; perceptions that women don't fit into the corporate culture; reluctance to give women key line positions important for advancement; women's home and family responsibilities; lack of mentoring and exclusion of women from the 'old boys' network';

and a work environment that values working long hours in an aggressive and competitive manner, among others. Interestingly, women in the labor union movement face the same barriers to their advancement as women in the private sector (Kirton and Healy, 2012).

Two themes run through these barriers. First, organizational cultures are problematic for women and discouraging of their career aspirations. Women are disadvantaged in male-created and male-dominated organizational cultures, and women have a hard time fitting into these cultures (Rutherford, 2001). Second, men seem to be part of the problem and not part of the solution (Cockburn, 1991). Organizations were created and designed by men for men (Marshall, 1984; Wacjman, 1998; Nye, 2012). Women are merely travelers in this male world. The culture of organizations is a reflection of patriarchy that exists in the wider society (Kimmel, 2009); organizations are therefore patriarchal as well. Culture serves to include some and exclude others (Rogers, 1988; McDowell, 1997; Rutherford, 2001, 2002, 2011). Organizational cultures are male dominated and masculine; they are better suited for men than for women (Wacjman, 1998). Women are excluded and marginalized in subtle and obvious ways. Women are less comfortable in these cultures and have more difficulties advancing careers in them. Women have more responsibility for 'second shift' work, to have career gaps for bearing and raising children, are more likely to work part-time at some point in their careers, have less time for socializing and informal networking after work, preferring not to go to bars, strip clubs and sports events, are more likely to be sexually harassed, and are perceived to be unable to relocate or to undertake international assignments, among other things.

Britton (1999) writes that rather than seeing organizations as gendered it is more accurate to view them as 'masculinized'. She observes that in masculinized organizations, skills identified with men are rewarded more than skills associated with women. Men and male organizations are viewed as ideal types. These masculinized (gendered) benefits to men are maintained through personal and impersonal ways such as policies, ideology, worker interactions, organizational structures, and the creation and maintenance of male and female identities.

Paris and Decker (2012) compared sex role stereotypes based on Schein's (1973) 'think manager, think male' framework among business students and non-business students in university. They hypothesized that business students would be less prone to the 'manager as male' stereotype given the recent attention to workforce diversity by business and business schools. They found, however, that business students more strongly supported the 'manager as male' stereotype than non-business students in university.

Eisaid and Eisaid (2012) also used Schein's 'think manager, think male' framework in comparing sex role stereotypes of the manager's job among students in Egypt and the USA. They found considerably more support in the 'manager as male' stereotype in Egypt (by both males and females) than in the USA, and that US males more strongly endorsed the 'manager as male' stereotype than US females.

These two studies suggest that 'think manager, think male' is still alive and well and likely exists worldwide. Interestingly, and relevant to this collection, business students more strongly endorsed this stereotype than non-business university students. The latter finding raises questions about the value of business education in addressing this stereotype and changing men from adversaries into allies in supporting women's career advancement (see Simpson, 2006; Kelan and Jones, 2010).

Tienari et al. (2013) conducted in-depth interviews with executive search consultants in three countries (Austria, Finland, and Sweden) and found that both male and female consultants, when it came to paring down their lists of potential applicants to one, resorted to 'think manager, think male' perspectives, resulting in 'then there was none' in the case of women. Women rarely made the shortlist and clients preferred the 'safe' choices (read men).

WOMEN AND MEN DISAGREE ON BARRIERS FACING WOMEN

Managerial and professional women and men do not agree on the barriers facing women in their careers. Women see the major barriers as the organizational culture and the attitudes and behaviors of their male colleagues; men see the barriers as not enough experience or time in the workplace, and family responsibilities (Ragins et al., 1998).

Organizational efforts to support the career development and advancement often fail because men deny that there is a problem, attacking the credibility of the change message and attacking the carriers of this message; refuse to accept responsibility for the change issue; refuse to implement change that has been agreed to; and act to dismantle change that has been implemented (Agocs, 1997).

Sandberg (2013) wants to diminish the 'internal barriers' that cause women to stall in their careers or not consider senior management positions. Only 21 of the Fortune 500 CEOs are women. She refers to this as a 'leadership ambition gap'. She writes that more women should work harder, not apologize for their ambitions, and stop blaming organizations for lack of advancement. Sandberg also noted the importance of a supportive husband. Easy for her to advocate as the Chief Operating Officer of Facebook with all her resources, but Sandberg doesn't address how women can combine both work involvement required in successful career advancement and being a parent. As Blair-Loy (2005) has shown, even successful women can be torn between their career commitments and their family commitments.

Sandberg's call for women to 'lean in' seems to blame the victims, blaming women for not trying 'hard enough' or not wanting the top jobs. Most companies are not meritocracies that reward individual effort and accomplishments. Women will benefit when more men (and most companies are run by men) reach out and support their talented, hard-working and ambitious women. No one ever succeeds on their own; everyone has been helped by someone else. Companies with more women in senior management are run by men who 'get it'.

Marissa Mayer was appointed CEO of Yahoo while pregnant, causing some writers to laud Yahoo for such an appointment. Mayer took two weeks off for childbirth and had a child care nursery built next to her office for her baby so she could put in long hours. Yahoo announced to all their workforce (26 February 2013) a stop to all their work-at-home arrangements; employees must now work in their offices or quit. Yahoo made this change to foster a more collaborative and innovative culture. What about creating on-site child care facilities for all Yahoo employees? This change at Yahoo created a heated conversation on how this change would hurt both women and men and whether it would make Yahoo more productive (Dowd, 2013). Some argued that this change would set back the causes of both working women and men.

NOTE TO KRISTOFF AND WUDUNN – WOMEN DON'T HOLD UP HALF THE SKY – YET

The results of the Catalyst 2012 survey of women on Financial Post 500 firms showed the following (Catalyst, 2013):

- In 2012, women held 18.1 percent of senior officer positions, a small increase over 17.7 percent in 2010.
- 30.3 percent of companies had no women senior officers in 2010 and this decreased to 29.8 percent in 2012.
- Companies with 40 percent or more women senior officers increased from 7.3 percent in 2010 to 8.7 percent in 2012.
- Companies with 25 percent women in senior officer jobs increased from 30.8 percent in 2010 to 31.4 percent in 2012.

Canadian figures (Tulk, 2013) showed the following:

- Women held 35 percent of management positions in 1993 and 36 percent in 2013.
- The number of women holding senior management positions in 1993 was 24 percent and this increased to 27 percent in 2013.

MALE PRIVILEGE

Although most men are unlikely to admit that they are over-privileged, some will admit that women are disadvantaged (McIntosh, 1989). This small group of men may work to lessen women's disadvantages providing this will not lessen their own advantages, but are unlikely to discuss the advantages they get from women's disadvantages (Crowley, 1993). Thus, male privilege is protected from being acknowledged, reduced or ended. Men have to give up the belief in meritocracy if they admit male privilege (Maier, 1994).

McIntosh (1989) distinguishes between earned entitlements and unearned entitlements, with male privilege being an example of the latter. Male privilege is 'like an invisible weightless knapsack of special provisions, assurances, tools, maps, guides, cookbooks, passports, visas, clothes, compass, emergency gear and blank checks' (ibid., p. 10). McIntosh in fact sees the term 'privilege' as too favorable since everyone would like to achieve a privileged state. Male privilege includes dominance, and the right to control. Here are some examples of male privilege: 'I will not have to work harder to prove myself as I am a man'; 'When I look at the people in senior management I am likely to see other men'; 'I can talk to other men without being accused of gossiping'; 'As a male I will not generally be worried about sexual harassment'; 'I can benefit from a system that assigns domestic and family responsibilities to women'.

When male privilege is identified, described, and acknowledged, men then become accountable for it (Maier, 1994). Most men then offer rationalizations that maintain 'business as usual'. These include: 'Yes, male privilege exists but it hasn't helped me'. 'Male privilege by itself can't explain the important roles that men play in the world'. 'Male privilege exists, but the system that created and sustains it is thousands of years old and cannot be changed'; 'I will make efforts to help women but I won't work to lessen men's privilege'.

DIMENSIONS OF CORPORATE MASCULINITY

> They [ambitious men] may not cease, but as a dog in a wheel, a bird in a cage,
> or a squirrel in a chain, so Budaeus compares them; they climb and climb still,
> with much labour, but never make an end, never at the top.
>
> (Robert Burton, *Anatomy of Melancholy*, 1621)

Organizations are characterized by rationality, instrumentality, analysis, emotional restraint, competitiveness, and self-sufficiency. Maier (1991) described men's behavior in organizations using the term 'corporate masculinity' and also included terms such as objectivity, competitiveness, adversarial, logic, and task oriented. Collinson and Hearn (1994) identified five practices of masculinity that were widespread and dominant in organizations: authoritarianism, paternalism, entrepreneurialism, informalism, and careerism:

- *authoritarianism* – intolerance of dissent, rejection of dialogue, use of coercive power and dictatorial control and unquestioned obedience;
- *paternalism* – an authoritative, benevolent, and wise father figure, use of power based on protected male authority;
- *entrepreneurialism* – competitive, hard working, totally dedicated to the task, tight deadlines;
- *informalism* – the 'old boys' network', socializing;
- *careerism* – upward mobility, career success, separation of work and family.

Maier (1991) sees corporate masculinity as having several kinds of dysfunctions. These include limiting men's managerial effectiveness since the best managers combine masculine and feminine characteristics; men need to get all their satisfaction from their work, resulting in long work hours and complete dedication to their jobs; men's self-esteem gets tied closely to the size of their incomes, organizational level, and external achievements.

Masculinity has its potential costs. Some writers have shown that rigidly adhering to masculinity norms has negative effects on the well-being of men (Goldberg, 1976; Pollack, 1998; Courtenay, 2001). Pleck (1995) outlines his gender role strain model for masculinity. Three broad themes underlie the ten propositions he lays out. First, large numbers of men experience failure in fulfilling male role expectations – they fall short. Second, even if men fulfill these expectations, the process of fulfilling these expectations and the outcomes themselves can be traumatic. Third, successfully fulfilling these work role expectations has undesirable side-effects for men and for others, such as low family involvement.

Ely and Meyerson (2008) were able to show a decrease in accidents on oil rigs by highlighting the dysfunctions of masculinity and encouraging oil rig employees to undertake less masculine behaviors such as not asking for help and not admitting when they didn't know something. Borman and Walker (2010) collected data from 118 Australian male university students, exploring the link between their conformity to masculinity norms and their perceived barriers to health care. Males indicating greater conformity to masculinity norms reported more barriers to health care.

THE LANGUAGE OF LEADERSHIP

Since organizations were designed by and for men, the language of leadership is also masculine. Men are more likely than women to talk in terms of 'I' than 'we'. Women use a more inclusive vocabulary. Men and women have different styles of communication (Annis and Gray, 2013), though one is not 'better' than the other. These differences should be acknowledged and celebrated as women and men learn to work together. In addition to some observed average communication differences between women and men, there is considerable overlap as well (Carothers and Reis, 2013), but women still tend to be overlooked when filling leadership roles. Men want to be promoted, show drive, and demonstrate this up the organization. Women who then sound like men are more likely to be promoted (Tannen, 1990). Yet, as Mehrabian (1981) documented, in terms of communication impact, words, the verbal part, accounted for only 7 percent of impact, 28 percent accounted for by tone, and 55 percent of impact accounted for by non-verbal behavior. Women are disadvantaged here as well. As young girls, women are socialized to not project authority by taking up physical space, to fit in, not seek attention, be quiet, and to consider whether others will like them. All these non-verbal behaviors reduce women's power.

MASCULINIZED ORGANIZATIONS AND THE BEHAVIOR OF WOMEN

As mentioned above, Britton (1999) suggested that working in masculinized workplaces subtly shapes the identities of women and men. These effects are sometimes harmful to women and to changing organizational cultures (Lutgen-Sandvik et al., 2011). For example, masculinized organizations encourage women to bully other women. Women bully other women at twice the rate they bully men, in part because women are more likely to work with other women. In addition, women who fail to conform to traditional gender roles trigger bullying. Women bully other women since they are an oppressed group. Women bully other women to get validation from men. Women bully other women to feel competent. Women that perform consistent with masculine traits tend to be respected by men. Women are expected to repress/not express negative feelings, but when these negative emotions build up they can be released in the form of women bullying other women. Women come to think they have to bully to compete for scarce resources such as career advancement. Thus, they come to reproduce behaviors common in masculinized workplaces. Ironically, women bullies are often seen as incompetent. When women bully women it takes attention away from the organizational characteristics that foster female aggression and oppression.

Women also sell themselves short when working with men in team contexts. Haynes and Heilman (2013) in a series of laboratory experiments found that women working in teams with men viewed their contributions to the team effort less favorably than they evaluated men's contributions, particularly on male tasks such as managing at an investment company. This did not happen when women were working only with other women on teams. The fact that women devalued their contributions when working with men likely limits their view of their own efficacy, competence, and power, and reduces their completion of challenging assignments and obtaining promotions.

Queen Bees and Women Undermining Other Women

A Queen Bee is a senior woman in a masculine organizational culture who has achieved career success by dissociating herself from her gender while contributing to the stereotyping of other women at the same time. To succeed, Queen Bees learn how to act like the men around them (Mavin, 2006a, 2006b, 2008). Queen Bees represent 'bad behavior' to other women in an organization. Queen Bees do not conform to either men's or women's stereotypes. The incongruity between managerial and gender roles can create tension between women, with some women being more critical than men of other women. Women can exhibit backlash against other women who have obtained or are seeking power and advancement in their workplaces.

Do Women Really Dislike Working with and for Other Women? Or Do We Just Believe They Do?

There has been some literature suggesting that women have more difficulty with, and dislike working with and for, other women (e.g., Tannenbaum,

2002; Holiday and Rosenberg, 2009). This is at odds with the belief women are supportive, nurturing, and caring. Unfortunately, no research has yet addressed this question directly. Sheppard and Aquino (2013) undertook an experiment in which 152 adult women and men read one of three different scenarios of conflict between two women, two men, and a woman and a man. They found that female–female conflict was perceived to have higher personal implications and more difficulty in relationship repair. In addition, lower levels of job satisfaction, less affective commitment, and higher turnover intentions were attributed to the woman–woman conflict scenario by these outside observers. These findings likely relate to beliefs that women have difficulty working with or for other women and influence women's promotion prospects.

COSTS TO WOMEN FOR BEING 'GOOD SOLDIERS'

Women bishops: Are we nearly there yet?

(Bumper sticker)

Employees engaging in organizational citizenship behaviors make a contribution to the success of their organizations. Organizational citizenship behavior (OCB) is voluntary, typically not recognized by the formal reward system, yet contributes to effective organizational functioning. OCBs have been divided into two types: communal and agentic. Sex-typed role expectations suggest that women engage in more communal OCB while men engage in more agentic OCB. Communal OCBs in an academic setting, for example, involve talking with colleagues, serving on committees, attending unit meetings, and attending major student events. Agentic OCBs included serving on a journal's editorial board, organizing meetings, and being an officer in a professional association. Engaging in OCBs is both time consuming and stressful, and although engaging in OCBs can enhance one's career it can take away from job performance.

In a study of faculty members at a major research university, Bergeron (2012) found (1) women engaged in more communal OCB but not more agentic OCB than men, (2) women engaged in more communal than agentic OCB, and (3) women received fewer benefits from their OCB investments than men. Eriksson and Lagerstrom (2012), using data from internet-based CVs of job hunters, found that women were less likely to job search in areas far away (in the same large metropolitan area, or further afield) from where they currently live. This resulted in fewer firm contacts, which they attribute to women's more restrictive search area.

MALE BACKLASH

Some men act in ways that reflect a 'backlash' against women (Goode, 1982; Astrachan, 1986; Faludi, 1991). There is evidence that masculine management can be dysfunctional as in the *Challenger* space disaster (Maier, 1997); that sexual harassment can be rampant in some organizations (Pope, 1993); that since men score higher on risk taking, greed, and materialism than women, men's behavior contributed to the recent financial meltdown; traditional masculinity (stigmatizing the feminine, seeking status and success, expressing anger and irritation, being tough, self-reliant, and over-confident, investing heavily in work) is associated with attitudes and behaviors that may diminish their psychological and physical health and well-being (Burke, 2002).

And the times are changing. Two stories appeared in the Toronto media four days apart in late November 2012. First, the Royal Canadian Mounted Police (RCMP), Canada's national police force, has faced a number of sexual harassment and discrimination claims from women over the past few years. The Federal Government minister responsible for the RCMP, Vic Toews, sent a letter to the head of the RCMP, which became public, asking him to produce a plan for increasing women's membership and advancement within the force by the end of 2012 (MacCharles, 2012). The plan would include targets but not quotas. This was followed by a story on women on corporate boards of directors, showing little progress in increasing their numbers, with more organizations now advocating the setting of targets and more individuals supporting the use of quotas (McFarland, 2012). It is likely that some male readers of these stories became a bit 'nervous' and others likely considered 'backlash thoughts' (Faludi, 1999).

Backlash Against Women's Progress

Burke (2014) considers three types of backlash against women's progress: backlash in the workplace, backlash in the wider society, and the question of why men in some countries hate women.

Backlash against agentic women in the workplace

Stereotypes dictate how women and men should behave. Most people believe in stereotypes even in the face of contrary evidence. A gender stereotype is a generalized belief about the qualities of women and men. Women are communal, nurturing, modest, focused on others; men are agentic, dominant, self-promoting, career oriented. Women's stereotypes illustrate a mismatch with desirable work behaviors and work roles, resulting in negative evaluations and discrimination (Heilman and Eagly, 2008). Even women's positive stereotyped attributes (such as warmth) are seen as inconsistent with the manager's job (see Schein's, 1973, 'think manager, think male' evidence). Characteristics associated with female gender role stereotypes do not fit the masculine organizational culture. Women are seen as less ambitious, less competent, and less competitive – less agentic – than men, and are less likely to be considered for hiring or promotion. Women who behave in agentic ways are also seen negatively for violating gender role prescriptions – an example of backlash (Phelan et al., 2008).

Heilman and Wallen (2010), in an experimental laboratory study, found that both women and men were penalized for success in areas that violated gender expectations, but the nature of the penalties differed. Men successful in female gender-typed jobs were seen as ineffectual and given less respect than women successful in the same job or men successful in gender-consistent jobs. Women, on the other hand, who were successful in male gender-typed jobs were more disliked and had their interpersonal skills criticized more than men in these same jobs. In addition, both women and men who violated gender norms were rated less preferable as managers. Thus, both women and men were punished for their successes when they violated gender expectations. Men who violate masculine gender role expectations (e.g., being communal) were also rated as less task competent and were less likely to be hired (Rudman, 1998; Rudman and Glick, 1999, 2001). Men who perform well in female domains (e.g., nursing, library science) are likely to be undermined by their male peers.

Backlash in the wider society

Men's movements in the wider society   Faludi (1991), in her ground-breaking book on backlash, noted that backlash against women's progress resulted in the development of a number of men's groups, which have been clustered under three labels: masculinist, anti-feminist, and pro-feminist:

- *Masculinist movement*. Men in these groups believe that feminism has gone too far. They demand equality for men and men's rights and fight against the male breadwinner role. They advocate for men to regain their masculinity and regain their dominant role in their families, in opposition to what they see as increasing feminization of men.
- *Anti-feminist movement*. Men in these groups represent backlash. They are against any measures that support women's equality, status, rights or opportunities.
- *Pro-feminist*. Men in these groups believe that men and women should enjoy the same privileges, opportunities, rights, roles, and

status in society. These men support women, countering toxic masculinity, are against rape, are against violence against women, encourage men to engage in healthy fathering; for these men, feminism has not yet gone far enough.

The first two men's movements have waned over the past decade while the third has grown in importance.

When women make progress some men respond by behaviors consistent with backlash in response to these gains (Faludi, 1999). In the early 1970s, a women's movement emerged to support women's work and career aspirations. This was followed by a men's movement. Some men's groups were partly against having the breadwinner role foisted on them, the need to be the financial provider, the need to work very long hours. Men were getting a raw deal as well. Some men believed that women were now being protected against discrimination in several arenas (schools, the workplace) by the government while men were not. Anti-male discrimination existed in the courts in cases of divorce and child custody (access by men to their children) and men having to serve in the army (Crowley, 2008).

Domestic violence   'Inter-partner violence (IPV) is a pattern of assaultive behaviors including one or more of the following – physical, sexual, psychological or economic coercion – inflicted by either a current or former marital or non-marital partner against intimate partners' (Saltzman et al., 2003, p. 3). It has been estimated that 5.3 million partner assaults occur annually in the USA, and about 41 percent to 61 percent of respondents from Asia and the Pacific Islands experience IPV during their lifetimes (Yoshima and Dabby, 2009). The National Violence Against Women survey reported that about 2.3 million assaults against women and 835 000 against men occur in a year (Tjaden and Thoennes, 2000). More women than men suffer serious injuries requiring medical attention, making IPV a leading cause of injury among women (Rennison and Wenchans, 2000; Ansara and Hindin, 2011).

IPV occurs at home but is more than just a significant domestic issue; it is also an organizational problem. IPV has direct costs such as lateness, absenteeism, turnover, and potential organizational liability and indirect costs such as reduced satisfaction, less commitment, a negative work climate, and lost productivity (Tolentino et al., 2011). Most victims of IPV are targeted at work because perpetrators know where they are, sometimes even working in the same organization. Most victims of IPV are employed (Farmer and Tiefenthaler, 2004). Unfortunately, most victims of IPV tend to keep these events private, afraid that disclosure will reflect badly on them. Efforts are being made to help both organizational and police first responders deal with such incidents as well as predicting the likelihood of future violence.

Mass shootings and male violence As this chapter was being written, Adam Lanza, a mentally disturbed 20-year-old, after killing his mother, entered an elementary school in Newtown, Connecticut and shot and killed 20 six- and seven-year-old male and female students, six teachers and himself. This was only the latest mass shooting in the USA undertaken by men; similar mass shootings have occurred in Norway, Canada, and Australia, among other countries, almost always by deranged and unstable men. The Newtown mass killing was the fourth in President Obama's first four-year term, all committed by young men. While more women now commit murder than previously, women never take part in mass shootings.

Backlash in societies in which men hate women

A 14-year-old girl in Pakistan, Malala Yousafzai, was shot by the Taliban for advocating that young girls be allowed to attend schools and obtain an education. She was in a coma but is now recovering. The Taliban indicated that should she survive they would attempt to kill her again. There are other countries (see Armstrong, 2012) in which girls are denied access to education, are forced into arranged marriages, where young girls undergo genital mutilating operations, where girls and women are raped with no punishment to the perpetrators, where women have acid thrown on them for rejecting a suitor's marriage proposal, and where female fetuses are aborted (India, Egypt, South Africa, China, Afghanistan, Pakistan). Why do men in some societies hate women? Giving up unearned male privilege is likely one possible answer.

Efforts to End Violence Against Girls and Women

Flood (2011) highlights the need to engage men and boys in ending violence against girls and women. He documents the increasing worldwide interest in involving boys and men in the prevention of violence against girls and women. These involve educational programs, men as targets in social marking initiatives, men as policy-makers and gatekeepers, and men as advocates and activists. Men have to be involved in these efforts since men perpetrate almost all of the violence against women. Aspects of masculinity and male dominance itself increase the likelihood of violence against women, and men themselves have a role and stake in preventing violence against women. It is important, however, that efforts to involve men are guided by a feminist agenda and are shaped by and accountable to women. Flood describes a spectrum of prevention methods, ranging from strengthening individual knowledge and skills (individual), community education (groups), educating trainers, professionals and providers of knowledge to others, building communities (collections of groups), changing organizational and workplace practices (organizational level), and influencing policy and legislation (various levels of government).

BUSINESS SCHOOL EDUCATION – THE SOLUTION OR THE PROBLEM?

Business schools have made efforts to increase the numbers of women in their student body, but these numbers have increased only slightly. But what seems to have changed is the way female and male MBA students viewed gender. Kelan and Jones (2010) intensively interviewed ten men and ten women enrolled on an elite MBA program about their views on gender in the program and in the wider business world. They reported two themes in their interviews related to gender: (1) male and female MBA students accept that male dominance in both domains was the 'way things are', 'the way the world is'; (2) gender did not matter to male and female students. The MBA model is masculine but this did not appear to bother MBA students. Kelan and Jones believe this to be an obstacle to progress on gender issues. Their data raise an important question for business education programs. How can they develop future business leaders who can respond to emerging needs in the workplace? They offer some 'obvious' and some 'subtle' strategies to advance this agenda. Their obvious strategies (p. 41) include:

- women's brochures depicting women;
- women's scholarships;
- women-only programs;
- women's centers;
- women-only recruitment events;
- women-in-business clubs.

Their 'subtle' strategies (p. 41) include:

- brochures depicting men and women in non-traditional working positions;
- rethinking how competences and concepts such as leadership are gendered;
- showing women in leading roles in case studies and as guest speakers;

- involving men in change;
- diversity awareness training for students and faculty;
- informal groups for women.

MASCULINITY AND THE FAMILY

> Today, while the titular head of the family may still be the father, everyone knows that he is little more than chairman, at most, of the entertainment committee.
>
> (Ashley Montague, British-American anthropologist, 1905–99)

Masculine ideology not only affects men but also affects women and children. Men working to fulfill the provider role have less time for their spouses/partners and children. Feinberg (1980) outlines some of the difficulties that children of high achievers face. These include excessively high standards, difficulty in being good enough and pleasing the father, and criticism for falling short. Sostek and Sherman (1977) undertook an eight-year study of children of executives, which examined their attitudes towards parents, and their own behavior. Most resented their parents, and they exhibited less achievement orientation, self-confidence, and pride in workmanship than did children serving as a control group. Children of executive parents complained about the need to rigidly comply with fathers' viewpoints. Brooks (1977) reported that children of executives were less interested in pursuing the same careers as their fathers. This partly reflected a rejection of their fathers' goals of money, status, and power. Only 15 percent of children whose fathers were in the top or middle management of Fortune 500 firms planned a corporate or business career. Piotrkowski (1978), in a study of work and family, found that children connected their fathers' jobs to their fathers' bad moods.

MEN AS ALLIES

A survey undertaken by the Simmons School of Management on women's experiences with women's networking groups indicated that they believed these efforts would be more useful if senior men were also included (see Williams, 2012). A study undertaken by Catalyst, a US-based women's advocacy group, found that women's advancement was hampered by unequal access to high-visibility jobs and international experience (Reaney, 2012). Catalyst studied 1660 male and female business school alumni of high-profile universities between 1996 and 2007 from several countries. Men worked on larger projects, had larger assignments, and more international exposure. Women got fewer of these critical experiences than men. More senior organizational men were the gatekeepers of these plum assignments.

And the shoe can also be on the other foot. The teaching staff at most public schools have been primarily white and female in Canada. It is also difficult to get a teaching job in Toronto today. A Toronto District School board, in an attempt to diversify teaching staff, targeted gender and race – men and racial minorities preferred. Female teachers were angered by the targeting of male and minority hires (Alphonso and Hammer, 2013; Hammer and Alphonso, 2013).

In addition, the major university degree seen as a prerequisite for career advancement, the MBA, itself does not do a good job in preparing women and men to work together in teams as equals and to work together to create an organizational culture that works for all when they leave school and enter the workplace (Simpson, 1996). The impetus for this volume is to increase the advancement of qualified managerial and professional women in organizations that were designed by men for men and are currently male dominated. Men currently in senior managerial roles may not have designed these organizations but are receiving the benefits from it.

IMPORTANCE OF THIS TOPIC

Issues of talent management and development, and human resource management more broadly, are slowly but surely gaining currency as organizational and government leaders strive for greater understanding on how to leverage performance in an increasingly demanding and competitive international environment. Coming to grips with a more diverse workforce, gender being a central feature of diversity, has become more important. Men seem to be part of the problem and a necessary part of the solution.

Every major academic association (e.g., Academy of Management, British Academy of Management, Administrative Science Association of Canada, American Psychological Association, Society for Industrial and Organizational Psychology) has a section devoted to women in management/gender/diversity. In addition, professional HR associations (e.g., Human Resources Professional Association of Ontario, Society for Human Resources) have demonstrated a major commitment to women in management/gender issues.

The business media increasingly cover stories about executive-level men who are attempting to change their organizational cultures to make them more welcoming of talented women. In addition, organizations in several countries that are making efforts to 'level the playing field' are being pro-filed. Some men and some organizations 'get it'.

Women are being seen as a critical source of talent. In Japan, only 0.8 percent of CEOs are women versus 10 percent in the UK. Less than 10 percent of Japanese managers are women versus 43 percent in the USA. Japan is facing a severe shortage of talent, and Japan does not encourage immigration, so to address the talent gap, it is vital for Japan to do a much better job in advancing qualified women. In addition, there is increasing evidence that women are more ethical than men (see Thiruvadi and Huang, 2011). An increasing number of North American organizations (e.g., McKinsey & Company and Bain & Company) are keeping contact with women who leave to have children, to recruit them to return. They generally offer flexible work arrangements in these efforts.

Women are increasingly being seen as drivers of the world economy. Silverstein and Sayre (2009a, 2009b) observe that women control $20 trillion in consumer spending and this figure is expected to increase. In addition, women earn about $13 trillion in total yearly income and this figure will also rise. Women make the major purchasing decisions in several areas (e.g., home furnishings, vacations, automobiles). Women represent the largest market opportunity in the world. Yet women get little help at home and are too often ignored by manufacturers and service providers. Women are likely to have more power in the future.

One can make the case that bringing about equal opportunities into the workplace would double the IQ of such countries. There are some countries where only small differences exist in male and female employment rates (e.g., Sweden, Denmark, France, Germany, the USA) while other countries have larger differences (e.g., Italy, Japan).

Eagly et al. (2003) undertook a meta-analysis of 45 studies that allowed a comparison of female and male leaders on transformational, transactional, and laissez-faire leadership styles. They found that female leaders were more transformational than male leaders, and female leaders also engaged in more contingent reward behaviors, a component of transactional leadership. Male leaders exhibited higher levels of other transactional-style behaviors (active and passive management by exception) and laissez-faire leadership. Although the differences were small, the results suggest that female leaders rated higher than male leaders in areas consistent with higher levels of effectiveness, whereas male leaders rated higher in areas of leadership that have negative or no relationship with effectiveness (Eagly and Carli, 2003).

DOES THE PRESENCE OF MORE WOMEN IN MANAGEMENT MATTER?

Stoker et al. (2012) considered employee gender, gender of one's manager, and the management gender ratio in relation to preference for masculine stereotyped managers. Data were collected from 3229 (67 percent men) respondents in the Netherlands. They found that although the general stereotype of a manager is masculine and most preferred a male manager to a female manager, female employees, female employees having a female manager, and employees working in organizations with a higher percentage of female managers had a stronger preference for feminine characteristics in managers and for female managers.

THE MYTH OF HAVING IT ALL

Why would anyone want to have it all? Where would they put it?
(Lily Tomlin, US comedienne)

To reject a high-flying career is not to reject aspiration. It is to refuse to succumb to a kind of madness.
(Judith Shulevitz, 'Sympathy for the stay-at-home mom: An argument about work, life, and the modern calendar', *The New Republic*, 21 March 2013)

Slaughter (2012) makes the case that 'women can't have it all right now' given the way organizations and work are structured. As a consequence, women feel guilty about giving their families and friends less commitment and attention than they would like to (Hewlett, 2003). Men also can't have it all. Interestingly, men rarely get asked how they 'juggle it all'.

Hewlett and Luce (2006) studied work and extra-work experiences of very successful and highly paid executives. Most were very work satisfied, received large salaries, a wide range of perks, interesting work, and recognition by their work colleagues. They were concerned about what their working 70 or more hours a week was doing to their emotional and physical health and what this work commitment was doing to their family relationships. Most indicated a desire to modestly reduce their working hours over the next five years.

There is increasing evidence that to continue to be successful, organizations will need to use the best talent they can attract and retain; a 'war for talent' (Michaels et al., 2001). Organizations, and society as a whole, cannot afford to waste the talents of half the population (Wittenberg-Cox and Maitland, 2008). Thus, attracting and developing talented and qualified women becomes a business case and not a fairness or gender case

(Wittenberg-Cox, 2010). Men in senior managerial roles need to become champions of these efforts. Their organizations will benefit, and the men themselves will benefit.

And some men do get it. We have observed that some men with daughters have become leaders in supporting women in their workplaces. Other men seem to have got it because it makes sound business sense. Significant progress in advancing women's careers will not be made until men get on board.

Can Anyone Have it All?

Two broad views emerged following the Marissa Mayer appointment: one positive and one negative. The positive view was that a talented woman can hold a high-powered demanding job and have a baby; the negative view was women should not expect to hold a high-powered demanding job and have a baby unless they only take a few weeks off work.

No one can have it all if all means being a child's primary caregiver, pursuing a demanding career and having a happy and satisfying marriage/ partnership. This entails being a full-time parent, a full-time careerist, and a full-time partner, with the difficulty of doing all of these things simultaneously. One obvious possibility is to do them sequentially, however. But gender differences exist here. Women can't have it all, yet they still have to do it all. Men rarely 'complain' about not having it all while some women do. Men choose to do significantly less housework and have less home responsibilities than do women. Ideally, men have to behave in different ways, shouldering more of the home and family duties and responsibilities. There is also a distinction between having a baby and being a mother or father. Marissa Mayer may in fact be behaving like most men.

Most managers and professionals work at least 50 hours a week, with some working 70 hours a week or more (Hewlett and Luce, 2006). More women and men are 'leaning back' rather than 'leaning in', giving up long work hours and the high levels of pay and perks for more flexibility, control, and balance (Major and Burke, 2013).

THE NEW REALITY

Here is a snapshot of the present, the new reality, for men, women, families, and organizations in an increasing number of developed and developing countries (Center for American Progress, 2009, 2010):

- Women are now ahead in academia.
- Women are slowly moving up the corporate hierarchy.
- More women are now the family breadwinners.
- More women are now choosing to stay single.
- Women now earn more than their male partners in 40 percent of couples.
- More women are the heads of single-parent households, leading to the rise of matriarchy, and an impact on men.
- Physical strength is no longer required in the vast majority of jobs; it is now a knowledge and service economy.
- There are increasing threats to men's self-image and what men will become in the future. More men are in jobs now using 'soft skills' service.
- Men still comprise the vast majority of CEOs and some people are still uncomfortable with women in power. But this too is slowly changing. It is not so much about the decline of men but about the rise of women. The educational system and the economy now fit the strengths of women. Women are more flexible; women have changed their roles much more so than men have. Men now have fewer options than women. There are fewer role models for men than for women, but some men are now more domestic minded.
- More men don't care who makes more money and who 'wears the pants'. Or do they?
- More men and boys now have or have had working mothers.
- It could be seen as not the end of men but the beginning of men. Men need to redefine what it now means to be a 'good man'. It is acceptable for men to now be involved fathers. This new reality seems to be leading more men to question whether there is more to life than just working. But men still need to do more at home and provide stronger support to their partners/spouses.

Wittenberg-Cox and Maitland (2008) make the case as to 'why women mean business':

- Women make 80 percent of the consumer goods purchasing decisions.
- Women comprise 60 percent of university graduates in North America and Europe.
- Companies with more women in leadership outperform those with few women in leadership.
- Companies with more women in leadership are better adapted to the new workforce.

- Countries that support women have higher birth rates and greater economic growth.

Kimmel (2009) believes some men are open to discussing such issues but they don't know how to take part in these discussions. Men want to know the 'new rules' for engaging women in the workplace. In this regard, the Good Men Project has been launched in Boston, focusing on issues of masculinity. Catalyst, a New York City-based organization promoting women in management has launched an online project called Men Advocating Real Change (MARC) to involve men in the discussion of women in management. Their organizations will attract and retain more qualified women. Second, their workplaces will be more reflective of the increased status of women in terms of their purchasing and decision-making power (Silverstein and Sayre, 2009a, 2009b). Third, their workplaces will potentially be more productive. Fourth, men supporting women will be contributing to a better future for these women, heightening men's generativity, thus making the work that men are doing more meaningful. Fifth, creating a culture more conducive to women's advancement will lessen the burden on men in terms of work hours, work–family tension, and improved psychological health (less anger, impatience, and time urgency).

There is another way that women's increasing success in education and the workforce may be benefitting men. Women's success may affect the expectations of men that they spend their working lives in jobs they did not want. Some men would be freed from the burdens of the 'provider role' as a result. As more women become free to pursue jobs and careers they like, more men may also become free to pursue jobs and careers that they like rather than being trapped in 'provider' jobs.

FEMINISM, FATHERING, AND MEN'S LIVES

There has been an increase in single-father households, stay-at-home fathers, and men taking parental leave upon the birth of a child. In addition, men now do a bit more of the home and household chores, but women still do more of the home care. A journal dedicated to fathering research, *Fathering: A Journal of Theory, Research and Practice about Men as Fathers* was first published in 2002.

Men's relations to fatherhood in general and to the new image of the caring and present father is evolving, influenced by changes in the portrayal of traditional masculinity (Dienhart, 1998; Deutsch, 1999). More men are taking paternity leave, a small percentage in some countries (the USA) and a larger percentage in other countries (Sweden). Men are generally contributing a bit more time to home and family responsibilities. Some men are leaving the workforce and becoming stay-at-home fathers. Parental leave is increasingly being divided between mothers and fathers where possible.

The good news is that we have developed a greater understanding of men, ways in which masculinity – the pros and cons – can be discussed, and how to go about changing the culture of organizations. These include organizational surveys of women's and men's work and career experiences, 360 degree feedback to identify helping and hindering attitudes and behaviors of managers, and ways to both make work more efficient and support women's advancement (Rapoport et al., 2002).

Several interrelated factors have contributed to the gains that women have made in the workforce. These include the emergence of feminism, a greater demand for labor in knowledge work where women can perform as well as men, more women in higher education, more people comfortable with women in the workforce and with women sometimes earning more than men, a greater availability of flexible work hours, work–family programs, and greater use of labor-saving technologies and appliances in the home. In addition, there is some evidence that younger men seem to be more supportive of organizational initiatives that improve quality of work life and support work–life integration.

But it gets complicated. Men exist and boys grow up in a gendered society that is reflected in the worlds of work and organizations. It is also important to consider the socialization experiences of both boys and girls in their wider social environment. Young men construct their social identity starting at a very young age (Kimmel, 2008). As boys grow up, many act immaturely (Cross, 2008) and even among some young men who go on to attend our best universities (e.g., Yale), they create what some feminists have called a 'rape culture'. Fraternity pledges at Yale walked around female dormitories shouting 'No means yes! Yes means anal!' (Beyerstein, 2011). Sexual assaults in the US military have taken on epidemic proportions. As many as 26 000 military members may have been sexually assaulted in 2012 (*Toronto Star*, 2013). More than 30 Air Force instructors are being investigated for assaults on trainees at a Texas military base. The number of reported sexual assaults increased 6 percent to 3374 in 2012. Ironically, the man heading up the Air Force's sexual assault prevention unit, Lt. Col. Jeffrey Krusinski, was arrested in May 2013 and charged with sexual assault, later changed to assault and battery (*The Telegraph*, 2013).

Given these observed differences in personal, organizational, and societal outcomes between men and women, we believe an emphasis on men in organizations and the way that masculine and male-dominated organizational cultures, policies, practices, and processes work to perpetuate inequality of opportunity warrants attention. But this must not be a 'male bashing' exercise. More men (and boys) need to become allies, supporters, and champions of women's position and place (Katz, 2006).

MEN AS FATHERS

No man on his deathbed ever said I wished I had spent more time at the office.
(Democrat Paul Tsongas when he resigned from the US Senate upon learning he had terminal health problems)

Fatherhood is in transition. Feminism and the women's movement have brought about changes in women's roles and aspirations. Although beginning a bit later, feminism and changes to women's roles are also contributing to changes in men's roles. The women's movement that resulted in more women pursuing both higher education and careers and more men being adversely affected by the economic recession were also contributing factors here. We now have more dual-career couples, more women earning more than their spouses/partners, changing family structures, changing career patterns, and changing values. Women fought for a place in the workplace and men are now striving for a place in both the workplace and at home. Women now realize that they can do what men do but women and men were slower in realizing that men can do what women can do. Fathers have been found to report higher levels of work–family conflict than working mothers, perhaps reflecting the fact that fathers generally worked more hours than working mothers (Harrington et al., 2011).

Harrington et al. (2010) interviewed 33 working fathers to better understand their views on being both workers and new/first-time fathers. Children ranged from 3 to 48 months old. Almost all had working spouses/partners. They found there was increasing pressure now on men not only to be 'providers' but also equal partners in co-parenting. Changes in women's situations and expectations were influencing men and fatherhood. Men in dual-career couples now reported an increase in work–life conflict. More men were thinking about and redefining their traditional gender-based roles, were happy as fathers, trying to spend more time with their children and to better support child parenting and home responsibilities. They seemed to be focusing less on work. They were surprised at how much time was needed to take care of children. For this group, a good father was someone who was both a provider and spent time with and loving their children. Most men said becoming a father was a life-changing event. Striving for a 50–50 division in caregiving usually fell short. There was a critical need to communicate and coordinate with their spouses/ partners. Most reported supportive bosses and some thought that their co-workers now saw them differently. Some men now had a different take on what constituted success. But women and men have different experiences. Men did not take leaves of absence, men did not generally use flexible work arrangements but tended to create informal flexibility.

Harrington et al. (2011) then extended their work to a larger sample of working fathers with at least one child under 18 (*n* = 963) who worked in four US-based large multinational organizations. They found that their sample was generally high on job satisfaction, wanted career advancement, were concerned about their job security given their current economic environment, worked long hours, were currently satisfied with their careers, used and valued flexible work arrangements, saw their roles as both providing financially and emotionally caring for their children – a good father provides love and emotional support, being present and involved in their children's lives, and were stewards, guides, and coaches. Men seemed to be interested in and embraced a 'new image' of being a father. Fathers took almost no time off at their children's birth – typically one week or less. Most felt confident in their ability to parent. Work interfered with family considerably more often than family interfered with work. Interestingly, family-to-work enrichment contributed to better work experiences and work-to-family enrichment contributed to men being better fathers and family members. Men wanted to be equal partners in caregiving but this was difficult to achieve; women almost always did more. Not surprisingly, men worked significantly more hours per week than did women (their partners). Spouse support was a large factor in helping men integrate their work with caregiving. Likewise, a supportive organizational environment (supervisors, co-workers, culture) made it easier to mesh work with family. A supportive organizational culture was associated with smoother work and family integration and higher levels of respondent job satisfaction.

They conclude with suggestions for employers. These include: more support for flexible work arrangements, offering benefits that directly support caregiving (on-site or off-site daycare, time off), recognizing fathers' caregiving responsibilities, getting to know and understanding the needs of new fathers, and creating a place where new fathers can talk with one another. Paid parental leave would be a benefit to both women and men.

Men who take time off work to care for children or elderly parents violate gender norms and are seen as less committed to their work, a 'flexibility stigma'. But men rarely argue for change and as a consequence they keep being punished for taking time off or using flexible work arrangements. But as more men do argue, this bias will diminish for both men and women. Williams (2012) argues that men are critical allies in the work–family debate.

Badalament (2013) notes that there is considerable evidence that a close father–child relationship is good for children and contributes to favorable physical and psychological health of fathers. Badalament offers the following practical ways in which men can be the best fathers they can:

- *Create a vision for fatherhood – a father's vision statement.* In 20 years what do you hope your child says about you?
- *Be the bridge between your own father and your children.* What positive features can you pass on to your children from your relationship with your father?
- *Establish a ritual dad time.* Create at least monthly a special time for a one-on-one with a child.
- *Know your children.* Be a skilled listener and keen observer of what is going on in your children's lives.
- *Be known to your children.* Let your children know what you were like at their age, what challenges you faced, how you had fun, among other things.
- *Take care of yourself.* Live the healthy life you want your children to lead.
- *Don't go it alone.* Talk to other parents – particularly other fathers. In this regard, Deloitte and Touche in Toronto has created a group called Deloitte Dads.

Badalament also offers practical ways in which women can support men in being the best fathers they can. These include:

- *Letting go.* Let fathers do more things – for better or worse – with their children without criticism.
- *See fathers as equals.* Even though fathers may do less or do things less than perfect make sure they have the information they need to know what is going on.
- *Speak up for what you want.* Talk with fathers if you think they could do things differently and 'better'.
- *Understand the legacy of your own father.* Your own views on fathering are likely affected by your relationship with your own father. Your husband is not your father.

WOMEN AS MOTHERS

Ladge et al. (2012) interviewed 30 professional women who were pregnant with their first child. Their pregnancies affected their professional and maternal identities and raised uncertainties for them. Women were uncertain as to how to maintain their professional identities given their growing maternal identity, and uncertain about how to manage the needs and priorities of being a working mother. The organizational context was an important source of information on the types of working mothers that were valued and accepted. Formal organizational policies and resources were important for women in combining their professional and maternal roles. In addition, spouse support made it easier for women to mesh their professional and maternal identities.

What else needs to be done to help both fathers and mothers manage both work and family? Slaughter (2012) laid out five mandates in order to bring about social change and be supportive of families:

- *Changing the culture of face time.* Women and men need to identify the available flexibility in their jobs and resist long hours of work and the bringing work home.
- *Revaluing family values.* Women and men need to be involved in their work while simultaneously being involved in their children's (and family) life.
- *Redefining the arc of successful careers.* Too often success is defined as who advances their career in the shortest amount of time. Slaughter argues that careers instead should be seen as a series of steps, some upward, some lateral, and some downward. In addition, since people are living longer, peaking one's career in the 50s instead of the 40s would support more balance in life.
- *Rediscovering the pursuit of happiness.* Women and men should include activities and experiences that enrich and bring joy to their lives and families. These should include self, family, community, and society at large.
- *Becoming an experimenting and innovating society.* Organizations need to be open to new ways of working that increase employee work engagement and retention, and these often involve greater flexibility. It is in an organization's best interests to be innovative in this regard.

USE OF FLEXIBLE WORK ARRANGEMENTS – BENEFITS OR PUNISHMENTS?

Leslie et al. (2012) showed in both field and laboratory studies that managers' interpretation of employee use of flexible work practices (productivity versus personal life attributions) affected their perceptions of employee commitment, which in turn affected later employee career success. Productivity attributions were a source of career premiums and personal life attributions were a source of career penalties. Since women are more likely than men to use these flexible work practices, it places a lot of influence in the 'eyes of the beholders' – more than likely men. Women who take even a little or no time off for children still encounter a 'maternal wall bias' that limits their career advancement. Mothers are less likely to be promoted and receive lower salaries. Female MBA graduates today are less likely to have children than graduates 20 years ago.

There are factors at work and at home that increase both men's and women's successful use of flexible work arrangements. Work factors include having supportive managers, managers who themselves have a balanced approach to work and family, and the presence of written policies that support work–family balance and parental leave. Home factors include parents working as a team to set and prioritize family goals, parents setting boundaries at work, and parents supporting each other. There are some factors at both home and work that support men's use and success with flexible work arrangements. Work factors include managers that support men's use of these arrangements, and male managers who themselves exemplify work–family balance and enrichment. Home factors include having partners that encourage fathers to take paternity leave, to spend lots of time with their children, and men who have other male role models of successfully using flexible work arrangements.

MORE MEN WANT WORK–FAMILY INTEGRATION AND THEY AREN'T GOING TO BE DENIED ANY MORE

Kolhatkar (2013), noting that an increasing number of young fathers are questioning the long work hours culture and its role in limiting their time with their children, suggests that these men may in fact make greater progress in addressing work–family issues than women have made to date. She describes an initiative at Deloitte Touche, Toronto called Deloitte Dads to help fathers achieve more time with their children. Other organizations, upon hearing about this effort, contacted Deloitte for more information.

Some women at Deloitte had earlier started a group called Career Moms to help mothers achieve greater balance in their lives without jeopardizing their work and careers.

MEN WHO 'GET IT'

The last thing Wall Street needs is a nursing mother.
(Comment made by US investor and billionaire Paul Tudor Jones, a married father with daughters, on 26 April 2013 at the University of Virginia Business School. Mississippi Governor Phil Bryant, at a *Washington Post* panel session on 4 June 2013, blamed the decline in the American educational system on working mothers)

There are obviously countless numbers of men who 'get it' and an increasing number of men becoming allies instead of obstacles. Avivah Wittenberg-Cox (2012), in her role as CEO of 20-first, an international gender consulting firm, wrote a blog profiling one such man. Paul Bulcke, appointed CEO of Nestlé in 2008, 'gets it'. Nestlé had done little to support women's advancement prior to his appointment, with only 3 percent of managers being women even though their 'shoppers' were 80 percent women. Bulcke put gender balance as the top priority for his top management team. He talked about gender balance regularly at management meetings. He produced a video showing why gender balance was important for the firm. But he did not set quotas. He did not assign this to HR; he did not see this as an HR issue but as a key business issue. He did not place a woman in charge of this initiative. Bulcke was the champion of this initiative. He began with a series of awareness sessions for all managers, starting at the top levels, as to why gender balance was critical to the continuing success of the firm. These sessions then cascaded down the organization. Considerable progress has been achieved in the support and advancement of women in Nestlé since he took office.

A full page appeared in the *Globe and Mail*, Canada's business newspaper, in which Bill Downe, CEO, Bank of Montreal, and Deborah Gillis, head of Catalyst Canada, made the case for why organizations should do more in supporting women. The Bank of Montreal has been seen as a leading Canadian organization in its efforts to advance qualified women to more senior levels.

In the UK, Cranfield University published the results of its 2012 audit of women on the corporate boards of directors of FTSE 100 and FTSE 250 organizations. Three men holding senior government or private sector organizational leadership positions were featured prominently in early pages – other examples of 'men who get it'. Interestingly the Cranfield results showed some modest gains in women's representation on UK corporate boards over the past two years.

Yet men who 'get it' do not always serve as leaders on gender issues. For some of these men, it is so obvious that it doesn't require selling or debate; the case has already been made. Other men prefer not to make a big public deal out of this. Instead they try to manage their own units in a gender-balanced way. Other men think that changes will happen naturally over time. They manage their own units in a gender-balanced way and think that all male managers do the same. Men who 'get it' can play a larger role in supporting women's advancement. They can become more active leaders on gender issues, can more actively 'sell' why supporting women as allies helps everyone, can inform other men how they went about changing the culture of their workplaces, and why having men champion these efforts is as powerful as having women take the lead (Prime and Moss-Racusin, 2009; Prime et al., 2009).

Men Doing Feminism

Universities and colleges began offering academic courses on feminism or women's studies a long time ago (Digby, 1998). Kimmel (1998) contends that men can 'do feminism' and support feminism, and a small number of men take courses in women's studies. These men are in a paradoxical position of being rare in the classroom yet are the subject (men and masculinity) of much of the discussion (Alilunas, 2011).

POTENTIALLY HELPFUL ACTIONS

The old boys' network is still alive and well. And it seems to work. It seems to help in making decisions, both directly business related as well as influencing the career development and advancement of others (and these can both obviously be related). The old boys' network has historically sponsored men. Lang (2011) believes that sponsorship is critical to closing the gender gap. Men's mentors are both more senior and more likely to sponsor these men for advancement. Women can get noticed by both achieving expected results and by promoting their achievements. But women are less likely to self-nominate and self-promoting women get penalized and punished. Lang believes that organizations need to recognize that the old boys' network needs to more actively sponsor women to advance their most talented managers and professionals.

Uzzi and Dunlap (2012) offer advice on how to make one's adversaries one's allies, not suggesting that all men are enemies of women.

Their advice is captured by the three Rs: redirection, reciprocity and rationality:

- Redirect any negative emotions you may have away from you. This may involve one-on-one discussions.
- Reciprocate by giving something to the other person.
- Use rationality/reason to identify and articulate what you need from the other person if you are to be successful at work. Strive for collaboration.

CONCLUSIONS

First, women have to want to be equal, and then men have to let them be.
(Rachel Cusk, feminist British writer, *The Globe and Mail*, 17 August 2012)

Women represent 50 percent of the population, comprise 60 percent of university graduates, and account for 60 percent of global spending. They have become a force to be reckoned with. Few women are advancing to the top levels of medium and large organizations despite efforts by organizations to create a more level playing field. We have come to know a lot about the barriers that women face in these organizations. Yet gender in organizations is always about women and never about men. Organizations were designed by men for men; men feel more comfortable in them and women feel less comfortable in them. Women often don't fit in. Socialization of boys/men and girls/women create gender role stereotypes and gender expectations. Yet young women seem to be faring better than young men in the wider society. Organizations need to make use of all the talent that is available to them if they are to be successful; they can't afford to under-utilize the talents of much of the population. For this to happen we need more men to become allies. Right now a small proportion of men are allies, most are passive observers, and a small proportion are obstacles to women's progress. We believe that when more men become allies of women it becomes a win-win experience for men, women, families, organizations, and society at large. The good news is that some men do 'get it'.

Baumeister (2012) writes that the top levels of organizations and society are occupied by men but the bottom levels are also predominantly occupied by men. Men are overly represented in prisons, in the military, in high accident industries such as mining, as work addicts, as alcoholics, as drug addicts, as perpetrators and victims of violence, and among the homeless. He attributes this to cultural values that 'exploit' men. Patriarchy developed, not to oppress women, but to capitalize on ways in which men and women differed, which produced a more effective society that raised the standard of living for all citizens. Baumeister suggests that relations between men and women have generally been more cooperative than antagonistic, that men and women are different in important ways (motivation, risk taking, nature of social relationships), that successful cultures/societies use these differences to outperform other cultures/societies, and that while some men have benefitted from these cultures other men have paid a huge price, along with women and families. We believe as he does that women and men are different but equal. We would also argue, however, that changes in patriarchy would bring benefits to men, women, and families; the more men become allies to women the better society becomes.

Patriarchy and rigid gender roles constrain both women and men. Women and men will benefit when more men become allies for change in the status quo. What we need is for both women and men to work together to bring about meaningful cultural change, which can liberate both to fulfill larger and critical roles in work and family. The status quo has several costs:

- For men: work addiction, long work hours, working in intense jobs, little leisure, restricted family involvement. Men more than women suffer from alcoholism and drug addiction, are more likely to commit suicide, are imprisoned at higher rates, and die at younger ages.
- For women: career frustration, not using their education and skills, little help at home.
- For families and children: little father involvement, less interest in pursuing jobs similar to those of their fathers.
- For organizations: women opting out, high turnover of women, a shortage of talent, high levels of work–family and family–work conflict, performance that falls short. Corporate masculinity has produced the *Challenger* space disaster and the 2008 financial crisis on Wall Street.
- For society: increased health care costs, organizations that are less effective than they might be. When more men become allies, there are potential benefits. Kolhatkar (2013), for example, in describing the formation of 'fathers' groups' in organizations, highlights some of these benefits.
- For men: more balance in their lives, better psychological and physical health, more family involvement, more caring fathers, more generativity through giving, helping, and sponsoring others. Men

who support gender equality are happier, healthier, live longer, have better lives, have better relationships with their friends, their wives, and their children.

- For women: more career progress, greater utilization of their talents and education, more help at home, more family contact, and satisfaction.
- For families and children: more contact, more satisfying role models.
- For organizations: less turnover, more attractive as employers, better attraction and utilization of talent, higher levels of success.
- For society: higher levels of satisfaction of employees, more successful organizations, lower health care costs.

Making advancing women's careers a strategic business initiative starts at the (typically male) CEO. But these efforts need to be focused on both women *and* men. Women do not need 'fixing'. Men need to embrace and support these efforts since men create the culture. Changing aspects of organizational culture requires that both women and men change. Unfortunately, few men see the need for themselves to change. Many men have little understanding of what a modern working woman represents.

Many organizations are making efforts to change their cultures from a command and control model to a flatter, more collaborative style. There is considerable evidence that women make greater use of collaboration, communication, listening, inspiration, and the use of 'we' instead of 'I' or 'me'. Having more women on board would increase the range of leadership styles and increase morale and performance as a by-product. Too many women, to get promoted, have chosen to behave like men. Unfortunately, these women are limited role models for younger women. Women and men are different in some fundamental ways and these differences should be valued and supported.

Men need to be more supportive of their spouses at home. When women leave the workforce they see their husbands/partners as important factors in these decisions. Men fall short in child care responsibilities, undertaking fewer home tasks, and their expectations that their spouses/partners will reduce their job, career or employment commitments. Few dual-earner relationships share housework evenly. When asked what men could do more of to help support and advance women's careers, Rosabeth Moss Kanter, professor at the Harvard Business School, answered 'the laundry' (Stewart, 2011).

NOTE

* Preparation of this chapter was supported in part by York University, Toronto, and Old Dominion University, Virginia. Carla D'Agostino assisted in its production.

REFERENCES

Acker, J. (1990), 'Hierarchies, jobs, bodies: A theory of gendered organizations', *Gender and Society*, **4**(2), 139–58.

Adams, R.B. and D. Ferreira (2009), 'Women in the boardroom and their impact on governance and performance', *Journal of Financial Economics*, **94**(2), 291–309.

Agocs, C. (1997), 'Institutionalized resistance to organizational change: Denial, inaction and repression', *Journal of Business Ethics*, **16**(9), 917–31.

Alilunas, P. (2011), 'The (in)visible people in the room: Men in women's studies', *Men and Masculinities*, **14**(2), 210–29.

Alphonso, C. and K. Hammer (2013), 'Targeting male, minority hires: an attempt to diversify', *Globe and Mail*, 20 February, A9.

Annis, B. and J. Gray (2013), *Work With Me: The 8 Blind Spots Between Men and Women in Business*, New York: Palgrave Macmillan.

Ansara, C. and M.J. Hindin (2011), 'Psychosocial consequences of intimate partner violence for women and men in Canada', *Journal of Interpersonal Violence*, **26**(8), 1628–45.

Armstrong, S. (2012), *Ascent of Women*, Toronto: Random House Canada.

Astrachan, A. (1986), *How Men Feel: Their Response to Women's Demands for Equality and Power*, Garden City: Anchor Books.

Badalament, J. (2013), *The Modern Dad's Dilemma*, Novata, CA: New World Library.

Barber, B.M. and T. Odean (2001), '"Boys will be boys": Gender overconfidence and common stock investment', *Quarterly Journal of Economics*, **116**(1), 261–92.

Barreto, M., M.K. Ryan and M.T. Schmitt (2009), *The Glass Ceiling in the 21st Century: Understanding Barriers to Gender Equality*, Washington, DC: American Psychological Association.

Baumeister, R.F. (2012), *Is There Anything Good About Men? How Cultures Flourish by Exploiting Men*, Oxford: Oxford University Press.

Bergeron, D.M. (2012), 'The stability of organizational citizenship behavior over time: Women as good soldiers', paper presented at the Annual Meeting of the Academy of Management, Boston. August.

Beyerstein, L. (2011), '"No means yes, yes means anal" frat banned from Yale', accessed 24 August 2013 at http://bigthink.com/focal-point/no-means-yes-yes-means-anal-frat-banned-from-yale.

Blair-Loy, M. (2005), *Competing Devotions: Career and Family Among Women Executives*, Boston, MA: Harvard University Press.

Blau, F.D. and L.M. Kahn (2006),'The U.S. gender pay gap in the 1990s: Slowing convergence', *Industrial and Labor Relations Review*, **60**(1), 45–66.

Borman, E.K.O. and G.A. Walker (2010), 'Predictors of men's health care utilization', *Psychology of Men and Masculinity*, **11**(2), 113–22.

Brammer, S., A. Millington and S. Pavelin (2009), 'Corporate reputation and women on the board', *British Journal of Management*, **20**(1), 17–29.

Britton, D.M. (1999), 'Cat fights and gang fights: Preference for work in a male-dominated organization', *Sociological Quarterly*, **40**(3), 455–74.

Brooks, P. (1977), 'Whatever happened to following in Dad's footsteps', *TWA Ambassador*, May.

Burke, R.J. (2002), 'Men, masculinity, and health', in D.L. Nelson and R.J. Burke (eds), *Gender, Work Stress and Health*, Washington, DC: American Psychological Association, pp. 35–54.

Burke, R.J. (2014), 'Individual, organizational and societal backlash against women', in R.J. Burke and D. Major (eds), *Men in Organizations: Allies or Adversaries to Women's Career Advancement*, Cheltenham, UK and Northampton, MA, USA: Edward Elgar Publishing, pp. 335–62.

Burke, R.J. and M.C. Mattis (2005), *Supporting Women's Career Advancement: Challenges and Opportunities*, Cheltenham, UK and Northampton, MA, USA: Edward Elgar Publishing.

Carothers, B.J. and H.T. Reis (2013), 'Men and women are from Earth: Examining the latent structure of gender', *Journal of Personality and Social Psychology*, **104**(2), 385–407.

Catalyst (1998), *Advancing Women in Business: Best Practices from the Corporate Leaders*, San Francisco, CA: Jossey-Bass.

Catalyst (2013), *Catalyst Census: Financial Post 500 Women Senior Officers and Top Earners*, New York: Catalyst.

Center for American Progress (2009), *The Shriver Report: A Woman's Nation Changes Everything*, Washington, DC: Center for American Progress.

Center for American Progress (2010), *Our Working Nation: How Working Women are Reshaping American's Families and Economy and What it Means for Policymakers*, Washington, DC: Center for American Progress.

Cockburn, C. (1991), *In the Way of Women: Men's Resistance to Sex Equality in Organizations*, London: Macmillan.

Collins, G. (2009), *When Everything Changed: The Amazing Journey of American Women from 1960 to the Present*, New York: Little, Brown and Company.

Collinson, D. and J. Hearn (1994), 'Naming men as men: Implications for work organization and management', *Gender, Work and Organization*, **1**(1), 2–22.

Connell, R. (2012), 'Neoliberal globalization, masculinity and gender justice', *World Financial Review*, March–April, 36–8.

Courtenay, W.H. (2001), 'Constructions of masculinity and their influence on men's well-being: A theory of gender and health', *Social Science and Medicine*, **50**(10), 203–17.

Cross, G. (2008), *Men to Boys: The Making of Modern Immaturity*, New York: Columbia University Press.

Crowley, J.E. (2008), *Defiant Dads: Father's Rights Activists in America*, Ithaca, NY: Cornell University Press.

Crowley, T. (1993), 'The lie of entitlement', in E. Buckwald, P.R. Fletcher and M. Roth (eds), *Transforming a Rape Culture*, Minneapolis, MN: Milkweed Press, pp. 341–54.

Davidson, M.J. and R.J. Burke (2011), *Women in Management Worldwide: Progress and Prospects*, Farnham, Hampshire, UK and Burlington, VT, USA: Gower Publishing.

Deutsch, F.M. (1999), *Having it All: How Equally Shared Parenting Works*, Cambridge, MA: Harvard University Press.

Dienhart, A. (1998), *Reshaping Fatherhood: The Social Construction of Shared Parenting*, Thousand Oaks, CA: Sage Publications.

Digby, T. (1998), *Men Doing Feminism*, New York: Routledge.

Dowd, M. (2013), 'Get off your cloud', *National Post*, 28 February, A14.

Eagly, A.H. and L.L. Carli (2003), 'The female leadership advantage: An evaluation of the evidence', *Leadership Quarterly*, **14**(6), 807–34.

Eagly, A.H., M.C. Johannesen-Schmidt and M.L. Van Engen (2003), 'Transformational, transactional and laissez-faire leadership styles: A meta-analysis comparing women and men', *Psychological Bulletin*, **129**(4), 569–91.

Eisaid, A.M. and E. Eisaid (2012), 'Sex stereotyping managerial positions: A cross-cultural comparison between Egypt and the USA', *Gender in Organizations: An International Journal*, **27**(2), 81–99.

Eisler, R. (2013), 'Economic and business as if caring matters: Investing in our future', *Career Development International*, **20**, 145–60.

Eisler, R., D. Loye and K. Norgaard (1995), *Women, Men, and the Global Quality of Life*, Pacific Grove, CA: Center for Partnership Studies.

Ely, R.J. and D. Meyerson (2008), 'Unmasking manly men', *Harvard Business Review*, **86**(7–8), 1–3.

Eriksson, S. and J. Lagerstrom (2012), 'The labor market consequences of gender differences in job search', *Journal of Labor Research*, **33**(3), 303–27.

Faludi, S. (1991), *Backlash: The Undeclared War Against American Men*, New York: Crown Publishers.

Faludi, S. (1999), *Stiffed: The Betrayal of the American Man*, New York: William Morrow.

Farmer, A. and J. Tiefenthaler (2004), 'The employment effects of domestic violence', *Research in Labor Economics*, **23**, 301–34.

Feinberg, M.R. (1980), *Corporate Bigamy: How to Reduce the Conflict Between Work and Family*, New York: Morrow.

Flood, M. (2011), 'Involving men in efforts to end violence against women', *Men and Masculinities*, **14**(3), 358–77.

Goldberg, H. (1976), *The Hazards of Being Male: Surviving the Myth of Masculine Privilege*, New York: New American Library.

Goode, W.J. (1982), 'Why men resist', in B. Thorne and M. Yalom (eds), *Rethinking the Family: Some Feminist Questions*, New York: Longman, Inc.

Hammer, K. and C. Alphonso (2013), 'School board's hiring policy singles out men, minorities', *Globe and Mail*, 19 February, A1, A12.

Harrington, B., F. Van Deusen and B. Humberd (2011), *The New Dad: Caring, Committed and Conflicted*, Boston, MA: Boston College Center for Work and Family.

Harrington, B., F. Van Deusen and J. Ladge (2010), *The New Dad: Exploring Fatherhood Within a Career Context*, Boston, MA: Boston College Center for Work and Family.

Haynes, M.C. and M.E. Heilman (2013), 'It had to be you (not me): Women's attributional rationalization of their contribution to successful joint work outcomes', *Personality and Social Psychology Bulletin*, **39**(7), 956–69.

Heilman, M.E. and A.H. Eagly (2008), 'Gender stereotypes are alive, well and busy producing discrimination', *Industrial and Organizational Psychology*, **1**(4), 393–8.

Heilman, M.E. and A.S. Wallen (2010), 'Wimpy men and undeserving of respect: Penalties for men's gender-inconsistent success', *Journal of Experimental Social Psychology*, **46**, 664–7.

Hewlett, S.A. (2003), 'Executive women and the myth of having it all', *Harvard Business Review*, **80**(4), 66–73.

Hewlett, S.A. and C.B. Luce (2006), 'Extreme jobs: The dangerous allure of the 70-hour work week', *Harvard Business Review*, **84**(12), 49–59.

Hewlett, S.A. and R. Rashid (2012), 'Winning the talent war in emerging markets: Women are the answer', *World Financial Review*, March–April, 40–44.

Holiday, E. and J. Rosenberg (2009), *Mean Girls, Meaner Women. Understanding Why Women Backstab, Betray and Trash-talk Each Other and How to Heal*, Charleston, NC: BookSurge, LLC.

Huse, M., S. Nielsen and I.M. Hagen (2009), 'Boards of directors, codetermination and women directors: Societal and business case CSR illustrations from Norway', *Journal of Business Ethics*, **89**(2), 581–97.

Hymowitz, K.S. (2011), *Manning Up: How the Rise of Women has Turned Men into Boys*, New York: Basic Books.

Kalleberg, A.L. and K.T. Leicht (1991), 'Gender and organizational performance: Determinants of small business survival and success', *Academy of Management Journal*, **34**(1), 131–61.

Katz, J. (2006), *The Macho Paradox: Why Some Men Hurt Women and How all Men Can Help*, Napierville, IL: Sourcebooks, Inc.

Kelan, E.K. and R.D. Jones (2010), 'Gender and the MBA', *Academy of Management Learning and Education*, **9**(1), 26–43.

Kennedy, J.A. and L.J. Kray (2013), 'Who is willing to sacrifice ethical values for money and social status? Gender differences in reactions to ethical compromise', *Social Psychological and Personality Science*, in press.

Kimmel, M. (1998), 'Who's afraid of men doing feminism?', in T. Digby (ed.), *Men Doing Feminism*, New York: Routledge, pp. 57–68.

Kimmel, M. (2008), *Guyland: The Perilous World Where Boys Become Men*, New York: Harper.

Kimmel, M. (2009), *The Gendered Society*, New York: Oxford University Press.

Kirton, G. and G. Healy (2012), *Gender and Leadership in Unions*, London: Routledge.

Kolhatkar, S. (2013), 'Men are people too', *Bloomberg Business Week*, 3–9 June, 58–63.

Kristoff, N.D. and S. WuDunn (2009), *Turning Oppression into Opportunity for Women Worldwide*, New York: Knopf.

Ladge, J.J., J.A. Clair and D. Greenberg (2012), 'Cross-domain identity transition during liminal periods: Constructing multiple selves as professional and mother during pregnancy', *Academy of Management Journal*, **55**(6), 1449–71.

Lang, I.H. (2011), 'Co-opt the old boy's club: Make it work for women', *Harvard Business Review Magazine*, November.

Leslie, L.M., C.F. Manchester, T-Y. Park and S.A. Mehng (2012), 'Flexible work practices: A source of career premiums or penalties', *Academy of Management Journal*, **55**(6), 1407–28.

Lutgen-Sandvik, P., E.A. Dickinson and K.A. Foss (2011), 'Priming, painting, peeling, and polishing: Constructing and deconstructing the women-bullying-woman identity at work', in S. Fox and T.R. Lituchy (eds), *Gender and the*

Dysfunctional Workplace, Cheltenham, UK and Northampton, MA, USA: Edward Elgar Publishing, pp. 136–59.

MacCharles, T. (2012), 'Public Safety Minister Vic Toews slams RCMP head Bob Paulson for inaction on gender bias', *Toronto Star*, 23 November, A1, A31.

Maier, M. (1991), 'The dysfunctions of "corporate masculinity": Gender and diversity issues in organizational development', *Journal of Management in Practice*, **8**, 49–63.

Maier, M. (1994), 'Save the males: Reflections on while male privileges in organizations', paper presented at the New York State Political Science Association, 48th annual meeting, Albany, NY, April.

Maier, M. (1997), 'Gender, equity, organizational transformation and Challenger', *Journal of Business Ethics*, **16**(9), 943–62.

Major, D.A. and R.J. Burke (2013), *Handbook of Work–Life Integration Among Professionals*, Cheltenham, UK and Northampton, MA, USA: Edward Elgar Publishing.

Marshall, J. (1984), *Women Managers: Travellers in a Male World*, Chichester: John Wiley.

Mavin, S. (2006a), 'Venus envy: Problematizing solidarity behavior and queen bees', *Women in Management Review*, **21**(4), 264–76.

Mavin, S. (2006b), 'Venus envy 2: Sisterhood, queen bee and female misogyny in management', *Women in Management Review*, **21**(5), 349–64.

Mavin, S. (2008), 'Queen Bees, wannabees, and afraid to bees: No more best enemies for women in management', *British Journal of Management*, **19**(S1), S75–S84.

McDowell, L. (1997), *Capital Culture: Gender at Work in the City*, Oxford: Blackwell.

McFarland, J. (2012), 'Women's work: From formal legal quotas to the power of moral suasion, companies grapple with a governance issue that has proven nettlesome – and for qualified women, frustrating. Diversity champions say there is more at stake than basic fairness', *Globe and Mail*, 26 November, B1, B6.

McIntosh, P. (1989), 'White privilege: Unpacking the invisible knapsack', *Peace and Freedom*, July–August, 10–12.

Mehrabian, A. (1981), *Silent Messages: Implicit Communication of Emotions and Attitudes*, Belmont, CA: Wadsworth.

Michaels, E., H.J. Handfield-Jones and B. Axelrod (2001), *The War for Talent*, Boston, MA: Harvard Business School Press.

Morrison, A.M. (1992), *The New Leaders*, San Francisco, CA: Jossey-Bass.

Nye, J. (2012), 'Leadership, power and contextual intelligence', *World Financial Review*, May–June, 2–4.

Paris, L.D. and D.L. Decker (2012), 'Sex role stereotypes: Does business education make a difference?', *Gender in Management: An International Journal*, **27**(1), 36–50.

Phelan, J., C. Moss-Racusin and L. Rudman (2008), 'Competent yet out in the cold: Shifting criteria for hiring reflect backlash toward agentic women', *Psychology of Women Quarterly*, **32**(4), 406–13.

Piotrkowski, C.S. (1978), *Work and the Family System*, New York: Free Press.

Pleck, J.H. (1995), 'The gender role strain paradigm: An update', in R.F. Levant and W.S. Pollack (eds), *A New Psychology of Men*, New York: Basic Books, pp. 11–32.

Pollack, W.S. (1998), *Real Boys*, New York: Henry Holt.

Pope, B.E. (1993), 'In the wake of Tailhook: A new order for the navy', in E. Buckwald, P.R. Fletcher and M. Roth (eds), *Transforming a Rape Culture*, Minneapolis, MN: Milkweed, pp. 158–73.

Prime, J. and C.A. Moss-Racusin (2009), *Engaging Men in Gender Initiatives: What Change Agents Need to Know*, New York: Catalyst.

Prime, J., C.A. Moss-Racusin and H. Foust-Cummings (2009), *Engaging Men in Gender Initiatives: Stacking the Deck for Success*, New York: Catalyst.

Ragins, B.R., B. Townsend and M.C. Mattis (1998), 'Gender gap in the executive suite: CEOs and female executives report on breaking the glass ceiling', *Academy of Management Executive*, **12**(1), 28–42.

Rapoport, R., L. Bailyn, J.K. Fletcher and B.H. Pruitt (2002), *Beyond Work–Family Balance: Advancing Gender Equity and Workplace Performance*, San Francisco, CA: Jossey-Bass.

Reaney, R. (2012), 'Unequal access to "hot jobs" obstructs women's careers: Report', *Globe and Mail*, 17 November, B18.

Rennison, C.M. and S. Wenchans (2000), *Intimate Partner Violence*, Washington, DC: Department of Justice, Office of Justice Programs, Bureau of Justice Statistics.

Rogers, B. (1988), *Men Only: An Investigation into Men's Organizations*, London: Pandora.

Rosin, H. (2012), *The End of Men and the Rise of Women*, New York: Riverhead Books.

Rudman, L.A. (1998), 'Self-promotion as a risk factor for women: The costs and benefits of counter-stereotypical impression management', *Journal of Personality and Social Psychology*, **74**(3), 629–45.

Rudman, L.A. and P. Glick (1999), 'Feminized management and backlash against agentic women: The hidden costs to women of a kinder, gentler image of middle managers', *Journal of Personality and Social Psychology*, **77**(5), 1004–16.

Rudman, L.A. and P. Glick (2001), 'Proscriptive gender stereotypes and backlash toward agentic women', *Journal of Social Issues*, **57**(4), 743–62.

Rutherford, S. (2001), '"Are you going home already?" The long hours culture. Women managers and patriarchal cultures', *Time and Society*, **10**(2/3), 259–76.

Rutherford, S. (2002), 'Organizational cultures, women managers and exclusion', *Women in Management Review*, **16**(8), 127–39.

Rutherford, S. (2011), *Women's Work, Men's Cultures: Overcoming Resistance and Changing Organizational Cultures*, London: Palgrave Macmillan.

Saltzman, L.E., J.L. Fanslow, P.M. McMahon and G.A. Shelley (2003), *Intimate Partner Violence Surveillance: Uniform Definitions and Recommended Data Elements*, Atlanta, GA: National Center for Injury Prevention and Control.

Sandberg, S. (2013), *Lean In: Women, Work and the Will to Lead*, New York: Alfred Knopf.

Sax, L. (2007), *Boys Adrift: The Five Factors Driving the Growing Epidemic of Unmotivated Boys and Underachieving Men*, New York: Basic Books.

Schein, V. (1973), 'The relationship between sex role stereotypes and requisite management characteristics', *Journal of Applied Psychology*, **57**(2), 95–1000.

Sheppard, L.D. and K. Aquino (2013), 'Much ado about nothing? Observers' problematization of women's same-sex conflict at work', *Academy of Management Perspectives*, **27**(1), 52–62.

Silverstein, M.J and T.K. Sayre (2009a), 'The female economy', *Harvard Business Review*, **87**(9), 46–53.

Silverstein, M.J. and T.K. Sayre (2009b), *Women Want More: How to Capture your Share of the World's Largest Market*, New York: Harper Collins.

Simpson, R. (1996), 'Does an MBA help women? Career benefits of the MBA', *Gender, Work and Organization*, **3**(2), 115–21.

Simpson, R. (2006), 'Masculinity and management education: Feminizing the MBA', *Academy of Management Learning and Education*, **5**(2), 182–93.

Slaughter, A-M. (2012), 'Why women still can't have it all', *Atlantic*, July–August, 84–102.

Sostek, A. and S. Sherman (1977), 'Report on children of executives', *Behavioral Science*, **8**, August.

Stewart, J.B. (2011), 'A C.E.O.'s support system, aka husband', *New York Times*, 4 November 2011.

Stoker, J.I., M. Van der Velde and J. Lammers (2012), 'Factors relating to managerial stereotypes: The role of gender of the employee and the manager and management gender ratio', *Journal of Business Psychology*, **27**(1), 31–42.

Tannen, D. (1990), *You Just Don't Understand: Men and Women in Conversation*, New York: Morrow.

Tannenbaum, L. (2002), *Catfight: Women and Competition*, New York: Seven Stories Press.

The Telegraph (2013), 'Soldier who coordinated US Army sexual assault prevention accused of "abusive sexual contact"', 15 May, accessed 24 August 2013 at http://www.telegraph.co.uk/news/worldnews/northamerica/usa/10057955/Soldier-who-coordinated-US-Army-sexual-assault-prevention-accused-of-abusive-sexual-contact.html.

Thiruvadi, S. and W.H. Huang (2011), 'Audit committee gender differences and earnings management', *Gender and Management: An International Journal*, **26**(7), 483–98.

Tienari, J., S. Merilainen, C. Holgersson and R. Bendl (2013), 'And then there are none: On the exclusion of women in processes of executive search', *Gender in Management: An International Journal*, **28**(1), 43–62.

Tjaden, P. and N. Thoennes (2000), *Extent, Nature and Consequences of Intimate Partner Violence*, Washington, DC: US Department of Justice, National Institute of Justice.

Tolentino, S.R., S.L.D. Restubug, K.L. Scott, P.R.M. Garcia and R.L. Tang (2011), 'Bringing home to work: Intimate partner violence, perceived organizational support, and outcomes', paper presented at the Annual Meeting of the Academy of Management, San Antonio, TX, August.

Toronto Star (2013), 'Sex assault in U.S. military on the rise: Air Force's head of prevention accused of groping woman', 8 May, A12.

Tulk, C. (2013), 'The gender gap', *Toronto Star*, 8 March, A23.

Uzzi, B. and S. Dunlap (2012), 'Make your enemies your allies', *Harvard Business Review Magazine*, May.

Wacjman, J. (1998), *Managing like a Man*, Cambridge, UK: Polity Press.

Williams, J.C. (2012), *Reshaping the Work–Family Debate: Why Men and Class Matter*, Boston, MA: Harvard University Press.

Wilson, N., M. Wright and A. Altanlar (2013), 'The survival of newly-incorporated companies and founding director characteristics', *International Small Business Journal*, **31**, in press.

Wittenberg-Cox, A. (2010), *How Women Mean Business*, Chichester: John Wiley.

Wittenberg-Cox, A. (2012), 'Gender in the multicultural corporation', HBR blog, 22 June 2012.
Wittenberg-Cox, A. and A. Maitland (2008), *Why Women Mean Business: Understanding the Emergence of Our Next Economic Revolution*, New York: John Wiley.
Yoshima, M. and C. Dabby (2009), *Facts and Stats: Domestic Violence in Asian, Native Hawaiian and Pacific Islander Homes*, San Francisco, CA: API Institute on Domestic Violence APIA Health Forum.

PART II

Masculinity and its discontents

2. The gender role socialization of boys to men

Ronald F. Levant and Thomas J. Rankin

INTRODUCTION

The purpose of this chapter is to review the literature on the gender role socialization of boys into men. We first put this domain of research and scholarship into context by discussing the gender role strain paradigm, which is the most influential theoretical framework in the psychology of men and masculinity. Attention is then given to the core construct of the gender role strain paradigm: masculinity ideologies. We discuss the varieties of masculinity ideologies and dominant ideology that informs the socialization of boys into men. After considering the types of strain posited by the gender role strain paradigm, we focus on trauma strain, which we use to frame the review of the literature on early childhood gender role socialization. In this review we focus on emotion socialization, and consider the trauma experienced by many boys as they are influenced to conform to the traditional masculine norm of restrictive emotionality. This then sets the stage for a discussion of the normative male alexithymia hypothesis, which posits that men reared to conform to traditional masculine norms will have difficulty becoming aware of and verbalizing their emotional experiences.

THE GENDER ROLE STRAIN PARADIGM

The gender role strain paradigm (GRSP; Pleck, 1981, 1995) is the most influential theoretical frame of reference in the psychology of men and masculinity (Cochran, 2010). It is an empirically oriented social constructionist perspective, distinct in its predominantly quantitative empiricism from other social constructionist perspectives on masculinity that have emerged in fields such as sociology (Connell and Messerschmidt, 2005) and discursive psychology (Edley and Wetherell, 1997). The GRSP views gender roles as entities that can change, as opposed to immutable biological characteristics. In contrast to biological entities, gender roles are instead seen as psychologically and socially constructed entities that bring both advantages and disadvantages. This is not to say that biological differences between men and women do not exist; rather, the GRSP posits that those biological differences of sex do not encompass 'masculinity' and 'femininity'. Instead, masculinity and femininity are socially constructed from social, psychological, and biological experience.

While there are intersex and pre-operative transsexual persons, sex is mostly a dichotomous variable, wherein one is either male or female. Gender, on the other hand, can be measured in a variety of ways and is a continuous variable. For example, gender can be measured as a set of stereotypical personality traits associated with each sex, in terms of the endorsement of, or conformity to, traditional masculine or feminine norms, and by the conflict or stress that one experiences while conforming to traditional norms. When any such measure of gender is administered to both men and women, there will be two distributions, one for men and one for women, with typically small mean differences and a great deal of overlap. Hence, while men will typically score higher on variables associated with men and masculinity and women will score higher on those associated with women and femininity, there will be many cases in which some women score higher on variables associated with masculinity than some men, and in which men score higher on variables associated with femininity than some women. This highlights, again, that gender is different from sex.

Pleck offered the GRSP as an alternative to the older gender role identity paradigm (GRIP). The GRIP dominated research on masculinity for 50 years, from 1930 to 1980. That perspective assumed that people have a powerful psychological need to form a gender role identity that matches their biological sex; furthermore, optimal personality development required that the correct gender role identity was formed. How completely a person adopted this traditional gender role determined the extent to which that 'inherent' psychological need was met. In other words, the development of appropriate gender role identity could be viewed as a failure-prone process: failure for men to achieve an appropriate masculine gender role identity was thought to result in homosexuality, negative attitudes towards women, and/or defensive hypermasculinity.

The GRIP paradigm sprung from the same philosophical roots as the 'essentialist' view of sex roles, namely, that there is a clear masculine 'essence' that is historically invariant for men (Bohan, 1997). Pleck (1981) provided a convincing demonstration that the GRIP poorly accounted for the observed data in many landmark studies on personality development; furthermore, he showed that such studies often arbitrarily reinterpreted the meaning of the data. For example, one of the most important studies in the GRIP concerned the relationship between sex typing and adjustment (Mussen, 1961); Pleck (1981, p. 86) pointed out that 'if a measure ordinarily indicating good adjustment occurs in non-masculine males, it is arbitrarily reinterpreted to indicate poor adjustment'.

Rather than the GRIP's essentialist position, the GRSP proposed a variety of propositions that went against the GRIP's historically invariant perspective. In contrast to the GRIP, for example, the GRSP argued that contemporary gender roles are often contradictory and inconsistent, and that the proportion of persons who violate gender roles is high. The GRSP posited that violation of gender roles led to condemnation by others and negative psychological consequences for the man or woman who violated those gender roles. Furthermore, the GRSP proposed that because of those negative consequences, actual violations of gender roles or imagined violations of gender roles both led people to over-conform to gender roles. Proponents of the GRSP believed that violating gender roles had more severe consequences for males than for females, and that certain prescribed gender role traits (e.g., restrictive emotionality) are often dysfunctional. Finally, the GRSP pointed out that each sex experienced gender role strain in its paid work and family roles, and that historical change caused gender role strain (Pleck, 1981, 1995).

In the GRSP, gender ideologies were beliefs about the roles thought to be appropriate for either males or females. Those roles were operationally defined by gender role stereotypes and norms. The dominant gender ideologies influenced how parents, teachers, and peers socialized children, and thus how children thought, felt, and behaved in regard to gender-salient matters (Pleck et al., 1994; Levant, 1996). Specifically, through social interactions resulting in reinforcement, punishment, and observational learning, masculinity ideologies informed, encouraged, and constrained boys (and men) to conform to the prevailing male role norms by adopting certain socially sanctioned masculine behaviors and avoiding certain proscribed behaviors (Levant, 2011). Gender roles and gendered behavior were thus thought to be the result of social cognition and social influence processes, instructed by gender ideologies. As noted above, this paradigm sprung from the same philosophical roots as social constructionism, in which notions of 'masculinity' and 'femininity' were relational, socially constructed, and subject to change (Bohan, 1997).

MASCULINITY IDEOLOGIES

Masculinity Ideology

Thompson and Pleck (1995) proposed the term 'masculinity ideology' to characterize the core construct in the body of research assessing attitudes toward men and male roles. Masculinity ideology was a radically different construct from the older notion of masculine gender role identity. Masculine gender role identity arose out of the GRIP, and 'presumes that masculinity is rooted in actual differences between men and women' (Thompson and Pleck, 1995, p. 130). This approach has attempted to assess the personality *traits* more often associated with men than women, using such instruments as the Bem Sex Role Inventory (BSRI; Bem, 1974) and the Personal Attributes Questionnaire (PAQ; Spence and Helmreich, 1978).[1] In contrast, studies of masculinity ideology took a *normative* approach, in which masculinity was viewed as a socially constructed set of gender norms for men. Whereas the masculine male in the identity/trait approach is one who *possesses* particular personality traits, the traditional male in the ideology/normative approach 'is one who endorses the ideology that men *should* have sex-specific characteristics (and women should not)' (Thompson and Pleck, 1995, p. 131; original emphasis). Thompson and Pleck (1995) summarized the evidence supporting the proposition that gender role identity and gender ideology are independent constructs and have different correlates.

Based on his classic ethnographic study of masculinity ideology, Gilmore (1990, pp. 2–3; emphasis added) suggested that 'there is something almost generic, something repetitive, about the criteria of man-playing, that underlying the surface variations in emphasis or form are certain convergences in concepts, symbolizations, and exhortations of masculinity in many societies but – and this is important – *by no means in all*'. Hence, a common set of standards and expectations was associated with the male role throughout most (but not all) of the world. These similarities derive from the fact that men perform the same social roles across almost all cultures: procreation (father), provision (worker), and protection (soldier). Therefore, virtually all societies must socialize boys to develop the set of characteristics that are necessary to perform the behaviors embedded in those roles. The exceptions that Gilmore found were the Tahitians and the Semai, 'virtually androgynous cultures [which] raise questions about the universal need for masculinity in male development, and . . . suggest that cultural variables may outweigh nature in the masculinity puzzle' (p. 201).

This dominant masculinity ideology defined the social norms for the male gender role. It was postulated to uphold existing gender-based power structures in the western world, specifically those that privilege men, and most often upper class, white, heterosexual, able-bodied, Christian men. This hegemonic masculinity concept has undergirded men's collective dominance over women, marginalized men of color and lower-class men, and subjugated sexual minority men (Connell and Messerschmidt, 2005).

Traditional Masculinity Ideology

In the USA, 'traditional masculinity ideology' was the dominant set of norms before the deconstruction of gender that took place beginning in the late 1960s. Traditional masculinity ideology contained 'a *particular* constellation of standards and expectations that individually and jointly have various kinds of negative concomitants' (Pleck, 1995, p. 20; original emphasis). However, this is not to deny that there is a diversity of masculinity ideologies in the contemporary United States.

Traditional masculinity ideology was thought to be a multidimensional construct. David and Brannon (1976) identified four components of traditional masculinity ideology: that men should not be feminine ('no sissy stuff'); that men should strive to be respected for successful achievement ('the big wheel'); that men should never show weakness ('the sturdy oak') and that men should seek adventure and risk, even accepting violence if necessary ('give 'em hell'). These dimensions were assessed by the Brannon Masculinity Scale, the first instrument developed for the assessment of traditional masculinity ideology (Brannon and Juni, 1984).

Masculinity Ideolog*ies*

The GRSP asserted that there is no single standard for masculinity nor is there an unvarying masculinity ideology. Rather, since masculinity is a social construction, ideals of manhood have differed for men of different social classes, races, ethnic groups, sexual orientations, life stages, and historical eras. Following Brod (1987) we therefore speak of masculinity ideolog*ies*. However, rather than looking for a completely different set of norms for each group, examining masculinity ideologies involves searching for differences in overall endorsement of and in the weighting of the norms of masculinity (Smiler, 2004).

In support of this view, despite the near universality of the dominant form of masculinity ideology, differences in overall endorsement and in the weighting of the norms have been found. Differences have included dimensions such as age, generation within a family, ethnicity, race, nationality, social class, geographic region of residence, sex, sexual orientation, and disability status (Thompson and Pleck, 1986; Pleck et al., 1994;

Levant et al., 1996, 1998, 2003a, 2003b; Levant and Majors, 1997; Wu et al., 2001; Levant and Richmond, 2007). Some variations in masculinity norms may reflect mere differences in 'emphasis or form' (Gilmore, 1990, p. 3), whereas others may reflect substantive differences in norms.

In the USA, male-dominated power structures have been weakened to some degree in different subcultures by the influence of feminism. This has resulted in new variants of masculinity ideology. In addition, some cultural variations in masculinity ideology appear to be based upon historical adaptations. For example, the acceptability of women making more decisions in the home and having employment outside of the home in the African American community may be the by-product of slavery (e.g., forced separation of families) and economic necessity (Lazur and Majors, 1995; Watkins et al., 2010). Still others, such as the 'cool pose' of young inner city African American men, may be a form of resistance to their marginalization by hegemonic masculinity (Majors and Billson, 1992).

TYPES OF MALE GENDER ROLE STRAIN

The gender role strain paradigm stimulated research on three different types of male gender role strain (Pleck, 1995). Pleck called these three types 'discrepancy strain', 'dysfunction strain', and 'trauma strain'. Discrepancy strain resulted when a man failed to live up to his internalized manhood ideal, which, among contemporary adult males, was often a close approximation of the traditional code of masculinity. Dysfunction strain occurred even when a man fulfilled the requirements of masculine norms, since many normatively masculine characteristics have negative side-effects on both men themselves and on those close to them. Finally, trauma strain resulted from harsh experiences with gender role socialization. This chapter focuses on trauma strain because it is most directly connected to the socialization of boys into men.

Trauma Strain

The concept of trauma strain was initially applied to certain groups of men whose experiences with gender role strain were thought to be particularly harsh. This included men of color (Lazur and Majors, 1995), professional athletes (Messner, 1992), veterans (Brooks, 1990), and survivors of child abuse (Lisak, 1995). It was also recognized that gay and bisexual men were normatively traumatized by male gender role strain by virtue of growing up in a heterosexist society (Harrison, 1995; Sanchez et al., 2010). Furthermore, while certain classes of men may have actually experienced trauma strain, another perspective emerged in the 1990s that viewed socialization under traditional masculinity ideology as *inherently* traumatic (Levant and Pollack, 1995).

GENDER ROLE SOCIALIZATION: THE ORDEAL OF EMOTION SOCIALIZATION

Males start out life more emotionally expressive than females, due to what seem to be biologically based differences from females. For example, Haviland and Malatesta (1981) reviewed data from 12 studies (11 of which were of neonates) and concluded that male infants were more emotionally reactive and expressive than their female counterparts. Specifically, the infants in those studies startled more easily, became excited more quickly, had a lower tolerance for tension and frustration, became distressed more quickly, cried sooner and more often, and fluctuated more rapidly between emotional states. Furthermore, Cunningham and Shapiro (1984, cited in Brody and Hall, 1993) found that infant boys were judged to be more emotionally expressive than infant girls; this was true even when the judges were misinformed about the infant's actual sex, thereby controlling for the effects of gender-role stereotyping on the part of judges. Finally, boys remained more emotional than girls at least until six months of age: Weinberg (1992, p. vii) found that six-month-old boys exhibited 'significantly more joy and anger, more positive vocalizations, fussiness, and crying, [and] more gestural signals directed towards the mother . . . than girls'.

Despite this initially higher level of emotional expressivity, boys in US culture were taught to tune out, suppress, and channel their emotions, whereas the emotion socialization of females encouraged their expressivity. Specifically, verbal expression of girls was different than that of boys by age two, while facial expression was different by age six. Dunn et al. (1987) found that two-year-old females refer to feeling states more frequently than do two-year-old males. Buck (1977) assessed the ability of mothers of four- to six-year-old boys and girls to accurately identify their child's emotional responses to a series of slides by observing their child's facial expressions on a TV monitor. The older the boy, the less expressive his face, and the harder it was for his mother to tell what he was feeling. Buck found no such correlation among the girls: their mothers were able to identify their emotions no matter what their age. Buck (p. 234) concluded that between the ages of four and six, 'boys apparently inhibit and mask their overt response to emotion to an increasing extent, while girls continue to respond relatively freely' (see also Allen and Haccoun, 1976;

Balswick and Avertt, 1977; Stapley and Haviland, 1989; Brody and Hall, 1993).

How can we account for this 'crossover in emotional expression' (Haviland and Malatesta, 1981, p. 16), such that boys start out more emotional than girls and wind up much less so? Using a social learning model, Levant and Kopecky (1995) proposed that four socialization influences result in the suppression and channeling of male emotionality. The mechanisms of emotion socialization include selective reinforcement, direct teaching, differential life experiences, and punishment. These mechanisms are employed by (1) mothers, (2) fathers, (3) both parents, and (4) peer groups:

1   *Mothers* work harder to manage their more excitable and emotional male infants (Tronick and Cohn, 1989; Kuebli and Fivush, 1992; Garner et al., 1997). They 'employ more contingent responding (and particularly contingent smiling) in playing with their sons. Mothers may go to special lengths to ensure that their sons are contented' (Haviland and Malatesta, 1981, p. 202). Mothers also control their own expressivity to 'preclude upsetting their [sons'] more fragile emotional equilibria' (ibid.). In contrast, mothers expose their infant daughters to a wider range of emotions than they do their sons (Malatesta et al., 1989).

2   *Fathers* take an active interest in their children after the thirteenth month of life (Lamb, 1977), and from that point on socialize their toddler sons and daughters along gender-stereotyped lines (Lamb et al., 1979; Greif et al., 1981; Siegal, 1987; Schell and Gleason, 1989; Garner et al., 1997), particularly when the father himself adhered to highly stereotyped beliefs about gender (Plant et al., 2000). Fathers interact more with infant sons than they do with daughters (Lamb, 1977). With older children, fathers engage in more verbal rough-housing with sons, and tend to speak more about emotions with daughters (Greif et al., 1981; Schell and Gleason, 1989). Fathers also express more disapproval to sons who engage in gender-inappropriate play (Langlois and Downs, 1980). Fathers focus greater attention on four-year-old to six-year-old girls' sadness and anxiety, while focusing more attention on boys' anger, thereby socializing each sex to behave in gender-stereotyped ways (Chaplin et al., 2005). Many adult men that the first author has counseled recalled experiences where their fathers made them feel deeply ashamed of expressing either vulnerable (i.e., sadness or fear) or caring/connection emotions (i.e., warmth or affection). This is consistent with research showing that fathers reward girls for expressing sadness or fear, while punishing

boys for expressing sadness or fear (Garside and Klimes-Dougan, 2002).

3 *Both parents* participate in the gender-differentiated development of language for emotions. While both mothers and fathers engage in conversations with their children about emotions, mothers' conversations about emotions are typically longer than those of fathers; in addition, mothers use more emotion words with their children than do fathers, and both mothers and fathers focus more on discussing feelings of sadness with girls than with boys (Fivush et al., 2000). Parents discourage their sons from learning to express vulnerable emotions; and, while they encourage their daughters to learn to express their vulnerable and caring/connection emotions, they discourage their expression of anger and aggression (Kuebli and Fivush, 1992; Casey and Fuller, 1994; Eisenberg et al., 1998).

It should be noted that females' language superiority also plays a role in their greater ability to express emotions verbally (Brody and Hall, 1993). Dunn et al. (1987) found that mothers used more emotion words when speaking with daughters than they did with sons. Fivush (1989) found that mothers spoke more about sadness with daughters than sons, and only spoke about anger with sons. With daughters, mothers discussed the experience of the emotion, whereas with sons they discussed the 'causes and consequences of emotions', which would serve to help sons learn to control their emotions. Greif et al. (1981) had parents 'read' stories to their children using wordless books, and videotaped and transcribed their conversations. Mothers talked about anger twice as frequently with sons as compared to daughters. Finally, Fuchs and Thelen (1988) found that school-aged sons expected their parents to react negatively to the expression of sadness, whereas school-aged daughters expected their mothers to react more positively to the expression of sadness than they would to anger.

Furthermore, both parents' participation in socializing boys to restrict their expression of emotion has consequences for boys' behavioral problems: both maternal and paternal negative reactions to boys' expression of negative emotions were associated with higher internalizing behaviors for boys (Engle and McElwain, 2011). Mothers also rewarded expression of negative emotions more than fathers did, while fathers were more likely to ignore negative emotions; fathers were likewise more punitive with their sons' expression of anger than were mothers (Klimes-Dougan et al., 2007). In general, boys are worse at emotional regulation than girls are (Bocknek et al., 2009), perhaps in part due to the factors discussed above.

4   Sex-segregated *peer groups* complete the job. Young girls typically
     play with one or two other girls, and their play consists of maintaining
     the relationship (by minimizing conflict and hostility, and maximizing
     agreement and cooperation) and telling each other secrets, thus fos-
     tering their learning skills of empathy, emotional self-awareness, and
     emotional expressivity. Whereas at age four, boys and girls display
     similar understandings of anger and sadness, by age seven – when
     peer groups become especially important – girls have a more nuanced
     understanding of both emotions and a greater ability to differenti-
     ate the causes of sadness versus anger (Hughes and Dunn, 2002).
     In contrast, young boys typically play in larger groups in structured
     games, in which skills such as learning to play by the rules, teamwork,
     stoicism, toughness, and competition are learned (Lever, 1976; Paley,
     1984; Maccoby, 1990). Another study (Crombie and DesJardins,
     1993, cited in Brody, 1994) found that boys experience direct com-
     petition in their play half of the time, whereas girls experience it very
     infrequently (less than 1 percent of the time). Boy culture is also noto-
     riously cruel to boys who violate male role norms, such as expressing
     vulnerable emotions, showing affection, or being unwilling to fight
     (Krugman, 1995).

The suppression and channeling of male emotionality by mothers,
fathers, and peer groups has several major consequences. First, men
develop a form of empathy that Levant and Kopecky (1995) referred to
as 'action empathy', which can be defined as the ability to see things from
another person's point of view, and predict what they will *do*. On the other
hand, men do not develop (as fully as do women) emotional empathy,
which can be defined as taking another person's perspective and being
able to know how they *feel* (Hall, 1978; Eisenberg and Lennon, 1983;
Brody and Hall, 1993). This empathy difference begins in childhood: for
example, girls reported feeling greater levels of personal emotional distress
than did boys when asked to imagine themselves in a victim's place for
morally relevant stories (e.g., imagining a child stealing another child's
ball) (Garner, 2012).

Second, through the suppression of male emotionality, men become
strangers to their own emotional life (Allen and Haccoun, 1976; Balswick
and Avertt, 1977; Stapley and Haviland, 1989; Brody and Hall, 1993;
Levant and Kopecky, 1995). Third, men experience and express more
aggression than women (Frodi et al., 1977; Eagly and Steffen, 1986) and
also tend to transform their vulnerable emotions into anger, which is
expressed aggressively (Long, 1987; Levant and Kopecky, 1995). Thus,
under the influence of traditional masculinity ideology, the emotion

socialization of boys can be an ordeal with traumatic consequences. Levant (1992) specifically proposed that mild-to-moderate alexithymia may result from the normative emotion socialization of boys, a process informed by traditional masculinity ideologies. This is the normative male alexithymia hypothesis, to which we now turn.

The Normative Male Alexithymia Hypothesis

Literally, alexithymia means 'without words for emotions'. Sifneos (1967) originally used the term to describe the extreme difficulty that certain psychiatric patients had in identifying and describing their feelings. This pattern was particularly evident in patients with psychosomatic illnesses, PTSD, substance use disorders, and chronic pain disorders (Levant et al., 2009a). The Toronto Alexithymia Scale (TAS; Bagby et al., 1994) has been the primary instrument used to measure alexithymia in clinical populations (Eid and Boucher, 2012).

In addition to the appearance of alexithymia in clinical populations, some symptoms of alexithymia have been seen in non-clinical settings; typically, symptoms in those settings have involved variability along a continuum of alexithymia symptoms. As a result, Levant (1992) proposed the 'normative male alexithymia' (NMA) hypothesis to account for a socialized pattern of restrictive emotionality influenced by traditional masculinity ideology. This hypothesis was that many men were discouraged as boys from expressing and talking about their emotions by parents, peers, teachers, or coaches – and that some were even punished for doing so. Therefore, those men neither developed a vocabulary for, nor an awareness of, many of their emotions.

The NMA hypothesis stemmed from work with research participants in the Boston University Fatherhood Project (Levant and Kelly, 1989), as well as with clients in Levant's clinical practice. In both of those settings, it took great difficulty and practice for many men to use words to describe their emotional states. Specifically, those men showed great deficits in identifying and expressing vulnerable feelings (such as sadness or fear) or feelings of attachment (such as fondness or caring). It may be the case that in certain environments – such as highly competitive ones – restricted emotionality may be adaptive in some ways. However, in most circumstances, alexithymic men often reported significant difficulties in their personal lives and presented with a variety of problems. These problems included substance abuse, sexual addiction, marital difficulties, domestic violence, and estrangement from their children (Levant and Kopecky, 1995).

Levant's clinical observations are consistent with a central tenet of the gender role strain paradigm (GRSP): namely, that men are influenced by society inasmuch as they were raised as boys to follow the norms of traditional masculinity. As was discussed above, one normative masculine role requirement is the restriction of emotional expression. Levant (1992, 1995, 1998) drew on the GRSP in theorizing that mild-to-moderate forms of alexithymia would afflict men more frequently according to the degree to which their socialization as boys was informed by traditional masculinity ideology. In other words, the larger impact that traditional masculinity ideology had on a man's upbringing, the larger chance that he would develop alexithymia. Indeed, the empirical research shows an association between the endorsement of traditional masculinity ideology and alexithymia in men: even after controlling for demographic differences, traditional masculinity ideology accounted for unique variance in male alexithymia (Levant et al., 2003b).

Males are not the only ones to experience alexithymia, however – females can also display alexithymic symptoms. Levant et al. (2006) reviewed 45 published studies that examined gender differences in alexithymia. Thirteen of the studies used a psychiatric or medical sample, while 32 studies were non-clinical (predominantly college students). Few studies using clinical samples found gender differences; however, the non-clinical samples did present some gender differences in alexithymia. Specifically, 17 of the 32 studies found males to be more alexithymic than females; one study found females to be more alexithymic than males; and 14 studies found no differences between males and females.

This narrative review, though, did not resolve the *magnitude* of the gender difference in alexithymia. Nor did it determine the extent of the difference between clinical and non-clinical samples, if any. To answer those questions, a meta-analysis of the alexithymia literature was required; this meta-analysis was conducted in Levant et al. (2009a). There was empirical support for gender differences: an effect size estimate based on 41 existing samples found consistent, although expectedly small, differences in mean alexithymia between women and men (*Hedges' d* = 0.22). In short, men exhibited higher levels of alexithymia. There were no significant moderator effects for clinical versus non-clinical population, though there were relatively few clinical samples; likewise, there were no moderator effects for alexithymia measure used, although there were relatively few non-TAS measures included in the meta-analysis.

Since the TAS does not specifically address normative male alexithymia, Levant et al. (2006) developed the Normative Male Alexithymia Scale. Evidence supporting the validity of the scale included analyses of gender differences, relations with other instruments, and incremental validity in predicting masculinity ideology. In addition, a clinical intervention to address NMA is currently underway: Levant (1998, 2006) developed a psychoeducational program for treating NMA, which was recently manualized as Alexithymia Reduction Treatment (ART). Assessment in a pilot study was promising (Levant et al., 2009b). Therefore, a randomized clinical trial of the efficacy of ART is planned; the study will examine the remediation of normative male alexithymia, as well as improving the uptake of therapy for male veterans suffering from PTSD.

NOTE

1. Although BSRI and the PAQ were initially intended to assess the personality traits differentially associated with men and women, subsequent research raised serious questions about the appropriateness of using the BSRI as a measure of self-perceived gender-linked personality traits (Choi et al., 2008), and the scales of the PAQ have been recast as Masculinity/Instrumentality and Femininity/Expressiveness (Helmreich et al., 1981).

REFERENCES

Allen, J.G. and D.M. Haccoun (1976), 'Sex differences in emotionality: A multidimensional approach', *Human Relations*, **29**(8), 711–22.
Bagby, R.M., J.D.A. Parker and G.J. Taylor (1994), 'The twenty-item Toronto Alexithymia Scale: I. Item selection and cross validation of the factor structure', *Journal of Psychosomatic Research*, **38**(3), 23–32.
Balswick, J. and C.P. Avertt (1977), 'Differences in expressiveness: Gender, interpersonal orientation, and perceived parental expressiveness as contributing factors', *Journal of Marriage and the Family*, **39**(1), 121–7.
Bem, S.L. (1974), 'The measurement of psychological androgyny', *Journal of Personality and Social Psychology*, **42**(4), 155–62.
Bocknek, E.L., H.E. Brophy-Herb and M. Banerjee (2009), 'Effects of parental supportiveness on toddlers' emotion regulation over the first three years of life in a low-income African-American sample', *Infant Mental Health Journal*, **30**(5), 452–76.
Bohan, J.S. (1997), 'Regarding gender: Essentialism, constructionism, and feminist psychology', in M.M. Gergen and S.N. Davis (eds), *Toward a New Psychology of Gender*, New York: Routledge.
Brannon, R. and S. Juni (1984), 'A scale for measuring attitudes about masculinity', *Psychological Documents*, **14**(1), 67–74.
Brod, H. (1987), *The Making of the Masculinities: The New Men's Studies*, Boston, MA: Unwin Hyman.
Brody, L. (1994), 'Gender, emotional expression, and parent–child boundaries', in R. Kavanaugh, B. Zimmerberg-Glick and S. Fein (eds), *Emotion: Interdisciplinary Perspectives*, New Jersey: Lawrence Erlbaum Associates.
Brody, L. and J. Hall (1993), 'Gender and emotion', in M. Lewis and J.M. Haviland (eds), *Handbook of Emotions*, New York: Guilford, pp. 447–60.

Brooks, G.R. (1990), 'Post-Vietnam gender role strain: A needed concept?', *Professional Psychology: Research and Practice*, **21**(1), 18–25.

Buck, R. (1977), 'Non-verbal communication of affect in preschool children: Relationships with personality and skin conductance', *Journal of Personality and Social Psychology*, **35**(4), 225–36.

Casey, R.J. and L.L. Fuller (1994), 'Maternal regulation of children's emotions', *Journal of Nonverbal Behavior*, **18**(1), 57–89.

Chaplin, T.M., P.M. Cole and C. Zahn-Waxler (2005), 'Parental socialization of emotion expression: Gender differences and relations to child adjustment', *Emotion*, **5**(1), 80–88.

Choi, N., D.R. Fuqua and J.L. Newman (2008), 'The Bem Sex-Role Inventory: Continuing theoretical problems', *Educational and Psychological Measurement*, **68**(5), 881–900.

Cochran, S.V. (2010), 'Emergence and development of the psychology of men and masculinity', in J.C. Chrisler and D.R. McCreary (eds), *Handbook of Gender Research in Psychology. Vol. 1: Gender Research in General and Experimental Psychology*, New York: Springer, pp. 43–58.

Connell, R.W. and J.W. Messerschmidt (2005), 'Hegemonic masculinity: Rethinking the concept', *Gender and Society*, **19**(6), 829–59.

Crombie, G. and M. DesJardins (1993), 'Predictors of gender: The relative importance of children's play, games, and personality characteristics', presented at the Biennial Meeting of the Society for Research in Child Development, New Orleans.

Cunningham, J. and L. Shapiro (1984), 'Infant affective expression as a function of infant and adult gender', unpublished manuscript, Brandeis University.

David, D. and R. Brannon (1976) (eds), *The Forty-nine Percent Majority: The Male Sex Role*, Reading, MA: Addison-Wesley.

Dunn, J., I. Bretherton and P. Munn (1987), 'Conversations about feeling states between mothers and their children', *Developmental Psychology*, **23**(1), 132–9.

Eagly, A.H. and V.J. Steffen (1986), 'Gender and aggressive behavior: A meta-analytic review of the social psychological literature', *Psychological Bulletin*, **100**(3), 309–30.

Edley, N. and M. Wetherell (1997), 'Jockeying for position: The construction of masculine identities', *Discourse and Society*, **8**(2), 203–17.

Eid, P. and S. Boucher (2012), 'Alexithymia and dyadic adjustment in intimate relationships: Analyses using the actor partner interdependence model', *Journal of Social and Clinical Psychology*, **31**(10), 1095–111.

Eisenberg, N. and R. Lennon (1983), 'Sex differences in empathy and related capacities', *Psychological Bulletin*, **94**(1), 100–31.

Eisenberg, N., A. Cumberland and T.L. Spinrad (1998), 'Parental socialization of emotion', *Psychological Inquiry*, **9**(4), 241–73.

Engle, J.M. and N.L. McElwain (2011), 'Parental reactions to toddlers' negative emotions and child negative emotionality as correlates of problem behavior at the age of three', *Social Development*, **20**(2), 251–71.

Fivush, R. (1989), 'Exploring sex differences in the emotional content of mother child conversations about the past', *Sex Roles*, **20**(11/12), 675–91.

Fivush, R., M.A. Brotman, J.P. Buckner and S.H. Goodman (2000), 'Gender differences in parent–child emotion narratives', *Sex Roles*, **42**(3–4), 233–53.

Frodi, A., J. Macaulay and P.R. Thome (1977), 'Are women always less aggressive than men: A review of the experimental literature', *Psychological Bulletin*, **84**(4), 634–60.

Fuchs, D. and M. Thelen (1988), 'Children's expected interpersonal consequences of communicating their affective state and reported likelihood of expression', *Child Development*, **59**(5), 1314–22.

Garner, P.W. (2012), 'Children's emotional responsiveness and sociomoral understanding and associations with mothers' and fathers' socialization practices', *Infant Mental Health Journal*, **33**(1), 95–106.

Garner, P.W., S. Robertson and G. Smith (1997), 'Preschool children's emotional expressions with peers: The roles of gender and emotion socialization', *Sex Roles*, **36**(11–12), 675–91.

Garside, R.B. and B. Klimes-Dougan (2002), 'Socialization of discrete negative emotions: Gender differences and links with psychological distress', *Sex Roles*, **47**(3–4), 115–28.

Gilmore, D. (1990), *Manhood in the Making: Cultural Concepts of Masculinity*, New Haven, CT: Yale University Press.

Greif, E.B., M. Alvarez and K. Ulman (1981), 'Recognizing emotions in other people: Sex differences in socialization', paper presented at meeting of the Society for Research in Child Development, Boston, MA.

Hall, J.A. (1978), 'Gender effects in decoding nonverbal cues', *Psychological Bulletin*, **85**(4), 845–57.

Harrison, J. (1995), 'Roles, identities, and sexual orientation: Homosexuality, heterosexuality, and bisexuality', in R.F. Levant and W.S. Pollack (eds), *A New Psychology of Men*, New York: Basic Books, pp. 359–82.

Haviland, J.J. and C.Z. Malatesta (1981), 'The development of sex differences in nonverbal signals: Fallacies, facts, and fantasies', in C. Mayo and N.M. Henly (eds), *Gender and Non-verbal Behavior*, New York: Springer-Verlag, pp. 183–208.

Helmreich, R.L., J.T. Spence and J.A. Wilhelm (1981), 'A psychometric analysis of the Personal Attributes Questionnaire', *Sex Roles*, **7**(11), 1097–108.

Hughes, C. and J. Dunn (2002), '"When I say a naughty word": A longitudinal study of young children's accounts of anger and sadness in themselves and close others', *British Journal of Developmental Psychology*, **20**(4), 515–35.

Klimes-Dougan, B., A.E. Brand, C. Zahn-Waxler, B. Usher, P.D. Hastings, K. Kendziora and R.B. Garside (2007), 'Parental emotion socialization in adolescence: Differences in sex, age and problem status', *Social Development*, **16**(2), 326–42.

Krugman, S. (1995), 'Male development and the transformation of shame', in R.F. Levant and W.S. Pollack (eds), *A New Psychology of Men*, New York: Basic Books, pp. 91–126.

Kuebli, J. and R. Fivush (1992), 'Gender differences in parent–child conversations about past emotions', *Sex Roles*, **27**(11–12), 683–98.

Lamb, M.E. (1977), 'The development of parental preferences in the first two years of life', *Sex Roles*, **3**(5), 475–97.

Lamb, M.E., M.J. Owen and L. Chase-Lansdale (1979), 'The father daughter relationship: Past, present, and future', in C.B. Knopp and M. Kirkpatrick (eds), *Becoming Female*, New York: Plenum, pp. 89–112.

Langlois, J.H. and A.C. Downs (1980), 'Mother, fathers, and peers as socialization agents of sex-typed play behaviors in young children', *Child Development*, **51**(4), 1217–47.

Lazur, R.F. and R. Majors (1995), 'Men of color: Ethnocultural variations of male gender role strain', in R.F. Levant and W.S. Pollack (eds), *A New Psychology of Men*, New York: Basic Books.

Levant, R. (1992), 'Toward the reconstruction of masculinity', *Journal of Family Psychology*, **5**(3–4), 379–402.

Levant, R.F. (1995), 'Toward the reconstruction of masculinity', in R.F. Levant and W.S. Pollack (eds), *A New Psychology of Men*, New York: Basic Books, pp. 229–51.

Levant, R. (1996), 'The new psychology of men', *Professional Psychology*, **27**(3), 259–65.

Levant, R. (1998), 'Desperately seeking language: Understanding, assessing and treating normative male alexithymia', in W. Pollack and R. Levant (eds), *New Psychotherapy for Men*, New York: John Wiley and Sons, pp. 35–56.

Levant, R.F. (2006), *Effective Psychotherapy with Men* (DVD and Viewers' Guide), San Francisco, CA: Psychotherapy.net.

Levant, R.F. (2011), 'Research in the psychology of men and masculinity using the gender role strain paradigm as a framework', *American Psychologist*, **66**(8), 762–76.

Levant, R.F. and J. Kelly (1989), *Between Father and Child*, New York: Viking.

Levant, R.F. and G. Kopecky (1995), *Masculinity Reconstructed: Changing the Rules of Manhood: at Work, in Relationships and in Family Life*, New York: Dutton.

Levant, R.F. and R.G. Majors (1997), 'An investigation into variations in the construction of the male gender role among young African American and European American women and men', *Journal of Gender, Culture, and Health*, **2**, 33–43.

Levant, R.F. and W.S. Pollack (eds) (1995), *A New Psychology of Men*, New York: Basic Books.

Levant, R.F. and K. Richmond (2007), 'A review of research on masculinity ideologies using the Male Role Norms Inventory', *Journal of Men's Studies*, **15**(2), 130–46.

Levant, R.F., R.G. Majors and M.L. Kelley (1998), 'Masculinity ideology among young African American and European American women and men in different regions of the United States', *Cultural Diversity and Mental Health*, **4**(3), 227–36.

Levant, R.F., R. Wu and J. Fischer (1996), 'Masculinity ideology: A comparison between U.S. and Chinese young men and women', *Journal of Gender, Culture, and Health*, **1**(3), 217–20.

Levant, R.F., R.J. Hall, C. Williams and N.T. Hasan (2009a), 'Gender differences in alexithymia: A meta-analysis', *Psychology of Men and Masculinity*, **10**(3), 190–203.

Levant, R.F., M.J. Halter, E. Hayden and C. Williams (2009b), 'The efficacy of Alexithymia Reduction Treatment: A pilot study', *Journal of Men's Studies*, **17**(1), 75–84.

Levant, R.F., A.C. Cuthbert, K. Richmond, A. Sellers, A. Matveev, O. Matina and M. Soklovsky (2003a), 'Masculinity ideology among Russian and U.S. young men and women and its relationship to unhealthy lifestyle habits among young Russian men', *Psychology of Men and Masculinity*, **4**(1), 26–36.

Levant, R.F., K. Richmond, R.G. Majors, J.E. Inclan, J.M. Rossello, M. Heesacker and A. Sellars (2003b), 'A multicultural investigation of masculinity ideology and alexithymia', *Psychology of Men and Masculinity*, **4**(2), 91–9.

Levant, R.F., G.E. Cook, S. Good, J. O'Neil, K.B. Smalley, K.A. Owen and K. Richmond (2006), 'Validation of the Normative Male Alexithymia Scale: Measurement of a gender-linked syndrome', *Psychology of Men and Masculinity*, **7**(4), 212–24.

Lever, J. (1976), 'Sex differences in the games children play', *Social Work*, **23**(4), 78–87.

Lisak, D. (1995), 'Integrating gender analysis in psychotherapy with male survivors of abuse', paper presented at the 103rd Annual Convention of the American Psychological Association, New York.

Long, D. (1987), 'Working with men who batter', in M. Scher, M. Stevens, G. Good and G.A. Eichenfield (eds), *Handbook of Counseling and Psychotherapy with Men*, Newbury Park, CA: Sage, pp. 305–20.

Maccoby, E.E. (1990), 'Gender and relationships: A developmental account', *American Psychologist*, **45**(4), 513–20.

Majors, R. and J.M. Billson (1992), *Cool Pose: The Dilemmas of Black Manhood in America*, New York: Lexington Books.

Malatesta, C.Z., C. Culver, J. Tesman and B. Shephard (1989), 'The development of emotion expression during the first two years of life', *Monographs of the Society for Research in Child Development*, **54**(1–2), 1–104.

Messner, M.A. (1992), *Power at Play: Sports and the Problem of Masculinity*, Boston, MA: Beacon Press.

Mussen, P. (1961), 'Some antecedents and consequents of masculine sex typing in adolescent boys', *Psychological Monographs*, **75**(2), 1–24.

Paley, V.G. (1984), *Boys and Girls: Superheroes in the Doll Corner*, Chicago: University of Chicago Press.

Plant, E.A., J.S. Hyde, D. Keltner and P.G. Divine (2000), 'The gender stereotyping of emotions', *Psychology of Women Quarterly*, **24**(1), 81–92.

Pleck, J.H. (1981), *The Myth of Masculinity*, Cambridge, MA: MIT Press.

Pleck, J.H. (1995), 'The gender role strain paradigm: An update', in R.F. Levant and W.S. Pollack (eds), *A New Psychology of Men*, New York: Basic Books, pp. 11–32.

Pleck, J.H., F.L. Sonenstein and L.C. Ku (1994), 'Problem behaviors and masculinity ideology in adolescent males', in R.D. Ketterlinus and M.E. Lamb (eds), *Adolescent Problem Behaviors: Issues and Research*, Hillsdale, NJ: Erlbaum, pp. 165–86.

Sanchez, F.J., J.S. Westerfeld, W.M. Liu and E. Vilain (2010), 'Masculine gender role conflict and negative feelings about being gay', *Professional Psychology Research and Practice*, **41**(2), 104–11.

Schell, A. and J.B. Gleason (1989), 'Gender differences in the acquisition of the vocabulary of emotion', paper presented at the annual meeting of the American Association of Applied Linguistics, Washington, DC.

Siegal, M. (1987), 'Are sons and daughters treated more differently by fathers than by mothers?', *Developmental Review*, **7**, 183–209.

Sifneos, P.E. (1967), 'Clinical observations on some patients suffering from a variety of psychosomatic diseases', *Proceedings of the Seventh European Conference on Psychosomatic Research*, Basel: Kargel.

Smiler, A.P. (2004), 'Thirty years after the discovery of gender: Psychological concepts and measures of masculinity', *Sex Roles*, **50**(1–2), 15–26.

Spence, J.T. and R.L. Helmreich (1978), *Masculinity and Femininity: Their Psychological Dimensions, Correlates, and Antecedents*, Austin, TX: University of Texas Press.

Stapley, J.C. and J.M. Haviland (1989), 'Beyond depression: Gender differences in normal adolescents' emotional experiences', *Sex Roles*, **20**(5–6), 295–308.

Thompson, E.H. and J.H. Pleck (1986), 'The structure of male norms', *American Behavioral Scientist*, **29**(5), 531–43.

Thompson, E.H. and J.H. Pleck (1995), 'Masculinity ideology: A review of research instrumentation on men and masculinities', in R.F. Levant and W.S. Pollack (eds), *A New Psychology of Men*, New York: Basic Books, pp. 129–63.

Tronick, E.Z. and J.F. Cohn (1989), 'Infant–mother face-to-face interaction: Age and gender differences in coordination and the occurrence of miscoordination', *Child Development*, **60**(1), 85–92.

Watkins, D.C., R. Walker and D.M. Griffith (2010), 'A meta-study of black male mental health and well-being', *Journal of Black Psychology*, **36**(3), 303–30.

Weinberg, M.K. (1992), 'Sex differences in 6-month-old infants' affect and behavior: Impact on maternal caregiving', doctoral dissertation, University of Massachusetts.

Wu, R., R.F. Levant and A. Sellers (2001), 'The influence of sex and social development on masculinity ideology of Chinese undergraduate students', *Psychological Science*, **24**, 365–6.

3. Taking the obvious apart: critical approaches to men, masculinities, and the gendered dynamics of leadership

David L. Collinson and Jeff Hearn

INTRODUCTION

For centuries and across many cultural traditions, the highly masculine and masculinized image of the heroic man has informed, shaped and characterized leadership practices and theories. The continuing dominance of men in leadership and leadership positions appears 'normal' or 'natural', and largely escapes critical analysis or commentary, even in progressive forums. Assumptions about the 'great man' of history (Carlyle, 1841; Hook, 1945) have defined who could be a leader, even who is a 'born leader', what a leader does and how they might enact leadership. Equally importantly, they have also specified, implicitly or explicitly, who would be excluded from leadership positions.

In contemporary organizations and societies, power, authority, and status are still frequently the preserve of particular men and specific masculinities. Men continue to predominate in senior organizational roles in ways that, in turn, often express and validate their masculinities and identities, while women's voices and identities are subordinated or excluded, especially at the highest leadership levels. Although in some countries women have increasingly entered middle management and certain well-established professions in recent years, this is far from universally so in all sectors and all parts of the world. Moreover, even when occupying leadership positions, women may still often be identified and marked as 'women leaders' or 'female leaders', and indeed their leadership may be seen and evaluated in relation to, typically as similar to or different from, more established, historical forms of men's leadership.

Assumptions embedded in many of the most influential forms of leadership, such as bureaucratic, charismatic and transformational variants, remain heavily saturated with dominant masculinity/ies. In the particular case of transformational leadership, this is especially ironic given the extensive debate on some women's tendencies towards and expertise in this specific leadership style, in contrast with transactional leadership. At the same time, men's status and power in the workplace has often reinforced their authority and control at home. The masculine ideal of the heroic leader that has predominated in the 'public' sphere of paid work and employment has often reflected and reinforced the male family breadwinner identity in the 'private' world of domesticity and the family. This is even the case with the long history of women's paid work and work outside the home, especially amongst working class, minority ethnic, racialized, migrant and rural women. These two sources of heroic masculine power and identity – home and paid work – typically reinforce each other. The power and control of (men) leaders and managers is often sustained by both the gendered segregation of jobs and the subordination of domestic labour (Hearn and Niemistö, 2012).

Before examining the dynamics of leadership in more detail and as a final word of introduction, we need to note that the relationship of 'leadership' and 'management' is complex and variable. There are several issues here: leadership and management framed as the practice of formal leaders/ managers or informal leaders/managers; leadership and management understood in terms of individuals' actions or as an organizational, social or political process(es); managers seen as leaders, or not, and vice versa; management seen as leadership, or not, and vice versa. In addition, there are significant cultural and linguistic differences in understandings of leadership and management, and their interrelations. Take, for example, the case of Finland where:

> [i]n Finnish, the term often used corresponding to 'management' is a generic term 'johtaminen', referring to both leading and managing; however, the exact meaning of the term compared to the English term remains somewhat obscure. A corresponding more accurate translation of 'management' into Finnish is reached by referring to 'management of issues', 'asioiden johtaminen'. 'Leadership' in Finnish is quite unproblematically translated as 'johtajuus', also often referring to the leading of people (Lämsä and Hautala, 2005). (Husu et al., 2011, p. vi)

Thus, the very ideas of 'leadership' and 'management', let alone other related notions, such as 'organizational control' or 'corporate strategy', are not innocent or transparent terms, but are culturally and linguistically variable in meaning and impact.

Against this general background, a wide range of critical studies highlight how gender, men and masculinities are important but frequently neglected features of organizational and societal leadership dynamics. So what are the implications of critical studies of men and masculinities for understanding the gendered dynamics of leadership? To begin to answer our own question, we very briefly outline some features of recent critical studies on men and masculinities (CSMM).

CRITICAL STUDIES ON MEN AND MASCULINITIES

The growth of critical studies on men and masculinities over recent decades (Kimmel et al., 2005; Flood et al., 2007; Cornwall et al., 2011) has considerable implications for how men, masculinities and leadership might be understood and analysed. CSMM is a wide-ranging set of perspectives that have a specific, rather than an implicit or incidental, focus on explicitly gendering of men and masculinities, in the light of feminist, gay and other critical gender scholarship. At the risk of generalization, CSMM see men and masculinities as socially constructed, produced, reproduced, and variable and changing across time (history) and space (culture), within and across societies, and through life courses and biographies. Relations, albeit differentially, to gendered power, and both the material and the discursive are emphasized in analysis, along with intersections of gender with other social divisions (Connell et al., 2005, p. 3). In our own approach, we favour CSMM that are historical, cultural, relational, materialist, deconstructive and anti-essentialist (Hearn and Pringle, 2006).

One of the most important set of influences on CSMM has come from what may be called 'masculinities theory', especially as propounded by Connell and colleagues (Carrigan et al., 1985; Connell, 1995; Connell and Messerschmidt, 2005). This broad theory is founded on: a power-laden concept of masculinities; emphasis on unequal relations between men, as well as men's unequal relations to women; attention to gay scholarship and sexual hierarchies; distinguishing hegemonic, complicit, subordinated and marginalized (and sometimes other) masculinities; highlighting contradictions and resistances; analysis of institutional/social, interpersonal and intrapsychic aspects of masculinities; and explorations of transformations and social change. While Gramscian theory has been a major force framing this theory, other influences include socialist feminism, critique of gender categoricalism, pluralism, intersectionality, practice theory, structuration theory and psychodynamics. Other scholars have developed this approach in various ways, interestingly often without reference to its initial Gramscian framing. Both these observations may explain its diverse appeal and its variable interpretation (Hearn, 2004). More recently, Connell and Messerschmidt (2005) have completed a re-evaluation of the concept of hegemonic masculinity and its various applications. In this revision they stress several key issues, including: a more holistic understanding of gender hierarchy; the importance of geography/ies of masculinities; return to an emphasis on social embodiment; and the dynamics of masculinities, contestation and democratization. These points are all, in different ways, relevant to analyses of men, masculinities and leadership dynamics.

Masculinities theory and theories of hegemonic masculinity have been applied in some empirical studies of leadership and management dynamics (e.g., Barrett, 1996; Poynting and Donaldson, 2005). Messerschmidt (1995) and Maier and Messerschmidt (1998) have argued that leaders' hegemonic masculinities, expressed especially through authoritarian practices and excessive risk-taking, were centrally implicated in the disastrous decision to launch the space shuttle *Challenger*. Their research demonstrates how crucial decision-making processes can reflect and reinforce dominant masculinities and leaders' power and control in organizational groups. At the same time, these former theories have themselves been subject to a range of critiques, including from studies of leadership and management (Collinson and Hearn, 1996, 2005; Whitehead, 1999; also see Kerfoot and Knights, 1993, 1996, 1998). First, there is often a lack of clarity in the concepts and meanings of masculinity and hegemonic masculinity: is hegemonic masculinity referring to cultural representations, everyday practices or institutional structures? Can it be reduced to a set of traits or practices? How does masculinity or hegemonic masculinity address the complexities of everyday action and resistance? Second, there are detailed empirical studies of how men behave and men talk about themselves that may complicate or contradict aspects of the theory (e.g., Wetherell and Edley, 1999). Third, there are more theoretical critiques: historical, poststructuralist, postcolonial, Gramscian (e.g., Howson, 2006).

Some critiques move the focus from masculinities, that is, specific masculinities, to men. Masculinities may change, but the power of men may shift little. Indeed, the very 'flexibility' of masculinity and elusiveness of patriarchy is part of the process through which men's power in leadership and management are often enacted and sustained. To address this means going beyond the analytical hegemony of hegemonic masculinity, as often used outside a Gramscian framing, to examine the hegemony of men: the simultaneous construction of men, individually, collectively and as a social category, and men's hegemonic domination in the gender order (Hearn, 2004). Thus, in analysing the gendered dynamics of leadership, we apply masculinities theory critically and with recognition of its limitations, as set out in these various critiques. The implications of critical studies of men and masculinities for understanding the key dynamics of leadership and organizational practices are potentially far-reaching.

THE GENDERED DYNAMICS OF LEADERSHIP

In the remainder of this chapter we consider some of the contemporary issues of gender dynamics of leadership in relation to men and masculinities. Drawing on and seeking to combine insights from critical studies of men and masculinities with the emergent perspective of 'critical leadership studies' (Collinson, 2011), the chapter highlights the following six key themes: mainstream gender and leadership approaches; power and control; multiplicity and diversity; contradictory resistances; hegemonic, heroic and post-heroic masculinities; and (dis)embodied and virtual dynamics.

Mainstream Gender and Leadership Approaches

Critical studies on men and masculinities raise important questions for studying leadership, management and organization. What might be called the 'mainstream gender and leadership' literature tends to focus primarily on whether women and men adopt similar or different (and better or worse) leadership styles (e.g., Rosener, 1990), and followers' preference for women or men, for different styles of leadership. Many researchers have argued that women are more relationship oriented and men more task oriented in their leadership, that men are more likely to adopt 'transactional' leadership styles, exchanging rewards or punishments for performance, using power from their organizational position/formal authority, and less likely to adopt person-oriented, transformational leadership (see Eagly and Johannesen-Schmidt, 2001). On the other hand, in some studies little difference is found (Boulgarides, 1984), perhaps as part of gender convergence, perhaps through common organizational experiences; and in some situations some women managers and leaders may be more achievement oriented than both men and other women (Donnell and Hall, 1980).

Despite well-recognized methodological problems with sex/gender differences and sex role approaches (Eichler, 1980; Carrigan et al., 1985), these perspectives continue to live on, especially in public, managerial and media discourses. They are especially popular in some popular business, governmental and international debates. They tend to reduce the problem of gender to variations in behaviour, not power and resources. On the other hand, empirical research shows that the gendered perception of leadership is not always as might be assumed. A recently published large-scale US national survey of over 60,000 women and men concluded that there is a 'cross-sex bias', one might say 'heterosexual bias', with women ranking men bosses more highly, and complementarily, men ranking women bosses more highly. An overall majority, 54 per cent, of participants claimed no preference for their boss's gender, but of the remaining men and women, a sizeable minority, preferred men bosses (Elsesser and Lever, 2011).

Sex differences and sex role approaches are not only about preferences and styles of doing leadership, but also gendered constructions of leadership. For example, men are reported as less likely than women to construe leadership in transformational terms, and to describe their own leadership as transformational, and moreover may be less likely to be described by others as transformational. Rather, they are more likely to be described as 'laissez-faire' or in terms of management-by-exception (Alimo-Metcalfe and Alban-Metcalfe, 2005). This raises the complex question of what it means to label leadership (or other activities) as masculine or feminine, male or female. There is an iterative, self-reproducing gendered process here by which labelling leadership as such solidifies what the masculine and the feminine might mean (Eichler, 1980; Clatterbaugh, 1998).

These kinds of sex/gender differences and sex role approaches to leadership have been problematized by critical feminist and pro-feminist writers. They have critiqued the tendency of (male) researchers to view leadership through stereotyped perspectives that underestimate the importance of gender (Calás and Smircich, 1991). Questioning the possible biological essentialism that can underpin such debates on the gender typing of leadership, critical feminist studies explore the gendered nature and gender relations of leadership, management and organization (Martin, 1990), focusing in particular on *both* the similarities and differences between men and women (Bacchi, 1990), and also between women *and* between men. Some also question these very categories, as in queer, transgender and intersexual approaches to organizations and management (Parker, 2002; Schilt, 2006; Davis, 2009).

Importantly, in most sex differences and sex role approaches there is little sense of the political and social conditions and contingencies of gendered power in leadership. Moreover, to find sex/gender differences (or not) does not explain gender power relations; for that there is a need to look to wider networks, relations and structures of power and control.

Dynamics of Power and Control

Recognizing that people are, arguably inherently, gendered beings in socially constructed ways, critical studies suggest that the power relations and dialectical relationships between men and women, between masculinity/ies and femininity/ies, as well as between paid employment and domestic work, are central issues when examining gender, men, masculinities and organizational leadership dynamics (Bligh and Kohles, 2008). Whereas power and gender are sometimes assumed to be separate, critical writers argue that they are inextricably linked (Scott, 1986). Bowring (2004) emphasizes that the binary and asymmetrical opposition between leaders and followers is itself reinforced by a gender dualism in which men are viewed as the universal, neutral subject and women as 'the other' (see Eichler, 1980). Bowring argues that we need to move towards the recognition of greater fluidity in leadership research including recognizing that people have multiple, interrelated and shifting identities.

Critical studies of men and masculinities in the workplace have revealed how both power and control (usually exercised by leaders and managers) and subordination and resistance (typically enacted by employees and followers) in organizational processes are often heavily shaped by specific dominant and subordinate masculinities. They demonstrate that the paid workplace, as well as the domestic sphere, is an important site for the reproduction of men's masculine power, identity and status: masculinity/ies can be embedded in formal organizational practices, for example, recruitment, through to more informal dynamics, for example, joking relationships. Similarly, critical feminist and pro-feminist studies of management and organization illustrate how certain gendered, ethnic and class-based, but still predominantly masculine, voices are routinely privileged in the workplace, whereas other, predominantly feminine, voices are marginalized (Ashcraft and Mumby, 2004).

Central to some men's valorization of 'work', power and control is also a close identification with machinery and technology (Cockburn, 1983; Hearn, 1992; Mellström, 2004). Masculine cultures at work, both managerial and non-managerial, can also be reproduced through men's sexuality and the sexual harassment of women. This includes the question of to what extent men managers intervene in harassment allegations (Collinson and Collinson, 1996), and to what extent tyrannical or laissez-faire management can actually facilitate bullying, harassment and other violations (Zapf and Gross, 2001; Salin, 2003; Hauge et al., 2007).

There is also growing interest in (men and women) followers' contribution to reproducing, reinforcing and challenging the asymmetrical nature of leadership dynamics (Collinson, 2006, 2011). Critical researchers have examined followers' conformity and compliance and thus the latter's tendency to reproduce leaders' power and status. Arguing that we have developed overly heroic and exaggerated views of what leaders are able to achieve, Meindl and colleagues (1985) were early critics of the tendency to 'romanticize leadership', where leaders are either solely credited for high organizational performance or, conversely, held personally responsible for workplace failures. They suggested that leaders' contribution to a collective enterprise is in fact inevitably somewhat constrained and closely tied to external factors outside a leader's control, such as those affecting whole industries. This analysis highlights the way that leaders, we would argue men leaders in particular, can be elevated and placed on a pedestal as somehow 'special', 'different' and worthy of great respect bordering on idolization. Having said that, followers may value heroic leaders who provide them with direction, meaning and security, thereby alleviating their own 'fear of freedom' (Fromm, 1977).

Various critical writers in leadership studies have examined how followers can often attribute exceptional, almost 'god-like' qualities to charismatic leaders through processes such as transference (Maccoby, 2007), fantasy (Gabriel, 1997), idealization (Shamir, 1999), projection (Shamir, 2007), seduction (Calás and Smircich, 1991) and reification (Gemmill and Oakley, 1992). Lipman-Blumen (2005) extended these arguments by analysing the 'allure of toxic leaders', where she contends that followers frequently seem to be fascinated by those who can be termed 'toxic leaders' despite, and possibly even because of, the latter's dysfunctional personal characteristics such as lack of integrity, insatiable ambition, enormous egos, arrogance, narcissism, reckless disregard for the effects of their actions on others and cowardice (Lipman-Blumen, 2005).

Although the gendered nature of these dynamics has typically remained implicit, the ways in which men and masculinity/ies are centrally implicated in followers' tendencies to elevate, imitate, emulate and romanticize other men in leadership positions is a crucially important dynamic (see Roper, 1996). This may be particularly so in the case of leaders who are perceived by their followers to be 'heroic' and rebellious change agents who challenge and transform the status quo. Suffice it to say here that the production of (men's) follower conformity to and romanticism of leaders, and thus a specific form of homosociality, is certainly one possible medium and outcome of asymmetric leadership dynamics, but there are other significant and more contested possibilities to consider as well.

Contradictory Resistances

In addition to studies that demonstrate how organizational power dynamics and their disciplinary/subordinating effects can be shaped and reinforced by dominant leadership and followership masculinities, critical research reveals that (employee/follower) resistance practices may also take (excessively) masculine forms. Oppositional workplace practices can reflect and reinforce both dominant and subordinate masculinities. Various studies reveal, for example, how male-dominated shopfloor counter-cultures are frequently characterized by highly masculine breadwinner identities, aggressive and profane forms of humour, ridicule and sarcasm, and the elevation of 'practical', manual work, sometimes in alliance with technical skills, as confirmation of working-class manhood (e.g., Collinson, 1992, 2000). Cockburn (1983) illustrates how male-dominated shopfloor counter-cultures and exclusionary trade union practices in the printing industry elevated men and masculinity while subordinating and segregating women. Research in female-dominated factories and offices suggests that women workers often engage in (feminine) counter-cultures characterized by similarly aggressive, joking and sexualized practices of resistance (e.g., Westwood, 1984).

Critical feminist studies also address the contradictory processes and outcomes of forms of workplace resistance that reflect, celebrate and reinforce dominant and/or subordinated masculinities. For example, Willis (1977) described how working-class 'lads' creatively constructed a counter-culture that celebrated their masculinity and the so-called freedom and independence of manual work. Yet, this counter-culture paradoxically facilitated the lads' smooth transition into precisely the kind of shopfloor work that then subordinated them for the rest of their working lives.

A small number of recent critical feminist studies suggest that it is not only followers but also those (broadly) defined as occupying leadership and management positions who may engage in (gendered forms of) resistance when seeking to promote organizational change (Meyerson, 2001; Sinclair, 2007; Zoller and Fairhurst, 2007; Ospina and Su, 2009). Ashcraft (2005) reveals how male airline captains engaged in subversive practices, but in this case their intentions were to undermine a change programme and to preserve their terms and conditions, and their masculine power and identity. Viewing the corporate enactment of a 'crew empowerment system' as a threat to their masculine authority and identity, pilots utilized numerous strategies to resist their loss of control, while also giving the appearance of supporting the change programme. These predominantly white professional men resisted the erosion of their masculine authority by giving the appearance of consent while actually engaging in subtle forms of resistance in order to retrieve control. Ashcraft illustrates how this masculine resistance can symbolically invert dominant values, but in ways that cut across emancipatory agendas, reinforcing the gendered status quo.

Hence, some critical studies also de-romanticize masculine forms of resistance by pointing to their potentially paradoxical processes and outcomes. They suggest that apparently oppositional practices that privilege masculinities may actually reinforce the very conditions of top-down control that stimulated resistance in the first place. Their focus on the consequences of employee resistance avoids the kind of overly romanticized interpretations that celebrate, rather than critically examine, oppositional practices that privilege specific masculinities.

These arguments in turn raise important questions about the gendered meanings of resistance, about who resists, how, why and when they do so, what strategies inform their practices, and what outcomes ensue. Critical feminist studies also raise important questions about how to theorize the multiple, simultaneous and potentially intersecting nature of leadership power dialectics and multiple masculinities. In addition to the gendered differences between men and women, inequalities between men and women, and between men, and between women, can all take multiple forms (shaped by, for example, class, ethnicity, age, disability, body, faith, sexuality, national origin) and different aspects of masculine power, inequality and identity may be reproduced by those in leadership positions in ways that can perpetuate disadvantage.

Masculinities: Hegemonic, Heroic or Post-heroic?

As noted at the outset of this chapter, critical feminist and pro-feminist studies have shown how romanticized notions of the heroic, 'tough' leader are often saturated with masculinity, that women continue to be largely excluded from senior positions (Sinclair, 1998, 2007) and that they can experience considerable hostility in male-dominated managerial cultures (Marshall, 1995). Critical studies of men and masculinities reveal the dominance of masculine assumptions in organizational cultures and practices generally, and in shaping the models, styles, language, cultures, identities and processes of leadership and management more particularly (Hearn, 1992, 2013; Collinson and Hearn, 1996). This approach highlights the importance of 'multiple masculinities' and how these are frequently shaped by class, race, ethnicity and further social divisions and intersections (Collinson and Hearn, 1994, 2009). Less often recognized are intersections of age, generation, (dis)ability, sexuality and embodiment more generally. Intersections of masculinities, gender and sexuality are of special interest, for example, in terms of the neglect of gay and non-heterosexual leadership, normalization of the confluence of men's heterosexuality and men's leadership, and some leaders' sexual abuses and sexual assaults, as in recent reports and allegations of several high-profile leaders in the media and popular entertainment industries in the UK, most infamously Jimmy Savile.

These various critiques raise further implications for analysis of the relations of men, masculinities and leadership. One set of implications concerns how different versions of men's leadership link with different masculinities. At least some forms of men's leadership can be interpreted within the frames of hegemonic masculinity or dominant masculinity. This is most obviously the case in relation to heroic models of (men's) leadership typically defined in terms of individualism, toughness, decisiveness

and quick, thrusting action. In this model of (men's) leadership, aggressiveness and competitiveness in the war-like conditions of 'the market',
(excessive) risk-taking, 'workaholism' and (excessive) self-belief are typically viewed as not only normal, but also desirable and legitimate qualities
that reflect and celebrate dominant, usually middle class, masculinities.
Routine organizational features like revenue and profit levels, performance figures, size of salary, office, and even the company car, can all be
used by men leaders to show their power and dominance while validating
themselves and their identities as 'high achievers', as distinctive men and
as successful family breadwinners. However, in taking for granted and/or
perpetuating such views within the literature, there are dangers of returning to a modified (male sex) role theory. As noted, there is a need to move
beyond analysis of men and leadership in terms of leadership styles.

The applicability, or not, of the concept of hegemonic masculinity
to leadership is complicated by the fact that the concept is often used
loosely and variably, sometimes as a form of masculinity, sometimes as
more general social processes. In this context, it is unclear whether it is
leadership through force or leadership through control of resources or by
example or by persuasion that would be hegemonic, or not. In considering the relationship of hegemonic masculinity and other masculinities to
leadership, one may ask: how do various *dominant/dominating* forms of
leadership interconnect with each other? How different forms of men's
leadership link with and relate to each other is difficult to specify. In one
sense it may seem that men's dominant, dominating or heroic leadership
is hegemonic. But we may question: are dominant images of men's leadership part of or illustrative of hegemonic masculinity or not? Similarly, not
all versions of men's dominant or dominating leadership rely on heroism.
To put this differently: is men's heroism in leadership or men's heroic
leadership so hegemonic in many contemporary organizations? Indeed,
why is heroism 'hegemonic' at all? So, is there a case for seeing tendencies
in men's contemporary leadership towards the post-heroic? Is post-heroic
leadership, emphasizing the development of subordinates' capabilities,
becoming hegemonic, especially within dispersed, project and network
organizing? How is hyper-optimism and exaggerated positivity used in
emerging forms of leadership and do these dynamics take masculine and
gendered forms (Collinson, 2012)? Thus, it is important to go beyond what
might appear obvious connections between (hegemonic) masculinity and
leadership.

A further aspect of the myth(s) of male/masculine heroic leaders is that
the image of competitive individualism they apparently promote is often
based on interdependencies, co-leaderships and shared, social or distrib-
uted dynamics. Accordingly, leaders are not islands and behind the public

image of isolated individuals at the top of hierarchies are whole gendered groups of gendered teams working to make the individual 'look good' and look as if they are an individual leader. Such human infrastructures are also very relevant in the cultivation of political leaders, in both politics and business. There are also important networks of collaboration and collusion, based, for example, on family, school, university, professional, regional ties, not only within but across organizations, that can further sustain individual leaders' power, status and identities.

Moreover, it is possible to change men's leader masculinities, heroic or otherwise, and for men to continue dominating in organizations, leadership and management. There are many different ways of being a 'successful', or dominant, man leader. To draw on an earlier analysis of men and management (Collinson and Hearn, 1994), some versions of men's leadership are strong on detail, and might be considered by some as relatively formal, even boring and pedantic: *bureaucratic* (cf. Weber, 1964). In contrast, some are entrepreneurial in style: *entrepreneurialism*; others are jolly and chummy: *informalism*, and some, perhaps many, are self-serving: *careerism*. Pronounced variations in men's leadership masculinities are also apparent in the political sphere, with dramatically different and more, or indeed less, 'successful' styles in public political life. Much of men's leadership is mundane, not dramatic (Martin, 2001). Indeed, some forms of men's leadership might exemplify complicit masculinity. Men's leadership, or indeed masculine leadership, should not be seen as one thing. It should not be reified.

Multiplicity, Diversity and Transnationalization

We have already noted the relevance of multiple masculinities in leadership, and this perspective highlights how by critically exploring the gendered nature of power relations and identity constructions, a rethinking of leaders, followers and contexts, as well as their dialectical interrelations, is necessary. Critical studies of men and masculinities highlight how gendered leadership dialectics are typically shaped by class, race, age and further social divisions and intersections. CSMM demonstrate that organizational power and resistance dynamics are inescapably situated within, and reproduced through multiple, intersecting and simultaneous differences and inequalities, especially those shaped by men and masculinities (Hearn and Collinson, 1994). This in turn raises complex questions about how to theorize the interrelations between multiple dialectics within particular gendered practices and contexts (Collinson, 2005, 2011). By raising and exploring such under-researched questions, particularly about gendered power and identity, critical studies of men and masculinities have the potential to broaden understanding of leadership dynamics, develop new forms of analysis and open up innovative lines of enquiry.

CSMM also highlight the significance of masculinity/ies in relation to other aspects of diversity and inequality in leadership dynamics, as well as the conceptual value of intersectionality, simultaneity and asymmetry (see Merrill-Sands and Holvino, 2003; Hearn and Collinson, 2006; Calás et al., 2010; Holvino, 2010). In addition to the theoretical challenges they pose for critical studies, these arguments highlight the need to develop more inclusive and integrated leadership practices that value multiplicity, diversity and difference (Mumby, 2005).

To some extent this emphasis can be traced to growing theoretical and practical interest in men, masculinities and leadership in the context of globalization, glocalization and transnationalization. In discussing this, Connell (1998) has proposed the notion of 'transnational business masculinity' as a frame for considering these conjunctions. This emphasizes individualism, lack of loyalty or very conditional loyalties to a specific corporation, international lifestyle, libertarian sexual and consumer tastes, and declining responsibility for others. This kind of masculinity can in turn be seen as legitimating global capitalism (see Connell and Wood, 2005; Elias and Beasley, 2009). At the same time, a variety of studies point to the diversity of forms of men transnational managers' lives in different parts of the world (Reis, 2004). Attention to transnational leadership is also prompted by theoretical and analytical challenges raised by debates on gender and intersectionality (Hearn, 2013).

(Dis-)Embodied and Virtual Dynamics

Increasingly, in contemporary contexts men's leadership can be seen as simultaneously gendered/intersectional, local/transnational and embodied/ virtual. In particular, the relation of embodiment and virtuality, not least through the use of ICTs in leadership, needs closer attention. There is growing research on both men's embodiment (Hearn, 2012) and virtual leadership (Boje and Rhodes, 2005; Zimmerman et al., 2008), but little on the everyday realities of men's embodied/virtual leadership practices.

In many ways leaders and men have typically been understood and have tended to understand themselves through a mind/body dualism, in which leaders are seen as inherently rational beings, somewhat detached and distant from their own, and others' (gendered) bodies. Leadership is frequently treated as an inherently disembodied process, concerned with strategy, vision and (changing) 'minds' (Gardner, 1996, 2006). Effective leaders are typically assumed to inspire and motivate followers primarily though cognitive processes of mental persuasion. While followers' bodies are often centrally implicated in the outcome of such processes, leaders and their practices are assumed to be almost entirely disembodied. Similarly, dominant conceptions of men and masculinity/ies indicate that men are often quite detached from their own bodies, especially in relation to illness (Connell, 1983; Jackson, 1990). We men are frequently reluctant to confront the possible fragilities of our bodies and to address the uncomfortable feeling that our bodies are not always under our control. We may often try, almost invariably unsuccessfully, to take distance from our own bodies (*pace* Hearn, 2012). In contemporary societies and organizations this 'double disembodiment' as leaders and as men can be compounded by new digital and virtual technologies that in multiple ways may exacerbate this deep-seated sense of mind/body separation that typically characterizes conventional conceptions of both leaders/leadership and men/masculinities. Furthermore the use of ICT and digital technologies can intensify (men) leaders' distance from followers, potentially compounding their tendency to view employees and customers simply as numbers on a spreadsheet.

In contrast, more critical approaches to both leadership/followership (Sinclair, 2005; Ropo and Sauer, 2008) and to men/masculinities increasingly emphasize that men's leadership needs to be understood as deeply embodied. Embodied approaches to men's leadership recognize the fundamental importance of bodies for understanding men and leadership. They are complicated by relations, sometimes contradictions, with virtual leadership practices, and the paradoxical play of the embodiment of the virtual, and the virtuality of embodiment. The characteristic features of ICTs – time/space compression, instantaneousness, asynchronicity, reproducibility of images, creation of virtual bodies, blurring of 'real' and 'representational', wireless portability, globalized connectivity, personalization – have numerous implications for 'smart masculinities' and 'smart leadership' – in which social contact, communication and leadership are de-humanized by efficient instrumentalism assisted by technological innovation and prosthetics. Quintessentially, 'smart' technological leader masculinity has been that personified by the founder and former CEO of Apple, Steve Jobs, combining managerial leadership, capitalist accumulation, personal charisma, technological aesthetics, virtuality, visuality and simplicity of sound bites, in particular, *buy it!* We might see in such dramaturgical performances (Sharma and Grant, 2011) a form of leadership as embodied love of technology, a 'natural', 'harmonious' prosthetics of men/masculinity, enacting a leadership transcending the embodied/virtual. The real and the virtual may coincide.

CONCLUSION

In making sense of the complex processes through which power is exercised in contemporary societies and organizations, we have sought in this chapter to problematize a key way of understanding and enacting leadership: namely through the notion of the heroic male (transformational) leader. Drawing on critical studies of both men/masculinities and of leadership/followership, we have examined these processes as they are articulated in the theory and practice of leadership. By deconstructing leadership, men and gender, we have questioned taken-for-granted assumptions about what it means to be 'a leader', 'a hero', and indeed 'a man'. Mainstream leadership and management, typically presented as 'gender neutral', remain structurally predominant forms of men's practices. The high status positions of leadership and management typically confer considerable power, influence and identity on specific men and particular masculinities. Yet, seeing 'men and leadership' as a specific gendered topic, arena of activity or research area is still rare. The 'man problem' remains obscure(d), partly because so much leadership is about men, yet is not recognized as such.

Having focused in this chapter on *asymmetric* gendered power relations, especially in relation to leaders/followers and men/women, we suggest there is also a need for more research on *horizontal* leadership power dynamics. There are a growing number of studies that highlight how competition and conflict between those in senior positions within and between competing organizations can have damaging organizational and personal effects (e.g., Gordon and Nicholson, 2008). This is illustrated by a study of the auto-destructive behaviour of the leaders of the major Scottish banks in the period 2005–08, where competition for positions of domination between senior men banking leaders distracted them from dealing with the global economic crisis and significantly contributed to the destruction of the banks themselves as independent institutions (Kerr and Robinson, 2011). Such studies of leader–leader relations and tensions are important but also need more explicitly and critically to focus on the ways that gender, men and masculinities are often centrally implicated in such leadership struggles for organizational and sector power and identity.

To move further beyond some of the more obvious links of leadership, men and masculinities, there is a need to attend to both debates within CSMM, and the major contextualizing questions of gender/ intersectionalities, the local/transnational and the embodied/virtual – and indeed beyond the binaries so easily suggested. Increasingly, men's leadership is likely to be, can become, and can be seen as simultaneously gendered/intersectional, local/transnational, embodied/virtual. And finally, and by no means least, these questions are of central importance both for organizational theory and social theory, and for changing men's practices of leadership away from enactments of sexism and reproductions of patriarchy.

REFERENCES

Alimo-Metcalfe, B. and J. Alban-Metcalfe (2005), 'Leadership: Time for a new direction?', *Leadership*, **1**(1), 51–71.
Ashcraft, K. (2005), 'Resistance through consent?', *Management Communication Quarterly*, **19**(1), 67–90.
Ashcraft, K. and D. Mumby (2004), *Reworking Gender: A Feminist Communicology of Organization*, London: Sage.
Bacchi, C. (1990), *Same Difference: Feminism and Sexual Difference*, London: Allen and Unwin.
Barrett, F. (1996), 'The organizational construction of hegemonic masculinity: The case of the US Navy', *Gender, Work and Organization*, **3**(3), 129–42.
Bligh, M. and J. Kohles (2008), 'The romance lives on: Contemporary issues surrounding the romance of leadership', *Leadership*, **3**(3), 343–60.
Boje, D.M. and C. Rhodes (2005), 'The virtual leader construct: The mass mediatization and simulation of transformational leadership', *Leadership*, **1**(4), 407–28.
Boulgarides, J.D. (1984), 'A comparison of male and female business managers', *Journal of Leadership and Organization Development*, **5**(5), 27–31.
Bowring, M.A. (2004), 'Resistance is not futile: Liberating Captain Janeway from the masculine–feminine dualism of leadership', *Gender, Work and Organization*, **11**(4), 381–405.
Calás, M. and L. Smircich (1991), 'Voicing seduction to silence leadership', *Organization Studies*, **12**(4), 567–602.
Calás, M., L. Smircich, J. Tienari and C.F. Ellehave (2010), 'Editorial: Observing globalized capitalism: Gender and ethnicity as entry point', *Gender, Work and Organization*, **17**(3), 243–7.
Carlyle, T. (1841), *Heroes and Hero Worship*, London: James Fraser.
Carrigan, T., R. Connell and J. Lee (1985), 'Towards a new sociology of masculinity', *Theory and Society*, **14**(5), 551–604.
Clatterbaugh, K. (1998), 'What is problematic about masculinities?', *Men and Masculinities*, **1**(1), 24–45.
Cockburn, C. (1983), *Brothers: Male Dominance and Technological Change*, London: Pluto.
Collinson, D.L. (1992), *Managing the Shopfloor: Subjectivity, Masculinity and Workplace Culture*, Berlin: Walter de Gruyter.
Collinson, D.L. (2000), 'Strategies of resistance: Power, knowledge and subjectivity in the workplace', in K. Grint (ed.), *Work and Society: A Reader*, Cambridge, UK: Polity Press, pp. 63–198.
Collinson, D.L. (2005), 'Dialectics of leadership', *Human Relations*, **8**(11), 1419–42.
Collinson, D.L. (2006), 'Rethinking followership: A post-structuralist analysis of follower identities', *The Leadership Quarterly*, **17**(2), 179–89.
Collinson, D.L. (2011), 'Critical leadership studies', in A. Bryman, D. Collinson,

K. Grint, B. Jackson and M. Uhl-Bien (eds), *The Sage Handbook of Leadership*, London: Sage, pp. 179–92.

Collinson, D.L. (2012), 'Prozac leadership and the limits of positive thinking', *Leadership*, **8**(2), 87–107.

Collinson, M. and D.L. Collinson (1996), 'It's only Dick: The sexual harassment of women managers in insurance sales', *Work, Employment and Society*, **10**(1), 29–56.

Collinson, D.L. and J. Hearn (1994), 'Naming men as men: Implications for work, organizations and management', *Gender, Work and Organization*, **1**(1), 2–22.

Collinson, D.L. and J. Hearn (eds) (1996), *Men as Managers, Managers as Men. Critical Perspectives on Men, Masculinities and Managements*, London: Sage.

Collinson, D.L. and J. Hearn (2005), 'Men and masculinities in work, organizations and management', in M. Kimmel, J. Hearn and R. Connell (eds), *Handbook of Studies on Men and Masculinities*, Thousand Oaks, CA: Sage, pp. 289–310.

Collinson, D.L. and J. Hearn (2009), 'Men, diversity at work, and diversity management', in M. Ozbilgin (ed.), *Equality, Diversity and Inclusion at Work: A Research Companion*, Cheltenham, UK and Northampton, MA, USA: Edward Elgar Publishing, pp. 383–98.

Connell, R. (1983), *Which Way Is Up?*, London and Boston: Allen & Unwin.

Connell, R. (1995), *Masculinities*, Cambridge, UK: Polity.

Connell, R. (1998), 'Globalization and masculinities', *Men and Masculinities*, **1**(1), 3–23.

Connell, R. and J.W. Messerschmidt (2005), 'Hegemonic masculinity: Rethinking the concept', *Gender and Society*, **19**(6), 829–59.

Connell, R. and J. Wood (2005), 'Globalization and business masculinities', *Men and Masculinities*, **7**(4), 347–64.

Connell, R., J. Hearn and M. Kimmel (2005), 'Introduction', in M. Kimmel, J. Hearn and R. Connell (eds), *Handbook of Studies on Men and Masculinities*, Thousand Oaks, CA: Sage, pp. 1–12.

Cornwall, A., J. Edström and A. Greig (eds) (2011), *Men and Development: Politicizing Masculinities*, London: Zed.

Davis, G. (2009), 'Mobilization strategies and gender awareness: An analysis of intersex social movement organizations', unpublished manuscript, Department of Sociology, University of Illinois at Chicago.

Donnell, S.M. and J. Hall (1980), 'Men and women as managers: A significant case of no significant differences', *Organizational Dynamics*, **8**(4), 60–77.

Eagly, A.H. and M.C. Johannesen-Schmidt (2001), 'The leadership styles of women and men', *Journal of Social Issues*, **57**(4), 781–97.

Eichler, M. (1980), *The Double Standard*, London: Croom Helm.

Elias, J. and C. Beasley (2009), 'Hegemonic masculinity and globalization: "Transnational business masculinities" and beyond', *Globalizations*, **6**(2), 281–96.

Elsesser, K.M. and J. Lever (2011), 'Does gender bias against female leaders persist? Quantitive and qualitative data from a large-scale survey', *Human Relations*, **64**(2), 1555–78.

Flood, M., J.K. Gardiner, B. Pease and K. Pringle (eds) (2007), *International Encyclopedia of Men and Masculinities*, London: Routledge.

Fromm, E. (1977), *The Fear of Freedom*, London: Routledge Kegan Paul.

Gabriel, Y. (1997), 'Meeting God: When organizational members come face to face with the supreme leader', *Human Relations*, **50**(4), 315–42.

Gardner, H. (1996), *Leading Minds*, London: Harper Collins.

Gardner, H. (2006), *Changing Minds*, Boston, MA: Harvard Business School.

Gemmill, G. and J. Oakley (1992), 'Leadership: An alienating social myth', *Human Relations*, **45**(2), 113–29.

Gordon, G. and N. Nicholson (2008), *Family Wars*, London: Kogan Page.

Hauge, L.J., A. Skogstad and S. Einarsen (2007), 'Relationships between work environments and bullying: Results of a large representative study', *Work and Stress*, **21**(3), 220–42.

Hearn, J. (1992), *Men in the Public Eye. The Construction and Deconstruction of Public Men and Public Patriarchies*, London: Routledge.

Hearn, J. (2004), 'From hegemonic masculinity to the hegemony of men', *Feminist Theory*, **5**(1), 49–72.

Hearn, J. (2012), 'Male bodies, masculine bodies, men's bodies: The need for a concept of gex', in B.S. Turner (ed.), *Routledge Handbook of Body Studies*, London: Routledge, pp. 307–20.

Hearn, J. (2013), 'Contextualizing men, masculinities, leadership and management: Gender/intersectionalities, local/transnational, embodied/virtual, theory/practice', in R. Simpson, R. Burke and S. Kumra (eds), *The Handbook of Gender in Organizations*, Oxford: Oxford University Press.

Hearn, J. and D.L. Collinson (1994), 'Theorizing unities and differences between men and between masculinities', in H. Brod and M. Kaufman (eds), *Theorizing Masculinities*, Newbury Park, CA: Sage, pp. 148–62.

Hearn, J. and D.L. Collinson (2006), 'Men, masculinities and workplace diversity/diversion: Power, intersections and contradictions', in A. Konrad, P. Prasad and J. Pringle (eds), *Handbook of Workplace Diversity*, London: Sage, pp. 299–322.

Hearn, J. and C. Niemistö (2012), 'Men, managers, fathers and home–work relations: National context, organisational policies, and individual lives', in P. McDonald and E. Jeanes (eds), *Men's Wage and Family Work*, London: Routledge, pp. 95–113.

Hearn, J. and K. Pringle, with members of CROME (2006), *European Perspectives on Men and Masculinities: National and Transnational Approaches*, London: Palgrave Macmillan.

Holvino, E. (2010), 'Intersections: The simultaneity of race, gender and class in organization studies', *Gender, Work and Organization*, **17**(3), 248–77.

Hook, S. (1945), *The Hero in History*, London: Secker and Warburg.

Howson, R. (2006), *Challenging Hegemonic Masculinity*, London: Routledge.

Husu, L., J. Hearn, A.-M. Lämsä and S. Vanhala (2011), 'Introduction – johdanto', in L. Husu, J. Hearn, A.-M. Lämsä and S. Vanhala (eds), *Women, Leadership and Management*, Helsinki: Edita, pp. v–viii.

Jackson, D. (1990), *Unmasking Masculinity: A Critical Autobiography*, London: Routledge.

Kerfoot, D. and D. Knights (1993), 'Management, masculinity and manipulation: From paternalism to corporate strategy in financial services in Britain', *Journal of Management Studies*, **30**(4), 659–79.

Kerfoot, D. and D. Knights (1996), '"The best is yet to come?" The quest for embodiment in managerial work', in D.L. Collinson and J. Hearn (eds), *Men as Managers, Managers as Men: Critical Perspectives on Men, Masculinities and Managements*, London: Sage, pp. 78–98.

Kerfoot, D. and D. Knights (1998), 'Managing masculinity in contemporary organizational life: A "man"agerial project', *Organization*, **5**(1), 7–26.

Kerr, R. and S. Robinson (2011), 'Leadership as an elite field: Scottish banking leaders and the crisis of 2007–2009', *Leadership*, **7**(2), 151–73.

Kimmel, M., J. Hearn and R. Connell (eds) (2005), *Handbook of Studies on Men and Masculinities*, Thousand Oaks, CA, Sage.

Lämsä, A.-M. and T. Hautala (2005), *Organisaatiokäyttäytymisen perusteet* [Organizational Behaviour], Helsinki: Edita.

Lipman-Blumen, J. (2005), *The Allure of Toxic Leaders*, Oxford: Oxford University Press.

Maccoby, M. (2007), *The Leaders We Need*, Boston, MA: Harvard Business School Press.

Maier, M. and J.W. Messerschmidt (1998), 'Commonalities, conflicts and contradictions in organizational masculinities: Exploring the gendered genesis of the Challenger disaster', *Canadian Review of Sociology and Anthropology*, **35**(3), 325–44.

Marshall, J. (1995), *Women Managers Moving On*, London: Macmillan.

Martin, J. (1990), 'Deconstructing organizational taboos: The suppression of gender conflict in organizations', *Organization Science*, **1**(4), 339–59.

Martin, P.Y. (2001), '"Mobilizing masculinities": Women's experiences of men at work', *Organizations*, **8**(4), 587–618.

Meindl, J., S.B. Ehrlich and J.M. Dukerich (1985), 'The romance of leadership', *Administrative Science Quarterly*, **30**(1), 78–102.

Mellström, U. (2004), 'Machines and masculine subjectivity: Technology as an integral part of men's life experiences', *Men and Masculinities*, **6**(4), 368–82.

Merrill-Sands, D. and E. Holvino, with J. Cummings (2003), 'Working with diversity: A focus on global organizations', in R. Ely, E. Foldy and M. Scully (eds), *Reader in Gender, Work and Organization*, Oxford and New York: Blackwell, pp. 327–42.

Messerschmidt, J.W. (1995), 'Managing to kill: Masculinities and the space shuttle Challenger explosion', *Masculinities*, **3**(4), 1–22.

Meyerson, D.E. (2001), *Tempered Radicals*, Boston, MA: Harvard Business School.

Mumby, D. (2005), 'Theorizing resistance in organization studies', *Management Communication Quarterly*, **19**(1), 19–44.

Ospina, S. and C. Su (2009), 'Weaving color lines: Race, ethnicity, and the work of leadership in social change organizations', *Leadership*, **5**(2), 131–70.

Parker, M. (2002), 'Queering management and organization', *Gender, Work and Organization*, **9**(2), 146–66.

Poynting, S. and M. Donaldson (2005), 'Snakes and leaders: Hegemonic masculinity in ruling-class boys' boarding schools', *Men and Masculinities*, **7**(4), 325–46.

Reis, C. (2004), *Men Managers in a European Multinational Company*, Mering and Munich: Rainer Humpp Verlag.

Roper, M. (1996), '"Seduction and succession": Circuits of homosocial desire in management', in D.L. Collinson and J. Hearn (eds), *Men as Managers, Managers as Men: Critical Perspectives on Men, Masculinities and Managements*, London: Sage, pp. 210–26.

Ropo, A. and E. Sauer (2008), 'Corporeal leaders', in D. Barry and H. Hansen (eds), *New Approaches in Management and Organization*, London: Sage, pp. 469–78.

Rosener, J.B. (1990), 'Ways women lead', *Harvard Business Review*, **68**(6), 119–25.

Salin, D. (2003), 'Ways of explaining workplace bullying: A review of enabling, motivating, and precipitating structures and processes in the work environ-ment', *Human Relations*, **56**(10), 1213–32.

Schilt, K. (2006), '"Just one of the guys?": How transmen make gender visible in the workplace', *Gender and Society*, **20**(4), 465–90.

Scott, J. (1986), 'Gender: A useful historical category of historical analysis', *American Historical Review*, **91**(5), 1053–75.

Shamir, B. (1999), 'Taming charisma for better understanding and greater useful-ness: A response to Beyer', *The Leadership Quarterly*, **10**(4), 555–62.

Shamir, B. (2007), 'From passive recipients to active co-producers: Followers' roles in the leadership process', in B. Shamir, R. Pillai, M.C. Bligh and M. Uhl-Bien (eds), *Follower-centered Perspectives on Leadership*, Greenwich, CT: Information Age, pp. ix–xxxix.

Sharma, A. and D. Grant (2011), 'Narrative, drama and charismatic leadership: The case of Apple's Steve Jobs', *Leadership*, **7**(1), 3–26.

Sinclair, A. (1998), *Doing Leadership Differently: Gender, Power, and Sexuality in a Changing Business Culture*, Victoria, Australia: Melbourne University Press.

Sinclair, A. (2005), 'Body possibilities in leadership', *Leadership*, **1**(4), 387–406.

Sinclair, A. (2007), *Leadership for the Disillusioned*, London: Allen and Unwin.

Weber, M. (1964), *The Theory of Economic and Social Organization*, London: Routledge and Kegan Paul.

Westwood, S. (1984), *All Day, Every Day: Factory and Family in the Making of Women's Lives*, London: Pluto Press.

Wetherell, M. and N. Edley (1999), 'Negotiating hegemonic masculinity: Imaginary positions and psycho-discursive practices', *Feminism and Psychology*, **9**(3), 335–56.

Whitehead, S. (1999), 'Hegemonic masculinity revisited', *Gender, Work and Organization*, **6**(1), 58–62.

Willis, P. (1977), *Learning to Labour: How Working Class Kids get Working Class Jobs*, Farnborough: Saxon House.

Zapf, D. and C. Gross (2001), 'Conflict escalation and coping with work-place bullying: A replication and extension', *European Journal of Work and Organizational Psychology*, **5**(2), 203–14.

Zimmerman, P., A. Wit and R. Gill (2008), 'The relative importance of leadership behaviours in virtual and face-to-face communication settings', *Leadership*, **4**(3), 321–37.

Zoller, H.M. and G.T. Fairhurst (2007), 'Resistance leadership: The overlooked potential in critical organization and leadership studies', *Human Relations*, **60**(1), 1331–60.

4. The imperative for servant-leadership: reflections on the (enduring) dysfunctions of corporate masculinity

Mark Maier

According to the power model, leadership is about how to accumulate and wield power, how to make people do things, how to attack and win. It is about clever strategies, applying pressure, and manipulating people to get what you want.
(Kent Keith, *The Case for Servant Leadership*, 2nd edition, 2012, p. 19)

Administration (n.), From the Latin, *ad* (to promote) and *ministrare* (service, as in 'to minister'). Literally, 'to promote service'.
(*Webster's Dictionary*)

Learn to lead in a nourishing manner.
Learn to lead without being possessive.
Learn to be helpful without taking the credit.
Learn to lead without coercion.
(John Heider, *The Tao of Leadership*, 1985, p. 19)

The wise and virtuous man is at all times willing that his own private interest should be sacrificed to the public interest of his own particular order or society.
(Adam Smith, *The Theory of Moral Sentiments*, 6th edition, 2009, VI.II.46)

INTRODUCTION

As the chapters in this volume underscore, despite significant strides towards gender equality in the workplace over the past 30–40 years, significant barriers remain. It is undeniable that women have made significant inroads in the public sphere of work. Where other contributions address the implications of the gendered nature of organizational culture (and family life) for women's advancement, I will focus here on the ways in which the gendered biases of our work and family spheres not only pose formidable barriers to women, but – paradoxically – also limit the life opportunities and leadership potential of men and seriously compromise both ethical decision-making in organizations and organizational performance. At the heart of this chapter is the question, 'Why should men work to transform and subvert a system that ostensibly privileges them?' We shall examine some of the fundamental assumptions of human behavior in organizations and explore how conventional forms of organizing (hierarchy, bureaucracy) and managing ('planning, organizing, directing, controlling') are not only masculine-gendered, but in fact undermine leadership and organizational effectiveness.

I will begin by elucidating some the primary dimensions of corporate masculinity (Maier, 1999), demonstrate the relevance of these dimensions to the work–family challenges facing men and women, highlight the salience of these dimensions in selected high-profile organizational dysfunctions (most notably the 1986 *Challenger* disaster, the 2003 *Columbia* accident, and the 2010 BP *Deepwater Horizon* oil spill), and close by articulating – and providing evidence in support of – a model of leading as a way of serving (servant-leadership) as a tried and tested – and inherently feminist – alternative paradigm for individual and organizational success.

'GREEDY ORGANIZATIONS', THE 'ACT AS THOUGH' PRINCIPLE AND THE WORK–FAMILY ROLE SYSTEM: THE STRUCTURAL FOUNDATIONS OF CORPORATE MASCULINITY

We begin our discussion of the dimensions of corporate masculinity with a reminder that the paid work role in modern society evolved in ways that legitimized the primacy – and dominance – of the organization in individual life. As Lewis Coser observed:

> The modern world continues to spawn organizations which ... make total claims on their members and which attempt to encompass within their circle the whole personality: These might be called greedy organizations, insofar as they seek exclusive and undivided loyalty and they attempt to reduce the claims of competing roles and status positions on those they wish to encompass within their boundaries. Their demands on the person are omnivorous. (Coser, 1974, p. 4)

A lasting consequence of the industrialization of society and its attendant sex segregation of human activity has been the creation of a bureaucratic social order grounded largely on norms conventionally ascribed to men. As David Morgan noted (1996), 'The more an organization conforms to the key dimensions of Weber's ideal type [bureaucracy], the more the organization will be masculinist in its composition and guiding assumptions' (p. 47). And, as Knights and Tullberg more recently observed (2012), 'To be a senior manager involves conquest, competition and control as performative elements in the process of doing masculinity in business life' (p. 390). The extent to which this world order is taken for granted is evident in the continued preoccupation with how to equalize women's participation in the occupational realm, without questioning the appropriateness – or viability – of such an orientation. It is interesting, though hardly surprising, that the male lifeworld – one that emphasizes individual career advancement and success – continues to be privileged as the objective for both men and women.

But this assumes women should imitate and embrace the conventional life patterns of men, without questioning whether this is a pattern worth emulating! It also assumes that men derive unilateral benefits from such an arrangement and should unquestioningly conform to that pattern. When I argue here that corporate masculinity is dysfunctional, I refer not only to the dysfunctional implications for women created by an 'ideology that naturalizes and justifies men's domination over women and . . . the unequal power relations sustained by this ideology [i.e., patriarchy]' (Kerfoot and Knights, 1993, p. 661, cited in Martin, 1996, p. 188), but draw special attention to its dysfunctions *for men.*

The conventional career pattern persists despite significant evidence that the type of participation required of men – especially those with children – is predicated on a parallel assumption that 'someone else' (read: spouse, partner, 'wife') would assume primary responsibility for one's family commitments. Among married couple families in the United States with children under 18 in 2009, both the husband and wife worked for pay in nearly three-fifths (!) of these families (58.9 percent) (US Bureau of Labor Statistics, 2012). And in a remarkable 30 percent of those two-earner families, women were the primary breadwinners (i.e., out-earn their husbands) (ibid.). It is clear that American companies structure their workers' days around an assumption that someone else is handling the home front, an assumption that is untenable – indeed, intensely stressful – for the great majority of American families.

Women's increased labor force participation – and the increasing participation of married mothers specifically – has caused a 'hairline fracture' in the structure of modern work, exposing a rift that is present but not immediately apparent in the underlying structural dilemma of the masculinist bias regarding the primacy of work and career in one's life.

Despite arguments to the contrary, it should be painfully obvious that the most successful of men under the prevailing masculine model of work were not 'self-made', but heavily dependent on the services of a stay-at-home spouse, or at least a partner who was willing to subordinate their career aspirations in favor of their family or to accommodate their husband's career, what Kanter originally articulated as 'the two-person career' (1977a). That may have been possible in 1948, when only about 17 percent of married mothers were in the labor force, but by 1995, that rate had increased to 70 percent (and seems to have leveled off at close to that rate). Since 1994, the proportion of women with school-age children who are participating in the labor force has remained steady at roughly 75 percent, providing further evidence of a structural limit in the gender accommodation of family to work (Cohany and Sok, 2007, p. 9).

In short, being married and having children is practically a job require-ment for men participating in the labor force; for women, those continue to be a liability, although less so in recent years than 20 or 30 years ago: the civilian labor force participation rate in the United States for young women (25–34) increased from 54 percent to 77 percent from 1975 to 2000. The par-ticipation rate for men in this age group held steady at around 95 percent. For those who were married with spouse present, the participation rate rose for young women from 48 percent to 71 percent; the rate for married men with spouse present stayed at 97 percent (DiNatale and Boraas, 2002, p. 5).

It should be noted that being married and having children is not neces-sarily an impediment to women's career advancement, although it leaves the issue of workplace flexibility unchallenged. As Facebook COO Sheryl Sandberg noted in her now-famous tome *Lean In* (2013):

> Of the twenty-eight women who have served as CEOs of Fortune 500 com-panies, twenty-six were married, one was divorced, and only one had never married. Many of these CEOs said they could not have succeeded without the support of their husbands, helping with the children, the household chores, and showing a willingness to move. (Sandberg, 2013, p. 110)

Note again the presumption of a single 'career primary' partner – in this case, female – and the presence of an attached-partner, in this case a husband – who is either willing to put his wife's career, or his family commitments, first. The 'male model of work' does not – cannot! – work for marriages in which both partners aspire to place career first, at least not careers in the masculinist form in which they have been (implicitly) defined. It is only slightly ironic that when I was in graduate school in the 1980s, the wry description of a 'two-career family' was one 'in which the woman held two jobs'.

The interdependence between work and family spheres – what Rosabeth Moss Kanter termed 'the Myth of Separate Worlds' (1977a) – is strong and persistent. Married men with a spouse present experience slightly higher promotion rates than never-married men. In contrast, married women had much lower rates of promotion than never-married women (Cobb-Clark and Dunlop, 1999). The demographic variable with the greatest apparent impact on promotion rates, Cobb-Clark and Dunlop note, is marriage and the presence of children: married men have promotion rates that are higher than those of never-married men, while the reverse holds true for women. 'It is striking', they observed, 'that never-married women reported having the same, or even higher, chances of being promoted than did other groups – even married men' (p. 35). As they further emphasized:

> Having a pre-school child was related to higher promotion rates for men, whereas the opposite was the case for women.. . . This differential may reflect the fact that men with young children feel they need to pursue a career more fervently to support their family. In contrast, women who have small children may direct more of their attention to their family and hence not their careers. (Cobb-Clark and Dunlop, 1999, p. 35)

It appears, therefore, that the work–family boundary continues to be what family researcher and men's studies pioneer Joseph Pleck once brilliantly described as 'asymmetrically permeable' (Pleck, 1977). One's family role is presumed to adversely limit one's work aspirations and opportunities if you are female, while the reverse holds true for men: one's work role is presumed to adversely limit one's family commitments if you are male! The boundary between the two spheres is permeable, albeit in opposite directions, depending which side of the 'gender divide' you are on. Although he described the gendered bias of this systemic connection over 35 years ago, it persists to this day. 'Regardless of employment status, wives were more likely than husbands to spend time in household activities' (Foster and Kreisler, 2012, p. 2). Married fathers, regardless of their wives' employment status, are 'less likely to engage in primary childcare on weekdays and spend less time providing childcare than married mothers did' (ibid., p. 6).

THE CONVENTIONAL ORGANIZATIONAL AND MANAGERIAL PARADIGM: DIMENSIONS OF CORPORATE MASCULINITY

It may well have been Virginia Schein who first made the explicit connection between management and masculinity when she introduced the 'think manager–think male' paradigm (1973). Appropriate forms of coordination and control in organizations have always been, and will always be, necessary to ensure individuals and units work together in the service of organizational goals. Yet since the advent of large-scale organizations in the nineteenth century, practitioners have tended to overemphasize the task/masculine side of the enterprise, with a concomitant – and enduring – neglect of the human/feminine side. In earlier work (Maier, 1992, 1999), I have elucidated the implicit gendered dimensions in the evolution of leadership theory. Here, I will address the gendered foundations for the prevailing model of organization and leadership and contrast with an alternative paradigm that has emerged and is evolving.

Table 4.1 summarizes the key dimensions of the conventional/dominant (masculinist) view of management and organization and contrasts it with a transformational feminist alternative. Table 4.2 articulates the model of leadership that arises from each contrasting paradigm.

To briefly explain the features of the dominant/conventional paradigm, the status quo is firmly anchored in the norms of 'corporate masculinity' (Maier, 1992, 1999). The organization is viewed as a hierarchical pyramid, organized under bureaucratic principles (Weber, 1946), in which power is asserted in a top-down manner and within which participants are expected to segment and subordinate their life interests to work and career. Since a primary goal is individual success and advancement, recognition and promotion by one's organizational superiors emerges as a critical factor in shaping individual choices. According to Block (1987), the consequent 'pyramidal politics' encourages participants to engage in a kind of 'myopic self-interest' in which 'playing it safe' and pleasing one's superiors becomes the key focus. Within the context of the work–family role system (Pleck, 1977), the organizational participant is presumed to be individualistically motivated by self-interest. From such egoistic presumptions, motivation is largely extrinsic, focusing on the allocation of raises and promotions.

Block's observations echo Robert Merton's (1957) analysis of the relationship between bureaucratic structure and personality, in which the conventional structure promotes 'over-conformity' (submissiveness) and rewards tendencies for 'ascendancy' (advancement). Merton was wise to point out that for all of purported advantages of bureaucratic structure (precision, reliability, efficiency), there are corresponding liabilities and limitations (e.g., lack of creativity, obedience and means–ends displacement – where the rules become ends in themselves).

The dominant values within this masculine framework include, first and foremost, a virtual obsession with the attainment of organizational objectives (goals, tasks, results), which are presumed to be promoted through efficiency, control, and the acknowledgement of managerial authority ... and the submission thereto by organizational subordinates. The core competencies necessary for success focus on a narrow technical rationality and task capability.

Table 4.1   Contrasting gendered paradigms of organization and management

	Dominant Paradigm: Management/Leadership	Emerging Paradigm: Servant Leadership
Gendered ethos	Masculine (Status quo patriarchy)	Feminine (Transformational feminism)
Organizational metaphor	Hierarchy – pyramid (Bureaucracy – top down)	Heterarchy – circular network (Web – inside out)
Self-to-other orientation	Individualistic – ME: Self 1st; Others 2nd	Collectivistic – WE: Others 1st; Self 2nd
Orientation to organization	Segmented 'Career 1st' Primacy of work	Holistic 'Life 1st' Life/work integration
Priority needs	Success and Power Ambition, individual achievement Status; Advancement (ranking); Money	Love and Connection Caring, shared accomplishment Affiliation; Connection (linking); Meaning
Motivational basis	Egoistic External; Materialistic	Altruistic Intrinsic; Actualization (of self and others)
Underlying values and guiding principles	Success (ends); Goal obsession – Results 1st Efficiency; Control; Authority: superiors 'lead' by wielding authority; subordinates 'follow' by submitting to authority; Use others	Service (means); Process emphasis – People 1st Effectiveness; Empowerment; Respect: People at all levels have the responsibility to lead and an obligation to respect others as they do so; Grow/develop others
Competencies stressed	Technical skills; Task capability; IQ; Narrow rationality (Denial of feelings)	Social- and Self-awareness; Relational capability; EQ; Emotional intelligence (Reason with feelings)

Table 4.2 Contrasting paradigms of leadership

	Dominant Paradigm: Management/Leadership	Emerging Paradigm: Servant-Leadership
Leadership icon	Leader as commander, hero (Control, direct, remain firm)	Leader as coach, servant (Enable, facilitate, be flexible)
Leadership platform (Stance)	Positional 'Power over' Lead through aggression: Coercive/intimidating/forcing; Enforce compliance; Maintain distance; Swift, decisive action – now! Anchored in fear	Personal 'Power with' Lead through affection: Persuasive/caring/ encouraging; Inspire commitment; Promote engagement; Foresight, thoughtful action Anchored in love
Leadership and influence strategies	Top-down/one-way; Managing as directing Coerce and intimidate; Critical; Deficit-focus Tops as 'superiors'; Bottoms as 'subordinates' (Submission to authority); Respect for chain of command/ obedience Please the boss – 'loyalty' Compliance and cowardice (In response to 'warrior tactics' by superiors to fulfill superior's vision)	Reciprocal/two-way; Leading as serving Connect and inspire; Appreciative inquiry Mutual respect Not positional authority; Dialogic; Collegiality; Respect for individuals Serve the mission – 'voice' Commitment and courage ('Warrior spirit' by all to advance mission and purpose)
Ultimate Leadership Objectives/ goal	Impose point of view; Advocate – win, prevail (Competitive) Career Advancement (individual) Profit (Organizational)	Mutual exploration and learning; Dialogue – exchange, understand (Collaborative) Living one's Purpose (individual) Promoting Purpose (organizational)

The model of leadership that arises from this paradigm is heavily imbued with norms of hegemonic masculinity (Koenig et al., 2011). The leader is seen as standing at the top of the organizational pyramid (or at least above one's subordinates), serving as commander and/or hero (McGee-Cooper and Looper, 2001). The leadership platform derives from one's managerial position in the hierarchy and an implied, if not overt, element of coercion by those in power and submission by those below. The leadership stance and resultant strategies within this conventional framework expects that people in powerful positions will maintain distance from those below them, enforce compliance with their directives, and be willing to take swift action (perceived as being decisive). Its stance is inherently aggressive. Interpersonally, one's strength as a leader is gauged by one's ability to impose one's point of view on others (prevailing and winning in competition), and a corresponding unwillingness to compromise or back down.

The ultimate objective from within this conventional worldview is – at the individual level – achievement, career advancement, material gain, the accumulation of power and status; at the organizational level: reaching organizational targets and goals and – especially – enhancing the corporate bottom line (short-term profit).

Yet despite its presumed benefits, there are significant flaws to this masculine organizational model and its vision of leadership. Ironically, it actually compromises individual and organizational performance. In the sections that follow I will highlight the ways in which this model is not only dysfunctional, but point out how it indeed violates innate human instincts and diminishes human happiness. If men are to replace their attachment to the corporate masculinity model in favor of a feminist alternative, they will need to understand 'What's In It For Me (WIIFM)?'

'WHY JOHNNY CAN'T LEAD . . .' ON THE DYSFUNCTIONS OF CORPORATE MASCULINITY

To begin with, the predominant model of organization and the managerial leadership behaviors it reinforces and rewards does not, in fact, maximize organizational performance. As Fred Luthans famously discovered in his pioneering research on 'real managers' (1988, 2013) the most effective managers engage in significantly higher levels of human-oriented and communication activities than their less effective counterparts. ('Effectiveness' was defined in Luthans's research as 'the perceived quantity and quality of the performance of a manager's unit and his or her work group members' satisfaction and commitment' [2013, p. 13] determined by an elaborate multiple-measures index.) Effective managers spent far more time engaging with their people, getting to know them, motivating them, sharing information with them, resolving conflicts, training them, developing them, recruiting and staffing for openings . . . as well as correcting and disciplining them when their performance was off-target.

Yet Luthans's research also unearthed some disturbing findings. Echoing Block's (1987) criticism of the limiting effects of pyramidal politics, Luthans found – meritocratic claims of organization notwithstanding – that the managers who were the most *effective* were not the ones who were most likely to be promoted! In a confirmation of the means–ends displacement in bureaucratic systems (Weber, 1946; Merton, 1957), Luthans found that *successful* managers – those who were most likely to be promoted and advance more swiftly in the organization – spent the *least* amount of time on human resource activities . . . and the most amount of time on politicking and networking! Consistent also with the points made earlier on the characteristics of the dominant model of organization (Table 4.1), Luthans observed that it:

> should be noted that many managers aspire to be successful rather than being effective. One reason is that personal pride and mobility are at stake.. . . . [A]lthough being successful as opposed to effective may seem less desirable to the organization, from an individual manager's perspective, it may be part of an effective career strategy. (Luthans, 2013, p. 13)

Indeed, Luthans stressed that – for effective managers – 'the least-relative contribution to the managers' measured effectiveness came from the networking activity.. . . . Human resource management activities had a strong relationship to effectiveness, but had the weakest relative relationship to success' (ibid.). These contrasting profiles, Luthans mused, 'may have significant implications . . . for understanding the performance problems facing today's organizations' (ibid., p. 14).

EXAMPLES OF MASCULINE MANAGERIAL DYSFUNCTION: THE NASA *CHALLENGER* AND *COLUMBIA* DISASTERS

A close study of the space shuttle *Challenger* and *Columbia* disasters – though 17 years and 66 missions apart – reveals striking parallels and direct connections to the dimensions of corporate masculinity enumerated above. The similarities between the twin catastrophies were so pronounced that the official Columbia Accident Investigation Board's final report (CAIB, 2003) devoted an entire section to dissecting the managerial actions that culminated in the death of the *Columbia* crew, entitled 'Echoes of Challenger.' The managerial critique offered by the CAIB represents, in essence, a ringing condemnation of a social system operating not abnormally, but absolutely normally – at least within the conventional paradigm of masculine management and organization that still (pre)dominates, and that produced not one, but two space shuttle disasters. Here is a brief synopsis of how managers and an organization operating 'normally' were, in fact, operating in ways that were masculine, deficient and dysfunctional . . . to the point of disaster.

Challenger failed in January 1986 because repeated attempts to alert key decision-makers of the inherent dangers of the Solid Rocket Boosters' O-ring sealing capability fell on deaf ears. Why? At the organizational level, middle-level managers were more preoccupied with meeting the timetable set by their bosses to accelerate the launch schedule from nine flights in 1985 to 15 flights in 1986 . . . and up to 24 by 1990, than with flight safety. Warnings that record cold temperatures at lift-off would compromise the ability of the rockets' O-rings to 'hold' and seal properly were also submerged because such news was anathema to managers' mental models: (1) that O-rings could not be a 'safety of flight' issue; and (2) that the space agency was already committed to bringing a secondary launch facility 'on line' at Vandenberg AFB in California . . . where cold temperatures in the range at issue on the *Challenger* launch (as low as 58 degrees) are commonplace. Hundreds of millions of dollars had been invested in that effort, and no one wanted to be responsible for bursting NASA's bubble . . . and confronting their bosses with the unwelcome news. William Lucas, the Marshall Center Director for NASA and the direct superior of Shuttle launch official Larry Mulloy, reportedly encouraged his subordinate to press for a 'go' decision: 'We get a little cold nip, and they want to shut the shuttle system down? I sure would like to see their reasons for that', Mulloy explained to me in a personal interview (Mulloy, 1991). One of the prescriptions of masculinity, after all, is 'no sissy stuff!' so Lucas was presenting an implicitly gendered challenge to the contractor through his subordinate manager.

In a famous telephone conference meeting between NASA and the rocket contractor Thiokol, NASA managers bristled at the suggestion of a low-temperature launch constraint: 'My God, Thiokol! When do you expect me to launch? – Next April?!' Unwilling to take the risk of alienating its major customer – and risking its sole-source contract – Thiokol reversed its 'no-launch' recommendation, even though its top experts were opposed. When asked why they did not even poll their engineers in a private caucus on the final decision, Thiokol managers asserted incredulously: 'We only polled the management people because we had already established that we were not going to be unanimous' (Maier, 2003).

The engineers, in this instance, were sidelined (1) because of their subordinated status and (2) because they could not provide objective evidence to prove the O-rings would fail. As Larry Mulloy, the Solid Rocket Booster manager for NASA put it, 'we were going to demand to know why and not accept it on the basis of some handwringing emotion' (Maier, 2003). Here we see the invocation of logic and rationality over emotions, which – ironically – was delivered during an intensely emotional tirade by the same manager.

Similarly, 17 years later, *Columbia*'s foam shedding problem presented an unwelcome challenge to NASA managers struggling once more to meet an organizationally imposed deadline of completing the core module of the International Space Station by 19 February 2004. So obsessed were NASA managers with meeting that projected target date, that all concerns with foam damage were interpreted within a mental model of a 'threat to schedule'. . . not as a threat to flight safety or human life. NASA's engineers' request to the Department of Defense to train one of its vaunted spy satellites onto the underbelly of the shuttle to assess the damage of the 'foam strike' that had hit the leading edge of the left-hand wing, was 'turned off' by their superiors who were more concerned with an apparent breach of protocol and procedure . . . that the request had not been 'vetted' through proper channels, reinforcing the masculine preoccupation with obeying one's chains of command and authority. Had the engineers' request – a request initiated in response to a managerial demand for a briefing on the implications of the 'foam hit' – been allowed to proceed, they would have discovered a hole larger than a basketball on the underside of the wing and would have been able to pull out all the stops in an Apollo 13 ('failure is not an option') type rescue effort. However, the NASA manager in charge, Linda Ham, simply asserted that even if there were a severe problem 'there is nothing we could do about it anyway' . . . setting in motion a catastrophic incidence of a self-fulfilling prophecy.

In its analysis of the twin disasters, the Columbia Accident Investigation Board (CAIB) found numerous structural and bureaucratic parallels, which resonate deeply with the masculine dimensions articulated in Tables 4.1 and 4.2: 'NASA's culture of bureaucratic accountability emphasized chain of command, procedure, following rules, and going by the book. The unintended negative effect: allegiance to hierarchy and procedure replaced deference to NASA engineers' technical expertise' (CAIB, 2003, p. 200). In further observations on 'History as Cause: Echoes of Challenger', CAIB found that NASA's structure and hierarchy 'blocked effective com-munication. Signals were overlooked, people were silenced, and useful information and dissenting views of technical issues did not surface at higher levels' (ibid., p. 201). The unstated subtext is that people were more concerned with meeting short-term goals and pleasing their bosses to protect their jobs, than with addressing the threat to human life posed by the foam hit. Rarely, if ever, were middle-level managers – in both tragedies – willing to put themselves at risk (organizationally speaking) by disappointing those above them by giving voice to their well-founded concerns. Fourteen astronauts paid with their lives for these managers' acquiescence to the norms of masculinity.

In both cases, 'what was communicated to parts of the organization was that O-ring erosion and foam debris were not problems' (ibid.). Had NASA been configured in ways less attuned to the masculine aspects of organization presented here, then both tragedies could – would – have been prevented.

Selected examples from two more recent events underscore the need to challenge the masculine-based structure of management and organizations. First, root cause analysis of the worldwide financial crisis of 2008 (from which we are still recovering at the time of writing) reveals that 'masculine fragilities' were a 'major condition of the excesses leading to the crisis' (Knights and Tullberg, 2012, p. 385), that is, in the banking executives' clamor to generate ever-higher levels of financial profit . . . and personal gain in the form of higher compensation and bonuses. This reveals the problematic nature of unbridled self-interest and a preoccupation with one's own (narrow) career advancement and personal material well-being. Second, the 2010 *Deepwater Horizon*/BP Macondo Well oil spill in the Gulf of Mexico was caused in part by a 'cowboy culture' (Hoffman, 2010). As the official investigation into the blowout revealed, 'While many technical failures contributed to the blowout, the Chief Counsel's team traces each of them back to an overarching failure of management' (Chief Counsel, 2011, p. 225). The managers' (masculine) obsession with goals, exacerbated by their inability to meet their proposed targets for schedule and cost efficiency, contributed to the failure, one in which 11 workers died and another 17 were seriously injured, and in which 5 million gallons of oil spewed into the Gulf until the well was finally sealed on 18 September . . . nearly six months after the explosion! What happened on 20 April was that a blowout preventer failed to plug the malfunctioning rig. Workers on the rig had been rushing to cap the well that had just been dug at a depth of 18 360 feet below the rig (and an astounding 13 000 feet below the ocean floor) so they could move the rig to another site. They were behind schedule, and over budget.

BP had scheduled the well drilling for 78 days at a cost of $96 million, but the real target was 51 days. By 20 April, the date of the calamitous explosion, the drill rig had been in position for 73 days. BP was leasing the *Deepwater Horizon* from Transocean at a rate of about $533 000.00 per day, the single greatest expense to BP for drilling the Macondo Well (ibid., p. 245). According to Mike Williams, Transocean's chief electronics technician, a BP manager was urging the crew to speed things along: 'Let's bump it up, let's bump it up', the manager said, as Williams told CBS's '60 Minutes' (Hoffman, 2010, p. 84). The 2011 *Chief Counsel's Report* of the National Commission on the BP *Deepwater Horizon* oil spill observed that BP employees made a number of decisions 'that increased risk and saved time' (Chief Counsel, 2011, p. 245): '*Understandable cost pressures drove decision making*' and decisions in the last month at Macondo were '*biased ... in favor of cost and time savings while increasing risk of a blowout*' (ibid., p. 242; emphasis original). Senior managers were evaluated on their ability to complete projects on schedule and under budget, and by 20 April the project was already 22 days behind its actual completion target. The masculine preoccupation with short-term organizational profit, the drive to please one's institutional superiors in the hierarchy (and/or fear of displeasing them), and the prospects for short-term individual gain through performance compensation bonuses were creating a perfect storm of pressures on the BP and Transocean managers on the scene.

Where a feminist orientation might have placed a higher premium on caution and human life, BP was notorious for its 'cavalier approach to safety' (Hoffman, 2010, p. 83). As Hoffman reported, according to the Center for Public Integrity, 'from June 2007 to February 2010, BP's refineries in Texas City (TX) and Toledo (OH) accounted for 829 of 851 industry-wide safety violations identified as "willful" by the Occupational Safety and Health Administration (OSHA)' ... and demonstrated what OSHA described as 'plain indifference to ... employee safety and health' (ibid.). The Macondo disaster – as the *Chief Counsel's Report* concluded, 'was not inevitable' (p. x).

TOWARDS A NEW PARADIGM OF ORGANIZATIONS: ENGENDERING LEADERSHIP FROM A FEMINIST PERSPECTIVE

One wonders why the task/production/control/authoritarian model of corporate masculinity predominates in organizations, when we have solid research evidence – from as far back as 50, and even 100, years ago, that a more feminine approach (participative, democratic, consensual, human-oriented) is actually more productive (McGregor [1957] 2001). Douglas McGregor, whose enduring contribution was to stress 'the human side of enterprise', was certainly not the first to lay claim to this (inherently feminine) territory. Mary Parker Follett, for example, in the 1920s – nearly 100 years ago – had already issued stinging critiques of Henri Fayol's (1916) and Frederick Winslow Taylor's (1911) perspectives on the primacy of managerial control, arguing that the wish to govern one's own life constituted 'the very essence of the human being' (Follett [1926] 2001, p. 155).

People, I have discovered, contribute to what they are connected to and some of the most important work that (feminist) leaders do is (1) to connect people to themselves (their own purpose), (2) to connect people to one another, (3) to connect people to them (the leader – which requires they know you care about them, not just as a 'worker', but as a fellow human being), and (4) to connect them to the organization's purpose ('how does what we do here – together – really matter?').

Such connections are irrelevant in the conventionally masculine managerial paradigm (emphasizing results, direction, control, prerogative), where the exigencies of pyramidal politics and organizational hierarchy induce organizational participants alike to 'follow in the footsteps' of their predecessors, encouraging both women and men to 'act like men'. Given the attendant dysfunctions just highlighted, it behooves us to lead and organize in fundamentally different ways, ways that emphasize service over self-interest (Greenleaf, 1991; Block, 2013) and create networks of collaboration over pyramids of control (Helgesen, 1990; Wheatley and Kellner-Rogers, 1996). John Zenger and Joseph Folkman, in their exhaustive study (2002) of 'extraordinary leaders', provide data from 400 000 360-degree assessments that substantiate that the most successful and effective leaders draw on both task and interpersonal competencies. They found, for example, that fully two-thirds (66 percent) of all leaders who were in the top quartile on both 'Focus on Results' and 'Focus on Interpersonal Skills' scored in the 90th percentile on overall leadership effectiveness. In contrast, only 13 percent of the leaders who were assessed in the top quartile of task results alone were also at the 90th percentile, and only 9 percent of those who were assessed at the top quartile of interpersonal skills alone were assessed at the 90th percentile in overall leadership effectiveness. Or, as Ken Blanchard and Norman Vincent Peale put it in their famous book, *The Power of Ethical Management* (1988, p. 106), 'managing only for profit is like playing tennis with your eye on the scoreboard and not on the ball'. It is not only possible to 'do well by doing good', but it may be that doing good is the foundation for doing well in the first place, as we find when we examine data beyond the individual managerial level.

At the institutional/organizational level, data from the Great Place to Work Institute, the research partner for *Fortune Magazine*'s annual 'Best Place to Work' survey provides a glimpse into the efficacy of following fundamentally feminine processes such as caring vs ranking, demonstrating respect vs insisting on authority, and being focused on purpose vs obsessed with profit. Twenty-five years of research and data from millions of employee surveys over that period reveal that companies that put people first – their own people, and their customers – actually outperform their competitors, whose focus is on results first. Over the past 15 years, for example, the cumulative stock market returns of the 'Great Places to Work' are three to four times greater than those of the S&P 500, and experienced 50 percent less turnover overall (Great Places to Work, 2013).

As we further examine Tables 4.1 and 4.2, we can see that a fundamentally different approach to organizing and leading is possible. This is not just a theoretical conjecture, but a reality. Organizations – and individuals – who follow these feminist principles (whether implicitly or explicitly) abound. The principal driver from a feminist perspective has to do with how we perceive our overriding purpose: is it to serve and advance ourselves, as the masculinist worldview promotes, or is it to serve others and bring out their best? Are members committed to a purpose beyond one's self?

In this alternate paradigm, metaphorically feminine gendered, the organization is perceived as a web of relationships, of which the titular leader is one player, but not the dominant one (quite literally). Leaders at all levels perceive their organizational lifeworld fundamentally in 'we' terms (vs 'me'), and see their work as but one meaningful component of their existence. They understand that they – and their colleagues – 'bring their whole selves to work', and seek to create space in those organizations where people can blend both high fulfillment with high performance (in that order). Their priority is on creating connections through love and care, and instilling a sense of shared accomplishment, never claiming credit for the efforts of others. As Jim Collins stressed in describing 'level 5 leaders' (2001), such leaders perceive success 'through a window', and perceive failure 'in the mirror:' When things go well, they credit their team; when things go wrong, the first place they look is within themselves. They are instinctively humble.

From a feminist perspective, emotional intelligence is regarded on par with technical intelligence, and in fact becomes increasingly important as one assumes greater and greater responsibility for managing the work of others (Goleman, 1995, 1998; Goleman et al., 2004). But above all, feminist organizations invert the priority of the dominant model: the principle purpose of feminist organizations is not to succeed, but to serve. Success is seen as derivative, a by-product, of service. To the extent that corporations deliver on that service, they earn profit. And though profit is essential to corporate survival, it cannot be confused with the corporation's reason for being, its core purpose. Organizations that cannot resolve that confusion operate blindly and implode dramatically. (Think: Enron, Worldcom, TYCO for other examples of the obsessive focus on the bottom line run amok.)

Arie de Geus, the legendary former head of worldwide planning for

Royal Dutch Shell, explained in *The Living Company* (1997) that this amounts to confusing a prerequisite for organizational survival with its reason for being: companies clearly require profit in the same way any living being requires oxygen. We require oxygen to stay alive, but the mere act of breathing it would never be construed as our purpose for being here, and, as Peter Senge and his associates point out in their best-selling *Fifth Discipline Fieldbook* (1994) every profit-making corporation has the purpose of making money, therefore focusing on that purpose, at the expense of others, distracts from an organization's competitive advantage; what makes it unique. This point has also been more recently corroborated in Collins and Porras's excellent research into companies of enduring greatness, those that are 'built to last' (1997).

Implications for Leadership

Robert Greenleaf put this challenge into stark relief when he first pro-posed that leading could be seen as a way of serving (1991), that for 'the servant as leader':

> it begins with a natural feeling that one wants to serve, to serve *first*. Then conscious choice brings one to aspire to lead. This is sharply different from the person who is *leader* first, perhaps because of the need to assuage an unusual power drive or to acquire material possessions. For this person it will be a later choice to serve – if the choice is made at all – after leadership has been estab-lished. (Greenleaf, 1991, p. 7; original emphasis)

The difference between these two archetypes for Greenleaf manifested itself in the extent to which – consistent with the masculine or feminine aspects of organizations model being elucidated here – other people's highest priority needs are being served. According to Greenleaf:

> The best test, and difficult to administer, is: Do those served grow as persons? Do they, *while being served*, become healthier, wiser, freer, more autonomous, more likely themselves to become servants? *And*, what is the effect on the least privileged in society; will they benefit, or at least, not be further deprived? (Ibid.; original emphasis)

Greenleaf's experience at AT&T and as founder in 1970 of the Center for Applied Ethics (now The Greenleaf Center for Servant Leadership), led him to some of the same conclusions that Douglas McGregor had reached about the transformative capability of putting people and their develop-ment first. But Greenleaf was ultimately more concerned not with narrow organizational performance per se, but with its implications for the kind of society that results. After all, since most people in the western world spend the majority of their waking hours devoted to the work sector, the quality of that experience would – according to Greenleaf – have the potential to transform society itself:

> If a good society is to be built, one that is more just and more caring and pro-viding opportunity for people to grow . . . the most effective way is to raise the performance-as-servants of *institutions*, and sanction natural servants to serve and lead. (Quoted in Frick and Spears, 1996, p. 5; emphasis added)

This shift in thinking and focus is consistent with the alternative (feminist) paradigm I have suggested by which organizations may operate. Indeed, if we compare organizations that are known exemplars of servant-leadership with the kind of high-performing organizations highlighted in Jim Collins's *Good to Great* study (2001), a very fascinating finding appears. Sipe and Frick did just that in their research in *The Seven Pillars of Servant Leadership* (2009). Where Collins's research team 'worked backwards' to discover, and then retroactively explain the sustained success of their 'great' companies – discovering that 'level 5 leadership' was a major con-tributing factor – Sipe and Frick started with the underlying value system of companies. They identified 11 corporations that were widely recognized for embracing the principles and practices of servant-leadership: AFLAC, FedEx, Herman Miller, Marriott Hotels, Medtronic, Men's Wearhouse, ServiceMaster, Starbucks, Southwest Airlines, Synovus Financial, and the TORO Company, and then set out to compare their performance with those that had been lauded in the *Good to Great* (GTG) study. They selected a ten-year period subsequent to the publication of *Good to Great* (i.e., 1994–2004), with the reasonable assumption that if a company had been truly great for 15 years (the Collins criterion), it should be able to remain so. Their findings are summarized in Table 4.3.

As Sipe and Frick report, when Collins and his research team sought a term to describe the outstanding but humble leaders that had helped make the 'great' results possible, 'servant-leader' was 'a serious contender' (Sipe and Frick, 2009, p. 2). This should not be surprising, since at the time GTG was being prepared for publication, the concept of servant-leader-ship had already been in circulation for 20 years. 'Some members of the team, however, "violently objected" to its connotations of "servitude" and "weakness"' (ibid.). 'Level 5 leadership' was not only less controversial, but allowed the team to put its own brand into the mix. Undeterred, when Sipe and Frick ran the results of their analysis, they made a startling dis-covery: 'servant-led companies are *even better than great!* . . . [producing] *far superior* financial results' (ibid.; original emphasis). (See also Melrose,

Table 4.3   The performance case for servant-led organizations

| | Financial Performance 1994–2004 (Average Pretax Portfolio Returns) | | |
	S&P 500	Good to Great Companies*	Servant-Led Companies**
% increase in portfolio performance	10.8	17.5	24.3

Note: *GTG (Collins, 2001) companies: Abbott, Circuit City, Gillette, Fannie Mae, Kimberly-Clark, Kroger, Nucor, Pitney Bowes, Walgreens, Wells Fargo; **Servant-led companies: AFLAC, FedEx, Herman Miller, Marriott Hotels, Medtronic, Men's Wearhouse, ServiceMaster, Starbucks, Southwest Airlines, Synovus Financial, TORO Company.

Source: Sipe and Frick (2009).

1995; Behar, 2007; Sisodia et al., 2007; Frick et al., 2008.)

INVITING PERSONAL REFLECTIONS ON LEADING AND MEANING

For the past 19 years in my work as creator and coordinator for the leadership studies programs at Chapman University, I have had countless occasions to engage undergraduate and graduate students as well as hundreds of participants in leadership development consulting projects in exercises that provide corroboration for the value abandoning our attachment to corporate masculinity in favor of a feminist orientation to leadership. Two of these may have particular significance to the foregoing discussion: 'Sources of Personal Meaning' and 'My Best Leadership'. I invite you to engage in them here, and to share them with your own clients, colleagues, and students.

Sources of Personal Meaning

When Rosabeth Moss Kanter suggested that the traditional career model expects professionals to 'act as though' they had no competing loyalties (1977b), she was raising a fact of life in organizations that we euphemistically tend to refer to as 'the real world'. And yet this 'act as though' principle does not accord with our own experience in the *real* world, that is, the reality of everyday life.

   To call this 'career success as life success' assumption into question, I have adapted an exercise shared with me by the then CEO of the Greenleaf Center for Servant Leadership, Dr. Kent Keith (personal communication, 2009). Kent told me he had used this exercise with thousands of participants in his conference presentations, keynotes, and leadership development programs over ten years, and I have now had the chance to replicate the same exercise with over 300 students in ten classes at the undergraduate and graduate levels, and in ten leadership development sessions with another 300 practicing managers. Consider Box 4.1, 'Sources

---

BOX 4.1   A DOZEN POSSIBLE SOURCES OF MEANING IN PEOPLE'S LIVES

Acquiring money/wealth	Living my values
Giving and receiving love	Being successful
Status	Family
Winning	Faith
Power/influence	Doing My Personal Best
Having a sense of accomplishment	Fame

Source: Keith (2009).

---

of Meaning' and take a moment to rank order or circle which ones *you* regard as sources of meaning in *your* life, those values or activities from which *you* derive your greatest sense of fulfillment.

In the thousands of people Keith has sampled with this methodology, and the 600 I have conducted this exercise with from 2009 to 2013, the results are remarkably, durably consistent. The values that rise to the top, without fail, are values anchored in an ethic of service, what Wharton School researcher Adam Grant has more recently (2013) termed "giver" values: family, giving and receiving love, having a sense of accomplishment, doing my personal best, and living my values. The ones that consistently place at or near the bottom when these dozen values are ranked are: fame, money/wealth, having power/influence, status and winning. According to Grant, these findings are virtually universal in cross-cultural studies, and classifies as "Taker Values" those latter ones (above) that Keith associates with the "Power Model". We need money to survive, to be sure, but we must not confuse it with providing our purpose in life. As Harvard Business Professor Mark Albion has suggested, there is a profound difference between 'making a living' and 'making a life' (Albion, 2000).

My Best Leadership Moment

The second exercise addresses the true nature of leadership, not the power model of leadership suggested by corporate masculinity. As deceptively simple as it is, it is also in many ways the most profound: take a 60-second break in your reading of this chapter to reflect on *your* personal best leadership moment; a time when you were leading at your absolute best! It could be at work, in your family, as a coach, in the community. Any time you stepped up as a 'leader' and attempted to influence a situation, somehow. Get a vivid mental picture of the situation, who you were with, what the context was, what challenge you were facing, what you were up to, what you did, what inspired you to do so, and so forth. Recall it fully, and make some notes on it here:

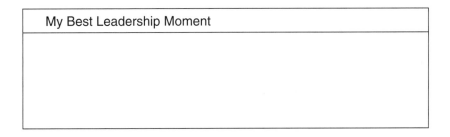

My Best Leadership Moment

When you reflect back to this time when you were leading at your absolute best, can you now identify who or what the *focus* of your leadership was at the time? What was the *intent* behind your leadership? This is a 'forced choice' question, because I want you to determine whether it was either (1) 'first, foremost, or fundamentally' about doing or getting something for *yourself* . . . or (2) 'first, foremost or fundamentally' about getting or doing something for *someone else* or *others*? Which is it? (1) . . . or (2)?

Think of this akin to the concept of a primary beneficiary: "Who was the intended *primary* beneficiary of your efforts in that 'best leadership moment': *yourself* . . . or the *others* you were leading?" It's not that you don't *both* benefit. Clearly you do, but it is the *directionality* of the benefit that I am getting at here: did others benefit because you did (first), or did you benefit because of what you did for them (first)?

In conducting this exercise with over 600 people across at least 15 different settings (keynotes, orientations, workshops, classes, etc.) I have found that in 90–95 percent of the cases, when we are leading at what we consider to be our own personal, absolute best, *we are serving others*. This inherently feminist leadership principle – when others do well, I do well

– does not only appear to be universal, but is evidently connected to the idea that we are, by nature, empathic and altruistic . . . not self-centered. Or, as scientific evidence increasingly suggests, survival of the kindest may explain our evolution as a species more than survival of the fittest (Decety and Ickes, 2009; DeWaal, 2009; Tomasello, 2009). Empathy and compassion, our concern for others, may be more powerful determinants of our mental and physical well-being and our success in life than aggression, competition, or self-interest (Goleman, 2006; Barasch, 2009; Keltner, 2009; Keltner et al., 2010). And those who lead from a foundation of "giver values" are increasingly emerging as those who are most successful in organizations, according to Grant's groundbreaking research (2013).

It also turns out that the more femininely attuned commitment to leading as a way of serving may help both men and women lead happier lives. Dr. Martin Seligman, one of the preeminent research psychologists of the twentieth century and a pioneer in the emerging field of 'positive psychology', suggests as much (2002). The author of over 20 books, perhaps his most significant contribution has been to discover the sources of 'authentic happiness'. Instead of following the traditional psychological approach of helping troubled people function normally again, Seligman studied people at the opposite end of the psychological spectrum: those who were deeply and consistently happy. He discovered that 'authentically happy' people (1) knew what they are really good at; they are aware of what Seligman calls their 'signature strengths', (2) they had concrete and frequent opportunities to use those strengths, and (3) most importantly, they did so in the service of something greater than themselves (Seligman, 2002; see also Achor, 2010; Martin, 2012).

Research indicates that we are at our happiest when we're serving others by doing what we have a passion for, and what we do best; when we are called upon to use our strengths (Rath, 2007; Rath and Conchie, 2008), our natural talents, in the service of something greater than ourselves. It is true, as Albert Schweitzer once remarked, that, 'Everyone must work to live, but the purpose of life is to serve and show compassion and the will to help others.' (cited in Keith, 2012, p. 3).[1] He also famously observed: 'I do not know what your destiny will be, but one thing I do know: The only ones among you who will be truly happy will be those who have sought – and found – how to serve' (ibid., p. 71).

NOTE

1. Actually, the more complete quote – as reflected on a plaque in one of the classroom buildings at Chapman University where Schweitzer is regarded as its 'guiding spirit' –

reads: 'Everyone must work to live, but the purpose of human life is to serve and show compassion and the will to help others. Only then have we become true human beings'.

REFERENCES

Achor, S. (2010), *The Happiness Advantage*, New York: Crown Business.

Albion, M. (2000), *Making a Life, Making a Living*, New York: Warner.

Barasch, M.I. (2009), *The Compassionate Life: Walking the Path of Kindness*, San Francisco, CA: Berrett-Koehler.

Behar, H. (2007), *It's Not About the Coffee: Leadership Principles from a Life at Starbucks*, New York: Penguin.

Blanchard, K. and N.V. Peale (1988), *The Power of Ethical Management*, New York: William Morrow.

Block, P. (1987), *The Empowered Manager: Positive Political Skills at Work*, San Francisco, CA: Jossey-Bass.

Block, P. (2013), *Stewardship: Choosing Service Over Self-interest*, 2nd edition, San Francisco, CA: Berrett-Koehler.

Bureau of Labor Statistics (2012), 'Wives who earn more than their husbands, 1987–2010; 1988–2011', *Annual Social and Economic Supplements to the Current Population Survey* (www.bls.gov/cps).

CAIB (2003), *Columbia Accident Investigation Board Report*, Washington, DC: US Government Printing Office.

Chief Counsel (2011), *Macondo, The Gulf Oil Disaster. Chief Counsel's Report*, Washington, DC: National Commission on the BP Deepwater Horizon Oil Spill and Offshore Drilling.

Cobb-Clark, D. and Y. Dunlop (1999), 'The role of gender in job promotions', *Monthly Labor Review*, **125**(12), 32–8.

Cohany, S.R. and E. Sok (2007), 'Trends in labor force participation of married mothers of infants', *Monthly Labor Review*, **130**(2), 9–16.

Collins, J. (2001), *Good to Great: Why Some Companies Make the Leap . . . And Others Don't*, New York: Harper-Collins.

Collins, J. and J. Porras (1997), *Built to Last: Successful Habits of Visionary Companies*, New York: HarperCollins.

Coser, L.A. (1974), *Greedy Institutions: Patterns of Undivided Commitment*, New York: Free Press.

Decety, J. and W. Ickes (eds) (2009), *The Social Neuroscience of Empathy*, Boston, MA: The MIT Press.

De Geus, A. (1997), *The Living Company: Growth Learning and Longevity in Business*, Chicago, IL: Longview.

DeWaal, F. (2009), *The Age of Empathy: Nature's Lessons for a Kinder Society*, New York: Crown Publishing Group.

DiNatale, M. and S. Boraas (2002), 'The labor force experience of women from "Generation X"', *Monthly Labor Review*, March, **125**(3), 3–15.

Fayol, H. (1916), *General and Industrial Management*, trans. C. Storrs, London: Pittman.

Follett, M.P. [1926] (2001), 'The giving of orders', in J.M. Shafritz and J.S. Ott, *Classics of Organization Theory*, 5th edition, New York: Harcourt Brace.

Foster, A.C. and C.J. Kreisler (2012), 'How parents use time and money', *US Bureau of Labor Statistics, Beyond the Numbers*, **1**(1), August, 1–8.

Frick, D. and L. Spears (1996), *On Becoming a Servant Leader: The Private Writings of Robert K. Greenleaf*, San Francisco, CA: Jossey-Bass.

Frick, D., D. Hoxeng and J. Panther (2008), *The Business Case for Servant Leadership*, Phoenix, AZ: Ken Blanchard Executive MBA Program.

Goleman, D. (1995), *Emotional Intelligence*, New York: Bantam.

Goleman, D. (1998), *Working with Emotional Intelligence*, New York: Bantam.

Goleman, D. (2006), *Social Intelligence: The Revolutionary New Science of Human Relationships*, New York: Bantam.

Goleman, D., R. Boyatzis and A. McKee (2004), *Primal Leadership: Learning to Lead with Emotional Intelligence*, Boston, MA: Harvard Business School Press.

Grant, A. (2013), *Give and Take: A Revolutionary Approach to Success.* New York: Penguin/Viking.

Great Place to Work (2013), 'The ROI on workplace culture', accessed 22 January 2013 at http://www.greatplacetowork.com/our-approach/what-are-the-benefits-great-workplaces.

Greenleaf, R. (1991), *The Servant as Leader*, Indianapolis: The Greenleaf Center.

Heider, J. (1985), *The Tao of Leadership: Leadership Strategies for a New Age*, Atlanta: Humanics.

Helgesen, S. (1990), *The Female Advantage: Women's Ways of Leadership*, New York: Doubleday.

Hoffman, C. (2010), 'How the blowout happened', *Popular Mechanics*, **187**(10), 76–87.

Kanter, R.M. (1977a), *Work and Family in the United States: A Critical Review and Agenda for Research and Policy*, New York: Russell Sage Foundation.

Kanter, R.M. (1977b), *Men and Women of the Corporation*, New York: Basic.

Keith, K. (2009), Personal communication, 21 September.

Keith, K. (2012), *The Case for Servant Leadership*, 2nd edition, Westfield, IN: The Greenleaf Center.

Keltner, D. (2009), *Born to be Good: The Science of a Meaningful Life*, New York: W.W. Norton and Company Inc.

Keltner, D., J. Marsh and J.A. Smith (eds) (2010), *The Compassionate Instinct*, New York: W.W. Norton and Company Inc.

Kerfoot, D. and D. Knights (1993), 'Management, masculinity and manipulation: From paternalism to corporate strategy in financial services in Britain', *Journal of Management Studies*, **30**(4), 659–77.

Knights, D. and M. Tullberg (2012), 'Managing masculinity/mismanaging the corporation', *Organization*, **19**(4), 385–404.

Koenig, A., A. Eagly, A. Mitchell and T. Ristikari (2011), 'Are leader stereotypes masculine? A meta-analysis of three research paradigms', *Psychological Bulletin*, **137**(4), 616–42.

Luthans, F. (1988), 'Successful vs. effective real managers', *Academy of Management Executive*, **2**(2), 127–32.

Luthans, F. (2013), 'Great leaders: An evidence-based approach', accessed 10 April 2013 at http://answers.mheducation.com/management/organizational-behavior/great-leaders-evidence-based-approach.

Maier, M. (1992), 'Evolving paradigms of management in organizations: A gendered analysis', *Journal of Management Systems*, **4**(1), 29–45.

Maier, M. (1999), 'On the gendered substructure of organization: Dimensions and dilemmas of corporate masculinity', in G. Powell (ed.), *Handbook of Gender and Work*, Thousand Oaks, CA: Sage, pp. 69–93.

Maier, M. (2003), *'A Major Malfunction . . .', The Story Behind the Space Shuttle Challenger Disaster*, 2nd edition [DVD and Instructional Materials], Albany: The Research Foundation of the State University of New York.

Martin, M.W. (2012), *Happiness and the Good Life*, Oxford: Oxford University Press.

Martin, P.Y. (1996), 'Engendering and evaluating dynamics: Men, masculinities and managements', in D. Collinson and J. Hearn, *Men as Managers, Managers as Men: Critical Perspectives on Men, Masculinities and Managements*, Thousand Oaks, CA: Sage, pp. 186–209.

McGee-Cooper, A. and G. Looper (2001), *The Essentials of Servant Leadership: Principles in Practice*, Waltham, MA: Pegasus.

McGregor, D. [1957] (2001), 'The human side of enterprise', in J.M. Shafritz and J.S. Ott, *Classics of Organization Theory*, 5th edition, New York: Harcourt Brace, pp. 179–84.

Melrose, K. (1995), *Making the Grass Greener on Your Side: A CEO's Journey to Leading by Serving*, San Francisco, CA: Berrett-Koehler.

Merton, R.K. (1957), *Social Theory and Social Structure*, Boston, MA: Free Press.

Morgan, D.H.J. (1996), 'The gender of bureaucracy', in D.L. Collinson and J. Hearn (eds), *Men as Managers, Managers as Men: Critical Perspectives on Men, Masculinities, and Managements*, Thousand Oaks, CA: Sage, pp. 43–60.

Mulloy, L. (1991), Personal communication, 15 May.

Pleck, J.H. (1977), 'The work–family role system', *Social Problems*, **24**(4), 417–27.

Rath, T. (2007), *StrengthsFinder 2.0*, New York: Gallup.

Rath, T. and B. Conchie (2008), *Strengths-based Leadership: Great Leaders, Teams, and Why People Follow*, New York: Gallup.

Sandberg, S. (2013), *Lean In: Women, Work and the Will to Lead*, New York: Knopf.

Schein, V.E. (1973), 'The relationship between sex role stereotypes and requisite management characteristics', *Journal of Applied Psychology*, **57**(2), 95–100.

Seligman, M. (2002), *Authentic Happiness*, New York: Free Press.

Senge, P., R. Ross, B. Smith, C. Roberts and A. Kleiner (1994), *The Fifth Discipline Fieldbook*, New York: Doubleday.

Sipe, J. and D. Frick (2009), *Seven Pillars of Servant Leadership: Practicing the Wisdom of Leading by Serving*, Mahwah, NJ: Paulist.

Sisodia, R., J. Sheth and D. Wolfe (2007), *Firms of Endearment: How World Class Companies Profit from Passion and Purpose*, New Jersey: Prentice Hall.

Smith, A. (2009), *The Theory of Moral Sentiments*, 6th edition/250th anniversary edition, New York: Penguin.

Taylor, F.W. (1911), *The Principles of Scientific Management*, New York: Horton.

Tomasello, M. (2009), *Why We Cooperate*, Boston, MA: MIT Press.

Weber, M. (1946), *From Max Weber: Essays in Sociology*, edited and trans. H.H. Gerth and C. Wright Mills, Oxford: Oxford University Press.

Wheatley, M. and M. Kellner-Rogers (1996), *A Simpler Way*, San Francisco, CA: Berrett-Koehler.

Zenger, J. and J. Folkman (2002), *The Extraordinary Leader: Turning Good Managers into Great Leaders*, New York: McGraw-Hill.

5. Relations, emotions and differences: re-gendering emotional labour in the context of men doing care

Ruth Simpson

INTRODUCTION

While there has been considerable work exploring how women perform emotional labour (e.g., Bolton and Boyd, 2003; Bolton, 2007), there has been less work on how men perform such 'caring' roles. Men in these contexts can face special difficulties, as 'feminine' discourses of service and care, which often carry a devalued status, collide with dominant conceptions of masculinity, and as organizational interactions and practices potentially reflect non-masculine ways of working. In this respect, as Sargent (2001) notes, men can be in a 'double bind'. If they perform masculinity through, for example, authoritarianism, emotional distance and control, their 'caring skills' are questioned; if they perform femininity through nurturance and care, their masculinity and their sexuality are called to account.

How do men manage these potential conflicts? How do men perform emotional labour so as to align meanings around care and masculinity and negotiate the often devalued status of such work? This chapter takes an explicitly gendered approach to consider how male nurses and primary (elementary) school teachers perceive and perform emotional labour and how they manage inherent conflicts in these gender-atypical roles. In this respect, the chapter is influenced by the work of both West and Zimmerman (2002) and Butler (1990), who argue that gender and gender differences are produced in everyday interactions and contexts in accordance with normative and localized conceptions of what it means to be a woman or a man. Gender is thus a 'situated doing' or performance. The chapter draws on literature on men working in non-traditional occupations as well as some findings from my own research (based on a study of male nurses and primary school teachers in Australia and the UK), to explore how men in these contexts 're-gender' emotional labour by drawing it into the masculine domain as well as how they draw on and activate sameness (e.g., to higher-status men) and difference (e.g., from women) to manage tensions between gender and their 'feminine' occupation.

The issue of men's experiences in non-traditional work is an interesting one given the prevalence of traditional assumptions concerning the supposed suitability of different types of work for women or men (Acker, 1990) and hence the strong 'sex typing' of jobs. Despite these assumptions that, for example, tend to consign emotional labour as 'women's work', there has been a trend for men and women to move into gender-atypical areas. For example, men now account for 10.9 per cent of nurses in the UK (Nursing and Midwifery Council, 2011) and 12 per cent of primary school teachers are male (Teaching Agency, 2013). However, while the proportion of women moving into 'male' jobs has increased, there has been a slower movement of men into traditionally 'female' jobs – perhaps reflective of the sacrifices in both pay and status, as well as the possibility of encountering disapproval from family and peers that can accompany these career decisions (Simpson, 2009). So while there is extensive literature on women who have previously been excluded from 'male' jobs and who have now moved into these male-dominated occupations (e.g., Kanter, 1977; Simpson, 1997, 2000; Cross and Bagilhole, 2002), less work has focused on the small but growing number of men who perform what could be seen as 'women's work'.

In exploring the ways in which men might perform emotional labour and how they manage the often conflicting meanings around care and masculinity, this chapter discusses three themes that have emerged from studies of such work: the creation of masculine spaces within a caring role; gendered divisions of emotional labour; and the masculinization of emotion through 'rational care' and the gift exchange. As background, the chapter begins with a discussion of the motives men may have for entering a non-traditional or 'caring' role and the links between emotional labour and masculinity.

CAREER ENTRY: SEEKERS, FINDERS AND SETTLERS

While research has demonstrated that women pursue male careers because they offer prestige, higher pay and opportunities for advancement (Chusmir, 1990; Galbraith, 1992), less is known about the entry decisions and career orientation of men in non-traditional occupations. The advantages for men in what are generally seen as 'women's jobs' are less clear cut, involving probable sacrifices in terms of pay and status as well as raising questions over their masculinity and suitability for the job (Bradley, 1993; Williams, 1993; Lupton, 2000; Simpson, 2009). Men therefore have less to gain and much to lose by choosing a non-traditional career.

Looking at the dynamics of entry into female-dominated occupations, Williams and Villemez (1993) differentiated between three broad groups of men: seekers who actively sought female-dominated jobs, finders who were looking for other types of work but who ended up in a non-traditional occupation, and leavers who were in 'female' jobs and left them. This typology has been further refined (Simpson, 2005) to include a further category of 'settlers'. Factors identifying each group include the location of the current occupation in respondents' scale of preferences, whether the occupation comprises a first or subsequent career, the nature of any previous occupation and relative levels of satisfaction compared to that job.

Thus, for seekers and settlers, current occupations are high on their preference scale and are 'first best' choices at the time the decision was made. By contrast, the decision to enter a non-traditional occupation is 'second best' for finders and involves some compromise around an alternative and preferred option (e.g., a decision to enter librarianship may be taken because of lack of necessary credentials in relation to the preferred choice of academia). The career decision of finders also has an unplanned element ('I just fell into it'). Settlers stand out in that the majority have undergone a career change and have moved out of careers that are radically different, in terms of sex type, from their current choice (e.g., management, engineering, finance, the army). After periods of dissatisfaction in their previous (more masculine sex-typed) roles, they frequently claim high levels of job satisfaction in their current occupation.

As a result, unlike seekers and finders, settlers prefer to remain close to professional practice at 'grass roots' level rather than adopting a careerist strategy and ascending the hierarchy into management (possibly because they have already rejected a competitive masculinist career model in their non-traditional occupational choice). They thus prioritize intrinsic over extrinsic rewards. In nursing and teaching, for example, settlers prefer to work closely with patients and to have responsibility for their own class at school in a context where seniority might remove them from this day to day professional contact. As I have argued elsewhere (Simpson, 2005, 2009), the common notion of 'fast track' or 'straight through' careers for men (e.g., Williams, 1993), where upward mobility is facilitated by assumptions of leadership capabilities associated with the masculine gender, may not therefore be representative for all men in these non-traditional roles.

Despite this, greater opportunities for promotion may present themselves as key motivating factors for some groups of men – as well as a possible desire for professional status not open to men in more 'masculine' occupations (Lupton, 2006). In accordance with the 'settler' category above, men may be motivated by a desire for fulfilment not available in male-sex-typed jobs (Chusmir, 1990). In short, while men in non-traditional careers are more likely than women to have leadership aspirations (Williams, 1993), they may also choose to develop the affective domain of their lives (Galbraith, 1992). These intrinsic elements may well be foregrounded in decisions to enter 'caring roles'.

GENDER AND EMOTIONAL LABOUR

Emotional labour has been defined as the ways individuals change or manage emotions to make them appropriate to a role or an expected organizational goal (Hochschild, 1983; Sturdy, 2002). The gendered nature of these roles and encounters has been highlighted by Hochschild's (1983) work on debt collectors and flight attendants. Following from this, as Lewis and Simpson (2007) argue, emotional labour can be seen as gendered in several key ways.

First, emotional labour has been associated with the sexual division of labour whereby men have traditionally been located within the world of (rational) production while women have been assigned to caring and nurturance in the private sphere of the home (Taylor and Tyler, 2000; Sturdy, 2002). The location of emotions in the private domain has led to their gendered connection with the domestic and with devalued femininity. This is in contrast to the rationality of the private domain, which has core assumptions with masculinity (Ross-Smith and Kornberger, 2004), so contributing to the hierarchical divisions between the rational and the emotional and between the public and private. As Sturdy (2002) has argued, these divisions have meant that emotions have been sidelined as 'irrational, private, inner sensations' largely associated with women.

The division between the private domain of home and the public domain of workplace compounds the already low status of 'natural' unskilled women's work. This brings us to the second and related gendered aspect of emotional labour, namely the belief that emotions and care are the 'natural' domains of women (Taylor and Tyler, 2000; Guerrier and Adib, 2004). It is assumed that women can 'do' service and care because they are women. Such work is therefore constructed (and hence concealed and devalued) as a 'natural' part of doing gender (Hall, 1993; Adkins, 2001). These assumptions about the natural abilities of women to use interpersonal skills and to perform care can influence how emotional labour is performed and managed. As Taylor and Tyler (2000) found in a study of the airline industry, women were judged by 'hard' and 'soft' standards, that is, getting a sale *and* interaction with customers, while men were only judged by the 'hard' standard of getting a sale. It was expected that women would draw on interpersonal skills necessary for successful service (and that they would put up with more 'hassle' from customers) because they were women. This has implications, in turn, for how such work is valued. As Fletcher (1999) points out, the attribution of relational activity as something that women are and not what they do 'disappears' any responsibility for reciprocity and for recognition. Such activities therefore remain devalued and often invisible within conceptions of work.

A third orientation towards gender and emotions constructs emotional labour as a cultural performance (e.g., Butler, 1994; Sass, 2000). Cultural performances are episodes through which members construct organizational reality (Williams, 2003) such as through performances of sociality and care. From West and Zimmerman's work (2002), gender can be seen as an accomplishment or a 'doing' that is acted out according to prevailing norms of what constitutes male and female. On this basis, as Hall (1993) points out, giving good service or care through emotional labour is part of 'doing' gender, involving culturally defined and gendered scripts. Therefore, the cultural performance of emotional labour is a gendered performance that in turn helps to construct and negotiate gender identities.

Finally, as the above suggests, emotional labour has been closely tied to notions of (gendered) service. Both foreground the needs of the 'consumer' and rely on social interaction where the boundaries between product and service provider are blurred. Characteristics of modern servanthood (being caring, polite and deferential) may be called upon to 'manage' (Bolton and Boyd, 2003) customer/client behaviour in an emotional labour context as well as expectations that have been heightened by general discourses of consumer sovereignty (Sturdy, 1998). The gendered nature of these roles and encounters has been highlighted by a body of research in the area, linking service to the 'natural' domain of women (Tyler and Abbott, 1998; Taylor and Tyler, 2000; Guerrier and Adib, 2004). Such work has explored the gendered consequences of giving 'good service' in the airline industry, how women 'do' service as overseas tour reps by conforming to 'patriarchally determined aesthetic codes of behaviour' (Guerrier and Adib, 2004); how gendered notions of servanthood infiltrate the delivery of service in banking (Forseth, 2005). Other work has explored strategies of resistance to expectations of deference (Bolton and Boyd, 2003) including the significance of bodily attributes such as size and voice (Forseth, 2005). From the above, women often have more service demands made of them than men (Macdonald and Sirianni, 1996) while men can draw on other voices and repertoires (e.g., of authority; of expert) to side-step both the practices and identity implications of such work.

EMOTIONAL LABOUR AND MASCULINITY

Much of the above work draws parallels between emotional labour and femininity. The 'feminine' nature of such work therefore has likely implications for men who occupy and perform these roles. For example, as Macdonald and Sirianni (1996) found, men are less likely to embrace the emotional demands, in particular the care-giving aspect of certain tasks because they do not fit their notion of gender-appropriate behaviour and, from Taylor and Tyler's (2000) study of flight attendants, men may tend to distance themselves from the 'niceness' demanded by the job. Equally, Hochschild (1983) found that men are more likely to adopt 'surface acting' whereby feelings displayed (e.g., friendliness of the smile) are 'put on' for the occasion so that the worker maintains a distance from the role. Other work (e.g., Alvesson, 1998; Lupton, 2000) suggests that in non-traditional or 'feminized' occupations, men engage in compensatory gendered practices (e.g., displays around the sexual appraisal of women based on masculine community) so as to minimize any non-masculine associations and to restore a dominating position. This can be achieved by emphasizing the male-associated and downplaying the female-associated elements of a job (Williams, 1993), through a preference for management or authority roles (Bradley, 1993) or for roles that require technical expertise and/or physical strength (Heikes, 1991; Simpson, 2004).

As Lupton (2000) found, men working in female-dominated occupations often fear feminization and stigmatization – feelings that may also influence the way that men perform emotional labour. In nursing, for example, men have been found to avoid the body proximity of female-associated general nursing care (Evans, 2002, 2004), preferring instead more gender-congruent specialist areas that involve high levels of technology (Dahl, 2005); in primary school teaching, as Sargent (2001) notes, men often practice a 'detached' form of care based around encouraging academic achievement as opposed to the more tactile 'maternal' care. This suggests a tension for men in caring roles generally, and in nursing and primary school teaching in particular, between the feminine nature of the job and dominant discourses of masculinity, with possible implications in terms of how, in both contexts, men approach and perform emotional labour.

MASCULINE SPACES WITHIN EMOTIONAL LABOUR

While emotional labour in the form of caring has been associated with femininity, in that it draws on feminine attributes of nurturing and service to others, studies suggest a traditionally drawn gendered division of labour within the caring role when such care is undertaken by men. Part of this division relates to choice of specialism within each profession. As Evans (2002) found, male nurses often gravitate towards mental health, seen as more demanding and 'masculine' with historical links with discipline, restraint and custodialism, and to accident and emergency, seen as more exciting and demanding than general nursing care. While there is less room for specialization within primary school teaching, most men in my study were involved in sport (Simpson, 2009) and took a special interest in the sporting development of male pupils.

These specialisms can offer opportunity to have more contact with higher-status men – a contact that could be affirming (in that it suggests a 'special relationship' or status) but that can also form the basis of tension and struggle. Thus, from my study, beyond a common male bonding around sport that served to break down status barriers, male nurses felt they were 'listened to' more readily by doctors so that the doctor–nurse relationship was more equal than when the nurse was a woman. Similarly, male head-teachers and male primary school teachers have been found to gravitate towards each other in an otherwise all female setting (Williams, 1993).

However, these alliances are not always problem free and can be a source of antagonism as men in non-traditional roles resist a subordinated identity through status-levelling tactics – seeking to undermine the authority of higher-status men. In other words, associations with femininity and men's marginal occupational status in a non-traditional role can render entry into the 'dominant centre' less than secure, leading to tension around the uncertain position in relation to this 'norm'. Thus, within the airline industry, male cabin crew can display antagonism towards the pilots in the flight deck – culturally associated with a superior and heterosexual masculinity (Simpson, 2005, 2009). From my study, male nurses were often dismissive of male doctors and recounted stories of how they put doctors 'in their place' – overturning norms of deference by openly challenging decisions made. This is captured in the quotes below:

> I've sent doctors out of my unit before – I've sent them off because I felt they were behaving inappropriately in front of my patients and I've said don't come back to my unit until you either apologize or you can conduct yourself appropriately.

I was at a meeting yesterday and there were three consultants just chit chatting away while I was trying to discuss something and I asked them if they could keep quiet and they just carried on chatting so I said if you don't **** shut up I'm going to walk out of here.

Therefore, while there is a tendency for men to create 'masculine spaces' within a caring role, often based on an alignment with higher-status men through a specialist status or through shared interests such as sport, these spaces can be sites of tension as men confront a privileged masculinity in the workplace.

A GENDERED DIVISION OF EMOTIONAL LABOUR

A gendered division of labour can also emerge within the caring role itself in terms of the type of emotional labour undertaken. For example, in teaching, men are often called upon to take on the role of disciplinarian and authority figure – while in nursing men are given more challenging and difficult tasks such as dealing with suicidal patients or breaking bad news to relatives. Similarly, they are assumed to have leadership capabilities – supported by wider divisions based on traditional notions of masculinity and femininity that tends to channel men into authoritarian roles or those demanding discipline and personal challenge. From Pierce (1995) and Brannen (2005) these activities may provide men with repertoires of 'doing' emotional labour and gender that, by drawing on displays of authority, expertise and control, can have positive identity implications. Women, by contrast, may perform emotional labour through traditional, devalued notions of passivity, service and care. This supports James's (1993) view that it is possible to identify 'differential divisions of emotional labour based on equal status work and deferential divisions of emotional labour which are characterized by submissions to authority' (p. 95). On this basis, the gendered division of emotional labour outlined above may imply deferential divisions in that the type of work performed by men has higher valuation and affords more resources for a positive sense of self.

'RATIONAL' CARE AND GIFT EXCHANGE

From my study, most male nurses and teachers perceived themselves to have relevant 'caring' skills and capabilities. However, they often presented themselves as emotional labourers in such a way as to afford those activities a higher value and a greater level of visibility. First, men often conferred a 'masculine' rationality on the skills required for the job, differentiating from the 'natural' capabilities of women while at the same time also differentiating themselves from what they saw as the 'emotional illiteracy' characteristic of other men. Second, there was a tendency for men to present their emotional labour as part of a 'gift exchange'.

In terms of the former, men often presented rationality and emotional distance as desirable for effective performance, thereby reframing discourses of care to privilege the masculine. Men, for example, described themselves as having 'a different form of compassion', caring in a more 'detached' way, as being 'more rational' and having 'more authority' than women. They saw themselves as able to deal with difficult or demanding situations without becoming 'over-emotional' – a 'female' tendency that was seen to interfere with the ability to meet the challenges of the job. One young Australian nurse described his approach working in palliative care:

> I'm not going to get too emotional with these guys [patients who are likely to die], I'm going to do whatever I can to help them without getting too close, and I know a lot of my female colleagues found it very hard because they got really emotional to patients, and on top of the work load as well. They just went home and cried every day and you know, if something happens to a patient they cry. I guess I try and distance myself as much as I can without putting the patient . . . making them uncomfortable.

Male teachers often presented themselves as being professionally oriented, focusing on the academic achievement of children, as opposed to perceptions of the maternal care offered by women:

> We're more results oriented and systems oriented . . . a large percentage of women are there because when they were young they loved kids, and without thinking, primary school teaching was the obvious career choice for them.

Men accordingly differentiated their attributes (disciplined, detached, professional) from those possessed by women (emotional, over-involved, maternal), employing masculine characteristics to 'add value' to caring skills and devaluing the motives of women by calling up their 'natural' role as child carers. At the same time, many men claimed a special status by seeking to maintain a distance from some common or traditional notion of masculinity (e.g., as being out of touch with emotions) – locating themselves within feminine discourses of care. In these instances men commented on and placed value on their 'feminine' side. Positioning themselves favourably against the masculine norm and by calling upon and activating discourses of 'new manhood', men thereby challenged the devalued status of relationality and, through a colonization of the feminine, helped to enhance the value of associated skills when practised by men. In this way, while the caring performed by women can be concealed and devalued through associations with essentialized notions of femininity, such work performed by men can be rendered visible and celebrated as an asset through claimed differences from women (more rational, more detached) as well as claimed differences from and privilege over other (i.e., traditionally masculine) men.

A further process of 'revaluing' concerns a tendency for men to present their work involving care as part of a gift exchange. From Bolton (2000), the gift exchange occurs when workers 'go the extra mile' – going beyond the call of duty in their caring role. This may include, for example, spending extra time with a child or mobilizing resources to assist a distraught relative. Here, male nurses in particular often presented their emotional labour skills in terms of a gift exchange, recounting examples of their ability to spend time with needy patients despite other work-related demands or to circumvent rules to satisfy individual wishes:

> I think that's partly why I'm a nurse . . . I also have a deep sense of nourishing that makes me able to empathize, like hold their hands and put patients' minds at rest – rather than sitting like a truck driver by the side of the bed . . . I went and I held her hand [a dying patient] and we talked about her job as a seamstress and I was quite happy to sit there doing all the things I had to do while talking about embroidery and crochet work because I think it's easy to talk to old ladies and put their minds at rest.

> What do I mean by care? Well, for me it's being able to do the best for the patient, and if that means breaking rules then so be it . . . so you've got to understand it from a patient's point of view . . . if a patient is obviously dying, he wants a cigarette, there's no point refusing him a cigarette. I would take him outside whereas my female colleagues would say 'no you're not allowed to smoke'. You try and give him a cigarette when they're going to die anyway. . . . Now, with the women he'll get a hard and fast, 'this is what's good for you' and that's it, that's the way . . . I don't feel that way. You tell me what's good for you, what you want – and I'll do it.

As the above quotes illustrate, some men present themselves as being able to offer time and support beyond the call of duty, while others combine philanthropic and maverick performances (doing that 'extra bit' for patients, circumventing rules and bureaucracy) to describe their care. Men thereby differentiate themselves from women and allowed the uptake of a more satisfying identity around independence and non-conformity. As Williams (2003) notes, fewer service demands can be made on men compared with women. It is expected that women will go beyond the call of duty in the service interaction so that, from Fletcher (1999), these 'extra services' are rarely recognized as such. On this basis, when men perform care, the effects may be more visible and it may be more likely that others see such labour (and that men see it themselves) as part of a gift exchange. Emotional labour is more likely to be seen as philanthropic and, relatedly, greater recognition is given when philanthropy is practised by men.

CONCLUSION

This chapter has explored how male nurses and primary school teachers both perceive and practice care. As we have seen, emotional labour skills are deeply gendered in that they are strongly associated with the 'natural' capabilities of women – rendering such work less visible and of lesser value. This led us to ask at the beginning of the chapter how men manage the tension and potential conflicts between the feminine nature of such work and the need to preserve or maintain masculinity. In other words, how do men perceive and perform emotional labour so as to align the often divergent meanings around care and masculinity and to negotiate the devalued status of such work?

As we have seen, many of these conflicts are negotiated through a 're-gendering' of care. This 'masculinization' of emotional labour has emerged in different ways. It can be seen in men's choice of specialist functions and preference for (or assignment to) more authoritarian and challenging roles – as well as in the way emotions and underlying skills and attributes are appropriated and expressed as part of 'masculinist' detachment and rationality. Here, some men embrace the demands of emotional labour but distance themselves from feminine associations in their rejection of 'over-involved' and 'over-emotional' and hence 'ineffective' care; others, particularly teachers, may practise a more 'distant' form of care through professionalism and a focus on academic performance – which is differentiated from devalued and naturalized maternalism. At this level, a masculinization of emotions can be seen to have occurred through the harnessing of emotional labour in the masculine project of rationality, efficiency and performance. In other words, emotions and emotional labour are colonized and brought into the masculine domain.

A 're-gendering' of emotional labour is also evident in the way service and care performed by men is presented and perceived, in Bolton's (2000) terms, as part of a 'gift exchange'. The notion of the 'gift' is gendered in the sense that men's care is more likely to be recognized as special and 'extra', while for women, 'going the extra mile' is part of femininity. Presenting care as a gift exchange can therefore be construed as masculine strategy in the sense that it enhances the value and visibility of such work – but only when it is undertaken by men. As we have seen, this can be combined with maverick (and masculine) performances around the mobilization of resources or the circumvention of bureaucracy. Together with the masculinization of skills and attributes associated with service and care discussed above, the location of activities around performance of such work within the gift exchange serves to render the work more visible and to increase the value of its skills and attributes.

This 're-gendering' of emotional labour can be seen as part of a broader trend. In other contexts, a masculinization of emotion has been associated with the current priority afforded to emotions in organizations, both as a source of competitive advantage in the service sector as well as a supposed essential component in successful management – increasingly oriented around empathy, cooperation and affiliation (see Lewis and Simpson, 2007). In terms of caring professions such as teaching and nursing it is evident in the masculinist discourses of quality and accountability that drive many of their practices (Simpson, 2009). These trends, linking emotions and emotional labour to competitiveness and performance may afford men gender-congruent spaces of meaning and repertoires of practices within a non-traditional role – spaces that, from Pierce (1995) and Brannen (2005), can be self-affirming rather than effacing and offer a positive sense of self.

Linked to the re-gendering of emotional labour is the significance of divisions and differentiation strategies for how men understand and perform care. In this respect, men draw on, activate and flatten difference (Simpson, 2009) as they manage the tensions in their caring role. Men activate difference from the 'natural' capabilities of women to 'revalue and reveal' skills and attributes. Men also activate difference from other men, drawing on discourses of 'new manhood', thereby further enhancing the specificity of their skills. Skills and attributes of emotional labour are therefore afforded special status through a colonization of the feminine and through differentiation strategies that separate such work from the capabilities of the majority of men. Men also resist difference, aligning themselves with higher-status men. However, the creation of these masculine spaces can be a source of tension as men confront a privileged masculinity in the workplace that may serve to heighten their 'devalued' status in a non-traditional role. In this respect, while women are frequently subordinated in organizations, the take-up of an inferiorized identity may be more difficult for men (Lupton, 2000; Simpson, 2004, 2005) – leading to struggles around the dominant centre. This points to the dynamic, often tension-ridden nature of difference and how it is activated (or de-activated) in managing gender in these contexts.

Overall, in taking a specifically gendered approach, this chapter has highlighted the ways in which men both perceive and perform care in the context of nursing and primary school teaching. In this respect, by highlighting processes of re-gendering and the significance of dynamics of difference, it has adopted an approach to gender and emotional labour that supports an understanding of both as continual performance or 'doing', along the lines of Hall (1993) discussed above. As we have seen, part of this 'doing' of difference involves 'cultural performances' (Hall, 1993) of emotional labour and care: men and women 'do' gender through emotional labour (women 'do' femininity through maternal care; men 'do' masculinity through displays of autonomy and detachment) while emotional labour is itself a gendered performance – suggesting feminine service and concern for relationships. This chapter has captured some of the complexities involved in these performances as men 'do' emotional labour and masculinity as well as some of the dynamics of doing difference in these work contexts. Further research will, I am sure, uncover other processes and meanings, as well as other interpretations, in the complex intersections that occur when men perform traditionally 'feminine' roles that require emotional labour and care.

REFERENCES

Acker, J. (1990), 'Hierarchies, jobs, bodies: A theory of gendered organization', *Gender and Society*, **4**(2), 139–58.

Adkins, L. (2001), 'Cultural feminisation: Money, sex and power for women', *Signs*, **26**(3), 669–95.

Alvesson, M. (1998), 'Gender relations and identity at work: A case study of masculinities and femininities in an advertising agency', *Human Relations*, **51**(8), 969–1005.

Bolton, S. (2000), 'Who cares? Offering emotion work as a "gift" in the nursing labor process', *Journal of Advanced Nursing*, **32**(3), 580–86.

Bolton, S. (2007), 'Emotion work as human connection: Gendered emotion codes in teaching primary children with emotional and behavioral difficulties', in P. Lewis and R. Simpson (eds), *Gendering Emotions in Organizations*, Basingstoke: Palgrave Macmillan.

Bolton, S. and C. Boyd (2003), 'Trolley dolly or skilled emotion manager? Moving on from Hochschild's *Managed Heart*', *Work Employment and Society*, **17**(2), 289–308.

Bradley, H. (1993), 'Across the great divide', in C. Williams (ed.), *Doing Women's Work: Men in Non-traditional Occupations*, London: Sage.

Brannen, M. (2005), 'Once more with feeling: Ethnographic reflections on the mediation of tensions in a small team of call centre workers', *Gender, Work and Organization*, **2**(5), 420–39.

Butler, J. (1990), *Gender Trouble: Feminism and the Subversion of Identity*, London: Routledge.

Butler, J. (1994), 'Gender as performance: An interview with Judith Butler', *Radical Philosophy*, No. 67, 32–9.

Chusmir, L. (1990), 'Men who make non-traditional career choices', *Journal of Counselling and Development*, **69**(1), 11–15.

Cross, S. and B. Bagilhole (2002), 'Girl's jobs for the boys? Men, masculinity and non-traditional occupations', *Gender, Work and Organization*, **9**(2), 204–26.

Dahl, R. (2005), 'Men, bodies and nursing', in D. Morgan, B. Brandth and E. Kvande (eds), *Gender, Bodies and Work*, Aldershot: Ashgate.

Evans, J. (2002), 'Cautious caregivers: Gender stereotypes and the sexualization of men nurses' touch', *Journal of Advanced Nursing*, **40**(4), 441–8.

Evans, J. (2004), 'Bodies matter: Men, masculinity and the gendered division of labor in nursing', *Journal of Occupational Science*, **11**(1), 14–22.

Fletcher, J. (1999), *Disappearing Acts: Gender Power and Relational Practices at Work*, Boston, MA: MIT Press.

Forseth, U. (2005), 'Gender matters? Exploring how gender is negotiated in service encounters', *Gender, Work and Organization*, **12**(5), 440–59.

Galbraith, M. (1992), 'Understanding the career choices of men in elementary education', *Journal of Educational Research*, **85**(4), 246–53.

Guerrier, Y. and A. Adib (2004), 'Gendered identities in the work of overseas tour reps', *Gender, Work and Organization*, **13**(3), 334–50.

Hall, E. (1993), 'Smiling, deferring and flirting: Doing gender by giving good service', *Work and Occupations*, **20**(4), 452–71.

Heikes, E. (1991), 'When men are the minority: The case of men in nursing', *The Sociological Quarterly*, **32**(3), 389–401.

Hochschild, A. (1983), *The Managed Heart*, Berkeley, CA: University of California Press.

James, N. (1993), 'Divisions of emotional labor: Disclosure and cancer', in S. Fineman (ed.), *Emotion in Organization*, London: Sage.

Kanter, R. (1977), *Men and Women of the Corporation*, New York: Basic Books.

Lewis, P. and R. Simpson (2007), *Gendering Emotions in Organizations*, Basingstoke: Palgrave Macmillan.

Lupton, B. (2000), 'Maintaining masculinity: Men who do women's work', *British Journal of Management*, **11**(S1), S33–S48.

Lupton, B. (2006), 'Explaining men's entry into female concentrated occupations: Issues of masculinity and class', *Gender, Work and Organization*, **13**(2), 103–28.

Macdonald, C. and C. Sirianni (1996), *Working in the Service Society*, Philadelphia: Temple University Press.

Nursing and Midwifery Council (2011), website accessed 24 April 2013 at http://www.nmc-uk.org/.

Pierce, J.L. (1995), *Gender Trials. Emotional Lives in Contemporary Law Firms*, Berkeley, CA: University of California Press.

Ross-Smith, A. and M. Kornberger (2004), 'Gendered rationality: A genealogical exploration of the philosophical and sociological conceptions of rationality, masculinity and organization', *Gender, Work and Organization*, **1**(3), 280–305.

Sargent, P. (2001), *Real Men or Real Teachers: Contradictions in the Lives of Men Elementary School Teachers*, Harriman, TN: Men's Studies Press.

Sass, J. (2000), 'Emotional labor as cultural performance: The communication of care giving in a nonprofit nursing home', *Western Journal of Communications*, **64**(3), 330–58.

Simpson, R. (1997), 'Have times changed? Career barriers and the token woman manager', *British Journal of Management*, **8**(S1), S121–S129.

Simpson, R. (2000), 'Gender mix and organizational fit: How gender imbalance at different levels of the organization impacts on women managers', *Women in Management Review*, **15**(1), 5–20.

Simpson, R. (2004), 'Masculinity at work: The experiences of men in female dominated occupations', *Work, Employment and Society*, **18**(2), 349–68.

Simpson, R. (2005), 'Men in non-traditional occupations: Career entry, career orientation and experience of role strain', *Gender, Work and Organization*, **12**(4), 363–80.

Simpson, R. (2009), *Men in Caring Occupations: Doing Gender Differently*, Basingstoke: Palgrave Macmillan.

Sturdy, A. (1998), 'Customer care in a consumer society: Smiling and sometimes meaning it?' *Organization*, **5**(1), 2–53.

Sturdy, A. (2002), 'Knowing the unknowable: A discussion of methodological and theoretical issues in emotion research in organization studies', *Organization*, **10**(1), 81–105.

Taylor, S. and M. Tyler (2000), 'Emotional labor and sexual difference in the airline industry', *Work Employment and Society*, **14**(1), 77–95.

Teaching Agency (2013), 'Record numbers of men teaching in primary schools – but more still needed', accessed 24 April 2013 at https://www.gov.uk/government/news/record-numbers-of-men-teaching-in-primary-schools-but-more-still-needed.

Tyler, M. and P. Abbott (1998), 'Chocs away: Weight watching in the contemporary airline industry', *Sociology*, **32**(3), 433–50.

West, C. and D. Zimmerman (2002), 'Doing gender', in S. Fenstermaker and C. West (eds), *Doing Gender, Doing Difference*, London: Routledge.

Williams, C. (ed.) (1993), *Doing Women's Work: Men in Non-traditional Occupations*, London: Sage.

Williams, C. (2003), 'Sky service: The demands of emotional labor in the airline industry', *Gender, Work and Organization*, **10**(5), 513–50.

Williams, L. and W. Villemez (1993), 'Seeker and finders: Male entry and exit in female dominated jobs', in C. Williams (ed.), *Doing Women's Work: Men in Non-traditional Occupations*, London: Sage.

6. Men, masculinity, well-being, and health*

Ronald J. Burke**

INTRODUCTION

Why do we need a chapter on men, masculinity, and health? Don't we know enough about them? It is true that although most research on work and health has involved men, the experiences of men as men have been virtually ignored (Hearn, 1994). In the 1970s and 1980s, attention was focused on women, spearheaded by scholars who called attention to the fact that increasing numbers of women were entering the workforce and women's roles were changing (Powell, 1999). In the mid-1990s, the focus shifted to men and men's roles, which are still undergoing sweeping changes (Levant, 1994).

The popular press has suggested that considerable confusion currently exists about men's roles (Kimmel and Messner, 1989). Questions such as 'What are men supposed to do?' and 'What do women want from men?' convey the general tenor of this uncertainty (Kimmel, 1993). Part of the confusion may be the result of pressures on men to exhibit behavior that conflicts with traditional notions of masculinity. Such pressures include those to commit to relationships, communicate one's deepest feelings, share in household responsibilities, nurture children, and to limit aggression and violence (Levant, 1994).

In addition, many men find it increasingly difficult to fulfill the expectations of the provider role. Historically, men have defined themselves by their work, a profession, and a paycheck (Kimmel, 1993, 1996). Now, men are having to redefine themselves as a result of women's influx into the workplace and the greater difficulties men face in working (acting as provider) as a result of corporate downsizing and restructuring. These forces require men to re-evaluate what it means to be a success at work and in the home, because the worker-provider role is no longer what it once was (Cohen, 1993; Faludi, 1999).

My intent in this chapter is to explore the topic of men, masculinity, and health. I am concerned that the chapter does not come across as

133

'male-bashing', because that is not my intent. Instead, I advocate a careful examination of the research evidence and consider the issue as part of men's life planning in the broadest sense. My objectives are to review and integrate a diverse body of research and writing; to identify what we know and don't know about men, masculinity, and health; and to suggest a research agenda for this under-studied area.

WHAT IS MASCULINITY?

The central construct in research that examines men and men's roles is masculinity ideology, which views masculinity as a socially constructed gender ideal for men (Thompson and Pleck, 1995). The roots of the masculine gender ideal are instilled through the socialization process.

West and Zimmerman (1991) describe gender as an achieved status, or an accomplishment constructed through psychological, cultural, and social means. While the terms 'male' and 'masculine' are used interchangeably there is a critical distinction between 'maleness', as a biologically determined state, and 'masculinity', a socially constructed state. In western societies, the shared cultural perspective of gender views women and men as naturally and clearly defined categories having distinctive psychological and behavioral characteristics based on their sex. Differences between women and men are seen as fundamental and enduring, supported by sexual division of labor, and clear definitions of women's and men's work. This division follows as a natural consequence of biological differences that form the basis for the observed differences in psychological, behavioral, and social outcomes (Korabik, 1999). These processes place unique pressures and expectations on men that influence men's work, private life, and health. For example, men historically have been judged on their ability to fill the breadwinner role (Ehrenreich, 1983, 1989), and by the size of their paychecks (Gould, 1974).

In general, contemporary adult men were socialized as boys to learn risk-taking, teamwork, assertiveness, and calmness in the face of danger, all of which are action skills. In contrast, contemporary adult women were socialized to learn emotional skills such as empathy, the ability to access and feel intense emotions, and the ability to express those emotions through both verbal and non-verbal means (Levant, 1995). Thus, traditional masculine and feminine ideology prevailed in the socialization process, and became reflected in adult behavior.

Because masculinity is a social construct, men's views of what constitutes masculinity vary widely. Despite this range of views, it is possible to identify what some refer to as traditional masculinity ideology (Pleck,

1995). Brannon (1976) identified four themes in traditional masculine ideology:

- No sissy stuff – avoid anything feminine.
- Be a big wheel – be powerful, strong, and competitive since men must be admired to be real.
- Be a sturdy oak – show no emotion.
- Give 'em hell – take risks, go for it, face danger, and demonstrate bravado.

Building on Brannon's four themes of the male role, Thompson and Pleck (1987) developed and validated a 57-item self-report questionnaire of the male sex role. Data were obtained from male college students. Factor analysis of their data yielded three prevailing attitudes: status – achieve status and others' respect; toughness – be mentally, physically, and emotionally tough and self-reliant; and anti-femininity – avoid stereotypically feminine attitudes and occupations. They concluded that men in their sample did not fully endorse traditional male norms.

More recently, Levant et al. (1992) described traditional masculine ideology as having seven dimensions: avoid anything feminine; restrict one's emotional life; display toughness and aggression; be self-reliant; work to achieve status above all else; adopt non-relational, objectifying attitudes toward sexuality; and fear and hate homosexuals.

IMPLICATIONS FOR MEN

In this section, we review the consequences of masculinity ideology, both positive and negative. Kaufman (1993) observes that the ways in which societies have defined male power for thousands of years have granted men access to great power and privilege but also caused them pain and insecurity. This pain remained hidden until the emergence of feminism. As women began to identify and challenge men's power and privilege, men felt under attack, vulnerable, confused, empty, and introspective.

There are many virtues to be found in men's masculinity: physical and emotional strength, sexual desire, the ability to operate under pressure, courage, creativity, intellect, self-sacrifice, and dedication to the task at hand (ibid.). Although these qualities exist in all humans, many of them become distorted in men. Some men work too hard, drink too much, are isolated and alienated from other men, distant from their children, and present a facade that all is well. Men's power is a source of both privilege and painful isolation.

Kaufman further contends that society's definition of masculinity creates a shell that protects men from the fear of not being manly. Ironically, it is almost impossible to live up to our society's image of masculinity and manhood. It should come as no surprise that many men have concerns about their ability to 'measure up' to this image. The development of a sense of what constitutes masculinity starts early in life for most men as they learn to discipline their bodies and unruly emotions. Men eventually come to accept relationships built on power and hierarchy (Butts and Whitty, 1993). Men generally learn to become leery of emotions, and to deny feelings and needs that are not considered masculine. Men come to suppress a range of emotions, needs, and possibilities, including nurturing, receptivity, empathy, and compassion, which are seen as inconsistent with the power of manhood. These are suppressed because they are associated with femininity. With the passage of time, men lose their ability to identify and express emotions. Sadly, men are often unaware they are behaving in this way (Jourard, 1964).

Brod (1987) also weighs the costs and benefits (economic, legal, social, and political) men obtain from patriarchy. The male role is associated with heart attacks, hypertension, ulcers, suicide, early death, and greater general life dissatisfaction (Harrison, 1978). Brod, like Kaufman, sees the possession of power (and privilege) as double-edged. Yet there are vested interests of the powerful and privileged in keeping the roots of their power and privilege secretive, since this is one way to remain powerful or privileged. Leaving men's lives unexamined is one way to keep men's power and privilege unexamined.

Kaufman (1993) cautions that there is a danger in placing undue emphasis on the costs, rather than the benefits, of masculinity. These benefits include the freedom to fully commit to the workplace, the luxury of a back-up resource on the home front (in many cases), the positive perception of a strong father figure, and the ability to achieve comfort and stability in their lives (Weiss, 1990), the exclusion of women, and the wider availability of privilege. Focusing on the downside of masculinity diverts attention away from the ways in which masculinity excludes and burdens women.

It is curious that although men seem to have all the power, many men feel powerless. There are two basic reasons for this apparent contradiction. First, only a small proportion of men meet the definition of masculinity. Second, there is discrimination among men on the basis of race, age, ethnicity, class, and sexual preference. Kaufman (1993) asserts that men's power comes with a high price in terms of pain, isolation, and alienation from both women and men. Yet an appreciation of this pain is important to understand men and masculinity. In addition, it sheds light on the ways men are socialized in society and on the process of gender acquisition.

The masculine role has been implicated in men's health (Courtenay, 2001). For example, the gap in life expectancy between males and females increased from two years in 1900 to eight years in 1988. Men also suffer heart attacks and ulcers at a consistently higher rate than do women. Harrison et al. (1989) estimate that three-quarters of men's early deaths are related to the male role. Men rarely ask for help with physical or emotional problems. Men internalize stress, more men cope with stress through use of alcohol, tobacco, and drugs, men take more unnecessary risks, and therefore have higher rates of accidental injury, and men are more successful at committing suicide (Jourard, 1964).

Males comprise the majority of many problem groups. Such groups include perpetrators of violence, sex offenders, substance abusers, victims of homicide, suicide, participants in fatal auto accidents, parents estranged from their children, and victims of stress-related illnesses (Levant, 1994). These problems affect not only men, but society as a whole. Many of these problems may be related in part to gender role strain.

GENDER ROLE STRAIN

Pleck (1995) provided an update on research relating to his 'gender role strain' model of masculinity (Pleck, 1981). Three broad ideas underlie the model's ten different propositions:

- A considerable number of males experience long-term failure to fulfill male role expectations. This is known as 'gender role discrepancy' or incongruity.
- Even if male role expectations are fulfilled, the process and/or the fulfillment itself is traumatic.
- The successful fulfillment of work role expectations leads to undesirable side-effects for men or for others (e.g., low family involvement). Three types of strain result: discrepancy, trauma, and dysfunction strain.

I will elaborate on gender role strain as a cost of masculinity when I consider implications later in the chapter.

Brannon and Juni (1984) reported that college males endorsing violence and adventure as important for men also reported being in fist fights. Among male college students, Thompson et al. (1985) found that greater endorsement of traditional masculinity was associated with having more power and engaging in less self-disclosure in heterosexual dating relationships. Perceptions of masculinity were also found to be related to college males' use of psychological violence in dating relationships (Thompson, 1990) and having myths about rape (Bunting and Reeves, 1983).

In a sample of teenage males, Pleck et al. (1993a, 1993b) noted that traditional attitudes toward male roles were associated with adolescent problem behaviors such as alcohol consumption, drug use, being picked up by the police, careless or negative attitudes towards condoms, and coercive sex.

HEALTH PROBLEMS

Men traditionally have difficulty maintaining positive health care in terms of nutrition, exercise, relaxation, and stress management. Men have been socialized to ignore the physical symptoms that lead to acute illness or chronic health problems. The male gender role depicts men as tireless achieving workers without limits. Some men have limited awareness of changes in their physiological processes, often because they are socialized to ignore them in order to get the job done. If a man cannot sense the signals from his body that all is not well, he is likely to become sick, exhausted, suffer heart attacks or premature death.

Since asking for help is associated with femininity, many men deny their physical problems. Goldberg (1977) believes that the basic bodily processes, attitudes, and behaviors that sustain life and maintain health are feminine, whereas the body-destroying attitudes and behaviors are masculine. Feminine characteristics men avoid include expressing emotions and pain, asking for help, attention to diet and alcohol consumption, self-care, dependence, and being touched. Masculine attitudes and behaviors include limited need for sleep, enduring pain, excessive alcohol consumption, poor eating habits, emotional independence, denial, and repression.

Masculine gender role stress has predicted negative psychosocial and somatic consequences in men (Eisler et al., 1988; Lash et al., 1990) including anger and anxiety (Eisler and Skidmore, 1987). Men's traditional gender role attitudes have been associated with attitudes supporting the use of physical force and marital violence (Finn, 1986). The masculine orientation was found to be correlated with self-reported drug use, aggressive behavior, dangerous driving following alcohol consumption, and delinquent behavior during high school (Mosher and Sirkin, 1984). Gender role conflict has been found to be negatively correlated with psychological well-being (Davis and Walsh, 1988), self-esteem, and intimacy

(Sharpe and Heppner, 1991). Gender role conflict has also been positively correlated with depression and anxiety (Good and Mintz, 1990; Sharpe and Heppner, 1991) and directly related to decreased likelihood of seeking help (Good et al., 1989).

In a sample of male college students, Sharpe and Heppner (1991) studied gender role conflict, sex role orientation, self-esteem, anxiety, depression, relationship intimacy, and relationship satisfaction. They found that gender role conflict was negatively correlated with self-esteem, relationship intimacy, and relationship satisfaction (partial support), but positively correlated with anxiety and depression. Surprisingly, gender role conflict was not correlated with masculinity.

Pollack (1998) provides a review of the 'costs' of masculinity. Men appear to be at risk from the moment of birth. Infant males are more likely to experience complications during labor and delivery and to have more birth defects than females. Boys often exhibit behavioral difficulties and learning difficulties in primary schools, and in middle school are less likely to have professional or career aspirations. Boys are nine times more likely to suffer from hyperactivity than girls and more than twice as likely to be suspended from school. Men are less likely to attend a university or graduate school than women. Compared to young women, young men are four times more likely to be victims of homicide and are five times more likely to kill themselves (ibid.).

Men suffer under a code of masculinity requiring them to be aggressive, dominant, achievement oriented, competitive, rigidly self-sufficient, adventure-seeking, willing to take risks, emotionally restrictive, and avoidant of all things feminine (Levant and Pollack, 1995; Mooney, 1995; Maier, 1999). This code is bound to influence men's health and longevity. The average life expectancy for males in North America is eight years shorter than that for women. Both Harrison (1978) and Waldron (1976) estimate that the difference in life expectancy between women and men is accounted for more strongly by sex role-related behaviors than biological or genetic factors. The traditional male role not only prevents men from seeking medical help in the early stage of illness and disease but also from paying attention to early warning signs of illness (Waldron and Johnson, 1976).

While women have shown higher rates of affective, anxiety, and somatic disorders, men have demonstrated higher rates of substance abuse and antisocial personality disorders (Landers, 1989). Such men are overly invested in work, emotionally unavailable to their families, and oblivious to the effects their lifestyle may have on their partners, their children, and their emotional and physical health (Brooks, 1992; Pleck, 1995). Men are rewarded for being competitive at work, where control of one's emotions, aggression, and assertiveness are considered 'effective' while expressing feelings of weakness and vulnerability are not (Kofodimos, 1993; Maier, 1999). Young boys suppress those skills that would better equip them to participate in adult intimate relationships and care for their emotional and physical needs.

Socially negative components of masculinity (aggressive or exploitative) have been found to be correlated with tendencies toward fighting (Spence et al., 1979) and alcohol and drug use (Snell et al., 1987). Mosher and Sirkin (1984) found that areas on their Hypermasculinity Inventory were correlated with self-reported drug use, aggressiveness, driving after drinking, and delinquent behavior. Helgeson (1990) noted that, among males with coronary heart disease, a masculinity scale predicted Type A behavior, poor health practices, impaired social networks, and was an overall predictive indicator of heart attack severity.

COSTS OF CORPORATE MASCULINITY

By the time boys reach the age of five, they are socialized into masculine role behavior (Paley, 1984). Boys are taught to believe they should be controlled, aggressive, competitive, loud, loyal, and self-directed. As boys move into their teens, they learn that to fill the masculine role they must also be providers and protectors of their families. These values are consistent with a social commitment to work and the tenets of corporate masculinity (Maier, 1991). As a consequence, men come to put work first and family second (Bardwick, 1984; Stroh and Reilly, 1999). They experience tension and stress from work overload, work–family conflict, and the discrepancy between what they say is important (family) and what they put energy toward (work). Few men have taken advantage of the Family and Medical Leave Act in the United States (Hawthorne, 1993); women still do the vast majority of second shift work (Hochschild, 1997). Men are sometimes unaware of their internal states and personal needs, given their tendency to fit with external demands, called a market orientation (Fromm, 1974, 1976). A majority of corporate men seem to be satisfied with their lives and life experiences but a minority feel trapped, alienated, and victimized. There is widespread pressure to achieve and to accumulate materialistic possessions in a capitalistic society. Corporate men's feelings of self-worth become linked to successfully overcoming challenges along the path of upward career mobility. These men must feel valued by others before they can value themselves (Korman and Korman, 1980).

The answer lies in freeing men from the requirements to be 'success objects' while filling the provider role. This involves breaking the masculine mold. This is challenging for a variety of reasons. Some men are unaware of how strongly they have been socialized. For them, giving up masculinity is a sign of weakness. New behavior will be uncomfortable for these men. Benefits of freedom from the masculine role include becoming a more effective manager, obtaining career and family balance, and becoming less work addicted.

Kofodimos (1993) suggests that the imbalance in the lives of American managers results from their basic character (masculinity). She notes the similarity of the character structure of male managers and the values and beliefs of organizations, which are consistent with a male model of success. Both external and internal forces operate so that individuals who capably manage large organizations lose control of their own lives. External forces include organizational pressures, values, and rewards. These forces are seductive, resulting in more time and energy being devoted to work with the accompanying neglect of family life. Internal forces include needs, wants, and drives.

Kofodimos implicates two broad polarities to explain men's escalating commitment of time and energy to work to the neglect of personal and family life. The first, striving for 'mastery', shows up for men in both work and family life. It embodies an emphasis on task accomplishment, rationality in decision-making, and viewing other people as resources for getting the job done. The second polarity, 'avoidance of intimacy', includes a lack of empathy and compassion, an unawareness of one's own and others' feelings, an unwillingness to be spontaneous and playful and an inability to admit weakness.

The imbalance resulting from mastery striving and intimacy avoidance has long-term costs. These include both difficulties in one's personal life (family crises, distant relationships) as well as failures in management (anger, intimidation over control, not asking for help, avoiding feedback), ultimately increasing stress levels and health care costs. Imbalances such as workaholism may affect entire families, with particular consequences for children (Burke, 2000). Corporate masculinity thus has costs not only for individual men but for organizations as well.

CORONARY-PRONE BEHAVIOR

The Type A behavior syndrome has captured considerable attention in medical and psychological research circles during the past three decades. An important series of studies has strongly implicated the Type A pattern in the pathogenesis of coronary heart disease (CHD), independent of standard risk factors such as age, hypertension, diet, and heredity generally associated with the condition (Friedman and Rosenman, 1974). Research evidence finds that Type A individuals' risk of developing CHD and of having fatal heart attacks is approximately twice that of Type Bs in the population.

Certain identifying elements of the Type A pattern include exaggerated expressions of achievement striving, a strong sense of time urgency and competitiveness, and an aggressive demeanor. The Type A individual is described as an unrelenting worker, dominated by the success ethic, eager to outperform others and to constantly better his productivity. A psychological vigilance, hurried and restless movements, polyphasic behavior, and overtones of free-floating hostility are other Type A features (Friedman and Rosenman, 1974). Type Bs are characterized as individuals displaying opposing behavioral characteristics, and having a more relaxed, calmer approach to life in general.

Type A behavior poses a threat to careers, personality, and life itself. Type A behavior threatens careers through impatience, anger, and burnout. Type A tendencies threaten personality by increasing interpersonal conflict, narrowing the possibilities for joy (limiting oneself to things that can be counted – becoming boring and dull). Finally, Type A threatens life by fostering the development of arterial disease and its association with cigarette smoking.

As opposed to their Type B counterparts, Type As work more hours per week, travel more days per year, take less vacation and sick time off work, and are more job involved and organizationally committed (Howard et al., 1977). Type As are more likely to experience high self-esteem at work (Burke and Weir, 1980). This encourages Type As to be more invested in and committed to their work than their Type B counterparts. Type As are not necessarily more satisfied in their jobs, however. Type A behavior has typically been found to bear no relationship to job satisfaction (Howard et al., 1977; Burke and Weir, 1980). Two questions still remain unanswered: (1) are Type As more productive or effective in their jobs than Type Bs; (2) are Type As more likely to be promoted (or found) at the top of organizations? The limited data that is available suggests that Type As were in fact more likely to receive greater organizational rewards than Type Bs (Mettlin, 1976). In addition, Type As were more likely to be promoted and to have higher performance ratings than Type Bs (Chesney and Rosenman, 1980). Kunnanatt (2004) studied 132 bank managers in India and reported that the vast majority displayed Type A behavior and those at higher levels and with better performance ratings exhibited higher levels of Type A behavior. In spite of this, Type As were generally not more satisfied in their jobs. Burke and Deszca (1982) reported that Type As were more likely to report mid-career experiences of personal and social alienation and pessimism, which Korman and Korman (1980) refer to as 'career success and personal failure', than Type Bs. Thus, although Type As invest more of themselves in their work role and report greater occupational self-esteem, they are not necessarily more satisfied in their jobs and run the risk of increased feelings of personal failure later in their careers.

Type As report less marital satisfaction, and a more adverse effect of their job demands on personal, home, and family lives (Burke and Weir, 1980). Spouses of Type A job incumbents agree with their husbands. They also report less marital satisfaction, and a more adverse effect of their partner's job demands on personal, home, and family lives (Burke et al., 1979). Thus, there probably is a link between Type A behavior and marital distress, and ultimately marital dissolution. It is also likely that Type A individuals are less involved with their children. Friedman and Rosenman (1974) provide anecdotal information that is consistent with the research conclusions that Type A individuals and their partners report a less satisfying home and family life.

It is interesting to note that the facets of Type A behavior are almost synonymous with traditional masculine ideology. Aggressiveness, competitiveness, and achievement striving are part of traditional masculinity. Anger and hostility, perhaps the most noxious components of Type A, are the common pathways for strong feelings among men (Pollack, 1998). Male gender role stress has been associated with anger and anxiety, which is consistent with higher Type A risk (Price, 1982; Eisler, 1995). Type A might well turn out to be 'Type M' for men because of its association with masculinity (Pollack, 1998).

Cohen and Reed (1985), in a study of 2187 Japanese men in the Honolulu Heart Program, reported that the prevalence rate of total CHD was found to be associated with Type A behavior, independent of other risk factors. Type A behavior was also found to be associated with levels of serum cholesterol, obesity, physical inactivity, and alcohol consumption.

Friedman and Booth-Kewley (1987) compared 50 middle-aged men who had heart attacks with 50 healthy controls. Type A behavior, particularly aspects related to emotional expression, was related to myocardial infarction, as were depression and anxiety.

Denollet (2000), in a study that included both women and men, reported that high levels of negative affect (the tendency to experience negative emotions) and social inhibition (the tendency to inhibit emotional expression in social interactions) were related to higher levels of hypertension.

More recent research has implicated anger as a key Type A characteristic in the etiology of CHD. Friedman and Ulmer (1984) used the acronym AIAI to capture this: Anger-Irritation-Aggravation-Impatience. Research undertaken by Williams et al. (1980), Shekelle et al. (1983), Dembrowski et al. (1989), Spicer and Hong (1991), Williams et al. (2000), Matthews et al. (2004), Whooley and Wong (2011), and research reviews and meta-analyses by Chida and Steptoe (2009) corroborate the anger/hostility and CHD association.

HEAVY WORK INVESTMENT

Schaef and Fassel (1988) conclude that addictive (greedy) organizations promote workaholism. Many men (and women) are structurally rewarded for colluding with addictive work systems. In these addictive organizations, destroying one's life and loved ones is acceptable if it produces something useful in the society. Schaef and Fassel argue that denial about worka-holism is pervasive because of an attachment to an economically based system, capitalism, and a social structure that supports this system (Fassel, 1990). Shortened work weeks coupled with increased leisure time have not been realized; in fact, the opposite is true. With increases in single-parent households and dual-income families, more people are caught in a time squeeze (Schor, 1991). The consequences of busy, time-pressured lives, while often ignored, are significant (see Robinson, 1998, for review).

Porter (1996) defines workaholism as 'excessive involvement with work evidenced by neglect in other areas of life and based on internal motives of behavior maintenance rather than requirements of the job or organization' (p. 71). She takes the position that an addictive pattern of excessive work impairs both immediate and long-term work performance. Consistent with other addictions such as alcoholism, Porter's review includes material on identity issues, rigid thinking, withdrawal, progressive involvement, and denial. Her definition has two elements: excessive involvement with work, and neglect of other areas of life. Workaholism makes it difficult to even think about anything other than work; family, friends, and self are neglected.

Burke (2000) compared self-reported work and psychological well-being outcomes of three types of workaholics: work enthusiasts, work addicts, and enthusiastic addicts. The three types of workaholics worked similar hours per week (approximately 55 hours on average). The work addicts, however, indicated significantly less satisfying work outcomes and poorer psychological well-being than did the two other workaholic types. What distinguished the work addicts from the other two groups were higher scores on feeling driven to work (the addictive-compulsive factor) and lower scores on work enjoyment.

This section considers issues around long work hours and excessive work investment. Long work hours and excessive work investment includes actual hours worked, overtime hours, 'face' time, workload, work intensity, and work addiction. Although the focus will be on the effects of these on individuals, effects are also present on families, workplaces, and innocent bystanders. It reviews the literature on the antecedents and consequences of working hours, work intensity, and work addiction, particularly among managers and professionals. The dependent variables associated with these include health-related illnesses, injuries, sleep patterns, fatigue, heart rate, and hormone level changes, as well as several work/non-work-life balance issues.

There is evidence that managers in industrialized countries are working more hours now than previously (Schor, 1991, 2003; Greenhouse, 2001). Working long hours may in fact be a prerequisite for achieving senior leadership positions (Wallace, 1997; Jacobs and Gerson, 1998). In addition, organizational downsizing efforts have increased the workloads of survivors (*Globe and Mail*, 2011).

The importance of focusing on work hours and work investment is multi-faceted. First, a large number of employees are unhappy about the number of hours they work (Jacobs and Gerson, 1998; Clarkberg and Moen, 2001; Dembe, 2005; MacInnes, 2005). Second, the amount of time demanded by work is an obvious and important way in which work affects other parts of one's life (Galinsky, 1999; Shields, 1999). Third, work hours are a widely studied structural output of employment (Adam, 1993). Fourth, the study of work hours and well-being outcomes has produced both inconsistent and complex results (Barnett, 1998).

New technology and job flexibility have facilitated working from home or outside the office, which has contributed to an increase in hours worked in North America (Golden and Figart, 2000). We have become a 24-hour society (Kreitzman, 1999). With more women now working, workers are increasingly married to other workers, making the family work week longer. In addition, smaller families also allow couples to work more.

People have expected an association of long working hours and adverse well-being consequences for over 100 years. These concerns were first raised during the Industrial Revolution in 1830 and in later years, and efforts were made to legislate limits in working hours to ten hours per day at that time (Golden, 2006).

Hewlett and Luce (2006) examined 'extreme jobs'. Jobs in which incumbents worked 70 hours a week or more were high wage earners, and had jobs with at least five characteristics of work intensity (e.g., unpredictable flow of work, fast-paced work under tight deadlines, inordinate scope of responsibility that amounts to more than one job, work-related events outside regular work hours, availability to clients 24/7, and a large amount of travel). They carried out surveys of high wage earners in the USA and high-earning managers and professionals working in large multinational organizations. In addition, they conducted focus groups and interviews to better understand the motivations for, and the effects of, working in these jobs. Their two surveys of high-earning managers and professionals revealed four characteristics that created the most intensity and pressure: unpredictability (cited by 91 percent of respondents), fast pace with tight deadlines (86 percent), work-related events outside business hours (66 percent), and 24/7 client demands (61 percent).

They concluded that managers and professionals were now working harder than ever. Of the extreme job holders, 48 percent said they were now working an average of 16.6 hours per week more than they did five years ago. And 42 percent took ten or fewer vacation days per year (less than they were entitled to) and 55 percent indicated that they had to cancel vacation plans regularly. Forty-four percent of their respondents felt the pace of their work was extreme.

But extreme job holders (66 percent in the US sample and 76 percent in the global sample) said that they loved their jobs. Several reasons were given for working these long hours: the job was stimulating and challenging (over 85 percent), working with high-quality colleagues (almost 50 percent), high pay (almost 50 percent), recognition (almost 40 percent), and power and status (almost 25 percent). In addition, increased competitive pressures, improved communication technologies, downsizings and restructurings resulting in few higher-level jobs, flattened organizational hierarchies, and values changes in the broader society supportive of 'extremes' also played a role (Wiehert, 2002).

Individuals holding 'extreme' jobs, however, had to let some things go. These included: home maintenance (about 70 percent), relationships with their children (almost 50 percent), relationships with their spouses/partners (over 45 percent), and an unsatisfying sex life (over 40 percent).

Extreme jobs were more likely to be held by men than women (17 percent versus 4 percent in the US sample; 30 percent versus 15 percent in the global sample). Women were more likely to be in jobs with high demands but working fewer hours. Women were not afraid of jobs having high levels of responsibility. Both women and men in extreme jobs indicated 'difficulties' with their children (acting out, eating too much junk food, under-achieving in school, too little adult supervision).

Most women (57 percent) in extreme jobs did not want to continue working as hard in five years (US sample), 48 percent of men felt the same way. Only 13 percent of women and 27 percent of men wanted to continue at this pace. The numbers were higher in the global survey: women, 80 percent, men 55 percent; and women, 5 percent and men, 17 percent.

WORK HOURS AND THEIR EFFECTS

A variety of outcome measures have been examined in connection with working long hours (van der Hulst, 2003). Most studies of long work hours have been conducted in Japan where '*karoshi*', sudden death due to long hours and insufficient sleep, was first observed. The Japanese coined this term to refer to deaths of individuals from overwork or working long work hours, and have actually defined such deaths (Kanai, 2006). Several hypotheses have been advanced to explain the relationship between long work hours and adverse health outcomes. Working long hours affects the cardiovascular system through chronic exposure to increases in blood pressure and heart rate (Buell and Breslow, 1960; Uehata, 1991; Iwasaki et al., 1998). Working long hours produces sleep deprivation and lack of recovery, leading to chronic fatigue, poor health-related behaviors, and ill health (Defoe et al., 2001; Ala-Mursjula et al., 2002; Liu and Tanaka, 2002). Working long hours makes it more difficult to recover from job demands and the stress of long work hours. Finally, working long hours has been associated with more errors and accidents (Schuster and Rhodes, 1985; Gander et al., 2000; Nachreiner et al., 2000; Loomis, 2005).

More specifically, the literature suggests that long hours are associated with adverse health effects and increased safety risk (Harrington, 1994, 2001; Cooper, 1996; Kirkcaldy et al., 1997; Spurgeon et al., 1997). Long work hours have been found to be associated with poor psychological health (Sparks et al., 1997; Borg and Kristensen, 1999; Kirkcaldy et al., 2000), excessive fatigue (Rosa, 1995) and burnout (Barnett et al., 1999). Several studies have also reported that long working hours are associated with more work–family conflict (Staines and Pleck, 1984; Galambos et al., 1995; Crouter et al., 1999, 2001; Galinsky et al., 2005), or fatigue, worrying, and irritability (Kluwer et al., 1996; Geurts et al., 1999; Grzywicz and Marks, 2000).

Between 1962 and 2002 there were 13 337 work-related highway deaths in the USA. In 2002, there were 808 truck driver deaths, 62 percent of highway accidents. The cost of a single work-related truck driver fatality in a highway incident was on average over $800 000. Costs to US society from truck driver incidents range from $316 million in 1992 to $506 million in 2000. Driver fatigue was a major factor in driver incidents, accounting for 31 percent of driver deaths. Forty-seven percent of drivers in New York State reported falling asleep at the wheel at least once during their career. To combat driver fatigue, drivers are limited in the number of hours they can drive each day or each week. Unfortunately 73 percent reported violating these limits, 56 percent of drivers worked more hours than they recorded, 23 percent of drivers worked 75 hours, and 10 percent more than 90 hours.

Dembe et al. (2005) examined the impact of overtime and extended working hours on the risk of occupational injuries and illnesses in a representative sample of working adults in the United States. They estimated the relative risk of long working hours per day, extended hours per week, long commute times, and overtime schedules on reporting a work-related injury or illness after controlling for age, gender, occupation, industry, and region. Data were collected from 10 793 workers between 1987 and 2000. After adjusting for these control factors, working in jobs with overtime schedules was associated with a 61 percent higher injury hazard rate compared to jobs without overtime. Working at least 12 hours per day was associated with a 32 percent increased hazard rate and working at least 60 hours per week was associated with a 23 percent increased hazard rate. A strong dose-response effect was observed, with the injury rate increasing in correspondence to the number of hours per day (or per week) in the worker's customary schedule. Job schedules with long working hours were not more risky because they are concentrated in inherently hazardous industries or occupations, or because people working long hours have more total time at risk for a work injury.

Van der Hulst et al. (2006) considered overtime, work characteristics (job demands, job control), and need for recovery in a large sample ($N =$ 1473) of Dutch municipal administration employees working full-time. The Effort-Recovery model (Meijman and Mulder, 1998) proposes that negative consequences of long working hours for health and well-being depends on the opportunities for recovery during the work day (internal recovery) and after work (external recovery). Working overtime reduces the time available for recovery. In addition, external recovery may be poor due to the spillover of work demands to one's home life. Finally, overtime is more likely to occur in demanding jobs, limiting opportunities for internal recovery. They examined four types of jobs: *low strain* – low demands, high control; *passive* – low demands, low control; *active* – high demands, high control; *high strain* – high demands, low control. Overtime was common for a majority of employees and in jobs having high demands. While there was no relationship between working overtime and need for recovery in the total sample, there was a significant and positive relationship between overtime hours and need for recovery in high strain jobs (high job demands, low control); there was also a relationship between overtime and need for recovery in active jobs (high demands, high control). Working conditions (high-demand jobs) influenced the relationship between overtime and need for recovery.

Caruso et al. (2004) reviewed the accumulating research evidence on the influence of overtime and extended work shifts on worker health and safety as well as worker errors, considering 52 studies in total. Overtime has increased in the United States from 1970 to 2000 (Rones et al., 1997; Hetrick, 2000). Overtime is defined as working more than 40 hours per week; extended work shifts are defined as shifts longer than eight hours. They found, in a majority of studies of general health that overtime was associated with poorer perceived general health, increased injury rate, more illness and increased mortality. A pattern of reduced performance on psychophysiological tests and injuries while working long hours, particularly very long shifts, was also noted. When 12-hour shifts were combined with more than 40 hours of work per week, more adverse effects were evident. Haenecke et al. (1998), in a study of 1.2 million German workers, found that the risk of workplace accidents increased during the latter portion (after the eighth hour) of a long work shift.

Van der Hulst (2003) found that long work hours was associated with adverse health, particularly cardiovascular disease, disability retirement, self-reported health problems and fatigue. She concluded that working more that 11 hours a day was associated with a three-fold risk of coronary heart disease and a four-fold risk of diabetes. In addition, working 60 or more hours a week was associated with a three-fold risk of disability retirement.

Van der Hulst's (2003) review showed that long work hours was associated with poorer physiological recovery; working long hours was associated with fewer hours of sleep. She suggested two possible pathways between long hours and health: insufficient recovery – a psychological recovery mechanism – and poor lifestyle behaviors – a behavioral lifestyle mechanism. Long work hours are believed to be associated with lifestyle choices such as smoking, coffee, and alcohol consumption, lack of exercise, and a poor (unhealthy) diet. These unhealthy behaviors produce physiological changes (e.g., high blood pressure, high levels of cholesterol, obesity, diabetes) and higher risk of coronary heart disease and poorer health in general. One perspective on why long work hours may be associated with reduced psychological well-being is the Effort-Recovery model (Meijman and Mulder, 1998) mentioned above. Working long hours is associated with short-term psychological costs that are irreversible. Individuals experience recovery when the work hours stop. Excessive work hours and insufficient recovery causes these negative effects to persist for a longer period of time or even become irreversible. Long work hours reduces the time of recovery as well as prolonging persistent and psychological demands.

Rissler (1977) studied the effects of high workload and overtime on heart rate and hormone levels during the rest and work hours. High workload was associated with higher levels of adrenaline and heart rate during evenings at home (rest periods) as well as feelings of fatigue and irritation. His results also indicated an accumulation effect of overtime on adrenaline levels. That is, it takes several weeks to return to normal (resting) values following several weeks of overtime.

Van der Hulst and Geurts (2001), in a study of 525 full-time employees of the Dutch Postal Service, found that working overtime was associated with negative work–home interference. Employees working overtime and reporting low rewards, indicated greater burnout, negative work–home interference, and slower recovery. Employees working overtime and experiencing a high pressure to work overtime, coupled with low rewards, had poorer recovery, more cynicism and negative work–home interference.

Major et al. (2002) in a study of 513 employees from one firm, found that hours worked per week was significantly related to work interference with family. Antecedents of hours worked included career identity, service, work overload, organizational expectations, self-reported financial needs, and non-job responsibilities (negatively). Parental demands were unrelated to hours worked; organizational rewards for time spent at work was respectively correlated (but weakly) with hours worked. Hours worked fully or partially related to the effects of many work and family characteristics on work interfering with family.

Nearly one-fifth of Canada's nurses admit to making occasional or frequent errors in giving medication to patients. Nurses working overtime, or where staffing and resources were inadequate, were more likely to report that a patient had received the wrong medication or dosage. In a 2005 study of 19 000 nurses, factors associated with medication errors included working overtime, work overload, and staffing shortages.

We undertook a longitudinal study of the effects of health care restructuring and hospital downsizing on the work and well-being of hospital-based nursing staff in the mid-1990s. Both job demands and work hours increased during these transitions. Nursing staff reported an increase in their work loads, sicker patients, along with increases in burnout and psychosomatic symptomatology (Burke and Greenglass, 2001). In addition, shift length, working more than eight hours, and working double shifts (back-to-back shifts) were significantly related to nurses' reports of nursing errors and injuries (Burke, 2003).

Rosa (1995) reported that overtime and fatigue were found to be associated with increases in back injuries, hospital outbreaks of bacterial infection, a three-fold increase in accidents after 26 hours of work and increased risk of safety violations in nuclear power plants, showing that long work hours does not just negatively affect the worker, it also puts a strain on overall workplace safety. Shimomitsu and Levi (1992) found that two-thirds of Japanese workers complain of fatigue, with '*karoshi*' or death from overwork, an important social concern. Moruyama et al. (1995) found long work hours to be associated with poor lifestyle habits such as heavy smoking, poor diet, and lack of exercise. Sparks et al. (1997) undertook a meta-analysis of 21 samples and found small but significant correlations between hours of work and physiological and psychological health symptoms.

FACE TIME

Some of the hours spent at work are unnecessary. Let's take 'face' time. We undertook a project with an international public accounting firm to determine why so few women achieved partnership and why valued and qualified women were leaving the firm. The emphasis on billable hours meant staff worked long hours. We also found that staff would remain in their offices, visible, until the Managing Partner went home. Then staff left though they could have left earlier. We heard of a staff member leaving an extra jacket on his chair with his office lights on while he attended a performance at a nearby theatre with his wife, then returning to his office to reclaim his jacket and turn out the lights.

WORK INTENSITY

Work intensity, on the other hand, is a construct that is not well developed in the literature (Green, 2004a, 2004b, 2005). It is generally conceptualized as an effort-related activity. In this regard, it is very similar to the 'work effort' concept discussed by Green (2001, p. 56) as: 'the rate of physical and/or mental input to work tasks performed during the working day . . . in part, effort is inversely linked to the "porosity" of the working day, meaning those gaps between tasks during which the body or mind rests'. Obviously, it would be difficult to measure such effort objectively; it can only be determined through self-reports, or extraordinarily well-controlled laboratory experiments. Burchell and Fagan (2004) used the 'speed of work' to mean work intensity, and reported that Europeans were working more intensely (2000 compared to 1991). Green (2001) focused on 'effort change' (respondents were asked to compare their current jobs with that of five years previously on items that included 'how fast you work', and 'the effort you have to put into your job'), and 'work effort' ('How much effort do you put into your job beyond what is required?' and 'My job requires that I work very hard'). He found that work effort had increased in Britain. While these are good starting points for conceptualizing work intensity, they measure only certain aspects of it. There is no research that attempts to capture a more extensive list of attributes.

Worrall and Cooper (1999), questioning over 1200 UK managers from 1997 to 1999, found that the pace of change had increased over these years. Managers now saw their jobs as more complex and fragmented. Managers in the 1999 survey had to deal with more information, to acquire a wider range of skills, and managed more staff. Seventy-six percent of these managers felt that the number of hours worked had a negative effect on their health. Clark (2005) comes to similar conclusions in a study of changes in job quality in OECD countries.

Adams and her colleagues (2000) have identified several factors leading to increased work intensification in nursing: shorter patient stays requires work to be done faster, more managerial responsibilities, need to cut costs, sicker patients, less student assistance, a lower ratio of qualified to unqualified nurses and fewer nurses, doctors working fewer hours so nurses have to fill this vacuum, and multi-skilling.

Ogbonna and Harris (2004) studied emotional labor as an element in work intensification among university lecturers. They conclude that emotional labor has increased due to heightened intensification of the academic labor process. They isolate some factors leading to the greater intensification of academic work (e.g., more students, higher workloads, increased scrutiny).

Green (2001), using various employee surveys conducted in the UK over almost a 20-year period, concluded that work effort has intensified since 1981. And between 1986 and 1997 there have been increases in the sources of pressure inducing hard work from employees. The most common sources of pressure were: one's own choice, fellow workers or colleagues, clients or customers, supervisors or bosses, pay incentives, and reports and appraisals (see also George, 1997 and Gallie, 2005).

Increases in work effort or intensity are represented in employees having less idle time (less time between tasks), having to work harder now, needing more skills (multi-skilling), greater use of performance goals and appraisals, use of total quality management and just-in-time processes, needing to work faster, having more deadlines, and having more responsibility (Green and McIntosh, 2001).

WORKAHOLISM AND WORK ADDICTION

Oates (1971, p. 4) defined a workaholic as 'a person whose need for work has become so excessive that it creates noticeable disturbance or interference with his bodily health, personal happiness, and interpersonal relationships, and with his smooth social functioning'. Others (see Killinger, 1991; Porter, 1996; Robinson, 1998) also define workaholism in negative terms. Most writers use the terms excessive work, workaholism, and work addiction interchangeably.

Types of Workaholics

Some researchers have proposed the existence of different types of workaholic behavior patterns, each having potentially different antecedents and associations with job performance, work and life outcomes. Scott et al. (1997) suggest three types of workaholic behavior patterns: compulsive-dependent, perfectionist, and achievement-oriented. They hypothesize that compulsive-dependent workaholism will be positively related to job performance and job and life satisfaction. Perfectionist workaholism will be positively related to levels of stress, physical and psychological problems, hostile interpersonal relationships, low job satisfaction and performance and voluntary turnover and absenteeism. Finally, achievement-oriented workaholism will be positively related to physical and psychological health, job and life satisfaction, job performance, low voluntary turnover and pro-social behaviors.

Spence and Robbins (1992) propose three workaholic profiles based on their workaholic triad notion. The workaholic triad consists of three concepts: work involvement, feeling driven to work because of inner pressures, and work enjoyment. These profiles were: (1) Work Addicts (WAs) who score high on work involvement, high on feeling driven to work and low on work enjoyment; (2) Work Enthusiasts (WE) who score high on work involvement, low on feeling driven to work and high on work enjoyment; (3) Enthusiastic Addicts (EA) who score high on all three workaholism components.

We compared the personal demographics, job behaviors, work outcomes, extra-work outcomes, and psychological health of the three types of workaholics proposed by Spence and Robbins (1992) in a series of studies:

Job behaviors
Burke (1999a) considered these relationships in a large sample of Canadian MBA graduates. First, there were no differences between WAs and WEs on hours worked per week or extra hours worked per week; workaholism types working significantly more hours and extra hours per week than did non-workaholism types. WAs reported higher levels of work stress, more perfectionism, and greater unwillingness

or difficulty in delegating than one or both of the other workaholism types.

Work outcomes

Burke (1999b) compared levels of work and career satisfaction and success among the workaholism profiles. WAs scored lower than WEs and EAs on job satisfaction, career satisfaction, and future career prospects, and higher than WEs on intent to quit.

Workaholism types and flow at work

Csikszentmihalyi (1990) uses the term 'optimal experience' to refer to times when individuals feel in control of their actions and masters of their own destinies. Optimal experiences commonly result from hard work and meeting challenges head on. Burke and Matthiesen (2004) found that journalists scoring higher on work enjoyment and lower on feeling driven to work because of internal needs indicated higher levels of flow or optimal experience at work. In this same study, Burke and Matthiesen found that WEs and EAs indicated higher levels of flow than WAs.

Psychological well-being

Burke (1999c) compared the three workaholism types on three indicators of psychological and physical well-being in a sample of 530 employed women and men MBA graduates. WAs had more psychosomatic symptoms than both WEs and EAs and poorer physical and emotional well-being than WEs.

Extra-work satisfactions and family functioning

Burke (1999d) compared the three workaholism types on three aspects of life or extra-work satisfaction: family, relationship, and community. The comparisons of the workaholism types on the three measures of life or extra-work satisfactions provided moderate support for the hypothesized relationships. WAs reported less satisfaction on all three extra-work satisfaction measures than did WEs and less satisfaction on one (family) than did EAs.

Individuals, families, organizations, and societies need to be concerned about the effects of long work hours, work intensity, and work addiction. These have been found to diminish employee well-being and health, levels of family functioning and organizational performance and increase social welfare and health care costs borne by society (Kirkcaldy et al., 2009). Healthy organizations and societies need healthy individuals and families; coming to grips with long work hours, intense and demanding jobs, and work addiction is an important start.

CAREER SUCCESS AND PERSONAL FAILURE

Korman and Korman (1980) highlighted and elaborated on the career success and personal failure phenomenon. Career success and personal failure is a syndrome that afflicts some managerial and professional men in mid-life and mid-career. Career success and personal failure refers to experiences reported among men who have attained an unquestionable level of success according to society's criteria (high occupational status, prestige, power and responsibility, substantial income, relative material worth, status in the community). However, concurrent with this experience of oneself as a career success is a growing disaffection with one's life as a whole. The individual feels victim to feelings of frustration, grief, loneliness, alienation, and despair, and to pressing questions about the meaning and direction of his life. The discrepancy between the individual's career identity with its external trappings and rewards, and the individual's more personal sense of self, creates varying degrees of psychological distress that demand resolution.

How Common are Career Success and Personal Failure Feelings?

The answer seems to be fairly common. Burke (1999d) asked 530 MBA graduates (278 men and 252 women) to respond to four questions developed by Korman and Korman (1980) to assess career success and personal failure feelings. Almost all worked full-time, most were married (80 percent), had children (70 percent), had achieved other professional designations such as the CFA, or CA designations (40 percent), and had incomes between $50 000 to $100 000 (50 percent). This group, on the whole, would be seen as 'successful' in their work and careers. Respondents provided considerable evidence indicating the presence of work and personal alienation typical of the career success and personal failure phenomenon.

Why should an individual who is so obviously successful in his career develop feelings of personal failure? One set of antecedents proposed by Korman and Korman results from new appreciations of life realities developed from particular work experiences. These include the realization that life demands are contradictory (one cannot necessarily have it all); the realization that one's view of cause–effect relationships was wrong; the realization that many of one's choices or decisions were made to please others; and the realization that one has few close friends and is basically alone. A second set of antecedents results from the male mid-life stage itself. These include an awareness of physical decline, advancing age, and goals that will never be achieved; changes in family and personal relationships among self and others; and increased feelings of obsolescence. The combination of these antecedents results in career-successful men feeling personally and socially alienated. With these feelings come a loss of work interest and dissatisfaction with one's job, career, or life in general. In turn, this leads to psychological distress and a desire to rearticulate a sense of purpose and meaning in one's life.

We typically assume that managers and professionals working in organizations are satisfied with their careers and extra-work aspects of their lives. They have status, prestige, interesting jobs, some degree of autonomy, and relatively high salaries. Korman et al. (1981) cite studies that challenge this rosy picture of managers and professionals. Instead these studies paint a picture of personally and socially alienated women and men.

These findings are important for several reasons. First, managers and professionals serve as important role models for others. Second, because managers and professionals have some discretion, these feelings of alienation can have negative effects on their work performance. Third, their negative feelings may color the views of others (subordinates, their children). Fourth, their experiences run counter to the commonly held belief that career success should be associated with life and personal satisfaction, causing some individuals to rethink their investments in careers. Korman et al. (1981), in two samples of MBA graduates, found support for their predicted antecedents of career success and personal failure feelings.

It seems that more people are wary of too much career investment and the costs of career success to some. Westman and Etzion (1990) had 23 management students and executives offer their reactions to four versions of a vignette describing a successful manager. Career success was seen as a major cause of personal failure due to hard work and long hours rather than the pursuit of material wealth. Thus individuals are aware of the costs of success (Evans and Bartolomé, 1980; LaBier, 1986).

Kofodimos defines balance as 'a satisfying, healthy and productive life that includes work, play, and love; that integrates a range of life activities with attention to self and to personal and spiritual development; and that expresses a person's unique wishes, interests, and values' (1993, p. xiii). Several factors have made the striving for balance a higher priority among some managers. These include the presence of more women in the workforce, increasing pressures for harder work and longer hours, the movement of baby-boomers into mid-life and management, and the realization by some that the simple-minded pursuit of career success has fallen short in providing happiness.

CHANGING MEN AND ORGANIZATIONS

There is increasing evidence that educational and counseling initiatives can prove useful in reducing the most lethal aspects of the male role. Friedman and his colleagues (Friedman and Rosenman, 1974; Friedman and Ulmer, 1984) indicate clearly that Type A behavior can be modified, resulting in a corresponding reduction in incidence of CHD. Friedman and Ulmer (1984) provide considerable information on ways to alleviate time urgency, free-floating hostility, and other self-destructive tendencies. Their program involves cognitive restructuring, behavior modification, self-monitoring, social support and reinforcement. On the opening day of their program, participants are given a list of ten freedoms, these freedoms constituting freedom from behavior patterns and attitudes that were putting their health and lives in jeopardy. These are (Friedman and Ulmer, 1984, p. 1565):

1 the freedom to overcome your insecurity and regain your self-esteem;
2 the freedom to give and receive love;
3 the freedom to mature;
4 the freedom to restore and enrich your personality;
5 the freedom to overcome and replace old hurtful habits with new life-enhancing ones;
6 the freedom to take pleasure in the experiences of your friends and family members;
7 the freedom to recall your past life frequently and with satisfaction;
8 the freedom to listen;
9 the freedom to play;
10 the freedom to enjoy tranquility.

Williams and Williams (1993) describe a program for controlling hostility, one of the key components of coronary-prone behavior (Williams, 1989). The major strategies involve learning how to deflect anger, improve relationships, and adopt positive attitudes. Johnston (1986) describes four approaches to reducing Type A behavior and the hostility component: stress management, cognitive therapy, cognitive-behavioral therapy, and beta-blockade.

There are also a number of workshops available allowing both men and women to confront the discontents of masculinity. Silverstein and Rashbaum (1994) offer one such workshop, titled 'The Courage to Raise Good Men'. The workshop questions traditional motives of manhood and encourages both mothers and fathers to refuse to sanction the emotional shutdown traditionally demanded of boys. Silverstein and Rashbaum also encourage a new way of valuing traditional 'feminine' behaviors such as empathy, nurturing, and compassion. As Kaufman (1993) writes, it is time to start 'cracking the armor'.

Achieving balance requires changes in both individuals and organizations. Kofodimos (1993) advocates, at the broadest level, that individuals change their approach to living, and that organizations review and change their norms, values, and practices. Individuals need to identify the allocation of time and energy that fits their values and needs. Organizations that support balance need to examine and redefine effective performance at work (to be more than hours worked per week) as well as redefine the notions of a career and career success.

Korman and Korman (1980) offer some suggestions for societal and organizational interventions that can be considered to reduce career success and personal failure experiences. First, with greater recognition of the existence of the problem, professionals in our society can develop programs explicitly designed to help individuals anticipate or resolve the problem of career success and personal failure. This may involve developing personal growth and life planning workshops, assessment centers, career and personal counseling facilities, and self-help materials, all specifically designed to aid individuals in coping with or preventing the severity of this experience.

Another intervention at the societal level might involve the educational system. Students in high schools and universities could be exposed to the different meanings of the word 'success'; to viable lifestyle options; to stages of adult development and their relevant tasks, issues and problems; to the interactive effects of work and family life; and to goal setting and career and life-planning activities. There is an obvious need to portray the reality of success more accurately. The societal model pushed so enthusiastically by schools offering business and corporate management development programs (i.e., hard work will bring success, success automatically creates the good life, the healthy life) grossly distorts the reality. As individuals begin their careers, unrealistic expectations can result in eventual disillusionment in mid-life, followed by psychosomatic symptoms, physical illness, alcoholism, and heart attacks. The costs of success must be presented if a balanced view is to be had.

Interventions at the organizational level are crucially important yet at the present time are virtually non-existent. Organizations are in a position to provide assessment and career planning programs for their employees and many do. Fortunately, there is a growing recognition that these kinds of programs make little sense without giving consideration to personal life needs and goals. In addition, it is impossible to ignore the fact that individuals' work life and personal life influence each other to a significant degree. It is not unreasonable to expect organizations to consider the impact they are having on the families of their employees; to understand the extent of that impact by surveys of both employees and their spouses; to providing adequate counseling facilities for employees and their families; and to take a more active role in involving and preparing families for the job and career changes that might affect them.

At an early stage in an individual's career, organizations can identify those who are prone to career success and personal failure. Every top management group knows who their workaholics and Type As are and can begin developing a program to educate these individuals on the possible effects such behavior could have on themselves and their families. Another interesting possibility for organizations is to make provisions for individuals to take sabbaticals, or to be assigned to special assignments that significantly change their day-to-day work and life patterns and free them to re-examine their life situation and gain new perspective.

CONCLUSIONS

Reconstructing or redefining masculinity requires social change. It must occur in early childhood, in schools, in the media (especially television), in universities, in organizations, and through government policies and initiatives. The current trend toward corporate and government restructuring has resulted in massive downsizing and job losses. Might these serve as stimuli for change? Some men may be forced out of the traditional breadwinner role, and some may adopt new definitions of masculinity as a result. Others, however, may respond with fear and a rigid adherence to traditional masculine ideology.

Brod and Kaufman (1994) suggest that contemporary men need to be open to women's presence and suppressed knowledge; consider men's lives and experiences as those of men and not humans in general; appreciate how men assume the privileges of a patriarchical society; become aware of how the masculine role oppresses women; and understand why it is so difficult for men to change. Theoretical understanding of men's experiences necessarily becomes personal understanding since it is men's lives that are being examined. It is men's responsibility to challenge an oppressive status quo through changes in men's personal lives as well as in ideas, structures, processes, and organizations.

Men who develop the capacity to provide a gender-sensitive empathic form of fathering may benefit in reducing levels of masculinity ideology. First, they can see the positive effects of their emotional commitment to their children's well-being, raising their children's self-esteem. Second, they can learn from their female partners how to better nurture. Robinson (1998) and Friedman and Ulmer (1984) provide useful insights on reducing the harmful habits of workaholism and Type A behavior respectively. Interestingly, Burke (1999e, 1999f) has found that the need to prove oneself is an individual difference characteristic associated with both levels of Type A behavior and work addiction.

How can men change? Men do not need to discard parts of themselves as much as they need to change them. Autonomy and aggressiveness are not negative unless they become extreme. These traits need to be tempered and balanced.

Orton (1993) defines social change as a process of unlearning gender-based and power-based behaviors that have proved harmful and then *relearning* respectful empowering behaviors that have no reference to gender. This process will take considerable time and practice to realize benefits from it. Orton believes that it is the job of men to point out to other men the dysfunctional aspects of traditional masculinity and support and model new behaviors.

Kimmel (1987) raises the question of how we can change those components of masculinity that limit 'men's development as healthy and fully responsive people'. He identifies three approaches: personal change by men; the creation of political organizations that communicate and lobby for change; and the emergence of broadly based social movements. He further suggests that men are changing, but points out that few do so in response to the downside and limitations of masculinity, but rather from pressures of external forces (e.g., the women's movement).

Brannon's four basic rules of manhood highlight the dilemma for men. These rules have limited men and channeled them away from whatever their real potential might have been. How can men free themselves from their prison? Suggestions include getting out of the corporate rat race; rejecting competition and aggression; and regaining emotional spontaneity. What was missing in all this was a new model of manhood.

Kimmel (1996) offers 'democratic manhood' as the model of masculinity of the future. Democratic manhood involves inclusion, fighting injustice based on difference, and private and public commitments. Men need to change themselves, foster relationships, and nurture their families. In addition, men need to challenge and remake social systems so that they and women will prosper.

NOTES

* Preparation of this chapter was supported in part by York University, Toronto. Carla D'Agostino produced the manuscript.
** I thank the American Psychological Association for permission to reprint parts of my earlier chapter (Burke, R.J. [2002], 'Men, masculinity and health', in D.L. Nelson and R.J. Burke (eds), *Gender, Work Stress and Health*, Washington, DC: American Psychological Association, copyright 2002 by the American Psychological Association; reproduced by permission).

REFERENCES

Adam, B. (1993), 'Within and beyond the time economy of employment relations: Conceptual issues pertinent to research on time and work', *Social Science Information*, **32**(2), 163–84.

Adams, A., J. Chase, S. Arber and S. Band (2000), 'Skill mix changes and work intensification in nursing', *Work, Employment and Society*, **14**(3), 541–55.

Ala-Mursjula, L., J. Vahtera, M. Kivimaki, M.V. Kevin and J. Penttij (2002), 'Employee control over working times: Associations with subjective health and sickness absences', *Journal of Epidemiology and Community Health*, **56**(4), 272–8.

Bardwick, J. (1984), 'When ambition is no asset', *New Management*, **1**, 22–8.

Barnett, R.C. (1998), 'Towards a review and reconceptualization of the work/family literature', *Genetic Social and General Psychology Monograph*, **124**(2), 125–82.

Barnett, R.C., K.C. Gareis and R.T. Brennan (1999), 'Fit as a mediator of the relationship between work hours and burnout', *Journal of Occupational Health Psychology*, **4**(4), 307–17.

Borg, V. and T.S. Kristensen (1999), 'Psychosocial work environment and mental health among traveling sales people', *Work and Stress*, **13**(2), 132–43.

Brannon, R. (1976), 'The male sex role: Our culture's blueprint for manhood and what it's done for us lately', in D. David and R. Brannon (eds), *The Forty-nine Percent Majority: The Male Sex Role*, Reading, MA: Addison-Wesley, pp. 1–48.

Brannon, R. and S. Juni (1984), 'A scale for measuring attitudes about masculinity', *Psychological Documents*, **14**(1), 6–7.

Brod, H. (1987), *The Making of the Masculinities: The New Men's Studies*, Boston, MA: Unwin Hyman.

Brod, H. and M. Kaufman (1994), *Theorizing Masculinities*, Thousand Oaks, CA: Sage.

Brooks, O.R. (1992), 'Gender-sensitive family therapy in a violent culture', *Topics in Family Psychology and Counseling*, **2**(4), 24–36.

Buell, P. and L. Breslow (1960), 'Mortality from coronary heart disease in Californian men who work long hours', *Journal of Chronic Disease*, **11**, 615–26.

Bunting, A.B. and J.B. Reeves (1983), 'Perceived male sex orientation and beliefs about rape', *Deviant Behavior*, **4**(3–4), 281–95.

Burchell, B. and C. Fagan (2004), 'Gender and the intensification of work: Evidence from the European working conditions survey', *Eastern Economic Journal*, **30**(4), 627–42.

Burke, R.J. (1999a), 'Workaholism in organizations: Measurement validation and replication', *International Journal of Stress Management*, **6**(1), 45–55.

Burke, R.J. (1999b), 'Are workaholics job satisfied and successful in their careers?', *Career Development International*, **26**, 149–58.

Burke, R.J. (1999c), 'Workaholism in organizations: Psychological and physical well-being consequences', *Stress Medicine*, **16**(1), 11–16.

Burke, R.J. (1999d), 'Workaholism and extra-work satisfactions', *International Journal of Organizational Analysis*, **7**(4), 352–64.

Burke, R.J. (1999g), 'Career success and personal failure feelings among managers', *Psychological Reports*, **84**(2), 651–3.

Burke, R.J. (1999e), 'Workaholism in organizations: The role of personal beliefs and fears', *Anxiety, Stress, and Coping*, **12**, 1–12.

Burke, R.J. (1999f), 'It's not how hard you work but how you work hard: Evaluating workaholism components', *International Journal of Stress Management*, **6**(4), 225–39.

Burke, R.J. (2000), 'Workaholism in organizations: Concepts, results and future research directions', *International Journal of Management Reviews*, **2**(1), 1–16.

Burke, R.J. (2003), 'Length of shift, work outcomes, and psychological well-being of nursing staff', *International Journal of Public Administration*, **26**(14), 1637–46.

Burke, R.J. and E. Deszca (1982), 'Type A behaviour and career success and personal failure', *Journal of Occupational Behaviour*, **3**(2), 161–70.

Burke, R.J. and E.R. Greenglass (2001), 'Hospital restructuring and nursing staff well-being: The role of perceived hospital and union support', *Anxiety, Stress and Coping*, **14**(1), 93–115.

Burke, R.J. and S. Matthiesen (2004), 'Workaholism among Norwegian journalists: Antecedents and consequences', *Stress and Health*, **20**(5), 301–8.

Burke, R.J. and T. Weir (1980), 'The Type A experience: Occupational and life demands, satisfaction and well-being', *Journal of Human Stress*, **6**(4), 28–38.

Burke, R.J., T. Weir and R.E. Duwors (1979), 'Type A behavior of administrators and wives' reports of marital satisfaction and well-being', *Journal of Applied Psychology*, **64**(1), 57–65.

Butts, D. and M. Whitty (1993), 'Why do men work? Money, power, success and deeper values', *Masculinities*, **1**, 35–53.

Caruso, C., F. Hitchcock, R. Dick, J. Russo and J.M. Schmitt (2004), *Overtime and Extended Work Shifts: Recent Findings on Illness, Injuries and Health Behaviors*, Publication No 2004-143, Cincinnati, OH: NIOSH Publications.

Chesney, M. and R.H. Rosenman (1980), 'Type A behavior in the work setting', in C.L. Cooper and R. Payne (eds), *Current Concerns in Occupational Stress*, New York: John Wiley, pp. 187–212.

Chida, Y. and A. Steptoe (2009), 'The association of anger and hostility with future coronary heart disease', *Journal of the American College of Cardiology*, **53**(11), 936–46.

Clark, A.E. (2005), 'Your money or your life: Changing job quality in OECD countries', *British Journal of Industrial Relations*, **43**(3), 377–400.

Clarkberg, M. and P. Moen (2001), 'The time squeeze: Is the increase in working time due to employer demands or employee preferences?', *American Behavioral Scientist*, **44**(7), 1115–36.

Cohen, J.B. and D. Reed (1985), 'The Type A behavior pattern and coronary heart disease among Japanese men in Hawaii', *Journal of Behavioral Medicine*, **8**(4), 343–52.

Cohen, T.E. (1993), 'What do fathers provide? Reconsidering the economic and nurturant dimensions of men as parents', in J. Hood (ed.), *Men, Work and Family*, Newbury Park, CA: Sage, pp. 1–22.

Cooper, C.L. (1996), 'Editorial, Working hours and health', *Work and Stress*, **10**, 1–4.

Courtenay, W.H. (2001), 'Constructions of masculinity and their influence on men's well-being: A theory of gender and health', *Social Science and Medicine*, **51**, 203–17.

Crouter, A.C., M.F. Bumpus, M.R. Head and S.M. McHale (2001), 'Implications of overwork and overload for the quality of men's family relationships', *Journal of Marriage and Family*, **63**(2), 404–16.

Crouter, A.C., M.F. Bumpus, M.C. Maguire and S.M. McHale (1999), 'Working parents, work pressures and adolescents' well-being: Insights into dynamics in dual career families', *Developmental Psychology*, **25**, 1453–61.

Csikszentmihalyi, M. (1990), *Flow: The Psychology of Optimal Experience*, New York: Harper Collins.

Davis, E. and W.B. Walsh (1988), 'Antecedents and consequences of gender role conflict: An empirical test of sex role strain analysis', paper presented at the 96th Annual Convention of the American Psychological Association, Atlanta, GA.

Defoe, D.M., M.L. Power, G.B. Holzman, A. Carpentieri and J. Schulkin (2001), 'Long hours and little sleep: Work schedules of residents in obstetrics and gynecology', *Obstetrics and Gynecology*, **97**(6), 1015–18.

Dembe, A.E. (2005), 'Long working hours: The scientific bases for concern', *Perspectives on Work*, **62**(Winter), 20–22.

Dembe, A.E., J.B. Erickson, R.G. Delbos and S.M. Banks (2005), 'The impact of overtime and long work hours on occupational injuries and illnesses: New evidence from the United States', *Occupational and Environmental Medicine*, **62**(9), 588–97.

Dembrowski, T.M., J.M. MacDougall, P.T. Costa and G.A. Grandits (1989), 'Components of hostility as predictors of sudden death and myocardial infarction in the Multiple Risk Factor Intervention Trial', *Psychosomatic Medicine*, **51**(5), 514–22.

Denollet, J. (2000), 'Type D personality: A potential risk factor refined', *Journal of Psychosomatic Research*, **49**(4), 255–66.

Ehrenreich, B. (1983), *The Hearts of Men: American Dreams and the Flight from Commitment*, New York: Anchor Press.

Ehrenreich, B. (1989), 'A feminist's view of the new man', in M. Kimmel and M.A. Messner (eds), *Men's Lives*, New York: Macmillan, pp. 34–43.

Eisler, R.M. (1995), 'The relationship between masculine gender role stress and men's health risk: The validation of a construct', in R.F. Levant and W.S. Pollack (eds), *A New Psychology of Men*, New York: Basic Books, pp. 207–25.

Eisler, R.M. and J.R. Skidmore (1987), 'Masculine gender role stress: Scale development and components factors in appraisal of stressful situations', *Behavior Modification*, **11**(2), 123–36.

Eisler, R.M., J.R. Skidmore and C.H. Ward (1988), 'Masculine gender-role stress: Predictor of anger, anxiety and health-risk behaviors', *Journal of Personality Assessment*, **52**(1), 133–41.

Evans, P. and F. Bartolomé (1980), *Must Success Cost So Much?*, New York: Basic Books.

Faludi, S. (1999), *Stiffed: The Betrayal of the American Male*, New York: William Morrow and Co.

Fassel, D. (1990), *Working Ourselves to Death*, San Francisco, CA: Harper.

Finn, J. (1986), 'The relationship between sex role attitudes and attitudes supporting marital violence', *Sex Roles*, **14**(5–6), 235–44.

Friedman, H.S. and S. Booth-Kewley (1987), 'Personality, Type A behavior, and coronary heart disease: The role of emotional expression', *Journal of Personality and Social Psychology*, **53**(4), 783–92.

Friedman, M. and R. Rosenman (1974), *Type A Behavior and Your Heart*, New York: Knopf.

Friedman, M. and D. Ulmer (1984), *Treating Type A Behavior and Your Heart*, New York: Alfred Knopf.

Fromm, E. (1974), *Man From Himself: An Inquiry into the Psychology of Ethics*, New York: Rinehart.

Fromm, E. (1976), *To Have Or To Be?*, New York: Harper and Row.

Galambos, N.L., H.A. Sears, D.M. Almeida and G. Kolaric (1995), 'Parents' work overload and problem behavior in young adolescents', *Journal of Research on Adolescence*, **5**(2), 201–23.

Galinsky, E. (1999), *Ask the Children: What America's Children Really Think About Working Parents*, New York: William Morrow.

Galinsky, E., J.T. Bond, S.S. Kim, L. Bachon, E. Brownfield and K. Sakal (2005), *Overwork in America: When the Way We Work Becomes Too Much*, New York: Families and Work Institute.

Gallie, D. (2005), 'Work pressure in Europe 1996–2001: Trends and determinants', *British Journal of Industrial Relations*, **43**(3), 351–75.

Gander, P.H., A. Merry, M.M. Millar and J. Weller (2000), 'Hours of work and fatigue-related error: A survey of New Zealand anaesthetists', *Anaesthesia and Intensive Care*, **28**(2), 178–83.

George, D. (1997), 'Working longer hours: Pressure from the boss or pressure from the marketers?', *Review of Social Economy*, **60**(1), 33–65.

Geurts, S., C. Rutte and M. Peeters (1999), 'Antecedents and consequences of work–home interference among medical residents', *Social Science and Medicine*, **48**, 1135–48.

Globe and Mail (2011), 'Heavier workloads from layoffs still not easing: poll', *Globe and Mail*, 12 March, B19.

Goldberg, H. (1977), *The Hazards of Being Male*, New York: New American Library.

Golden, L. (2006), 'How long? The historical economic and cultural factors behind: Working hours and overwork', in R.J. Burke (ed.), *Research Companion to Working Hours and Work Addiction*, Cheltenham, UK and Northampton, MA, USA: Edward Elgar Publishing, pp. 36–57.

Golden, L. and D.M. Figart (2000), *Work Time: International Trends, Theory and Policy Perspectives*, London: Routledge.

Good, G.E. and L.B. Mintz (1990), 'Gender role conflict and depression in college men: Evidence for compounded risk', *Journal of Counseling and Development*, **69**(1), 17–21.

Good, G.E., D.M. Dell and L.B. Mintz (1989), 'Male role and gender role conflict: Relations in help seeking in men', *Journal of Counseling Psychology*, **36**(3), 295–300.

Gould, R.E. (1974), 'Measuring masculinity by the size of a paycheck', in J. Pleck and J. Sawyer (eds), *Men and Masculinity*, Englewood Cliffs, NJ: Prentice-Hall, pp. 96–100.

Green, F. (2001), 'It's been a hard day's night: The concentration and intensification of work in late twentieth-century Britain', *British Journal of Industrial Relations*, **39**(1), 53–80.

Green, F. (2004a), 'Why has work effort become more intense?', *Industrial Relations*, **43**(4), 709–41.

Green, F. (2004b), 'Work intensification, discretion, and the decline in well-being at work', *Eastern Economic Journal*, **30**(4), 615–25.

Green, F. (2005), *Demanding Work: The Paradox of Job Quality in the Affluent Economy*, Princeton, NJ: Princeton University Press.

Green, F. and S. McIntosh (2001), 'The intensification of work in Europe', *Labour Economics*, **8**(2), 291–308.

Greenhouse, S. (2001), 'Report shows Americans have more "labor days"', *New York Times*, 1 September, A6.

Grzywicz, J.G. and N. Marks (2000), 'Reconceptualizing the work–family interface: An ecological perspective on the correlates of positive and negative spillover between work and family', *Journal of Occupational Health Psychology*, **5**(1), 111–26.

Haenecke, K., S. Tiedemann, F. Nachreiner and H. Grzech Sukalo (1998), 'Accident risk as a function of hour at work and time of day as determined from accident data and exposure models for the German working population', *Scandinavian Journal of Work, Environment and Health*, **24**(S3), S43–S48.

Harrington, J.M. (1994), 'Working long hours and health', *British Medical Journal*, **308**(6944), 1581–2.

Harrington, J.M. (2001), 'Health effects of shift work and extended hours of work', *Occupational and Environmental Medicine*, **58**(1), 68–72.

Harrison, J.C. (1978), 'Warning: The male role may be hazardous to your health', *Journal of Social Issues*, **34**(1), 65–86.

Harrison, J.C., J. Chin and T. Ficarrotto (1989), 'Warning: Masculinity may be dangerous to your health', in M.S. Kimmel and M.A. Messner (eds), *Men's Lives*, New York: Macmillan, pp. 296–309.

Hawthorne, F. (1993), 'Why family leave shouldn't scare employers', *Institutions Investor*, **27**, 31–4.

Hearn, J. (1994), 'Changing men and changing managements: Social change, social research and social action', in M. Davidson and R.J. Burke (eds), *Women in Management: Current Research Issues*, London: Paul Chapman, pp. 192–209.

Helgeson, V.S. (1990), 'The role of masculinity as a prognostic predictor of heart attack severity', *Sex Roles*, **22**(11), 755–76.

Hetrick, R. (2000), 'Analyzing the recent upward surge in overtime hours', *Monthly Labor Review*, **123**(2), 30–33.

Hewlett, S.A. and C.B. Luce (2006), 'Extreme jobs: The dangerous allure of the 70-hour work week', *Harvard Business Review Magazine*, December, 49–59.

Hochschild, A.R. (1997), *The Time Bind: When Work Becomes Home and Home Becomes Work*, New York: Metropolitan/Henry Holt and Company.

Howard, J.M., D.A. Cunningham and P.A. Rechnitzer (1977), 'Work patterns associated with Type A behavior: A managerial population', *Human Relations*, **36**(9), 825–36.

Iwasaki, K., T. Sasaki, T. Oka and N. Hisanaga (1998), 'Effect of working hours on biological functions related to cardiovascular system among salesmen in a machinery manufacturing company', *Industrial Health*, **36**(4), 361–7.

Jacobs, J.A. and K. Gerson (1998), 'Who are the overworked Americans?', *Review of Social Economy*, **56**(4), 442–59.

Johnston, D.W. (1986), 'Can and should Type A behavior be changed?', *Postgraduate Medical Journal*, **62**(730), 785–8.

Jourard, S.M. (1964), 'Some lethal aspects of the male role', in S.M. Jourard, *The Transparent Self*, Princeton, NJ: Van Nostrand, pp. 46–55.

Kanai, A. (2006), 'Economic and employment conditions, *karoshi* (work to death) and the trend of studies on workaholism in Japan', in R.J. Burke (ed.), *Research Companion to Working Time and Work Addiction*, Cheltenham, UK and Northampton, MA, USA: Edward Elgar Publishing, pp. 158–71.

Kaufman, M. (1993), *Cracking the Armour: Power, Pain and the Lives of Men*, Toronto: Viking.

Killinger, B. (1991), *Workaholics: The Respectable Addicts*, New York: Simon and Schuster.

Kimmel, M.S. (1987), *Changing Men: New Directions in Research on Men and Masculinity*, Newbury Park, CA: Sage.

Kimmel, M.S. (1993), 'What do men want?', *Harvard Business Review*, **71**(6), 50–63.

Kimmel, M.S. (1996), *Manhood in America*, New York: The Free Press.

Kimmel, M.S. and M.A. Messner (1989), *Men's Lives*, New York: Macmillan Publishing Company.

Kirkcaldy, B., A. Furnham and R. Shephard (2009), 'The impact of working hours and working patterns on physical and psychological health', in S. Cartwright and C.L. Cooper (eds), *The Oxford Handbook of Organizational Well-being*, Oxford: Oxford University Press, pp. 303–35.

Kirkcaldy, B.D., R. Levine and R.J. Shephard (2000), 'The impact of working hours on physical and psychological health of German managers', *European Review of Applied Psychology*, **50**(4), 443–9.

Kirkcaldy, B., R. Trimpop and C. Cooper (1997), 'Working hours, job stress, work satisfaction and accident rates among medical practitioners, consultants and allied personnel', *International Journal of Stress Management*, **4**(2), 79–87.

Kluwer, E.S., J.A.M. Heesink and E. van den Vliert (1996), 'Marital conflict about the division of household labor and paid work', *Journal of Marriage and the Family*, **58**(4), 958–69.

Kofodimos, J. (1993), *Balancing Act*, San Francisco, CA: Jossey-Bass.

Korabik, K. (1999), 'Sex and gender in the new millennium', in G.N. Powell (ed.), *Handbook of Gender and Work*, Thousand Oaks, CA: Sage, pp. 3–16.

Korman, A. and R. Korman (1980), *Career Success and Personal Failure*, New York: Prentice-Hall.

Korman, A.K., U. Wittig-Berman and D. Lang (1981), 'Career success and personal failure: Alienation in professionals and managers', *Academy of Management Journal*, **24**(2), 342–60.

Kreitzman, L. (1999), *The 24-hour Society*, London: Profile Books.

Kunnanatt, J.T. (2004), 'Type A behavior pattern and managerial performance: A study among bank executives in India', *International Journal of Manpower*, **24**(6), 720–34.

LaBier, D. (1986), *Modern Madness: The Emotional Fallout from Success*, Reading, MA: Addison-Wesley.

Landers, S. (1989), 'In U.S., marital disorders affect 15 percent of adults', *APA Monitor*, **20**, 16.

Lash, S.J., R.M. Eisler and R.S. Schulman (1990), 'Cardiovascular reactivity to stress in men: Effects of masculine gender role stress appraisal and masculine performance challenge', *Behavior Modification*, **14**(1), 3–20.

Levant, R.E (1994), 'The new psychology of men', *Professional Psychology: Research and Practice*, **27**(3), 259–65.

Levant, R.E (1995), 'Toward the·reconstruction of masculinity', in R.E Levant and. W. S. Pollack (eds), *A New Psychology of Men*, New York: Basic Books, pp. 229–51.

Levant, R.E. and W.S. Pollack (1995), *A New Psychology of Men*, New York: Basic Books.

Levant, R., F. Hirsch, L. Celentano, E. Cozza, T. Hill, S. MacEachern and M. Schnedeker et al. (1992), 'The male role: An investigation of norms and stereotypes', *Journal of Mental·Health Counseling*, **14**, 325–37.

Liu, Y. and H. Tanaka (2002), 'Overtime work, insufficient sleep, and risk of non-fatal acute myocardial infarction in Japanese men', *Occupational Environmental Medicine*, **59**(7), 447–51.

Loomis, D. (2005), 'Long work hours and occupational injuries: New evidence on upstream causes', *Occupational and Environmental Medicine*, **62**(9), 588–97.

MacInnes, J. (2005), 'Work–life balance and the demands for reduction in working hours: Evidence from the British Social Attitudes Survey 2002', *British Journal of Industrial Relations*, **43**(2), 273–95.

Maier, M. (1991), 'The dysfunctions of "corporate masculinity": Gender and diversity issues in organizational development', *Journal of Management in Practice*, **8**, 49–63.

Maier, M. (1999), 'On the gendered structure of organization: Dimensions and dilemmas of corporate masculinity', in G.N. Powell (ed.), *Handbook of Gender and Work*, Thousand Oaks, CA: Sage, pp. 69–93.

Major, V.S., K.J. Klein and M.G. Erhart (2002), 'Work time, work interference with family, and psychological distress', *Journal of Applied Psychology*, **87**(3), 427–36.

Matthews, K.A., B.B. Gump, K.F. Harris, T.L. Haney and J.C. Barefoot (2004), 'Health behaviors predict cardiovascular mortality among men enrolled in the Multiple Risk Factor Intervention Trial', *Circulation*, **109**(1), 66–70.

Meijman, T.F. and G. Mulder (1998), 'Psychological aspects of workload', in P. Drenth, H. Thierry and C. DeWolff (eds), *Handbook of Work and Organizational Psychology Vol. 2, Work Psychology*, 2nd edition, Hove, UK: Psychology Press, pp. 5–33.

Mettlin, C. (1976), 'Occupational careers and the prevention of coronary-prone behavior', *Social Science and Medicine*, **10**, 367–72.

Mooney, T.F. (1995), 'Cognitive behavior therapy for men', in R.F. Levant and W.S. Pollack (eds), *A New Psychology of Men*, New York: Basic Books, pp. 57–82.

Moruyama, S., K. Kohno and K. Morimoto (1995), 'A study of preventive medicine in relation to mental health among middle-management employees. Part 2. Effects of long working hours on lifestyles, perceived stress and working-life satisfaction among white-collar middle-management employees', *Nippon Elseigaku Zasshi* (*Japanese Journal of Hygiene*), **50**, 849–60.

Mosher, D.L. and M. Sirkin (1984), 'Measuring a macho personality constellation', *Journal of Research on Personality*, **18**(2), 150–63.

Nachreiner, F., S. Akkermann and K. Haenecke (2000), 'Fatal accident risk as a function of hours into work', in S. Hornberger, P. Knauth, G. Costa and S. Folkard (eds), *Shift Work in the 21st Century*, Frankfurt: Peter Lang, pp. 19–24.

Oates, W. (1971), *Confessions of a Workaholic: The Facts about Work Addiction*, New York: World.

Ogbonna, E. and L.C. Harris (2004), 'Work intensification and emotional labor among UK university lecturers: An exploratory study', *Organization Studies*, **25**(7), 1185–203.

Orton, R.S. (1993), 'Outside in: A man in the movement', in E. Buckwald, P.R. Fletcher and M. Rother (eds), *Transforming a Rape Culture*, Minneapolis, MN: Milkweed Editions, pp. 237–46.

Paley, V.G. (1984), *Boys and Girls: Superheroes in the Doll Corner*, Chicago: University of Chicago Press.

Pleck, J.H. (1981), *The Myth of Masculinity*, Cambridge, MA: MIT Press.

Pleck, J.H. (1995), 'The gender role strain paradigm: An update', in R.F. Levant and W.S. Pollack (eds), *A New Psychology of Men*, New York: Basic Books, pp. 11–32.

Pleck, J.H., F.L. Sonenstein and L.C. Ku (1993a), 'Masculinity ideology: Its impact on adolescent males' heterosexual relationships', *Journal of Social Issues*, **49**(3), 11–29.

Pleck, J.H., F.L. Sonenstein and L.C. Ku (1993b), 'Attitudes toward male roles among adolescent males: A discriminant validity analysis', *Sex Roles*, **30**(7–8), 481–501.

Pollack, W.S. (1998), *Real Boys*, New York: Henry Holt.

Porter, G. (1996), 'Organizational impact of workaholism: Suggestions for researching the negative outcomes of excessive work', *Journal of Occupational Health Psychology*, **1**(1), 70–84.

Powell, G.N. (1999), *Handbook of Gender and Work*, Thousand Oaks, CA: Sage.

Price, V.A. (1982), *Type A Behavior Pattern: A Model for Research and Practice*, New York: Academic Press.

Rissler, A. (1977), 'Stress reactions at work and after work during a period of quantitative overload', *Ergonomics*, **20**, 13–16.

Robinson, B.E. (1998), *Chained to the Desk: A Guidebook for Workaholics, their Partners and Children and the Clinicians Who Treat Them*, New York: New York University Press.

Rones, P.L., R.E. Ilg and J.M. Gardner (1997), 'Trends in hours of work since the mid-1970s', *Monthly Labor Review*, **120**(4), 3–14.

Rosa, B.R. (1995), 'Extended work shifts and excessive fatigue', *Journal of Sleep Research*, **4**(S2), S51–S56.

Schaef, A.W. and D. Fassel (1988), *The Addictive Organization*, San Francisco, CA: Harper.

Schor, J. (1991), *The Overworked American: The Unexpected Decline of Leisure*, New York: Basic Books.

Schor, J.B. (2003), 'The (even more) overworked American', in J. deGraaf (ed.), *Take Back Your Time*, San Francisco, CA: Berrett-Koehler, pp. 6–11.

Schuster, M. and S. Rhodes (1985), 'The impact of overtime work on industrial accident rates', *Industrial Relations*, **24**(2), 234–46.

Scott, K.S., K.S. Moore and M.P. Miceli (1997), 'An exploration of the meaning and consequences of workaholism', *Human Relations*, **50**(3), 287–314.

Sharpe, M.J. and P.P. Heppner (1991), 'Gender role, gender role conflict, and psychological well-being in men', *Journal of Counseling Psychology*, **38**(4), 323–30.

Shekelle, R.B., M. Gale, A.M. Ostfeld and O. Paul (1983), 'Hostility, risk of coronary heart disease, and mortality', *Psychosomatic Medicine*, **45**(2), 109–14.

Shields, M. (1999), 'Long working hours and health', *Health Reports*, **11**(2), 33–48.

Shimomitsu, T. and L. Levi (1992), 'Recent working life changes in Japan', *European Journal of Public Health*, **2**, 76–96.

Silverstein, O. and B. Rashbaum (1994), *The Courage to Raise Good Men*, New York: Viking.

Snell, W.E., S.S. Belk and R.C. Hawkins (1987), 'Alcohol and drug use in stressful times: The influence of the masculine role and sex-related personality attributes', *Sex Roles*, **16**(7–8), 359–73.

Sparks, K., C. Cooper, Y. Fried and A. Shirom (1997), 'The effects of hours of work on health: A meta-analytic review', *Journal of Occupational and Organizational Psychology*, **70**(4), 391–409.

Spence, J.T. and A.S. Robbins (1992), 'Workaholism: Definition, measurement, and preliminary result', *Journal of Personality Assessment*, **58**(1), 160–78.

Spence, J.T., R.L. Helmreich and C.K. Holahan (1979), 'Negative and positive components of psychological masculinity and femininity and their relationship to self-reports of neurotic and acting-out behaviors', *Journal of Personality and Social Psychology*, **37**(10), 1673–82.

Spicer, J. and B. Hong (1991), 'Interpreting coronary-prone behavior: Relationships among Type A behavior, hopelessness, anger management and social contact', *Psychology and Health*, **5**(3), 193–202.

Spurgeon, A., J.M. Harrington and C. Cooper (1997), 'Health and safety problems associated with long working hours: A review of the current position', *Occupational and Environmental Medicine*, **54**(6), 367–75.

Staines, G.L. and J.H. Pleck (1984), 'Non standard work schedules and family life', *Journal of Applied Psychology*, **69**(3), 515–23.

Stroh, L.H. and A.H. Reilly (1999), 'Gender and careers: Present experiences and emerging trends', in G.N. Powell (ed.), *Handbook of Gender and Work*, Thousand Oaks, CA: Sage, pp. 307–24.

Thompson, E.H. (1990), 'Courtship violence and the male role', *Men's Studies Review*, **7**(3), 4–13.

Thompson, E.H. and J.H. Pleck (1987), 'Reformulating the male role', in M.S. Kimmel (ed.), *Changing Men*, Newbury Park, CA: Sage, pp. 25–36.

Thompson, E.H. and J.H. Pleck (1995), 'Masculine ideology: A review of research instrumentation on men and masculinities', in R.F. Levant and W.S. Pollack (eds), *A New Psychology of Men*, New York: Basic Books, pp. 129–63.

Thompson, E.H., C. Grisanti and J.H. Pleck (1985), 'Attitudes toward the male role and their correlates', *Sex Roles*, **13**(7–8), 413–27.

Uehata, T. (1991), 'Long working hours and occupational stress-related cardiovascular attacks among middle aged workers in Japan', *Journal of Human Ergonomics*, **20**(2), 147–53.

van der Hulst, M. (2003), 'Long work hours and health', *Scandinavian Journal of Work, Environment and Health*, **2**, 171–88.

van der Hulst, M. and S. Geurts (2001), 'Associations between overtime and psychological health in high and low reward jobs', *Work and Stress*, **156**, 227–40.

van der Hulst, M., M. van Veldenhoven and D. Beckers (2006), 'Overtime and need for recovery in relation to job demands and job control', *Journal of Occupational Health*, **48**(1), 11–19.

Waldron, I. (1976), 'Why do women live longer than men?', *Journal of Human Stress*, **2**(5), 1–13.

Waldron, I. and S. Johnson (1976), 'Why do women live longer than men?', *Journal of Social Stress*, **2**(2), 19–29.

Wallace, J.E. (1997), 'It's about time: A study of hours worked and work spillover among law firm lawyers', *Journal of Vocational Behavior*, **50**(2), 227–48.

Weiss, R.S. (1990), *Staying the Course: The Emotional and Social Lives of Men Who Do Well at Work*, New York: Free Press.

West, C. and D.H. Zimmerman (1991), 'Doing gender', in J. Lorber and S.A. Farrel (eds), *The Social Construction of Gender*, Newbury Park, CA: Sage, pp. 13–37.

Westman, M. and D. Etzion (1990), 'The career success/personal failure phenomenon as perceived in others: Comparing vignettes of male and female managers', *Journal of Vocational Behavior*, **37**(2), 209–24.

Whooley, M.A. and J. Wong (2011), 'Hostility and cardiovascular disease', *Journal of the American College of Cardiology*, **58**(12), 1229–30.

Wiehert, I.C. (2002), 'Job insecurity and work intensification: The effects on health and well-being', in B.J. Burchell, D. Lapido and F. Wilkinson (eds), *Job Security and Work Intensification*, London: Routledge, pp. 57–74.

Williams, R. (1989), *The Trusting Heart: Great News about Type A Behavior*, New York: Random House.

Williams, R. and V. Williams (1993), *Anger Kills*, New York: Random House.

Williams, J.E., C.C. Paton, I.C. Siegler, M.L. Eigenbrodt, F.J. Nieto and H.A. Tyroler (2000), 'Anger proneness predicts coronary heart disease risk: Prospective analysis from the Atherosclerosis Risk in Communities (ARIC) Study', *Circulation*, **101**(17), 2034–9.

Williams, R.B., T.L. Haney, K.L. Lee, Y.H. Kong, J.A. Blumenthal and R.E. Whalen (1980), 'Type A behavior, hostility, and coronary atherosclerosis', *Psychosomatic Medicine*, **42**(6), 539–49.

Worrall, L. and C.L. Cooper (1999), *Quality of Work Life Survey*, London: Institute of Management.

7. The causes and consequences of workaholism

Shahnaz Aziz and Benjamin Uhrich

INTRODUCTION

Workaholism, a progressive and compulsive disorder, is a common term in popular culture that describes individuals who are addicted to work. Often, people view so-called 'workaholics' as hardworking employees who are devoted to their careers. In fact, many individuals believe that being a workaholic is a requirement to having a successful career. Over the last several decades, the concept of workaholism has become an accepted way of life and engrained in the culture of North America.

Workaholism has a positive connotation in our society and, as Spruell (1987, p. 44) put it, 'workaholism is the most rewarded addiction in our culture'. With all of the interest surrounding workaholism and its prevalence in North America, it is surprising that there is still a dearth of empirical research on this topic. There are several reasons for this neglect that are thematic in the workaholism literature. First, researchers have failed to agree on a unified definition for workaholism (Scott et al., 1997; Burke, 2001b; Buelens and Poelmans, 2004). Second, the most commonly used measures of workaholism are methodologically flawed and often criticized for their lack of validity and reliability (McMillan et al., 2002; Ersoy-Kart, 2005). Last, researchers have not been able to impress upon society that the behavioral component of workaholism, working excessively, can lead to negative outcomes. Instead, organizations prefer that their employees work longer hours, which presumably leads to financial gains for both the organization and the employee.

The term 'workaholism' was first used by Oates (1971), who described it as the 'addiction to work, the compulsion or the uncontrollable need to work incessantly' (p. 1). Since then, researchers have attempted to refine the definition with mixed results. Contrary to the commonly held belief that workaholics are desirable employees, most researchers today see workaholism as having negative effects on both the employee and the organization (e.g., Burke, 2000a; Aziz and Zickar, 2006). Many researchers have focused on developing a better understanding of the ante-cedents and correlates of workaholism in order to predict and understand its consequences (e.g., Burke, 2001a; Burke et al., 2006). Clearly, more research is needed in this area in order to minimize the negative impact of workaholism.

In this chapter, we will first provide an overview of workaholism, followed by a discussion on the antecedents and consequences of worka-holism, and, finally, a brief synopsis on workaholism's association with gender.

OVERVIEW OF WORKAHOLISM

Despite the use of the term 'workaholism,' researchers have struggled to agree on what comprises the construct. Is workaholism simply an extreme case of an already recognized construct such as work involvement or organizational commitment? Researchers have attempted to answer this question and have come to different conclusions. Some believe that work-aholics can have a positive influence on organizations, as workaholics are committed, hardworking employees (Machlowitz, 1980) – employers who adopt this view seek to attract, develop, and retain this type of worker. Yet many others view workaholism negatively (e.g., Porter, 1996; Burke, 2000a). If it is true that workaholics are perfectionists who are unable to delegate work and work cooperatively with others, then, given the global trend to work more in teams, they are unlikely to be productive members of an organization. From this perspective, employers should avoid worka-holics and discourage an organizational culture of workaholism. Clearly, these two contrasting viewpoints can make choosing an organizational strategy difficult. While there is disagreement on whether workaholism is a desirable or undesirable trait in organizations, most researchers currently view it as an addictive work behavior that interferes with an individual's health, happiness, and/or personal relationships (Robinson, 1996; Burke, 2000a; Aziz and Zickar, 2006).

The most widely used and agreed upon definition of workaholism was developed by Spence and Robbins (1992). They measured three distinct components of workaholism: work involvement, work drive, and work enjoyment. Work involvement is the extent to which individuals commit themselves to a project and make constructive use of their time. Work drive is the individual's internal motivation to work. Work enjoyment is the pleasure that comes from working. These facets were considered to be independent of one another, as a person could be high on one com-ponent, yet low on another. Using a cluster analysis technique, Spence and Robbins divided employees into six worker types; they defined the workaholic as high on work involvement and work drive, but low on work enjoyment.

Vodanovich and Piotrowski (2006) expanded on previous delineations and conceptualized workaholism as a syndrome that moves through progressively worse stages. In its early stage, workaholic behaviors form as a result of individual differences, responsibilities, and stress. At this stage, the behaviors exist but they do not disrupt the workaholic's daily functioning. Eventually, these behaviors intensify and become recurrent, to the point where they do interfere with the individual's functioning. When the full syndrome has emerged, work reinforces the individual's behavior and consumes the individual's life, rendering him or her dysfunctional (Fassel, 1990). In this latest stage, the workaholism syndrome causes one to neglect all other aspects of his or her life including family, relationships, and personal health (Vodanovich and Piotrowski, 2006).

Workaholism as an Addiction

Workaholism has been compared to other addictions, such as alcoholism (Porter, 1996). As our understanding of workaholism has increased in breadth and complexity, its ties to alcoholism have only strengthened. Researchers have demonstrated commonalities between the two constructs by explaining how workaholism can lead to the neglect of other interests, identity issues, rigid thinking, withdrawal, and denial (ibid.).

'Addiction' is a term that describes excessive, persistent behavior that leads to negative consequences (ibid.). Workaholics' maladaptive behavioral patterns are driven by compulsions to work and they think about work excessively, to the point where they neglect personal activities and experience negative health and work-related consequences. Many people believe that being a workaholic simply means working more hours per week than the average full-time employee—Mosier (1983) defined workaholics as those who work at least 50 hours per week. However, McMillan et al. (2002) found that hours worked did not significantly correlate with workaholism, leading them to conclude that hours worked should not define workaholism alone. People work unusually long hours for many different reasons (e.g., deadlines, pressure from a supervisor). In brief, workaholics have an intense, internal drive to work that leads to a neglect of other interests and negative consequences—it is this intense, internal drive that is the crux of workaholism.

As workaholics give in to their addiction to work, other aspects of their lives usually tend to suffer, resulting in work–life imbalance—an occupational stressor based on the amount of time spent at work, a lack of energy available after work for non-work-related activities, and a strain between the demands of work life and personal life (Fisher et al., 2009). Porter (1996) asserts that it is work drive, not work involvement, which causes workaholics to neglect other interests. This symptom of workaholism is included in the diagnostic criteria for other addiction disorders in the DSM-IV-TR (American Psychiatric Association, 2000). Working longer hours inevitably takes away from time that could be spent pursuing hobbies, being with family and friends, or enjoying other activities that comprise a balanced life. Having work–life balance is necessary because the time spent with family and friends or doing other enjoyable activities serves as a psychological and physical recovery period that is crucial to avoiding health problems caused by work stress (Schaufeli et al., 2009a). Workaholism and work–life imbalance have been shown to strongly correlate in several studies (Aziz and Zickar, 2006; Aziz et al., 2010b), with work drive being the workaholic dimension that most strongly correlates with work–life imbalance (Bonebright et al., 2000; Aziz and Zickar, 2006).

ANTECEDENTS OF WORKAHOLISM

There has been a rising interest in establishing the personal and environmental factors that may contribute to the development of workaholism. The number of potential antecedents that lead to workaholism has grown, so researchers must decide which ones are paramount, how they influence each other, and if they directly or indirectly cause workaholism. Ng et al. (2007) asserted that dispositions, socio-cultural experiences, and behavioral reinforcements directly affect workaholism, but they did not propose that any interaction occurred between the three different groups of antecedents. Liang and Chu (2009) proposed that personality traits, personal inducements (e.g., intrinsic work values), and organizational factors (e.g., peer competition) directly affect workaholism, and the impact of personality traits on workaholism is moderated by both personal inducements and organizational factors.

McMillan and O'Driscoll (2008) explained the development of workaholism using the biopsychosocial model—a model that has increased in favorability among the medical community over the past 30 years (Suls and Rothman, 2004). The biopsychosocial model explains the development of a broad range of physical and mental illnesses through the interaction of their biological, psychological, social, and macrocultural variables. McMillan and O'Driscoll show that a complex model, such as the biopsychosocial model, is necessary when explaining the causes of workaholism because individual theories (e.g., behavior theory, cognitive theory, systems theory of the workplace) are too simplistic on their own. We feel the biopsychosocial model is the most accurate framework for explaining the development of workaholism for several reasons: (1) it can incorporate all of the different antecedents that have been proposed in the workaholism literature, (2) it hypothesizes that all of the antecedents may interact with each other, and (3) it does not weigh the importance of one group of antecedents over another. In this section, we will review the most prevalent antecedents of workaholism, but a discussion regarding the nature of the interaction between the antecedents is beyond the scope of this chapter.

Personality Trait Antecedents

Personality traits serve as dispositions that can be triggered by certain environments or circumstances, leading to an addiction (Eysenck, 1997); workaholism is not an exception to this well-established fact. Determining which traits and behaviors are most crucial to the development of workaholism has been a challenging task for researchers. Perfectionism, obsessive-compulsiveness, Type A personality, and the Big 5 personality traits have been a focal point in discussions on the relationship between workaholism and personality—we review the theoretical and empirical research regarding these traits in the following paragraphs.

Perfectionism and obsessive-compulsive personality traits share common beginnings and lead to similar outcomes—both originate from a need to control their environment and lead to controlling behaviors (Robinson, 2007). Perfectionism potentially precedes its more behaviorally extreme counterpart – Killinger (1991) states, 'Perfectionism clearly is not a positive trait but a curse that leads to a compulsive need to be successful and to create a persona that broadcasts success' (p. 21). Spence and Robbins (1992) found that, in both men and women samples, perfectionism was more highly correlated with work drive than with the other dimensions of the workaholism triad (i.e., work enjoyment and work involvement); this finding has been replicated in samples of Canadian MBA graduates (Burke and Fiksenbaum, 2009a) and Australian psychologists (Burke and Fiksenbaum, 2009b).

Regarding obsessive-compulsive personality traits, Ng et al. (2007) cite obsessive-compulsive personality disorder (OCPD) as a key dispositional trait of workaholism and Naughton (1987) postulates that workaholism is simply OCPD expressed in the workplace. The connection between these two disorders has also been supported empirically. Aziz et al. (2010a) found that all three dimensions of Spence and Robbins's (1992) workaholism triad predicted obsessive-compulsive behavior, in which work drive had the strongest relationship with obsessive-compulsive behavior.

Workaholics have a strong desire for upward mobility and are sensitive to external rewards, so it is not surprising that achievement-oriented personality traits, such as Type A personality, are also considered antecedents of workaholism. There is significant overlap between individuals with Type A personality and workaholics—both are burdened by high stress because of their hard-driving, urgent, impatient approach to life (Robinson, 1996). Type A children and adult workaholics show strikingly similar behavioral characteristics, suggesting that Type A behaviors in childhood may be temperamental antecedents to the development of workaholism in adulthood (Steinberg, 1985). Robinson (1999) found that people with a high risk for work addiction scored higher on the Type A Self-report Inventory and several subscales of the Jenkins Activity Scale (e.g., hard driving and competitive, speed, and impatience) than people with a medium or low risk for work addiction.

The Big 5 personality traits (i.e., openness to experience, conscientiousness, extraversion, agreeableness, and neuroticism) are the most heavily researched personality traits by psychologists, so it is not surprising that their relationships with workaholism have been explored. Using Spence and Robbins's (1992) triad of workaholism in a sample of American employees from different work settings, Aziz and Tronzo (2011) found that conscientiousness and agreeableness were positively related to work involvement, while conscientiousness and openness to experience were positively related to work drive. Also, agreeableness, conscientiousness, and openness to experience were positively related to work enjoyment, while neuroticism was negatively related to it. Researchers note that being able to identify personality dispositions that lead to the development of workaholism may aid practitioners when selecting new hires.

Environmental Antecedents

Research published in the counseling literature proposes that workaholism originates from an upbringing in a dysfunctional family and is carried into adulthood (Robinson, 1996). Families that produce work addicts fall at two ends of a spectrum, with seemingly 'perfect families' on one end and 'chaotic families' on another (Robinson, 2007). In seemingly perfect families, children are subjected to strict rules, rigid schedules, and high expectations. The children yearn for their parents' attention, which they believe is contingent on their performance. This cycle is self-perpetuating—the better the child performs, the higher the parents' expectations are the next time, and the child adopts the new expectations—leading to more compulsive and achievement-striving behavior (Machlowitz, 1980). In chaotic families, children are sometimes forced into adult roles where they either have to fend for themselves or even take care of a parent (i.e., parentification). This type of environment can cause children to lose their feelings of control and they soon start overcompensating by trying to control everything around them. When these children grow up, they bring their need for control into the workplace. In a study on workaholism's association with current family functioning, the high-risk workaholic group perceived their family as currently having more problem-solving issues, greater communication problems, less clearly defined family roles, lower affective responsiveness, a lack of affective involvement (i.e., family members value other member's activities and interests), and more problematic general family functioning than the low-risk workaholic group (Robinson and Post, 1997). Since it is widely accepted that one's personality develops during childhood, which is dramatically influenced by family life, then family life undoubtedly plays a role in the development of workaholism.

Cognitive Antecedents

A workaholic's compulsive tendencies to work may be driven by irrational or extreme beliefs. Burke (2000b) has identified three such beliefs, each accompanied by a particular fear, which may lead to workaholism. The first belief is that people must prove themselves through laudable accomplishments or risk being judged as unsuccessful by themselves or others. This fear of being judged unsuccessful may push a person into an achievement-striving behavior pattern that is a fundamental characteristic of workaholism. A second belief is that no universal moral principle exists, which increases the probability of people taking justice into their own hands. A third belief is that people must strive against others to get their fair share because the desired resources in life are limited. These last two beliefs may lead to the competitive, and sometimes hostile behavior that is prevalent in both workaholism and Type A personality (Robinson, 1999).

These beliefs and fears were shown to be related to workaholism using survey data gathered on full-time working professionals. The work drive component of Spence and Robbins's measure (1992) positively correlated with all three beliefs and fears, while work enjoyment negatively related to all of them. It is notable that the work drive component had stronger correlations with the three beliefs and fears than work enjoyment. These findings were supported by subsequent cross-cultural studies with samples of Turkish managers and professionals, Australian psychologists, and Canadian MBA graduates (Burke and Koksal, 2002; Burke et al., 2003; Burke and Fiksenbaum, 2009a).

Robinson (2007) suggests that workaholism is perpetuated by low self-esteem. Workaholics are achievement-oriented individuals and their compulsion to work serves as a mechanism to ease their deeply rooted insecurities—the more they work, the more accomplishments they accrue, and the better they feel about themselves (Fassel, 1990; Robinson, 2007). This behavior can be tied to the self-concept problems that workaholics share with alcoholics (Byers et al., 1990) and substance abusers (Kitano, 1989). Even though self-esteem would appear to be an important anteced-ent of workaholism (Ng et al., 2007; Liang and Chu, 2009), this relation-ship has rarely been investigated, although one study did find that work addicts scored significantly lower on a measure of self-esteem than the other participants (Burke, 2004).

Biological Antecedents

Biological factors can help explain the development of workaholism through the medical model of addiction (McMillan et al., 2001). Some authors have theorized that workaholics may be addicted to their own adrenaline (Hatcher, 1989; Fassel, 1990). Hatcher (1989) observed that work addicts enjoy being in control and aware of their surroundings, both of which are easily enhanced by the adrenaline rush they receive from working hard. Kiechel (1989) described how workaholics' excessive working patterns may be motivated by the emotional rush they receive from being rewarded for hard work. Even though the emotional and adrenaline rushes come from two different sources in the examples above, both show how hard work can directly or indirectly physiologically affect individuals, pushing them towards work addiction.

Robinson (1996) states that workaholics likely 'get adrenaline highs from their work binges and experience hangovers as they come down' (p. 447). Indeed, several authors have postulated that workaholics can experience an adrenaline rush when working, followed by depression, anxiety, headaches, sleeplessness, and other withdrawal symptoms when not at work (Fassel, 1990; Porter, 1996; Robinson and Kelley, 1998; McMillan et al., 2001). McMillan et al. (2001) observe that there have been no studies to date that have empirically tested the fluctuation of chemicals in the body to support this notion, so clinical observations are the only proof of these physiological reactions (Robinson, 1989; Fassel, 1990).

Organizational Antecedents

Some researchers have espoused that workaholism is primarily a psycho-logical problem and is merely enabled, not caused, by sociological forces (e.g., technology, organizational structures; Robinson, 2007). However, most researchers agree that organizations and global work trends may have a large impact on the development of workaholism, yet very little research has investigated the extent of such influences (Ng et al., 2007; Liang and Chu, 2009). The following subsections review the theoretical connections and empirical studies that have linked organizational influences and global work trends to the development of workaholism.

Organizational culture
An organizational culture that promotes workaholic behavior will likely cause work–life balance problems for employees; similarly, a culture that encourages work–life imbalance may also create workaholic employees. An organization's values play a key role in setting the organization's culture. Research has shown that employees of organizations with values that support work–life balance feel less driven to work and more work enjoyment; employees of organizations that value work–life imbalance feel more driven to work and less work enjoyment (Burke, 2001c). In a follow up study, Burke and Fiksenbaum (2009a) found that employees who scored higher on a workaholism scale were working for organizations that showed less support for their employees' work–life balance.

Most research purports that while there are many innovative strategies companies can use to help employees balance their work and personal lives, if the leadership within the company does not encourage them to take advantage of such benefits, then the benefits are useless (Major et al., 2008). Support to use work–family benefits should come from the supervisor in order to be taken seriously—this statement is supported by a study which found a negative relationship between work drive and supervisor support (Schaufeli et al., 2009a). These findings support Schaef and Fassel's (1988) assertion that a workaholic culture is cold and impersonal, and close relationships are minimized or even discouraged in such environments.

Another primary characteristic of a workaholic culture is a competitive environment (Liang and Chu, 2009). These types of cultures can be created when an organization implements reinforcement systematically, such as a 'winner-takes-all' reward system (Ng et al., 2007), or by giving an annual bonus only to the top-performing percentile of employees. If such systems are believed to allocate rewards based on an employee's input rather than output, they may further increase workaholic behavior patterns. For instance, Landers et al. (1996) demonstrated how professional organizations that use the number of hours an employee works per week to make decisions regarding salaries or promotions can induce a 'rat race'–studying law firms, they showed that as an employee's work hours decreased, support for their promotion also declined. This type of incentive system creates an overly competitive environment where employees work an inefficient number of hours, leading to stress and workaholism.

Organizational climate

The climate of an organization is an employee's perception of the workplace environment and it may have large effects on one's workplace behavior and job satisfaction (Ashforth, 1985), making it a relevant construct to the workaholism literature. Johnstone and Johnston (2005) explored the associations between workaholism and organizational climate, measured by four dimensions—work pressure, involvement, co-worker cohesion, and supervisor support. They found that employees who perceived their work climates to be highly supportive, cohesive, involving, and low in pressure were more likely to enjoy their work, while those who perceived high pressure in their workplace were more intensely driven to work. Thus, an organizational climate that could potentially promote and maintain workaholism within employees is perceived as being highly pressured, where there is little commitment and support from co-workers and managers.

Job characteristics

Job characteristics describe the demands and pressure put on an employee in the work environment. Time pressure, loss of control, and emotional demands may worsen one's perfectionist, compulsive behavior (Greenberger et al., 1991), as well as increase an employee's work efforts (Greenberger and Strasser, 1991). Moreover, after working excessively long and challenging hours for extensive periods of time, individuals might get used to the hectic, intense schedule and feel guilty or experience withdrawal symptoms when not working (Porter, 1996; Ng et al., 2007). Furthermore, in a sample of Dutch medical residents, Schaufeli et al. (2009a) found that workaholics—residents who worked both excessively and compulsively—perceived more job demands (e.g., scored higher on work overload, work–family conflict, organizational/mental/emotional demands) and less job resources (i.e., reported less support from colleagues, job control, coaching, opportunities to learn, and feedback) than other residents. Regardless of the 'chicken before the egg' problem involving workaholism and job characteristics, research has shown that jobs characterized by high demands with little control might contribute to workaholism.

Technology

The fact that technology may facilitate a person's addiction to work is not a new idea (Fraser, 2001). A study of 2,300 executives from 75 countries found that 80 percent of the executives used mobile devices for work, 77 percent believed the mobility afforded by the devices enhanced work–life balance, and about 33 percent said they found the devices addictive (Korn/ Ferry International, 2006). Addiction to work and addiction to technology (i.e., technophilia; Korac-Kakabadse et al., 2001) can be mutually reinforcing behaviors—a technophiliac can justify owning and using technology devices because of heavy work demands and a workaholic can more easily work away from the office. Workaholics cannot stop thinking about work and want to work all of the time, and the mobility of devices like BlackBerries and computer tablets gives them the means to do so more easily. In a qualitative study, supervisors not only acknowledged the interplay of long work hours with information communication technology, but they also noticed placing expectations on their employees to do the same (Porter and Kakabadse, 2006). To conclude, longitudinal research should be conducted using validated measures of workaholism and technology to determine the direction of the relationship between these two addictions: does workaholism further promote an addiction to technology or does technophilia encourage an addiction to work?

CONSEQUENCES OF WORKAHOLISM

Although workaholic behaviors may occasionally lead to positive outcomes in the short run (e.g., positive affect at work: Baruch, 2011; career success in terms of promotions: Burke, 2001b; job satisfaction and career satisfaction: Ng et al., 2005), the majority of research on workaholism has shown that it has harmful consequences to employees, the people who are close to them, and the organization as a whole (Ng et al., 2007). Research has shown that, compared to non-workaholics, workaholics experience higher amounts of stress, perfectionism, worse mental and physical health, and poorer social relationships in the long run (Bonebright et al., 2000; Ng et al., 2007). In addition, workaholics exhibit more irritability, self-neglect, and impatience, as well as have difficulty participating in leisurely activities (Robinson, 1996).

Self

Workaholics' excessive work behavior, combined with their inability to psychologically detach from work, cripples their ability to enjoy life outside of work. For instance, workaholics tend to have greater work–life imbalance and work stress (Aziz and Zickar, 2006), more work–family conflict (Bakker et al., 2009; Shimazu et al., 2011), and significantly less life satisfaction and purpose in life (Bonebright et al., 2000) than non-workaholics. These consequences of workaholism all serve as major stressors, impairing one's mental health and physical well-being (Burke, 2001a; Ng et al., 2007). Several studies have shown that workaholics experience more stress-induced illnesses (Bonebright et al., 2000), chronic fatigue (Tyler, 1999), increased anxiety levels (Caproni, 1997), and psychological distress (Shimazu et al., 2011) than non-workaholic employees.

Working excessive hours and enduring chronic stress negatively impact physical health, so it is not surprising that workaholism eventually takes a toll on the physical well-being of employees. Shimazu et al. (2010) concluded that workaholism has a direct relationship with ill health, which is supported by other studies that have empirically shown that workaholics report more health complaints than non-workaholics (Kanai et al., 1996; Chamberlin and Zhang, 2009). Workaholics tend to work much longer hours than other employees, resulting in poor health-related behavior due in part to higher work stress as well as insufficient time to recover from work because of their lack of leisure and exercise (Taris et al., 2005). According to Burke and Cooper (2008), long work hours are thought to be associated with adverse health behaviors, such as smoking, coffee and alcohol consumption, lack of exercise, decreased sleep, weight gain, and a poor (unhealthy) diet—indeed, simply working long hours is linked to more physical illnesses (Sparks et al., 1997). These unhealthy behaviors often result in long-term physiological changes, such as high blood pressure and cholesterol, obesity, diabetes, coronary heart disease, and poorer general health (Burke and Cooper, 2008).

Excessive working can lead to burnout, which is a syndrome of emotional exhaustion, depersonalization, and reduced personal accomplishment (Maslach et al., 2001). In fact, Schaufeli et al. (2009b) found an indirect relationship between workaholism and burnout, as both have relationships with inter-role conflict. Furthermore, van Beek et al.'s (2011) findings suggest that workaholic employees experience more burnout. Similarly, workaholics may also experience brownouts, where they may forget conversations or trips taken due to mental exhaustion and obsession with work (Robinson, 1996). Other symptoms of workaholism include fatigue, anxiety, depression, anger, mood swings, loss of sleep, and hopelessness (Seybold and Salomone, 1994; Robinson, 1998; Robinson et al., 2001a).

Others

Not only does workaholism have adverse consequences for individuals who experience the addiction, it also affects their family members, friends, co-workers, and other individuals who are associated with the workaholic (Porter, 1996). Family members of workaholics have typically indicated feelings of loneliness, low self-esteem, abandonment, isolation, and feelings of being unloved (Robinson, 1998). Similarly, due to the workaholic's poor communication, Robinson (2000) found evidence of familial problems, such as the inability of family members to solve problems effectively, family roles being unclear, and less emotional involvement in the relationships of workaholics. A study conducted by Robinson and Kelley (1998) revealed that children of workaholic fathers have a greater probability of having mental health issues later in life, scoring higher on depression, external locus of control, and anxiety.

Workaholics usually sacrifice personal relationships for work, which explains their problems with communication, family roles, and emotional attachment (Bakker et al., 2009). Essentially, due to the excessive time and energy workaholics spend on work, workaholism can result in poorer social relationships outside of work and has been found to be detrimental to intimate relationships (Robinson and Post, 1997; Porter, 2001). For example, workaholism is related to greater marital problems (Robinson et al., 2001b) and higher work–family conflict (Bonebright et al., 2000). The spouses of workaholics report having less positive feelings and a greater external locus of control, when compared to spouses of non-workaholics (Seybold and Salomone, 1994; Robinson et al., 2001a). More recently, Yaniv (2011) found that workaholism contributes to marital estrangement.

Organization

Several negative organizational consequences could also occur as a result of the presence of workaholic behaviors. For instance, employers may find themselves faced with increased health care costs that are associated with health issues, which may develop as a result of workaholism. They might also experience a loss in productivity due to absenteeism, in that employees suffering from health-related issues are more likely to be absent than healthy employees, as well as increased short-term disability (Rodbard et al., 2009).

Due to stress and possible burnout, long-term consequences for the organization are likely through a decline in individual performance, increases in health- and accident-related expenses, and higher turnover rates (Maslach and Jackson, 1981; Homer, 1985). Furthermore, workaholics' performance standards are unrealistically high, thereby making it challenging for them to trust that their colleagues will perform to such high standards (Porter, 1996). Due to their perfectionistic nature, workaholics typically do not delegate work to colleagues and tend to work more independently, which may lead them to think they are indispensable to the organization and drive them to work even harder. These perfectionistic tendencies can cause the deterioration of gains from collaborative work by creating a competitive atmosphere in the workplace, which in turn could be detrimental to the effectiveness of the overall organization by causing further damage to co-worker relationships (Porter, 1996). Additionally, Galperin and Burke (2006) found that employees with a high work drive, a component of workaholism, were more likely to be involved in organizational deviant acts toward co-workers (e.g., public embarrassment), which further impacts organizational effectiveness. In sum, workaholism can lead to detrimental outcomes for organizations by driving up employee health-related costs and through workaholics' counterproductive work behaviors.

WORKAHOLISM AND GENDER

The importance of gender roles in shaping work patterns and behaviors has been underestimated. Therefore, there has been a relatively recent stream of research that has examined gender and workaholism. However, as discussed below, results of the few empirical studies have been mixed. Some research has found that gender is independent of workaholism, while other studies suggest they are related.

Aziz and Cunningham (2008) investigated the role of gender on workaholism, work stress, and work–life imbalance. They hypothesized that female workaholics would have more work–life imbalance due to the multiple roles women play in families and perhaps more work stress due to role overload and work–life imbalance. On the other hand, they predicted men would be higher on workaholism and work more hours if they are considered 'good providers' (i.e., the only or chief breadwinners). However, work–life imbalance and work stress were correlated with workaholism equally for both genders, and men and women did not significantly differ on workaholism. Also, gender was not found to moderate the relationship between workaholism and work stress or work–life imbalance, suggesting there has been a substantial shift in gender roles and identity over the years. Perhaps work–family roles are changing and the once traditional roles of men and women may not predominate in today's workforce; women may be taking a more career-minded view by becoming career-oriented caregivers, while men are sharing the care-giving role by becoming more family-oriented as their wives go to work (Harpaz and Snir, 2003). Thus, Aziz and Cunningham suggest that intervention programs should focus on decreasing workaholism in both men and women.

Based on a study conducted in the Netherlands, the relationships between workaholism and work–family conflict, social support, and relationship satisfaction are not affected by gender (Bakker et al., 2009). One possible explanation for the similarity between genders in this study is that the participants were young, educated couples with very young children, implying that the couple may share many family responsibilities. On a related note, Burgess et al. (2006) and Russo and Waters (2006) suggest that if a relationship does exist between gender and workaholism, it may be weak at best. Furthermore, Burke (1999) investigated workaholism and related variables and found no significant gender differences. Similarly, Taris et al. (2005) examined the potential link between workaholism and gender, but they did not find any support for such an association. In line with these research findings, Johnstone and Johnston (2005) found that males and females did not significantly differ on either of Spence and Robbins's (1992) work drive or work enjoyment facets of workaholism.

Burke and Matthiesen (2009) investigated possible gender differences in Spence and Robbins's (1992) three facets of workaholism (i.e., work involvement, work drive, work enjoyment) in a sample of Norwegian journalists. Their results indicated that females scored higher on the work drive component compared to males. However, given that the sample was comprised of journalists, it is questionable whether these findings are generalizable to other occupations. Additionally, Shimazu et al. (2011) recently conducted a study on workaholism among Japanese dual-earner couples. They found that partners of workaholics were more likely to report family-to-work conflict, although this finding was only true of female workaholics. Perhaps this is because in Japanese culture, dual-earner couples have already adapted to their roles in accordance with the good provider model—women may have adapted to men working long hours, but men might not have adapted to women working long hours. To ameliorate some of the negative effects of workaholism, Shimazu et al. suggest targeting workaholic women, whom in this population appear to show more harmful outcomes related to workaholism than men. In sum, consensus regarding the relationship between gender and workaholism has yet to be reached in that findings from the limited research on this topic have been mixed.

REFERENCES

American Psychiatric Association (2000), *Diagnostic and Statistical Manual of Mental Disorders*, 4th edition, text rev., Washington, DC: APA.

Ashforth, B.E. (1985), 'Climate formation: Issues and extensions', *Academy of Management Review*, **10**(4), 837–47.

Aziz, S. and J. Cunningham (2008), 'Workaholism, work stress, work–life imbalance: Exploring gender's role', *Gender in Management: An International Journal*, **23**(8), 553–66.

Aziz, S. and C.L. Tronzo (2011), 'Exploring the relationship between workaholism facets and personality traits: A replication in American workers', *The Psychological Record*, **61**(2), 269–86.

Aziz, S. and M.J. Zickar (2006), 'A cluster analysis investigation of workaholism as a syndrome', *Journal of Occupational Health Psychology*, **11**(1), 52–62.

Aziz, S., K.L. Wuensch and H.R. Brandon (2010a), 'A comparison among worker types using a composites approach and median splits', *The Psychological Record*, **60**(4), 627–42.

Aziz, S., C.T. Adkins, A.G. Walker and K.L. Wuensch (2010b), 'Workaholism and work–life imbalance: Does cultural origin influence the relationship?', *International Journal of Psychology*, **45**(1), 72–9.

Bakker, A.B., E. Demerouti and R. Burke (2009), 'Workaholism and relationship quality: A spillover-crossover perspective', *Journal of Occupational Health Psychology*, **14**(1), 23–33.

Baruch, Y. (2011), 'The positive wellbeing aspects of workaholism in cross cultural perspective: The chocoholism metaphor', *The Career Development International*, **16**(6), 572–91.

Bonebright, C.A., D.L. Clay and R.D. Ankenmann (2000), 'The relationship of workaholism with work–life conflict, life satisfaction, and purpose in life', *Journal of Counseling Psychology*, **47**, 469–77.

Buelens, M. and S.A.Y. Poelmans (2004), 'Enriching the Spence and Robbins' typology of workaholism: Demographic, motivational and organizational correlates', *Journal of Organizational Change Management*, **17**(5), 440–58.

Burgess, Z., R.J. Burke and F. Oberklaid (2006), 'Workaholism among Australian psychologists: Gender differences', *Equal Opportunity International*, **25**(1), 48–59.

Burke, R.J. (1999), 'Workaholism in organizations: Gender differences', *Sex Roles*, **41**(5–6), 333–41.

Burke, R.J. (2000a), 'Workaholism in organizations: Psychological and physical well-being consequences', *Stress Medicine*, **16**(1), 11–16.

Burke, R.J. (2000b), 'Workaholism in organizations: The role of beliefs and fears', *Anxiety, Stress and Coping*, **13**(1), 53–64.

Burke, R.J. (2001a), 'Predictors of workaholism components and behaviors', *International Journal of Stress Management*, **8**(2), 113–27.

Burke, R.J. (2001b), 'Workaholism components, job satisfaction, and career progress', *Journal of Applied Social Psychology*, **31**(11), 2339–56.

Burke, R.J. (2001c), 'Workaholism in organizations: The role of organizational values', *Personnel Review*, **30**(6), 637–45.

Burke, R.J. (2004), 'Workaholism, self-esteem, and motives for money', *Psychological Reports*, **94**(2), 457–63.

Burke, R.J. and C.L. Cooper (2008), *The Long Work Hours Culture: Causes, Consequences, and Choices*, Bingley, UK: Emerald Group Publishing Limited.

Burke, R.J. and L. Fiksenbaum (2009a), 'Work motivations, satisfactions, and health among managers: Passion versus addiction', *Cross-cultural Research*, **43**(4), 349–65.

Burke, R.J. and L. Fiksenbaum (2009b), 'Work motivations, work outcomes, and health: Passion versus addiction', *Journal of Business Ethics*, **84**(2), 257–63.

Burke, R.J. and H. Koksal (2002), 'Workaholism among a sample of Turkish managers and professionals: An exploratory study', *Psychological Reports*, **91**(1), 60–68.

Burke, R.J. and S. Matthiesen (2009), 'Workaholism among Norwegian journalists: Gender differences', *Equal Opportunities International*, **28**(6), 452–64.

Burke, R.J., Z. Burgess and F. Oberklaid (2003), 'Predictors of workaholic behaviors among Australian psychologists', *The Career Development International*, **8**(6), 301–8.

Burke, R.J., S. Matthiesen and S. Pallesen (2006), 'Personality correlates of workaholism', *Personality and Individual Differences*, **40**, 1223–33.

Byers, P.H., L.M. Raven, J.D. Hill and J.E. Robyak (1990), 'Enhancing the self-esteem of inpatient alcoholics', *Issues in Mental Health Nursing*, **11**(4), 337–46.

Caproni, P.J. (1997), 'Work/life balance: You can't get there from here', *Journal of Applied Behavioral Science*, **33**(1), 46–56.

Chamberlin, C.M. and N. Zhang (2009), 'Workaholism, health, and self-acceptance', *Journal of Counseling and Development*, **87**(2), 159–69.

Ersoy-Kart, M. (2005), 'Reliability and validity of the Workaholism Battery (Work-BAT): Turkish Form', *Social Behavior and Personality*, **33**(6), 609–18.

Eysenck, H.J. (1997), 'Addiction, personality, and motivation', *Human Psychopharmacology: Clinical and Experimental*, **12**(S2), S79–S87.

Fassel, D. (1990), *Working Ourselves to Death*, San Francisco, CA: Harper-Collins.

Fisher, G.G., C.A. Bulgar and C.S. Smith (2009), 'Beyond work and family: A measure of work/nonwork interference and enhancement', *Journal of Occupational Health Psychology*, **14**(4), 441–56.

Fraser, J.A. (2001), *White-collar Sweatshop: The Deterioration of Work and its Rewards in Corporate America*, New York: W.W. Norton and Company, Inc.

Galperin, B.L. and R.J. Burke (2006), 'Uncovering the relationship between workaholism and workplace destructive and constructive deviance: An exploratory study', *The International Journal of Human Resource Management*, **17**(2), 331–47.

Greenberger, D.B. and S. Strasser (1991), 'The role of situational and dispositional factors in the enhancement of personal control in organizations', in L.L. Cummings and B.M. Staw, *Research in Organizational Behavior, Vol. 13*, Greenwich, CN: JAI Press, p. 111.

Greenberger, D.B., G. Porter, M.P. Miceli and S. Strasser (1991), 'Responses to inadequate personal control in organizations', *Journal of Social Issues*, **47**(4), 111–28.

Harpaz, I. and R. Snir (2003), 'Workaholism: Its definition and nature', *Human Relations*, **56**(3), 291–319.

Hatcher, A.S. (1989), 'From one addiction to another: Life after alcohol and drug abuse', *Nurse Practitioner*, **14**(11), 13–20.

Homer, J.B. (1985), 'Worker burnout: A dynamic model with implications for prevention and control', *System Dynamics Review*, **1**(1), 42–62.

Johnstone, A. and L. Johnston (2005), 'The relationship between organizational climate, occupational type and workaholism', *New Zealand Journal of Psychology*, **34**(3), 181–8.

Kanai, A., M. Wakabayashi and S. Fling (1996), 'Workaholism among employees in Japanese corporations: An examination based on the Japanese version of the workaholism scales', *Japanese Psychological Research*, **38**(4), 192–203.

Kiechel, W. III (1989), 'The workaholic generation', *Fortune*, **119**(8), 50–62.

Killinger, B. (1991), *Workaholics: The Respectable Addicts*, New York: Simon and Schuster.

Kitano, H.H.L. (1989), 'Alcohol and drug use and self-esteem: A sociocultural perspective', in A.M. Mecca, N.J. Smelser and J. Vasconcellos (eds), *The Social Importance of Self-esteem*, Berkeley, CA: University of California Press, pp. 294–326.

Korac-Kakabadse, A., N. Korac-Kakabadse and A. Kouzmin (2001), 'Leadership renewal: Towards the philosophy of wisdom', *International Review of Administrative Sciences*, **67**(2), 207–28.

Korn/Ferry International (2006), '38% of executives surveyed believe they spend too much time connected to mobile devices', press release, accessed 8 September 2013 at http://www.kornferry.com/PressRelease/3428.

Landers, R.M., J.B. Rebitzer and L.J. Taylor (1996), 'Rat race redux: Adverse selection in the determination of work hours in law firms', *American Economic Review*, **86**(3), 329–48.

Liang, Y. and C. Chu (2009), 'Personality traits and personal and organizational inducements: Antecedents of workaholism', *Social Behavior and Personality: An International Journal*, **37**(5), 645–60.

Machlowitz, M.M. (1980), *Workaholics: Living with Them, Working with Them*, Reading, MA: Addison-Wesley.

Major, D.A., T.D. Fletcher, D.D. Davis and L.M. Germano (2008), 'The influence of work–family culture and workplace relationships on work interference with family: A multilevel model', *Journal of Organizational Behavior*, **29**(7), 881–97.

Maslach, C. and S. Jackson (1981), 'The measurement of experienced burnout', *Journal of Occupational Behavior*, **2**(2), 99–113.

Maslach, C., W.B. Schaufeli and M.P. Leiter (2001), 'Job burnout', *Annual Review of Psychology*, **52**(1), 397–422.

McMillan, L.H.W. and M.P. O'Driscoll (2008), 'The wellsprings of workaholism: A comparative analysis of the explanatory theories', in *The Long Work Hours Culture: Causes, Consequences and Choices*, Bingley, UK: Emerald Group Publishing Limited, pp. 85–111.

McMillan, L.H.W., M.P. O'Driscoll, N.V. Marsh and E.C. Brady (2001), 'Understanding workaholism: Data synthesis, theoretical critique, and future design strategies', *International Journal of Stress Management*, **8**(2), 69–91.

McMillan, L.H.W., E.C. Brady, M.P. O'Driscoll and N. Marsh (2002), 'A multifaceted validation study of Spence and Robbins' (1992) Workaholism Battery', *Journal of Occupational and Organizational Psychology*, **75**(3), 357–68.

Mosier, S.K. (1983), 'Workaholics: An analysis of their stress, success and priorities', unpublished Master's thesis, University of Texas at Austin.

Naughton, T.J. (1987), 'A conceptual view of workaholism and implications for career counseling and research', *The Career Development Quarterly*, **35**(3), 180–87.

Ng, T.W., K.L. Sorensen and D.C. Feldman (2007), 'Dimensions, antecedents, and consequences of workaholism: A conceptal integration and extension', *Journal of Organizational Behavior*, **28**(1), 111–36.

Ng, T.W.H., L.T. Eby, K.L. Sorensen and D.C. Feldman (2005), 'Predictors of objective and subjective career success: A meta-analysis', *Personnel Psychology*, **58**(2), 367–408.

Oates, W. (1971), *Confessions of a Workaholic: The Facts about Work Addiction*, New York: World.

Porter, G. (1996), 'Organizational impact of workaholism: Suggestions for researching the negative outcomes of excessive work', *Journal of Occupational Health Psychology*, **1**(1), 70–84.

Porter, G. (2001), 'Workaholic tendencies and the high potential for stress among co-workers', *International Journal of Stress Management*, **8**(2), 147–64.

Porter, G. and N.K. Kakabadse (2006), 'HRM perspectives on addiction to technology and work', *Journal of Management Development*, **25**(6), 535–60.

Robinson, B.E. (1989), *Work Addiction*, Deerfield Beach, FL: Health Communications.

Robinson, B.E. (1996), 'The psychosocial and familial dimensions of work addiction: Preliminary perspectives and hypotheses', *Journal of Counseling and Development*, **74**(5), 447–52.

Robinson, B.E. (1998), 'The workaholic family: A clinical perspective', *The American Journal of Family Therapy*, **26**(1), 65–75.

Robinson, B.E. (1999), 'The Work Addiction Risk Test: Development of a tentative measure of workaholism', *Perceptual and Motor Skills*, **88**(1), 199–210.

Robinson, B. (2000), 'Workaholism: Bridging the gap between workplace, sociocultural, and family research', *Journal of Employment Counseling*, **37**(1), 31–48.

Robinson, B.E. (2007), *Chained to the Desk: A Guidebook for Workaholics, Their Partners and Children, and the Clinicians Who Treat Them*, 2nd edition, New York: New York University Press.

Robinson, B. and L. Kelley (1998), 'Adult children of workaholics: Self-concept, anxiety, depression, and locus of control', *The American Journal of Family Therapy*, **26**(3), 223–38.

Robinson, B.E. and P. Post (1997), 'Risk of work addiction to family functioning', *Psychological Reports*, **81**(1), 91–5.

Robinson, B.E., J.J. Carroll and C. Flowers (2001a), 'Marital estrangement, positive affect, and locus of control among spouses of workaholics and spouses of nonworkaholics: A national study', *The American Journal of Family Therapy*, **29**(5), 397–410.

Robinson, B.E., C. Flowers and J.J. Carroll (2001b), 'Work stress and marriage: A theoretical model examining the relationships between workaholism and marital cohesion', *International Journal of Stress Management*, **8**(2), 165–75.

Rodbard, H.W., K.M. Fox and S. Grandy (2009), 'Impact of obesity on work productivity and role disability in individuals with and at risk for diabetes mellitus', *American Journal of Health Promotion*, **23**(5), 353–60.

Russo, J.A. and L.E. Waters (2006), 'Workaholic worker type differences in work–family conflict: The moderating role of supervisor support and flexible work scheduling', *Career Development International*, **11**(5), 418–39.

Schaef, A.W. and D. Fassel (1988), *The Addictive Organization*, New York: Harper and Row Publishers.

Schaufeli, W.B., A.B. Bakker, F.M.M.A. van der Heijden and J.T. Prins (2009a), 'Workaholism among medical residents: It is the combination of working excessively and compulsively that counts', *International Journal of Stress Management*, **16**(4), 249–72.

Schaufeli, W.B., A.B. Bakker, F.M.M.A. van der Heijden and J.T. Prins (2009b),

'Workaholism, burnout and well-being among junior doctors: The mediating role of role conflict', *Work and Stress*, **23**(2), 155–72.

Scott, K.S., K.S. Moore and M.P. Miceli (1997), 'An exploration of the meaning and consequences of workaholism', *Human Relations*, **50**(3), 287–314.

Seybold, K.C. and P.R. Salomone (1994), 'Understanding workaholism: A review of causes and counseling approaches', *Journal of Counseling and Development*, **73**(1), 4–9.

Shimazu, A., W.B. Schaufeli and T.W. Taris (2010), 'How does workaholism affect worker health and performance? The mediating role of coping', *International Journal of Behavioral Medicine*, **17**(2), 154–60.

Shimazu, A., E. Demerouti, A.B. Bakker, K. Shimada and N. Kawakami (2011), 'Workaholism and well-being among Japanese dual-earner couples: A spillover-crossover perspective', *Social Science and Medicine*, **73**(3), 399–409.

Sparks, K., G.L. Cooper, Y. Fried and A. Shirom (1997), 'The effects of hours of work on health: A meta-analytical review', *Journal of Occupational and Organizational Psychology*, **70**(4), 391–408.

Spence, J.T. and A.S. Robbins (1992), 'Workaholism: Definition, measurement, and preliminary results', *Journal of Personality Assessment*, **58**(1), 160–78.

Spruell, G. (1987), 'Work fever', *Training and Development Journal*, **41**, 4–45.

Steinberg, L. (1985), 'Early temperamental antecedents of adult Type A behaviors', *Developmental Psychology*, **21**(6), 1171–80.

Suls, J. and A. Rothman (2004), 'Evolution of the biopsychosocial model: Prospects and challenges for health psychology', *Health Psychology*, **23**(2), 119–25.

Taris, T.W., W.B. Schaufeli and L.C. Verhoeven (2005), 'Workaholism in the Netherlands: Measurement and implications for job strain and work-nonwork conflict', *Applied Psychology: An International Review*, **54**(1), 37–60.

Tyler, K. (1999), 'Spinning wheels', *HR Magazine*, **44**(9), 34–9.

van Beek, I., T.W. Taris and W.B. Schaufeli (2011), 'Workaholic and work engaged employees: Dead ringers or worlds apart?', *Journal of Occupational Health Psychology*, **16**(4), 468–82.

Vodanovich, S.J. and C. Piotrowski (2006), 'Workaholism: A critical but neglected factor in O.D.', *Organization Development Journal*, **24**(2), 55–60.

Yaniv, G. (2011), 'Workaholism and marital estrangement: A rational-choice perspective', *Mathematical Social Sciences*, **61**(2), 104–8.

PART III

Gendered organizational cultures and male privilege

8. Gendered organizational cultures, structures and processes: the cultural exclusion of women in organizations

Sarah Rutherford

> Business remains a world created by males for males.
> (Jeremy Isaacs, a former chief executive of Lehman Brothers, quoted in
> Wittenberg-Cox and Maitland, 2008, p. 13)

INTRODUCTION

I was greeted with utmost courtesy and respect when I entered the boardroom for the first time. Most of the men were genuinely very nice people and made an effort to make me feel at home. In reality, the only women who had ever entered that room were the waitresses who served lunch during board meetings. We were all a bit nervous. I felt conscious that I had been allowed into this elite powerful group and felt I had to do everything I could to fit in. Drinks were served and I tried to join in the small talk. I could do it quite well – I was brought up by a father who was in the City (financial district of London) and had worked there in my school and college holidays and as a graduate and then as a City journalist. I was familiar with the tastes, interests and lifestyles of these men. I wouldn't have been there if I was not. But there was no mistaking, I had crashed an all male party and would have to work hard to gain acceptance.

In this chapter I am going to explore the ways in which most organizational cultures develop around the interests of men – the dominant group – and in the process may exclude and/or marginalize outsiders. Why women are considered outsiders is outside the scope of this chapter but a fact that we too often take as a given rather than examine why – and that includes organizations. The dominant group is defined not solely by numbers but also by access to resources – and is still in most of public life, men. Identifying the link between men, power and organizational culture helps to highlight the persistent resistance to real change. My research and subsequent book (Rutherford, 2011) on the different constituents of gendered cultures reveals the myriad ways in which gendered cultures, structures and processes may act to exclude and or marginalize women in the workplace.

The 'invisibility' of masculinity continues to permit certain practices, processes and discourses to remain unchallenged. By breaking down culture into its constituents we are able to identify and research these specific practices and discourses that, while appearing to be gender neutral and 'fair', are actually exclusionary to women and imbued with a masculine bias. I write as a practitioner as well as an academic, and will use data from both areas of my work as well as my own experience as being an outsider in a powerful group to illustrate these subtle and not so subtle exclusionary practices. In my original research I had two case studies: an airline and an investment bank, and I use data from this research in the chapter (Rutherford, 1999, 2001a, 2001b, 2011).

Looking back it was astonishing that an investment bank, albeit a small one, such as this took me on as a non-executive director. Despite having some City background my main work was now that of an academic/ diversity consultant, an unknown field to them but described in the press and by all other board members as 'employee relations'. I was the 'different' employee – friendly board member, an appointment greatly influenced by the Higgs Report (2003) on corporate governance, which recommended that UK corporate boards widened their skills and experience of members.

In academic terms my presence around the boardroom table at that time in the firm's history and culture represented some disruption to the dominant culture, which may or may not have had resonance throughout the organization. I know I was at least held up as a role model – but in the main nothing changed. Ongoing gender processes continue to adapt and accommodate changes and even when numbers change, cultural barriers shift to protect the dominant group from the entry of outsiders. Organizations that have spent literally millions on diversity interventions in a quest to create a more inclusive culture find they are still battling with the same issues 25 years later. Like my presence on a male board, the 'disruption is usually not complete, nor fully shared by everyone, leaving traces of the old gender order to co-exist with an emerging newer and more complex notion of gender at work' (Benschop et al., 2012, p. 4).

The reason for starting this chapter with a personal story of my work experience is to illustrate the subtle and normality of masculine cultures that are only exposed by the arrival of women, who for the most part, like me, try to fit in, all too pleased to have found themselves there in positions of relative power. On the surface there was no overt sexist behaviour, no discrimination, the odd crude remark was followed by a swift apology and I was treated with respect. Yet I was aware of my 'otherness', my outsider status. I didn't know the informal rules, the codes of conversation. I was outspoken in my views and gave too much of myself away but I only found this out later.

In the 2010 *Gender Gap Report* for which organizations from 30 countries took part, a masculine patriarchal corporate culture was the second most cited barrier to women's progress. Very often we are left with this description of culture as male/masculine, which does not help in identifying specific exclusionary practice. I will discuss some characteristics of cultures as well as outline a model for breaking down culture into constituents that can meaningfully be applied to research and practice.

CULTURAL EXCLUSION

All organizations have been exposed as being gendered (Acker, 1990) and all organizational cultures and all aspects of culture are gendered (Itzin, 1995; Martin, 2002). Kanter's classic *Men and Women of the Corporation* (1977) showed the importance of cultural practices in the career of managers and detailed many of the rites and rituals of life at Insco. Cynthia Cockburn was one of the first to identify the importance of cultural practices and resistance to equal opportunities in organizations (Cockburn, 1991) and link these directly with the behaviour of men, and I have further explored some of the issues she raises in her book.

Cultures protect interests, create boundaries and act as closure to outsiders. Some cultures are comfortable and some are not and some are not meant to be. The more sought after, the more prestigious or the more highly paid the work, the fewer the women. This is not a coincidence. Maddock (1999) gives a materialist analysis of gender and culture in public sector organizations and refers to gender cultures, saying that 'male cultures vary from organization to organization but there are common themes, one of which is that . . . men continue to underrate and undervalue women in general' (p. 192).

Academics and practitioners alike have been discussing the centrality of organizational culture to the exclusion and marginalization of women in the workplace (Kanter, 1977; Cockburn, 1991; McDowell, 1997; Wacjman, 1998) and academics have been linking men, masculinity and organizational culture for many years too (Collinson, 1992; Hearn, 1992; Hearn and Parkin, 1995). In the world of organizational change at a time when most formal barriers to women's equality in the workplace have been dismantled, cultural barriers are blamed for remaining marginalization and exclusion.

In order to discuss and define these cultural barriers we need a good understanding of what organizational culture is, its function and how any of its exclusionary characteristics can be identified. Much of culture is intangible and we need to be clear about the ways it is reproduced and how to identify its processes.

CHARACTERISTICS OF ORGANIZATIONAL CULTURE

There were early criticisms of writers who defined culture as residing in the minds of people, in their values and attitudes, thus neglecting behaviour and practice and removing it from the original meaning – a concept borrowed by organizational theories from anthropology. Now, more commonly, management writers include both beliefs and behaviours. It is also a dynamic process. Every day when people work they produce cultures. This means that culture changes all the time and may even lend itself to being disrupted. 'While people are working they are not just producing goods and services, pay packets and careers, they are also producing culture' (Cockburn, 1991, p. 134).

A psychodynamic approach to culture pays more attention to internal instincts, childhood issues and the need to stave off anxiety. This is useful when we look at resistance to culture change. Members of a group or organization produce forms of behaviour that will be psychologically advantageous to them under the conditions imposed by the environment: 'Culture is developed as a result of the group producing forms of behaviour that are advantageous to them under the conditions imposed by their holding environment' (Stapley, 1991, p. 43).

From this it may be supposed that businesses develop cultures that best serve their interests, reduce anxiety and facilitate whatever function or task is at hand and protect from invasion from outsiders. My own research found that management style is indeed heavily influenced by the type of business/work engaged in – more so than by gender (Rutherford, 2001a).

All human beings develop cultures, whether we are talking about an exercise class that meets weekly, a group of holiday-makers in a resort, or the workplace. We create rituals and methods of communication that serve our group and may keep others out. However, organizational cultures can also be dysfunctional, that is, narcissistic leadership can lead to corporate disasters, as the fall of British tycoons like Fred Goodwin, former Chief Executive of Royal Bank of Scotland and Robert Maxwell can testify. And, in terms of gender, for example, there may be no external opposition to the presence of women at board level yet on a deeper level there may well be anxiety based on early experiences, for example, fear of masculinity being challenged, mother issues and so on, which result in a reluctance to include women into their own group. The Catalyst Research, *Engaging Men in Gender Initiatives*, showed that 74 per cent of male interviewees identified fear as a barrier to men's support of gender equality – fear of loss of status, fear of making mistakes and fear of other men's disapproval.[1]

Organizations are also open systems and will be affected by societal dynamics. They do not operate in a goldfish bowl although some of the corporate literature pays little attention to what is going on outside. People bring in to an organization values and attitudes from the wider society. This means that if women are devalued in wider society, then there is a steep hill to climb for organizations to ensure that they are valued at work. As Kelan points out, 'changes in gender relations and changes in the workplace are entwined' (2009, p. 182).

Half-articulated problems will lead to partial solutions. Most organizations keen to effect real change in gender understand that all their employees may be expected to hold values and attitudes that may be at odds with wider society. Overt sexism was part and parcel of some areas of work 25 years ago (perhaps in some pockets it still is) but generally the corporate world no longer tolerates it. But challenging wider gender issues such as power and the history of domination goes beyond the legal minimum and many organizations stop short of going into this territory.

Cultures develop to protect the interests of the dominant group. Boundaries will be drawn (anthropology spends a lot of time looking at boundaries) to exclude outsiders, for, 'what is important is the way culture is constructed as a boundary device to mark off insiders from outsiders; the privileged from the unprivileged; men from women; and "us" from "them"' (Grint, 1995, p. 166).

Regarding culture as an observable aspect of human behaviour lays emphasis on the realities of symbolic boundaries. Not only do they exist as conceptual distinctions in persons' minds, they are also publicly visible in the manner in which social interaction occurs, in discourse and in tangible objects. Resources are expended in creating and maintaining them and many social activities may be understood as efforts to shorten eroded boundaries to redefine cultural distinctions or as symptoms of ambiguous frameworks. Identifying these activities is a concrete task to which cultural analysis can be applied (Wuthnow et al., 1984, p. 246). For example, emphasizing women's difference, whether biological or psychological (something that the diversity discourse has encouraged), is one way of keeping the boundaries clear.

Seeing culture as practice enables us to highlight its role in boundary marking and exclusion. It is also appropriate to see that resources are expended on creating and maintaining them. In most organizations men on the whole have more access to these resources than women and can redefine cultural distinctions. An example of this in management theory may be the translation of women's propensity to manage intuitively by emotion, which used to be considered a risk and a negative attribute, into 'emotional intelligence', a much-vaunted management 'skill' to be learned and not associated with women at all.

Work in change management regarding culture and gender is seriously hampered by the limiting discourse of diversity, whose definition has been imposed and agreed upon and become the dominant discourse replacing and discarding notions of inequality, social justice and feminism. Terminology and language of this topic don't happen by chance – language is power.

All cultures include some members while excluding others. In-groups keep outsiders out. Employees may be included in some parts of the culture and excluded from others at the same time. Organizations have many subcultures within them. In the diversity world then we have the paradox of wanting to change cultures to be inclusive when one of their very purposes is to exclude outsider groups. Why women are outsiders regardless of their position in the organization needs to be discussed in this organizational space.

So, a summary of the characteristics of organizational culture may include the following:

- It is a psychosocial process.
- Every culture is gendered.
- Every culture and subculture is unique.
- Cultures are developed to exclude and protect the interests of the dominant group.
- Culture is a dynamic process and thus open to change.
- It is influenced by conscious and unconscious processes.

DEFINITION OF ORGANIZATIONAL CULTURE

Having established that organizational cultures usually act in the interests of the dominant group we can now go on to look at the definition of culture and the ways in which it may be expressed. Much of the women-in-management and gender diversity literature refers to culture but stops short of defining it. However, the meaning, definition and impact of culture on organizations have been thoroughly discussed in the managerial literature (Trompenaars, 1993; Brown, 1995; Sackmann, 1997; Schein, 2010) although gender has been neglected. I wanted an approach/ definition of culture that was able to incorporate many of the issues facing women at work so I took in the debates on women in management, sexual harassment, same/difference, work/life, old boy networks and brought them within the ambit of culture. This was both for theoretical reasons and practical ones. In this way, instead of seeing each issue as a somehow separate/discrete area that could be dealt with on its own, they can all instead be seen to be one constituent of organizational culture.

There are a multitude of different definitions for a researcher to take but drawing on Strati (1992), like Gherardi (1995) and developed during my research, I take organizational culture to be the symbols, beliefs and patterns of behaviour of organizational members. It is expressed in the management style, work philosophies, language and communication, dress, physical artefacts, informal socializing and temporal structuring of work, and in the gender awareness and expression of sexuality. The background of an organization will also inform its culture (see Figure 8.1).

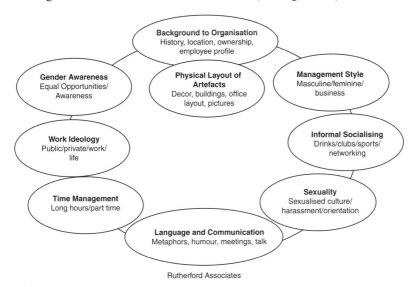

Figure 8.1   A model of organizational culture

GENDERED CULTURES

The following section will give a short summary of the different constituents of culture that are gendered and highlight the role men play in developing them and the ways in which these may act to exclude or marginalize women. I use examples from the case studies of my research. The first organization, Airco, is a large UK airline with five main divisions – marketing, finance, cabin services, human resources and cargo – each with their own cultures and large enough to be a separate company. The second case study was a UK investment bank, Investco, which is no longer independent. The main divisions were broking, corporate finance and fund management. I also use examples of companies I have come across in my consultancy work as well as my own experience in the corporate world.

Background

An organization's culture is also heavily influenced by its past and its environment. Historically, almost all organizations were founded by men. Schein showed that a founder of a company has the opportunity to build in their own values and attitudes (Schein, 2010). If the company is successful these will remain until they are challenged by a change in the environmental situation or new leadership. Subsequent leaders then have their own opportunity to influence the culture. Littlewoods, a UK mail order company, was founded by the late Sir John Moores, who was a strong advocate of equality, with the result that Littlewoods was at the forefront of equality for many years. The Cadbury family were Quakers and this influenced the culture, which emphasized social responsibility, throughout their company's history. Katherine Corish, founder and chairperson of Sysdoc Group, wanted to create a company with strong family values and this has been built into its ethos of allowing flexibility of work for all employees.

Every organization is located within an industry that itself has its own culture, and this will also have a bearing. A relatively new industry like marketing will not be imbued with a long history of male-only practices and traditions, as is the case in older industries like engineering or banking. I found that the culture of Airco was heavily influenced by the location of the airline offices, which were at an airport, and so employees were constantly reminded of their business. They were also isolated from any different types of businesses and activities, as everyone around them worked in the airline industry. This made work life more intense and urgent. Airco's culture was also influenced by the fact that it had developed out of the

RAF and still carried military overtones, obviously masculine. Its military beginnings had left traces of military life, such as the importance of rank and status. It had been state-owned and then privatized, and was still very bureaucratic. It was also heavily unionized, which again informed aspects of the management style and culture, particularly in cargo, which had a history of difficult employment relations (Rutherford, 2011).

Buildings and Artefacts

Corporate values are expressed clearly through architecture and artefacts (Gabriel, 1999). In my case study, the bank Investco, the interior décor implied power, money and men. The head office lay in the heart of the City and was of classic architecture, with a plain, marbled reception area. The meeting rooms got larger and smarter the higher up the building you went – the seventh floor was corporate finance, smart mahogany table, lovely views and tea brought in porcelain cups. Many of the big City institutions are now based in Canary Wharf – its iconic skyline a symbol of the wealth and power contained in the skyscraper glass buildings, no longer held back by family holdings or even traditional banking functions, the opportunities for profit endless – unbridled greed for profit encased in rocket-shaped buildings – the sky was indeed the limit until the credit crisis revealed the vulnerability within.

One highly successful property company has a very understated head office, which looks more like a garage than a building. This symbolizes a lean business focused on the bottom line with restraint on costs. Clients often walk straight past the building but once in, know where they are, as they are greeted not by a garage mechanic but by an attractive female receptionist.

The bank that I joined as a non-executive director was located in the heart of the City, hidden behind Bishopsgate and approached by a cobbled road into a courtyard with a well. The building was a converted mill and 'stylish', contemporary without being cold. There was a lot of art because one of the original founders loved modern art. The boardroom was very modern, unlike the dark austere boardrooms usually associated with banks. This lightness and airiness suited me – I felt comfortable in it. The chief executive had bought the table, which was a beautiful pale maple round table, again unusual for this type of building, and artefacts were reflecting the ethos of the bank – somewhat marginalized from the big banks as it was small and independent, a free spirit, a little non-conformist and modern in its outlook on business. Indeed, their own marginalization may have been one of the reasons that they had allowed me entry in the first place.

GENDER AWARENESS

Organizational awareness of gender is a constituent of organizational culture as attitudes to gender pervade the workplace and influence the men and women who work there. We can ask the questions – what is the level of awareness around the issues of women working and is there a culture of equality in this workplace? The history of equal opportunities/diversity policies may act as an indicator of gender awareness (Rutherford, 1999). However, organizations may be gender aware without an equal opportunity policy and this would be transmitted through the attitudes expressed by men and women in the organization. The dominant group will control the discourse on gender – what may or may not be said about gender in an organization. There may be an equality or diversity policy, there may be an organizational view that women are the same as men, or different and need help.

Airco was overtly gender aware with a highly developed equal opportunities policy and Investco had so far ignored gender issues. An effort to create a culture of equality, where equal opportunities are strongly backed by senior management, creates a better working environment for women (Rutherford, 1999). A historically male culture, like Investco, which denies gender difference, and operates under free market mechanisms, masks that gender inequality is exclusionary to women (ibid.). In Airco, women's grievances were channelled through the discourse of equal opportunities, and were accepted, up to a certain point, as organizational issues. In the bank there was no such available discourse and women's grievances were individualized. The hegemonic discourses of biological and psychological difference prevailed in the bank to justify the scarcity of women and this was accepted by many of the women themselves. A culture that represents women as 'naturally' wanting to be at home or 'exceptional' to work in certain areas – like corporate finance, or at senior levels or combining work and family – is exclusionary to women.

Organizations with a long history of diversity and equality and those that have a more recent strong commitment are now developing a more sophisticated corporate discourse on gender. New ways of working, different management styles and inherent bias in workplace structures and practices have widened the debates and are enabling a small challenge to existing male cultures that was not possible before.

WORK IDEOLOGY – THE PUBLIC/PRIVATE DIVIDE

The purpose of including this as a constituent of organizational culture is to make visible what always goes invisible – the assumptions about the meaning of work and where it takes place. It is important to explore how the separation of home (private) and work (public) may pervade an organizational culture and have an impact on men and women in different ways, both in a material sense and through the gendered representations that this dualism brings about. The public/private divide has been an important focus for research into gender and organizations (Lewis, 1996; Halford et al., 1997; Massey, 1997). Historically, women have been associated with the private and men the public. An organization's culture indicates whether this divide is marked or being challenged, and whether it is being challenged on behalf of women only or for both women and men. There is quite an emphasis on 'being yourself at work' or even 'bringing yourself to work' in the diversity field right now. Arguably, this is part of the public/ private divide. How much of yourself can you bring to the workplace? The recent turn to well-being, wellness and happiness is testament to the problems that organizations face if the private is left at the office front door. However, recent years have seen an erosion of the boundaries of home and work going the other way with the advent of technology. Employees are now often expected to be available after work hours at home, through mobile phones and laptops, and so on.

In my work life I have experienced both extremes. As a journalist on a female-dominated newspaper there wasn't much we didn't know about one another – relationships, children, illnesses, and so on, were all out in the open. Many would say this was unprofessional and some wouldn't like it. But that was the way it was. This aspect of the culture worked for us – the dominant group in our department – but perhaps for the few men there it was not comfortable.

As a non-executive director many years later, private lives were firmly left out of the boardroom – I knew this and when I was going through a messy divorce I never spoke of it to any other board member or allowed it to affect my ability to attend meetings and so forth. My father died and I never spoke of it. The chairperson, a widower for some time, got married and didn't think it relevant to tell us till afterwards. This was not too hard as it was a part-time role but I would have found it very difficult to work full-time in an environment that failed to recognize the 'other side of life'.

Many organizations fail to acknowledge that many employees go home to another job. This is the 'life' part of work/life balance, a concept that has many gendered assumptions in it. Many women and some men have to disguise the fact that there are serious demands on their time and energy when they are not at work. In the past many men had their home lives looked after for them, and at the top of organizations this is still most often the case. Those that have caring responsibilities bring useful skills into organizations. Juggling three small children and a demanding job requires many useful skills that are for the most part neither acknowledged nor valued within an organization.

MANAGEMENT STYLE

Management style is an important constituent of organizational culture and is often cited as being a barrier to women's progress at work. Debates on women's different ways of communicating and behaving at work are currently very popular in the West but too often neglect the role of status. People's status influences the way they behave and communicate, and how they are treated (Cameron, 2007).

In the equality and diversity field, management style has been much debated as a possible issue that contributes to women not achieving progress on a par with men, usually because women find they have to adapt to the prevailing style that is not naturally their own. The other side of this argument is that organizations do not value women's styles. Indeed, in the recent research, *What Holds Women Back* by Opportunity Now (2010), nearly half (48 per cent) of all women respondents cite personal style differences as a barrier to progress. However, any debate on styles must take place within a theoretical framework that acknowledges inequalities of power, and economic and patriarchal interests.

The dominant model of professional management from its inception excluded the symbols of femininity and promoted characteristics of a type of exemplary masculinity (typically white middle class). These management practices assumed a gender-neutral professional norm, as have male-orientated patterns of behaviour in the workplace. Middle class women were at that time confined to the domestic sphere where their work was reproduction. Because paid work was – and still is – the main social arena in which men act out their needs for status, authority, power influence and material rewards, it has been argued that organizations are structured to protect male power and reward masculinity accordingly.[2] Even when the status of a job has been downgraded, preserving the masculinity of a job is important.[3] Men's ability to hold on to management as a male domain is rooted in men's ability to construct the cluster of skills that make up management as being rooted in masculinity. This has got harder to do as women have developed the same skills and gained the same qualifications as men. Far from being an objective economic fact, skill is often an ideological category imposed on certain types of work by virtue of the sex and power of the workers who perform it.

At different points in time, women's sameness to men or women's difference from men have been highlighted and both have been given as reasons for women's lack of progress in senior management. Certain attributes may be privileged at some times and not others. As we have seen in other areas of culture, the discourse of management and management style will be ultimately determined by the dominant group. This may explain why despite the much-vaunted age of the woman heralded by writers like Sally Hegelson in the *Female Advantage* and others[4] we have yet to see women's skills held in high demand in the higher echelons of organizations. In another example, women's emotionality was regarded as a handicap in organizational life until it was co-opted and turned into a management 'skill' by men and called emotional intelligence.

I identified a number of styles in the different divisions of my case studies and concluded that it was the business of the division that most influenced management style not the gender of the manager. However, women in the study did feel they managed differently and better than male managers but that this was not recognized by the companies. Neither was it recognized by male managers.

So, management style in my research was not in itself an indicator of women's unsuitability for senior management. However, the naturalization and hence lack of recognition of women's skills, combined with prevailing management's focus on status, visibility and networking, could be construed as a form of closure to women managers, particularly at senior levels. When women displayed styles associated with masculinity, transactional, vocal, assertive, the women are then deemed unfeminine (Rutherford, 2001a).

A focus on difference rather than sameness has gathered pace, encouraged by the diversity discourse in which the rhetoric is all about celebrating difference. However, difference doesn't seem to be celebrated very much when the majority of gender diversity programs are aimed at 'enhancing' or adding to women's skills to equip them better for the journey to the top. Leadership development, confidence building, and mentoring schemes are offered as women seem to be 'naturally' lacking what is required to progress to senior leadership. They need to be more vocal, ask for what they want, boast about their successes, and so on. Many of these particular characteristics on offer to women can arguably be attributed to problematic aspects of masculinity rather than necessary attributes to success in management. While women play so little part in determining exactly the style of conducting business they have little chance in displaying the 'right' skills.

The alarming popularity of neuroscience takes things a stage further, claiming that women are innately different and therefore cannot change. This leaves the key very much in the hands of the dominant group to say whether or not they want these 'unchangeable' attributes or not, and if so where. The difference approach, encouraged by the new 'neurosexism' as Cordelia Fine has called it (Fine, 2010, p. 154), can be seen as a resistance to equality. The exaggeration of difference acts to strengthen boundaries that are being crossed all the time by women.

Rather than seeing women's difference as the reason for lack of progress, might we see men's indifference to or reluctance/refusal to acknowledge the value that women bring in the ways in which they manage, and/or the insistence that particular characteristics are a requirement for successful leadership as a means of resistance? The valuing of certain styles over others may be construed as exclusionary to women who do not display those styles.

Communication and language can be considered as part of management style or investigated as a separate cultural constituent. The type of language and humour used in the workplace can reveal a lot about gender relations. I have mentioned that while on the bank board there were apologies when swear words slipped out or the conversation turned a bit 'blue'. This in itself is a reminder that you are an outsider and talk would be different if you were not there. Male bonding often involves swearing and sexual language (often denigrating to women) and serves to shore up a particular type of masculinity (Gruber and Morgan, 2005).

I still felt left out of discussions about golf, horse racing and other City folk (men) mainly because I didn't have much to say about these topics. Men and how they talk and what about have emerged in research as unintentionally or intentionally excluding to women present and/or marginalizes them to the position of listener, outsider. Much of business language involves the use of sexual language, sports language and war language, most of which are quite alien to women who do not use these in their everyday discourse.

TIME MANAGEMENT – THE LONG HOURS CULTURE

The concept of a long hours culture is now widely accepted and as such I include it as one of my constituents of organizational culture. At first glance, time management and the long hours culture seem to be gender neutral – there are no innate talents and skills in men that cannot be matched by women – stamina and energy are equally shared out. But it has an indirect effect on women in the workplace, in as much as women still take primary responsibility for child care and household management and thus the burden of working long hours adds to the pressure they already have managing both family and career. Men benefit from being the dominant group that can determine working hours – although this is often blamed on 'clients', global environment and other outside factors – and also very often from having their domestic needs taken care of by a woman.

Organizations and their divisions can be analysed to see what kind of hours people work and why. How important are the hours? Is it workload or just visibility and availability? A recent court case concluded that a banker should be expected to work 14 hours a day even though she had four children because she earned so much money.[5] In both organizations in my research, senior management worked on average one hour longer than other managers (average time for senior managers was 10.4 hours per day). There was almost a requirement of omnipresence for senior managers, which in turn set the standards for the managers who worked for them. Divisions varied as to the hours worked, with the most elite division in Investco, corporate finance, working the longest hours. One of the male directors there said to me, 'I don't mind women working here as long as they put in the hours' (Rutherford, 2001b, p. 272). 'It seems to be the culture of the company. It seems to me, if I am honest, an expectation that people, particularly if you've got to manager level, that people will work a 12-hour day' (Male Manager, Marketing, Airco; ibid., p. 265).

It is not surprising that far fewer senior women, in both case studies, had children than did men. There is then a convergence of this new masculinity (Massey, 1997) with the interests of the organization, as this aspect of culture is readily manipulated by management. Men are more likely to be able to work the long hours that are required for the most senior jobs because they do not carry primary responsibility at home. Time here can be seen as a resource to which more men than women have access to. These patriarchal interests may converge with business interests in that people supposedly work longer and are more productive: 'If I leave at 5.30 pm my output will be a lot less than someone who is working until 7 pm' (Female Manager, Cargo, Airco; Rutherford, 2001b, p. 265).

My research findings suggest that in areas of prestige and high status, for example the senior levels of all organizations and in corporate finance in banks, the long hours culture may act as a form of closure to exclude women. At a time when women can offer almost everything that men can in terms of ability, skills and experience, time becomes an important differentiating feature that makes men appear more suitable than women.

INFORMAL SOCIALIZING

Work groups bond and develop their mutual ties in many ways but one important way is through informal networking and socializing. Kanter's epic tale of Indsco in her book *Men and Women of the Corporation* (1977) charts the terrain of the informal side of organizational life where alliances are built, reputations managed and organizational resources traded. Another aspect of an organization's culture that may appear gender neutral, informal socializing and networking have been shown to be a barrier to women's progress in organizations (Opportunity Now, 2010). In their research on women retail managers, Tomlinson et al. (1997) found that their interviewees highlighted the significant, subjective and political processes at work. They (women managers) stressed the need to engage in political manoeuvres and game playing. The authors said that, despite their equal numbers at entry points, women remained poorly represented at senior levels, suggesting that 'subjective and informal processes were important determinants of women and men's progress' (ibid., p. 218). There is becoming a current crisis among professional services firms in the UK as they have been recruiting at least 50 per cent women at graduate level for many years – and that has increased to over 60 per cent in some firms – yet women are still grossly under-represented at partnership level. Two key reasons that I hear as a consultant are networking and the men's club, together with the long hours required. And, of course, much of this networking is done after hours.

Exclusion from the informal side of work, then, may mean being left in the dark about imminent promotions, not being given frank performance appraisals, or not understanding the significance of particular meetings. More importantly, friendships are forged through the informal network, often crossing barriers of official seniority. Whatever the formal rules of bureaucracy, in business it is friends and contacts that give you the final edge. The importance of informal rules is particularly relevant when it comes to promotion and selection. As soon as people reach general management, companies start looking for someone who can oil the wheels, who can bring in other business and contacts, someone who will socialize with the right people, who is pleasant to go drinking with or to introduce to others. It is not hard to see why men may score higher here than women. In most organizations, the stage has been set by men for many years and the actors know their parts well. Newcomers have to learn their lines if they want to take part and pay attention to how the lead actors interact. Collinson et al. (1990) discovered the importance of informal relationships in their research on discrimination in recruitment. The high degree of informality in the use of selection channels and criteria was supplemented in several insurance companies by the use of job interviews conducted in the pub:

> The idea is to see how you shaped up informally, in a social situation, to see how you handle yourself over a couple of drinks and an informal chat. If you can operate on a sporting level and have a good chat, that's the sort of thing they're looking for. (Recent Recruit; Collinson et al., 1990 p. 144)

Although the above was written over 20 years ago, my own more recent research found that informal socializing is alive and well. A recent client expressed some frustration with the difficulties women who were mothers were finding in doing client entertaining. He said it was vital to spend out-of-hours' time with clients to nurture relationships. In my Investco research the most senior woman in corporate finance refused to do client entertaining because of her family life and she delegated it to a trusted colleague.

Male bonding, which often involves specifically excluding women and often denigrating them (Gruber and Morgan, 2005), occurs both within and outside organizations. Looking at how and why men exclude women in wider social settings gives us more insight into what happens informally within organizations. Although the old boys' network usually refers to the informal relationships of senior managers within and outside their organizations, the boys start young:

> I joined my accounting firm on a large grad scheme that was hugely male dominated in my department, corporate finance. I have found this to be both an advantage and a disadvantage. It is an advantage in the sense that as one of the only girls it is easier to stand out, have people remember you and also to network. However, I feel restricted from certain social activities such as the evenings in the pub watching the football, golf holidays and the occasional trip to gentlemen's clubs on a night out! My male peers are able to do all these things with our male seniors, which is something I feel I miss out on. (Female trainee accountant, aged 26; Rutherford, 2011, p. 146)

As I experienced in the boardroom, a senior HR manager at Airco expressed the view that:

> [t]here is still an unsaid, some sort of comfort that men have around each other that they don't have around women. There are still golf days, there are still boys' nights out, still a strong sense of male affinity that you sense rather than necessarily see. (Female senior manager in HR at Airco; ibid., p. 161)

Informal networks and their exclusionary power are an important area when analysing an organization's culture and its impact on women

(Marshall, 1984; Cockburn, 1991; Rigg and Sparrow, 1994) and the ways in which they may promote exclusion or inclusion. I include it in my model of organizational culture (Figure 8.1) – in some organizations it will play a big part and in others may not. Certain industries set a lot of store by socializing with clients and networking (in UK property, finance and law firms to name but a few). In her study of women managers, Trudy Coe (1992) found that the greatest barrier to women in management was the existence of a 'men's club'. It is therefore important to investigate the reasons for informal networking and socializing and the ways in which these may directly or indirectly exclude women. Informal life may include the following – networking, mentoring, socializing after hours (including forms of sexual entertainment), both corporate and with colleagues, and sport. In this way it is possible to gauge the ways in which managers may use informal channels to further their careers, see how important this form of networking is and to examine the potentially exclusionary aspects of this side of work life. Failure to be included in the informal networks of an organization means exclusion from a wealth of potential business information and client contact, and can have severe consequences on career progression, as well as isolation and personal distress. The importance of informal life at work is often not really felt until a person reaches a senior position and it is very hard for a woman to research because so much of it goes on behind the scenes. Women managers are very often unaware of their exclusion and many organizations have introduced formal networks for women and other under-represented groups as a way of counterbalancing their exclusion. But these as well as the formal mentoring and sponsorship schemes lack the power because of their formality. They may go some way to encourage women and provide support but cannot replicate the power of the informal relationships and networks that drive so much of business.

SEXUALITY

Deleted from the bureaucratic model, sex, like emotion, cannot be deleted from human beings. Most organizational discussions on sexuality focus on sexual harassment or in recent years on sexual orientation, as these two interests are specifically targeted by the law. But all organizational cultures will express something about sex as well as gender. It has been illegal to discriminate on the grounds of sexual orientation in the UK since 2003 and there have been huge changes in the acceptance and inclusion of mostly gay men in some organizations.[6] Sexual harassment, meaning unwanted sexual conduct or creating an intimidating environment, is also illegal but sits uneasily within the diversity framework, carrying as it does more negative notions of power and inequality. Training on sexual harassment usually concentrates on concepts of dignity and respect rather than questioning the dominance of a type of male heterosexuality that objectifies women. Arguably, targeting women (harassment) and lesbians and gay men for scrutiny over-sexualizes both groups, perpetuating the belief that it is only their presence in organizations that is sexual. Heterosexual men (apart from the odd 'rogue' male), who are by far the most dominant sexual group in organizations, are not considered a problem.

A few years on from the first analysis of sexual harassment,[7] some academics began to see sexuality like emotion as part and parcel of organizational life. Hearn and Parkin (1995) described it as being a fundamental, but neglected, structuring principle of organizational life,[8] and that it could also be seen a subtext of organizational life. Sexuality, like other hitherto hidden gendered aspects of organizational life, was revealed like other taken-for-granted norms as privileging male experience and interpretation.

I chose to theorize and analyse cultures as being sexualized in different ways. I include sexuality in my list of cultural constituents and see it as a resource on which men may or may not draw as necessary in order to dominate/control/marginalize women.

In my research in both Airco and Investco no one complained about the sexual language and humour. Even though many of the working environments in which women work could be construed as intimidating under the law, there is a general resistance to labelling behaviours, particularly if they are normative, as sexual harassment – as if the naming of such would expose the woman as being the outsider (Mott and Condor, 1997).

Sexualized cultures may or may not be misogynistic. Sexual harassment may take place in areas that do not appear to be overtly sexualized at all. Not all male-dominated workplaces are sexually harassing – in the hallowed halls of corporate finance in Investco there was hardly a woman to be found but the environment was polite and restrained. However, the overt or exaggerated heterosexualization of a culture can be readily identified by those who visit it or inhabit it. It is evidenced by the prolific use of sexual humour and banter. Employees and even commentators most probably refer to these type of cultures as 'masculine' or 'macho', not sexual. Employees may seem impervious to the implicit disrespect of these cultures towards women. Thomas and Kitzinger have discussed some of the reasons for this 'normalizing' of sexual harassment by both men and women (Thomas and Kitzinger, 1997). This type of culture reminds women that they do not really belong in this workplace. One way of normalizing harassment is to treat the wolf whistles and similar kinds of everyday harassment as manifestations of the normal process of establishing a masculine identity.

In the cabin services division of Airco, the dominant sexuality was not presumed to be heterosexuality on account of the high numbers of gay men in that division. The impact for women managers there was interesting . . . they themselves felt less scrutinized and freer to express their own sexuality. Also, a higher percentage of women than in any other division reported excellent relations between men and women, and fewer women than in any other department (apart from HR) said that they dressed to avoid sexual attention. Could the presence of large numbers of gay men in a division dilute or displace some of the sexual attention that is paid towards women in organizational environments? Because the sexuality is not presumed heterosexual, women's presence in the workplace does not seem to be breaking the 'symbolic gender order' (Rutherford, 2011, p. 183).

As one area of life where men dominate women (Walby, 1990) sexuality is controlled and defined by men (Pringle, 1989; Adkins, 1995). Aggressively heterosexualized cultures are undoubtedly exclusionary to women yet individual harassment may occur in the most 'feminine' of cultures. Indeed, in Airco the highest rates of sexual harassment occurred in the marketing department where the senior managers were nearly 50 per cent women. None of my respondents had reported any incident of harassment, despite nearly all of them having experienced recurring incidents. A sexualized harassing culture may act as a means of closure to women because of the discomfort of working in that kind of environment. A culture that allows individualized harassment to go unreported is also excluding, as it leads to the individual women themselves often having to leave rather than speak up.

There are unquestionably bigger questions around the increasing sexualization of women in wider society and how this affects the workplace. These are challenging issues that men both in and out of organizations need to debate with themselves and with women. If women are objectified sexually in wider society it is no wonder that many feel they have to make a considerable effort to desexualize themselves at work (Rutherford, 2011). Sexualizing women can reduce women to 'bodies', which are at the disposal of men. It devalues and demeans women at a time when intellectually, educationally, and in many other ways, women are gaining equality with men.

CONCLUSION

From the above analysis we can see that men do indeed hold the key to change for women in the workplace, for 'those in positions of leadership and power have much more influence on what is and is not done and how things are done' (French, 1995, p. 55). As the dominant group, men have more resources from which to draw to reproduce the organizational cultures in which they can flourish. This may require excluding outsiders from coming in to their territory – we can see cultures here acting as closure to areas of power and privilege. One or two may enter but the cultural conditions will be such as to ensure not too many. In different places, in different organizations, the exclusionary elements will be different. In one, long hours leading to difficulties for women who are mothers, in another homo-sociability and the consequences of being out of the loop, in another the emphasis on types of skills not shown by women and the devaluing of others that may be, in another the reluctance to acknowledge the 'other side of life', making combining work and life impossible or painful to achieve. None of these things seem 'discriminating'. Many will see them as normal and the way things are. But increasingly, women and some men are starting to reveal the bias inherent in most of our working systems and organizational life. To understand the resistance to change we also have to acknowledge the reluctance to concede power and privilege. Some years ago now John Varley, a former chief executive of Barclays Bank PLC wrote in the preface of an Opportunity Now report:

> Change is uncomfortable; sharing power, if you want to think about it that way, is uncomfortable. No wonder then that our heads of diversity often feel they are swimming upstream. We have the duty and the power to make that journey much easier. (Rutherford, 2004, p. 4)

Men and leaders are beginning to realize that changing organizational culture in order to make workplaces fit for men and women's lives may involve giving something up – power. The link between culture and power is rarely made in the world of diversity because it is too threatening. Recently, when I was discussing diversity strategy with the head of HR at a large law firm, he warned me to be 'careful as to how you bring up the question of gender targets with the board . . . they are not likely to vote for something that may do them out of a job!' He had inadvertently summed up the whole dilemma of asking the dominant group to create an inclusive culture when theirs serves them very well.

Nearly 20 years ago, Kate French (1995), noting that organizations in their structures, their working arrangements and modes of service delivery continued to serve the interests of men, asked whether men want to share their locations of power and influence with women. And she concluded: 'I remain dissatisfied with progress. I am left with the question of what to do about men' (French, 1995, p. 54). Many of us are still asking that question in 2013.

NOTES

1. Prime and Moss-Racusin (2009).
2. Collinson and Knights (1986).
3. Collinson and Knights (1986).
4. Hegelson (1990); Rosener (1990); Fagenson (1993).
5. The case of *Sykes* v. *JP Morgan*: see *The Guardian* at http://www.theguardian.com/uk/2000/jan/13/colinblackstock1.
6. For information on the work done in organizations on sexual orientation see UK lobby group Stonewall at www.stonewall.org.uk.
7. Farley (1978); MacKinnon (1979); Rubinstein (1987); Sex Discrimination Act 2005; Equality Act 2010.
8. Hearn et al. (1989).

REFERENCES

Acker, J. (1990), 'Hierarchies, jobs and bodies: A theory of gendered organizations', *Gender and Society*, **4**(2), 139–58.
Adkins, L. (1995), *Gendered Work: Sexuality, Family and the Labour Market*, Buckingham: Open University Press.
Benschop, Y., J. Helms Mills, A. Mills and J. Tienar (2012), 'Gendering change: The next step', *Gender, Work and Organization*, **19**(1), 1–9.
Brown, A. (1995), *Organisational Culture*, London: Pitman.
Cameron, D. (2007), *The Myth of Mars and Venus*, Oxford: Oxford University Press.
Cockburn, C. (1991), *In the Way of Women: Men's Resistance to Sex Equality in Organizations*, London: Macmillan.
Coe, T. (1992), *Key to the Men's Club; Opening the Doors to Women in Management*, Corby, Northants: Institute of Management.
Collinson, D.L. (1992), *Managing the Shopfloor: Subjectivity, Masculinity and Workplace Culture*, Berlin: Walter de Gruyter.
Collinson, D. and D. Knights (1986), 'Men only: Theories and practice of job segregation in insurance', in D. Knights and H. Wilmot (eds), *Gender and the Labour Process*, Aldershot: Gower.
Collinson, D.L., D. Knights and M. Collinson (1990), *Managing to Discriminate*, London: Routledge.
Fagenson, E. (1993), 'Diversity in management: Introduction and importance of women in management', in E. Fagenson (ed.), *Women in Management – Trends, Issues and Challenges in Managerial Diversity*, Newbury Park, CA: Sage.

Farley, L. (1978), Sexual Shakedown: *The Sexual Harassment of Women on the Job*, New York: McGraw Hill.

Fine, C. (2010), *The Delusion of Gender: The Real Science Behind Sex Differences*, London: Icon.

French, K. (1995), 'Men and locations of power: Why move over?', in C. Itzin and J. Newman (eds), *Gender, Culture and Organisational Change: Putting Theory into Practice*, London: Routledge, pp. 54–66.

Gabriel, Y. (ed.) (1999), *Organizations in Depth*, London: Sage.

Gherardi, S. (1995), *Gender, Symbolism and Organizational Cultures*, London: Sage.

Grint, K. (1995), *Management: A Sociological Introduction*, Oxford: Polity Press/ Blackwell.

Gruber, J.E. and P. Morgan (eds) (2005), *In the Company of Men: Male Dominance and Sexual Harassment*, Boston, MA: Northeastern University Press.

Halford, S., M. Savage and A. Witz (1997), *Gender, Careers and Organisations*, Basingstoke: Macmillan.

Hearn, J. (1992), *Men in the Public Eye: The Construction and Deconstruction of Public Men and Public Patriarchies*, London/New York: Routledge.

Hearn, J. and W. Parkin (1995), *Sex at Work: The Power and the Paradox of Organization Sexuality*, Brighton: Wheatsheaf.

Hearn, J., D. Sheppard, P. Tancred-Sheriff and G. Burrell (eds) (1989), *The Sexuality of the Organisation*, London/Beverly Hills, CA: Sage.

Hegelson, S. (1990), *The Female Advantage – Women's Ways of Leadership*, New York: Doubleday.

Higgs, D. (2003), *Review on the Role and Effectiveness of Non-executive Directors*, accessed 4 September 2013 at http://www.ecgi.org/codes/documents/higgsreport.pdf.

Itzin, C. (1995), 'The gender culture in organisations', in C. Itzin and J. Newman (eds), *Gender, Culture and Organisational Change: Putting Theory into Practice*, London: Routledge.

Kanter, R. (1977), *Men and Women of the Corporation*, New York: Basic Books.

Kelan, E. (2009), *Performing Gender at Work*, Basingstoke: Palgrave Macmillan.

Lewis, S. (1996), 'Rethinking employment: An organizational culture framework', in S. Lewis and J. Lewis (eds), *The Work–Family Challenge: Rethinking Employment*, London: Sage, pp. 1–19.

Mackinnon, C. (1979), *Sexual Harassment of Working Women: A Case of Sex Discrimination*, New Haven, CT: Yale University Press.

Maddock, S. (1999), *Challenging Women: Gender, Culture and Organization*, London: Sage.

Marshall, J. (1984), *Women Managers – Travellers in a Male World*, Chichester: John Wiley.

Martin, J. (2002), *Organizational Culture: Mapping the Terrain*, London: Sage Publications.

Massey, D. (1997), 'Masculinity, dualisms and high technology', in N. Duncan (ed.), *Body Space*, London: Routledge, pp. 109–25.

McDowell, L. (1997), *Capital Culture – Gender at Work in the City*, Oxford: Blackwell.

Mott, H. and S. Condor (1997), 'Sexual harassment and the working lives of secretaries', in A. Thomas and C. Kitzinger (eds), *Sexual Harassment: Contemporary Feminist Perspectives*, Buckingham: Open University Press, pp. 49–91.

Opportunity Now (2010), *What Holds Women Back: Women and Men's Perceptions of the Barriers to Women's Progression*, accessed 5 September 2013 at http:// www.bwmb.org/upload/docs/What%20holds%20women%20back%20-%20Bar riers_to_Work.pdf.

Prime, J. and C.A. Moss-Racusin (2009), *Engaging Men in Gender Initiatives: What Change Agents Need to Know*, New York: Catalyst.

Pringle, R. (1989), *Secretaries Talk: Sexuality, Power and Work*, London and New York: Verso.

Rigg, C. and J. Sparrow (1994), 'Gender, diversity and working styles', *Women in Management Review*, **9**(1), 9–16.

Rosener, J. (1990), 'Ways women lead', *Harvard Business Review*, **68**(6), 119–25.

Rubinstein, M. (1987), *The Dignity of Women at Work. A Report on the Problem of Sexual Harassment in the Member States of the European Community*, Directive V/4/2/87, October, Brussels: European Commission.

Rutherford, S. (1999), 'Equal opportunities – making a difference', *Women in Management Review*, **14**(6), 212–19.

Rutherford, S. (2001a), 'Any difference? An analysis of gender and divisional management styles in a large airline', *Gender, Work and Organization*, **8**(3), 326–45.

Rutherford, S. (2001b), 'Are you going home already? The long hours culture, women managers and patriarchal closure', *Time & Society*, **10**(2–3), 259–76.

Rutherford, S. (2004), *Diversity Dimensions*, London: Opportunity Now.

Rutherford, S. (2011), *Women's Work, Men's Cultures: Overcoming Resistance and Changing Organizational Cultures*, Basingstoke: Palgrave Macmillan.

Sackmann, S. (1997), *Cultural Complexity in Organizations*, London: Sage.

Schein, E.H. (2010), *Organizational Culture and Leadership*, San Francisco, CA: Jossey-Bass.

Stapley, L. (1991), *Personality of the Organization: A Psycho-dynamic Explanation of Culture and Change*, London: Free Association Books.

Strati, A. (1992), 'Organizational culture', in G. Szell (ed.), *Concise Encyclopedia of Participation and Co-management*, Berlin: De Gruyter.

Thomas, A. and C. Kitzinger (1997), *Sexual Harassment: Contemporary Feminist Perspectives*, Buckingham: Open University Press.

Tomlinson, F., A. Brockbank and J. Traves (1997), 'The feminization of management? Issues of "sameness" and "difference" in the roles and experiences of female and male retail managers', *Gender, Work and Organization*, **4**(4), 218–30.

Trompenaars, F. (1993), *Riding the Waves of Culture: Understanding Cultural Diversity in Business*, London: Nicholas Brealey.

Wacjman, J. (1998), *Managing Like a Man: Women and Men in Corporate Management*, Cambridge, UK: Polity Press.

Walby, S. (1990), *Theorizing Patriarchy*, Oxford: Blackwell.

Wittenberg-Cox, A. and A. Maitland (2008), *Why Women Mean Business: Understanding the Emergence of our Next Economic Revolution*, Chichester: Wiley.

Wuthnow, R., J. Davidson Hunter, J. Bergeson and E. Kurzweil (eds) (1984), *Cultural Analysis: The Work of Peter L. Berger, Mary Douglas, Michel Foucault and Jürgen Habermas*, London: Routledge.

9. Is this a man's world? Obstacles to women's success in male-typed domains

Suzette Caleo and Madeline E. Heilman

INTRODUCTION

Today, women remain under-represented in many traditionally male fields. Although this disparity has declined in the past decades, it remains especially apparent in high-level positions. Women, for instance, comprise only 4 percent of Fortune 500 CEOs, 20 percent of full professors in the natural sciences, and 11 percent of engineers (Catalyst, 2013a; National Science Foundation, 2013). In accounting for the lack of women in these areas, researchers argue that gender stereotypes play a major role in inhibiting women's career progress (Eagly and Karau, 2002; Heilman, 2012). In this chapter, we discuss the ways in which stereotypes not only create barriers for women attempting to prove their worth in male-typed domains, but also generate further difficulties for those women who have already done so. We also consider a growing body of evidence that documents the kinds of obstacles that women encounter when working in traditionally male jobs – barriers that restrict their advancement prior to, during, and after demonstrating their success.

Decades of research support the notion that stereotypical beliefs about men and women exist in the workplace (Heilman et al., 1989; Schein, 2001), and recent evidence suggests that these stereotypes continue to persist (Hentschel et al., 2013). In short, the content of gender stereotypes dictates that men are agentic (e.g., achievement oriented, dominant, aggressive, and ambitious) and that women are communal (e.g., relationship oriented, warm, kind, and interpersonally sensitive). These descriptors are also oppositional in nature, suggesting that men are viewed as lacking communality, and that women are viewed as lacking agency.

Although gender stereotypes can create limitations in all contexts, they are especially harmful to women within male-typed occupations and fields – work contexts that often are the most prestigious, high-paying, and sought after. Traditionally, the 'maleness' of a given context is dictated by the perception that a greater proportion of men work in that area (Pazy and Oron, 2001). It also is defined by the extent to which it is thought to require stereotypically male qualities and behaviors (White and White, 2006; Gaucher et al., 2011). These two determinants of gender-type are closely intertwined, with studies suggesting that people tend to ascribe more masculine attributes to male-dominated occupations and more feminine attributes to female-dominated occupations (e.g., Cejka and Eagly, 1999).

Male-typed contexts encompass an array of jobs, positions, and industries, including executive leadership, upper management (Lyness and Heilman, 2006), and STEM fields (Ceci et al., 2009). Although distinct in their scope, each of these areas appears to necessitate characteristics that are congruent with stereotypes about men and incongruent with stereotypes about women. This disparity between female stereotypes and the requirements needed for success is key to understanding the challenges that women face in male-typed contexts. Also important is a further discussion of the properties of gender stereotypes.

STEREOTYPES AS DESCRIPTIVE AND PRESCRIPTIVE

Researchers have established that gender stereotypes have both descriptive and prescriptive properties (Burgess and Borgida, 1999; Heilman, 2001; Eagly and Karau, 2002), with descriptive stereotypes describing what men and women are like and prescriptive stereotypes prescribing what men and women should be like. Thus, whereas descriptive stereotypes dictate that men *are* agentic and women *are* communal, prescriptive stereotypes designate that men *should be* agentic and women *should be* communal. Given these differences, descriptive and prescriptive stereotypes operate through different mechanisms and thereby create distinct consequences for women in the workplace.

Descriptive stereotypes play a role in producing negative expectations about women's performance in male-typed domains. These expectations are created when people consider stereotypical perceptions about women alongside the attributes that are thought necessary for success in male-typed fields. The resulting 'lack of fit' (Heilman, 1983, 2012) promotes the expectation that women are not equipped to succeed in those contexts. In turn, prescriptive stereotypes establish normative expectations for how men and women should behave. As a result, women are derogated when they act in ways that run contrary to female stereotypes. This potential derogation creates a predicament for women who aim to do well in male-typed domains by exhibiting the masculine attributes regarded as essential for success. It is also detrimental to women who have already exhibited their competence.

We contend that both descriptive and prescriptive stereotypes create obstacles for women's success in male-typed domains. However, because they operate through distinct mechanisms, we also argue that they introduce difficulties for women in various ways and at various stages of their careers. In the subsequent sections, we consider the biases created by each of these stereotypes and how they present challenges for women in traditionally male fields.

BIAS RESULTING FROM DESCRIPTIVE STEREOTYPES

Decades ago, researchers established that gender stereotypes tend to describe men as agentic and women as communal (Bakan, 1966; Broverman et al., 1972). Although women's standing in the workplace has markedly improved since then, continued inquiries suggest that descriptive stereotypes about men and women are far from extinct, persisting across culture (Williams and Best, 1990), time (Heilman et al., 1989; Schein, 2001), and context (Heilman et al., 1995). In a recent study, Hentschel et al. (2013) surveyed a diverse sample of male and female respondents, who rated men as significantly more agentic than women and women as significantly more communal than men.

On their own, descriptive stereotypes do not necessarily suggest negative consequences for women. Rather, their use becomes particularly problematic for those who work in male-typed contexts. The 'lack of fit' model (Heilman, 1983, 2012) suggests that negative expectations about women's performance develop due to an incongruity between what people perceive women to be like and what they regard as the necessary requirements for success in male-typed fields. Thus, the theory outlines two components that perpetuate gender discrimination against women: the first is the gender-type of the task, job, or industry, and the second is the degree to which stereotypes about women are accessible.

Whereas female stereotypes are regarded as incompatible with the supposed prerequisites for male-typed fields, such a mismatch does not occur for women in female- or neutral-typed domains. Accordingly, the evidence suggests that discrimination against women in work settings is specific to male-dominated fields. Lyness and Heilman (2006), for example, found that women were evaluated more negatively than men in male-typed line jobs, but not in staff jobs. Furthermore, Pazy and Oron (2001) found that women were rated less favorably than their male counterparts in units that were heavily male, but not in units that had a greater representation of women.

If male-typed fields seem to necessitate masculine attributes, then conditions that heighten reliance on female stereotypes are likely to contribute to a greater lack of fit. Indeed, research suggests that negative expectations arise more frequently when a woman's gender is made salient and her femininity is emphasized. Specifically, emphasizing certain attributes, such as motherhood (Heilman and Okimoto, 2008) or physical attractiveness (Heilman and Saruwatari, 1979; Heilman and Stopeck, 1985), encourages people to characterize women in more stereotypical terms and consequently evaluate them less favorably in male-typed positions. Organizational and group-level factors also increase the salience of women's gender. For example, women who have token or minority status are not only viewed more stereotypically (Kanter, 1977), but they also are less likely to be promoted (Sackett et al., 1991). Thus, having more men in a male-dominated field not only suggests that people will attribute more masculine attributes to it (Cejka and Eagly, 1999), but it also suggests that women who enter those fields may be viewed as more stereotypically female (Kanter, 1977), thus heightening a lack of fit.

When there is a lack of correspondence between these two components, negative expectations about women's performance likely arise. Women, who are typically characterized as stereotypically female, are considered to lack the qualifications needed to thrive in male-typed positions, and this belief sets the expectation that women will underperform in those contexts. Once in place, stereotype-based expectations can bias the processing of information in various ways, as people are likely to filter incoming information in a way that fits their beliefs. Indeed, research demonstrates that existing expectations can influence which pieces of information people attend to (Johnson and Judd, 1983; Swim and Sanna, 1996), what they recall (Fiske and Neuberg, 1990), and how they interpret the information they receive (Kunda et al., 1997). In the end, these biases translate into inequities in the recruitment, selection, compensation, and promotion of women.

The Influence of Ambiguity

Ambiguity is commonplace in most work settings and often pervades the decision-making process in organizations. Unfortunately, these widespread uncertainties further allow stereotype-based expectations to color the evaluation of women in male-typed fields, as information processing becomes even more susceptible to distortion when people need to 'fill in the blanks'. Specifically, evaluators tend to put stereotype-based expectations to use when information is subjective, unclear, or unstructured (Heilman and Haynes, 2008). Thus, unless a woman exhibits her competence in an unequivocal light, she will tend to be viewed as less competent than her male counterparts. Below, we describe findings that illustrate the role that various kinds of ambiguity play in the evaluation of women.

Ambiguity in quantity and quality of information
Research suggests that the amount of information available during the evaluation process is linked to biased thinking. When evaluators lack sufficient information, they are likely to rely on their expectations to form impressions (Davison and Burke, 2000). However, abundant information is not enough to diminish reliance on stereotype-based expectations; the quality of that information is also critical. In order to reduce discriminatory assessments, the information provided must be specific, job-relevant, and diagnostic of success (Swim et al., 1989; Davison and Burke, 2000). Thus, if organizations are to curb discrimination, they must ensure that evaluators can draw from information that is adequate in quantity and quality.

Ambiguity in evaluative criteria
Ambiguity also can emerge as a result of the standards used to judge the quality of employees' performance. Specifically, judgment criteria that are subjective and abstract leave more room for interpretation than those that are objective and concrete. One example lies in the evaluation of personal characteristics relative to actual work behaviors. Specifically, research suggests that supervisors tend to rate interpersonal and communication competence less reliably than productivity and work quality (Viswesvaran et al., 1996).

Vague criteria also allow evaluators to redefine the extent to which certain performance outcomes are regarded as critical to the assessment of performance. Several studies indicate that people shift their standards to overstate the importance of criteria that favor men and understate the importance of criteria that favor women (Norton et al., 2004; Uhlmann and Cohen, 2005). Thus, ambiguous criteria provide evaluators with widespread flexibility in their interpretation of employee performance, thereby offering opportunity to rely on biased assessments.

Ambiguity in evaluative structure
Managers evaluate employee performance over time, and this continuous process presents uncertainty in how to weight and combine multiple pieces

of information. Research suggests that managers are likely to rely on existing expectations when appraising employees' performance (Manzoni and Barsoux, 1998; Heslin et al., 2005), and evaluators can similarly hold on to stereotype-based expectations when evaluating women over several points in time. Indeed, findings from recent studies (Caleo and Heilman, 2011; Manzi et al., 2012) indicate that people differentially update their impressions of men and women over time. Following a decrement in performance, previously successful women were evaluated as less competent than previously successful men. In turn, improvements in performance had a less beneficial effect on the evaluations of previously unsuccessful women. A third study further supports the notion that stereotype-based expectations only affect women in male contexts. Although people reconciled changes in performance differently for men and women in male-typed fields, male and female targets in female-typed settings were comparably evaluated as their performance improved or declined.

Ambiguity in group work

The prevalence of group work within organizations can inadvertently promote ambiguity concerning the source of performance. These collective contexts create situations in which individual contributions become blurred, thereby encouraging the use of stereotype-based expectations to determine responsibility for the work outcome. Thus, women who work on projects in male-typed fields stand the chance of either losing credit to their male counterparts or being charged with more blame (Heilman and Haynes, 2005; Caleo and Heilman, 2010). The presence of this effect, termed 'attributional rationalization' (Heilman and Haynes, 2005), is dependent on various conditions. Specifically, recent research suggests that women only receive less credit than men when their collaborator is male and when the joint work is conducted in male-typed fields (Heilman and Caleo, 2013).

Summary of Descriptive Bias

The evidence reviewed above is clear in its implications – descriptive stereotypes perpetuate the expectation that women are not as competent as men in male-typed fields. Yet, other barriers loom large for women in male contexts, and some of them arise as women attempt to overcome the problems created by descriptive stereotypes. In the next section, we discuss how prescriptive stereotypes present further challenges for women who try to disprove negative expectations about their performance.

BIAS RESULTING FROM PRESCRIPTIVE STEREOTYPES

As described above, people perceive that success in male-typed domains necessitates masculine attributes. Thus, one potential path to success could be to demonstrate stereotypically male qualities and behaviors. Although doing so might disprove the expectation that women are not suited for success in male tasks, the adoption of masculine attributes creates a new predicament for women. Because such behaviors run contrary to prescriptive stereotypes, women who exhibit stereotypically male actions are seen as violating gender-normative expectations. Therefore, when women attempt to surpass the burden introduced by descriptive stereotypes, they encounter a new set of obstacles presented by prescriptive stereotypes (Rudman, 1998). In this section, we discuss how prescriptive stereotypes impede women's progress by provoking negative reactions and by limiting the type and scope of performance-relevant behaviors that women enact in male-typed fields.

Whereas descriptive stereotypes dictate what men and women are like, prescriptive stereotypes dictate what men and women should be like. Thus, they create expectations that men should be agentic and women should be communal. Because prescriptive stereotypes reflect *shoulds* and *oughts*, researchers have likened them to social norms (Cialdini and Trost, 1998; Eagly and Karau, 2002). When people violate social norms, they are punished for doing so, and prescriptive stereotypes function similarly. Specifically, women who act in counter-stereotypical ways are penalized for not conforming to gender-normative expectations (Eagly and Karau, 2002; Heilman, 2012).

It is clear that descriptive and prescriptive stereotypes operate through different mechanisms. However, do they yield different consequences? The evidence suggests that they do. In creating negative expectations about women's performance, descriptive stereotypes promote the conclusion that women are not as competent as men (Heilman, 2012). In contrast, women who fail to abide by prescriptive stereotypes encounter personal derogation (ibid.). Because they act in ways that are regarded as antithetical to female stereotypes, they are thought to lack communality, and this perception fuels their depiction as cold, manipulative, pushy, and selfish (Heilman, 2001). Women who violate prescriptive stereotypes, like most violators of social norms, are also disliked (Heilman et al., 2004). Thus, prescriptive stereotypes generate penalties to social attractiveness that descriptive stereotypes do not. Although women's competence might not be questioned when they violate normative expectations (ibid.), their character certainly is. Yet, the dislike and personal derogation of women can also result in decrements to organizational success. Heilman et al. (2004), for example, found that people who are disliked – regardless of gender – receive fewer recommendations for raises and promotions than those who are liked. Thus, the reduced social attractiveness and likability brought on by violated prescriptive stereotypes can also lead to inequities for women in all stages of the career process.

Penalties for Exhibiting Stereotypical Male Behaviors

Women face obstacles in proving that they are competent in male-typed domains. In an attempt to show they have what it takes, they are punished for exhibiting agentic attributes and behaviors. Below, we review evidence that illustrates how women can be penalized for engaging in the stereotypically masculine behaviors that are thought to be required for success in male-typed domains.

Striving for male-typed careers

An essential step to achieving success in male-typed fields involves expressing both interest and ambition. Yet, women can encounter obstacles for doing so. Having intentions to achieve power, for example, can facilitate ascension into leadership and high-level positions. However, such power-seeking intentions are regarded as incongruent with female stereotypes (Rudman et al., 2001). Recent research suggests that women are evaluated unfavorably for expressing intentions to seek power. Okimoto and Brescoll (2010) found that female, but not male politicians were penalized when they exhibited power-seeking intentions. They also found that these results were explained by perceived deficits in communality. Thus, women who exhibit a goal that is essential to success in upper-level positions tend to be viewed as lacking femininity and are consequently derogated.

Women can also be penalized simply for having actively pursued a male-typed career. Results of a recent study (Pierre and Heilman, 2013) indicated that women were more disliked, characterized as more unpleasant, and considered less desirable as a boss when they had aggressively sought their male-typed position than when they were in the position as a result of circumstances beyond their control. As with the power-seeking research reported above, the perception that women intentionally pursue positions and roles that violate gender prescriptions seems to fuel negative reactions to them.

Self-promotion and negotiation

Self-promotion can also be regarded as a behavior that is necessary for success in male-typed contexts. In fact, both men and women tend to engage in greater self-promotion when discussing stereotypically male topics (Thomson, 2006). Given its masculine connotations, self-promotion is also a behavior that runs contrary to female stereotypes of modesty and self-effacement. Indeed, existing research indicates that when women advocate for themselves, they are negatively evaluated for doing so (Rudman, 1998). This finding also applies to negotiation, where women encounter penalties for negotiating on their own behalf (Bowles et al., 2007; Amanatullah and Morris, 2010). If women are to gain comparable outcomes in male-typed fields, they must negotiate for better outcomes; however, doing so could potentially backfire.

Communication
Effective communication allows individuals to exert influence on others – an undertaking that is essential to upward mobility in organizations. Because men may be viewed as having greater legitimacy and expertise than women in male-typed fields (Carli, 2001), the use of influence is imperative for women, who may need to work harder than men to demonstrate their legitimacy in male contexts. Yet, the possibility of stereotype violation presents a double bind for women. Although direct styles of communication may yield greater legitimacy, research suggests that women who communicate with a task-oriented style are not only liked less, but also are less persuasive than those who communicate using a people-oriented style (Carli et al., 1995). Although likability is a major determinant of influence for women (ibid.), the use of tentative and people-oriented styles may not result in increased legitimacy, and may even serve to confirm existing female stereotypes.

In addition, research suggests that women are subject to penalties not only due to their style of communication, but also due to the amount that they communicate. Brescoll (2012) examined the effects of volubility on the evaluations of male and female CEOs. She found that female executives who freely and frequently offered their opinions were rated more negatively than those who tended to hold back their thoughts. In turn, male executives were rewarded for their volubility; those who talked often were evaluated more favorably than those who did not. Although recent research suggests that there are merits to leaders listening to their followers (Grant et al., 2011), restraining thoughts can potentially eliminate opportunities for women in male-typed domains where men are rewarded for being forthright and outspoken. In addition, inaction could further reinforce female stereotypes of timidity, as well as stereotype-based expectations of incompetence.

Assertiveness

Assertiveness – the tendency to defend or speak out for one's own interests – is a stereotypically male characteristic that has been linked to leadership emergence and effectiveness (Lord et al., 1986; Bass, 1990). Yet, men and women are regarded differently when engaging in comparable levels of assertiveness. Specifically, women who engage in assertive behaviors are regarded less favorably than men (Costrich et al., 1975). Recent research supports the pervasiveness of this phenomenon – when asked to predict reactions to those who advocated for themselves when mistreated, demeaned, or overlooked in the workplace, people expected women to be reacted to with greater negativity than men (Battle, 2008).

Penalties for Success in Male-typed Contexts

Women do not need to explicitly adopt stereotypically male qualities and behaviors in order to face penalties. They also encounter personal derogation and dislike when they merely display competence and success in male-typed settings. Thus, women who manage to overturn the stereotype-based expectations created by descriptive stereotypes meet an additional obstacle – disapproval and derogation incited by success in male contexts. Such impediments could account for the finding that promotion becomes more difficult for women as they move up the organizational hierarchy (Lyness and Judiesch, 1999). They can also account for the unique set of labels ascribed to successful women leaders, such as ice queen, iron maiden, dragon lady, and witch.

Why are women in male-typed fields derogated and disliked for their success? Typically, when people demonstrate achievement, they intimate that they possess the necessary characteristics to succeed. In the case of male-typed positions, that requisite attribute is agency – a job requirement that is congruent with male stereotypes and incongruent with female stereotypes. Thus, highly successful women in male contexts send a signal that they are highly agentic (Rudman et al., 2012) and lacking in communality (Heilman and Okimoto, 2007). These inferences, which run contrary to prescriptive stereotypes about women, consequently incite penalties. In fact, changing these inferences by providing information about successful women's communality can reduce the negative effects of success (ibid.).

Both evidence and theory suggest that women are only subject to penalties for success in male-typed fields. Because success outside of male contexts does not necessitate agentic attributes, successful women in those areas would not be at odds with gender prescriptions. Indeed, several studies indicate that women are punished for their accomplishments in male-typed domains, but not in female-typed domains (Heilman et al.,

2004; Heilman and Wallen, 2010). Thus, success itself is not problematic for women. Rather, it is success in male-typed areas that implies a violation of prescriptive gender stereotypes. For women in these domains, unequivocal signs of competence and accomplishment provoke dislike and negative characterizations, which can eventually jeopardize continued or sustained career success.

Women Keeping Their Own Behavior in Check

Prescriptive stereotypes damage women's prospects in male-typed fields by not only spurring derogation and dislike towards them, but also by limiting and discouraging certain sets of behaviors. Because women face negative consequences for gender norm violation, some of them try to prevent these penalties by avoiding stereotypically male behaviors (Moss-Racusin and Rudman, 2010). This can take the form of self-limiting behavior or self-censorship. Indeed, various studies suggest that women who fear backlash are less likely to self-promote (ibid.), negotiate on their own behalf (Amanatullah and Morris, 2010), be assertive (Battle, 2008), and freely express their opinions (Brescoll, 2012). Although this strategy allows women to avoid social disapproval, it also results in sets of behaviors that disadvantage both women, who should be able to use a wide array of behaviors to prove their worth, and organizations, which might miss out on their female employees' full potential.

IMPLICATIONS

The research discussed in this chapter bears important implications for male-typed jobs, organizations, and industries. Within these 'male' contexts, incongruities exist between descriptive female stereotypes and the attributes perceived to be required for success and between prescriptive female stereotypes and the behaviors actually necessary for success. Together, both sources of bias create a discriminatory and unwelcoming environment for women. Thus, male-typed organizations not only risk violating workplace fairness, but they also stand a chance of losing important talent. Smith et al. (2013), for example, found that women in male-dominated fields perceive themselves as exerting more effort than their peers, which drives a weakened sense of belonging and motivation. Therefore, the barriers discussed above could also make it difficult for male-dominated industries to retain talented women. Adopting strategies to reduce these impediments is necessary if male-typed organizations wish to maintain both equity and competitive advantage.

Achieving a full understanding of the processes that drive gender bias facilitates the creation of strategies that could reduce discrimination in male-typed settings. First, the components of the 'lack of fit' model hint at possible solutions. By reframing the attributes associated with success in male-typed fields, organizations can alter the gender-type of certain jobs – a solution that would not only reduce negative expectations of incompetence, but also make it possible for women to exhibit the requisite attributes for success without penalty. They also can enact strategies to minimize the activation of gender stereotypes, such as clustering women into units rather than isolating them as tokens. Top management could also work against the discriminatory effects of descriptive gender stereo-types by making efforts to eliminate ambiguity from their selection and appraisal practices. Such efforts could involve providing abundant infor-mation, adopting uniform standards, and engaging in frequent, periodic feedback.

Motivating employees to be accurate can also counteract the biases dis-cussed in this chapter. Both transparency and accountability in decision-making can force employees to engage in more thoughtful information processing that reduces reliance on gender stereotypes. Finally, encourag-ing and creating outcome interdependence among employees can inhibit the use of stereotypes. In situations where decision-makers' outcomes are contingent on those of the employee being evaluated, they will exhibit greater motivation to assess the person solely on the basis of talent.

Ironically, the implementation of these suggestions, which are targeted towards those who direct and implement organizational policies and pro-cedures in male-typed settings, is likely to depend on men. Men not only occupy a greater proportion of positions in male-dominated fields, but also comprise the majority of top managers in those contexts (Catalyst, 2013b). Thus, it is critical that men come to understand the difficulties women face in male-typed workplaces and be motivated to do something about it. Only by understanding the processes underlying gender bias and the conditions that encourage its occurrence can current leaders – male as well as female – be in a position to combat it.

CONCLUSION

In this chapter we discussed the varied and often conflicting obstacles that women face in male-typed occupations and fields. Descriptive ste-reotypes, which designate what men and women are like, spur expec-tations that women do not perform well in male-typed contexts and promote gender bias in evaluative decisions. In turn, attempts to disprove these stereotype-based expectations result in a violation of prescriptive stereotypes. Because stereotypically male attributes are antithetical to expectations of appropriate female behavior, women who engage in masculine behaviors are derogated and disliked, making the stereotypically male actions needed for success 'unavailable' to women. Prescriptive stereotypes also create problems for women who have already proven their accomplishments in male-typed settings, as the success itself is viewed as incongruent with the dictates of female stereotypes.

Overall, the evidence makes it clear that these obstacles are specific to male-typed contexts and are less prevalent, if at all present, in other domains. Thus, more work is needed to continue uncovering the conditions that create barriers to women's progress in male gender-typed jobs, organizations, and industries. In understanding the processes that thwart women's success in male fields, we can generate solutions to eliminate these obstacles and move toward creating a workplace that maximizes the talents of all – whether male or female.

REFERENCES

Amanatullah, E. and M. Morris (2010), 'Negotiating gender roles: Gender differences in assertive negotiating are mediated by women's fear of backlash and attenuated when negotiating on behalf of others', *Journal of Personality and Social Psychology*, **98**(2), 256–67.

Bakan, D. (1966), *The Duality of Human Existence*, Chicago, IL: Rand McNally.

Bass, B.M. (1990), *Bass and Stogdill's Handbook of Leadership: Theory, Research, and Managerial Applications*, New York: Free Press.

Battle, W. (2008), 'Women's inhibition of self-advocacy: Avoiding the consequences of gender deviance', unpublished dissertation.

Bowles, H.R., L. Babcock and L. Lai (2007), 'Social incentives for gender differences in the propensity to initiate negotiations: Sometimes it does hurt to ask', *Organizational Behavior and Human Decision Processes*, **103**(1), 84–103.

Brescoll, V.L. (2012), 'Who takes the floor and why: Gender, power, and volubility in organizations', *Administrative Science Quarterly*, **56**(4), 622–41.

Broverman, I.K., S.R. Vogel, D.M. Broverman, F.E. Clarkson and P.S. Rosenkrantz (1972), 'Sex-role stereotypes: A current appraisal', *Journal of Social Issues*, **28**(2), 59–78.

Burgess, D. and E. Borgida (1999), 'Who women are, who women should be: Descriptive and prescriptive gender stereotyping in sex discrimination', *Psychology, Public Policy, and Law*, **5**(3), 665–92.

Caleo, S. and M.E. Heilman (2010), 'Who gets the credit and who gets the blame? Differential reactions to men's and women's joint work', paper presented at the annual meeting of the Society for Industrial and Organizational Psychology, Atlanta, GA.

Caleo, S. and M.E. Heilman (2011), 'The role of gender stereotypes in revising performance appraisal judgments', paper presented at the annual meeting of the Society for Industrial and Organizational Psychology, Chicago, IL.

Carli, L.L. (2001), 'Gender and social influence', *Journal of Social Issues*, **57**(4), 725–41.

Carli, L.L., S.J. LaFleur and C.C. Loeber (1995), 'Nonverbal behavior, gender, and influence', *Journal of Personality and Social Psychology*, **68**(6), 1030–41.

Catalyst (2013a), 'Women CEOs of the Fortune 1000', accessed 6 September 2013 at http://www.catalyst.org/knowledge/women-ceos-fortune-1000.

Catalyst (2013b), 'Women in male-dominated industries and occupations in U.S. and Canada', accessed 10 May 2013 at http://www.catalyst.org/knowledge/women-male-dominated-industries-and-occupations-us-and-canada.

Ceci, S.J., W.M. Williams and S.M. Barnett (2009), 'Women's underrepresentation in science: Sociocultural and biological considerations', *Psychological Bulletin*, **135**(2), 218–61.

Cejka, M.A. and A.E. Eagly (1999), 'Gender stereotypic images of organizations correspond to the sex segregation of employment', *Personality and Social Psychology Bulletin*, **25**(4), 413–23.

Cialdini, R. and M. Trost (1998), 'Social influence: Social norms, conformity, and compliance', in D. Gilbert, S. Fiske and G. Lindzey (eds), *The Handbook of Social Psychology, Vol 2*, 4th edition, Boston, MA: McGraw-Hill, pp. 151–92.

Costrich, N., J. Feinstein, L. Kidder, J. Marecek and L. Pascale (1975), 'When stereotypes hurt: Three studies of penalties for sex-role reversals', *Journal of Experimental Social Psychology*, **11**(6), 520–30.

Davison, H.K. and M.J. Burke (2000), 'Sex discrimination in simulated employment contexts: A meta-analytic investigation', *Journal of Vocational Behavior*, **56**(2), 225–48.

Eagly, A.H. and S.J. Karau (2002), 'Role congruity theory of prejudice toward female leaders', *Psychological Review*, **109**(3), 573–98.

Fiske, S. and S. Neuberg (1990), 'A continuum of impression formation, from category-based to individuating processes: Influences of information and motivation on attention and interpretation', in M. Zanna, *Advances in Experimental Social Psychology, Vol. 23*, Orlando, FL: Academic Press, pp. 1–74.

Gaucher, D., J. Friesen and A.C. Kay (2011), 'Evidence that gendered wording in job advertisements exists and sustains gender inequality', *Journal of Personality and Social Psychology*, **101**(1), 109–28.

Grant, A., F. Gino and D.A. Hofmann (2011), 'Reversing the extraverted leadership advantage: The role of employee proactivity', *Academy of Management Journal*, **54**(3), 528–50.

Heilman, M.E. (1983), 'Sex bias in work settings: The lack of fit model', *Research in Organizational Behavior*, **5**, 269–98.

Heilman, M.E. (2001), 'Description and prescription: How gender stereotypes prevent women's ascent up the organizational ladder', *Journal of Social Issues*, **57**(4), 657–74.

Heilman, M.E. (2012), 'Gender stereotypes and workplace bias', *Research in Organizational Behavior*, **32**, 113–35.

Heilman, M.E. and S. Caleo (2013), 'Who's to praise and who's to blame? Reactions to men's and women's joint work', unpublished manuscript.

Heilman, M.E. and M.C. Haynes (2005), 'No credit where credit is due: Attributional rationalization of women's success in male–female teams', *Journal of Applied Psychology*, **90**(5), 905–16.

Heilman, M.E. and M.C. Haynes (2008), 'Subjectivity in the appraisal process: A facilitator of gender bias in work settings', in E. Borgida and S. Fiske (eds), *Beyond Common Sense: Psychological Science in the Courtroom*, Mahwah, NJ: Lawrence Erlbaum Associates, pp. 127–55.

Heilman, M.E. and T.G. Okimoto (2007), 'Why are women penalized for success at male-typed tasks? The implied communality deficit', *Journal of Applied Psychology*, **92**(1), 81–92.

Heilman, M.E. and T.G. Okimoto (2008), 'Motherhood: A potential source of bias in employment decisions', *Journal of Applied Psychology*, **93**(1), 189–98.

Heilman, M.E. and L.R. Saruwatari (1979), 'When beauty is beastly: The effects of appearance and sex on evaluations of job applicants for managerial and nonmanagerial jobs', *Organizational Behavior and Human Decision Processes*, **23**(3), 360–72.

Heilman, M.E. and M.H. Stopeck (1985), 'Attractiveness and corporate success: Different causal attributions for males and females', *Journal of Applied Psychology*, **70**(2), 379–88.

Heilman, M.E. and A.S. Wallen (2010), 'Wimpy and undeserving of respect: Penalties for men's gender-inconsistent success', *Journal of Experimental Social Psychology*, **46**(4), 664–7.

Heilman, M.E., C.J. Block and R.F. Martell (1995), 'Sex stereotypes: Do they influence perceptions of managers?', *Journal of Social Behavior and Personality*, **10**(6), 237–52.

Heilman, M.E., C.J. Block, R.F. Martell and M.C. Simon (1989), 'Has anything changed? Current characterizations of males, females and managers', *Journal of Applied Psychology*, **74**(6), 935–42.

Heilman, M.E., A.S. Wallen, D. Fuchs and M.M. Tamkins (2004), 'Penalties for success: Reactions to women who succeed at male gender-type tasks', *Journal of Applied Psychology*, **89**(3), 416–27.

Hentschel, T., M.E. Heilman and C. Peus (2013), 'Have perceptions of women and men changed? Gender stereotypes and self-ratings of men and women', poster presented at the annual meeting of the Society for Personality and Social Psychology.

Heslin, P.A., G.P. Latham and D. VandeWalle (2005), 'The effect of implicit person theory on performance appraisals', *Journal of Applied Psychology*, **90**(5), 842–56.

Johnson, J.T. and C.M. Judd (1983), 'Overlooking the incongruent: Categorization biases in the identification of political statements', *Journal of Personality and Social Psychology*, **45**(5), 978–96.

Kanter, R.M. (1977), *Men and Women of the Corporation*, New York: Basic Books.

Kunda, Z., L. Sinclair and D. Griffin (1997), 'Equal ratings but separate meanings: Stereotypes and construal of traits', *Journal of Personality and Social Psychology*, **72**(4), 720–34.

Lord, R.G., C.L. de Vader and G.M. Alliger (1986), 'A meta-analysis of the relation between personality traits and leadership perceptions: An application of validity generalization procedures', *Journal of Applied Psychology*, **71**(3), 402–10.

Lyness, K.S. and M.E. Heilman (2006), 'When fit is fundamental: Performance evaluations and promotions of upper-level female and male managers', *Journal of Applied Psychology*, **91**(4), 777–85.

Lyness, K.S. and M.K. Judiesch (1999), 'Are women more likely to be hired or promoted into management positions?', *Journal of Vocational Behavior*, **54**(1), 158–73.

Manzi, M.F., S. Caleo and M.E. Heilman (2012), 'Improvement in performance but little change in evaluation: The tenacity of stereotype-based expectations about women', poster presented at the annual meeting of the Society for Personality and Social Psychology.

Manzoni, J.F. and J.L. Barsoux (1998), 'How bosses create their own poor performers: The set-up-to-fail syndrome', *Harvard Business Review Magazine*, March, 101–13.

Moss-Racusin, C. and L.A. Rudman (2010), 'Disruptions in women's self-promotion: The backlash avoidance model', *Psychology of Women Quarterly*, **34**(2), 186–202.

National Science Foundation (2013), 'Women, minorities, and persons with disabilities in science and engineering: 2013', accessed 10 May 2013 at http://www.nsf.gov/statistics/wmpd/.

Norton, M.I., J.A. Vandello and J.M. Darley (2004), 'Casuistry and social category bias', *Journal of Personality and Social Psychology*, **87**(6), 817–31.

Okimoto, T.G. and V.L. Brescoll (2010), 'The price of power: Power-seeking and backlash against female politicians', *Personality and Social Psychology Bulletin*, **36**(7), 923–36.

Pazy, A. and I. Oron (2001), 'Sex proportion and performance evaluation among high-ranking military officers', *Journal of Organizational Behavior*, **22**(6), 689–702.

Pierre, G. and M.E. Heilman (2013), 'Negating responsibility for gender stereotype violation: Its salutary effect for women', unpublished manuscript.

Rudman, L.A. (1998), 'Self-promotion as a risk factor for women: The costs and benefits of counterstereotypical impression management', *Journal of Personality and Social Psychology*, **74**(3), 629–45.

Rudman, L.A., A.G. Greenwald and D.A. McGhee (2001), 'Implicit self-concept and evaluative implicit gender stereotypes: Self and ingroup share desirable traits', *Personality and Social Psychology Bulletin*, **27**(9), 1164–78.

Rudman, L.A., C.A. Moss-Racusin, J.E. Phelan and S. Nauts (2012), 'Status incongruity and backlash effects: Defending the gender hierarchy motivates prejudice toward female leaders', *Journal of Experimental Social Psychology*, **48**(1), 165–79.

Sackett, P.R., C.L. Dubois and A.W. Noe (1991), 'Tokenism in performance evaluation: The effects of work group representation on male–female and black–white differences in performance ratings', *Journal of Applied Psychology*, **76**(2), 263–7.

Schein, V.E. (2001), 'A global look at psychological barriers to women's progress in management', *Journal of Social Issues*, **57**(4), 675–88.

Smith, J.L., K.L. Lewis, L. Hawthorne and S.D. Hodges (2013), 'When trying hard isn't natural: Women's belonging with and motivation for male-dominated fields as a function of effort expenditure concerns', *Personality and Social Psychology Bulletin*, **39**(2), 131–43.

Swim, J.K. and L.J. Sanna (1996), 'He's skilled, she's lucky: A meta-analysis of observers' attributions for women's and men's successes and failures', *Personality and Social Psychology Bulletin*, **22**(5), 507–19.

Swim, J.K., E. Borgida, G. Maruyama and D.G. Myers (1989), 'Joan McKay vs. John McKay: Is there a case for gender biased evaluations?', *Psychological Bulletin*, **105**(3), 409–29.

Thomson, J. (2006), 'The effect of topic of discussion on gendered language in computer-mediated communication discussion', *Journal of Language and Social Psychology*, **25**(2), 167–78.

Uhlmann, E.L. and G.L. Cohen (2005), 'Constructed criteria: Redefining merit to justify discrimination', *Psychological Science,* **16**(6), 474–80.

Viswesvaran, V., D.S. Ones and F.L. Schmidt (1996), 'Comparative analysis of the reliability of job performance ratings', *Journal of Applied Psychology*, **81**(5), 557–74.

White, M.J. and G.B. White (2006), 'Implicit and explicit occupational stereotypes', *Sex Roles*, **55**(3–4), 259–66.

Williams, J. and D. Best (1990), *Measuring Sex Stereotypes: A Multination Study*, revised edition, Beverly Hills, CA: Sage Publications.

10. Unspeakable masculinities in business schools

Elisabeth Kelan

INTRODUCTION

The under-representation of women in business schools is widely acknowledged. The top ten schools of the *Financial Times* (FT) MBA ranking 2013 have on average 34 per cent women in their MBA classes (*Financial Times*, 2013). Business schools are in consequence an ideal place to change the male domination of business. However, rather than challenging the male dominance of business, business schools seem to be a reflection of current business. For change to happen in business schools it is important to look beyond the confines of numerical representation of women in business schools and instead focus on practices that maintain gender inequalities in business schools and those that can potentially destabilize it. Research on the changing nature of gender inequality has indicated that gender is increasingly becoming unspeakable (Gill, 2013). The unspeakability of gender inequality means that gender is often acknowledged but not seen as important any more. This poses the challenge to researchers to find new ways to render gender speakable. In a business school context it is certain practices of masculinity that permeate business schools.

The aim of this chapter is to explore how masculine practices could be rendered speakable in business schools. First, a brief review of the literature on women and gender in business school is offered. Second, the silencing of gender in business school is discussed based on specific research and linked to the notion of the unspeakability of gender. The next section then starts shifting the focus on men and masculinity by exploring how doing and undoing masculinity can be explored. The fourth section draws on interviews in a business school to expose certain practices of masculinity. The conclusion summarizes the finding and highlights future research directions to explore masculine practices in business school.

BUSINESS SCHOOLS – A MAN'S WORLD?

It has by now been widely established by research that business has been designed by men and for men (cf. Acker, 1990; Calás and Smircich, 1991; Wajcman, 1998). In consequence most approaches to women in business have attempted to fit women into systems and structures that were not designed with them in mind. The traditional training ground for aspiring business leaders are business schools in general and the MBA programmes of those business schools specifically. As mentioned in the introduction, the top ten schools of the *Financial Times* MBA ranking 2013 have on average 34 per cent women in their MBA classes (*Financial Times*, 2013). Training to be one of the future business leaders is an experience with a tilted gender balance.

The impetus for many business schools to change their gender representation is often linked to the business case. Business schools have realized that women are a potential growth market and started marketing their programmes specifically to women. Many business schools run women-only information sessions or even women-only courses and started offering scholarships to women. Others try to run MBA programmes part-time to allow mothers to join (Shellenbarger, 2008). The limited success of those initiatives is often attributed to the fact that most MBA programmes are suited to junior professionals with three to five years of work experience, which means most people will be in their late 20s when they start an MBA. This coincides with many women starting to think about motherhood and the limitations that might bring for a return on investment of an MBA (Sinclair, 1995).

More importantly, this changes little of the fact that studying for an MBA in most cases means an immersion into a masculine culture. Men dominate business schools not only numerically but also culturally. As business schools mirror the world of business, it is in a sense not surprising that key values are more aligned with traditional concepts of hegemonic masculinity. Hegemonic masculinity refers to a dominant form of masculinity that is characterized by competition, risk-taking and aggressiveness (Connell, 1995; Connell and Messerschmidt, 2005; Connell and Wood, 2005). It has been shown that the values permeating the MBA experience share much in common with the values of hegemonic masculinity (Sinclair, 1995). Competition, instrumentalism and individualism dominate in the classroom and heavy drinking and extreme sports are valued outside the classroom (ibid.). The same research also indicates that hegemonic masculinity is performed in the classroom by overruling women, dismissing their comments and giving them clerical tasks (ibid.). Similar studies have supported this (Simpson, 1996; MacLellan and Dobson, 1997; Smith, 1997;

Catalyst, 2000; Simpson et al., 2005). Business schools are thus training women to manage like men or 'surrogate males' (Kilduff and Mehra, 1996, p. 118) and to survive in business culture that is dominated by values of masculinity.

While much previous research has lamented the shortage of women in business schools, business schools themselves have tried to make superficial changes to make women feel more welcome. However, academic research has continually highlighted that a core issue of women not joining business school is the culture that they find in those business schools. For change in regard to the proportion of women in business school to happen, the culture of business schools needs to change.

SILENCING OF GENDER IN BUSINESS SCHOOL

While women are still outnumbered by men in business school and find the culture of business schools potentially alienating, gender is surprisingly not something that is regularly seen as problematic. Research I conducted with ten male and ten female full-time MBA students in a leading business school in the United Kingdom has traced how MBA students talk in interviews about gender in business school (Kelan and Dunkley Jones, 2010). The study shows how female MBA students are heavily invested in the status quo in business school. They accept the experiences in business school as a reflection of how the world of business is and to succeed in it, they better start playing the game like a man (ibid.).[1]

When asked about the scarcity of women in business school, many MBA students voiced that women are under-represented in the world of business as well and business schools as such only mirror the business world. MBA students regularly referred to the fact that the percentage of women in business school was similar or even compared favourably to what they had experienced in the workplace. The business school setting therefore appeared as not unusual and merely a reflection of the outside world. An example is Emma who was asked about whether it is problematic that business school is dominated by men's experiences:

> *Emma:* Um (.).[2] Um yeh, I mean, yeh, most of the case studies are about men, but that's just the way the world *is*.

Rather than expecting business schools to lead the way and have more women present than in business, the scarcity of women was normalized as just how business is. This denies any impetus for change.

While much research has pointed to the fact that the case studies used in business schools are dominated by men (Sinclair, 1995), this in turn was not seen as problematic by MBA students. MBA students often equated the dominance of men in business school as preparing them well for the environments they are going to find once they graduate. One female MBA student for instance insisted:

> *Frances:* (0.6). If you want to do business, you have to learn to play business like a man.

What is happening through statements like this is that business is constructed as an endeavour for men. It is also constructed as a game that one has to learn. One way of learning the game Frances suggests is through an MBA degree.

My research has shown that the gender order in business school is not questioned by most MBA students (Kelan and Dunkley Jones, 2010). The male dominance in business school is even constructed as useful to train MBA students in an environment that resembles the business world most closely. To be inculcated into the business culture, it is necessary to learn business based on the prevailing norms. The masculine content of those norms is rarely considered as problematic. Instead, female MBA students seem to accept that this is the world of business they are going to enter and that they have to learn to play the game like a man.

At the same time many MBA students also insisted that gender in fact does not matter in business school. Female MBA students, for instance, said that gender like nationality was not something that she 'registered' anymore and that thus no longer plays a major role. Another female MBA student talked about how the numerical representation of women did not play a role in daily interactions. Male MBA students similarly suggested that gender did not matter on an interactional level and that they would find it deeply problematic to increase the representation of women through a quota that was regularly constructed as a move that decreases quality of students. It was more commonly assumed that women just do not apply to enter business school. Thereby the under-representation of women in business school is seen as a choice on the side of women rather than as supported by structures that make business schools unwelcoming places for women.

The study also highlighted an interesting dynamic around the Women in Business Club. The Women in Business Club in this business school creates one of the few spaces dominated by women. The purpose of the Club was mainly to create a network for women rather than pursuing any gender change within the business school or wider business. Although most women were members of the Club, the main purpose of joining was access to recruiters and to discuss what was termed 'women's special responsibilities', that is, with regard to children. However, most women were cautious and made clear that they did not want to appear as extreme and radical by constructing men and women as different groups. Those descriptions can be taken as euphemistic for being a feminist, which was not a desired identity construction (Edley and Wetherell, 2001; Scharff, 2012). MBA students preferred a view where people pretended to be individuals rather than men and women. Moreover, they disliked it if gender issues were discussed in organized settings, which were described as sessions for whining and taking issues too personally.

The female MBA students tried very hard to be just one of the students in the generic form. Gender was ignored as much as possible in an attempt to avoid being singled out as different. Female MBA students invested in not seeing gender. This move might be explained by their wish to safeguard a rather large financial investment in their future that might be jeopardized by acknowledging that gender has an influence on their potential future success.

MBA students work very hard to make gender issues appear as irrelevant. This is in line with research on post-feminism, which has shown that feminism is constructed as an out-dated concept that has lost its relevance in modern times (cf. Coppock et al., 1995; McRobbie, 2004; Gill, 2007). Here liberatory discourses like feminism are obsolete because gender equality is supposedly achieved (Coppock et al., 1995; McRobbie, 2008; Scharff, 2012). In order to achieve this, an awareness of gender is displayed and simultaneously disavowed (Gill, 2007). Gill has termed this 'unspeakable inequality', where a repudiation of gender inequality is required to pretend that it is individual agency rather than external structures that shape individual changes (Gill, 2002, 2013).

DOING AND UNDOING MASCULINITY

Much research on gender in business school has focused on those who are the under-represented groups in business schools, that is, women. Comparatively little attention has been paid to exploring how positions of power are maintained in business schools. Much research on men and masculinities has tried exactly this: making practices of men and masculinity visible by analysing them to establish how they unfold their power.

Unmasking masculinity is an important move but in itself not without problems (Ely and Meyerson, 2008). Whilst studies on gender regularly include men as a comparative group (Wajcman, 1998), men have emerged as a focus of research attention in their own right. Research has shown that men often profit from patriarchy and therefore resist gender change (Kanter, 1977; Yuval-Davis, 1985; Cockburn, 1991). These approaches follow a rather static view of manhood.

A sizeable body of research has also explored masculinities in organizations, which presumes a more fluid and situative understanding of gender. Masculinities can be divided into hegemonic masculinity, as the dominant form of masculinity, and various subjugated forms of masculinities (Connell, 1995). It has been argued that hegemonic masculinity is performed in male groups through serious games (Meuser, 2001). Defining masculinity is, however, not a straightforward endeavour. Very often masculinity as a practice is linked to a male body, thus creating masculinity as something that men do (MacInnes, 1998). However, it has also been argued that masculinity is something that women can equally perform in the form of female masculinity (Halberstam, 1998). Research on organizations has used masculinities to show how men enact their identities in the work context (Kondo, 1990; Kerfoot and Knights, 1993; Salzinger, 1997; Collinson and Hearn, 2005; Connell and Wood, 2005; Cross, 2012). It has also been argued that in business a specific form of masculinity, which is called transnational business masculinity, holds sway (Connell and Wood, 2005). This transnational business masculinity is shaped by the insecurities, uncertainties and changes that require an increasing management of the self (Connell and Wood, 2005).

Enacting masculinity can be seen as a way of doing gender (Jurik and Siemsen, 2009). In recent years change and continuity with regard to gender relations have been analysed using the lens of doing and undoing gender. Approaches that see gender as a social practice and a 'doing' have started to focus more on behavioural patterns that sustain gender inequality. Emerging from poststructuralist (Butler, 1990) and ethnomethodological (West and Zimmerman, 1987) traditions, approaches to doing gender and gender as a doing stress the fluidity of gender practices and how these daily interactions sustain gender inequality (Gherardi, 1994; Gherardi and Poggio, 2001; Kelan, 2009). It has, for instance, been shown that in areas where men and women do similar work, gender difference is established through the wearing of different uniforms (Hall, 1993). Studies reveal that even in so-called feminized areas of work such as advertising, gender difference is re-established by different degrees of femininity. Men in advertising are seen as feminized, but their female colleagues accentuate their femininity even more through displays of hyper-femininity (Alvesson, 1998). These mechanisms of re-ordering gender when the gender order has been broken have been described as ways of practising gender (Gherardi, 1994). The perspective of practising gender combines an understanding of organizational structures with an emphasis on how gender identities and relations are shaped by everyday interactions (Kelan, 2009).

In order to explore how masculinity is done, a few studies have shown how fathers (Nentwich, 2008) and men working in dangerous workplaces (Ely and Meyerson, 2010) are doing and undoing gender. The latter highlights male workers' interactions on oil platforms. The research explores how masculinity is performed in relation to the technical and emotional domains: the technical domain included, for instance, making a mistake and the emotional domain contained, for instance, a concern for others (ibid.). Normally, men in dangerous workplaces are seen as displaying forms of masculinity that stress strength and emotional detachment but this research has shown that particularly in dangerous situations, workers made themselves vulnerable in service of safety and effectiveness. This was interpreted as undoing gender because normative ideas of doing masculinity were suspended. Such behaviour was mediated by the organizational culture, which stressed safety.

If one is interested in changing gender practices, the undoing of masculinity might be particularly insightful in exploring how gender change in organizations and business schools can happen. Masculinities can be performed in non-hegemonic ways to foster greater gender equality. Men can counteract hegemonic masculinity that stresses aggression and competition and is supported by denigrating women in the workplace (Connell and Wood, 2005) by enacting different behaviour. For this, it would be required to study practices of masculinity in business school in greater detail in order to expose those practices that foster hegemonic masculinity and those that challenge it.

EXPOSING MASCULINITIES IN BUSINESS SCHOOL (AND BEYOND)

One way to change gender relations in business school is thus to disrupt the mechanisms that create hegemonic masculinity. This can be achieved through making those masculine practices that preserve hegemonic power speakable. In order to illustrate one approach of how exposing masculine practices in business school might look, I will draw on some examples that arose from my research on business schools. As argued above, many interviewees struggled with the unspeakability of gender in business school. However, one interviewee in particular talked about masculine practices, Yatin. Yatin was unusual in the sense that he as a man was very outspoken about gender inequality and other forms of diversity and practices of inclusion and exclusion. He did not silence gender but started to expose practices of hegemonic masculinity:

Yatin: It's a very masculine school, I think just because most of the students are men, so there is a certain. . .

Elisabeth: What makes it masculine?

Yatin: (hhh). I mean you're in a sort of like, I don't want to like necessarily drop this, there's a, there's an aggression, there's a sort of like, I mean, there's mostly men here, right? So there's a lot of like that kind of like frat boy mentality that seems to be here. Do you know what I mean by frat boy mentality? . . . It's kind of like the guy mentality, you know, like, 'Where'd you go out last night?' 'Oh, I got wasted or played rugby or like I hooked up with this'. There's just a lot of that here. . . But yeh, there's a loud sort of extroverted aggression that seems to be in some of the classes and there's the stereotypical qualities of masculinity are sort of highlighted in that respect and not balanced very well, so. . .

Yatin describes the culture of the business school as masculine. He specifies that this masculinity is expressed through aggression and what he labels a 'frat boy mentality'. This mentality seems to be shaped by going out and presumably drinking heavily, sexual encounters and playing rugby. These practices are, as outlined in previous research, one expression of hegemonic masculinity in business schools (Sinclair, 1995). Yatin continues:

Yatin: It just seems like there *definitely* seems like there's a lot more like machoism than I'm sort of used to.

Elisabeth: And how do you find this machoism for you, do you find it ok or do you find it difficult to deal with or. . .?

Yatin: Ehh, it's fine, I mean, I'm not typically your very aggressive person, so it's something that I find rather bizarre and funny to watch. . . Yeh, I mean, it's, it's, it is what it is. I mean, you sort of, you know, I'm a man so you can play the game if you need to, but it isn't necessarily something that I identify with all the time. But you know, this is kind of life too, right?

Yatin makes clear here that he does not appreciate the aggressive machoism that he confronts in business school but he also states that he can play the game. Like in the previous examples the metaphor of a game is used to describe business interactions but here more concretely those that are saturated with masculinity. As Yatin is perceived as a man, he can join in the games if he wishes to. He uses an example to explain what he means:

Yatin: And there's a lot of business environments that I think there'd be a lot more of that sort of macho camaraderie than other environments, which I don't necessarily like very much, but that's kind of how it works. . . Yeh, I mean, I remember one business seminar that I was on and there was sort of six guys there and they started ogling. . . we were sort of in a restaurant and they sort of started just making comments about women that passed by and I was like, 'Look, you guys, this is inappropriate right now, I mean, we're at a business dinner. Granted, it's after work but, you know, I don't really think we should be talking about things like this, it's just sort of. . .'

Elisabeth: And how did they react to that?

Yatin: Um, they were taken aback and it was awkward after that, and it was tense, and I wasn't put into that business situation again. So it was to my detriment, to be honest. But, I mean, it just wasn't something I felt particularly comfortable with and I didn't particularly like where it was going. . . And I threw a wrench in that and they didn't really know how to deal with me throwing a wrench in that.

What Yatin here explains is how he broke the practices of hegemonic masculinity in a business meeting by pointing out that it was inappropriate to comment on the attractiveness of women who walked by the group of business men in a restaurant. By saying that he was uncomfortable with the comments, he broke the silence around those practices of masculinity. However, this behaviour was not without repercussion: Yatin was not invited to such dinners in the future and therefore missed out on networking opportunities outside work. This shows the punitive consequences of undoing gender (Butler, 2004):

Yatin: And I mean, I kn-, I see how it works, right, I mean, I've been in business negotiations and development where you play that 15 minute game of like, 'Yeh, my golfing' and, you know, 'My wife' and just stuff like that, and it's stupid to be honest, but that's how the bonding works and then they create the relationships after that. And I'm not very good at that game, so. . .

For Yatin the male bonding that he has observed in the workplace happens through comments about golfing or talking about the wife, which also connotes heterosexuality. Yatin appears to be aware of those dynamics but after the experiences at the dinner, he seems cautious to expose the masculine practices that contribute to male bonding because it might lead to him being isolated. By not exposing these masculine practices, he allows them to continue. Even though he realizes what happens the normative forces that support the masculine practices in this situation make it difficult for Yatin to break his silence. Breaking the silence is likely to have negative consequences for him and might jeopardize the success of the business negotiation.

Apart from Yatin, some of the female MBA students referred to masculine practices in business school. Helen, for instance, talked about a member of the team to which she was assigned:

Helen: Someone (.) I work with kind of seems to have an attitude towards women of what I'd think of as a sort of a 14-year-old boy and he's constantly making references to body parts and, you know, if ever we, you know, have to do anything he's always talking about naked women; he downloaded porn during one exercise.

The practices of masculinity that Helen refers to are largely of a sexualized nature and presumably designed to construct Helen as a woman:

> *Helen:* I've noticed that if I say something he will almost disagree with me instantly but if then someone who's male in the group says the same thing as me he'll happily adopt the views as long as it comes from him.

Helen here refers to a classic form through which masculinity is practised that means to ignore comments from women. Helen reflects in other parts of the interview on her personal agency to deal with this form of discrimination but she does not reflect on more systematic ways to counteract these masculine practices. However, following on from Yatin's intervention in the business dinner situation described above, it would be possible that another male team member of Helen's group would expose the masculine practices. This could happen, for instance, by making clear that Helen had made the point beforehand to ensure that she receives full credit for her comment.

These examples indicate how hegemonic masculine practices can be made visible and potentially be undone. They also illustrate how individuals who break the gender norm often suffer punitive consequences by not winning business by being excluded from further interactions. Making masculine practices visible is therefore an uncomfortable experience for male change agents but their work might contribute to the fact that those practices become not only visible but also unwanted.

CONCLUDING THOUGHTS

A central concern of this chapter was to render masculine practices in business school speakable. Research on women in business schools has highlighted not only the numerical domination of men but also how the culture of business schools themselves is masculine, which potentially alienates women. Drawing on empirical research on how MBA students talk about gender in business school, it was shown how gender is silenced. The male dominance in business school is constructed as a useful vehicle to train future business leaders for a male-dominated business world. MBA students accept the male domination of business schools as a true and accurate reflection of how the business world is. For women to succeed, they need to learn to play the game like a man. MBA students also tried to repudiate gender as much as possible, claiming that it no longer mattered. This resonated strongly with the notion of unspeakable inequalities (Gill, 2013) where gender inequality is acknowledged but simultaneously made irrelevant. The chapter continued to argue that masculine practices need to be discussed to make them speakable to change how gender is done in business schools. Examples of how masculine practices are used to create hegemonic masculinity through serious games and how it can be disrupted were discussed with a view to show how these practices of masculinity can be disrupted. While women often cannot even enter the game to compete for masculinity, men can play the game and also potentially disrupt those practices. However, disrupting masculine practices often carries punitive consequences for those who initiate them.

The chapter has argued that further research is needed to understand the practices of how hegemonic masculinity is created in business school. Research would need to highlight the detailed interactional practices that lead to the accomplishment of masculinity in a business school and business setting. This can, for instance, be achieved through video-supported observation that allows a fine-grained analysis of those interactions (Heath et al., 2010). Although important, research should not stop at documenting and analysing those practices that stabilize hegemonic masculinity. Instead, it should be highlighted how an undoing of masculinity in business and business schools might look. Exposing such change practices has the potential to disrupt masculine business practices by making them speakable. In sum, the chapter has offered a review of research on gender in business schools as well as a research trajectory that should indicate how gender change might come about through further research on doing and undoing of business masculinity.

NOTES

1. Most of the quotes used in this chapter have been published in Kelan and Dunkley Jones (2010).
2. The transcription system is an adaptation and simplified version of the Jefferson system, where (.) is a short, notable pause; (0.6) (see Frances below) is an exactly timed longer pause (more than 5 seconds, here 6 seconds); and (hhh) (see Yatin below) is an audible exhalation.

REFERENCES

Acker, J. (1990), 'Hierarchies, jobs, bodies: A theory of gendered organizations', *Gender & Society*, **4**(2), 139–58.
Alvesson, M. (1998), 'Gender relations and identity at work: A case study of masculinities and femininities in an advertising agency', *Human Relations*, **51**(8), 969–1005.

Butler, J. (1990), *Gender Trouble: Feminism and the Subversion of Identity*, London: Routledge.

Butler, J. (2004), *Undoing Gender*, London: Routledge.

Calás, M.B. and L. Smircich (1991), 'Re-writing gender into organizational theorizing: Directions from feminist perspectives', in M. Reed and M. Hughes (eds), *Rethinking Organization: New Directions in Organization Theory and Analysis*, London: Sage, pp. 227–53.

Catalyst (2000), *Women and the MBA: Gateway to Opportunity*, New York: Catalyst.

Cockburn, C. (1991), *In the Way of Women: Men's Resistance to Sex Equality in Organizations*, London: Macmillan.

Collinson, D.L. and J. Hearn (2005), 'Men and masculinities in work, organizations, and management', in M.S. Kimmel, J. Hearn and R.W. Connell (eds), *Handbook of Studies on Men & Masculinities*, London: Sage, pp. 289–310.

Connell, R.W. (1995), *Masculinities*, Cambridge, UK: Polity.

Connell, R.W. and J.W. Messerschmidt (2005), 'Hegemonic masculinity: Rethinking the concept', *Gender & Society*, **19**(6), 829–59.

Connell, R.W. and J. Wood (2005), 'Globalization and business masculinities', *Men and Masculinities*, **7**(4), 347–64.

Coppock, V., D. Haydon and I. Richter (1995), *The Illusions of 'Post-Feminism' – New Women, Old Myths*, London: Taylor and Francis.

Cross, J. (2012), 'Technological intimacy: Re-engaging with gender and technology in the global factory', *Ethnography*, **13**(2), 119–43.

Edley, N. and M. Wetherell (2001), 'Jekyll and Hyde: Men's construction of feminism and feminists', *Feminism & Psychology*, **11**(4), 439–57.

Ely, R.J. and D. Meyerson (2008), 'Unmasking manly men', *Harvard Business Review*, **86**(7/8), 20.

Ely, R.J. and D.E. Meyerson (2010), 'An organizational approach to undoing gender: The unlikely case of off shore oil platforms', *Research in Organizational Behavior*, **30**, 3–34.

Financial Times (2013), 'Global MBA Ranking 2013', accessed 6 September 2013 at http://rankings.ft.com/businessschoolrankings/global-mba-ranking-2013.

Gherardi, S. (1994), 'The gender we think, the gender we do in our everyday organizational lives', *Human Relations*, **47**(6), 591–610.

Gherardi, S. and B. Poggio (2001), 'Creating and recreating gender order in organizations', *Journal of World Business*, **36**(3), 245–59.

Gill, R. (2002), 'Cool, creative and egalitarian? Exploring gender in project-based new media work in Europe', *Information, Communication and Society*, **5**(1), 70–89.

Gill, R. (2007), 'Postfeminist media culture: Elements of a sensibility', *European Journal of Cultural Studies*, **10**(2), 147–66.

Gill, R. (2013), 'On not saying the "S" word: Postfeminism, entrepreneurial subjectivity and the repudiation of sexism among cultural workers', Social Politics, in press.

Halberstam, J. (1998), *Female Masculinity*, London: Duke University Press.

Hall, E.J. (1993), 'Waitering/waitressing: Engendering the work of table servers', *Gender & Society*, **7**(3), 329–46.

Heath, C., J. Hindmarsh and P. Luff (2010), *Video in Qualitative Research*, London: Sage.

Jurik, N.C. and C. Siemsen (2009), '"Doing gender" as canon or agenda', *Gender & Society*, **23**(1), 72–5.

Kanter, R.M. (1977), *Men and Women of the Corporation*, New York: Basic Books.

Kelan, E.K. (2009), *Performing Gender at Work*, Basingstoke: Palgrave.

Kelan, E.K. and R. Dunkley Jones (2010), 'Gender and the MBA', *Academy of Management Learning & Education*, **9**(1), 26–43.

Kerfoot, D. and D. Knights (1993), 'Management, masculinity and manipulation: From paternalism to corporate strategy in financial services in Britain', *Journal of Management Studies*, **30**(4), 659–77.

Kilduff, M. and A. Mehra (1996), 'Hegemonic masculinity among the elite – power, identity, and homophily in social networks', in C. Cheng (ed.), *Masculinities in Organizations*, London: Sage, pp. 115–29.

Kondo, D.K. (1990), *Crafting Selves: Power, Gender, and Identity in a Japanese Workplace*, Chicago: The University of Chicago Press.

MacInnes, J. (1998), *The End of Masculinity*, Buckingham: Open University Press.

MacLellan, C. and J. Dobson (1997), 'Women, ethics, and MBAs', *Journal of Business Ethics*, **16**(11), 1201–9.

McRobbie, A. (2004), 'Post-feminism and popular culture', *Feminist Media Studies*, **4**(3), 255–64.

McRobbie, A. (2008), *The Aftermath of Feminism: Gender, Culture and Social Change*, London: Sage.

Meuser, M. (2001), 'Zur kolletiven Konstruktion hegemonialer Männlichkeit' ['The collective construction of hegemonic masculinity'], in D. Janshen and M. Meuser (eds), *Schriften des Essener Kollegs für Geschlechterforschung*, Essen College Publications, pp. 4–32.

Nentwich, J.C. (2008), 'New fathers and mothers as gender troublemakers? Exploring discursive constructions of heterosexual parenthood and their subversive potential', *Feminism & Psychology*, **18**(2), 207–30.

Salzinger, L. (1997), 'From high heels to swathed bodies: Gendered meanings in Mexico's export-processing industry', *Feminist Studies*, **43**(3), 549–74.

Scharff, C. (2012), *Repudiating Feminism*, Farnham: Ashgate.

Shellenbarger, S. (2008), 'The mommy M.B.A.: Schools try to attract more women', accessed 6 September 2013 at http://online.wsj.com/article/SB121918306439554611.html?mod=todays_us_nonsub_pj.

Simpson, R. (1996), 'Does an MBA help women? Career benefits of the MBA', *Gender, Work & Organization*, **3**(2), 115–21.

Simpson, R., J. Sturges, A. Woods and T. Altman (2005), 'Gender, age, and the MBA: An analysis of extrinsic and intrinsic career benefits', *Journal of Management Education*, **29**(2), 218–47.

Sinclair, A. (1995), 'Sex and the MBA', *Organization*, **2**(2), 295–317.

Smith, C.R. (1997), 'Gender issues in management education: A new teaching resource', *Women in Management Review*, **12**(3), 100–104.

Wajcman, J. (1998), *Managing Like a Man*, Oxford: Blackwell.

West, C. and D.H. Zimmerman (1987), 'Doing gender', *Gender & Society*, **1**(2), 125–51.

Yuval-Davis, N. (1985), 'Front and rear: The sexual division of labor in the Israeli Army', *Feminist Studies*, **11**(3), 649–75.

11. Male backlash: penalties for men who violate gender stereotypes

Corinne A. Moss-Racusin

INTRODUCTION

Imagine that you are a man working a grueling job on an offshore oil rig. The hours are long, the labor is difficult, and the workplace culture on the rig is based around a set of clearly defined masculine norms. You and your fellow (all male) employees have been trained not to complain about rough physical conditions, to 'tough it out' when you experience injuries, and that the job requires consistently enacting your masculinity by demonstrating your strength, taking risks, and proving your superior technical skills. Simply put, this is not a professional environment in which it is acceptable to ask for help or admit weaknesses.

Under these circumstances, what do you do when a piece of equipment begins to malfunction, and you have not received training on the proper way to fix it? What if you get a migraine headache while you're operating potentially dangerous equipment, and your vision is compromised? If you know your co-worker is running a high fever and may be jeopardizing the safety of the entire crew, do you inform your superior? In each case, you may refrain from asking for help or reporting a serious illness due to fear of negative reactions from others for failing to behave 'like a man.'

As discussed below, the extreme macho culture of this type of work setting ultimately creates an organizational climate that encourages unnecessary risk-taking, and penalizes cooperative strategizing and harm reduction. As a result, hyper-masculine stereotypes dictating men's acceptable behavior – and the penalties associated with breaking them – carry serious consequences for organizations. For example, after studying the effects of strict masculine stereotypes on a large oil company, researchers concluded that pressures to constantly appear tough and fearless (or face the consequences) were responsible for high accident rates (Ely and Meyerson, 2008). After introducing an intervention in which management encouraged employees to ask for help when necessary, acknowledge the toll of workplace stress, and downplay the importance of masculine strength displays (i.e., reducing the threat of penalties for failing to adhere to masculine stereotypes), the company's accident rate plummeted by 84 percent (ibid.). This suggests that not only can pressures to uphold masculine stereotypes harm organizations, but that removing penalties for men who deviate from these expectations can have measurable, positive outcomes. In this way, companies have a vested interest in understanding the ways in which masculine stereotype compliance (and negative reactions targeting men who do not comply) may undermine workplace goals.

Although a large body of research has investigated negative reactions to women who violate gender stereotypes (see Rudman and Phelan, 2008, for a review), comparatively little work has considered the consequences of *men's* stereotype violations. In this chapter, I begin by describing the nature of gender stereotypes and outlining the consequences of hyper-masculine stereotype compliance for men's health, relationships, aggressive behavior, and egalitarianism. I will then briefly review the research on penalties for stereotype-violating women, and discuss the growing body of literature on penalties for stereotype-violating men. Utilizing the status incongruity hypothesis (Rudman, Moss-Racusin, Phelan & Nauts, 2012), I will also explore the processes driving penalties against men and women who violate gender stereotypes. Finally, I will identify remaining questions and highlight promising unexplored areas for further inquiry. Throughout this chapter, I focus my discussion on findings and implications of particular relevance for organizations.

THE CONTENT OF MASCULINE GENDER STEREOTYPES

Despite some perceptions that gender stereotypes have relaxed over time (Good and Moss-Racusin, 2010), immediately recognizable stereotypes regarding men's and women's roles and behaviors remain remarkably pervasive (Rudman and Glick, 2008). Moreover, research on 'dynamic stereotypes' projects that the content of these stereotypes is unlikely to change even 50 years in the future (Diekman, Goodfriend and Goodwin, 2004). Across eras and cultures, women have been viewed as *communal* (i.e., nurturing, modest, other oriented), while men have been perceived as *agentic* (i.e., dominant, self-promoting, career oriented; Williams and Best, 1990; Prentice and Carranza, 2002; Rudman et al., 2012a). Specifically, men are thought of as possessing more 'leadership ability' and 'business sense,' and being more aggressive, assertive, and ambitious than women (Rudman et al., 2012a). Men are also expected to control their emotions, be comfortable taking large risks, and demonstrate consistent self-reliance (Mahalik et al., 2003). Additionally, gender stereotypes portray men as higher in power and status relative to women, and thereby serve to legitimize existing professional hierarchies (Eagly, 1987; Glick and Fiske, 2001; Ridgeway, 2001).

Men are aware of these stereotypes, and experience significant pressure to adhere to them. For example, Prime and Moss-Racusin (2009) conducted a series of interviews with men in organizations, and identified four primary components of workplace masculine stereotypes that are typically enforced within western professional cultures. These components were supported by the existing research literature, and consisted of requirements to (1) avoid behaving in any way that could be construed as feminine, or enacting female stereotypes (Rudman and Fairchild, 2004; Bosson, Prewitt-Freilino and Taylor, 2005; Rudman, Mescher and Moss-Racusin, 2013); (2) 'be a winner' by attaining status, power, and professional prestige (Mahalik et al., 2003; Kimmel, 2004); (3) show no weaknesses or 'chinks in the armor' by demonstrating constant vigilance and emotional and physical toughness (Derlega and Chaiken, 1976; Brescoll and Uhlmann, 2008); and (4) be a 'man's man' or 'one of the boys' by complying with masculine stereotypes and fitting in with other male peers who can provide career advancement (Williams, 2000). One male employee summed up many of these stereotypic professional expectations by noting:

> There's a script that many men have been fed, inculcated, reward[ed] by, around suck-it-up, act tough, don't let them see you sweat, show no chinks in the armor . . . I call it, 'acquired male answer syndrome', [where] if asked a definitive question, [I] give a definitive answer, whether I know what I'm talking about or not . . . along the way, I lost myself – who I really am – because I think I was caught in this myth of being male or acting male. (Prime and Moss-Racusin, 2009, p. 9)

THE HIGH PRICE OF MASCULINE GENDER STEREOTYPE ADHERENCE

As the above quote implies, research suggests that there are many serious consequences associated with strict adherence to traditional male gender stereotypes. Indeed, across a wide variety of behaviors, men who comply with masculine gender stereotypes pay a steep price. Of importance, stereotypes calling for men to demonstrate physical strength and toughness can paradoxically undermine their mental and physical health (Levant and Pollack, 1995), with obvious implications for their workplace productivity, attendance, and job performance. For example, masculine stereotype compliance is linked to men being more likely than women to engage in over 30 risky health behaviors (such as smoking, drinking and driving, and missing routine health screenings and doctors appointments; Courtenay, 2000a, 2000b). These risky behaviors contribute to men's life expectancy being seven years shorter than women's, and to men's higher death rates for all 15 leading causes of death (ibid.). Additionally, stereotypic expectations for men's self-reliance and stoicism (even when grappling with difficult events) are linked to men's elevated levels of depression and psychological distress (Hayes and Mahalik, 2000; Magovcevic and Addis, 2008). Moreover, these stereotypes serve as barriers to men's help-seeking behavior, contributing to their low rates of utilizing needed mental and physical health services (Addis and Mahalik, 2003). Indeed, when interviewed, one male employee explained:

> I think one of the disadvantages of being male is that I have bought the myth that I can do anything, if I dream it. And, as a result, it's taking me continued work to have to ask for help and support from others, particularly other men . . . I sit there and struggle with stuff when I really don't need to. I think that lowers my life expectancy and other men's life expectancy. (Prime and Moss-Racusin, 2009, p. 9)

Thus, pressures to adhere to masculine stereotypes have consequences for men's mental and physical well-being, ultimately undermining their ability to contribute to their organizations as effectively as possible.

Relatedly, strict adherence to masculine stereotypes can undermine men's interpersonal skills (Pollack, 1999), which are essential tools for functioning well within organizations. For example, forming and maintaining successful relationships as well as communicating clearly with others are often identified as critical workplace skills. However, men's compliance with traditional stereotypes was associated with less satisfying and functional interpersonal relationships (as rated by both men themselves as well as their female relationship partners; Burn and Ward, 2005). Additionally, stereotypic expectations that men demonstrate dominance and immodesty are linked to men's propensity to sexually harass (Berdahl, 2007) and enact violence against women (Parrott and Zeichner, 2003; Reidy, Shirk, Sloan and Zeichner, 2009).

Indeed, pressure on men to defend their masculinity can lead to several aggressive forms of behavior with organizational consequences. Multiple studies have demonstrated that masculinity itself is viewed as 'precarious', in that it is a more elusive and impermanent state compared to femininity (e.g., Vandello, Bosson, Cohen, Burnaford and Weaver, 2008; Weaver, Vandello, Bosson and Burnaford, 2010). As such, men must re-establish their threatened manhood consistently, often by means of aggressive displays that could potentially lead to workplace disruptions or poor professional decision-making (Bosson and Vandello, 2011). For example, men whose masculinity had been challenged engaged in more aggressive behavior (e.g., punching a pad with greater force) and were more likely to choose to participate in a violent over a non-violent task relative to men whose masculinity was not threatened, in order to re-establish masculine stereotype compliance (Bosson, Vandello, Burnaford, Weaver and Wasti, 2009). In an even more organizationally relevant task, men under masculinity threat made much riskier financial decisions (such as placing larger but unwarranted bets during a gambling game and pursuing a lower immediate payoff instead of waiting for a larger payoff later) than those who had not been threatened (Weaver, Vandello, & Bosson, in press). This indicates that demands to repeatedly re-establish one's masculine stereotype compliance have serious consequences for men's aggressive workplace behavior, and may undermine their abilities to make appropriate financial decisions.

Finally, masculine stereotype compliance reduces men's egalitarianism within organizations, including undermining support for corporate diversity and inclusion practices. For example, expectations for male power and success are associated with men's 'resistance towards policies, programs and initiatives undertaken by organizations to promote the hiring and advancement of marginalized employees (e.g., women, people of color, the handicapped, aboriginal people')' (Burke and Black, 1997, p. 934). Additionally, 'zero-sum' thinking (i.e., the perception that progress for women necessarily represents a threat to men) consistent with stereotypic expectations that men must hold positions of power predicted male managers' reduced interest in taking a diversity and inclusion training course (Prime, Moss-Racusin and Foust-Cummings,, 2009). Finally, men who experienced a threat to their masculinity demonstrated higher levels of prejudice (i.e., reported more fear, hostility, and discomfort) against gay men than men whose masculinity had not been threatened (Glick, Gangl, Gibb, Klumpner and Weinberg, 2007). Thus, not only do masculine stereotypes undermine men's support for corporate diversity initiatives, but are also associated with biased and unprofessional behaviors that may leave organizations vulnerable to litigation.

In sum, compliance with hyper-masculine stereotypes is associated with a host of negative consequences for men's mental and physical health, interpersonal relationships, aggressiveness, and egalitarian behavior. These outcomes are concerning for men themselves, but in each case, also present obvious impediments for successful workplace functioning. For these reasons, it seems useful to encourage men to feel free to deviate from strict masculine stereotype adherence, sidestepping the negative associated consequences. However, the penalties for violating male gender

stereotypes can be equally (if not more) severe than the risks associated
with stereotype compliance. Below, I discuss the consequences of gender
stereotype violations.

BACKLASH FOR GENDER STEREOTYPE VIOLATIONS

What happens when people 'break the gender rules' by violating traditional stereotypes regarding masculinity and femininity? Key to answering this question is the fact that gender stereotypes can take two distinct
forms. 'Descriptive' stereotypes state what men and women are thought
to be like, while 'prescriptive' stereotypes go a step further to dictate the
rules for acceptable behavior (Eagly, 1987; Burgess and Borgida, 1999;
Heilman, 2001; Eagly and Karau, 2002; Prentice and Carranza, 2002;
Rudman et al., 2012a, 2012b; see Table 11.1 for a description of all categories of gender stereotypes discussed in the current chapter, as well as
their implications for backlash). That is, whereas descriptive stereotypes
specify 'how women and men actually are', prescriptive stereotypes dictate

*Table 11.1   Categories of gender stereotypes, with associated status
rankings and implications for backlash*

Type	Description	Content	Status Ranking	Lead to Backlash When Violated?
Men's descriptive	Describe how men are thought to be			
Women's descriptive	Describe how women are thought to be			
Men's prescriptive	Dictate how men must behave	Agentic (Independent, leadership ability)	High	✔
Men's proscriptive	Dictate how men must not behave	Weak (Insecure, naive)	Low	✔
Women's prescriptive	Dictate how women must behave	Communal (Warm, sensitive to others)	Neutral	✗
Women's proscriptive	Dictate how women must not behave	Dominant (Demanding, ruthless)	High	✔

'norms about behaviors that are suitable for each – how women and men *should* be' (Heilman, 2001, p. 659; emphasis in original). For example, the descriptive stereotype that women *are* nurturing and supportive is contrasted with the prescriptive stereotype that women *must behave* in ways that are nurturing and supportive (Eagly, 1987; Burgess and Borgida, 1999); similarly, the descriptive stereotype that men typically are aggressive and assertive is related to the prescriptive stereotype that men *should* exhibit aggressive, assertive behavior (Rudman et al., 2012a).

Of importance, whereas descriptive stereotypes can be overridden with clear contrary evidence, prescriptive stereotypes are robust to new information (Gill, 2004). That is, although interacting with a woman who is not particularly nurturing or a man who does not appear to be aggressive may lead individuals to revise their descriptive stereotype (i.e., acknowledging that all women or men, on average, do not necessarily possess these traits), their prescriptive stereotypes are likely to remain intact (i.e., they are still likely to believe that this individual woman *should* be nurturing, or that this particular man *should* be aggressive; Gill, 2004; Rudman, Moss-Racusin, Glick and Phelan, 2012). In this way, the prescriptive 'gender rules' governing men's and women's behavior remain intact and are perpetuated.

When men and women break these gender rules by clearly behaving in ways that violate prescriptive gender stereotypes, they risk *backlash*, or social and economic penalties (Rudman, 1998; Rudman and Glick, 1999, 2001; Rudman et al., 2012a, 2012b). Backlash typically consists of prejudice (i.e. social penalties), which in turn leads to discrimination (i.e., economic penalties); that is, stereotype violators are often treated unfairly by others because they are disliked (Burgess and Borgida, 1999; Heilman, 2001; Rudman et al., 2012a). Within organizations, prejudice may manifest as social ostracism, lack of access to informal mentoring channels and social capital, and even workplace bullying; discrimination can take the form of not being hired, failure to advance, inequitable pay, and wrongful termination (Rudman and Phelan, 2008; Moss-Racusin, Dovidio, Brescoll, Graham and Handelsman, 2012). In these ways, backlash can serve to limit individuals' free expression, policing behavior with the threat of prejudice and discrimination and perpetuating the existing status quo (Rudman and Fairchild, 2004; Rudman et al., 2012a, 2012b).

The vast majority of existing research on backlash has focused on penalties for stereotype-violating women. For example, Rudman (1998) demonstrated that when women violated gender stereotypes by self-promoting, they overcame descriptive stereotypes depicting women as less competent and competitive than men (e.g., Broverman, Vogel, Broverman, Clarkson and Rosenkrantz, 1972) and were rated as equivalently qualified relative

to identical men. However, because self-promotion also violates prescriptive stereotypes calling for women to be modest and self-effacing
(Moss-Racusin and Rudman, 2010), women experienced organizationally
relevant backlash for this behavior. Specifically, they were rated as less
socially attractive (i.e., experienced prejudice) as well as less hireable for
a high-pressure job (i.e., encountered discrimination; Rudman, 1998).
Similarly, women who violated gender stereotypes by demonstrating
success in a male gender-typed job were acknowledged as competent,
but experienced backlash in the form of interpersonal derogation (prejudice) and poor evaluations and low recommendations for organizational
reward allocations (discrimination) relative to identical men (Heilman,
Wallen, Fuchs and Tamkins, 2004). Additionally, 'power-seeking intentions' (i.e., expressing a purposeful, carefully planned goal to pursue and
obtain a position of power) lead to backlash in the form of weakened
voting support for a female but not identical male candidate, in part
because these power-seeking intentions were at odds with female (but not
male) gender stereotypes (Brescoll and Okimoto, 2010). In sum, backlash
places women in a powerful 'catch-22': they must choose between being
viewed as unqualified (and thus, unhireable) if they do not violate female
prescriptive stereotypes, or being viewed as unlikeable (and thus, unhireable) as a result of backlash when they do.

MEN'S CATCH-22: BACKLASH FOR VIOLATING HARMFUL MASCULINE STEREOTYPES

Although the vast majority of work on backlash has examined reactions to
stereotype-violating women, there is a growing body of work on penalties
against 'gender-deviant' men (i.e., those who do not comply with traditional gender stereotypes). Researchers have begun to investigate how
backlash for violating strict, hyper-masculine stereotypes places men in a
unique dilemma distinct from the catch-22 experienced by gender-deviant
women. Specifically, men are trapped between the 'rock' of the high costs
to their health, relationships, and egalitarianism associated with masculine stereotype compliance, and the 'hard place' of potential backlash for
violating these prescriptive stereotypes. In this way, the threat of backlash
against gender-deviant men curtails challenges to the status quo, reinforcing traditional hyper-masculine stereotypes and perpetuating unprofessional workplace behavior (Rudman and Fairchild, 2004). Thus, male
backlash has critical implications for organizational functioning.

Men encounter backlash for a variety of behaviors that violate masculine gender stereotypes. One domain particularly likely to result in

backlash for men is emotional self-disclosure, or any expression of weakness or emotional vulnerability. For example, not only are men who violate stereotypes by working in the traditionally female field of nursing perceived to be more at risk for harassment and rejection than female nurses (Cherry and Deaux, 1978), but results of a large survey of 6485 nurses indicated that male nurses were actually more likely than female nurses to suffer workplace bullying (Erikson and Einarsen, 2004). When men violate traditional stereotypes by self-disclosing a troubling personal problem (e.g., a recent serious car accident resulting in the death of a family member), they are viewed as less well adjusted than an identical woman and a man who did not disclose his personal problem (Derlega and Chaiken, 1976). Similarly, a man who behaved passively with a mental health counselor was rated as more in need of therapy than an identical woman, and a male patient who behaved dependently with his therapist was viewed as less likeable and suffering from more serious emotional problems than an identical female patient (Costrich, Feinstein, Kidder, Marecek and Pascale, 1975). These results suggest that men experience harsh penalties when they reveal emotional weaknesses or seek help for personal problems. Of importance, backlash for emotional disclosure can serve as a powerful barrier to men's interpersonal communication in the workplace, particularly surrounding personal issues that may interfere with work but could be managed successfully with appropriate support.

Men are also likely to encounter backlash for possessing skills or occupying roles typically associated with women. For example, men who were described as having scored well on a test measuring 'feminine knowledge' (including domains such as child care, cooking, and baking) were subsequently sabotaged by their peers, preventing their chances to earn subsequent financial rewards (Rudman and Fairchild, 2004). When men were self-effacing in a job interview (i.e., used hedging language such as 'I'm no expert, but. . .' and avoided direct eye contact), they were rated as less competent and worthy of being hired compared to self-effacing women and self-promoting men (Rudman, 1998). Additional research has found similar effects with men who behave more overtly modestly on job interviews (e.g., answering the question, 'What kind of salary do you expect?' with the response, 'Well, if I should be lucky enough to get the position, I'm sure you'd offer me a fair wage. You know, whatever the going rate is for someone with my skills and experience'; Moss-Racusin, Phelan and Rudman, 2010; see also Rudman and Glick, 1999, 2001).

Additional work suggests that the nature of backlash against stereotype-violating men may differ in important ways from that directed at gender-deviant women. More specifically, a man who was successful in a traditionally feminine professional role (i.e., employee relations counselor) suffered a 'wimpiness' penalty (Heilman and Wallen, 2010). Specifically, the stereotype-violating male employee relations counselor suffered penalties in the form of being viewed as a less effectual leader, was afforded less respect, and was rated as a less desirable boss than an identical woman or a gender-consistent man (i.e., a financial advisor). Finally, relative to control targets, men who requested a family leave (an action stereotypically associated with women; Brescoll Glass and Sedlovskaya, 2013) were viewed as poor workers, encountered organizational penalties (such as salary reductions and demotions) and were less eligible for important rewards (such as raises and promotions; Rudman and Mescher, 2013).

Backlash is also likely to ensue when men interact with women in ways that challenge traditional organizational gender hierarchies. For example, men who violate the traditional status hierarchy by working as subordinates for female construction site supervisors were conferred lower organizational status and paid almost $20 000 per year less than the identical female subordinate (Brescoll, Uhlmann, Moss-Racusin and Sarnell 2012). Additionally, merely working on teams with women can result in low third party and self-rated performance assessments for men (West, Heilman, Gullett, Moss-Racusin and Magee, 2012).

Of great importance for effective workplace functioning, men are at risk for backlash when they offer help and mentoring to talented women, or more broadly, when they support workplace diversity initiatives (Prime and Moss-Racusin, 2009; Prime et al., 2009). Many of the male employees interviewed by Prime and Moss-Racusin (2009) reported fears of negative repercussions for championing their talented female colleagues and supporting gender-fair workplace policies. In particular, men expressed concern that backlash for violating male stereotypes by supporting female colleagues and workplace diversity policies would manifest as challenges to their masculinity itself, and even allegations that they might be gay. Specifically, one man stated:

> The other thing that is major that keeps us from wandering into this topic is our fear of breaking rank, our fear of what's going to happen if I stand up and support this and start challenging my white man[hood]. Well, first of all, some men are afraid of being seen as gay. If you're a white male you must be gay because you're so actively adamant about diversity. (Prime and Moss-Racusin, 2009, p. 15)

Similarly, another male employee noted:

> What are men who are identified with 'women's issues' or men who are, publicly or privately, seen as supporting . . . equality and women's challenges to men's power – what are some of the words you've heard to describe those men?

It's always – their manhood is undermined. They're not real men. They're a wimp. They're . . . whipped. Their heterosexuality is questioned. These are all really powerful policing mechanisms that keep men silent. (Ibid., p. 15)

Experimental research speaks to the reality of these concerns, and to the power of backlash to shape men's behavior within organizations. For example, men responded negatively and resisted performing stereotypically feminine behaviors (such as talking with friends about emotions) to the extent that they believed they might be perceived as gay, even though enacting these behaviors provided psychological benefits (Bosson et al., 2005). Even more relevant to an organizational context, men who expressed gender egalitarian beliefs encountered backlash, in that they were more likely to be stigmatized as feminine, weak, and likely to be gay relative to control targets (Rudman et al., 2013). Thus, men are at risk for severe forms of backlash when they support female colleagues and egalitarian policies in the workplace. In this way, the very real threat of backlash may undermine men's equitable treatment of talented female employees and their full participation in organizational diversity and inclusion initiatives.

Taken together, these results suggest that male backlash powerfully shapes men's behavior within organizations. Because men encounter penalties when they disclose their vulnerabilities, demonstrate valuable skills traditionally associated with women, and challenge the established gender hierarchy by supporting female colleagues, backlash likely interrupts efficient organizational functioning in each of these domains. However, until recently, little was understood regarding the motivational underpinnings or processes responsible for backlash. Recent research has begun to identify what leads people to administer backlash, and the specific components of stereotype violations that result in penalties against gender-deviant men.

UNDERSTANDING BACKLASH: THE STATUS INCONGRUITY HYPOTHESIS

Why do people penalize gender stereotype violators? To answer this question, one further subdivision of stereotyping categories is necessary. While stereotypes can be *prescriptive* (specifying how men and women should behave), they can also be *proscriptive* (outlining how men and women should not behave; Prentice and Carranza, 2002; Moss-Racusin et al., 2010; Rudman et al., 2012a, 2012b). More specifically, women are forbidden from expressing dominance traits (such as being aggressive, intimidating, dominating, and arrogant), while men may not express traits associated with weakness (such as being emotional, naive, weak, and insecure; Rudman et al., 2012a). Thus, while prescriptive stereotypes require that women be communal and men be agentic, proscriptive stereotypes dictate that women *not be dominant* and men *not be weak*. These prescriptive and proscriptive stereotypes for both men and women comprise the four sets of gender rules governing acceptable behavior, violations of which are associated with backlash.

However, until recently, the specific mechanisms and motivations responsible for backlash remained unclear. Two central questions underscore the ways in which gender stereotype violations lead to backlash:

Q1: Which specific gender stereotype violations result in backlash?

That is, does backlash result from violations of prescriptive stereotypes, proscriptive stereotypes, or both – and do the same gender rule violations result in backlash for gender-deviant men and women? Answering these critical questions would identify the types of behavior that are associated with penalties for men and women, and perhaps even more importantly, the types of behavior that may be gender atypical, but do not initiate backlash. For example, if backlash against women results from violations of communality prescriptions and dominance proscriptions, then women must ensure that they are both sufficiently communal and that they are not excessively dominant, or risk penalties. However, if backlash stems only from violations of prescriptions, then women would only need to ensure that they are not insufficiently communal in order to avoid backlash, and could feel free to engage in the dominant behavior that is essential to advance their careers (e.g., Rudman et al., 2012b). Conversely, if proscriptive stereotype violations result in female backlash, then women should avoid perceptions that they are excessively dominant, but would not need to be simultaneously overly concerned about appearing insufficiently communal (Rudman et al., 2012a).

If male backlash is the result of both prescriptive and proscriptive stereotype violations, then men must ensure that they are viewed as both sufficiently agentic and that they are not seen as excessively weak. However, if only prescriptive stereotypes are to blame, then men need only be concerned with fulfilling expectations of agency, but could experience important latitude to express some inevitable human weaknesses, with important mental health benefits as a result (e.g., Moss-Racusin et al., 2010). Conversely, if only proscriptive stereotypes result in backlash, then men may relax their concerns to relentlessly demonstrate agency, as long as they do not actively appear weak. Thus, it was critical to pinpoint the specific gender rule violations responsible for backlash against stereotype-violating men and women.

Q2: Why are people motivated to administer backlash when they observe a gender stereotype violator?

Simply put, the reasons why gender stereotype violations result in backlash are not immediately clear. The copious evidence reviewed thus far clearly reveals that when men and women 'break the gender rules' by violating stereotypes, they encounter backlash. But for some time, the specific reasons why observers find gender-deviant men and women to be so distressing – and are thus motivated to penalize them with severe forms of backlash – remained elusive.

Research on the status incongruity hypothesis (SIH) suggests that the answers to both of these core questions center on issues of status. That is, gender-deviant behavior not only violates the roles that men and women are expected to enact (e.g., Eagly and Karau, 2002), but also violates the status positions that men and women are expected to occupy (Moss-Racusin et al., 2012; Rudman et al., 2012a, 2012b; Rudman and Mescher, 2013). Thus, the SIH predicts that backlash fundamentally functions to police and reinforce the existing gender status hierarchy, punishing women who seek to take on too much power and men who give their power away. Because motivations to uphold the existing social system are powerful, pervasive, and often operate outside of conscious awareness (Jost and Banaji, 1994; Jost, Banaji and Nosek, 2004), men and women are equally likely to penalize gender deviants (e.g., Phelan, Moss-Racusin and Rudman, 2008; Rudman and Phelan, 2008). Thus, research testing the SIH suggests that only the gender stereotypes linked to status result in backlash, and that motivations to uphold the existing gender status hierarchy are responsible for backlash against gender-deviant men and women.

A1: Only status-linked stereotype violations lead to backlash

Because status violations are responsible for backlash, only gender stereotypes that are fundamentally linked to perceptions of status for women and men result in backlash. Rudman et al. (2012a) measured the extent to which the four sets of gender stereotypes are associated with status (see Table 11.1). Results indicated that for women, proscriptions against dominance (i.e., what women must not be) were associated with high status, whereas prescriptions requiring communality (i.e., what women must be) were viewed as neutral in status. Experimental tests confirmed that only violations of dominance proscriptions result in backlash for women. Thus, women must avoid enacting dominance, because it is associated with high status and thus challenges the existing hierarchy. However, because communal behavior is not associated with status, failing to be communal did not have backlash consequences for women (Rudman et al., 2012a, 2012b).

However, the nature of male backlash is quite different. For men, violations of both status-linked prescriptions and proscriptions are linked to status, and thus lead to backlash. Agency prescriptions (i.e., what men must be) were linked to high status, while dominance proscriptions (i.e., what men must not be) were linked to low status (Moss-Racusin et al., 2010; Rudman et al., 2012a). Experimental evidence confirmed that male backlash results from violations of both agency prescriptions and dominance proscriptions. Men must enact high-status agentic behavior while simultaneously being vigilant to avoid any displays of low-status weakness, because both would challenge the existing gender hierarchy. Thus, because male backlash stems from violations of both prescriptive and proscriptive stereotypes (compared to only proscriptive violations resulting in female backlash), men's acceptable range of behaviors is even narrower than women's (Moss-Racusin et al., 2010; Rudman et al., 2013). As a result, men in organizations must be constantly on guard to appear both sufficiently high in status and not excessively low in status. The fact that, for men, both gender rules have status implications – and thus result in backlash – may help to shed light on why manhood is a more precarious state than womanhood, and in turn, why men often respond aggressively against threats to their masculinity (Bosson and Vandello, 2011).

A2: Defending the gender hierarchy motivates backlash

The results outlined above support the SIH's central argument that backlash functions to uphold the existing status hierarchy. By extension, the core motivation driving people's tendency to respond to stereotype violators with backlash should be their desire to defend the current system (Jost and Banaji, 1994; Jost, Banaji and Nosek; 2004). Indeed, Rudman et al. (2012a, Study 3) determined that the strength of observers' system-justifying beliefs predicted their propensity to administer backlash to gender-deviant women. That is, individuals who were most chronically invested in upholding the existing social system were the most likely to penalize women who posed a threat to it. Providing more direct experimental evidence, backlash was most severe when observers experienced a threat to the existing social system. In contrast, when observers did not feel that the existing system was threatened, they were less likely to administer backlash against gender-deviant women (Rudman et al., 2012a, Study 4). Future work should directly test the idea that backlash against gender-deviant men is also motivated by a desire to defend the existing gender status quo.

Taken together, these results support the status incongruity hypothesis and suggest that a pervasive, automatic desire to defend the existing gender hierarchy motivates backlash against gender deviants. In so doing, this research shed light on the processes underlying negative reactions to people who violate our shared assumptions about how men and women should behave, in two main ways. First, these results identify the specific gender stereotype violations that are culpable in backlash. Because only gender stereotypes linked to status result in penalties, gender-deviant women are penalized for their excessive dominance, rather than their insufficient communality. In contrast, gender-deviant men must walk an even narrower tightrope, facing backlash both for insufficient agency and excessive weakness.

Additionally, the SIH sheds light on the motivator behind backlash effects. Because people are fundamentally driven to uphold the existing social structure even when doing so is not necessarily in their best interest (Jost and Banaji, 1994; Jost et al., 2004), they are likely to penalize men and women who deviate from their assigned positions in the social hierarchy (Moss-Racusin et al., 2010; Rudman et al., 2012a, 2012b; Rudman et al., 2013). For organizations, this suggests that backlash will continue to plague male employees who violate traditional gender stereotypes by behaving in ways that are discordant with the high-status roles they are expected to occupy, even when this behavior is in the best interests of the company.

UNANSWERED QUESTIONS AND SUGGESTIONS FOR FUTURE RESEARCH

The work reviewed in this chapter represents significant progress in understanding penalties directed against men who violate gender stereotypes, and how this backlash directly impacts organizations. However, the existing research highlights compelling unanswered questions, and points toward fruitful areas for further inquiry.

Notably, future work should seek to determine whether backlash differentially affects men from various social groups. The vast majority of existing research has focused on backlash directed against gender-deviant men who are white (Rudman et al., 2012b), and typically described in terms that would likely lead observers to assume that they are heterosexual and middle or upper class. The few experiments that serve as exceptions to this rule suggest that backlash (and indeed, gender stereotypes themselves) may function noticeably differently for gender deviants from different racial groups. For example, black NFL players who celebrated after

touchdowns were penalized significantly more so than identical white athletes, suggesting that high-status dominance displays may be proscribed
(and thus, result in backlash) for black but not white men (Hall and
Livingston, 2012). This finding is consistent with the SIH; because black
men have traditionally occupied a lower rung on the status hierarchy relative to white men, it follows that their dominance displays should be met
with corrective backlash. Of importance, these findings reveal opposite
reactions to black and white men, suggesting that the established literature
on gender stereotype content (e.g., men must be dominant) may apply
predominately or solely to white targets.

Indeed, some research has suggested that the gender rules may be completely reversed for black targets. In another experiment, black female and
white male leaders did not encounter backlash for dominant workplace
behavior (i.e., chastising a subordinate for their poor performance, and
directly discussing a plan for improvement; Livingston, Rosette and
Washington, 2012). These results run contrary to established findings
demonstrating backlash against dominant (white) women (e.g., Rudman,
1998). In contrast, black male leaders and white female leaders did receive
backlash for this stereotype-violating behavior, again contradicting past
research indicating that (white) men do not encounter backlash for
dominance (and in fact, are penalized when they *fail to be dominant*; Moss-
Racusin et al., 2010). This suggests that in a reversal from the previous
literature, black males appear to be penalized for dominance, while black
women appear to have more latitude for this behavior. Additionally, initial
research examining reactions to dominant Asian employees indicated that
male and female Asian targets were equally likely to encounter backlash
for violating the racial proscription against Asian dominance (Berdahl
and Min, 2012). In this case, it appears that a racial stereotype may be
equally applied to group members of both genders, or that race-based
backlash may have masked the effect of backlash based on gender. In
either case, there was no evidence that female Asian employees were penalized for their dominant behavior more so than their male counterparts.

Taken together, these findings highlight the pressing need for additional
programs of research investigating the impact of individuals' social group
memberships on the backlash they may (or may not) encounter when
violating stereotypes. Future work should seek to determine how prescriptive and proscriptive stereotypes for men and women vary for different
racial groups, and how these differing gender rules lead to diverse rates
of backlash. Additionally, research has yet to investigate whether gender
stereotypes and backlash vary as a function of social identities beyond racial
group membership, such as sexuality, class, education level, and so on.

As a broader point, additional work studying backlash from an intersectional perspective is urgently needed. When researchers have examined reactions to non-white targets, they have largely investigated the impact of various social categories (such as race and gender) on judgments and treatments of individuals in parallel, rather than taking an intersectional perspective to examine the simultaneous impact of both racial and gender group membership within the same study (e.g., Gonzalez, Blaton and Williams, 2002; Goff, Thomas, and Jackson, 2008; Purdie-Vaughns and Eibach, 2008; Wilton, Good, Moss-Racusin and Sanchez, 2013). This paucity of intersectional research is particularly detrimental for work on backlash, which draws upon basic social categorization processes to shed light on person perception, prejudice, and discrimination. As illustrated by the reversal of traditional backlash effects for black employees discussed above, arriving at a complete understanding of penalties against gender deviants is impossible without considering their simultaneous membership in multiple social groups.

Future research should also attempt to identify whether there are circumstances in which gender-deviant men are shielded from some elements of backlash in response to stereotype violations. For example, some research has found that men who behave modestly are disliked, but are not less likely to be hired, relative to comparable women (i.e., that they experience social but not economic penalties, whereas gender-deviant women experience both; Moss-Racusin et al., 2010). This raises the possibility that men's elevated status as a group may buffer them from the most severe forms of backlash under some circumstances. However, it remains unknown whether these findings would generalize to other circumstances, and whether prejudice would lead to different forms of workplace discrimination over time. That is, even if a modest man is initially hired for a position, being disliked could pose serious impediments to workplace productivity and advancement over the course of his career. In any case, the status incongruity hypothesis argues that status (rather than role) violations are responsible for backlash. If this is accurate, then men should have latitude to engage in behavior that violates some gender role expectations, as long as they are perceived to be high in status. For example, future research should examine whether a male CEO who engages in stereotypically feminine activities (e.g., baking, knitting) might avoid backlash by virtue of his high-status position, whereas the identical stereotype-violating behavior might be judged harshly when enacted by a low-status male assistant in the same company. If the SIH's process predictions are correct, then congruent (i.e., high) status may serve as a buffer against backlash for men's role-incongruent (i.e., stereotypically feminine) behavior.

Finally, research should test a variety of intervention strategies that might effectively reduce backlash against stereotype-violating men, in order to enable them to freely engage in the full range of behaviors that are currently restricted by backlash for violating hyper-masculine stereotypes. To my knowledge, no existing research has tested intervention strategies that might protect men from the effects of backlash. However, one study has identified a buffering factor that alleviates the negative impacts of backlash against gender-deviant women. Specifically, female MBA students who were high on self-monitoring (i.e., the ability to accurately assess social situations and to project situationally appropriate responses; Snyder and Gangestad, 1986) avoided backlash for aggressiveness and actually received more promotions than comparable male students and low self-monitoring women over an eight-year period (O'Neill and O'Reilly, 2011). This suggests that being attuned to social cues and tempering stereotype-violating behavior with stereotype-consistent behavior may be a route out of backlash. However, the specific impression management strategy employed by high self-monitors to avoid backlash (as well as whether good self-monitoring skills can be trained) remains unknown, and should be investigated by future research. The question of whether self-monitoring would be similarly effective for gender-deviant men has also yet to be tested.

Additional work should seek to develop inventive strategies that enable both men and women to express the full range of human behavior without fear of backlash. This is particularly critical for men, who face a powerful catch-22 in choosing between the consequences associated with hyper-masculine stereotype compliance and backlash for its violation. Organizations – which are populated by men driven to risky financial decisions, ineffective communication strategies, and anti-egalitarian behavior by pressure to adhere to hyper-masculine stereotypes – have an explicit investment in identifying remedies for backlash.

CONCLUSIONS

Because gender stereotypes largely confer high levels of power and privilege on men relative to women (Eagly, 1987; Ridgeway, 2001), their detrimental effects on men often remain overlooked (Pollack, 1999). However, just as researchers have identified the ways in which gender-stereotyping processes constrain women's behavior and progress, it is critical to recognize the ways in which male gender stereotypes can powerfully limit men's free expression. Indeed, pressure to adhere to hyper-masculine stereotypes presents men with an unattainable ideal. When men attempt to uphold this unrealistic masculinity, there are serious consequences for their health, relationships, and the organizations they serve. When they instead resist the pressures to conform to masculine stereotypes, they risk severe backlash, and endanger their professional advancement. As a result, organizations should strive to gain a better understanding of the ways in which workplace masculinity pressures, coupled with the threat of backlash, can powerfully undermine the performance of male employees. Because organizations have a vested interest in optimal productivity, efficient communication, high morale and thoughtful decision-making, backlash must be identified and targeted, such that all employees – both male and female – are no longer prevented from reaching their full potential.

REFERENCES

Addis, M.E. and J.R. Mahalik (2003), 'Men, masculinity, and the contexts of help seeking', *American Psychologist*, **58**(1), 5–14.

Berdahl, J.L. (2007), 'Harassment based on sex: Protecting social status in the context of gender hierarchy', *Academy of Management Review*, **32**(2), 641–58.

Berdahl, J.L. and J. Min (2012), 'Prescriptive stereotypes and workplace consequences for East Asians in North America', *Cultural Diversity and Ethnic Minority Psychology*, **18**(2), 141–52.

Bosson, J.K. and J.A. Vandello (2011), 'Precarious manhood and its links to action and aggression', *Current Directions in Psychological Science*, **20**(2), 82–6.

Bosson, J.K., J.L. Prewitt-Freilino and J.N. Taylor (2005), 'Role rigidity: A problem of identity misclassification?', *Journal of Personality and Social Psychology*, **89**(4), 552–65.

Bosson, J.K., J.A. Vandello, R.M. Burnaford, J.R. Weaver and S.A. Wasti (2009), 'Precarious manhood and displays of physical aggression', *Personality and Social Psychology Bulletin*, **35**(5), 623–34.

Brescoll, V.L. and T.G. Okimoto (2010), 'The price of power: Power seeking and backlash against female politicians', *Personality and Social Psychology Bulletin*, **36**(7), 923–36.

Brescoll, V.L. and E.L. Uhlmann (2008), 'Can an angry woman get ahead? Gender, status conferral, and workplace emotion expression', *Psychological Science*, **19**(3), 268–75.

Brescoll, V.L., J. Glass and A. Sedlovskaya (2013), 'Ask and ye shall receive? The dynamics of employer-provided flexible work options and the need for public policy', *Journal of Social Issues*, **69**(2), 367–88.

Brescoll, V.L., E.L. Uhlmann, C.A. Moss-Racusin and L. Sarnell (2012), 'Masculinity, status and subordination: Why working for a stereotype violator causes men to lose status', *Journal of Experimental Social Psychology*, **48**(1), 354–7.

Broverman, I.K., S.R. Vogel, D.M. Broverman, F.E. Clarkson and P.S. Rosenkrantz (1972), 'Sex-role stereotypes: A current appraisal', *Journal of Social Issues*, **28**(2), 59–78.

Burgess, D. and E. Borgida (1999), 'Who women are, who women should be:

Descriptive and prescriptive stereotyping in sex discrimination', *Psychology, Public Policy, and Law*, **5**(3), 665–92.

Burke, R.J. and S. Black (1997), 'Save the males: Backlash in organizations', *Journal of Business Ethics*, **16**, 933–42.

Burn, S.M. and Z.A. Ward (2005), 'Men's conformity to traditional masculinity and relationship satisfaction', *Psychology of Men and Masculinity*, **6**(4), 254–63.

Cherry, F. and K. Deaux (1978), 'Fear of success versus fear of gender-inappropriate behavior', *Sex Roles*, **4**(1), 97–101.

Costrich, N., J. Feinstein, L. Kidder, J. Marecek and L. Pascale (1975), 'When stereotypes hurt: Three studies of penalties for sex-role reversals', *Journal of Experimental Social Psychology*, **11**(6), 520–30.

Courtenay, W.H. (2000a), 'Engendering health: A social constructionist examination of men's health beliefs and behaviors', *Psychology of Men and Masculinity*, **1**(1), 4–15.

Courtenay, W.H. (2000b), 'Behavioral factors associated with disease, injury, and death among men: Evidence and implications for prevention', *The Journal of Men's Studies*, **9**(1), 81–142.

Derlega, V.J. and A.L. Chaiken (1976), 'Norms affecting self-disclosure in men and women', *Journal of Consulting and Clinical Psychology*, **44**(3), 376–80.

Diekman, A.B., W. Goodfriend and S. Goodwin (2004), 'Dynamic stereotypes of power: Perceived change and stability in gender hierarchies', *Sex Roles*, **50**(3/4), 201–15.

Eagly, A.H. (1987), *Sex Differences in Social Behavior: A Social-role Interpretation*, Hillsdale, NJ: Lawrence Erlbaum Associates.

Eagly, A.H. and S.J. Karau (2002), 'Role congruity theory of prejudice toward female leaders', *Psychological Review*, **109**(3), 573–98.

Ely, R.J. and D. Meyerson (2008), 'Unmasking manly men', *Harvard Business Review*, **86**(7/8), 1–3.

Erikson, W. and S. Einarsen (2004), 'Gender minority as a risk factor of exposure to bullying at work: The case of male assistant nurses', *European Journal of Work and Organizational Psychology*, **13**(4), 473–92.

Gill, M.J. (2004), 'When information does not deter stereotyping: Prescriptive stereotyping can foster bias under conditions that deter descriptive stereotyping', *Journal of Experimental Social Psychology*, **40**(5), 619–32.

Glick, P. and S.T. Fiske (2001), 'An ambivalent alliance: Hostile and benevolent sexism as complementary justifications of gender inequality', *American Psychologist*, **56**(2), 109–18.

Glick, P., C. Gangl, S. Gibb, S. Klumpner and E. Weinberg (2007), 'Defensive reactions to masculinity threat: More negative affect toward effeminate (but not masculine) gay men', *Sex Roles*, **57**(1–2), 55–9.

Goff, P.A., M.A. Thomas and M.C. Jackson (2008), '"Ain't I a woman?" Towards an intersectional approach to person perception and group-based harms', *Sex Roles*, **59**(5–6), 392–403.

Gonzales, P.M., H. Blanton and K.J. Williams (2002), 'The effects of stereotype threat and double-minority status on the test performance of Latino women', *Personality and Social Psychology Bulletin*, **28**(5), 659–70.

Good, J.J. and C.A. Moss-Racusin (2010), '"But, that doesn't apply to me": Teaching college students to think about gender', *Psychology of Women Quarterly*, **34**(3), 418–21.

Hall, E.V. and R.W. Livingston (2012), 'The hubris penalty: Biased responses to "celebration" displays of black football players', *Journal of Experimental Social Psychology*, **48**(4), 899–904.

Hayes, J.A. and J.R. Mahalik (2000), 'Gender role conflict and psychological distress in male counseling center clients', *Psychology of Men and Masculinity*, **1**(2), 116–25.

Heilman, M.E. (2001), 'Description and prescription: How gender stereotypes prevent women's ascent up the organizational ladder', *Journal of Social Issues*, **57**(4), 657–74.

Heilman, M.E. and A.S. Wallen (2010), 'Wimpy and undeserving of respect: Penalties for men's gender-inconsistent success', *Journal of Experimental Social Psychology*, **46**(4), 664–7.

Heilman, M.E., A.S. Wallen, D. Fuchs and M.M. Tamkins (2004), 'Penalties for success: Reactions to women who succeed at male gender-typed tasks', *Journal of Applied Psychology*, **89**(3), 416–27.

Jost, J.T. and M.R. Banaji (1994), 'The role of stereotyping in system-justification and the production of false-consciousness', *British Journal of Social Psychology*, **33**(1), 1–27.

Jost, J.T., M.R. Banaji and B.A. Nosek (2004), 'A decade of system justification theory: Accumulated evidence of conscious and unconscious bolstering of the status quo', *Political Psychology*, **25**(6), 881–919.

Kimmel, M.S. (2004), *The Gendered Society*, New York: Oxford University Press.

Levant, R.F. and W.S. Pollack (1995), *A New Psychology of Men*, New York: Basic Books.

Livingston, R.W., A.S. Rosette and E.F. Washington (2012), 'Can an agentic black woman get ahead? The impact of race and interpersonal dominance on perceptions of female leaders', *Psychological Science*, **23**(4), 354–8.

Magovcevic, M. and M.E. Addis (2008), 'The masculine depression scale: Development and psychometric evaluation', *Psychology of Men and Masculinity*, **9**(3), 117–32.

Mahalik, J.R., B.D. Locke, L.H. Ludlow, M.A. Diemer, R.P.J. Scott, M. Gottfried and G. Freitas (2003), 'Development of the conformity to masculine norms inventory', *Psychology of Men and Masculinity*, **4**(1), 3–25.

Moss-Racusin, C.A. and L.A. Rudman (2010), 'Disruptions in women's self-promotion: The backlash avoidance model', *Psychology of Women Quarterly*, **34**(2), 186–202.

Moss-Racusin, C.A., J.E. Phelan and L.A. Rudman (2010), 'When men break the gender rules: Status incongruity and backlash against modest men', *Psychology of Men and Masculinity*, **11**(2), 140–51.

Moss-Racusin, C.A., J.F. Dovidio, V.L. Brescoll, M. Graham and J. Handelsman (2012), 'Science faculty's subtle gender biases favor male students', *Proceedings of the National Academy of Sciences*, **109**(41), 167–79.

O'Neill, O.A. and C.A. O'Reilly (2011), 'Reducing the backlash effect: Self-monitoring and women's promotions', *Journal of Occupational and Organizational Psychology*, **84**(4), 825–32.

Parrott, D.J. and A. Zeichner (2003), 'Effects of hypermasculinity on physical aggression against women', *Psychology of Men and Masculinity*, **4**(1), 70–78.

Phelan, J.E., C.A. Moss-Racusin and L.A. Rudman (2008), 'Competent yet out in the cold: Shifting criteria for hiring reflect backlash towards agentic women', *Psychology of Women Quarterly*, **32**(4), 406–13.

Pollack, W.S. (1999), *Real Boys*, New York: Henry Holt and Company.

Prentice, D.A. and E. Carranza (2002), 'What women and men should be, shouldn't be, are allowed to be, and don't have to be: The contents of prescriptive gender stereotypes', *Psychology of Women Quarterly*, **26**(4), 269–81.

Prime, J. and C.A. Moss-Racusin (2009), *Engaging Men in Gender Initiatives: What Change Agents Need to Know*, New York: Catalyst.

Prime, J., C.A. Moss-Racusin and H. Foust-Cummings (2009), *Engaging Men in Gender Initiatives: Stacking the Deck for Success*, New York: Catalyst.

Purdie-Vaughns, V. and R.P. Eibach (2008), 'Intersectional invisibility: The distinctive advantages and disadvantages of multiple subordinate-group identities', *Sex Roles*, **59**(5–6), 337–91.

Reidy, D.E., S.D. Shirk, C.A. Sloan and A. Zeichner (2009), 'Men who aggress against women: Effects of feminine gender role violation on physical aggression in hypermasculine men', *Psychology of Men and Masculinity*, **10**(1), 1–12.

Ridgeway, C.L. (2001), 'Gender, status, and leadership', *Journal of Social Issues*, **57**(4), 627–55.

Rudman, L.A. (1998), 'Self-promotion as a risk factor for women: The costs and benefits of counterstereotypical impression management', *Journal of Personality and Social Psychology*, **74**(3), 629–45.

Rudman, L.A. and K. Fairchild (2004), 'Reactions to counterstereotypic behavior: The role of backlash in cultural stereotype maintenance', *Journal of Personality and Social Psychology*, **87**(2), 157–76.

Rudman, L.A. and P. Glick (1999), 'Feminized management and backlash toward agentic women: The hidden costs to women of a kinder, gentler image of middle managers', *Journal of Personality and Social Psychology*, **77**(5), 1004–10.

Rudman, L.A. and P. Glick (2001), 'Prescriptive gender stereotypes and backlash toward agentic women', *Journal of Social Issues*, **57**(4), 732–62.

Rudman, L.A. and P. Glick (2008), *The Social Psychology of Gender: How Power and Intimacy Shape Gender Relations*, New York: Guilford.

Rudman, L.A. and K. Mescher (2013), 'Penalizing men who request a family leave: Is flexibility stigma a femininity stigma?', *Journal of Social Issues*, **69**(2), 322–40.

Rudman, L.A. and J.E. Phelan (2008), 'Backlash effects for disconfirming gender stereotypes in organizations', in A.P. Brief and B.M. Staw (eds), *Research in Organizational Behavior, Vol. 4*, New York, Elsevier, pp. 61–79.

Rudman, L.A., K. Mescher and C.A. Moss-Racusin (2013), 'Reactions to gender egalitarian men: Perceived feminization due to stigma-by-association?', *Group Processes and Intergroup Relations*, **16**, 572–599.

Rudman, L.A., C.A. Moss-Racusin, J.E. Phelan and S. Nauts (2012a), 'Status incongruity and backlash effects: Defending the gender hierarchy motivates prejudice against female leaders', *Journal of Experimental Social Psychology*, **48**, 165–79.

Rudman, L.A., C.A. Moss-Racusin, P. Glick and J.E. Phelan (2012b), 'Reactions to vanguards: Advances in backlash theory', in P.G. Devine and E.A. Plant (eds), *Advances in Experimental Social Psychology, Vol. 45*, San Diego: Academic Press, pp. 167–227.

Snyder, M. and S. Gangestad (1986), 'On the nature of self-monitoring: Matters of assessment, matters of validity', *Journal of Personality and Social Psychology*, **51**(1), 125–39.

Vandello, J.A., J.K. Bosson, D. Cohen, R.M. Burnaford and J.R. Weaver (2008), 'Precarious manhood', *Journal of Personality and Social Psychology*, **95**(6), 1325–39.

Weaver, J.R., J.A. Vandello and J.K. Bosson (2013), 'Intrepid, imprudent, or impetuous? The effects of gender threats on men's financial decisions', *Psychology of Men and Masculinity*, **14**(2), 184–91.

Weaver, J.R., J.A. Vandello, J.K. Bosson and R.M. Burnaford (2010), 'The proof is in the punch: Gender differences in perceptions of action and aggression as components of manhood', *Sex Roles*, **62**(3), 241–51.

West, T.V., M.E. Heilman, C.A. Moss-Racusin, R. Gullett and J.C. Magee (2012), 'Building blocks of bias: Gender composition predicts male and female group members' evaluations of each other and the group', *Journal of Experimental Social Psychology*, **48**(5), 1209–12.

Williams, J. (2000), *Unbending Gender: Why Family and Work Conflict and What To Do About It*, New York: Oxford University Press.

Williams, J.E. and D.L. Best (1990), *Measuring Sex Stereotypes: A Multination Study*, Newbury Park, CA: Sage.

Wilton, L.S., J.J. Good, C.A. Moss-Racusin and D.T. Sanchez (under review), 'Communicating diversity and bias: The role of institutional diversity statements on performance expectations for women of color', *Psychology of Women Quarterly*.

12. Stereotype threat impacts on women in the workforce

Valerie N. Streets and Hannah-Hanh D. Nguyen

INTRODUCTION

The perceived and actual impacts of gender stereotypes on women's life and work outcomes have long been described and evidenced in the broad interdisciplinary literature on stigmatization and discrimination (see Major and O'Brien, 2005). Gender stereotypes about women are consisted of socio-cultural beliefs about women's characteristics (as compared with those of men's): (1) women are inherently kind, warm, caring, nurturing, agreeable, sensitive, and sympathetic (i.e., being *communal*; Heilman, 2001), and (2) women should not be ambitious, competitive, outspoken, independent, and assertive or aggressive because those are men's characteristics (i.e., being *agentic*; Burgess and Borgida, 1999; Heilman, 2001). Gender-based stereotypes are also composed of negative stigmas about women's inferior abilities or capabilities, such as their lack of aggression and competence to lead a military in a national crisis (e.g., Huddy and Terkildsen, 1993), and their underperformance in mathematics and science fields compared with men (e.g., Spencer et al., 1999), a phenomenon known as stereotype threat (Steele and Aronson, 1995).

In this chapter, we will first present the classic definition of stereotype threat as affecting women's intellectual ability, and then focus on possible impacts of negative stereotype consequences in work- and career-related areas. Those impacts may include a hindrance or an obstacle to women's entering the workforce, choosing a career, and/or advancing with their career. Throughout the chapter, we will review the empirical literature of interest based on three conceptual premises that may facilitate or exacerbate the stereotype threat effects of women's career issues whenever appropriate: (1) when a challenging task is inconsistent with female gender stereotypes; (2) when a woman is made aware of her devalued gender membership in a stereotyped career domain, and/or (3) when environmental factors also reinforce female gender stereotypes. When possible, we will also review suggested intervention tactics in the literature, particularly those involving the role of men (a constant source of outgroup social comparison for women), that might either neutralize said stereotype threat effects or promoting self-efficacy among women in the workforce.

BACKGROUND OF STEREOTYPE THREAT

Definition

Stereotype threat was first introduced in the literature by Steele and Aronson (1995). According to the authors, stereotype threat occurs when a common negative stereotype exists regarding one's demographic group, and that stereotype indicates to targets that any of their features or behaviors that conform to the stereotype are characteristic of them. Simply put, members of groups targeted by negative stereotypes (e.g., women; minorities) are at risk for confirming those stereotypic ideas as true of themselves. In their meta-analysis on the experimental evidence of stereotype threat effects on cognitive performance of several stereotyped groups (i.e., women and minority test takers), Nguyen and Ryan (2008) noted that stereotype threat can be triggered in a blatant fashion, via explicit presentation of stereotypical information, or in a subtle manner through the simple acknowledgement of one's sociodemographic identity. Women would, paradoxically, experience more performance decline when stereotype threat was triggered subtly than when a blatant cue was introduced to the testing environment.

Why Does Stereotype Threat Occur?

A number of empirical findings have emerged regarding the operational mechanisms that underlie the performance decrements associated with stereotype threat. The research is largely clustered into three types of processes: physiological, emotional, and cognitive. Ultimately, no single mechanism has been deemed a genesis; rather there is situational support for all of them.

Physiological mechanism
A variety of measures have been used to gauge physiological arousal among stereotype-threatened individuals. Croizet et al. (2004) used heart rate measures as an indication of stereotype threat; the researchers found that participants within a stereotype threat condition experienced a

sharper increase in their heart rate, and maintained a higher heart rate, than those not threatened. Such outcomes are indicative of heightened mental load and anxiety caused by stereotype threat. Victims of stereotype threat also displayed a greater level of skin conductance and reduced skin temperature, and other signs of physiological arousal under stereotype threat (Osborne and Walker, 2006). Arousal increases with task difficulty: Blascovich et al. (2001) found increased blood pressure among stereotype-threatened participants on more challenging test questions.

Emotional mechanism

From an emotional standpoint, stereotype threat effects have been partially explained by negative thoughts and feelings of dejection (Keller and Dauenheimer, 2003). Cadinu et al. (2005) tested this assertion by asking participants who completed a math test to engage in a thought-listing technique: stereotype-threatened women listed a greater number of negative thoughts about the test and mathematics in general than did those not threatened. Such thoughts and emotions can then lead to lowered performance expectations, which correspond with self-handicapping via reduced effort, and worse task performance (Stangor et al., 1998; Stone, 2002; Cadinu et al., 2003).

Cognitive mechanism

Recent research suggests that the aforementioned mechanisms act in tandem to deplete one's available cognitive resources (Beilock et al., 2007). For example, Schmader and Johns (2003) assessed the short-term memory system that controls, regulates, and retains task-relevant information of women exposed to stereotype threat within a math test context. Specifically, they measured women's short-term memory with a word recall task and found that threatened women exhibited both lower math scores and poorer recall than did non-threatened participants. This reduced working memory capacity can then diminish stereotype threat victims' ability to regulate their attention and behavior when needed (Inzlicht et al., 2006).

Which Women are Most Vulnerable to Stereotype Threat?

A number of individual factors place women at a greater risk for stereotype threat effects. Three general categories of influences have emerged from the research literature: (1) one's stereotype awareness, (2) level of identification, and (3) level of empowerment.

Stigma consciousness

Chronic awareness of one's stigmatized status resulting from a stereotype was introduced by Pinel (1999) as stigma consciousness. Brown and Pinel (2003) found that, under conditions of stereotype threat, women high in stigma consciousness regarding their math abilities performed worse on a math test than did women low on the construct. This pattern becomes especially problematic if any endorsement of the stereotypes is present, as women who subscribe to gender stereotypic beliefs are especially susceptible to stereotype threat effects (Schmader et al., 2004).

Gender and domain identification

Women can either identify with their gender or with the domain of ability in question. Researchers have found that gender identification, or a sense of deep attachment to one's gender group and characteristics of that group, tends to affect women threatened on math tasks (e.g., Marx et al., 2005). Women with high levels of gender identification are most adversely affected when the task is framed in such a way that it questions the ability of women as a group rather than that of the individual (Wout et al., 2008).

Domain identification, or the amount of value one places on achievement within a given area, has been shown to be positively related to stereotype threat effects (Aronson et al., 1999). For example, Keller (2007) found that women who strongly identified with the domain of mathematics and cared about succeeding within that realm showed greater performance decrements under stereotype threat than did women who did not view math as a critical component of their self-concept. Furthermore, Nguyen and Ryan (2008) showed that women who are only moderately identified with the math domain suffer more from the effect of stereotype threat than did those highly identified with math. Perhaps highly math-identified women have a built-in level of stereotype reactance (i.e., acting in the opposite direction of the stereotype because they perceive the stereotype as a limit to their freedom and ability to perform; see Kray et al., 2001).

Empowerment

Women also vary on the degree to which they feel empowered against negative stereotypes. Much of this occurs because of one's locus of control, or the amount that a woman attributes her experiences to her own actions. Women with an internal locus of control (i.e., assuming responsibility for her actions) are more susceptible to stereotype threat (Cadinu et al., 2006). Additionally, proactive personality (i.e., a stable inclination to affect change and resist situational constraints; Bateman and Crant, 1993) is positively related to stereotype threat sensitivity. Specifically, more proactive women are less interested in pursuing careers in a field in which a negative stereotype exists for them (Gupta and Bhawe, 2007). These findings may seem counterintuitive, as more empowered individuals might be expected to buck negative stereotypes more effectively than women with less empowerment. However, perhaps empowered women have a greater investment in performing well. Thus, the stakes are higher and the situation becomes more threatening.

CAREER DECISIONS AND ENTRY

In this section, we focus on the role of stereotype threat in shaping the careers of women, specifically as women begin to embark upon the career decision-making and initiation processes. Essentially, in the early phases of women's career development, stereotype threat plays a major role in two distinct ways. First, stereotype threat has been consistently linked to domain avoidance and (lowered) career aspirations (Steele et al., 2002; Davies et al., 2005). In other words, the presence of stereotype threat within a given field or career path may cause women to become less inclined to pursue that route, avoiding the risk of not being able to perform well and thus confirming the stereotypes. Second, stereotype threat causes actual performance decrements for women (Steele and Aronson, 1995), hindering the chance for women to gain valuable achievements and qualifications for certain jobs as do men. We will consider both of these effects within career contexts in which negative stereotypes about women exist. Special attention will be paid to science, technology, engineering, and mathematics (STEM) fields, as these are the target of most stereotype threat research involving women.

Avoidance of Male-dominated Domains

Expected devaluation
One of the earliest ways stereotype threat can affect women's career development is through its impact on career aspirations and decisions. This relationship largely exists through a social identity threat, which occurs when women recognize the potential for being devalued in a given field because of their gender. The devaluation is expected because women are aware of the negative stereotypes that surround their identity (i.e., they lack leadership aptitude; Crocker et al., 1998). Social identity threat then leads to stereotype threat effects by creating apprehension among threatened individuals that they will confirm the stereotypes, thereby validating their devaluation (Steele et al., 2002). This fact translates to less female interest in a male-dominated career, because they expect to be in

the minority, and because they perceive themselves as having fewer abilities than men as far as work tasks in that field are concerned (Murphy et al., 2007).

Additionally, such pessimistic expectations can compromise the job interview performance of women who do pursue jobs in male-dominated fields and organizations. Research has established that in situations where the stakes are high and the need to succeed is great, such as in the context of standardized tests and job interviews (Kray et al., 2001; Frantz et al., 2004; Marx et al., 2005), individuals become more vulnerable to stereotype threat effects on their performance.

Domain disidentification

STEM in higher education provides an excellent exemplification of this pattern. According to the National Science Foundation (2013), 33 percent of freshman women declare or intend to declare a STEM major, with most of those women enrolling in social and life sciences, whereas 44 percent of freshman men report current enrollment or intent to enroll in a STEM major, with a fairly even distribution among departments. The gender disparity is more pronounced in terms of retention, with men almost doubling the number of STEM degrees that women earn (NSF, 2013). Much of this is believed to be attributable to women's disidentifying themselves from these domains (Steele, 1997).

Rather than denying themselves the opportunity to further their education, women who feel threatened in this domain often choose to switch to academic areas that are not surrounded by negative gender stereotypes: Steele et al. (2002) administered questionnaires to female freshman and senior college students, inquiring about their academic experiences. They found that women in male-dominated majors (i.e., STEM majors) reported greater feelings of threat related to negative gender stereotypes and a higher likelihood of changing their majors. Furthermore, women report a decreased interest in pursuing math following subtle reminders of their gender (Steele and Ambady, 2006), thereby indicating that stereotypes do not need to be made explicit to affect women within male-dominated contexts.

Decreased sense of belongingness

Stereotype threat also reduces women's sense of belonging and persistence within stereotyped fields or domains (e.g., in math fields; Good et al., 2012). A sense of belonging to a STEM domain is important for women because the feeling of belongingness can override achievement and performance in determining one's intentions to pursue or remain within that field (Steele, 1997). For example, Rattan and Dweck (2010) found that, as women's experience of math-related stereotype threat increased, their subsequent sense of belonging decreased, which in turn predicted women's poorer math grades.

Moreover, stereotype threat in the form of unbalanced gender representation in the workplace can prevent women from joining a male-dominated organization. For example, Murphy et al. (2007) showed videos promoting a math, science, and engineering department, which was either balanced in the numbers of men and women, or featured men outnumbering women. The researchers found that after watching the gender-unbalanced video, women displayed either a lack of interest in that department, or became highly anxious when thinking about joining that department.

Intervention tactics
The phenomenon of women avoiding male-dominated careers and/or workplace can be rectified through organizations actively reducing any emphasis of female stereotypes, enhancing women's gender and/or domain identities in the workplace. For example, organizations can encourage women job incumbents or female job candidates to focus on the characteristics that make them unique and valuable to the career domain or the organization that women may see as male-dominated. While this intervention tactic has yet to be explored in applied settings, Ambady and colleagues (2004) demonstrated its effectiveness in overcoming stereotype threat effects on math test performance. Women who were asked to reflect on their strengths and weaknesses and provide individuating information (i.e., characteristics that make them unique) prior to completing a math test did not suffer threat-induced performance decrements. Such positive priming allows targets of stereotype threat to consider themselves as individuals rather than as part of a stereotyped group.

Underperformance and Reduced Qualifications

Women are aware of stereotypes of their ineptitude within STEM fields (Jones et al., 1984) and leadership domains (Eagly et al., 1995). While such awareness often limits their willingness to pursue those areas, it can also hamper their performance within those areas and domains, thus diminishing their ability to succeed in those fields. As mentioned above, such stereotypes detract from women's sense of belonging within those domains, which in turn increases their performance anxiety and decreases their self-efficacy (Good et al., 2012). These internal states create a breeding ground for performance inhibitions among women in the workplace.

Environmental prompts of stereotype threat

Stereotype threat effects can happen without much prompting, particularly in male-dominated contexts. Merely asking women to indicate their gender before completing a task for which their performance is negatively stereotyped can elicit performance effects (Steele and Aronson, 1995; Yopyk and Prentice, 2005; McGlone and Aronson, 2006). For example, Danaher and Crandall (2008) found that when women were asked to report their gender prior to taking an Advanced Placement calculus exam, they performed worse than when they were asked to indicate their gender *after* completing the test. Specifically, the authors found an additional 5.9 percent of the women could have been expected to pass the exam had they been asked to provide their gender after the exam. Researchers have also shown that interacting with outgroup members (i.e., men; Marx and Goff, 2005) or being administered a task by an outgroup member (Stone and McWhinnie, 2008) are also detrimental to performance.

Findings of stereotype threat leading to women's underperformance indicate that women may be adversely affected in negatively stereotyped domains, such as in STEM fields, whether or not their interest and aspiration levels are impacted. Taken together, the studies cited above provide evidence to support the notion that stereotype threat creates a performance decrement among women. When such decrements are aggregated over time, threatened women may gradually lose the opportunity to develop critical task-related abilities and qualifications (e.g., credentials, experiences), and could eventually fall behind men in terms of having the capability to succeed within a given field such as in STEM areas.

Intervention tactics

As with targets' avoidance of stereotypically masculine domains, women's underperformance, reduced capabilities, and fewer qualifications can potentially be alleviated via a reduced emphasis on gendered identities. Rosenthal et al. (2007) found that when women are asked to list similarities between themselves and men in a testing group, they expected themselves to perform better on a math test, and actually performed that well, compared with women who were not asked to do so. Although it is still unclear whether or not real-world companies can apply this intervention tactic successfully to alleviate stereotype threat for women, organization researchers can certainly test the intervention tactic, for instance, by emphasizing values and required skills and characteristics that are gender neutral in the workplace. If female employees are primed to consider themselves through such a lens, they may be less likely to be attuned to stereotypical attitudes and expectations within the workplace.

CAREER OBSTACLES

Once women enter the workforce, stereotype threat is likely to remain a barrier on their career path. By affecting women's work attitudes, levels of identification with their careers, and behavior in the workplace, stereotype threat can continually shape women's career experiences in a negative direction. Here we give attention to each of the above ways that stereotyping would color women's experiences at work.

Effects on Women's Work Attitudes

While stereotype threat is often discussed with regard to its effects on task performance, it can also carry considerable implications for one's attitudes and career outlook. According to Roberson and Kulik (2007), regardless of personal beliefs or previous experiences, employees are aware of stereotypes that could potentially be applied to them. Further, upon entering a new organizational context, employees are left to wonder whether their supervisors and co-workers use such stereotypes in judging their work performance. Such concerns prove most problematic for employees who value and identify closely with their work and its quality (ibid.). These concerns do carry performance implications, as individuals exposed to superiors who are perceived to be prejudiced tend to perform worse than those exposed to neutral supervisors (Adams et al., 2006). For female employees, these effects are often exacerbated in male-dominated organizations: being in the minority, or in extreme cases, the sole woman in a work unit may lead women to underperformance per stereotype threat theory as previously mentioned. Inzlicht and Ben-Zeev (2000) demonstrated that women completing stereotyped tasks tend to suffer performance decrements that are proportionate to the number of men present. For this reason, unmanaged diversity in the workplace has been linked to low morale, high turnover rates, low job satisfaction, and interpersonal conflict (Tsui et al., 1992; Niemann and Dovidio, 1998; Jehn et al., 1999).

Reduced Work Identification

Disengagement
Awareness of negative stereotypes often leads to coping mechanisms in which targets protect their self-esteem by disengaging from the domain in question (Crocker and Major, 1989). Disengagement is understood as a detachment of one's self-esteem from one's performance in a stereotyped domain; in other words, an individual's self-worth is not at all predicated upon personal successes and/or failures within that domain. Additionally,

it is a contextual response, meaning that it occurs mainly in domains where poor performance (of the stereotyped individual) is anticipated (Major et al., 1998). Conversely, if those targeted by stereotype threat do not disengage, they may alter their self-evaluations. For example, girls had far lower assessments of their math ability than did boys who had equivalent math test scores (Eccles, 1998).

Feedback discounting
Disengagement can be detrimental both to the employee and the organization in that it can often result in the discounting of feedback. Stereotype threat contributes to a distrust in one's environment; when stereotypes are perceived to influence judgments within the organization, feedback and performance evaluations are seen as less credible (Roberson et al., 2003). In such cases, feedback is not viewed as indicative of one's ability or worth to the organization (Major and Crocker, 1993). While this has yet to be empirically explored for women at work, research on racial bias has shown that bias priming would result in greater feedback discounting among African Americans (Major et al., 1998).

This coping tactic can also be applied to one's personal identity (i.e., identity bifurcation), such that stereotype-threatened individuals distance themselves from group identities that may jeopardize their favorable evaluations of their own abilities. For example, women working within male-dominated contexts (e.g., engineering) stray from maintaining a stereotypically feminine appearance, engaging in flirtatious behavior or gossip, and expressing an interest in starting a family (Pronin et al., 2004).

Intervention tactics
Rather than fostering such coping mechanisms, organizations can look to combat stereotype threat by placing an emphasis on high standards while also providing assurance that employees have the capability to meet them. Cohen et al. (1999) found that pairing negative feedback with standards and assurance that the targeted individual can achieve those standards can eliminate perceptions of bias in superiors. Furthermore, coupling feedback with standards and encouragement was found to be preventative of threat-induced declines in motivation and disidentification with the domain. These findings have yet to be applied outside of a laboratory setting, but can easily be put into practice within an organizational context to bolster motivation and identification in situations that may otherwise breed stereotype threat effects.

Behavioral Implications

Avoiding challenging tasks

Stereotype threat also serves as a career obstacle for women in that it shapes how they may behave in the workplace. First, women who are targeted by negative stereotyping challenges are less likely to seize and overcome these challenges. The more a task is considered difficult, the more severely stereotype threat affects task performance (Spencer et al., 1999). This is particularly problematic for female employees and organizations alike, as task challenge is a recommended way to avoid boredom and increase learning and job involvement among workers (Greenberg, 1996). However, targets of stereotype threat or anticipated stereotyping are inclined to avoid challenging situations (Roberson and Kulik, 2007).

Deficient negotiation skills

Such avoidance can perpetuate the wage gap that women have long experienced, which is partly attributable to women's deficient skill of salary negotiation (e.g., Stuhlmacher and Walters, 1999; Babcock and Laschever, 2008). Stereotype threat is known to affect women during negotiation tasks. For example, in 2001, Kray and colleagues demonstrated that when gender stereotypes were activated prior to a negotiation, men experienced performance advantages whereas women suffered a disadvantage. Further, associating negotiation success with stereotypically masculine skills (e.g., problem solving) or gender-neutral skills (e.g., demonstrating patience) hindered women's performance in mixed-gender groups (Kray et al., 2002). While it would be inappropriate to blame stereotype threat for the existence of gendered pay inequities, the fact that it has been demonstrated within negotiation contexts presents an additional hurdle to women seeking pay equality in the workplace.

CAREER ADVANCEMENT AND LEADERSHIP

As briefly mentioned above, one particular consequence of stereotype threat on women in the workforce is that female stereotypes may hinder a woman's career advancement in male-dominated occupations, either by reducing their interest in pursuing leadership positions in organizations, and/or diminishing their self-efficacy in such positions. In this section, we will review relevant empirical evidence in the broad literature of women leadership and the (limited) stereotype threat literature on women's career advancement. Specifically, we will focus on two aspects of stereotype threat conditions pertaining to career development of women in the workforce: (1) when female gender stereotypes are incongruent with the selection criteria of leader roles, and (2) when the saliency of minority group membership (i.e., being a woman in a man's world) is heightened. Relevant career advancement and leadership-related outcomes for women will be considered in this context (e.g., career progress; career aspiration; entrepreneurial intentions; leadership self-efficacy; leadership domain identification), and recommendations based on the literature of stereotype threat will be integrated throughout this section when appropriate.

Incongruities between Women Stereotypes and Leadership Requirements

Disfavored as leaders

The theory of stereotype threat posits and evidences that individuals of a minority group may underperform on high-stakes tasks or domains the criteria of which are portrayed as too difficult or atypical for their social group to succeed (Steele, 1997). This applies to women facing the demanding requirements of leadership or supervisory positions, particularly in male-dominated occupations, simply because there appears to be an incongruence between female gender stereotypes and the characteristics of leadership roles (i.e., traditionally male). The phrase 'think manager–think male' (coined by Schein et al., 1996) succinctly summarizes this phenomenon.

In fact, Eagly and Karau (2002) reviewed the broad literature of prejudice towards female leaders and found that female leaders were perceived less favorably than males as either a leader or a leadership candidate; women assumingly have less ability to lead an organization than men because their inherent female characteristics (e.g., nurturing) are inconsistent with those of the typical leader role (e.g., aggressive). In the stereotype threat literature, Bergeron et al. (2006) and Gupta and colleagues (2007, 2008) provided preliminary experimental evidence supporting gender–work incongruent stereotypes. Bergeron et al. told women who were role-playing a manager that their predecessor had been either a man (with a stereotypically male, aggressive managerial style) or a woman (whose managerial style was stereotypically nurturing). Facing the implied inconsistency between the job requirements (being male and aggressive) and their gender characteristics, women in the 'male manager' group performed worse on the assigned managerial tasks than both women in the control group and men in either condition.

Likewise, Gupta and Bhawe (2007) described the characteristics of typical entrepreneurs as either gender neutral (i.e., creative, steady, generous, and well-informed) or male stereotypical (i.e., aggressive, risk-taking, and autonomous) to a group of female business students. The dependent variable was women's intentions to pursue entrepreneurship, which has been found to be positively associated with masculine characteristics and negatively related to feminine characteristics (Fagenson and Marcus, 1991; Ahl, 2006). As predicted, women's entrepreneurial intentions were lower under the male stereotype condition but only for women whose personality was characterized as proactive (i.e., willing to act to change environments; Crant, 1995). One consequence of such inconsistency is that it becomes difficult for women to be perceived as good leadership material, and to succeed in that capacity (Eagly and Karau, 2002).

Intervention tactics
On the other hand, removing male stereotypical characteristics from managerial and leadership positions may constitute an effective stereotype threat removal tactic; for example, according to Carnes et al. (2005), when the National Institutes of Health eliminated a stereotypically male attribute (i.e., risk-taking) from their selection criteria for NIH Director's Pioneer Awards, not only did the number of applications by female scientists increase substantially, but also did the number of female recipients. In other words, one effective intervention that organizations can adopt is to be mindful and use gender-neutral language as much as possible in describing high-stakes criteria as far as talent management programs and/ or leadership effectiveness evaluations are concerned (Burgess et al., 2012).

Saliency of Minority Status of Female Leaders

The broad literature of female leadership has long acknowledged the scarcity of positive female role models and mentors for aspiring women in the workplace (Noe, 1988; Levinson et al., 1991; Growe and Montgomery, 1999), which in turn becomes a stereotype threat trigger itself. Indeed, simply reminding females that few women are top leaders has successfully activated a gender-based stereotype threat (see Hoyt and Blascovich, 2007, 2010).

Isolation status
The reasons are two-fold. First, the minority status of women (e.g., in leadership positions) becomes more salient to both male and female stakeholders when women find themselves isolated from female peers (i.e., as a token minority or having the 'solo' status; see Inzlicht and Ben-Zeev, 2000; Sekaquaptewa and Thompson, 2003), making those women more susceptible to gender identity threat.

Social comparison

Second, women in the workplace are likely to engage in the process of social comparisons (see Festinger, 1954), particularly with men, to gain self-knowledge and evaluate themselves in an organizational setting (Isobe and Ura, 2006). Unfortunately, the broad literature on gender differences in organizational status has long established that men are typically advantageous in career progress compared with their female counterparts (e.g., having a higher salary; enjoying faster promotions; working on better value-added tasks than women; Heilman, 2001; Carter and Silva, 2010), a fact that is a direct result of discrimination and preferential treatment favoring males in the workplace.

Reduced self-confidence

Recently, von Hippel et al. (2011) provided evidence that such social comparisons were sufficient to incur women's stereotype threat feelings, which were in turn detrimental to their self-confidence in the likelihood of reaching their career advancement goals. Specifically, the researchers asked female workers in the legal (male-dominated) field whether they had thought of their career progress in comparison to that of men in their organization. Von Hippel et al. found that women who engaged in comparisons with male colleagues reportedly felt less confident that they would successfully climb the corporate ladder than those who did not, a result explained by their heightened stereotype threat perception. Burnette et al. (2010) also evidenced that women's leadership self-efficacy (i.e., beliefs in general capabilities to lead; Murphy, 2001) was significantly diminished as a response to a female stereotype threat trigger. Those women's lower self-efficacy, in turn, resulted in lower self-evaluation of their leadership potentials.

Intervention tactics

There are several implications for interventions based on those findings. First, organizations may reduce such stereotype threat effects by promoting a *gender identity safety* context in their company, engaging both male and female stakeholders and across organizational hierarchy levels (Burgess et al., 2012). Unlike the aforementioned gender threat loaded context (i.e., low female representation), a gender identity-safe work environment is defined as an organization's valuing diversity and with high female representation (Purdie-Vaughns et al., 2008). Such a goal is achievable: the percentage of female managers in the United States has increased from 15.6 percent in 1960 to 51.5 percent in 2012 (Catalyst, 2013). However, it may be unrealistic to expect a rapid adjustment in the (disproportional) male–female leadership ratio in the short term.

The stereotype threat literature suggests an alternative: companies should promote explicit messages about the ability of men and women being equally effective leaders, which is also considered a tactic of identity safety for women (Davies et al., 2005; Wayne et al., 2010). For example, Davies et al. (2005) asked women to self-select the role of a leader or a non-leader in a group task (i.e., leadership aspiration). Prior to that, those women had read a job advertisement with either a sexist tone (the stereotype threat condition) or a neutral tone (the control group). Further, half of the women in the stereotype threat group received an 'identity safety' statement (i.e., men and women performing equally well as leaders in the said group task). Interestingly, the 'identity-safe' women consequently nominated themselves as group task leaders to a greater extent than those reading the sexist advertisement only, and at the same rate as that of the control group.

Second, although stereotype threat could reduce leadership self-efficacy or confidence as mentioned above, an organizational strategy of proactively enhancing women's leadership self-efficacy may buffer the effect of gender-based stereotype threat on their identification with the leadership domain. Hoyt and colleagues provided some indirect evidence to support this recommendation (Hoyt, 2005; Hoyt and Blascovich, 2007, 2010). For example, Hoyt (2005) exposed her 'stereotype threat' female participants to (fictitious) data that shows men are more effective leaders than women. Leadership self-efficacy was assessed both before and after the gender threat trigger. The researcher found that, surprisingly, women who received the gender stereotype message but had a higher level of leadership self-efficacy coming into the experience reported a greater tendency of identifying themselves as leaders (i.e., desiring a leader position; evaluating themselves as a leadership-oriented person), whereas those with lower self-efficacy were not interested in being a leader. Given that the higher the number of previous leadership role experiences is, the greater one would report leadership self-efficacy (e.g., McCormich et al., 2002), and that the advantages of having a mentor at the workplace include more job satisfaction, greater career opportunities and promotion rate, as well as better recognition (e.g., Fagenson, 2006), organizations that wish to create an identity-safe, threat-free environment and intentionally develop women's managerial careers may do well to foster professional mentorship and leadership programs targeting female high potentials.

CONCLUSION

The objective of this chapter is to review the literature of stereotype threat effects applying to women performing tasks in general and women in the workplace in particular. As such, the literature on stereotype threat implies two notions about men's role in this process. (1) Men can directly activate stereotype threat on women's job performance by endorsing gender stereotypes about a woman's career choice, her capability to handle task challenges or lead her work unit or the organization, for instance. In that light, men may serve the role of adversary to women within this context. However, (2) stereotype threat does not require the active involvement of men to incur; men's existence within the workplace can often be sufficient means to trigger stereotype threat effects on their female colleagues. Even when some men hold more egalitarian views, they can still perpetuate gender stereotype threat merely by serving as a (superior) comparison group for women who hold similar positions but may encounter pay inequity or restrictive upward career mobility. While it is still a new area of research, we have outlined a number of potential intervention tactics to reduce stereotype threat effects for women in their career development. To the extent that men (and organizations) become aware of the problem and choose to actively engage in pro-women practices such as de-emphasizing gender stereotypes and creating a sense of gender identity safety, they can become allies to women as they work to overcome stereotype threat effects.

REFERENCES

Adams, G., D.M. Garcia, V. Purdie-Vaughns and C.M. Steele (2006), 'The detrimental effects of a suggestion of sexism in an instruction situation', *Journal of Experimental Social Psychology*, **42**(5), 602–15.

Ahl, H. (2006), 'Why research on women entrepreneurs needs new direction', *Entrepreneurship Theory and Practice*, **30**(5), 595–621.

Ambady, N., S.K. Paik, J. Steele, A. Owen-Smith and J.P. Mitchell (2004), 'Deflecting negative self-relevant stereotype activation: The effects of individuation', *Journal of Experimental Social Psychology*, **40**(3), 401–40.

Aronson, J., M.J. Lustina, C. Good, K. Keough, C.M. Steele and J. Brown (1999), 'When white men can't do math: Necessary and sufficient factors in stereotype threat', *Journal of Experimental Social Psychology*, **35**, 29–46.

Babcock, L. and S. Laschever (2008), *Women Don't Ask: Negotiation and the Gender Divide*, Princeton, NJ: Princeton University Press.

Bateman, T.S. and J.M. Crant (1993), 'The proactive component of organizational behavior: A measure and correlates', *Journal of Organizational Behavior*, **14**(2), 103–18.

Beilock, S.L., R.J. Rydell and A.R. McConnell (2007), 'Stereotype threat and working memory: Mechanisms, alleviation, and spillover', *Journal of Experimental Psychology: General*, **136**(2), 256–76.

Bergeron, D.M., C.J. Block and A. Echtenkamp (2006), 'Disabling the able: Stereotype threat and women's work performance', *Human Performance*, **19**(2), 133–58.

Blascovich, J., S.J. Spencer, D.M. Quinn and C.M. Steele (2001), 'African Americans and high blood pressure: The role of stereotype threat', *Psychological Science*, **12**(3), 225–9.

Brown, R.P. and E.C. Pinel (2003), 'Stigma on my mind: Individual differences in the experience of stereotype threat', *Journal of Experimental Social Psychology*, **39**(6), 626–33.

Burgess, D. and E. Borgida (1999), 'Who women are, who women should be: Descriptive and prescriptive gender stereotyping in sex discrimination', *Psychology, Public Policy, and Law*, **5**(3), 665–92.

Burgess, D.J., A. Joseph, M. van Ryn and M. Carnes (2012), 'Does stereotype threat affect women in academic medicine?' *Academic Medicine*, **87**(4), 506–12.

Burnette, J.L., J.M. Pollack and C.L. Hoyt (2010), 'Individual differences in implicit theories of leadership ability and self-efficacy: Predicting responses to stereotype threat', *Journal of Leadership Studies*, **3**(4), 46–56.

Cadinu, M., A. Maass, M. Lombardo and S. Frigerio (2006), 'Stereotype threat: The moderating role of locus of control beliefs', *European Journal of Social Psychology*, **36**(2), 183–97.

Cadinu, M., A. Maass, A. Rosabianca and J. Kiesner (2005), 'Why do women underperform under stereotype threat? Evidence for the role of negative thinking', *Psychological Science*, **16**(7), 572–8.

Cadinu, M., A. Maass, S. Frigerio, L. Impagliazzo and S. Latinotti (2003), 'Stereotype threat: The effect of expectancy on performance', *European Journal of Social Psychology*, **33**(2), 267–85.

Carnes, M., S. Geller, E. Fine, J. Sheridan and J. Handelsman (2005), 'NIH Director's Pioneer Awards: Could the selection process be biased against women?' *Journal of Women's Health*, **14**(8), 684–91.

Carter, N.M. and C. Silva (2010), *Pipeline's Broken Promise*, New York: Catalyst, accessed 8 September 2013 at http://www.catalyst.org/knowledge/pipelines-broken-promise.

Catalyst (2013), 'Women in management in the United States, 1960–present', accessed 8 September 2013 at http://www.catalyst.org/knowledge/women-management-united-states-1960-present.

Cohen, G.L., C.M. Steele and L.D. Ross (1999), 'The mentor's dilemma: Providing critical feedback across the racial divide', *Personality and Social Psychology Bulletin*, **25**(10), 1302–18.

Crant, J.M. (1995), 'The Proactive Personality Scale and objective job performance among real estate agents', *Journal of Applied Psychology*, **80**(4), 532–7.

Crocker, J. and B. Major (1989), 'Social stigma and self-esteem: The self-protective properties of stigma', *Psychological Review*, **96**(4), 608–30.

Crocker, J., B. Major and C.M. Steele (1998), 'Social stigma', in D. Gilbert and S. Fiske (eds), *The Handbook of Social Psychology, Vol. 2*, pp. 504–53.

Croizet, J.C., G. Despres, M.E. Gauzins, P. Huguet, J.P. Leyens and A. Meot (2004), 'Stereotype threat undermines intellectual performance by triggering a disruptive mental load', *Personality and Social Psychology Bulletin*, **30**(6), 721–31.

Danaher, K. and C.S. Crandall (2008), 'Stereotype threat in applied settings reexamined', *Journal of Applied Social Psychology*, **38**(6), 1639–55.

Davies, P.G., S.J. Spencer and C.M. Steele (2005), 'Clearing the air: Identity safety moderates the effects of stereotype threat on women's leadership aspirations', *Journal of Personality and Social Psychology*, **88**(2), 276–87.

Eagly, A.H. and S.J. Karau (2002), 'Role congruity theory of prejudice toward female leaders', *Psychology Review*, **109**(3), 573–98.

Eagly, A.H., S.J. Karau and M.G. Makhijani (1995), 'Gender and the effectiveness of leaders: A meta-analysis', *Psychological Bulletin*, **117**(1), 125–45.

Eccles, J.S. (1998), 'Perceived control and the development of academic motivation', *Monographs of the Society for Research in Child Development*, **63**(2–3), 221–31.

Fagenson, E.A. (2006), 'The mentor advantage: Perceived career/job experiences of protégés versus non-protégés', *Journal of Organizational Behavior*, **10**(4), 309–20.

Fagenson, E.A. and E.C. Marcus (1991), 'Perceptions of the sex-role stereotypic characteristics of entrepreneurs: Women's evaluations', *Entrepreneurship Theory and Practice*, **15**(4), 33–48.

Festinger, L. (1954), 'A theory of social comparison processes', *Human Relations*, **7**(2), 117–40.

Frantz, C.M., A.J. Cuddy, M. Burnett, H. Ray and A. Hart (2004), 'A threat in the computer: The race implicit association test as a stereotype threat experience', *Personality and Social Psychology Bulletin*, **30**(12), 1611–24.

Good, C., A. Rattan and C.S. Dweck (2012), 'Why do women opt out? Sense of belonging and women's representation in mathematics', *Journal of Personality and Social Psychology*, **102**(4), 700–717.

Greenberg, J. (1996), *The Quest for Justice on the Job: Essays and Experiments*, Thousand Oaks, CA: Sage Publications.

Growe, R. and P. Montgomery (1999), *Women and the Leadership Paradigm: Bridging the Gender Gap*, ERIC Clearinghouse.

Gupta, V.K. and N.M. Bhawe (2007), 'The influence of proactive personality and stereotype threat on women's entrepreneurial intentions', *Journal of Leadership and Organizational Studies*, **13**(4), 73–85.

Gupta, V.K., D.B. Turban and N.M. Bhawe (2008), 'The effect of gender stereotype activation on entrepreneurial intentions', *Journal of Applied Psychology*, **93**(5), 1053–61.

Heilman, M. (2001), 'Description and prescription: How gender stereotypes prevent women's ascent up the organizational ladder', *Journal of Social Issues*, **57**(4), 657–74.

Hoyt, C.L. (2005), 'The role of leadership efficacy and stereotype activation in women's identification with leadership', *Journal of Leadership and Organizational Studies*, **11**(5), 2–14.

Hoyt, C.L. and J. Blascovich (2007), 'Leadership efficacy and women leaders' responses to stereotype activation', *Group Processes and Intergroup Relations*, **10**(4), 595–616.

Hoyt, C.L. and J. Blascovich (2010), 'The role of leadership self-efficacy and stereotype activation on cardiovascular, behavioral and self-report responses in the leadership domain', *The Leadership Quarterly*, **21**(1), 89–103.

Huddy, L. and N. Terkildsen (1993), 'The consequences of gender stereotypes for women candidates at different levels and types of office', *Political Research Quarterly*, **46**(3), 503–25.

Inzlicht, M. and T. Ben-Zeev (2000), 'A threatening intellectual environment: Why females are susceptible to experiencing problem-solving deficits in the presence of males', *Psychological Science*, **11**(5), 365–71.

Inzlicht, M., J. Aronson, C. Good and L. McKay (2006), 'A particular resiliency to threatening environments', *Journal of Experimental Social Psychology*, **42**(3), 323–36.

Isobe, C. and M. Ura (2006), 'Effects of intergroup upward comparison, trait self-esteem, and identity shift on state self-esteem and affect in upward comparison with in-group members', *Asian Journal of Social Psychology*, **9**(1), 50–58.

Jehn, K.A., G.B. Northcraft and M.A. Neale (1999), 'Why differences make a difference: A field study of diversity, conflict and performance in workgroups', *Administrative Science Quarterly*, **44**(4), 741–63.

Jones, E.E., A. Farina, A.H. Hastorf, H. Marcus, D.T. Miller and R.A. Scott (1984), *Social Stigma: The Psychology of Marked Relationships*, New York: W.H. Freeman.

Keller, J. (2007), 'Stereotype threat in classroom settings: The interactive effect of domain identification, task difficulty and stereotype threat on female students' math performance', *British Journal of Educational Psychology*, **77**, 323–38.

Keller, J. and D. Dauenheimer (2003), 'Stereotype threat in the classroom: Dejection mediates the disrupting threat effect on women's math performance', *Personality and Social Psychology Bulletin*, **29**(3), 371–81.

Kray, L.J., A.D. Galinsky and L. Thompson (2002), 'Reversing the gender gap in negotiations: An exploration of stereotype regeneration', *Organizational Behavior and Human Decision Processes*, **87**(2), 386–410.

Kray, L.J., L. Thompson and A. Galinsky (2001), 'Battle of the sexes: Gender stereotype confirmation and reactance in negotiations', *Journal of Personality and Social Psychology*, **80**(6), 942–58.

Levinson, W., K. Kaufman, B. Clark and S.W. Tolle (1991), 'Mentors and role models for women in academic medicine', *Western Journal of Medicine*, **154**(4), 423–6.

Major, B. and L.T. O'Brien (2005), 'The social psychology of stigma', *Annual Review of Psychology*, **56**(1), 393–421.

Major, B. and J. Crocker (1993), 'Social stigma: The consequences of attributional ambiguity', in D. Mackie and D.L. Hamilton (eds), *Affect, Cognition and Stereotyping: Interactive Processes in Group Perception*, San Diego, CA: Academic Press.

Major, B., S. Spencer, T. Schmader, C. Wolfe and J. Crocker (1998), 'Coping with negative stereotypes about intellectual performance: The role of psychological disengagement', *Personality and Social Psychology Bulletin*, **24**(1), 34–50.

Marx, D.M. and P.A. Goff (2005), 'Clearing the air: The effect of experimenter race on target's test performance and subjective experience', *British Journal of Social Psychology*, **44**(4), 645–57.

Marx, D.M., D.A. Stapel and D. Muller (2005), 'We can do it: The interplay of construal orientation and social comparisons under threat', *Journal of Personality of Social Psychology*, **88**(3), 432–46.

McCormich, M.J., J. Tanguma and A.S. Lopez-Forment (2002), 'Extending self-efficacy theory to leadership: A review and empirical test', *Journal of Leadership Education*, **1**(2), 34–48.

McGlone, M.S. and J. Aronson (2006), 'Stereotype threat, identity salience, and spatial reasoning', *Journal of Applied Developmental Psychology*, **27**(5), 486–93.

Murphy, S.E. (2001), 'Leader self-regulation: The role of self-efficacy and multiple intelligences', in R.E. Riggio and S.E. Murphy (eds), *Multiple Intelligences and Leadership*, Mahwah, NJ: Lawrence Erlbaum Associates, pp. 163–86.

Murphy, M.C., C.M. Steele and J.J. Gross (2007), 'Signaling threat: How situational cues affect women in math, science, and engineering settings', *Psychological Science*, **18**(10), 879–85.

National Science Foundation (2013), *Women, Minorities, and Persons with Disabilities in Science and Engineering: 2013*, Special Report NSF 13-304, Arlington, VA, accessed 12 September 2013 at http://www.nsf.gov/statistics/wmpd/.

Nguyen, H.H.D. and A.M. Ryan (2008), 'Does stereotype threat affect test performance of minorities and women? A meta-analysis of experimental evidence', *Journal of Applied Psychology*, **93**(6), 1314–34.

Niemann, Y.F. and J.F. Dovidio (1998), 'Relationship of solo status, academic rank, and perceived distinctiveness to job satisfaction of racial/ethnic minorities', *Journal of Applied Psychology*, **83**(1), 55–71.

Noe, R.A. (1988), 'Women and mentoring: A review and research agenda', *Academy of Management Review*, **13**(1), 65–78.

Osborne, J.W. and C. Walker (2006), 'Stereotype threat, identification with academics, and withdrawal from school: Why the most successful students of colour might be most likely to withdraw', *Educational Psychology*, **26**(4), 563–77.

Pinel, E.C. (1999), 'Stigma consciousness: The psychological legacy of social stereotypes', *Journal of Personality and Social Psychology*, **76**(1), 114–28.

Pronin, E., C.M. Steele and L. Ross (2004), 'Identity bifurcation in response to stereotype threat: Women and mathematics', *Journal of Experimental Social Psychology*, **40**(2), 152–68.

Purdie-Vaughns, V., C.M. Steele, P.G. Davies, R. Ditlemann and J.R. Crosby (2008), 'Social identity contingencies: How diversity cues signal threat or safety for African Americans in mainstream institutions', *Journal of Personality and Social Psychology*, **94**(4), 615–30.

Rattan, A. and C.S. Dweck (2010), 'Who confronts prejudice? The role of implicit theories in the motivation to confront prejudice', *Psychological Science*, **21**(7), 952–9.

Roberson, L. and C.T. Kulik (2007), 'Stereotype threat at work', *The Academy of Management Perspectives*, **21**(2), 24–40.

Roberson, L., E.A. Deitch, A.P. Brief and C.J. Block (2003), 'Stereotype threat and feedback seeking in the workplace', *Journal of Vocational Behavior*, **62**(1), 176–88.

Rosenthal, H.E., R.J. Crisp and M.W. Suen (2007), 'Improving performance expectancies in stereotypic domains: Task relevance and the reduction of stereotype threat', *European Journal of Social Psychology*, **37**(3), 586–97.

Schein, V.E., R. Mueller, T. Lituchy and J. Liu (1996), 'Think manager–think male: A global phenomenon?' *Journal of Organizational Behavior*, **17**(1), 33–41.

Schmader, T. and M. Johns (2003), 'Converging evidence that stereotype threat reduces working memory capacity', *Journal of Personality and Social Psychology*, **85**(3), 440–52.

Schmader, T., M. Johns and M. Barquissau (2004), 'The costs of accepting gender differences: The role of stereotype endorsement in women's experience in the math domain', *Sex Roles*, **50**(11/12), 835–50.

Sekaquaptewa, D. and M. Thompson (2003), 'Solo status, stereotype threat, and performance expectancies: Their effects on women's performance', *Journal of Experimental Social Psychology*, **39**, 68–74.

Spencer, S.J., C.M. Steele and D.M. Quinn (1999), 'Stereotype threat and women's math performance', *Journal of Experimental Social Psychology*, **35**(1), 4–28.

Stangor, C., C. Carr and L. Kiang (1998), 'Activating stereotypes undermines task performance expectations', *Journal of Personality and Social Psychology*, **75**(5), 1191–7.

Steele, C.M. (1997), 'A threat in the air: How stereotypes shape intellectual identity and performance', *American Psychologist*, **52**(6), 613–29.

Steele, C.M. and J. Aronson (1995), 'Stereotype threat and the intellectual test performance of African Americans', *Journal of Personality and Social Psychology*, **69**(5), 797–811.

Steele, J.R. and N. Ambady (2006), '"Math is Hard!" The effect of gender priming on women's attitudes', *Journal of Experimental Social Psychology*, **42**(4), 428–36.

Steele, J., J.B. James and R.C. Barnett (2002), 'Learning in a man's world: Examining the perceptions of undergraduate women in male-dominated academic areas', *Psychology of Women Quarterly*, **26**(1), 46–50.

Stone, J. (2002), 'Battling doubt by avoiding practice: The effects of stereotype threat on self-handicapping in white athletes', *Personality and Social Psychology Bulletin*, **28**(12), 1667–78.

Stone, J. and C. McWhinnie (2008), 'Evidence that blatant versus subtle stereotype threat cues impact performance through dual processes', *Journal of Experimental Social Psychology*, **44**(2), 445–52.

Stuhlmacher, A.F. and A.E. Walters (1999), 'Gender differences in negotiation outcome: A meta-analysis', *Personnel Psychology*, **52**(3), 653–77.

Tsui, A.S., T.D. Egan and C.A. O'Reilly III (1992), 'Being different: Relational demography and organizational attachment', *Administrative Science Quarterly*, **37**(4), 549–79.

von Hippel, C., M. Issa, R. Ma and A. Stokes (2011), 'Stereotype threat: Antecedents and consequences for working women', *European Journal of Social Psychology*, **41**(2), 151–61.

Wayne, N.L., M. Vermillion and S. Uijtdehaage (2010), 'Gender differences in leadership amongst first-year medical students in the small group setting', *Academic Medicine*, **85**(8), 1276–81.

Wout, D., H. Danso, J. Jackson and S. Spencer (2008), 'The many faces of stereotype threat: Group- and self-threat', *Journal of Experimental Social Psychology*, **44**(3), 792–9.

Yopyk, D.J.A. and D.A. Prentice (2005), 'Am I an athlete or a student? Identity salience and stereotype threat in student-athletes', *Basic and Applied Social Psychology*, **27**(4), 329–36.

13. Barriers to women in science: examining the interplay between individual and gendered institutional research cultures on women scientists' desired futures*

Susan Schick Case and Bonnie A. Richley

INTRODUCTION

Much is known about women working in organizations. Research continues to focus on factors hindering and helping women throughout their career trajectories, revealing an ongoing and pervasive dissatisfaction about equity and opportunity along with the importance of professional development and institutional change. Prior investigations indicate women working in environments that are male-centric (men have the power, privilege, and are in the majority) are subject to disparate treatment and gender-specific barriers negatively impacting their ability to reach professional goals. In the last decade minimal progress has been made in recruiting and retaining women in the sciences. Those 'successful' in these fields, persevering and not dropping out, often experience frustrations and dilemmas negatively affecting the quality of their careers. They make enormous personal sacrifices, often working harder than their male counterparts in order to prove themselves in difficult circumstances (MacLachlan, 2006; Rosser, 2006).

What remains to be understood is how the interplay of individual and institutional dynamics impact women's career choices, job satisfaction, fulfillment, and retention in areas where they continue to leave in record numbers or continue to be under-represented such as in the field of academic science.[1] What problems do the women who persevere experience? What barriers continue to thwart their progress of full participation in science?

Prior research in the sciences reveals a high attrition rate for women following the post-doctoral experience that is not sufficiently explained.[2]

Until recently, much research emphasized women's perceptions, expectations, and choices focusing on helping women fit into existing science departments. Women were construed as 'the problem' in need of change (Bystydzienski and Bird, 2006), an approach increasingly shown to be inappropriate for increasing the numbers of women in science (Preston, 2004; Burke and Mattis, 2007; Stewart et al., 2007; Bilimoria and Liang, 2012).

High-level administrators from the most prestigious US universities acknowledge that organizational resistance to change and the persistence of systemic barriers existing for women will take significant changes in institutional policies and procedures as well as within the fields of science for women's full participation (Rosser, 2006; Burke and Mattis, 2007; Ely and Rhode, 2010). Changes to fully embrace women are needed. The ADVANCE program, initiated by NSF in 2001, was established to encourage institutional solutions to increase women's participation in science, technology, engineering, and management (Bilimoria and Liang, 2012).

This exploratory study focuses on women in the post-doctoral phase of their careers. Post-doctoral scholars hold a doctoral degree and are engaged in a temporary period of mentored research and scholarly training for the purpose of acquiring the professional skills needed to pursue a career path of his or her choosing in science. It is a critical stage in the academic pipeline, the period after which they are more likely to quit academic science just before their transition to principle investigator (PI) as a scientist (Martinez et al., 2007). The study provides a unique vantage point for understanding barriers within organizational cultures and work practices experienced, as well as how their experience is influenced by individual identity, gender, and family situation. We examine work practices that create painful conflicts between women and desired notions about work-in-life integration impacting success and fulfillment, offering insight into the sensemaking process of women during a time when they are focused on actively constructing their desired future.

BARRIERS TO WOMEN IN SCIENCE

Working in a Gender Zone: Women and Identity

'Gender is one of the most basic constructs by which individuals define themselves' (Philpot et al., 1997, p. 35), providing sensemaking for understanding who they are in the world, who they hope to be, and what they can be expected to accomplish. The differential socialization of men and women forms a major barrier to the career success of women scientists, with barriers that men do not face and privileges that women do not have (Philipsen, 2008). Ingrained gender attributes provide limitations as well as opportunities:

> In American society, women are expected to be nurturing, emotional, and cooperative, and serve in the capacity of wife and mother and provide a sense of family for children and spouses. Men, on the other hand, are trained to be aggressive, competitive, logical, and self-reliant and to serve in the role of protector and provider. (Philpot et al., 1997, pp. 41–2)

Women in science have few role models whose styles are feasible or congruent with their self-concepts: 'acting like a man' or 'acting like a woman' diminishes credibility (Ibarra and Petriglieri, 2007, p. 19; Ely and Rhode, 2010, p. 394).

Gendered theories create awareness of the complex roles and responsibilities comprising women's lives. It is equally important to understand that many women include in their identity the relationships and connections they have to others (Miller, 1976; Chodorow, 1978; Case and Thompson, 1995; Belenky et al., 1997). It is this fundamental link between self and other, and the accompanying expectations about tending to those relationships that prohibit women from segregating their lives into distinct spheres, professional and personal. Because of the complexity of women's identity and associated relational responsibilities and needs, women continuously seek ways to 'function and find satisfaction in both work and personal life' and to achieve what is now being referred to as 'work–life integration' (Rapoport et al., 2002, p. 17).

Juxtaposing a woman's need to be in relationship with others, the socialized demands of her role as 'caretaker', and her desire to develop a professional identity when the workplace culture may be 'aligned with traditional images of masculinity such as autonomy, assertiveness, competition, and heroic action' (ibid., p. 28) makes it possible to recognize that women working in male-centric domains experience a daily battle as competing desires collide. The impact of this environment on women's lives can be most fully observed in 'organizational cultures that glorify employees who work as if they had no personal-life needs or responsibilities, silence personal concerns and make it difficult to recognize or admit the costs of overwork' (ibid., p. 31). Such gender biases affect capacities for developing an identity as woman and scientist.

Women's under-representation is at least partly attributable to such traditional gender expectations and practices (Eagly and Carli, 2007). We do not know the impact on women's lives when they work in environments in direct opposition to how they see themselves. We also do not understand how a male-gendered culture influences women in the process of creating a professional identity.

Working in Male-centric Organizations: Tokenism and Cultural Gender Schemas

Differential structures of opportunity and power block many women's access and advancement in organizations (Kanter, 1977; Reskin, 1988; Ridgeway, 1993). Some women persevere and succeed in spite of barriers because their level of commitment kept them working through the challenges (Preston, 2004). But barriers experienced through routine practices of how science is done continue to shape their development and subsequent experiences. Research demonstrates that women working in male-centric cultures experience additional deterrents to success based solely on gender including tokenism (Kanter, 1977), gender stereotyping in workplace interactions (Williams, 2010), and sex-role spillover (Gutek and Cohen, 1987).

Many women in science are often the only woman in a lab or one of few in their field. This singularity or tokenism is an influential characteristic of the structure of their organizations. Predictable problems include social isolation, extreme visibility and scrutiny, and little feedback, affecting attitudes, achievement, and the frequency and quantity of interpersonal contact between majority members and tokens (Kanter, 1977; National Academy of Sciences, 2006). Stereotypical roles are exacerbated in such contexts where men are dominant. The result of the skewed sex composition is that the dominant group's ideology establishes the norm that ultimately supports a hegemonic system (Gutek and Morasch, 1982).

When a woman is one of few, difficulties often result. They are perceived and treated differently from others in a work setting, feel a need to work harder to be taken seriously, accomplish more to be recognized, and make fewer mistakes compared to other members (Kanter, 1977). Solos are more likely to be subjected to stereotyping, scrutiny, and negative judgment, experiencing greater internal stress (Thompson and Sekaquaptewa, 2002). This means the practices and procedures through which post-docs are recruited, processed, and deemed successful (or not) advantage men and constructions of masculinity over women and constructions of femininity (Acker, 1992; Bystydzienski and Bird, 2006). Small but consistent differences in evaluation, often caused by gender bias, have sustained and substantial impact on careers (National Academy of Sciences, 2007). For women scientists to succeed, they not only have to be competent in their knowledge and skills, but also behave consistent with masculine norms (Burke, 2007). More women than their male counterparts drop out of these fields. Among those persevering, many experience difficulties and obstacles as they pursue their science careers.

Typical token dynamics occur when proportional under-representation is less than 15 percent, including performance pressures due to extreme visibility and scrutiny, exaggeration of differences between the tokens and the majority, and stereotyping or generalizing characteristics of tokens (Kanter, 1977). Token dynamics diminish when workforce participation of minority group members in influential positions within a system form a critical mass of more than 35 percent (Kanter, 1977; Yoder, 1994). When women scientists become a significant minority they begin to be viewed through more individualistic and less stereotyped lenses.

Gender stereotypes are not just descriptive of how women are, but are also prescriptive, demanding particular ways that women are to behave. Women who behave out of role are punished (Heilman et al., 2004). Those who stay have found a place in a male-centric, often unwelcoming environment, in which men find a more natural fit, left to navigate these treacherous waters without guidance from a mentor or role model. They frequently shoulder the additional burdens of both work and family. For some, passion still burns, but they need to continually focus on issues involving an exclusionary scientific workplace (Preston, 2004).

Liang and Bilimoria (2007) examined the everyday experiences of the disproportionately few women faculty in academic STEM disciplines in research universities. They found women faculty less likely to achieve career advancement in a climate where 'everything is negotiable', with side deals and unequal application and transparency in rules, policies, procedures, and practices. Women felt isolated, lacking role models, mentoring, and an influential sponsor (Etzkowitz et al., 2000); they had to work harder and accomplish more to earn their reputation and credibility, with disproportionate service and teaching pressures. In sum, the women faculty faced a 'chilly climate', driven in part by the attitudes of male colleagues and administrators. This was described as 'unwelcoming, marginalizing, tough, isolating, male-dominated, and silencing' (p. 322).

Even successful tenured women scientists at MIT found themselves effectively invisible and marginalized within their departments and excluded from participating in significant decisions. They had thought that gender discrimination was only a problem of previous generations and were surprised that the playing field was not level for them either, with a sense of marginalization growing as their careers advanced (Bailyn, 2003, 2006).

Not unlike the military and politics, academic science is a gendered institution (Acker, 1992). Its rules and practices are based on the life experiences and characteristics of men, even if the rules and practices appear to be neutral with respect to gender. Stereotypes maintain socially defined roles, creating a relationship between gender and behaviors promulgating sex-role spillover defined as 'the carryover of gender-based roles into the work setting' (Gutek and Cohen, 1987, p. 97).

Even in an audience overwhelmingly composed of female scientists, scholars, government and university administrators, unconscious bias and implicit associations confirmed views that science is masculine and home and family is feminine (Greenwald and Krieger, 2006). This influences evaluations and productivity, limiting opportunities, undermining motivation and the continuance of previously desired careers in science (National Academy of Sciences, 2006).

Virginia Valian uses the term 'gender schemas' to refer to 'a set of implicit or unconscious hypotheses about sex differences that affect our expectations of men and women, our evaluations of their work, and their performance as professionals' (Valian, 1999, p. 2). Both women and men hold the same gender schemas developed in early childhood, affecting our reactions to women and men. These gendered assumptions about ideal workers and ideal work are often invisible, rooted in the historic separation of spheres of masculine paid work and female domestic work, maintained through beliefs and cultural assumptions underpinning workplace practices and giving priority to workplace demands (Rapoport et al., 2002).

The underlying function of sex stereotypes embedded within these gender schemas and role definitions exerts control on behavior (Unger and Crawford, 1992; Worell and Remer, 1992). Implicit 'rules for success' in today's workplace are closely aligned with traditional images of masculinity (Rapoport et al., 2002). Madeline Heilman's work on 'lack of fit' has demonstrated that if the predominant model is that scientists are male, then women somehow do not fit if they seem like women; but if they try to fit by acting like men, they are not much liked and that does not work either (2001).

This is what Barbara Gutek called sex-role spillover (Gutek and Morasch, 1982). People have implicit expectations that men are going to act like men and women act like women in the workplace. 'Sex roles are more stereotypical and more problematic' when there are 'relatively low proportions of senior women' (Ely, 1995; Bystydzienski and Bird, 2006). In organizations with few women in positions of power, gender is very salient and negatively affects women lower in the organizational ranks, despite the currently more balanced representation at those levels in many of the fields of science. The science workforce resembles a foreign landscape for many women who enter it. Low proportions of women increase the role of implicit gender stereotyping, impacting performance opportunities and evaluation. Due to unconscious assumptions held about women, the tendency, by both men and women, is to overvalue the work of men and undervalue that of women (evaluation bias) (Valian, 1999; Burke, 2007).

The legacy of traditional gender stereotypes remains. Male and female careers in the sciences follow different trajectories (National Academy of Sciences, 2006). The expectation of how women should behave creates a double standard and a classic double bind: too aggressive, not tough enough; what appears assertive in a man appears abrasive in a woman (Case, 1994, 1995). Gender determines what is expected, socially permitted, and valued about men and women in a particular context. This legacy of gender stereotypes subjects aspiring female scientists to higher standards, needing more output to be rated as competent as men (Burke, 2007; Williams, 2010), and more ongoing constraints than their male counterparts (Rudman and Correll, 2001; Ely and Rhode, 2010). Rosser (2006) found this to be one of the major problems faced by women in science.

In studies involving women scientists, many recall times they felt disrespected or treated inappropriately because of their gender, leading to fewer connections to potential mentors or less interesting assignments (Preston, 2004; Rosser, 2006; Burke and Mattis, 2007; Stewart et al., 2007; Bilimoria and Liang, 2012). Low numbers led to isolation, outsider status, lack of camaraderie, and difficulty gaining credibility from peers and administrators, access to networks, and opportunities. Social isolation is one of the reasons that even single women without children who are in the bench sciences consider leaving academia (Mason and Goulden, 2002).

Traditional gender expectations and practices continue to shape people's experiences throughout their careers. This is especially prevalent when women occupy traditionally male roles (Heilman et al., 2004). The cultural lens is distorted by bias (Rhode and Kellerman, 2007). For example, men's predominance in positions of organizational power, together with differences in men and women's social and professional networks, give men more access to information and support (Burt, 1992; Ibarra, 1992; Podolny and Baron, 1997). Women in traditionally male-dominated settings have a difficult time breaking into the 'old boys' loop of advice and professional development opportunities (Ragins, 1998). Prejudices based on deep-rooted stereotypes continue to create gender conflicts in the practice of science.

Gendered Institutional Norms: The Male Model of Science

Masculine norms predominate in the scientific workplace, rooted in assumptions about heroic individualism, dictating how people should act within their organizations. Work practices and rewards and the formal and informal criteria used to determine excellence reflect implicit beliefs that the success and reputation of institutions depends on attracting, retaining, and supporting 'intellectual stars'. These giants publish quality research in leading academic journals as part of an ethic of academic individualism (Rapoport et al., 2002, p. 45).

Strong cultural barriers and rigid stereotypes of what constitutes a successful person in science continue. The assumption about academic 'stars' governs systems of recognition and evaluation, favoring publishing in elite journals above all other criteria for success. Women post-docs occupy many of the support positions that enable the 'individual' achievement of academic stars. Their contributions go unrecognized (Fletcher, 1999) as the norms focus on 'single mindedness', 'exclusive devotion', and 'aggressive self-promotion' (Dean and Fleckenstein, 2007), not on collaboration.

The dominant group that controls institutional roles has power and status that determine institutional norms and influences what the organizational culture accepts as life style, work style, and expected beliefs (Bystydzienski and Bird, 2006, p. 6). They indicate traditional male values of hierarchy, challenge, competition, and independence persist in fields largely filled with men, hence when women enter these male spaces they are confronted with a culture and structures that many of them (and some men) find bothersome, and at worst, excluding or hostile. The problem of exclusion is compounded by organizational structures and practices reflecting and supporting men's experiences (Rapoport et al., 2002; Bailyn, 2006). Women's progress is thwarted by limited opportunity in such male-dominated structures. Even with gender equity gaining ground, lingering prejudicial attitudes result in unconscious and subtle forms of discrimination (Preston, 2004; Williams, 2010).

The norms of commitment and competence

The most gendered assumptions permeating science are linked to commitment and competence (Rapoport et al., 2002). The implicit male standard is devotion to scientific investigation to the exclusion of all other aspects of life (Noble, 1992; Preston, 2004; Burke, 2007). Excessive work hours are entrenched (Drago, 2007). The traditional concept of the ideal worker is about commitment. Personal sacrifices are expected. Do whatever it takes to get the job done. Spend much time at work and be seen. The image of scientists in the lab at all hours of the night and weekend is not far from what is demanded (Dean and Fleckenstein, 2007). Commitment to work is manifested by this singular devotion to work unencumbered with family responsibilities, designed around masculinity and men (Williams, 2010).

It is assumed that people really serious about a career in science will make work the highest priority in life, demonstrating unlimited commitment to science, with personal life secondary. This gendered experience places constraints on men's involvement in family life, even if they want to be involved and leads to negative assumptions about the commitment of mothers in particular (Correll et al., 2007). Women are disadvantaged by the out of sync convergence of their biological and professional clocks and the escalating time demands of their research. It is difficult to pursue care of a family, especially during the very demanding early years of a career. Thus, women who want to have a family, or social life, and do not wish to sacrifice it all for work, are made to feel their desire to have a life outside of science renders them unfit for scientific careers (Preston, 2004; Bystydzienski and Bird, 2006).

The factor most detrimental to career progression for women scientists was family status, with women particularly disadvantaged if they had children, with no similar pattern found for men (Xie and Shauman, 2003; National Academy of Sciences, 2006). The motherhood penalty included powerful schemas about parenthood, including perceptions of less competence and commitment (Correll et al., 2007; Williams, 2010). Family formation (marriage and childbirth) accounts for the greatest exiting of academic research women scientists (Goulden et al., 2009; Rosser and Taylor, 2009), partly because of the separate spheres assumption that the jobs of scientists are best suited to real scientists, not 'mothers' (Williams, 2010).

In Rosser's (2006) study, to understand the most significant issues, challenges, and opportunities facing 450 women scientists in their careers, she found balancing career with family was mentioned by close to 88 percent of them, including the issues of dual careers as well as children. Eighty-three percent of women scientists with doctorates have academic partners who are also scientists, compared with only 54 percent of male peers (Schiebinger et al., 2008), creating further work–life difficulties.

The increasing pace and competitiveness of organizational life, coupled with technological advances, has created a culture of expected constant accessibility, blurring the boundaries between home and work. Technology has made it easier to work from home and harder not to work there when not at the workplace. Nonetheless, labs require women to be present at irregular hours. Rising work commitments with longer hours lead to stress and being too busy off the job. Post-doctoral women who are scrambling to build their careers while simultaneously raising children have difficulty finding time for activities beyond the workplace to forge professional relationships. Expectations for mothering and reasonable standards of co-parenting are in conflict with the expected primary commitment in science to one's work.

A second gendered assumption that permeates science is the ideal worker image of competence. This values stereotypical masculine ways of working that are individualistic, competitive, and self-promoting (Rapoport et al., 2002). Members of status groups tend to associate with one another and exclude outsiders. Although men report that they do not oppose hiring a woman if she has the qualifications (Galen and Palmer, 1994) the dilemma may be in how men perceive who is qualified, competent, and according to what standards, with implicit bias prevalent and a devaluation of feminine attributes like relational skills (Fletcher, 1999; Valian, 1999; Bagenstos, 2007; Correll et al., 2007; National Academy of Sciences, 2007).

The 'Old Boys' Club' – Influence and Legitimacy

Research demonstrates that age, sex, and race determine the distribution of power, influence, and prestige among members of dominant groups (Berger et al., 1972). This dynamic creates what is commonly referred to as the 'old boys' club', an informal but powerful collective of like individuals who either explicitly or implicitly signal whether full membership in an organization is granted or denied. Embedded sex role expectations contribute to the persistence of gendered institutions (Acker, 1992).

Particular institutional-level problems lead to a lack of gender equity, diversity, and inclusion in STEM fields. Fifty-two percent of women in the STEM workforce quit their jobs, with most leaving during their mid- to late thirties (Hewlett et al., 2008). The explanation they provide includes under-representation and isolation, like being the lone woman on a team or site; lack of a critical mass of women faculty at all ranks and in leadership positions; unequal employment opportunities with lack of clarity about career paths and possibilities; job segregation involving disproportionate numbers of women in non-tenure track or less valued academic career paths; inequitable treatment and devaluing through stereotyping, excessive scrutiny, biased evaluations that lead to a hostile macho culture; unequal access to resources and compensation; a system of reward emphasizing risk taking; extreme work pressures; and the differential effects of conflicts between work and life/family demands for women and men scientists (Hewlett et al., 2008; Bilimoria and Liang, 2012).

Conflating the idealized masculine with being an 'ideal' scientist often results in the persistence of dysfunctional, outdated, and ineffective practices that are routinized and rarely questioned. In order to secure legitimacy a process of strict conformity is applied including for expected behavior (Scott, 1987). Gender bias occurs in such closed systems that self-replicate dominant value, behaviors, and ideologies (Perrow, 1986, pp. 157–77).

Academic science norms demand total focus on work, producing extreme pressure in early career stages coinciding with women's child-bearing years. Women continue to shoulder the major burden of house-hold responsibilities (Ely and Rhode, 2010; Williams, 2010), engaging in twice as much child care as men (Bianchi et al., 2006). Women cite lack of support in child care and other domestic tasks and unlike men, they lack support of spouses who are at home full-time, or working part-time (Williams, 2000, 2010).

Gender bias does not look like what we thought discrimination looked like (Bailyn, 2006). It is very difficult to balance post-doctoral demands and motherhood, resulting in many women who leave (Wasserman, 2000; Preston, 2004). When women scientists have been asked to identify the most significant issues and challenges they faced as they planned their careers, pressures in balancing career and family remained the most significant barrier identified by these women. They continually struggle over the timing and rearing of children, with an expectation of a substantial career penalty when and if they have children (Burke, 2007). Xie and Shauman (2003) identified motherhood as the factor most likely to preclude a woman in science from advancing in an academic career. Discrimination is triggered by family responsibilities once scientists become mothers (Williams and Segal, 2003; Biernat et al., 2004).

Barriers to Work–Life Balance

Marriage and family is the major barrier to women in science. The 'maternal wall' metaphor (Swiss and Walker, 1993) has been used by Joan Williams to show particular maternal wall patterns that impact women (Williams, 2010) as part of what is now described as family responsibilities discrimination (Bornstein and Williams, 2008).

Maternal wall patterns described by Williams include: (1) jobs defined around masculine patterns with workers selected who are 'single minded'; (2) role incongruity where you can not be both a mother and a full-time scientist; (3) prescriptive stereotyping (she shouldn't worry about her work, but should focus on her family); (4) attribution bias (an absent man is presenting a paper; an absent woman is taking care of her kids); and (5) leniency bias in which women are held to higher standards than men.

Marriage and family have quite different effects on the careers of men and women in science, negatively affecting career outcomes for women as they try to balance these. It is the most important factor differentiating labor force participation of male and female scientists, a difference that disappears when comparing single men and single women (Long, 2001). The two-body problem of dual career families and its job restrictions of less mobility was also important since many of these women were married to other scientists, many more senior than they were (Rosser, 2006; Burke, 2007).

Without offering the same paid parental leave to fathers as to mothers the effect is to entrench unequal family responsibilities, perpetuating unequal workplace opportunities (Ely and Rhode, 2010). There is a differential career effect of marriage and the presence of young children, with it spurring the career advancement of men but slowing it for women (Xie and Shauman, 2003; Drago, 2007). In order to change the status quo it is important to understand how gender identity salience results in disparate treatment against women working in predominantly male cultures.

Even today, women on highly competitive academic career tracks marry at lower rates than men faculty, are childless at higher rates, report having fewer children than they would like, and are more likely to divorce than women on lower-level academic posts to minimize family commitments that interfere with career progress (Drago, 2007; Williams, 2010).

The pressure-filled road to a full-time science job involves 'tunnel vision' and heavy time commitments to publish, write grants, and put in long hours in the lab. This has often caused women to second-guess their career choice, abandon their desire to have children, or ultimately leave the field (June, 2012) at twice the rate of men (Preston, 2004).

In this study we turn to the experience of women post-doctoral bench scientists in order to understand factors most important to their lived experience that impact their ability to create their desired futures. The question central to the study is: 'What are the individual and institutional forces experienced by women working in a male-centric environment?' The second question is embedded in the first and asks: 'How do these dynamics impact the projected desired futures of these women?' We then speculate about how women might succeed and how organizations might assist them. There are clearly individual, organizational, and societal consequences if barriers remain.

METHODS

The research design is an inductive exploratory study to understand the interplay of individual and institutional forces experienced by women in a male-centric environment and how this impacts their desired futures. The study is situated in basic sciences, primarily within medical schools or medically based research institutions due to their high attrition rate for women and a predominance of men in higher-level positions. The overall study is guided by feminist research practice in service of promoting social change for women, using thematic analysis for data interpretation.

Our method enables a fuller understanding of the experience of the participants in the wholeness of their lives and how this guides future choices (Reinharz, 1992; Hesse-Biber and Leavy, 2007).

At its core, feminist research aims 'to create theories grounded in the actual experiences and language of women by investigating women's lives and experience in their own terms' (Humm, 1989, p. 242). Following DeVault, our study is grounded in 'women's standpoint . . . [that] does not imply that all women share a single position or perspective' (1999, p. 60) but rather seeks to learn from the variation between the individual and the collective as well as from the similarities, gaining access to their ideas, thoughts, and memories in their own words rather than those of the researcher (Reinharz, 1992; DeVault and Gross, 2012; Harding, 2012). A qualitative approach supports the exploratory nature of the study allowing for collection of descriptive data. Further, it is used to uncover and understand a phenomenon about which little is known (Strauss and Corbin, 1990). Semi-structured interviews allowed participants to respond conversationally, answer questions out of order, digress, and speak as long as they wanted as a way to more fully understand their 'lived experiences' (Hesse-Biber and Leavy, 2007, p. 118) both in the context of their work and life and how they made sense of it.

The interviewer, mindful of the relationship between herself and the respondent during the process, probed for additional information by asking new questions throughout the interview, supporting and encouraging the respondent without pushing her own agenda into the conversation. This enabled a more accurate understanding of the participants' experience. At times the interviewer offered her own stories or insights, freely entering the conversation, creating common ground, fostering shared learning, and reducing the hierarchy of power and authority issues often present in interviews. Through a collaborative interview process the interviewer and participant worked together to create a thorough understanding of the participant's experience as a woman working in the bench sciences (Gersick and Kram, 2002; Hesse-Biber, 2012).

Sample Selection

The study utilized purposive sampling to 'select unique cases that are especially informative . . . [involve a] difficult-to-reach specialized population . . . [and] to identify particular types of cases for in-depth investigation' (Neuman, 1997, p. 206). Since we were concerned with in-depth understanding, a small sample was desired to look at the process and meanings individuals attributed to their situation, not necessarily to make generalizations (Hesse-Biber, 2012). Participants were chosen from the basic

medical sciences for two reasons: (1) the importance of basic research as
'the engine that drives medical advances' and the centrality of the field
to human life (Centofanti, 2000, p. 1); and (2) the fact that four times as
many men as women with doctorates (in science and technology) hold
full-time faculty positions in US research institutions (Trower and Chait,
2002, p. 35). The women in our sample were in non-tenure post-doctoral
teaching and/or research positions funded by 'soft' or short-term funding.

Utilizing purposeful sampling, potential participants were identified
at a major Midwestern research university using the online directory and
the search phrases 'research associate' and 'post-doctoral fellowship'.
The directory provided information on 462 post-doctoral researchers on
campus including those employed at an affiliate university hospital. Based
on our research criteria (gender, degree field, citizenship, and physical
location) a list of potential participants to contact was completed. Men,
foreign students, and women not doing research in basic sciences were
eliminated. This resulted in 46 women scientists within the population.

Women post-doctoral researchers are typically between 24 and 34 years
of age, the period of early adulthood when many begin to think about
marriage and children (Newman and Newman, 1999). This is also the
time when researchers are expected to focus on their work if they hope
to become successful scientists. The post-doctoral experience provides
an opportunity to learn more about the salience of career, family, and
environment to women researchers, knowing already that familial obligations affect women differently than men. Controlling for this particular
age group resulted in a sample size of ten. Because of the limited number
of women at the initial site, another major Midwestern hospital was
contacted for access, with three more participants engaged. With only 13
women signed up for the study a 'call for participants' was made via an
online journal affiliated with a top-tier journal in the sciences. Seventy-two
women from across the country responded to the request. From this group
14 women working at major research institutions across the United States,
who best matched the rest of the sample, agreed to participate. The final
sample for our study included 24 participants. Their career aspirations
and educational investments matched those of the most ambitious men.

Table 13.1 shows the demographic data of participants in this study.
Fourteen of the 24 were married (59 percent), two were engaged (9
percent), and seven (30 percent) had children ranging from newborn to age
six. Participants were 28–35 (average age was 31, median, 35); years with
time in post-doctoral positions ranging from eight to 78 months, averag-
ing 37 months. At least seven of the women had been in their positions for
four or more years. Ten were single and 14 married, with half the married
women having one to three children, all five years or younger. At the

Table 13.1   Demographic data of sample

Age	Marital Status	Children	Post-doc (Months)	Projected Career Path	University
32	Single	N	30	Research	Yale
28	Married	N	21	Research	Vanderbilt
30	Single	N	8	Research	Harvard
31	Single	N	48	Research	Cleveland Clinic Foundation
35	Married	N	78	Research	Case Western Reserve
35	Married	Y	78	Research	Case Western Reserve
31	Married	N	60	Research	Case Western Reserve
35	Married	Y	36	Research	Case Western Reserve
34	Married	Y	72	Research	Case Western Reserve
31	Single	N	24	Research	Baylor
33	Married	N	24	Research	UC San Diego
32	Married	Y	48	Teaching	Case Western Reserve
35	Married	Y	60	Teaching	Cleveland Clinic Foundation
34	Married	N	24	Teaching	Case Western Reserve
32	Married	Y	42	Teaching	Case Western Reserve
34	Single	N	24	Teaching	Cleveland Clinic Foundation
31	Engaged	N	14	Teaching	New York University
32	Single	N	18	Teaching	Vanderbilt
35	Married	N	24	Teaching	Case Western Reserve
28	Single	N	12	Industry	National Institute of Health
29	Married	N	42	Industry	UC Los Angeles
31	Married	Y	36	Industry	Dana Farber Cancer Institute
35	Engaged	N	36	Industry	Case Western Reserve
33	Single	N	18	Industry	Georgetown

time of the study their projected career paths were research (46 percent), academic teaching (33 percent), and industry (21 percent). Participants were interviewed from 12 different research institutions across the United States within the bench sciences including fields of genetics, neuroscience, pharmacology, immunology, biochemistry, infectious diseases, oncology, and biology (cancer, molecular, developmental, and reproductive).

All the women in the sample were bright, talented at science, with a strong desire to be successful, move ahead in their fields and develop a professional life compatible with their personal values. These women were 'survivors' who had successfully finished top-level doctoral programs, moving onto post-docs, the next important step to establishment of their independence as scientists.

Procedure

Interviews were conducted to document these post-doctoral women's experiences, concerns, illuminating gender-based stereotypes and biases, and realities often hidden and unarticulated, exploring issues of particular concern to their lives. Eleven participants were interviewed face to face and 13 by phone, with each tape-recorded interview lasting 1½ to 2 hours. The interviewer had no problem establishing rapport, even with those interviews conducted by telephone. No apparent differences appeared in the quality or length of in-person or phone interviews.

Thematic analysis was used to generate codes that could be uniformly applied to the data to maximize differentiation between the subsamples (Boyatzis, 1998). Individual interviews were analyzed using each question as the unit of coding with probes considered part of the question. Codes were only counted once, in either the interview question or the probe, to avoid double coding. Since the study was designed to capture differences and commonalities in the post-doctoral sample, the codes were also used to determine shared themes across groups. The overall design was intended to elicit stories to learn how the participants made sense of what they experienced in their research environment and how these experiences impacted future career choice. Participants were free to draw and reflect upon past and present events.

Analysis Process

All interviews were transcribed. From the sample, using projected career paths (research, teaching, and industry), three interviews were randomly selected from each of the three projected career groups to form a subsample of nine used to develop the themes, clusters, and codes. The data from these nine interviews were then reduced by highlighting only relevant information and then reduced again by reconfirming all data was true to the syntax and context stated by the participants.

This reduced data was organized by interview questions on a chart. The themes were abstracted, placed in clusters, and a matrix developed identifying the themes within each cluster. The cluster themes were again verified with the outlined data in the original nine interviews to ensure the context of the participants' responses was maintained. Themes were then compared across each interview within the three groups separately. Those themes that did not resurface from the comparison were removed while others that emerged were included. Twelve coding categories emerged. Reliability using an independent coder was established at an IRR of 89.9 percent, which exceeded the requirement of 80 percent. After establishing reliability, the codes were applied to the remaining interviews.

Additional analysis of the data was completed, comparing the women in clusters based on the level of stated care-giving responsibilities they had: single (eight), engaged (two), married (seven), and married with children (seven). This was examined to see how they navigated their post-doctoral experience when they were trying to have it all: both a career and a family.

FINDINGS

Overview

The findings of this study are based on the interviews of 24 women in various stages of their post-doctoral experiences. At the time of the study all women were working in research institutions. Although the sample size is limited, it permits deep analysis of the data, providing a vantage point to understand individual differences and shared experiences. The intent is to understand the lived experience of women post-doctoral researchers and to identify the key influences that inform their sensemaking with regard to identity, career/life choices, and notions of success and fulfillment. This study provides insight about how the interplay of individual and institutional factors affects choices in career track (i.e., academic research, teaching, industry) and sheds new light on what is understood about the experience referred to as the leaky pipeline.

The findings are presented to depict the progression of the raw data from concepts to themes, codes, and clusters through discussion, a data structure, and quotes from the interviews. The culmination of the analysis is a model representing the post-doctoral experience.

Women in Science and the Post-doctoral Experience

The post-doctoral experience is marked by three key interconnecting dynamics experienced within the post-doctoral transition: (1) self-awareness, (2) contextual engagement, and (3) future orientation (see Figure 13.1). Figure 13.2 shows the emerged data structure with its themes, codes, and clusters. What follows the figures is a discussion of each cluster.

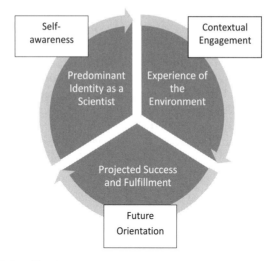

Figure 13.1   Key interconnecting events

Self-awareness and Predominant Identity as a Scientist

Self-awareness is the ability used by our post-docs to perceive and interpret aspects of their personality, behavior, emotions, motivation, and thought processes during their post-doctoral experience. It was a key process hallmarked by conscious attention to the aspects of their environment and lived experience that gave the most meaning to their predominant identity as a scientist. Participants articulated how certain skills, roles, and experiences became more salient to them, leading to an ongoing mindful assessment of what they most liked or disliked. This process of thoughts and interpretation of experiences provided critical data that helped them shape the image of their life in the future after the post-doctoral experience. This mindful process led to enhanced clarity as they selected a career track either as an academic researcher, teacher or moving into industry. The choice of career track related to the interplay of their predominant identity as a scientist, their experience of the environment and their desired future. Participants' responses reflected individual preferences coded as pragmatic and relational orientations that support their personal notion of success as a scientist.

Pragmatic
A pragmatic orientation focuses on skills, abilities, and a desire to contribute to the field by publishing in top-tier journals, presenting at

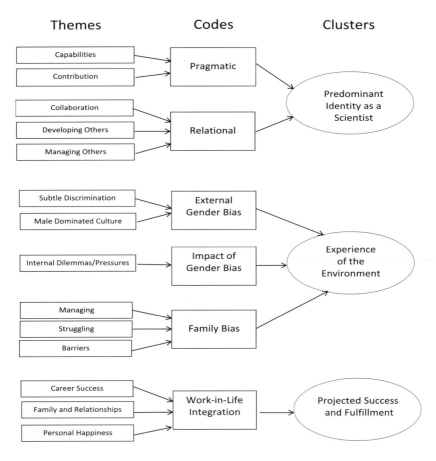

Themes   Codes   Clusters

Figure 13.2   Data structure

conferences, and gaining the respect of peers. This profile most resembles the traditional markers of success in academic science. This orientation is supported by two related themes that emerged from the data: (1) capabilities and (2) contribution. Capabilities is coded as emphasizing a focus on developing good writing skills, communicating clearly, business acumen, patience, persistence, and attention to detail. Contribution signifies a focus on publishing in reputable journals, the quantity of publications, the overall quality of their research, and the desire to achieve a reputation as a respected scientist. Below are representative quotes from the data indicating a pragmatic orientation:

> You have to be really good at communicating your results to people, either putting them into a graph, or displaying them in some way. You have to be able to quickly and concisely communicate your experiences to other people [and] to be good at networking.

> I would say that being a successful scientist would mean publishing in high-profile, peer-reviewed journals, having more than one NIH grant or other sources of funding, having several people working in your lab, having an exciting research environment in your lab, of which you are the head . . . and being well respected by your peers. Therefore you'd be recognized as being that by being on editorial boards of different scientific journals or other kinds of boards for the NIH, doing peer review and grants. And for my own personal measure of success I would hold myself to similar standards.

Relational

A relational orientation demonstrates a desire to be in connection with others through teaching, mentoring, or collaborating by being a part of a team and by being a good role model. A relational focus may also be expressed as a wish to supervise or manage others in the work environment. Three themes supported this code: (1) collaboration, (2) developing others, and (3) managing others. 'Collaboration' is defined as a desire to work with others and is best described as a team approach to science. 'Developing others' places a high value on teaching and mentoring, especially students, and to provide a nurturing and supportive environment conducive to learning. 'Managing others' involves positions that require supervising or directing work in a lab setting. Participants who indicated a relational orientation reflect the importance of being connected to others as key to their identity as a successful scientist across all three themes:

> I would broaden that definition [of success] to go beyond just productivity measured in publications or measured in lab work. I would include other things like your commitment to teaching people, and also working with your colleagues, if you can mentor another person. And you could even extend it even more than that, with interaction with family or community.

> I would very much enjoy working with graduate students and I would make it a high priority to be mentoring people, and teaching them how to write papers, and how to write grants.

> Having people in the lab that you can support and you can supply them with opportunities.

The 'developing others' category was not exclusively coded for women focused on a teaching career. Six of 11 women (54 percent) projecting a research career and three of the five women (60 percent) going into industry were also coded for 'developing others'. This finding suggests that women, irrespective of career choice, value and enjoy mentoring, teaching, and interacting with students, and the significance of relationships in their lives as scientists.

Contextual Engagement and Experience of the Environment

'Contextual engagement' describes the participants' direct and indirect experience and sensemaking of their environment as a woman in science. 'Experience of the environment' focuses on the individual in interaction with others within science and considers such factors as the salience of gender, organizational culture, and family-related issues. Our analysis revealed the impact of the behavior and actions of others (external forces) involving gender and family-related biases that had negative consequences on their lives and careers. These experiences included intentional and unintentional acts of discrimination against an individual and/or references to children, child rearing, or family issues as demonstrating a lack of commitment to science. Participants across all three career paths expressed a collective awareness of working in a culture that disadvantages women. When participants were asked to consider barriers to success for women in science within the environment, three codes emerged: (1) external gender bias, (2) impact of gender bias, and (3) family bias.

External gender bias
This code represents discriminatory standards and acts against a woman scientist by others in the environment. Two themes emerged from our analysis that reveals gender bias: (1) subtle discrimination and (2) male-dominated culture. 'Subtle discrimination' is defined as acts against women that are intentional and unintentional; visible but often unnoticed; communicated both verbally and behaviorally; and appear to be situational (Benokraitis and Feagin, 1986). Fifty-eight percent of the participants articulated acts of subtle discrimination, revealing that even in the early stages of their careers they were aware, or were developing an awareness, of the disparate treatment in science against women similar to that experienced by those more senior:

> Okay, there is a slight undertone. Not everybody perceives a woman at first impression . . . capable of making it to the top.

> Men basically saying, 'Women can't do this, women can't do that'. Some of it comes back to us to prove ourselves, which on some level is kind of annoying, proving yourself over and over again. I look around me and I see how much easier it is for men with less effort to basically be seen in a different way.

I personally haven't experienced it but I have seen it happen, where women aren't necessarily given tenure before a man is even though they've done more work and you see that all the time.

'Male-dominant culture' is defined as an environment where men outnumber women and are the primary owners of power and privilege. The behavior exhibited in the environment reflects often unconscious, preferential treatment toward males and toward those who behave in ways that favor the dominant culture. All 11 women projecting a career in research described their environment reflecting cultural norms and values favoring men. Six of eight women (75 percent) considering a teaching track and four of five (80 percent) who were considering industry reported the impact of male-dominant culture on their experiences. Variations on the impact of the 'old boys' club' was a continuous refrain throughout the interviews:

I mean traditionally there are a lot of men and there is an old boys' network and they help each other out. There's a lot of politics involved in science too and if you're in the old boys' network, or some network, of course you have an advantage of other people who aren't.

And the guy sitting next to me who doesn't really understand the applications of tools, and basically puts things together, he gets referred to as Dr. Such-and-Such, and I many times don't even get introduced to people.

It's very much an old boys' club . . . an unwillingness to let other people be part of that club on some level.

Impact of gender bias

This code is defined as the impact on participants experiencing gender bias. The theme to emerge from the data is labeled 'internal/dilemmas/ pressures' and represents the negative outcomes on the individual as a result of this external gender bias. These descriptions include how sense is made of the bias, how it is experienced as a woman within the environment, and the different treatment/standards placed on her. This code also includes an expressed understanding or belief that the salience of their gender results in 'extreme expectations' for their performance on the job when compared to what is required of men in the same position:

Confidence, determination, hard work . . . women might need more, I guess that, that's the only distinction I would make.

I think that, unfortunately still in science, women I think need to work a little harder, need to portray confidence a little more. Not that they don't work hard enough but I think . . . that they might need to do more work to get the same recognition.

The threshold for validity is maybe higher than for men. So you need to maybe publish 15 papers instead of eight.

The 'impact of gender bias' was coded for eight of 11 women (73 percent) projecting a research path, six of eight (75 percent) who focused on teaching, and four of five (80 percent) interested in industry. These findings demonstrate an awareness of the salience of gender bias as well as the impact of this disparate treatment on their daily work life making it more difficult for them to succeed. The data suggest participants experience an additional burden on them as scientists with being a woman 'affecting everything'. They had to continually 'live up to higher expectations' and were 'having to prove themselves more than men'.

Family bias

Beyond gender bias, participants also reported 'family bias', defined as how children and family impacted their careers and life in general. Three major themes emerged from the analysis: (1) managing, (2) struggling, and (3) barriers. 'Managing' refers to the need for additional support from the institution to deal with family responsibilities:

Women who have children use more support . . .with pay, with full pay . . . they cannot remove your position for one year . . . so this is actually exceptionally supportive to a woman.

Because it is very demanding, and certainly at the early stages, you're not paid well enough to have other people do the things that you need to do. So you're not paid well enough to have a full-time nanny or a full-time housekeeper, and all this kind of stuff. People who work in other professions where they're expected to work incredibly hard, at least they have the financial resources to pay other people to get the other stuff done in their life.

'Struggling' highlights difficulties experienced from the organizational environment with regard to pregnancy, raising children, and tending to family life. Participants across all three career paths reported challenges or difficulties experienced within their environments with regard to each of these. For those participants choosing research, ten of 11 (91 percent) were coded for 'struggling'. All eight women projecting teaching were similarly coded; and four of five (80 percent) hoping to go into industry acknowledged difficulties presented within their post-doctoral environments of trying to have both a family and a career in science:

Because I feel so restricted in being able to balance out the other areas of my life, it makes me more resentful of work, just in general. Which makes it more difficult for me to go to work on a daily basis and do what I need to do. Because I feel like it's sucking every ounce of my life out of me.

Because I feel, when I look back now, I think that this is a terrible career choice for a family. On the other hand, I feel like if I hadn't pursued this I wouldn't be fulfilling my own personal goals. So I'm constantly wrestling with these two identities, one as a wife and mom, and one as a scientist as well.

I've heard of examples from people who say that when they've told their advisor that they're pregnant, he's threatened to cut off their health insurance. I don't think that's true for men. I think they [men] automatically sort of see this [family] as a distraction from their [a women scientist's] research.

The third theme emerging with regard to family bias is 'barriers'. Barriers represent experiences within the work environment suggesting that family life creates obstacles to achieving career success:

And you did not get pregnant in his lab, he made it clear.

The barriers in terms of family – it becomes an excuse for why they [women] can't really be successful.

[They said]'Well we hired this female faculty, but now she wants to have a baby! We knew this wouldn't work'.

I do feel that it is not a field that makes it very easy for women. It is not very accommodating if they decide to have children or if they want to have a life outside of your work.

Seven of 11 women (64 percent) planning a research career stated that children or family life would negatively impact their career success, with six of the seven already married and three of them with children. For those on a teaching path, six of eight (75 percent) mentioned this as 'barriers'. Five of the six were married; three had children. Only two of five (40 percent) seeking a career in industry felt this was a salient theme, but both were the only married women in this group, with one having a child. Married women and those who already had children were extremely aware of family bias barriers to career advancement and success. Some who were still single also recognized the patterns. Most of these women indicated they had not or would not ask for resource support concerning family life responsibilities from their institutions for fear of it further jeopardizing the perception of them as 'real scientists'.

Projected Success and Fulfillment

Our inquiry included juxtaposing the participants' notion of success against how success is defined in the larger community of science. Our analysis found individual differences around some themes as well as shared themes that spoke of a more inclusive notion of success involving concepts of relationship, personal satisfaction, and wanting healthy work-in-life integration as part of their envisioning a fulfilling life. Because of our interest in the wholeness of their lives we asked the question, 'How do you define success in your own terms?'

Since participants are in the process of their post-doctoral experience and simultaneously constructing their ideal future the third cluster to emerge from the data is projected success and fulfillment coded as 'work-in-life integration'. The importance of work-in-life integration became figural when asked, 'Are there other things that you need in order to have a life that feels fulfilled?' All participants but one stated the importance of work–life balance/integration as a critical part of what they envisioned as a fulfilled life. Participants spoke of attending to their feelings as a source of data for gauging their success, rather than merely using markers of external validation. This code is defined as the desire to achieve both a successful and a happy life. Three themes were developed from the data: (1) career success, (2) family and relationships, and (3) personal happiness:

> A definition of success for me personally is a balance for me of various aspects of my life. And I think that some of the trick is finding how to achieve the right level of success in each area, so that you have enough of yourself to invest in the other areas.

> I would like to be in a job that I find fulfilling and one that makes me personally happy, that's stimulating and interesting. But that also allows me to have a life outside of just a career.

> Feeling happy with what I'm doing and still enjoying things. Then personally, that's more successful than if I'm just gritting my teeth and sucking it up and continuing on some path.

A Model of the Post-doctoral Experience Transition Zone

The information garnered from the participants and the data organized as clusters, codes, and themes that emerged from the analysis show that the post-doctoral experience is an interactive and recursive process involving experiencing, sensemaking, and deciding. At play are three key dynamics involving self-awareness, contextual engagement, and future orientation represented as a conceptual model shown in Figure 13.3.

DISCUSSION

Virtually all the women in our study were united in their love of science and desired to continue with sustained interest in the field that initially attracted them to be scientists. Most would have loved nothing better than to pursue this love through research and/or teaching in academia. It is clear that obstacles for women in science were embedded in the way that academic science was organized and practiced, with its rules and policies interacting with gender. This imposed different demands on women that impacted their desired sense of what success entailed for them so they would achieve personal fulfillment. All these women, across institutions, shared descriptions of living in the post-doctoral transition zone.

The Transition Zone

Our study reveals that even at this early stage of career development and before full membership has been obtained in an organization, these women are experiencing barriers similar to those of women further along in academia, with the biological demands of childbirth conflicting with the timing of their ideal career. This is a period for them of pressure, stress, and vulnerability. It was difficult for these women to reconcile the demands of science with those of their private lives. Many felt they did this poorly, leading to 'not much of a private life'. They spoke of setting priorities and making sacrifices. All acknowledged that what they were trying to do took incredible effort.

These women post-doctoral researchers were engaged in a complex interaction of observation, word-of-mouth, lived experience or anticipation of biases within this unique learning environment that invariably influenced their career path from the beginning of their post-doctoral experience until they end up in what 'emerged' as the career that fits who they are as women and the type of gendered life they wanted to live.

The women in our study provide insight into their experience in a transitional environment. Science is tied to the environment of work: signals, resources, reward schemas, and networks of communication. This includes processes of appraisal, collegial interaction, work climate, and collaborative opportunities. The environment does not operate uniformly, neutrally, or androgynously within the same setting.

Little is known about women in transition zones during their

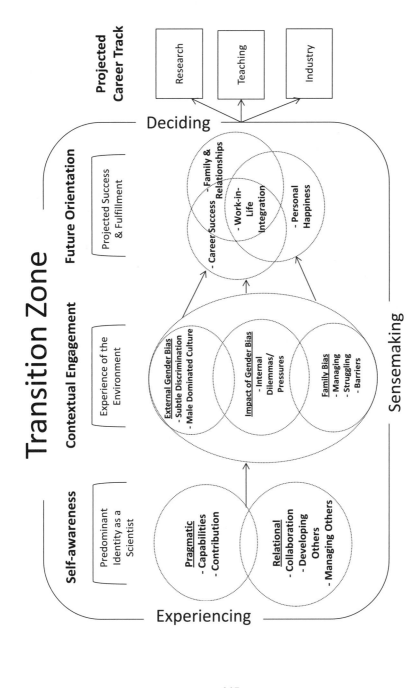

Figure 13.3   The post-doctoral experience transition zone

careers. This critical period is defined in our paper as a period in time where formal membership in an organization is being considered and the individual is engaged in a learning process of exploration about the fit between self, environment, and a desired future. This process is shaped by the experience encountered, the sensemaking in relation to these experiences, and their decisions based on both the experiences and sensemaking in this transition zone. Most interestingly, the decision whether to stay in research or go into teaching, or industry is a decision to align their passions as scientists to be successful in their chosen field. These women were not leaving science as the 'leaky pipeline' metaphor suggests occurs. Instead they found other venues in which to be scientists.

The women in this study are in essence 'free agents' and have not obtained or accepted full membership in the organization. The study offers insight into the period prior to an individual obtaining full membership in an organization that is not just an adaptation process (Ibarra, 1999) but both adaptive and selective. This 'adapting-selecting' process is unique to transition zones. What we know from our data is that the transition zone still involves a persistent and ongoing struggle for many, as well as a great joy in their life and a critical source of fulfillment as they do science. We need to understand post-doctoral support to lesson the internal as well as the external struggle. This transition point to full-time labor force participation is a critical point at which more women are lost to science than men are lost (Long, 2001).

There needs to be cognizance of three unconscious norms (ideal worker, motherhood, and individualism) that shape our views of work, family, and life spheres and the expectations we have of others and ourselves (Drago, 2007). In this study the ideal worker is described as what participants project will lead to success and fulfillment in this environment. They predominantly reject for themselves that to be a scientist you must be totally committed to career, working endlessly and at all hours for periods of years and decades at a stretch, with high rewards achieved only for this type of commitment.

Motherhood is described in the work environment as a struggle or barrier that has to be managed since commitment to family or other care-giving is viewed as deviating from the ideal worker norm. On the other hand, these women simultaneously said that motherhood, family, and other forms of care-giving should be part of the life they envision of success and fulfillment. They rejected the continual encroachment of work responsibilities into personal time, making the amount of time spent working and even simply being at work the definition of commitment. They felt extremely committed and passionate about their science, yet realized that the system favored individuals with few other commitments. For those with children there was guilt because the norm of motherhood puts high demands on these women in terms of care-giving.

Finally, individualism is described as how they perceive the identity of a scientist (as single-mindedly devoted and self-promoting), and the type of scientist they do not want to be (pragmatic vs relational). They wanted to collaborate in the creation of new science knowledge and teach and develop future scientists.

Norms can be challenged and transformed with thought, organization, and effort. But people need to recognize and pay attention to how they strongly operate in our workplaces. As a young woman academic stated:

> I think women have an issue proving they're committed period. [And] it's always bizarre to me that I could have gone through four years of college, five years of graduate school, nine years as a post-doctoral fellow . . . and . . . I'm in my sixth year here now working my butt off, and people are wondering about my commitment . . . I don't think men get that. (Drago and Colbeck, 2003)

This research adds to documentation about how institutions both exclude and include women in science. The purpose was to understand institutional obstacles and barriers that forced choices and decisions leading to many women leaving the system, trying to fulfill their scientific research interests and career and life goals through other paths. The questions asked about success, fulfillment, projected career path and how gender is experienced in science enabled development of a more comprehensive picture of the participants' lives during this critical transition point in their career. We learned what is most important to them as scientists, as women, and in the totality of their lives.

Findings provided insight into the individual career decision process involving how gender was experienced and interpreted in a male-centric culture, demonstrating the significant role that being a woman continued to have on daily lived experiences and how gender salience impacted their plans for the future. Together, these two overarching areas provide information about the post-doctoral 'transition zone' for women, marked by a period of psychological squeezing and internal sensemaking, suggesting an environment heavily laden with institutional gender bias and forced family struggles, juxtaposed by a feeling of powerlessness and vulnerability. These women understand, based on signals in their environment, that being different from the norm and being labeled uncommitted has negative, lasting career consequences.

Many of the women reported being treated differently than male counterparts and living under a shroud of doubt about their ability to 'do science' and 'make it to the top as a woman'. Most of the post-docs showed keen understanding of where the Academy stands relative to the necessary sacrifices participants must make in terms of family life. But there was ambivalence by some about acknowledging 'the old boys' club' as a reality for them, impacting their demonstration as capable scientists. They believed in science as objective and its system based on merit. They bought into the ideal worker norm that dominates science. They wanted to fit in without 'woman' being relevant.

Work-in-life Integration

Even though women bear the brunt of challenges arising from working in male-dominated STEM fields, efforts to make the workplace more family-friendly will keep falling short as long as women are the face of work–life balance efforts. If the work of 'caring' (child care and parent care) continues to be seen as women's work rather than human work, there will be an ongoing cost to women, to science, and to society. Janet Koster, Executive Director of the Association for Women in Science stated, 'Let's stop pointing the finger at women by putting a "baby" Band-Aid on the problem' (June, 2012, p. 29).

Is it a values problem? Men do appear to be more willing to forgo a 'balanced life' in order to have a scientific career than women (Valian, 2006). There are long-standing cultural norms concerning work, family, and gender roles. These need changing. A culture shift is slowly occurring, with men beginning to demand changes around work/family. A recent survey of 4225 scientists and researchers found work–family balance elusive for men as well as women, with almost 40 percent of men unhappy with the way their work life meshes with their personal life in contrast to 50 percent of the women who felt that way (June, 2012). Both men and women are struggling with the issue of family responsibility and its effects on their scientific careers (Preston, 2004; Philipsen, 2008). Preston (2004) found that taking care of ailing parents is also increasing, with evidence that it was responsible for an exit from science for some. The issue is structural and atmosphere-related.

Participants spoke of balance as a goal where they could equally accommodate their time to both career and family demands. But work balance is a myth that is impossible to achieve. No one can equally split their time between multiple spheres that need attending to: work, family, community, personal. As long as balance is the goal, people, especially women, will feel some sense of dissatisfaction. What is necessary is the understanding that to build a successful career and to have a personal life is more about weaving work into one's life in an integrated way. We call this work-in-life integration. It challenges the ideal worker assumption about totally work-involved employees, segregating personal and family life from work life, with work given the priority in ways that increase the conflict between work and the rest of life.

This is not just a woman's issue. It involves family and care-giving as well as personal development and healthy living. Women are still the main care-takers of the young, and increasingly of the elderly. Women scientists need to deal with the personal issues of their lives more than their male colleagues because they are still the main care-givers (Dean and Fleckenstein, 2007), which results in different trade-offs in how they allocate their time. The mistaken notion of the ability to balance work and family has contributed to our current care-giving crisis.

The vision of integration moves away from idealized gender images in the division of labor. Social norms get masked as individual choices. You choose work or family. But it is impossible to have it all with the way work is organized around stereotypical male employees with no significant responsibilities outside the workplace. This continues to be a major obstacle for people combining work and family.

The goal of work-in-life integration is to maintain the ability to combine interests and responsibilities outside of work with a productive work life. Work is part of one's life; not life the work one does. Work-in-life integration enables control over when, where, and how you work, leading to being able to enjoy an overall positive quality of life. Each woman should not have to beat a solitary path through littered impediments in order to find a way to have a satisfying life and career success. The path needs to meander, allowing flexibility and freedom of movement, with ample rest stops fitting a work-in-life perspective. The issue of meaningful and rewarding science as part of life recognizes that individual priorities may differ, but that men and women should be able to experience work and personal life in an integrated way.

More generally, work-in-life-integration addresses concerns of everyone: single, couples with no children, and working parents. It recognizes that scientists lead multidimensional lives and that these dimensions are not readily compartmentalized.

Projected Success and Fulfillment

It was important for these women to find a path for themselves that led to their own definition of being successful, leading to fulfillment in the life they were creating. This had to fit who they were and who they wanted to become. None of these women were rejecting work. They were rejecting the 'all-or-nothing workplace' (Williams, 2010, p. 30).

When sharing their individual definitions of success, most of the women included the importance of relationships such as the developing of others as well as personal satisfaction. This extension to their definition of success supports previous research about the tension individuals experience working in cultures defined by male notions of success (Rapoport et al., 2002) including research by Case and Thompson (1995) that women often include more 'relationship-oriented definitions' of achievement in their overall concepts of success, wanting to achieve in 'multiple arenas of their life', not just in their career (p. 159).

As post-docs they became increasingly aware of the difficulties of integrating personal life and parenting with a career as a scientist. We don't believe that women in science select themselves out. They often felt invisible, discounted, left out, whittled down – half in, half out. This experience was both subtle and explicit. It accumulated from many points of origin. It felt like institutional assault, a psychological infliction, a forced choice rather than a freely made choice. The experience of working in such a climate could be continually humiliating, like a low-grade infection, cumulative in its power.

Today, more women entering the sciences are unwilling to give up motherhood for a scientific career. They want to be able to have both. These women continue to confront academic norms demanding total focus on their work and especially extreme pressure in early career stages during their 20s and 30s when their careers demand the most time, coinciding with their child-bearing years.

There is a profound sense of imbalance. Women's biological clock limits their reproductive years. Professional women often put family commitments on hold until their career is established, forcing a choice between pregnancy, childbirth, and child care, and a fast track career. Forty percent of the women in a survey conducted by The Association of Women in Science indicated that they short-circuited their child-bearing plans (June, 2012). Composing a career within a life is especially difficult for those who choose family and motherhood in their earlier years. Equality is largely a mirage.

We think the questions we should be asking are more on the constraints on excellence: structural and cultural barriers to the recognition and demonstration of achievement in multiple arenas of one's life. Structural factors include arrangements and practices in the workplace that cause men and women to be treated differently even when they have the same qualifications and work orientations. We know more about supply-side factors that account for productivity and differences between men and women scientists than we do about the impact of specific structural barriers and cultural stereotypes on the shaping of women's identity, fulfillment, and careers. There has been an increase in university implementation of more family-friendly policies and practices (especially those few universities participating in ADVANCE National Science Foundation programs) such as stopping the tenure clock for parental or other family-related reasons and postponing the time when faculty can come up for tenure (Philipsen and Bostic, 2010). This is not enough. Some provide on-site day care, elder care support, and facilitate dual career employment (Rosser, 2006; Philipsen and Bostic, 2010). This is still insufficient. In a recent survey by The Association of Women in Science, one-third of the researchers who took advantage of work–life initiatives believed it damaged their careers (June, 2012).

There is also a need for more flexible schedules and meaningful part-time positions including part-time tenure track possibilities. Time is an issue for post-doc women, especially when they have children. Work time is not infinitely expandable, nor are all times of the day equally available for work. Flexibility is an illusion in early career years when scientists are putting in 60–70 hours a week to demonstrate needed commitment and competence. Policies are not enough. Initiatives and programs aimed at removing barriers have to be sensitive to the needs of diverse women and men including their systemic socialization into the profession.

Ostensibly gender-neutral policies like a seven-to-ten-year clock require women to show early promise during their prime reproductive years. Even if programs are available for work/family issues, few women take advantage of them. They believe, with reason, that any limitation in their hours of availability will jeopardize their career prospects (Rhode and Williams, 2007). These supposed family-friendly policies are embedded in institutional workplace structures with norms designed to weed out all but the most dedicated employees with 'star' potential, so women who take advantage of such policies to accommodate family care-giving responsibilities are seen as less serious and committed to science in contrast to their male colleagues (National Academy of Sciences, 2006). Those who succeed often rely on 'avoidance behaviors', strategies used to escape penalties in the workplace for employees who take on (or merely admit to having) care-giving responsibilities.

Many women spoke of feeling the need to hide pregnancies as long as possible because of the connotations by more senior scientists of a lack of work commitment if pregnant. Wearing baggy clothes to hide the pregnancy was linked to this view: 'if you become pregnant there is a definite change in how they will treat you. You are not taken seriously anymore' (Preston, 2004, p. 148). The issue of pregnancy will always be a factor as long as it is equated with a lack of commitment. All women are subject to this accusation that they are not as serious about science as their male counterparts, seeking to fit the mold of the ideal worker norm, often sacrificing family commitments, and forgoing outside interests.

Societal and organizational structures supporting women's willingness to reduce or suspend their workforce participation carries an unwelcome by-product. These structures reinforce assumptions about women's lesser career commitment, leading to perceptions of them as less worthy of mentoring, training, and challenging assignments (Rhode and Williams, 2007). These assumptions are buttressed by other cognitive biases. People are more likely to notice and recall information that confirms prior stereotypes than information that contradicts them; dissonant data get filtered out (Festinger, 1957). For example, if a Principal Investigator assumes a working mother will sometimes give priority to her family over her science, they will more easily remember the times she left early than the times she stayed late. Women's attrition reinforces stereotypes about women's lesser commitment and creates a self-perpetuating cycle of gender inequalities.[3]

Organizations need to find ways to help women successfully have both marriage and children and a career that is intellectually challenging and offering high levels of responsibility just as men can have. Bias against care-giving has led women to employ strategies to avoid damaging their career, including sacrificing having children and/or marriage, deflecting attention from or hiding family commitments for achievement of career success or avoidance of career-damaging punishment. Not surprisingly, women are more likely to leave their positions because of this (National Academy of Sciences, 2006; Williams, 2010).

In a 2003 study by Drago and Colbeck on faculty use of bias-avoidance behaviors, they found that 19 percent of men and almost 33 percent of women declined the opportunity of a reduced workload or to take parental leave because they feared adverse repercussions if they did not appear dedicated to their career. Just under one-fifth of faculty fathers and mothers did not stop the tenure clock for a new child even if it would have helped. Because of the need to appear committed, many faculty mothers took no time off or just a day or two after giving birth because they believed that the appearance of commitment was so important. Almost half of mothers reported missing important events in their children's lives in order to be taken seriously at work as an academic, whereas only one-third of fathers reported this.

Perceptions largely determine what is possible in different life spheres because they are embedded in established structures, relationships, and ways of doing things, and exert powerful influence over people's sense of identity and self-esteem (Rapoport et al., 2002). Gender assumptions and stereotypes based on separation of spheres constrain the choices of women and men. Both should be able to experience all parts of their lives in an integrated way.

Experience of the Environment

Our findings demonstrate the significant role that gendered identity has on the daily experience of women in science impacting the professional and personal spheres of their lives. Widely held cultural stereotypes about gender impact perceptions of the quality and performance of men and women, not only by employers, but also in the ways men and women perceive themselves. Tokens are expected to work harder, are scrutinized more severely, expected to behave as if they are not different from the majority, and their problems (which differ from the majority) are seen as insignificant or a burden to the organization.

In hierarchical systems the closer one is to the top of the organization the more commonly rewards are determined by subjective criteria and the more powerful the informal system (Case, 1990). In science, one advances via a sponsor. The question becomes, 'What is done in the organization to ensure that women with potential are able to achieve excellence?' Women should not have to aspire to male standards and conform to male values in order to achieve.

The effects of gender, professional culture, and social expectations on the evolving roles of men and women are a dilemma in trying to craft an integrated life. There is both a need for systemic changes in institutional actions, directions, structures, and processes, and for transformational change affecting values, assumptions, ideologies, and beliefs that people have about science and their organizations, shaping attitudes, priorities, and actions (Fox, 2008). Women cannot be changed to fit academic institutions and traditional ways science is done. Success needs to be created in ways that do not pose continual conflicts between work and the rest of life (Wylie et al., 2007).

The workplace environment is communicated through policies and practices that assume that faculty members are not primary care-givers for others, and they can rely on others to take care of those responsibilities in their lives (Xie and Shauman, 2003; Preston, 2004). Academic science prevents many women from meaningful integration of their professional and personal selves. Whereas motherhood is a career liability for women, for men, fatherhood is a career asset (Williams, 2010). Nonetheless, family responsibilities discrimination penalizes mothers, potential mothers, and fathers who seek an active role in family care.

Preston (2004) found that 80 percent of women scientists mentioned at least one lost career opportunity to accommodate a husband or children.

Fifty percent of married women without children mentioned similar sacrifices to accommodate a husband's career. None felt they made conscious decisions to advance their career at the expense of their family. Of those single and childless women scientists, most had not faced the conflicting pulls from family and work except sacrificing a relationship that could have led to marriage in order to advance a career.

Being a woman is 'a better predictor of inequality than such variables as age, religion, intelligence, achievements, or socioeconomic status' (Benokraitis, 1997, pp. 6–7). To bring about change, organizational norms limiting career choices and opportunities to those who seek fulfillment through commitments to both work and personal life need challenging (Rapoport et al., 2002). Women who face 'family responsibilities discrimination' experience gender stereotyping in the ways jobs are defined, standards to which they are held, and in assumptions made about competence and commitment. The forms of discrimination reported are often subtle, sometimes intentional, or unintentional, but with implications that negatively affect experience.

Yet, in spite of the challenges particular to women, our participants were committed to their chosen field of science, not opting out completely, but in many cases choosing other venues in which they could contribute their passion for science like teaching or industry. The 'pipeline theory' focuses on increasing the number of women in science without questioning why the pipeline works as it does, or the context in which it is situated (Hammonds and Subramanian, 2003). The 'leaky pipeline' is in part an institutionally imposed construction based on a linear male version of success in science, focusing on the continual moving upwards in a career done 'my way or no way', with no points for exiting and re-entry.

The findings from our study suggest an ongoing interplay between individual and institutional factors negatively affecting women's daily life and their desired futures when they work in male-centric science environments. Decision-making is inherently a political process, influenced by the distribution of power among groups with differing and often conflicting interests. There are many harmless-looking 'micro-inequities'. These interfere with work, exacting costly tolls on self-confidence and relationships (Lenhart and Evans, 1991; Benokraitis, 1997).

Barriers today are much more subtle than they were earlier in the century. For example, most faculty scientists intend to treat their male and female post-doctoral students alike. But this seeming equality actually works against women because they are expected to behave in ways that are contrary to socially constructed stereotypes and preferences of many women, including cooperation, relational interactions, and sharing experiences that are all part of their identity.

Academic female scientists are troubled over isolation they experience associated with science and voice this discontent more than men do (Preston, 2004; Rosser, 2006). Lack of personal contact and further lack of communication between science, personal relationships, and emotions links to significant gender-related differences in desired social interaction and fulfillment (Case, 1994; Eagly, 2004). Many want to help others and work with people, preferring a career like teaching.

Structural changes can allow for better work-in-life integration and retention of women as research scientists. But these changes alone will have little effect on the subtle and largely unrecognized social psychological processes that occur linked to gendered stereotypes about women's and men's roles and occupations (Benokraitis, 1997). Institutions must demonstrate their belief that scientists can combine a high level of professional achievement with family life.

Contrary to the popular view of the scientist as a lone practitioner spending countless hours in the lab, the practice of science today involves teams of academic scientists applying for grants and working together on research and publications. Despite this reality, many women do not benefit from such collaborative efforts, as they are excluded from departmental networks (Etzkowitz et al., 2000; MacLachlan, 2006; Rosser, 2006).

This study demonstrates that women are not leaving the sciences entirely, but instead finding other arenas where their norms and expectations are more aligned with personal identities and desired futures, or as one participant stated, 'I'm going to leave and I'm going to be successful where I know I can be successful'.

IMPLICATIONS

This research extends existing studies in three ways: (1) it involves participants in transition zones; (2) individuals who are not accepted as full-time, regular members of organizations; and (3) work-in-life integration.

We discovered that these women envisioned three different career paths: research, teaching, and industry. What we don't know is to what extent their post-doctoral experience influenced their choice of path and how it carries over to influence them in their new environment. It is clear that these women post-doctoral scientists navigate a different societal and organizational terrain from their male counterparts, a terrain deeply rooted in cultural ambivalence. This ambivalence about women emerges in organizational structures and practices, as well as individual attitudes. The double bind that women face shapes their experiences and identities as scientists. Women think about their careers in the context of their whole lives. Obstacles to career achievement that arise in their personal lives need addressing, as well as maintaining a focus on both work and family life. These dynamics end up limiting their choices and capacity to exercise all their potential as scientists and human beings.

The pipeline analogy for increasing women in science is an inappropriate one. It takes a linear view, with one entry point through education and one exit point with no re-entry possibilities. Career success is continuing along the pipeline, ending with recognition as a distinguished scientist. As described, there are not varied entry points and branch points that occur in actual pipeline systems. You enter at one point, and if you exit at any of the transition points, there is no way back in.

Women's experience along their science journey is an interactive process beginning during their educational experiences. Becoming a scientist, and remaining one, is a process of individual experience, self-awareness and sensemaking, coupled with information and knowledge obtained observing the climate and treatment of women, through informal communication, and direct contact with the science 'grapevine' where women learn what is in store for them the longer they remain in science through others' stories. As scientists they walk on a tightrope juggling gender tensions continually.

NOTES

*   Presented at the Work and Family Researchers Network Conference, New York City, 14 June 2012. Partially supported by the National Science Foundation ACES (Academic Careers in Science and Engineering) CWRU ADVANCE Opportunity Grant.
    This chapter is an extended version of the research with post doc women scientists. A shortened paper appeared as Case & Richley, "Gendered Institutional Research Cultures in Science: The Post-doc Transition for Women Scientists", *Community, Work, and Family*, 16 (3), August 2013, 327–49.
1. This study refers only to women in the biological bench sciences.
2. This phenomenon is often called the 'leaky pipeline' and signifies the increased departure of women from the sciences after each phase of their careers, especially during graduate school (Sindermann, 2001).
3. In a study conducted at the Center for Work Life Policy of some 3000 highly educated Americans, nearly four in ten women reported voluntarily leaving the workforce at some point in their career. The same proportion reported sometimes choosing a job with lesser compensation and fewer responsibilities than qualified for to accommodate family responsibilities. Only one in ten men reported leaving the workforce for family (Hewlett and Luce, 2005).

REFERENCES

Acker, J. (1992), 'From sex roles to gendered institutions', *Contemporary Sociology*, **21**(5), 565–9.

Bagenstos, S.R. (2007), 'Implicit bias, "science", and antidiscrimination law', *Harvard Law and Policy Review*, **1**, 477–93.

Bailyn, L. (2003), 'Academic careers and gender equity: Lessons learned from MIT', *Gender, Work, and Organization*, **10**(2), 137–53.

Bailyn, L. (2006), *Breaking the Mold: Redesigning Work for Productive and Satisfying Lives*, Ithaca, New York: Cornell University Press.

Belenky, M.F., B.M. Clinchy, N.R. Goldberger and J.M. Tarule (1997), *Women's Ways of Knowing*, New York: Basic Books.

Benokraitis, N.V. (1997), 'Sex discrimination in the 21st century', in N.V. Benokraitis (ed.), *Subtle Sexism: Current Practice and Prospects for Change*, Thousand Oaks, CA: Sage.

Benokraitis, N.V. and J.R. Feagin (1986), *Modern Sexism: Blatant, Subtle, and Covert Discrimination*, Englewood Cliffs, NJ: Prentice Hall.

Berger, J., B. Cohen and M. Zelditch (1972), 'Status characteristics and social interaction', *American Sociological Review*, **37**(3), 241–55.

Bianchi, S., J. Robinson and M. Milkie (2006), *Changing Rhythms of American Family Life*, New York: Russell Sage Foundation.

Biernat, M., F.J. Crosby and J.C. Williams (2004), 'The maternal wall', *Journal of Social Issues*, **60**(4), 675–83.

Bilimoria, D. and X. Liang (2012), *Gender Equity in Science and Engineering: Advancing Change in Higher Education*, New York: Routledge.

Bornstein, S. and J. Williams (2008), 'The evolution of "Fred": Family responsibilities discrimination and developments in the law of stereotyping and implicit bias', *Hastings Law Journal*, **59**(6), 1–58.

Boyatzis, R.E. (1998), *Transforming Qualitative Information*, Thousand Oaks, CA: Sage.

Burke, R.J. (2007), 'Women and minorities in STEM: A primer', in R.J. Burke and M.C. Mattis (eds), *Women and Minorities in Science, Technology, Engineering, and Mathematics*, Cheltenham, UK and Northampton, MA, USA: Edward Elgar Publishing, pp. 3–27.

Burke, R.J. and M.C. Mattis (2007), *Women and Minorities in Science, Technology, Engineering, and Mathematics: Upping the Numbers*, Cheltenham, UK and Northampton, MA, USA: Edward Elgar Publishing.

Burt, R. (1992), *Structured Holes*, Cambridge, MA: Harvard University Press.

Bystydzienski, J.M. and S.R. Bird (2006), *Removing Barriers: Women in Academic Science, Technology, Engineering, and Mathematics*, Bloomington, IN: Indiana University Press.

Case, S.S. (1990), 'Communication styles in higher education: Differences between academic men and women', in L. Welch (ed.), *Women in Higher Education: Changes and Challenges*, New York: Praeger.

Case, S.S. (1994), 'Men and women at work: Gender differences in communication styles', in M. Davidson and R. Burke (eds), *Women in Management: Current Research Issues*, London: Paul Chapman, pp. 135–66.

Case, S.S. (1995), 'Gender, language, and the professions: Recognition of wide-verbal repertoire speech', *Studies in Linguistic Sciences*, **25**(2), 149–92.

Case, S.S. and L. Thompson (1995), 'Gender differences in student development', in R.E. Boyatzis, S.S. Cowen and D.A. Kolb (eds), *Innovation in Professional Education*, San Francisco, CA: Jossey-Bass, pp. 135–66.

Centofanti, M. (2000), 'Hopkins launches institute for basic medical sciences', *UniSci*, 1–4.

Chodorow, N. (1978), *The Reproduction of Mothering*, Berkeley, CA: University of California Press.

Correll, S.J., S. Benard and I. Paik (2007), 'Getting a job: Is there a motherhood penalty?', *American Journal of Sociology*, **112**(5), 1297–338.

Dean, D.J. and A. Fleckenstein (2007), 'Keys to success for women in science', in R.J. Burke and M.C. Mattis (eds), *Women and Minorities in Science, Technology, Engineering, and Mathematics*, Cheltenham, UK and Northampton, MA, USA: Edward Elgar Publishing, pp. 28–46.

DeVault, M.L. (1999), *Liberating Method: Feminism and Social Research*, Philadelphia: Temple University Press.

DeVault, M.L. and G. Gross (2012), 'Feminist qualitative interviewing: Experience, talk, and possibilities', in S.N. Hesse-Biber, *The Handbook of Feminist Research: Theory and Praxis*, 2nd edition, Los Angeles, CA: Sage, pp. 206–36.

Drago, R.W. (2007), *Striking a Balance: Work, Family, Life*, Boston, MA: Dollars and Sense.

Drago, R. and C. Colbeck (2003), *Final Report for the Mapping Project: Exploring the Terrain of U.S. Colleges and Universities for Faculty and Families*, University Park, PA: Pennsylvania State University.

Eagly, A.H. (2004), 'Few women at the top: How role incongruity produces prejudice and the glass ceiling', in D. van Knippenberg and M.A. Hogg (eds), *Identity, Leadership and Power*, London: Sage.

Eagly, A.H.L. and Carli (2007), 'Overcoming resistance to women leaders', in B. Kellerman and D. Rhode (eds), *Women and Leadership: The State of Play and Strategies for Change*, San Francisco, CA: Jossey-Bass, pp. 27–148.

Ely, R.J. (1995), 'The power in demography: Women's social constructions of gender identity at work', *Academy of Management Journal*, **38**(3), 589–634.

Ely, R.J. and D.L. Rhode (2010), 'Women and leadership: Defining the challenges', in N. Nohria and R. Khurana (eds), *Handbook of Leadership Theory and Practice*, Boston, MA: Harvard Business Press, pp. 377–410.

Etzkowitz, H., C. Kemelgor and B. Uzzi (2000), *Athena Unbound: The Advancement of Women in Science and Technology*, New York: Cambridge University Press.

Festinger, L. (1957), *Theory of Cognitive Dissonance*, Stanford, CA: Stanford University Press.

Fletcher, J.K. (1999), *Disappearing Acts: Gender, Power and Relational Practice at Work*, Cambridge, MA: MIT Press.

Fox, M.F. (2008), 'Institutional transformation and the advancement of women faculty: The case of academic science and engineering', in J.C. Smart, *Higher Education: Handbook of Theory and Research*, Dordrecht: Springer Science + Business Media B.V., pp. 73–103.

Galen, M. and A.T. Palmer (1994), 'White, male and worried', *Business Week*, 31 January, 50–51.

Gersick, C.J.G. and K.E. Kram (2002), 'High-achieving women at midlife: An exploratory study', *Journal of Management Inquiry*, **11**(2), 104–29.

Goulden, M., K. Frasch and M.A. Mason (2009), 'Staying competitive: Patching America's leaky pipeline in the sciences', Center for American Progress, accessed 2 January 2012 at http://www.americanprogress.org/issues/2009/11/women_and_sciences.html.

Greenwald, A.G. and L.H. Krieger (2006), 'Implicit bias: Scientific foundations', *California Law Review*, **94**(4), 945–67.

Gutek, B.A. and A.G. Cohen (1987), 'Sex ratios, sex role spillover, and sex at work: A comparison of men's and women's experiences', *Human Relations*, **40**(2), 97–115.

Gutek, B.A. and B. Morasch (1982), 'Sex-ratios, sex-role spillover, and sexual harassment of women at work', *Journal of Social Issues*, **38**(4), 55–74.

Hammonds, E. and B. Subramanian (2003), 'A conversation on feminist science studies', *Signs: A Journal of Women in Culture and Society*, **28**(3), 923–44.

Harding, S. (2012), 'Feminist standpoints', in S.N. Hesse-Biber (ed.), *The Handbook of Feminist Research: Theory and Praxis*, 2nd edition, Los Angeles, CA: Sage, pp. 46–64.

Heilman, M. (2001), 'Bias in evaluation of women leaders. Description and prescription: How gender stereotypes prevent women's ascent up the organizational ladder', *Journal of Social Issues*, **57**(4), 657–75.

Heilman, M.A., A. Wallin, D. Fuchs and M. Tamkins (2004), 'Penalties for success: Reactions to women who succeed at male gender-typed tasks', *Journal of Applied Psychology*, **89**(3), 416–27.

Hesse-Biber, S.N. (2012), *The Handbook of Feminist Research: Theory and Praxis*, 2nd edition, Los Angeles, CA: Sage.

Hesse-Biber, S.N. and P.L. Leavy (2007), *Feminist Research Practice: A Primer*, Thousand Oaks, CA: Sage.

Hewlett, S. and C. Luce (2005), 'Off-ramps and on-ramps: Keeping talented women on the road to success', *Harvard Business Review*, **83**(3), 43–54.

Hewlett, S., C. Luce, L. Servon, L. Sherbin, P. Shiller, E. Sosnovich and K. Sumberg (2008), *The Athena Factor: Reversing the Brain Drain in Science, Engineering and Technology*, Boston, MA: Harvard Business School Publishing.

Humm, M. (1989), *The Dictionary of Feminist Theory*, 2nd edition, Columbus, OH: Ohio State University Press.

Ibarra, H. (1992), 'Homophily and differential returns: Sex differences in network structure and access in an advertising firm', *Administrative Science Quarterly*, **37**(3), 422–47.

Ibarra, H. (1999), 'Provisional selves: Experimenting with image and identity in professional adaptation', *Administrative Science Quarterly*, **44**(4), 764–91.

Ibarra, H. and J. Petriglieri (2007), 'Impossible selves: Image strategies and identity threat in professional women's career transitions', Working Paper, INSEAD.

June, A.W. (2012), 'Work–life balance is out of reach for many scientists, and not just women', *The Chronicle of Higher Education*, 23 March, A29.

Kanter, R.M. (1977), *Men and Women of the Corporation*, New York: Basic Books.

Lenhart, S. and S. Evans (1991), 'Sexual harassment and gender discrimination: A primer for women physicians', *Journal of the American Medical Women's Association*, **46**(3), 77–82.

Liang, X. and D. Bilimoria (2007), 'The representation and experience of women faculty in STEM fields', in R.J. Burke and M.C. Mattis (eds), *Women and Minorities in Science, Technology, Engineering, and Mathematics: Upping the Numbers*, Cheltenham, UK and Northampton, MA, USA: Edward Elgar Publishing, pp. 317–33.

Long, J.S. (2001), *From Scarcity to Visibility: Gender Differences in the Careers of Doctoral Scientists and Engineers*, Washington, DC: National Academy Press.

MacLachlan, A.J. (2006), 'The graduate experience of women in STEM and how it could be improved', in J.M. Bystydzienski and S.R. Bird (eds), *Removing Barriers: Women in Academic Science, Technology, Engineering, and Mathematics*, Bloomington, IN: Indiana University Press, pp. 237–53.

Martinez, E.D., J. Botos, K.M. Dohoney, T.M. Geiman, S.S. Kolla, A. Olivera, Y. Qui, G.V. Rayasam, D.A. Stavreva and O. Cohen-Fix (2007), 'Falling off the academic bandwagon', *EMBO Reports*, **8**, 977–81, accessed 18 June 2011 at http://www.nature.com/embor/journal/v8/n11/full/7401110.html.

Mason, M.A. and M. Goulden (2002), 'Do babies matter? The effect of family formation on the lifelong careers of academic men and women', *Academe*, November/December.

Miller, J.B. (1976), *Towards a New Psychology of Women*, Boston, MA: Beacon Press.

National Academy of Sciences (2006), *Biological, Social and Organizational Components of Success for Women in Academic Science and Engineering*, Washington, DC, National Academies Press.

National Academy of Sciences (2007), *Beyond Bias and Barriers: Fulfilling the Potential of Women in Academic Science and Engineering*, Washington, DC: National Academies Press.

Neuman, W.L. (1997), *Social Research Methods: Qualitative and Quantitative Methods*, 3rd edition, Needham Heights, MA: Allyn and Bacon.

Newman, B. and P. Newman (1999), *Development Through Life: A Psychosocial Approach*, 7th edition, Belmont, CA: Wadsworth Publishing Company.

Noble, D. (1992), *A World Without Women: The Christian Clerical Culture of Western Science*, Oxford: Oxford University Press.

Perrow, C. (1986), *Complex Organizations: A Critical Essay*, New York: McGraw-Hill.

Philipsen, M. (2008), *Challenges of the Faculty Career for Women: Success and Sacrifice*, San Francisco, CA: Jossey-Bass.

Philipsen, M. and T. Bostic (2010), *Helping Faculty Find Work–Life Balance: The Path Toward Family-friendly Institutions*, San Francisco, CA: Jossey-Bass.

Philpot, C.L., G.R. Brooks, D.D. Lusterman and R.L. Nutt (1997), *Bridging Separate Gender Worlds: Why Men and Women Clash and How Therapists Can Bring them Together*, Washington, DC: American Psychological Association.

Podolny, J. and J. Baron (1997), 'Resources and relationships: Social networks and mobility in the workplace', *American Sociological Review*, **62**(5), 673–93.

Preston, A.E. (2004), *Leaving Science: Occupational Exit From Scientific Careers*, New York: Russell Sage.

Ragins, B. (1998), 'Gender and mentoring relationships: A review and research agenda in the next decade', in G. Powell (ed.), *Handbook of Gender and Work*, Thousand Oaks, CA: Sage, pp. 347–71.

Rapoport, R., L. Bailyn, J.K. Fletcher and B.H. Pruitt (2002), *Beyond Work–*

Family Balance: Advancing Gender Equity and Workplace Performance, San Francisco, CA: Jossey-Bass.

Reinharz, S. (1992), *Feminist Methods in Social Research*, New York: Oxford University Press.

Reskin, B. (1988), 'Bringing the men back in: Sex differentiation and the devaluation of women's work', *Gender and Society*, **2**(1), 58–81.

Rhode, D. and B. Kellerman (2007), 'Women and leadership: The state of play', in B. Kellerman and D. Rhode (eds), *Women and Leadership: The State of Play and Strategies for Change*, San Francisco, CA: Jossey-Bass, pp. 1–64.

Rhode, D. and J. Williams (2007), 'Legal perspectives on employment discrimination', in F. Crosby, M. Stockdale and A. Ropp (eds), *Sex Discrimination in the Workplace*, Santa Cruz, CA: University of California.

Ridgeway, C. (1993), 'Gender, status and the social psychology of expectations', in P. England (ed.), *Theory on Gender/Feminism on Theory*, New York: Aldine Press, pp 175–98.

Rosser, S.V. (2006), 'Using POWRE to ADVANCE: Institutional barriers identified by women scientists and engineers', in J.M. Bystydzienski and S.R. Bird (eds), *Removing Barriers: Women in Academic Science, Technology, Engineering, and Mathematics*, Bloomington, IN: Indiana University Press, pp. 69–92.

Rosser, S.V. and M.Z. Taylor (2009), 'Why are we still worried about women in science?' *Academe*, **95**(3), 327–46.

Rudman, L. and S. Correll (2001), 'Prescriptive gender stereotypes and backlash toward agentic women', *Journal of Social Issues*, **57**(4), 743–62.

Schiebinger, L., A.D. Henderson and S.K. Gilmartin (2008), 'Dual-career academic couples: What universities need to know', Clayman Institute for Gender Research, Stanford University, accessed 8 September 2013 at http://gender.stanford.edu/dual-career-research-report.

Scott, W.R. (1987), 'The adolescence of institutional theory', *Administrative Science Quarterly*, **32**(4), 493–511.

Sindermann, C.J. (2001), *Winning the Games Scientists Play: Strategies for Enhancing your Career*, Cambridge, MA: Perseus.

Stewart, A.J., J.E. Malley and D. LaVaque-Manty (2007), *Transforming Science and Engineering: Advancing Academic Women*, Ann Arbor, MI: University of Michigan Press.

Strauss, A. and J. Corbin (1990), *Basics of Qualitative Research*, Newbury Park, CA: Sage Publications.

Swiss, D.J. and J.P. Walker (1993), *Women and the Work/Family Dilemma*, New Jersey: John Wiley.

Thompson, M. and D. Sekaquaptewa (2002), 'When being different is detrimental: Solo status and the performance of women and racial minorities', *Analysis of Social Issues and Public Policy*, **2**(1), 183–203.

Trower, C. and R. Chait (2002), 'Faculty diversity: Too little for too long', *Harvard Magazine*, **104**(4), 33–98.

Unger, R. and M. Crawford (1992), *Women and Gender: A Feminist Psychology*, Philadelphia, PA: Temple University Press.

Valian, V. (1999), *Why So Slow? The Advancement of Women*, Cambridge, MA: MIT Press.

Valian, V. (2006), 'Beyond gender schemas: Improving the advancement of women in academia', in J.M. Bystydzienski and S.R. Bird (eds), *Removing Barriers:*

Women in Academic Science, Technology, Engineering, and Mathematics, Bloomington, IN: Indiana University Press, pp. 320–32.

Wasserman, E.R. (2000), *The Door in the Dream: Conversations with Eminent Women in Science*, Washington, DC: Joseph Henry.

Williams, J. (2000), *Unbending Gender: Why Family and Work Conflict and What To Do About It*, New York: Oxford University Press.

Williams, J. (2010), *Reshaping the Work–Family Debate: Why Men and Class Matter*, Cambridge, MA: Harvard University Press.

Williams, J. and N. Segal (2003), 'Beyond the maternal wall: Relief for family care-givers who are discriminated against on the job', *Harvard Women's Law Journal*, **26**, 77–162.

Worell, J. and P. Remer (1992), *Feminist Perspectives in Therapy: An Empowerment Model for Women*, London: John Wiley and Sons.

Wylie, A., J.R. Jakobsen and G. Fosado (2007), 'Women, work, and the academy: Strategies for responding to "post-civil rights era" gender discrimination', New York: Barnard Center for Research on Women, accessed 12 January 2012 at http://faculty.washington.edu/aw26/WorkplaceEquity/BCRW-WomenWorkAcademy_08.pdf.

Xie, Y. and K.A. Shauman (2003), *Women in Science: Career Processes and Outcomes*, Cambridge, MA: Harvard University Press.

Yoder, J.D. (1994), 'Looking beyond numbers: The effects of gender status, job prestige, and occupational gender-typing on tokenism processes', *Social Psychology Quarterly*, **57**(2), 150–59.

14. Individual, organizational, and societal backlash against women*

Ronald J. Burke**

INTRODUCTION

As someone who has researched and written about women in management for over 20 years, I am often asked for comments on various related topics by media outlets. Recently I was asked to comment on why women were less willing than men to put themselves up for promotion when qualified. I indicated that more women than men may not see a managerial job in their self-identity, they may be more risk averse than men to take a chance, and even when they put themselves forward they are less likely to get the promotion because of the 'think manager, think male' stereotype that exists. Several readers responded, mostly male, with many indicating that women were less qualified, that supporting such women was another example of social engineering, efforts to support women forced women to become more like men, and I was a leftist. A female friend, Leah Eichler, writes a weekly column for the newspaper, the *Globe and Mail*, on women in management issues. At a lunch to discuss possible themes for her column she indicated that she frequently gets 'hate mail' from male readers. Backlash is alive and well and living in Canada.

In 2012, Anita Sarkeesian started a modest fundraising campaign on the internet to raise money to produce a free series on stereotypes of women in video games (Fernandez-Blaunce, 2012). She began to get death threats, comments on her gender and race, and on Wikipedia, someone replaced her picture with a pornographic one. Then death and rape threats were made against her. A game called 'Beat up Sarkeesian', which allowed individuals to beat her virtual face into a bloody pulp soon followed. A feminist tweeter tweeted against this game and she also received death and rape threats. Gaming is a male-dominated culture.

Events that transpired on 6 December 1989 at the University of Montreal make this connection with the larger context. Marc Lépine, blaming women and particularly feminist women for ruining his life, entered a classroom at the University of Montreal's engineering building, forced the men present to leave and shot the women. In a suicide note, Lépine wrote that feminists wanted to keep the advantages of women while trying to also take those of men. Lépine screamed, 'You're all a bunch of feminists,' as he went on his rampage. Lépine likely acquired his attitudes from messages he took away from the society around him. Thus, we need to understand the sources of male backlash and begin to tackle it at all levels of society, from primary schools to senior management level, if we want to reduce such incidents in the future.

This chapter reviews the literature on male backlash in organizations, in the wider society, and cultures in which men hate women. It defines backlash, explores its causes, symptoms, and consequences, who is more likely to exhibit it, and proposes initiatives for addressing and reducing backlash. Backlash may be on the increase in organizations as men increasingly face challenges in the workplace, and in society at large (increasing unemployment, less success in school and university). Some writers (Hymowitz, 2011; Rosin, 2012) have suggested that men are becoming an endangered species, supporting the notion or concern that men are increasingly unfairly disadvantaged. Others (Sax, 2007; Kimmel, 2008) have described the ways that young men are increasingly squandering their skills and talents.

Surprisingly, very little research attention has been devoted to understanding backlash, although stories about it have appeared in the media, acclaimed books have addressed the issue (Faludi, 1991, 1999), and individuals responsible for leveling the organizational playing field have observed it. Faludi (1999) writes that women experience more backlash in male-dominated professions such as the military, policing, and fire-fighting. Faludi (1999) describes the experiences of Shannon Faulkner, the first woman admitted to The Citadel Military College of South Carolina and some faculty members of that military college (previously all male students). The college at first tried to keep her out. At The Citadel, calling a male cadet a 'woman' was the ultimate put down. Newly arrived women faculty received abuse from cadets. Some women faculty members did not put their names on their office doors, fearing abuse. Another woman faculty member was told she was a prime example of why women should not be allowed at The Citadel. Still another woman faculty member was called a 'pussy' and a 'fucking bitch'. Another woman received death threats on her student evaluations. Some women faculty were forced to move when their phone numbers, e-mails and addresses were made public. Shannon Faulkner eventually quit The Citadel after only a week, suffering from emotional and physical distress. Other female cadets admitted later suffered harassment as well. Two other young women withdrew in 1996 after male cadets sprayed profanity and derogatory messages in their residences. Faludi (1999) also chronicles changes that men experienced during these times in other industries (manufacturing, aerospace) undergoing transitions that threatened their security and livelihoods, causing some men to feel threatened.

My motivations for writing this chapter come from several sources. First, I was intrigued by isolated stories and reports on male backlash in the popular press, and in particular, the number of letters to the editor from aggrieved males. Second, Faludi's book (1991) pulled together instances of backlash in a wide variety of areas and provided an historical overview of the phenomenon. Third, my involvement with four organizations in bringing about workplace changes to support the career advancement of women has highlighted how difficult efforts towards the creation of a level playing field can be. One of these projects provided an opportunity to glimpse, first-hand, the reactions of several groups of men towards such efforts. Fourth, more research evidence had emerged in the past two decades about men's reactions to affirmative action, competent and agentic women, and men working in female-dominated occupations (Cohn, 1973/74; Astrachan, 1998). Finally, we have achieved greater knowledge of the ways that girls and women have been and are being treated in other parts of the world.

Creating a level playing field in the workplace means working towards a workplace where no one is advantaged or disadvantaged based on their group membership (e.g., women). Not everyone supports a level playing field, however (Cockburn, 1981; Rossi, 2004). Creating a level playing field may be threatening to some, particularly those who have historically been advantaged (e.g., men). The use of quotas in affirmative action or employment equity is viewed as discriminatory by many men and threatening to them. Men say that less qualified women would get preferential treatment, and some women say that these practices may raise questions about the qualifications of women being advanced. Typically, they convey a preference for hiring females and non-white males for jobs or changing job qualifications in an effort to include more females and non-white males.

Backlash occurs when members of the historically privileged group react negatively to efforts to assist members of the historically disadvantaged groups. Backlash is a form of resistance men exhibit towards policies, programs, and initiatives undertaken by groups, organizations, and governments to promote the hiring and advancement of women. Backlash can be overt or covert and occur on many fronts. It has been noted that backlash occurs against women and men using particular work–family programs (Rothansen et al., 1998; Hayashi, 2001; Haar et al., 2004), against affirmative action (Taylor, 2000; Fobanjong, 2001), and against agentic women (Rudman and Glick, 1999, 2001).

Faludi (1991), writing that male backlash has a long history, sees it as a recurring phenomenon such that every time women make some progress backlash occurs. Backlash then is a reaction to progress or change. Faludi believes that backlash was stronger in response to the women's movement of the 1970s. First, in the 1970s the feminist movement argued strongly for equality. Second, increasing economic uncertainty made it harder for men to fulfill the breadwinner/provider role. Third, preference was sometimes given to the hiring of women. Fourth, men saw women making inroads into what was earlier a male-only or male-dominated domain. Fifth, some organizations began examining their workplace cultures to identify potential barriers to women's career progress and initiate efforts to overcome these. Sixth, in a time of change, uncertainty, and confusion men became more anxious, resentful, and fearful. More recently, concerns about political correctness have added fuel to the backlash fire; some men now feel muzzled. Politically incorrect words or behaviors and telling off-colored jokes might get one censured. These factors have become increasingly important today.

Backlash has consequences for women, men, and their organizations. Relationships between women and men can become tenser. Backlash by men confirms some women's beliefs in the primitive attitudes of some men towards women. Male backlash can strengthen the bonds between men. Male backlash can also heighten and sharpen whatever differences exist between men and women; men and women inhabit two different worlds.

Male backlash can also affect women's relationships with other women. Women get divided into those who have 'made it' in a male system and those who have not. Successful women may not support the women's movement, successful women may opt out of their careers, and women who have not yet made it may be less interested in career advancement.

Backlash also has negative effects on individual and organizational performance. Energy gets invested in tension, anger, resentment, frustration, and recrimination. Men attempt to undermine organizational efforts to support women. Morrison (1992) found that male backlash was identified as the biggest problem organizations faced in their efforts to support women's advancement. A female colleague and I presented some 'gender in the workplace' sessions at a large financial services firm in several different Canadian cities. Some of the top male managers in their Vancouver office at first indicated they would not attend this session, but did attend when 'required to' by higher-level executives in the Toronto head office.

Faludi (1991) suggests that backlash is likely to be expressed by two groups of men. One group is blue-collar workers who are less educated, more authoritarian in their attitudes, and more threatened by economic and social change. The global economic recession that started in 2008, with the ensuing downsizing and job losses, certainly added to this group's reactions, with the possibility that more professional men who lost their jobs joined them. The second group includes younger professional men who face increased competition from women both in their education and upon university graduation, and some professional men over 40 who have been passed up for promotion. A new group may also be emerging in much of the industrialized world today. This group includes young men, 18 to 30, many of whom have college or university education, who are unable to find jobs, or jobs that utilize their education, skills, and training. Recent university graduates in Canada take jobs as baristas at Starbucks – not meant as a putdown of Starbucks.

During this time, men felt 'stiffed' and 'betrayed' (Faludi, 1999) by events outside their control. The benefits of male privilege that suggested that the 'sky was the limit' for men were now less likely to be realized. Some men were in crisis. Some of these men reacted by engaging in spouse abuse, alcoholism, and backlash against women and visible minorities. Some men were feeling powerless in the face of changes in their lives and environments; they were no longer in control and in charge. To be a 'real man' one must be in control and *feel* that one is in control. This is the image of masculinity (Faludi, 1999). Women were also demanding more say and this was troubling to these men. Some men lost the ability or possibility of fulfilling the provider role and being appreciated and respected as a result. Ironically their situation was similar to that of many women during this time.

Backlash is also likely to occur as a result of other changes in the environment. Here are two current examples. First, in order to increase the number of qualified women serving on corporate boards of directors, some countries (e.g., Spain, Norway) have introduced quotas that companies will have to meet. This will increase levels of concern among some men. Second, some police forces are trying to recruit officers that more closely reflect their policing communities (more women, more visible minorities, more multilingual officers). A white male knowing only one language will have a more difficult time being hired.

DEFINITION OF AND REASONS FOR BACKLASH

Backlash can be defined as any form of resistance men exhibit towards policies, programs, and initiatives undertaken by organizations to promote the hiring and advancement of marginalized employees (e.g., women, people of color, the disabled, aboriginal people). This resistance can take many forms – both overt and covert.

Goode (1982) distinguishes two kinds of resistance typically shown by men. First there are men who historically paid lip service to equality, but now disapprove of the way equality is being concretely applied. Second, there are men who never believed in equality and now oppose it openly because it is no longer just a trivial threat. Goode reserves the term backlash for the first group, those who now feel negatively about a policy they once thought was desirable. We believe the term covers both kinds of male resistance.

We believe that backlash is not generally a male conspiracy at a conscious level. Men who exhibit backlash may be unaware of their attitudes, behavior, and roles, or if they are aware, do not realize the impact of their attitudes. Women have optimistically believed that once they demonstrated the merits of their case, male hostility to their claims and rights would disappear. Faludi (1991) concludes that unfortunately women have always been disappointed.

Faludi (1991) believes that backlash is stronger now, though negative views on women's progress have always existed. She proposes several reasons for this. First, beginning with feminism, in the 1970s, women have argued voraciously for equality. The anti-feminist backlash has been unleashed not by women's achievement of full equality – but by the increased possibility that they may get it. Male backlash is an indication that women may have really had an effect (Faludi, 1991).

Second, there are now more challenges and obstacles to men's economic and social welfare, to their abilities to fulfill the male provider and breadwinner role, and ultimately to their masculinity (Goode, 1982; Pleck, 1987; Hymowitz, 2011; Rosin, 2012). These include:

- retrenchment and decline in organizations, leading to fewer employment opportunities;
- slower growth in organizations, leading to fewer promotions;
- increased competition for jobs and promotions;
- smaller wage increases, leading to a decreasing standard of living;
- a politically correct environment that fosters male-bashing;
- increased media attention to the notion of unfair advancement of women;
- increasing number of corporate and government initiatives supporting change (e.g., employment equity, diversity training).

Manhood is measured by power, wealth, and success, and unfortunately for men it is becoming harder to measure up. Kimmel (1993) writes that American men fear other men because they may be seen by them as less than manly. Since men derive much of their identity from the workplace, and it is increasingly more difficult for men to satisfy these needs, more men will feel like failures, inadequate and powerless. Women and non-white men serve as a convenient target at which to direct those frustrations, anxieties, and anger.

Third, there are indications that women are/may be increasingly advantaged. This shows up in a variety of ways. When a job is posted, it is likely to state that applications from women (and other non-traditional groups) are particularly encouraged and that the firm is committed to employment equity. In addition, there have been a few well-publicized announcements of positions specifically available only to women. Other well-publicized stories have covered the hiring of women over men (e.g., police, fire-fighters, admissions to medical school, Ontario College of Art, the Ontario government advertisement).

Fourth, men are now sensing that, though not yet an endangered species, they may be becoming a minority. They are becoming increasingly aware of changing workforce demographics. In addition, if they examine the statistics carefully, women are slowly but surely making inroads and may even be gaining. We have found in most of our research and consulting sites, that although more men than women currently receive promotions, the percentage of women receiving promotions during the past five years has increased at a faster rate than the percentage of men. Some men now realize that the world around them has become more competitive. Men have historically only competed with other men; now men have to compete with an increasing number of women as well.

Fifth, some organizations are actively engaged in diagnosing their work environments to better understand the experiences of women (and men) and to identify barriers to women's (and men's) advancement. In an attempt to level the playing field these leading-edge firms are initiating policies and programs that involve removing advantages and exclusive privileges men have always had, as well as providing women with greater support. Backlash may be fostered by the very practices used to advance women (and other non-traditional employees).

Sixth, it is obviously a time of change, and change – usually coupled with ambiguity, confusion, and frustration – makes people anxious. In light of changing roles and changing rules, some men report greater fear and resentment. Organizational discussion of targets or quotas, the increasingly popular establishment of women's groups, and the perception that women can now be placed on the 'fast track' leaves many men feeling passed over, ignored or excluded. In addition, backlash has also been observed against employees and company policies and programs that benefit some but not others. Thus elder-care benefits, which tend to be used more by women than men (though only a small number of women), are seen as an example of injustice by those not having a use for them.

HOW STRONG AND PERVASIVE IS MALE BACKLASH?

There are little data that address this question. Astrachan (1986), in a seven-year-long study of American males' attitudes in the 1980s, reported that only 5 to 10 percent of the men he surveyed supported women's demands for equality. A later survey of about 3000 men (American Male Opinion Index, 1988) reported that only about 25 percent of men supported the women's movement. The majority favored traditional roles for women. As is often the case, men paid lip service to fairness, equal pay, and working women until it was their wife that wanted to work. Faludi (1991) suggests that even these few men have in fact lost interest in feminist concerns. The pressure of male backlash is likely to reduce this support even further. As a result, the attitudinal gap between women and other women continues to widen as more women come to support the goals of the push for equality.

The major challenge to men – and men in the workplace – has come from feminism (Ferguson, 1984). Feminism was concerned with the oppression of women, and power and authority relationships in the wider patriarchal society. Feminists have cast men in management and masculine management as problematic. It is harder now to accept only men in management, and masculine management as the natural order of things. Men have responded to this critique in a variety of ways: hostility coupled with backlash, indifference, and in some cases with an openness to the possibilities for change and even motivation to change.

Begging the issue of whether male backlash is ever warranted, it is understandable to the extent that men perceive that women are making increasing gains, that women are hired and/or promoted though they lack qualifications or have lesser qualifications than men who are not hired (merit has gone by the board), and that relatively more women are being promoted. Backlash may be a rational response to perceptions of reverse discrimination.

Backlash may also be irrational and an over-reaction since although more men than women continue to be promoted, men are still likely to be responsible for making the hiring and promotion decisions, and discriminations have always had to be made between similarly qualified applicants (e.g., men) using not only formal criteria (i.e., merit) but other factors as well. When one looks at the scarcity of women at the top levels of most organizations, the cry of 'save the males' seems premature.

CONSEQUENCES OF BACKLASH

Male backlash has consequences for women, men, and organizations. Male backlash influences the relationship between men and women, resulting in increased tension between them. Male backlash confirms some women's views of the Neanderthal attitudes of some men. These men 'don't get it' and women may perceive them as the enemy. Male backlash solidifies the bonds between some men; they are under siege; they are an endangered species; they are now being discriminated against. This period, characterized by confusion, ambiguity, change, fear, and attacks on male identity and masculinity, has increased some men's introspection and supported a growing interest in men's movements (Bly, 1990; Keen, 1991; Lee, 1991). Women become the enemy for making men aware of the unfairness of the system. Men become suspicious of women if their firm has a women's group. The differences between women and men, the idea that they belong to two different worlds, become reinforced (Tannen, 1990; Gray, 1993).

The recent writing and debate centering on political correctness can also be interpreted in the context of male backlash. Men now feel muzzled; previously acceptable conversation and behavior is now seen by some in bad taste. If men display 'politically incorrect' words or behaviors they may be singled out and punished. This serves to drive those conversations and actions underground. Solidarity between some men is heightened as they decry the new and venerate the old. Tensions between men and women are heightened, particularly by men who encounter women who support their concerns about the negative effects of the politically correct environment.

Male backlash also has an effect on organizations in a variety of insidious ways. Considerable energy may get dissipated in tension, anger, resentment, and frustration. Men may rebel against and undermine organizational efforts to support women's career advancement.

The following vignettes provide illustrations of male backlash we have observed in four Canadian organizations. These observations were made in the early 1990s and the situation for women has likely improved since then. First is a national professional services firm with a 2200-person workforce, 50 percent of whom are women. This firm is part of an international public accounting organization. Although women made up half of the new professional hires, at the time only 5 percent of the partnership were women. In focus groups exploring barriers to women's advancement, women stated that male colleagues were critical of their participation in this activity and had told some of them not to gripe. One senior manager indicated that he would not take part in these sessions but was 'forced' to attend.

Second is a financial services firm with a 35 000-person workforce, 75 percent of whom were females. Some professional and managerial women belonging to a corporate women's network of about 150 chose not to reveal their membership in the network with male colleagues for fear of criticism. Some women believed that other women who were active in the creation of this group suffered setbacks in their careers as a result of their participation.

Third is a computer manufacturing firm with an 8000-person work-force, 25 percent of whom were female. Some men and women were criti-cal of the formation of a women's advisory council.

Fourth, is another financial services firm employing over 30 000 people, of whom approximately 75 percent were female. The firm had few senior female executives and has become concerned with barriers to advance-ment faced by women. As a result it has undertaken a diagnosis of this issue and one method of gathering data has been a series of focus groups. The male-only groups have revealed considerable feelings of anxiety and anger by men, resulting in expressions of backlash. First, although some of the men acknowledged the absence of women at senior levels, few thought women at their levels faced any unique barriers. Second, when asked to identify benefits they hoped would come out of this diagnostic effort, many stated that they hoped that reverse discrimination would not be endorsed or undertaken. Several believed that women have already been given preferential treatment. For example, when asked specifically about what would help their career, the first answer given by a man in human resources was a 'skirt'. They shared a perception that promotion decisions were no longer based on merit, and moreover, membership in a designated group, such as 'an MBA in a wheelchair' was a distinct advan-tage in one's career. The group believed the bank was under pressure to unfairly favor non-traditional groups from two sources. First, they were under the erroneous perception that the employment equity law must now be interpreted as hiring, supporting, and promoting quotas in order to achieve a 50–50 distribution of men and women at the senior levels of the organization. Second, they believed that the firm was buckling under to political correctness pressure to maintain its image as a good corporate citizen. Focus groups we conducted with women and with men in the same organization have supported the following conclusions. Women and men want organizations to make personnel decisions based on merit. Women believe that past decisions have not always been merit-based. Men believe that current personnel decisions are becoming less merit-based.

Burke (2005) explored backlash in a large Canadian financial services organization, part of an international operation. Data were collected from

1962 women and 480 men using anonymously completed questionnaires. In general, men were at higher organizational levels than were women. Backlash was operationalized by employee views on how much their organization had done to support the advancement of our designated groups – women, disabled, aboriginals, and racial/visible minorities – too much, about right, and too little. Women more strongly indicated that their organization had done less to support women than men did and men more strongly indicated that their organization had done more to support aboriginals than women did. Males more strongly endorsing backlash ('the organization had done too much'), had longer organizational tenures, and tended to be at lower organizational levels. Men believing that their organization had done too much and women, indicating that their organization had done too little, generally indicated less satisfying work and organizational outcomes as well (organizational identification, teamwork, supervisor satisfaction, career prospects). Thus, backlash has potentially important work and organizational consequences.

WHO IS LIKELY TO EXHIBIT BACKLASH?

As mentioned above, Faludi (1991) suggested that backlash is more likely to be expressed by two groups of men. The first are blue-collar workers. These men are typically less educated, less egalitarian men (more authoritarian) in their attitudes and more threatened by societal changes – those involving women in particular. The second group she identifies are men who are younger baby-boomers. These men face increasing competition in a more demanding world that offers fewer rewards. It will be more difficult for these men to achieve economic success and satisfy the provider role than their predecessors. Goode (1982) wrote that older men, less educated men, white men, and men living in rural areas will have more negative reactions. Our work also indicates that older men who have been passed over (over 40, less educated) will have more negative attitudes towards women's equality and progress.

DO TWO WRONGS MAKE A RIGHT?

Some men will admit that women have been discriminated against in the past. But these same men will respond that men are now being discriminated against. As a result of their perceptions of feminism, some men believe they are viewed as the enemy. Male-bashing, in their opinion, has become the order of the day. Some men believe they are prejudged as sexist, and that men are held responsible for creating and maintaining a sexist system. And to the extent to which these men perceive this to be the case, the question is then asked 'Do two wrongs make a right?'

Men resist the notion that they should be bashed or punished for a system that they did not create. An important distinction needs to be made between male-bashing that truly bashes males from male-bashing that calls into question the white male system that gives more privilege (i.e., unearned advantage). In addition, men's reactions to male-bashing deflect attention away from the ways in which men benefit/have benefitted and ways in which the playing field might be leveled.

There is an emerging consensus in North America that the setting of goals or quotas to redress past wrongs, termed reverse discrimination by some, is still discrimination, however laudatory the intended consequences. Efforts are now underway to remove or weaken the legislative support for employment equity initiatives. The effects of such efforts on the continued advancement of women in the workplace is an open question at this point.

BACKLASH AGAINST AGENTIC WOMEN AND WIMPY MEN

Gender stereotypes exist and have consequences (Heilman and Eagly, 2008). Although the stereotypes of women make them appear 'nicer' than men (more positive) they are still often the victims of prejudice. Women's stereotypes illustrate a mismatch with desirable work behaviors and work roles, resulting in negative evaluations and discrimination. Even women's positive stereotyped attributes (warmth) are seen as inconsistent with the manager's job (see Schein's, 1973, 'think manger, think male' evidence). There is considerable support for stereotyping: it is just world phenomenon – the world is just and fair. People get what they deserve. They do not see flaws/problems in stereotyping others or a need to improve their situation. This is the way things are.

Heilman and Wallen (2010), in an experimental laboratory study, found that both women and men were penalized for success in areas that violated gender expectations, but the nature of the penalties differed. Men successful in female gender-typed jobs were seen as ineffectual and given less respect than women successful in the same job or men successful in gender-consistent jobs. Women, on the other hand, who were successful in male gender-typed jobs, were more disliked and had their interpersonal skills criticized more than men in these same jobs. In addition, both women and men who violated gender norms were rated less preferable as managers.

Thus, both women and men were punished for their successes when they violated gender expectations.

Backlash has been defined as 'social and economic sanctions for counterstereotypical behaviors' (Rudman and Fairchild, 2004, p. 157). The backlash effect functions to maintain a stereotype and most stereotypes are negative. The function of a stereotype is to make the in-group feel superior by derogating and excluding others. Both women and men share gender schemas as a result of socialization.

Women who display traits associated with successful managers, such as self-confidence, assertiveness, and dominance have been shown to be punished for violating the feminine gender stereotype of submissiveness, supportiveness, and relationship sensitivity (Eagly et al., 1992; Eagly and Karau, 2002). Rudman and Glick (2001) call these sanctions the 'backlash effect'. Backlash has been found to be stronger against women in masculine jobs or positions (Chatman et al., 2008) and against women displaying masculine behaviors (Heilman et al., 2004). Women face a double bind. When they display masculine traits expected of managers – the male stereotype – they violate the female gender stereotype and are negatively evaluated (Heilman et al., 1989). In addition, masculine women, while seen as more competent than feminine women, are seen as less socially skilled, less likeable, and less likely to be promoted (Rudman and Glick, 2001).

Managerial and professional women need to be agentic to counteract the lack of fit between their gender and leadership roles, yet when they do so they get punished, face prejudice and hiring discrimination, all examples of backlash that exist throughout their careers (Phelan and Rudman, 2010). This raises an impression management dilemma for women: women need to look competent, tough, and decisive but they may not look feminine enough.

It has been suggested that self-monitoring, individual skills in accurately reading social situations, and exhibiting behaviors appropriate to the situation might reduce the backlash effect. Self-monitoring is beneficial to both men and women but perhaps even more important for women. O'Neill and O'Reilly (2011) suggest that self-monitoring was associated with the absence of backlash effects typically shown against agentic women.

Women are aware of potential backlash. Thus, they respond by 'hiding', which confirms gender stereotypes, exhibit less deviant behavior, which serves to maintain the status quo. Not surprisingly there are gender differences in self-promotion. Self-promotion is, however, important for career success. In a longitudinal study of MBA graduates, O'Neill and O'Reilly (ibid.) found that women who were more masculine, as well as scoring higher on self-promotion, received more promotions. But self-promotion violates gender prescriptions for women to be nice, modest, and other-oriented. A fear of backlash results in less self-promotion by women, resulting in less/slower career progress, being less goal focused, and engaging in less goal pursuit. Women may be more willing to promote their female peers since this does not engender backlash. When women are seen as competent and agentic they are seen as violating gender roles (Rudman and Glick, 2001). Backlash occurs when individuals violate gender stereotypes; backlash undermines competent agentic women.

Backlash also affects some men. Men who violate masculine gender role expectations (e.g., being communal) were also rated as less task competent and were less likely to be hired (Rudman, 1998; Rudman and Glick, 1999, 2001). Men who perform well in female domains (e.g., nursing, library science) are likely to be undermined by their male peers. Men are also punished for violating gender stereotypes.

Thus, both males and females are in a double bind. If either violates gender expectations or stereotypes they get punished. Agentic women get punished; passive women do not advance in their careers. Passive men (self-disclosing, success in female domains, supporting fairness) get punished; agentic men succeed in their careers but face psychological and health issues, and overwork, and are less willing or able to ask for help. There is thus backlash for disconfirming gender stereotypes: not being hired, not promoted, paid less, evaluated less favorably, negative attitudes towards women, and a negative workplace climate overall.

Rudman and Phelan (2008) also showed that when women and men deviated from gender role stereotypic expectations both women and men experienced backlash (were punished). Rudman et al. (2012) developed the status incongruity hypothesis (SIH) to explain the observed backlash. Moss-Racusin et al. (2010) found backlash reflected in bias against modest (atypical) men. Modest men were seen as violating men's prescriptions related to low status by showing weakness and uncertainty as well as agentic men's prescriptions related to high status by violating the demonstration of confidence and ambition. Backlash resulted from status violations that likely pressure some men to conform to masculine expectations and stereotypes.

Judge et al. (2012), in four studies, reported that disagreeable men (who confirm gender stereotypes) earned more money than women and agreeable men (who disconfirmed gender stereotypes). Nice guys and gals do finish last. And disagreeable women were not advantaged.

Brescoll et al. (2012), in two studies, found that male subordinates of a gender deviant (i.e., a female supervisor working in a masculine domain or a male supervisor working in a feminine domain) were accorded lower status and paid less than male subordinates working for supervisors in gender-congruent roles (a female supervisor in a feminine domain and a male supervisor working in a male domain). Interestingly, the status and reactions to female subordinates working for a gender-atypical supervisor were unaffected. Male subordinates who were able to establish their masculine credentials did not suffer any loss of status or pay.

Heilman et al. (1996), using a sample of 162 male undergraduates, carried out an experiment to study the experience of how unfair treatment affects the reactions of non-beneficiaries of sex-based preferential selection and hiring, with measures of task satisfaction and feelings towards the beneficiaries. Prosocial aspects of the work setting, the basis for selection (merit versus preference), and the abilities of the beneficiaries (superior, equal, inferior, unknown) were assessed as well. Preferential selection was found to often produce negative reactions from non-beneficiaries, but these effects were moderated by the abilities of the beneficiaries and aspects of perceived unfairness.

PREDICTORS OF THE BACKLASH EFFECT

I conclude that the prevalence and depth of male backlash is a function of societal, organizational, and personal characteristics. Personal characteristics predictive of male backlash would include such factors as age, level of education, organizational level, career progress compared to personal organization, age norms, career satisfaction, years in present position, early socialization about male and female roles, ethnic group membership, attitudes towards women, and attitudes toward equity.

Organizational characteristics predictive of male backlash would include type of industry, recent experiences of company growth versus decline, promotion opportunities, amount of government regulation and attention to employment equity (numbers), presence of initiatives (i.e., policies and/or programs) supporting women's career advancement, motivations for initiating such programs, credibility of senior management on equity issues, education and skill levels in the workforce, number and location of women in the organization and the existence of women's groups in the organization.

Societal factors predictive of male backlash would include aspects of the macro-economy such as expansion, visibility of equity issues among the general public, visibility of male backlash symptoms among the general public and number and significance of events celebrating women's achievements or struggles.

MEN'S MOVEMENTS

Although the focus of this chapter is on male backlash in organizations, behavior in organizations reflects attitudes and values of the broader society. Some men's groups believe that protection from discrimination against men is not being provided to them though women in the west are generally given such protection. In their view, anti-male discrimination is rampant from the government, in the courts, and in schools. Men are more likely to be conscripted into the army, be victims of violence, be imprisoned, lose custody of their children, and commit suicide. Men's liberation groups see pain and distress in men's lives.

In the early 1970s, a women's movement emerged to support women's work and career aspirations. This was followed by a men's movement (or movements). Early reactions to feminism and the women's movement were negative and dismissive. Men had and have a need to resist feminism. This movement was also partly against having the breadwinner role foisted on them, the need to be the financial provider, the need to work very long hours – men felt they were getting a raw deal as well. There was a need for men's liberation from these demands. Faludi believes that in the 1980s as a result of male backlash, women lost some rights.

Three kinds of men's movements have been identified: pro-feminist, masculinist, and anti-feminist:

- *Pro-feminist*. These groups believe that men and women should enjoy the same privileges, opportunities, rights, roles, and status in society. Men's real power lies in supporting women's liberation. Masculinity should be cooperative not competitive. Power should be shared equally by women and men. Men should be good fathers and express their feelings. Men in these groups support women and believe that women's liberation has not gone far enough. These groups were the last of the three to start and are now the largest.
- *Masculinist*. Men in these groups believe that men suffer from gender discrimination and burdens from the provider role. The 'mythopoetic' men's movement encouraged men to reclaim their natural barbaric manhood that feminism suppressed. This movement places women and men in opposition, encouraging men to be more aggressive, more dominant, less emotionally expressive. These masculine traits, however, are associated with sexual assaults against women, suicide, depression, and alcoholism. The more power that women have, the less power that men have: equality is seen as a zero-sum game, and that with more women now working and better education, high public support, state concessions, legal reforms, there is

family breakdown, less husband/father authority, a diminished role as provider for men. Traditionalists oppose feminist goals, calling for outmoded gender relations – men dominant, women submissive. They resist change that threatens the traditional personal authority of men. It is ok for women to work but not in ways that undermine male authority. There is a loss of patriarchal privilege.

- *Anti-feminist (the backlash)*. These men are against all measures that support women's equality, status, rights or opportunities. The changes made to support women have gone too far. The Promise Keepers Christian organization for men claimed that feminism had corrupted society, damaged the traditional nuclear family, supported women working outside the home, encouraged gay liberation, and prevented men from leading their families and government (Sommers, 2000). Fathers' rights groups (Crowley, 2008) want reforms of child support and child custody, a few concerned about the way that work hours reduce fathers' time with their children. Such men's groups can also provide valuable sources of social support and information to help men navigate their new circumstances (Metz, 1968). They help men develop healthier ways of responding to their situation and learn skills for dealing with their children and former spouses/partners. Interestingly, promoting greater gender equality both inside and outside the home will enhance men's/fathers respect to a level equal to women's/mothers respect that currently exists in society, but these groups don't consider the structural inequalities that exist in society, and domestic violence that affects women's and men's lives.

The latter two men's movement groups started as an individual and small movement, grew modestly and are now in decline. Faludi's critique of these last two men's movements (1991) noted the inconsistency between their two major complaints: (1) feminism has ruined women's lives and (2) women have never had it so good.

Men have a choice: be dragged kicking and screaming into the future or they go willingly. Men who support gender equality are happier, healthier, live longer, have better lives, have better relationships with their friends, their wives, and their children.

NOW THE BAD NEWS

Discrimination Against Women

I would like to get behind the numbers and focus on the tangible 'flesh and blood' experiences of women and men in several countries through events and stories reported in the media. It should be clearly noted that my sample of stories and events is non-random and may not represent the experiences of women and men in the workplace worldwide. These stories mostly appeared in Toronto newspapers and obviously did not contain examples of successes experienced by women in many countries as well as difficulties faced by women in these same countries. And while my interest to date has focused on managerial and professional women for the most part, relatively elite, educated, successful and privileged women, my stories also include the experiences of women and men in general. There seems to be support for the conclusion that in some societies men hate women.

Mazin al-Shihan, director of a city agency in Baghdad developed a plan to pay men to marry Iraqi war widows. Here is his rationale: 'If we give the money to the widows, they will spend it unwisely because they are uneducated and they don't know about budgeting. But if we find her a husband, there will be a person in charge of her and her children for the rest of their lives'.

Only 18 percent of Afghan women can now read or write. This prevents them from undertaking even the simplest tasks such as counting money. The Taliban banned all girls' education from 1996 to 2001 when they were in power. Taliban recruits were attacking girls' schools as this chapter was being written. Girls' education in Afghanistan suffered a setback in May 2009 when schools north of Kabul were attacked with gas, sending almost 150 students to hospital. Frightened parents were now keeping their daughters at home.

A Saudi Arabian man, aged 50, married an eight-year-old girl in the summer of 2008 against the wishes of her mother. The man was a friend of the girl's father and was paid $16 000 in return. The girl was granted a divorce from the man in mid-2009. Saudi Arabia, though receiving criticism from many countries for this practice, still permits child marriages. However, they have now raised the age to 14.

Violence Against Women

George Sodini went into a gym in Pennsylvania with guns and ammunition and killed three women, wounding nine others before committing suicide (August, 2009). Sodini developed a hatred for women as a result of his difficulties in meeting women and developing a long-term relationship with them.

A Saudi judge, speaking at a conference on domestic violence told the audience that a man had the right to slap his wife if she spent money wastefully and said that women were equally to blame for increased spousal abuse. These remarks, while not an element of their law, carry weight since Saudi judges, who are also Islamic clerics, are respected.

An eight-year-old girl in Phoenix was raped by four young boys from Liberian families. The girl's father, also from Liberia, said he did not want his daughter back (July, 2009).

Culturally Approved Violence Against Women

As this chapter was being written, a 23-year-old female student was gang raped by six young men in Delhi on 16 December 2012. She later died while in hospital from the injuries suffered during this savage attack. The six assailants have been captured, charged and convicted of murder. This incident, widely condemned worldwide, placed increased scrutiny on rape and other types of sexual assaults and harassment endured by Indian women. There were 95 000 pending rape cases in 2011 with only 15 percent making it to trial (Pokharel et al., 2013). It sometimes takes ten years for a rape case to reach the courts. In addition, most rapes are likely unreported. Some sitting legislators in India's government were themselves facing rape charges. The Indian government seems insensitive to issues of women's safety. As a result India seems indifferent to sexualized violence. Millions of Indian women live in fear of violence, from groping, leering, to rape, in this patriarchal culture. Police are either uninterested in following up rape cases or are lacking the skills to do the job. Aulakh (2012) lists the indignities women in India are subjected to starting before birth (sex-selective abortions, forced into marriages before the legal age of 18, sexual assaults and rape, a majority of male and female adolescents believing that a husband is justified in beating up his wife under certain circumstances, and life-long discrimination).

The lawyer for three of the men charged in this gang rape has resorted to 'blaming the victim'. The lawyer remarked that he never heard of a 'respected lady' being raped in India (Macaskill, 2013), adding that the couple should not have been out on the streets at night and the male companion should have defended the woman. Macaskill quotes an Indian politician saying that rapes only occur in Indian cities not villages since women in cities adopt western lifestyles.

Four weeks after this vicious rape, seven men were arrested following another rape of a 29-year-old female, again on a bus in India (Sharma,

2013). In addition, a 33-year-old man was arrested with the rape and murder of a nine-year-old girl. The man committed this rape seven months after being released from prison following conviction for the rape and murder of another young girl in 2003.

Rape is about power over another rather than sex. As Indian women became more independent, strong willed, career oriented and educated, this threatened some men in their patriarchal culture. For this culture to begin to change, it must start with changes in men's attitudes, beginning in childhood. The prevalence of rape in India is having an effect on women working in the IT sector. Many women hold jobs there and they are increasingly concerned about their safety since shift work is common. Patriarchy in India will be difficult to change. It will require at least two generations of men to realize that women are equal and should be treated accordingly. It must start in homes where girls will be valued as much as boys, boys and girls are given the same education, and parents invest as much in their sons and daughters. Equality of women and men must be accepted or little will change.

Sexual violence has been widespread in Eastern Congo for several years (York, 2012). Thirty-seven percent of men interviewed in a UN survey said they had raped a woman. This has become routine behavior for many men. Twenty-two percent of women and 9 percent of men were victims of sexual violence according to this survey. Forty-eight women are being raped every hour in the Congo. In addition, thousands of women are raped in South Africa each year (Malala, 2013; Porter, 2013) and in Zimbabwe. Homes in South Africa include 'rape doors', sliding jail doors that divide a house so intruders cannot reach residents. In Egypt, Tahrir Square has become a gang rape site (Ward, 2013).

In South East Asia, acid attacks, almost always female victims, are the result of dowry demands, domestic disputes, and revenge when young women spurn marriage proposals or sexual advances (Aulakh, 2013). Aulakh lists the following statistics: 1500 annual acid attacks worldwide; 34 114 Bangladeshi victims between 1999 and 2011; 1500 Pakistani attacks reported since 2000; 382 Ugandan victims between 1985 and 2011; 342 Cambodian victims since 1990; and 153 Indian attacks between 2002 and 2010.

In the Sudan, ten women were flogged in public for wearing trousers in violation of the country's strict Islamic law. One of these women, Ludna Hussein, pursued her case in court to expose the violent treatment of women in her country (July, 2009). Other countries having similar laws include Saudi Arabia, Pakistan, Iran, and the most conservative areas of Afghanistan. Afghanistan (August 2009) is considering a law in which women can be denied food and money if they do not have sex with their husbands. An earlier version of this law allowed men to rape their wives if they refused sex (in the Shiite community).

About 200 women in Turkey die each year as a result of honor killings (Mojad and Abdo, 2004). In some parts of the country, Turkish women dishonor their families by wearing tight clothes, having unauthorized contact with young men, or falling victim to rape. Some women are buried alive with their hands tied behind their backs. Others are locked in a room, given rat poison, a rope, or a gun and told to kill themselves to spare a family member from legal retribution. Honor killing is part of a larger culture of gendered or patriarchal violence, which is a global phenomenon common in Middle Eastern and South Asian countries. Honor-related violence is sometimes given legal sanction in the form of lighter sentences or complete leniency. Honor crimes are premeditated and often involve several family members following considerable planning. Both religion and culture are likely related to such violence.

Honor killings, including violence against women termed 'ideological terrorism' have taken place in Canada (Tripp, 2012), but these have also taken place in Muslim, Sikh, Hindu, and South Asian Christian communities. Women have been killed for engaging in premarital sex, extra-marital sex, and being the victims of a sexual assault. These acts, reflecting gender bias, an imbalance of power, and efforts to control, enforce what men believe women should be doing.

An Afghan family living in Montreal has been charged with the murder of four women including three of their daughters. The parents charged, along with a son, were upset and angered by one of their daughters dating a young man from Pakistan that they did not approve of (July 2009).

Attacks in schools in Afghanistan by the Taliban (May 2009) have meant more parents keeping their daughters at home. Malala Yousafzai, a 14-year-old girl in Afghanistan, was shot in the head by the Taliban, but luckily survived, for advocating that girls be allowed to go to school. Afghan women are concerned (February 2010), that efforts to include the Taliban in the Karzai government will set back some of the recent gains made by Afghan girls and women. There has been a sharp increase in the number of Afghan women, mainly in their early 20s, who are increasingly turning to suicide to deal with the violence and brutality they face in their daily lives.

Hypocritically, Muslim men from the Gulf States go to Bahrain where they can drink alcohol and use the services of prostitutes.

'How did 100 000 000 women disappear?' This was a headline in the *Toronto Star*, Saturday, 6 June, 2009. The United Nations Population Fund stated that over 60 million girls are 'missing' from various countries in Asia. Researchers have discovered that the ratio of women to men in developing countries and in some cultures fell below average (India, sub-Saharan Africa). Hundreds of millions of women in these countries are dead – victims of violence, discrimination, and neglect. These women are dead because their lives were given little value; the strongest indication of discrimination. These women were denied access to health care, food, and social services. The United Nations estimates that the number of 'missing' girls in the world is about 200 million (Izri, 2012). Some women murdered their babies to protect them from a life of poverty and violence, but wealthier families also prefer sons. Female infanticide has been a concern in India and China for several years. As families from India immigrate to Canada, this practice is slowly taking root there (Kay, 2012). Much of this excess mortality also occurs later in life: 66 percent in India, 55 percent in China, and 83 percent in sub-Saharan Africa (e.g., from HIV/AIDS, suicide, murder, not given hospital care when sick).

IMPLICATIONS

There are some tangible signs of progress, though uneven, and indications of stalling and back-sliding. More women are now in the workforce. More women are getting the necessary education and experience to equip them for success in the workforce. The fact that we are still chronicling 'firsts', however, is disappointing.

The bad news includes evidence showing little and slow progress in women's career advancement, some back-sliding, lots of words but little action or follow-through, along with a series of worldwide events that highlight some deeply rooted societal biases against women, fatal in specific instances. Kristoff and WuDunn (2009) describe a hatred towards women that seems to be present in some countries. Very few organizations have undertaken initiatives to support the advancement of women in most of the world's countries (Davidson and Burke, 2011).

My focus on managerial and professional women reflected, in part, my affiliation with leading schools of business and management. Our female students might someday become successful managers and professionals. In addition, I live in Canada, a developed industrialized and advanced country. Women in my country, while facing unique challenges because of their gender, are also supported in several important ways. This legitimate emphasis, however, blinded me to the reality of a significantly larger number of women in the workplace worldwide. In addition, appreciating the reality and experiences of these women in a wider range of countries highlighted the huge challenges these women face and how addressing these obstacles is also likely to advance the cause of their more educated and privileged 'sisters'. The work and life experiences of women in several countries in the developing world indicated many distressing features (bias, hostility towards women, huge restrictions on their choices). Sadly, women worldwide still lack basic rights such as education, freedom from violence, opportunities to pursue taken-for-granted life options, and justice in the workplace.

I had assumed that supporting the advancement of women into management and professional jobs would influence the experiences of women in all walks of life. This does not seem to have happened. Perhaps supporting women facing hatred, hostility, and discrimination represents a more fruitful starting point that might, in time, influence the numbers of women in management and the professions.

Several of the 'bad news' articles came from particular countries (e.g., Afghanistan, Saudi Arabia). My intention is not to single out these countries or their religions but rather paint a picture of women's experiences worldwide. I hope, in time, that the circumstances in these, and other countries, will change to provide a higher quality of life and access to more opportunity among women and girls in these countries.

I believe that efforts must be made along at least two inter-related tracks simultaneously if greater progress for women worldwide is to be realized. One track involves a continuation of our efforts to support the education and advancement of women into managerial and professional jobs. Burke and Black (1997) offer suggestions on how individuals and organizations might address and reduce backlash. The second track is to tackle the pervasive negative attitudes, behaviors, and hatred that face women worldwide.

It is no coincidence that countries among the least prosperous in the world display the greatest hatred for their women. Landes (1999) suggests that the best indicators of an economy's growth potential are the legal rights and status of its women. He writes that denying women deprives a country of both labor and talent while undermining the motivation to achieve of boys and men. Boys and men who believe they are superior and entitled do not need to learn and achieve.

BROADENING OUR RESEARCH AND ACTION AGENDA: CHERISHING AND REVERING WOMEN

Efforts need to be made at the macro-level (societal) before significant progress will be seen at the levels of individual women (Hearn, 1994). In addition, obstacles and barriers must be tackled at several levels simultaneously. These include education beginning in the early formative years, and socialization in families and schools.

On the research front, there is an urgent need to undertake projects on the experiences of women, not only in management but at all levels and walks of life (and including men as well) that include a small number of countries and also examine indicators of country/society cultural values (Emerich et al., 2004; Burke, 2009). The work of Hofstede (1980, 1998), and the GLOBE project (House et al., 2004) have identified some of these cultural values (e.g., masculinity, egalitarianism).

We must continue to put pressure on our government leaders to support women in all countries of the world. Institutions such as the United Nations, World Bank, International Monetary Fund, International Labour Organization, and the Organisation for Economic Co-operation and Development need to support such initiatives by collecting statistics on the experiences of all women in various countries.

NOTES

*   Preparation of this manuscript was supported in part by York University, Toronto.
** I acknowledge the friends and colleagues that I have had the pleasure of working with on these issues over the years: Tamara Weir, Mary Mattis, Carol McKeen, Debra Nelson, Lyn Davidson, and Mark Maier. And all of our daughters and sons. Carla D'Agostino prepared the manuscript.

REFERENCES

American Male Opinion Index (1988), New York: Conde Nast Publications.
Astrachan, A. (1986), 'How men feel: Their response to women's demands for equality and power', Garden City, NY: Anchor Books.
Astrachan, A. (1998), *How Men Feel: Their Responses to Women's Demands for Equality and Power*, New York: Anchor Press.
Aulakh, R. (2012), 'Indian women rising up against a culture of violence', *Toronto Star*, 20 December, A1, A26.
Aulakh, R. (2013), 'The scars of hate: New laws have helped Bangladesh sharply cut acid attacks. But the disfiguring violence thrives in South Asia, where it costs $1 to wreck a life', *Toronto Star*, 12 January.
Bly, R. (1990), *Iron John*, Reading, MA: AddisonWesley.
Brescoll, V.L., E.L. Uhlmann, C.A. Moss-Racusin and B. Sarnell (2012), 'Masculinity, status and subordination: Why working for a stereotype violator causes men to lose status', *Journal of Experimental Social Psychology*, **48**(1), 354–7.
Burke, R.J. (2005), 'Backlash in the workplace', *Women in Management Review*, **20**(3), 165–76.
Burke, R.J. (2009), 'Cultural values and women's work and career experiences',

in R.S. Bhagat and R.M. Steers (eds), *Culture, Organizations, and Work*, Cambridge, UK: Cambridge University Press, pp. 442–61.

Burke, R.J. and S. Black (1997), 'Save the males: Backlash in organizations', *Journal of Business Ethics*, **16**(9), 933–42.

Chatman, J., A.D. Boisnier, S. Spataro, C. Anderson and J. Berdahl (2008), 'Being distinctive versus being conspicuous: The effects of numeric status and sex-stereotyped tasks on individual performance in groups', *Organizational Behavior and Human Decision Process*, **107**, 141–60.

Cockburn, C. (1981), *In the Way of Women: Men's Resistance to Sex Equality in Organizations*, London: Macmillan.

Cohn, J. (1973/74), 'Coping with affirmative action backlash', *Business and Society Review/Innovation*, **8**, 14–25.

Crowley, J.E. (2008), *Defiant Dads: Fathers' Rights Activists in America*, Ithaca, NY: Cornell University Press.

Davidson, M.J. and R.J. Burke (2011), *Women in Management Worldwide: Progress and Prospects*, Surrey: Gower Publishing.

Eagly, A.H. and S.J. Karau (2002), 'Role congruity theory of prejudice toward female leaders', *Psychological Review*, **109**(3), 573–98.

Eagly, A.H., M. Makhijani and B. Klonssky (1992), 'Gender and the evaluation of leaders: A meta-analysis', *Psychological Bulletin*, **111**(1), 3–22.

Emerich, C.G., F.L. Denmark and D.N. Den Hartog (2004), 'Cross-cultural differences in gender egalitarianism', in R.J. House, P. Hanges, M. Javidan, P.W. Dorfman and V. Gupta (eds), *Culture, Leadership and Organizations. The GLOBE Study of 62 Societies*, Thousand Oaks, CA: Sage, pp. 343–93.

Faludi, S. (1991), *Backlash: The Undeclared War Against American Women*, New York: Crown Publishers.

Faludi, S. (1999), *Stiffed: The Betrayal of the American Man*, New York: William Morrow.

Ferguson, K. (1984), *The Feminist Case Against Bureaucracy*, Philadelphia, PA: Temple University Press.

Fernandez-Blaunce, K. (2012), 'Feminist blogger faces a games backlash', *Toronto Star*, 11 July.

Fobanjong, T. (2001), *Understanding the Backlash Against Affirmative Action*, Hauppauge, NY: Nova Science Publishers.

Goode, W.J. (1982), 'Why men resist', in B. Thorne and M. Yalom (eds), *Rethinking the Family: Some Feminist Questions*, New York: Longman.

Gray, J. (1993), *Men are from Mars, Women are from Venus*, New York: Harper.

Haar, J.K., C.S. Spell and M.P. O'Driscoll (2004), 'The backlash against work–family benefits. Evidence from New Zealand', *Compensation and Benefits Review*, **35**(1), 26–34.

Hayashi, A.M. (2001), 'Mommy track backlash', *Harvard Business Review*, **79**(3), 33–42.

Hearn, J. (1994), 'Changing men and changing managements: Social change, social research and social action', in M.J. Davidson and R.J. Burke (eds), *Women in Management: Current Research Issues*, London: Paul Chapman Publishing, pp. 192–211.

Heilman, M.E. and A.H. Eagly (2008), 'Gender stereotypes are alive, well and busy producing discrimination', *Industrial and Organizational Psychology*, **1**(4), 393–8.

Heilman, M.E. and A.S. Wallen (2010), 'Wimpy and undeserving of respect:

Penalties for men's gender-inconsistent success', *Journal of Experimental Social Psychology*, **46**(4), 664–7.

Heilman, M.E., W.F. McCullough and D. Gilbert (1996), 'The other side of affirmative action: Reactions of non-beneficiaries to sex-based preferential selection', *Journal of Applied Psychology*, **81**(4), 346–57.

Heilman, M.E., C.J. Block, R.F. Martell and M.C. Simon (1989), 'Has anything changed? Current characterizations of men, women and managers', *Journal of Applied Psychology*, **74**(6), 935–42.

Heilman, M.E., A. Wallen, D. Fuchs and M. Tamkins (2004), 'Penalties for success: Reactions to women who succeed at male gender-typed tasks', *Journal of Applied Psychology*, **89**(3), 416–27.

Hofstede, G. (1980), *Culture's Consequences: International Differences in Work-related Values*, Newbury Park, CA: Sage Publications.

Hofstede, G. (1998), *Masculinity and Femininity: The Taboo Dimension of National Cultures*, Newbury Park, CA: Sage Publications.

House, R.J., P.J. Hanges, M. Javidan, P.W. Dorfman and V. Gupta (2004), *Culture, Leadership and Organizations: The GLOBE Study of 62 Societies*, Thousand Oaks, CA: Sage.

Hymowitz, K.S. (2011), *Manning Up: How the Rise of Women has Turned Men into Boys*, New York: Basic Books.

Izri, T. (2012) '"It's a girl": The 3 deadliest words in the world', *Toronto Star*, 15 November.

Judge, T.A., A. Livingston and C. Hurst (2012), 'Do nice guys – and gals – really finish last? The joint effects of sex and agreeableness on income', *Journal of Personality and Social Psychology*, **102**(2), 390–407.

Kay, B. (2012), 'The "war on women" that dares not speak its name: Every year thousands of female fetuses are killed through sex-selective abortion in this country – not that feminists seem to care', *National Post*, 19 December, A17.

Keen, S. (1991), *Fire in the Belly: On Being a Man*, New York: Bantam Books.

Kimmel, M. (1993), 'Clarence, William, Iron Mike, Tailhook, Senator Packwood, Spur Posse, Magic. . .and us', in E. Buchwald, J.R. Fletcher and M. Roth (eds), *Transforming a Rape Culture*, Minneapolis, MN: Milkweed, pp. 156–78.

Kimmel, M. (2008), *Guyland: The Perilous World Where Boys Become Men*, New York: Harper.

Kristoff, N.D. and S. WuDunn (2009), *Turning Oppression into Opportunity for Women Worldwide*, New York: Knopf.

Landes, D.S. (1999), *The Wealth and Poverty of Nations: Why Some are so Rich and Some so Poor*, New York: Norton.

Lee, J. (1991), *At My Father's Wedding: Reclaiming our True Masculinity*, New York: Bantam Books.

Macaskill, A. (2013), 'Gang rape victim's fault: Indian lawyer: Never heard of "respected lady" being attacked', *National Post*, 10 January, A9.

Malala, J. (2013), 'In this war against women, everyone loses', *Globe and Mail*, 21 February, A17.

Metz, C.V. (1968), *Divorce and Custody for Men: A Guide and Primer Designed Exclusively to Help Men Win Just Settlements*, New York: Doubleday and Company.

Mojad, S. and N. Abdo (2004), *Violence in the Name of Honour: Theoretical and Political Challenges*, Istanbul: Bilgi University Press.

Morrison, A.M. (1992), *The New Leaders*, San Francisco, CA: Jossey-Bass.

Moss-Racusin, C.A., J.E. Phelan and L.A. Rudman (2010), 'When men break the gender rules: Status incongruity and backlash against modest men', *Psychology of Men and Masculinity*, **11**(2), 140–51.

O'Neill, O.A. and C.A.O. O'Reilly (2011), 'Reducing the backlash effect: Self-monitoring and women's promotions', *Journal of Occupational and Organizational Psychology*, **84**(4), 825–32.

Phelan, J.E. and L.A. Rudman (2010), 'Reactions to ethnic deviance: The role of backlash in racial stereotype maintenance', *Journal of Personality and Social Psychology*, **99**(2), 265–81.

Pleck, J.H. (1987), 'The contemporary man', in M. Scher, M. Stevens, G. Good and G.-A. Eichenfield (eds), *Handbook of Counseling and Psychotherapy with Men*, London: Sage, pp. 119–33.

Pokharel, K., V. Agarwal and S. Anand (2013), 'Murder charges filed against alleged rapists', *Globe and Mail*, 4 January, A9.

Porter, C. (2013), 'In South Africa simply being a woman spells premonition for attack', *Toronto Star*, 10 September, A10.

Rosin, H. (2012), *The End of Men and the Rise of Women*, New York: Riverhead Books.

Rossi, S.E. (2004), *The Battle and Backlash Rage On: Why Feminism Cannot Be Obsolete*, New York: Xlibris Corporation.

Rothansen, T.J., J.A. Gonzalez, N.E. Clarke and L.L. O'Dell (1998), 'Family-friendly backlash fact or fiction? The cost to organizations on-site child care centers', *Personnel Psychology*, **51**(3), 685–706.

Rudman, L.A. (1998), 'Self-promotion as a risk factor for women: The costs and benefits of counter-stereotypical impression management', *Journal of Personality and Social Psychology*, **74**(3), 629–45.

Rudman, L.A. and K. Fairchild (2004), 'Reactions to counter stereotypic behavior: The role of backlash in cultural stereotype maintenance', *Journal of Personality and Social Psychology*, **87**(2), 157–76.

Rudman, L.A. and P. Glick (1999), 'Feminized management and backlash against agentic women: The hidden costs to women of a kinder, gentler image of middle managers', *Journal of Personality and Social Psychology*, **77**, 1004–16.

Rudman, L.A. and P. Glick (2001), 'Proscriptive gender stereotypes and backlash toward agentic women', *Journal of Social Issues*, **57**(4), 743–62.

Rudman, L.A. and J.E. Phelan (2008), 'Backlash effects for disconfirming gender stereotypes in organizations', in A.P. Brief and B.M. Staw (eds), *Research in Organizational Behavior, Vol. 4*, New York: Elsevier, pp. 61–79.

Rudman, L.A., C.A. Moss-Racusin, J.E. Phelan and S. Nauts (2012), 'Status incongruity and backlash effects: Defending the gender hierarchy motivates prejudice toward female leaders', *Journal of Experimental Social Psychology*, **48**, 165–79.

Sax, L. (2007), *Boys Adrift: The Five Factors Driving the Growing Epidemic of Unmotivated Boys and Underachieving Young Men*, New York: Basic Books.

Schein, V.E. (1973), 'The relationship between sex role stereotypes and requisite management characteristics', *Journal of Applied Psychology*, **57**(2), 95–100.

Sharma, A. (2013), 'Six arrested in second India bus gang rape', *National Post*, 14 January, A1, A12.

Sommers, C.H. (2000), *The War Against Boys: How Misguided Feminism is Harming Our Young Men*, New York: Simon and Schuster.

Tannen, D. (1990), *You Just Don't Understand: Men and Women in Conversation*, New York: Morrow.

Taylor, E. (2000), 'Critical race theory and interest convergence in the backlash against affirmative action. Washington State and Initiative 200', *Teachers College Record*, **102**(3), 539–60.

Tripp, R. (2012), *Without Honour: The True Story of the Shafia Family and the Kingston Canal Murders*, Toronto: HarperCollins.

Ward, O. (2013), 'Battling a culture of harassment', *Toronto Star*, 19 February, A4.

York, G. (2012), 'Rape rampant in chaotic Congo: Nearly 1700 assaults perpetrated by armed men in two of Congo's eastern provinces in the first half of this year, UN report says', *Globe and Mail*, 11 December, A3.

PART IV

Men as allies: signs of progress

15. How can men and women be allies in achieving work–family balance? The role of coping in facilitating positive crossover

Michael L. Litano, Dante P. Myers and Debra A. Major

INTRODUCTION

As dual-earner couples have become the norm, once well-defined partner life roles (i.e., breadwinner or homemaker) have become more ambiguous. Concurrently, what it means to achieve work–family balance lacks a singular definition; instead, ideal 'balance' is individually defined. Balancing work and family is a challenge that both men and women confront, but are they allies in facing this challenge? In this chapter we argue that the answer to this question largely hinges on the extent to which men and women's efforts to manage work–family conflict and to find balance are aligned. To the extent that men and women engage in coping strategies that stimulate each other's well-being, they become allies in combating work–family conflict and in achieving their own personal balance.

The chapter is presented in three sections. In the first, we define work–family conflict and facilitation, the two primary precursors of work–family balance. In the second, we review the ways in which men and women can be both adversaries and allies in influencing each other's well-being via crossover effects. We conclude this chapter by arguing that the key determinant of whether men and women are allies or adversaries in achieving work–family balance depends on the extent to which each partner engages in work–family coping strategies that facilitate positive crossover.

THE WORK–FAMILY INTERFACE

Broadly construed, 'work' and 'family' are considered the two primary domains or spheres of life (Major, 2007). Spillover refers to the transfer process of positive and negative experiences, moods, and attitudes between two domains (i.e., work and home) within the same individual (Crouter, 1984; Bolger et al., 1989). In the work–family interface, this spillover between the work and family domains has generally been characterized negatively as work–family conflict (e.g., Greenhaus and Beutell, 1985) and more recently, positively as work–family facilitation (e.g., Frone, 2003) and enrichment (Greenhaus and Powell, 2006).

Work–Family Conflict

Greenhaus and Beutell (1985) defined 'work–family conflict' as 'a form of interrole conflict in which the role pressures from the work and family domains are mutually incompatible' (p. 77). Two separate forms of interference have been recognized as components of work–family conflict (Gutek et al., 1991). Work interference with family (WIF) transpires when the work role demands required of an employee hinder his or her ability to perform at home in the family role. Family interference with work (FIW) occurs when one's responsibilities at home get in the way of work performance. Work–family conflict has negative consequences in both the family life and occupational domains. Research has shown that high work–family conflict has been linked to reduced physical health and mental health, including increased body mass index (BMI), cholesterol, alcohol use and depression (Grzywacz and Bass, 2004; van Steenbergen and Ellemers, 2009; Wang et al., 2010). Furthermore, increased work–family conflict has been linked to reduced job and life satisfaction (Kossek and Ozeki, 1998) and increased marital dissatisfaction (Bedeian et al., 1988).

Work–Family Facilitation

Conversely, 'work–family facilitation' refers to the extent to which participation in one life domain (i.e., home) is enhanced by the acquisition or development of experiences, skills, and opportunities in another life domain (i.e., work; Frone, 2003). Similar to work–family conflict, work–family facilitation can be described as bi-directional, such that involvement in the work domain may facilitate participation at home, or participation in the home domain may facilitate involvement at work. More specifically, Wayne and colleagues (2007) define work–family facilitation as 'the extent to which an individual's engagement in one life domain (i.e., work/family) provides gains (i.e., developmental, affective, capital, or efficiency) which contribute to enhanced functioning of another life domain (i.e., family/work)' (p. 64). In this definition, individual engagement is considered to reflect the degree of one's involvement in a particular domain, during which the individual experiences and acquires developmental (e.g., knowledge), affective (e.g., emotional), capital (e.g., economic assets) and efficiency (e.g., increased attention) 'gains' (Carlson et al., 2006). Facilitation occurs when gains from one domain improve effectiveness in another domain. Though related, work–family conflict and work–family facilitation are distinct constructs that do not represent counterparts to each other, but rather represent two key antecedents to work–family balance (Frone, 2003).

Work–Family Balance

Balance in one's work and family lives refers to achieving fulfilling experiences in both the work and family domains while expending resources sensibly across both roles (Kirchmeyer, 2000). Personal balance differs within and between individuals and does not necessarily imply equal investments across domains. Balance, in this case, means achieving a personally defined harmony among life roles. Major and Litano (2013) characterized it as a form of 'adaptability' that enables individuals to pursue desired goals in the changing landscape of their work and personal life. At a given point, for example, this could entail focus on one's education and career, whereas at another point, family and personal life may be emphasized. Such adaptive transitions play out over the course of a day as well as over the life course (cf. Ashforth et al., 2000; Rusconi et al., 2013). Balance is facilitated by support from extended family, friends, a spouse, or an employer (e.g., Greenhaus and Parasuraman, 1994; Carlson and Perrewé, 1999; Major et al., 2008). Work–family balance is a dynamic and continuous objective that is enhanced when work–family conflict is minimized and work–family facilitation is maximized (Frone, 2003).

While Frone's (2003) conceptualization captures the intra-personal processes of positive and negative spillover and the resulting work–family balance at the individual level, it neglects spillover between individuals within a couple. 'Crossover' research addresses the question, 'Does one partner's positive or negative spillover affect the work–family balance of the other partner?' The answer is a resounding 'yes' and reveals the ways in which men and women can be considered adversaries and allies in the effort to effectively manage work–family conflict, promote work–family facilitation, and develop work–family balance.

NEGATIVE AND POSITIVE CROSSOVER EFFECTS

Whereas spillover is an intra-individual process between domains, crossover is an inter-individual process that occurs between two closely related individuals (Westman, 2001). In the work–family interface, crossover represents the process by which one partner's positive or negative states of well-being transfer and affect the well-being of the other partner (Westman, 2001; Demerouti et al., 2005). Building upon the previous definition, Westman et al. (2009) suggested that crossover may apply to emotions, moods, feelings or dispositions. Westman (2001) and Westman and Vinokur (1998) recognized three non-exclusive mechanisms that describe the crossover process: direct and indirect crossover, and common stressors. 'Direct crossover' occurs when the positive or negative experience that transfers between two partners is produced by a direct empathetic reaction. For example, stress in one partner causes an empathetic reaction in the other that results in his or her increased levels of stress. 'Indirect crossover' effects occur when an additional variable (such as partner support) mediates the crossover process. Stress may influence one's own coping strategies as well as the coping strategies of his or her partner, ultimately influencing partner stress. Lastly, crossover may appear to occur when 'common stressors' in the same environment affect both partners; this effect is considered spurious (Westman, 2001, 2006).

Although the majority of crossover research tends to concentrate on the negative experiences that transfer between partners, the degree to which men and women can transfer positive experiences to each other may enhance their individual pursuits of work–family balance. The following sections of this chapter will discuss the literature focusing on the negative and positive crossover of experiences in the work–family interface. We will then examine how men and women may intentionally facilitate work–family balance in one another, while also realizing their own optimal balance.

Evidence of Men and Women's Adversarial Relationship: Negative Crossover

Negative crossover is the label applied to the undesirable outcomes that partners transfer to one another. Such outcomes include: mood, depression, dissatisfaction, physical illness, work–family conflict, and burnout/exhaustion (Westman, 2001). In this section, we examine crossover research on work–family conflict and burnout/exhaustion, two primary contributors to work–family balance.

Work–family conflict

The relationship between men and women can be construed as adversarial to the extent that they induce one another's work–family conflict through crossover effects. Hammer et al.'s (1997) study examined the effects of work and family variables (i.e., work salience, perceived work schedule flexibility, and family involvement) on partners' work–family conflict in dual-earner couples. Bi-directional crossover effects of work–family conflict were found to occur between men and women in dual-earner couples. Partners' work–family conflict accounted for more variance in one's own work–family conflict than the other work and family variables examined. Additionally, the results indicated that women's work salience is a significant predictor of men's work–family conflict, such that as women were more involved with and placed a higher priority on their own career, their partners' level of work–family conflict increased. In fact, the crossover effects of partners' work and family variables accounted for similar levels of variance in men's work–family conflict as did men's own spillover effects from these variables. Ultimately, both men and women's work–family conflict was found to cross over and to predict their partners' levels of work–family conflict, suggesting a downward spiral of negative crossover between partners.

Hammer et al. (2003) also found significant bi-directional crossover effects for work–family conflict on organizational withdrawal behaviors in dual-earner couples. Specifically, wives' family-to-work conflict positively predicted the number of interruptions husbands reported at work. Furthermore, husbands' family-to-work conflict predicted wives' increased work tardiness. These findings suggest that one's work–family conflict can have significant implications for a partner's participation in other roles, including work. Through crossover, work–family conflict has been shown to have negative intra-individual and inter-individual effects in dual-earner couples.

Negative crossover of work–family conflict also affects how satisfied partners are with their relationships. Matthews et al. (2006) examined the presence of crossover effects between work-to-relationship conflict and relationship tension in dual-earner couples. Their results suggested that individual perceptions of partners' work-to-relationship conflict were positively related to personal reports of relationship tension. How a partner's work-to-relationship conflict is perceived seems to act as a device through which personal work-to-relationship conflict impacts experiences of relationship tension. Additionally, men reported greater relationship tension when their partners reported higher levels of work-to-relationship conflict. This study suggests that how one perceives a partner's work–family conflict affects the tensions they feel in their relationship.

Men and women can play an adversarial role even when attempting to ameliorate each other's stressors. Westman and Etzion (2005) found evidence for this paradox while examining the bi-directional crossover of work–family conflict between partners after controlling for job and family stressors. Job stressors were positively related to work–family conflict for both partners, whereas family stressors were only related to work–family conflict for wives. Furthermore, women benefited from their husbands' social support to buffer the effect of their job stress, and husbands benefited from their wives' support concerning family stress. Interestingly, a reverse buffering effect was found for wives' job-related support. The support husbands received from their spouses concerning job issues amplified the positive relationship between their job stress and work–family conflict. A possible explanation for this phenomenon is that husbands may perceive their wives' concerns about their own job stressors as a reinforcement of their inability to cope themselves. As a result, work–family conflict increases despite supportive partner intentions.

The demands of the home and work domains promote adversarial roles by allowing work–family conflict to cross over between partners. For example, Bakker et al. (2008) found support for a spillover–crossover model of job demands, exhaustion, and work–family conflict in dual-earner couples. For men and women, job demands were positively related to their reported work–family conflict as well as their partner's perceived work–family conflict. High levels of job demands were also linked to an increased chance of bringing work home and prioritizing work over family. This opens the door to a domino effect that may ultimately increase the conflict between partners. Specifically, as job demands cause partners to prioritize work over family, this may create an unequal division of responsibilities within the household, which then engenders role conflict for each partner. Home demands were positively related to family–work conflict and ultimately predicted work-related exhaustion.

Burnout/exhaustion

The crossover of exhaustion or burnout between men and women is another barrier to work–family balance. As Frone (2003) notes, work–family balance is more than the absence of work–family conflict, rather balance is achieved through a combination of low work–family conflict and high work–family facilitation. Work–family facilitation is contingent upon work engagement. Burnout and exhaustion suggest an extreme lack of work engagement. Burnout refers to a psychological syndrome of emotional exhaustion and cynicism or depersonalization (Maslach, 1993). Exhaustion is the fatigue one experiences in response to extended exposure to high job demands (Bakker and Demerouti, 2007), and cynicism refers to lack of job interest and job meaningfulness (Bakker et al., 2002). Research has examined the outcomes of burnout for individuals (i.e., negative health outcomes) and the negative effects it has as it crosses over between partners and between co-workers.

Bakker et al. (2005) found support for the bi-directional crossover of burnout between men and women. Results showed that one's exhaustion and cynicism levels cross over and significantly predict partner exhaustion and cynicism. Thus, both negative work experiences and negative affect derived from work cross over and influence partner burnout. The negative crossover effects of burnout may also lead to reduced partner health and contribute to depressive feelings. Bakker (2009) conducted two studies among medical residents and teachers examining the crossover effects of burnout on partner health. His findings suggest that burnout is negatively related to reported health and also crosses over to influence partners' health. Furthermore, the crossover of burnout was shown to have a positive relationship with self-reported depression and partner depression. Not only can burnout cross over from one spouse to the other, but it may negatively affect partner physical and mental health.

Bakker et al. (2009a) examined the relationship between workaholism, work–family conflict, and relationship quality in dual-earner couples. Results demonstrated that workaholism was positively related to work–family conflict, which was in turn a significant negative predictor of partners' perceived social support. Because workaholism includes compulsive overworking (Robinson, 1997) it implies a risk of fatigue (exhaustion/burnout) in response to these demands. Therefore, these results illustrate increased relationship turmoil as work is over-prioritized.

The crossover of burnout also has the capacity to influence negative spousal interactions. An adversarial relationship between men and women can be exacerbated by social undermining behaviors as burnout crosses over. For example, Westman et al. (2001) investigated job insecurity and the crossover of burnout between spouses working within the same Israeli organization. Results demonstrated a direct crossover effect of burnout from husbands to wives, but not from wives to husbands. Westman and colleagues (2001) suggested this unilateral crossover effect may be attributable to gender differences in coping and/or work–family focus. Additionally, men and women's burnout was a strong predictor of social undermining behavior toward the opposite partner. These results suggest that conflict may arise within partner relationships as antagonistic interaction is amplified in response to both partners experiencing the psychological strain of burnout.

Just as the crossover of burnout has negative effects between partners, men and women may be adversaries in the workplace to the extent that burnout crosses over between co-workers. In Bakker et al.'s (2009b) review of the crossover literature, they discuss numerous studies that demonstrate the crossover of burnout between co-workers. Research has acknowledged that burnout/exhaustion crosses over from teams to individual team members (e.g., Westman and Bakker, 2008) and between co-workers (Bakker et al., 2006). Furthermore, Bakker et al. (2009b) outline conditions that may facilitate the crossover of burnout between co-workers, including: susceptibility to contagion, frequency of interaction, and similarity with the source. Bakker and Schaufeli (2000) demonstrated that practitioners and teachers who were susceptible to emotions expressed by their colleagues were more likely to experience burnout; in addition, they found that when the frequency of conversations between teachers and their colleagues who experience burnout were high, they were more likely to catch the negative attitudes of their colleagues. In regard to similarity, Bakker et al. (2007) found that soldier similarity in profession and status to the stimulus person moderated the crossover of burnout, such that cynicism was especially pronounced among those closest in rank. The possibility of crossover between co-workers increases as more of the discussed conditions are present, and in turn, adverse effects on employee burnout become imminent. Aside from the one study that examined the crossover of burnout among husbands and wives who were employed by the same organization (Westman et al., 2001), no research to our knowledge has examined gender differences in the crossover of burnout/exhaustion between co-workers, or the impact that the gender composition of the organization and occupation may have on crossover effects. Research in these areas will help to clarify whether the adversarial (or cooperative) roles men and women assume in their pursuit of work–family balance are contingent on domain-related factors.

Men and Women as Allies: Positive Crossover

As discussed in the previous section, the majority of crossover research has focused on negative effects, such as job burnout (Bakker et al., 2005), distress (Westman, 2001), and work–family conflict (e.g., Hammer et al., 2003; Westman and Etzion, 2005). More recently, research has begun to explore positive crossover effects and how the work–family interface is affected. Men and women can be allies in each other's efforts to balance work and family to the degree that positive well-being transfers in both domains (Bakker et al., 2009b; Kinnunen et al., 2013). At home, positive experiences felt by one partner may allow for similar states to transmit to the other partner, initiating an upward spiral of positive transfer. At work, positive crossover between employees, teams, and supervisors may lead to an increase of perceived work resources, which ultimately facilitates positive crossover in the home domain as well (e.g., Demerouti, 2012).

Positive crossover between partners

Researchers have examined the positive effects of crossover in the home domain. For example, research has suggested men's life satisfaction crosses over and positively affects that of their wives (Demerouti et al., 2005). It has also been shown that positive work–family spillover crosses over and reduces depressive symptoms in one's partner over time (Hammer et al., 2005). In addition, this positive work–family spillover has a greater impact on partner depression levels than on one's own depressive symptoms. Perhaps most notable is the finding that positive work–family spillover had a greater effect than work–family conflict (a type of negative spillover) on the depressive symptoms of one's partner. The results from this study suggest that positive experiences in the work–family interface may have a stronger impact on partner outcomes than negative experiences. This is especially pertinent when considering work–family balance as a product of reduced conflict and increased facilitation.

Researchers have examined the crossover effects of work engagement (Bakker et al., 2005), an antecedent of work–family facilitation. Schaufeli et al. (2002) defined work engagement as a positive work-related mentality consisting of vigor, dedication, and absorption. These authors describe 'vigor' as work-related investment, energy, and persistence; 'dedication' as a work-related sense of involvement, significance, and enthusiasm; and 'absorption' as deep, work-related attentiveness and engrossment. Work engagement is related to, but distinct from job burnout. While they reflect opposing constructs, they do not represent polar ends of a continuum. Bakker et al. (2005) tested the bi-directional crossover effects of two dimensions of work engagement, vigor and dedication between partners and found that engagement was positively related to partner levels of engagement. Furthermore, their results suggested that the strength of positive crossover effects is similar to that of negative crossover effects (e.g., job burnout). Bakker and Demerouti (2009) also found that work engagement crossed over between partners when men were more likely to embrace the psychological perspectives of others. As a result of these crossover effects, co-workers reported that both in-role (e.g., role-defined work obligations) and extra-role (e.g., helping behaviors) job performance increased. Together, the results from these studies suggest that high work engagement transfers between partners and may ultimately influence performance at work. However, no research to our knowledge has examined how family engagement might transfer between partners and thereby affect work–family facilitation and work–family conflict. Considering family engagement is especially apposite given that the family domain is more permeable than the work domain, a situation known as asymmetrical boundary permeability (Pleck, 1977). Indeed, research suggests that work interferes with the family domain at a greater frequency than family interferes with the work domain (Frone et al., 1992). On the other hand, this asymmetrical boundary permeability between the work and family domains might indicate that a similar relationship would occur in terms of work and family resources. Thus, increasing one's own work resources may also benefit partner well-being through crossover effects.

For example, Demerouti (2012) tested a spillover-crossover model by which one partner's work resources spilled over to affect his or her individual energy levels through work self-facilitation. Domain-specific self-facilitation transpires when resources accumulated in one domain stimulate functioning and/or affect during time allotted to personal leisure. Demerouti's (2012) spillover-crossover model specifically examined the roles of work and family self-facilitation. The energy levels of one individual increase from his or her allocation of work resources, such as social support and autonomy, through work self-facilitation. These amplified energy levels then cross over and influence the perceived home resources of his or her partner and stimulate his or her energy levels through family self-facilitation. Thus, the resources that each partner individually accumulates affect his or her own personal balance, and also his or her partner's balance through crossover effects.

Similarly, Song et al. (2008) found spillover and crossover effects of positive and negative moods between the work and family domains. Men and women may be allies in achieving work–family balance by attaining resources from the work domain and separately transferring them to the family domain. The attainment and crossover of positive states of well-being are particularly germane to achieving work–family balance as these positive experiences have been shown in some research to outweigh the impact of negative crossover (e.g., Hammer et al., 2005).

Positive crossover in the workplace
Though research on positive crossover has been limited, studies have generally examined crossover effects among men and women in domestic partnerships. Work–family balance involves multiple life domains, therefore positive crossover effects among those engaged in work relationships are also relevant. Indeed, several studies have shown that work engagement transfers between employees and their co-workers, work teams, and supervisors.

Bakker and Xanthopoulou (2009) examined the daily crossover of work engagement between 62 co-worker dyads. On days when an employee exhibited high vigor, the work engagement of his or her co-worker was positively related. This effect was moderated by the frequency of dyad communication by phone, e-mail, or in person, such that the more often the dyad communicated the stronger the crossover relationship. Ultimately, this positive crossover resulted in increased self-reported job performance for the dyads high in work engagement. Similarly, Bakker et al. (2006) surveyed 85 teams of Royal Dutch officers to examine how work engagement and burnout may cross over from work teams to individual members. Results suggested that men and women who worked in highly engaged groups reported higher levels of individual work engagement including vigor, dedication, and absorption, regardless of team size and the frequency of interactions between team members. The individual level increases in work engagement facilitated higher energy levels in team members.

Positive experiences also have been shown to cross over from a supervisor to his or her subordinates (Carlson et al., 2011). Findings from Carlson and her colleagues (2011) indicate that supervisors' work–family enrichment influences subordinate work–family enrichment through the perception of a family-friendly work environment. The authors suggest that supervisors with high levels of work–family enrichment are more likely to empathize with their employees' aspirations for work–family balance, thus indirectly influencing employee work–family enrichment through a supportive work environment. As suggested in previous literature (e.g., Demerouti, 2012), it may be reasonable to posit that the work resources obtained from supervisor–subordinate crossover may then stimulate the positive transfer of resources between partners in the home domain, creating an upward spiral of positive crossover. We advocate exploring this possible phenomenon for future research, where the focal employee acts as a mediator of his or her partner's and supervisor/co-workers' indirect crossover effects. Research in this area would provide an indication as to how extensively crossover effects may extend.

FACILITATING POSITIVE CROSSOVER THROUGH INTENTIONAL COPING

Through positive crossover, men and women can enhance each other's well-being in both the home and work domains, and facilitate each other's work–family balance. Despite Westman's (2001) three proposed mechanisms, the crossover literature provides inadequate evidence to support how these processes are controlled (Kinnunen et al., 2013). The recent emphasis on positive crossover raises questions regarding what determines the positive or negative nature of these effects. Put more simply, what regulates the valence of effects that cross over between men and women? We propose that the answer to this question is determined largely by intentional efforts to facilitate positive crossover. For example, negative (or less positive) crossover seems to occur without intent; rarely would one expect an individual to purposely transfer negative states of well-being (i.e., burnout, exhaustion, work–family conflict) to his or her significant other. On the other hand, we contend that positive (negative) crossover effects are enhanced (mitigated) when an individual actively engages in work–family coping.

Cramer (1998) differentiated coping from other defense mechanisms such that individuals employ coping strategies 'with the intent of managing or solving a problem situation' (p. 921), whereas defense mechanisms transpire without conscious intentionality. Consistent with Folkman and Lazarus's (1980) seminal work, coping in the work–family literature has been conceptualized as either problem- or emotion-focused and episodic or preventive in nature (c.f. Thompson et al., 2007; Major and Morganson, 2011). Problem-focused coping involves reacting to conflict by directing action at its cause, while emotion-focused coping involves managing one's emotions in response to a stressor (Thompson et al., 2007). Episodic and preventive coping differ in that the former involves managing conflicts as they arise, whereas the latter refers to a proactive approach to preemptively impede conflict. Major and Morganson (2011) proposed preventive problem-focused coping to be the most effective form of work–family coping. Similarly, we propose preventive problem-focused coping to be most effective at enabling positive crossover between men and women due to its anticipatory and intentional nature. Because preventive coping strategies aim to alleviate future conflicts, the intentional employment of these strategies may determine the extent to which men and women can be allies in achieving work–family balance. Indeed, research has provided supportive evidence for the crossover of coping strategies between partners. A survey of police officers and their spouses found bi-directional crossover effects of one's coping strategies to influence the other's well-being (Beehr et al., 1995). The researchers examined the men and women's engagement in four coping strategies (problem-focused, emotion-focused, religiosity, and rugged individualism) and the effects that coping had on three potential strains: divorce potential, drinking behavior, and suicidal thoughts. Results suggested that one's coping strategy may be influenced by the strategy of his or her significant other. Furthermore, problem-focused coping was found to be most effective in reducing divorce potential for both the officers and their spouses. The inclusion of spousal responses in a predominantly male sample of police officers (91 percent) helps to strengthen evidence of both a direct influence on the coping strategy employed, and an indirect effect between one's own strain and his or her partner's strain. In fact, Westman (2001) suggested that coping strategies can directly influence partner stress or mediate the relationship between one's stress and his or her partner's stress. Examining the preventive or episodic nature of the coping strategy employed by an individual and his or her spouse may shed further light on how men and women can purposely facilitate positive outcomes in one another.

Employing preventive coping strategies to manage future conflict is particularly important considering that many of the resources that enhance the prospect of positive crossover seem to be constrained by domain context (e.g., job autonomy, opportunity for development; Bakker and Geurts, 2004; Bakker, 2005). Additionally, employees have little control over organizational policies that contribute to their (im)balance, such as teleworking, on-site child care, and schedule flexibility (e.g., Thompson et al., 1999; Major and Cleveland, 2007). When family-friendly benefits that promote work–family balance are available, they are often underutilized due to concern for career consequences (Thompson et al., 1999). For example, a survey of female university employees found that 77 percent were afraid that the use of maternity leave would hinder their professional advancement (Finkel et al., 1994).

When men and women are proactive and collaborative in their use of preventive coping strategies they may enable each other's pursuit of work–family balance. For example, male and female co-workers may discuss work and family affairs to help nurture a family-friendly and supportive work environment; in turn, co-workers may be more empathetic and accommodating of each other's work–family needs, reducing the likelihood of future conflict. Actively seeking co-worker social support provides a wealth of job resources that act to buffer the negative effects of burnout, exhaustion, and work–family conflict (Constable and Russell, 1986; Major et al., 2008), which have been shown to cross over at home and work. Men and women can be allies in facilitating work–family balance as positive states of well-being cross over indirectly through the presence of a family supportive work environment. We propose these crossover effects will spill over to other life domains and may then cross over to one's partner, resulting in a more expansive crossover model than has been presented in the literature thus far.

Men and women in supervisor–subordinate relationships can also be allies to the extent that the employee intentionally negotiates his or her role responsibilities to meet his or her desired work–family balance (Major and Morganson, 2011). Leader–member exchange (LMX) theory illustrates the quality of the supervisor–subordinate relationship (Graen and

Uhl-Bien, 1995). LMX theory suggests that the leader (supervisor) and follower (subordinate) participate in a social exchange process in which a mutually beneficial and influential relationship develops. As subordinates complete in role and extra-role duties, they distinguish themselves from other employees and are more likely to be provided with resources that support their work–family balance needs. A relationship high in LMX is mutually beneficial for both parties, as subordinate work outcomes typically improve as a result of greater negotiating latitude and schedule flexibility (Duchon et al., 1986; Dunegan et al., 1992), which also enhance work–family coping (Major and Morganson, 2011).

Idiosyncratic deals, or 'i-deals', may also facilitate work–family coping. I-deals refer to special employment terms negotiated between an individual employee and employer that are intended to benefit both parties (Rousseau et al., 2006). I-deals are a proactive method that employees may use to negotiate for accommodations to enhance work–family balance (Rousseau et al., 2006; Major and Litano, 2013). Major et al. (2013) proposed a model of work–family coping that focuses on i-deal negotiation as a process that employees intentionally utilize to prevent and manage work–family conflict. While these arrangements benefit both the individual employee and the supervisor, the effects of an employee's role negotiation may extend to men and women outside of this relationship. As the employee is able to better accommodate familial responsibilities, his or her partner may benefit from reduced conflict via crossover effects and as distribution of family responsibilities becomes more ideal. Furthermore, successful arrangements may encourage supervisors to accommodate other employees' work–family balance needs, creating a shared perception of a family-friendly work environment. Thus, men and women can be allies in achieving work–family balance by taking an active approach to negotiate their work roles, which may then promote positive crossover between agents at both work and home.

At home, men and women often work as 'allies' by sharing household tasks and child care responsibilities. Pleck's (1977) concept of asymmetrical boundary permeability suggests that the home domain is more permeable than the work domain, possibly due to less structured role demands. Thus, men and women may have the greatest opportunity to influence their collective work–family balance at home. Impromptu and fluid role agreements between partners may be more common than in the workplace due to a mutual environment with similar family-related demands and resources. For example, if a husband or wife is required to stay late at work, preventing him or her from performing an immediate family obligation (i.e., driving a child to soccer practice), the other partner may assume this role for the benefit of the family. Because many family-related demands are shared among partners, they are more likely to accommodate one another when conflicts arise.

Research has found partner (spousal) support to positively impact many work–family outcomes, including conflict and facilitation (van Daalen et al., 2006; Karatepe and Bekteshi, 2008). Van Daalen and colleagues (2006) found support from one's partner or spouse to be the strongest negative antecedent of family interference with work, and research by Westman and Etzion (2005) suggests that partner support may act to alleviate the negative crossover effects of work–family conflict. In the extant literature, proactively seeking social support at work or home is considered an adaptive work–family coping mechanism (Frone, 2003; Major and Litano, 2013). Men and women are allies at home to the extent that they actively support one another emotionally and through shared responsibilities. Partners may benefit from explicitly sharing their perceptions of ideal work–family balance in the present and in the future, to provide the family with an opportunity to strategically anticipate how future conflicts could be managed. These strategies may help to promote positive crossover between partners while mitigating negative crossover effects, including work–family conflict, resulting in optimal work–family balance.

CONCLUSIONS

Although one's experience of work–family balance is personal, it is affected by many different agents in all life domains. The crossover literature has largely focused on how men and women play adversarial roles in managing the work–family interface, but recently researchers have focused attention on positive crossover effects. We argue that an individual's work–family coping efforts can influence the positive or negative nature of crossover effects. Men and women become allies in their pursuit of work–family balance when they intentionally change their circumstances to be congruent with work–family needs. In turn, positive states of well-being influence closely related others' states of well-being, resulting in a virtuous cycle of positive crossover effects at home and at work and ultimately in a sense of work–family balance.

REFERENCES

Ashforth, B.E., G.E. Kreiner and M. Fugate (2000), 'All in a day's work: Boundaries and micro role transitions', *Academy of Management Review*, **25**(3), 472–91.

Bakker, A.B. (2005), 'Flow among music teachers and their students: The crossover of peak experiences', *Journal of Vocational Behavior*, **66**(1), 26–44.

Bakker, A.B. (2009), 'The crossover of burnout and its relation to partner health', *Stress and Health*, **25**(4), 343–53.

Bakker, A.B. and E. Demerouti (2007), 'The job demands–resources model: State of the art', *Journal of Managerial Psychology*, **22**(3), 309–28.

Bakker, A.B. and E. Demerouti (2009), 'The crossover of work engagement between working couples: A closer look at the role of empathy', *Journal of Managerial Psychology*, **24**(3), 220–36.

Bakker, A.B. and S.A.E. Geurts (2004), 'Toward a dual-process model of work–home interference', *Work and Occupations*, **31**(3), 345–66.

Bakker, A.B. and W.B. Schaufeli (2000), 'Burnout contagion processes among teachers', *Journal of Applied Social Psychology*, **30**(11), 2289–308.

Bakker, A.B. and D. Xanthopoulou (2009), 'The crossover of daily work engagement: Test of an actor–partner interdependence model', *Journal of Applied Psychology*, **94**(6), 1562–71.

Bakker, A.B., E. Demerouti and R.J. Burke (2009a), 'Workaholism and relationship quality: A spillover-crossover perspective', *Journal of Occupational Health Psychology*, **14**(1), 23–33.

Bakker, A.B., E. Demerouti and M.F. Dollard (2008), 'How job demands affect partners' experience of exhaustion: Integrating work–family conflict and crossover theory', *Journal of Applied Psychology*, **93**(4), 901–11.

Bakker, A.B., E. Demerouti and W.B. Schaufeli (2002), 'Validation of the Maslach burnout inventory-general survey: An internet study', *Anxiety, Stress and Coping*, **15**(3), 245–60.

Bakker, A.B., E. Demerouti and W.B. Schaufeli (2005), 'The crossover of burnout and work engagement among working couples', *Human Relations*, **58**(5), 661–89.

Bakker, A.B., H. van Emmerik and M.C. Euwema (2006), 'Crossover of burnout and engagement in work teams', *Work and Occupations*, **33**(4), 464–89.

Bakker, A.B., M. Westman and W.B. Schaufeli (2007), 'Crossover of burnout: An experimental design', *European Journal of Work and Organizational Psychology*, **16**(2), 220–39.

Bakker, A.B., M. Westman and H. van Emmerik (2009b), 'Advancements in crossover theory', *Journal of Managerial Psychology*, **24**(3), 206–19.

Bedeian, A.G., B.G. Burke and R.G. Moffett (1988), 'Outcomes of work–family conflict among married male and female professionals', *Journal of Management*, **14**(3), 475–91.

Beehr, T.A., L.B. Johnson and R. Nieva (1995), 'Occupational stress: Coping of police and their spouses', *Journal of Organizational Behavior*, **16**(1), 3–25.

Bolger, N., A. DeLongis, R.C. Kessler and E.A. Schilling (1989), 'Effects of daily stress on negative mood', *Journal of Personality and Social Psychology*, **57**(5), 808–18.

Carlson, D.S. and P.L. Perrewé (1999), 'The role of social support in the stressor–strain relationship: An examination of work–family conflict', *Journal of Management*, **25**(4), 513–40.

Carlson, D.S., K.M. Kacmar, J.H. Wayne and J.G. Grzywacz (2006), 'Measuring the positive side of the work–family interface: Development and validation of a work–family enrichment scale', *Journal of Vocational Behavior*, **68**(1), 131–64.

Carlson, D.S., M. Ferguson, K.M. Kacmar, J.G. Grzywacz and D. Whitten (2011), 'Pay it forward: The positive crossover effects of supervisor work–family enrichment', *Journal of Management*, **37**(3), 770–89.

Constable, J.F. and D.W. Russell (1986), 'The effect of social support and the work environment upon burnout among nurses', *Journal of Human Stress*, **12**(1), 20–26.

Cramer, P. (1998), 'Coping and defense mechanisms: What's the difference?' *Journal of Personality*, **66**(6), 919–46.

Crouter, A.C. (1984), 'Spillover from family to work: The neglected side of the work–family interface', *Human Relations*, **37**(6), 425–41.

Demerouti, E. (2012), 'The spillover and crossover of resources among partners: The role of work–self and family–self-facilitation', *Journal of Occupational Health Psychology*, **17**(2), 184–95.

Demerouti, E., A.B. Bakker and W.B. Schaufeli (2005), 'Spillover and crossover of exhaustion and life satisfaction among dual-earner parents', *Journal of Vocational Behavior*, **67**(2), 266–89.

Duchon, D., S.G. Green and T.D. Taber (1986), 'Vertical dyad linkage: A longitudinal assessment of antecedents, measures, and consequences', *Journal of Applied Psychology*, **71**(1), 56–60.

Dunegan, K.J., D. Duchon and M. Uhl-Bien (1992), 'Examining the link between leader member exchange and subordinate performance: The role of task analyzability and variety as moderators', *Journal of Management*, **18**(1), 59–76.

Finkel, S.K., S. Olswang and N. She (1994), 'Childbirth, tenure, and promotion for women faculty', *Review of Higher Education*, **17**(3), 259–70.

Folkman, S. and R.S. Lazarus (1980), 'An analysis of coping in a middle-aged community sample', *Journal of Health and Social Behavior*, **21**, 219–39.

Frone, M.R. (2003), 'Work–family balance', in J.C. Quick and L.E. Tetrick (eds), *Handbook of Occupational Health Psychology*, Washington, DC: American Psychological Association, pp. 143–62.

Frone, M.R., M. Russell and M.L. Cooper (1992), 'Prevalence of work–family conflict: Are work and family boundaries asymmetrically permeable?', *Journal of Organizational Behavior*, **13**(7), 723–9.

Graen, G.B. and M. Uhl-Bien (1995), 'Relationship-based approach to leadership: Development of leader–member exchange (LMX) theory of leadership over 25 years: Applying a multi-level multi-domain perspective', *The Leadership Quarterly*, **6**(2), 219–47.

Greenhaus, J.H. and N.J. Beutell (1985), 'Sources of conflict between work and family roles', *Academy of Management Review*, **10**(1), 76–88.

Greenhaus, J.H. and S. Parasuraman (1994), 'Work–family conflict, social support and well-being', in M.J. Davidson and R.J. Burke (eds), *Women in Management: Current Research Issues*, London: Paul Chapman, pp. 213–29.

Greenhaus, J.H. and G.N. Powell (2006), 'When work and family are allies: A theory of work–family enrichment', *The Academy of Management Review*, **31**(1), 72–92.

Grzywacz, J.G. and B.L. Bass (2004), 'Work, family, and mental health: Testing different models of work–family fit', *Journal of Marriage and Family*, **65**(1), 248–61.

Gutek, B.A., S. Searle and L. Klepa (1991), 'Rational versus gender role explanations for work–family conflict', *Journal of Applied Psychology*, **76**(4), 560–68.

Hammer, L.B., E. Allen and T.D. Grigsby (1997), 'Work–family conflict in dual-earner couples: Within-individual and crossover effects of work and family', *Journal of Vocational Behavior*, **50**(2), 185–203.

Hammer, L.B., T.N. Bauer and A.A. Grandey (2003), 'Work–family conflict and work-related withdrawal behaviors', *Journal of Business and Psychology*, **17**(3), 419–36.

Hammer, L.B., J.C. Cullen, M.B. Neal, R.R. Sinclair and M.V. Shafiro (2005), 'The longitudinal effects of work–family conflict and positive spillover on depressive symptoms among dual-earner couples', *Journal of Occupational Health Psychology*, **10**(2), 138–54.

Karatepe, O.M. and L. Bekteshi (2008), 'Antecedents and outcomes of work–family facilitation and family–work facilitation among frontline hotel employees', *International Journal of Hospitality Management*, **27**(4), 517–28.

Kinnunen, U., J. Rantanen and S. Mauno (2013), 'Crossover and spillover between family members and work and family roles', in D.A. Major and R.J. Burke (eds), *Handbook of Work–Life Integration Among Professionals*, Cheltenham, UK and Northampton, MA, USA: Edward Elgar.

Kirchmeyer, C. (2000), 'Work-life initiatives: Greed or benevolence regarding workers' time?' in C.L. Cooper and D.M. Rousseau (eds), *Trends in Organizational Behavior: Time in Organizational Behavior, Vol. 7*, Chichester: Wiley, pp. 79–94.

Kossek, E.E. and C. Ozeki (1998), 'Work–family conflict, policies, and the job–life satisfaction relationship: A review and directions for organizational behavior–human resources research', *Journal of Applied Psychology*, **83**(2), 139–49.

Major, D.A. (2007), 'Work–life balance', in S.G. Rogelberg (ed.), *Encyclopedia of Industrial and Organizational Psychology, Vol. 2*, Thousand Oaks, CA: Sage, pp. 888–92.

Major, D.A. and J.N. Cleveland (2007), 'Strategies for reducing work–family conflict: Applying research and best practices from industrial and organizational psychology', in G.P. Hodgkinson and J.K. Ford (eds), *International Review of Industrial and Organizational Psychology, Vol. 22*, Chichester: John Wiley and Sons, Ltd.

Major, D.A. and M.L. Litano (2013), 'The role of adaptability in work–family conflict and coping', in D. Chan (ed.), *Responding to Changes at Work: New Directions in Research on Individual Adaptability*, New York: Taylor and Francis Group.

Major, D.A. and V.J. Morganson (2011), 'Coping with work–family conflict: A leader–member exchange perspective', *Journal of Occupational Health Psychology*, **16**(1), 126–38.

Major, D.A., H.M. Lauzun and M.P. Jones (2013), 'New directions in work–family coping research', in J.H. Greenhaus and M. Maestro (eds), *Expanding the Boundaries of Work–Family Research: A Vision for the Future*, New York: Palgrave Macmillian, pp. 193–211.

Major, D.A., T.D. Fletcher, D.D. Davis and L.M. Germano (2008), 'The influence of work–family culture and workplace relationships on work interference with family: A multilevel model', *Journal of Organizational Behavior*, **29**(7), 881–97.

Maslach, C. (1993), 'Burnout: A multidimensional perspective', in W.B. Schaufeli, C. Maslach and T. Marek (eds), *Professional Burnout: Recent Developments in Theory and Research. Series in Applied Psychology. Social Issues and Questions, Vol. 7*, Philadelphia, PA: Taylor and Francis, pp. 19–32.

Matthews, R.A., R.E. Del Priore, L.K. Acitelli and J.L. Barnes-Farrell (2006),

'Work-to-relationship conflict: Crossover effects in dual-earner couples', *Journal of Occupational Health Psychology*, **11**(3), 228–40.

Pleck, J.H. (1977), 'The work–family role system', *Social Problems*, **24**(4), 417–27.

Robinson, B.E. (1997), 'Work addiction and the family: Conceptual and research considerations', *Early Child Development and Care*, **137**(1), 77–92.

Rousseau, D.M., V.T. Ho and J. Greenberg (2006), 'I-deals: Idiosyncratic terms in employment relationships', *Academy of Management Review*, **31**(4), 977–94.

Rusconi, A., P. Moen and A. Kaduk (2013), 'Career priorities and pathways across the (gendered) life course', in D.A. Major and R.J. Burke (eds), *Handbook of Work–Life Integration Among Professionals*, Cheltenham, UK and Northampton, MA, USA: Edward Elgar.

Schaufeli, W.B., M. Salanova, V. González-Romá and A.B. Bakker (2002), 'The measurement of engagement and burnout: A two sample confirmatory factor analytic approach', *Journal of Happiness Studies*, **3**(1), 71–92.

Song, Z., M.D. Foo and M.A. Uy (2008), 'Mood spillover and crossover among dual-earner couples: A cell phone event sampling study', *Journal of Applied Psychology*, **93**(2), 443–52.

Thompson, C.A., L.L. Beauvais and K.S. Lyness (1999), 'When work–family benefits are not enough: The influence of work–family culture on benefit utilization, organizational attachment, and work–family conflict', *Journal of Vocational Behavior*, **54**(3), 392–415.

Thompson, C.A., S.A.Y. Poelmans, T.D. Allen and J.K. Andreassi (2007), 'On the importance of coping: A model and new directions for research on work and family', in P.L. Perrewé, D.C. Ganster (eds), *Exploring the Work and Non-work Interface (Research in Occupational Stress and Well-Being, Vol. 6)*, pp. 73–113.

van Daalen, G., T.M. Willemsen and K. Sanders (2006), 'Reducing work–family conflict through different sources of social support', *Journal of Vocational Behavior*, **69**(3), 462–76.

van Steenbergen, E.F. and N. Ellemers (2009), 'Is managing the work–family interface worthwhile? Benefits for employee health and performance', *Journal of Organizational Behavior*, **30**(5), 617–42.

Wang, M., S. Liu, Y. Zhan and J. Shi (2010), 'Daily work–family conflict and alcohol use: Testing the cross-level moderation effects of peer drinking norms and social support', *Journal of Applied Psychology*, **95**(2), 377–86.

Wayne, J.H., J.G. Grzywacz, D.S. Carlson and K.M. Kacmar (2007), 'Work–family facilitation: A theoretical explanation and model of primary antecedents and consequences', *Human Resource Management Review*, **17**(1), 63–76.

Westman, M. (2001), 'Stress and strain crossover', *Human Relations*, **54**(6), 717–51.

Westman, M. (2006), 'Crossover of stress and strain in the work–family context', in F. Jones, R.J. Burke and M. Westman (eds), *Work–Life Balance: A Psychological Perspective*, New York: Psychology Press, pp. 163–84.

Westman, M. and A.B. Bakker (2008), *Crossover of Burnout Among Health Care Professionals*, New York: Nova Science.

Westman, M. and D. Etzion (2005), 'The crossover of work–family conflict from one spouse to the other', *Journal of Applied Social Psychology*, **35**(9), 1936–57.

Westman, M. and A.D. Vinokur (1998), 'Unraveling the relationship of distress levels within couples: Common stressors, empathic reactions, or crossover via social interaction?' *Human Relations*, **51**(2), 137–56.

Westman, M., P. Brough and T. Kalliath (2009), 'Expert commentary on work–

life balance and crossover of emotions and experiences: Theoretical and practice advancements', *Journal of Organizational Behavior*, **30**(5), 587–95.

Westman, M., D. Etzion and E. Danon (2001), 'Job insecurity and crossover of burnout in married couples', *Journal of Organizational Behavior*, **22**(5), 467–81.

16. Engaging men through inclusive leadership

Jeanine Prime, Mike Otterman and Elizabeth R. Salib

INTRODUCTION

In an era where talent is fast superseding capital as a key driver of economic growth (Florida et al., 2012), twenty-first-century leaders face a critical challenge: leveraging the full pool of available talent – both women and men. To thrive in this new talent economy, businesses cannot afford to ignore any one gender. They must develop leaders with the inclusive skills needed to fully utilize the talents of women and men equally. Seeing their economic competitiveness at risk, many countries are squarely focused on increasing women's participation in business, passing legislation – including quotas – intended to increase gender diversity on corporate boards. Many businesses are keenly aware of the stakes involved, and are taking their own measures to address leadership gender gaps. But too often their tactics fall short – many focus singularly on women and their choices to the exclusion of men and their role in maintaining the status quo. This is unfortunate, as men have a critical part to play in closing gender gaps. Even though men overwhelmingly retain the greatest positions of power and influence in business, they are often overlooked in organizational efforts to drive change. By excluding men from the focus and development of strategies to attenuate gender disparities, businesses are missing an important opportunity to effect change. This chapter will outline the causes of gender disparities in business and what organizations can do to better engage men in closing them by fostering inclusive leadership. A lot is at stake: by engaging men in creating more equal workplaces, companies are not just addressing gender inequity problems, but creating better leaders, stronger businesses and more fulfilling lives for both women *and* men.

GENDER INEQUALITY IN BUSINESS: THE LANDSCAPE

The International Labour Organization called the increasing proportion of women in the global workforce 'one of the most striking phenomena of recent times' (International Labour Organization, 2004, p. 1). Others have called the mass arrival of women into the workplace 'a quiet revolution' (*Economist*, 2011). Women's labor force participation surpasses 50 percent in some countries (International Labour Organization, 2012) and in several industrialized nations, women account for more than half of all workers in management and professional occupations (Bureau of Labor Statistics, 2011).

A second 'quiet revolution' has occurred in the realm of education: for decades American women have been earning more Bachelor's degrees and Master's degrees, and more recently doctorates, than men (National Center for Education Statistics, 2011). Women are also increasingly earning MBAs – accounting for almost 40 percent of MBA degrees awarded in the USA and Canada (Graduate Management Admission Council, 2012). The trend of women attaining similar or higher levels of education relative to men is expected to continue. Taken together, it's clear that women represent a highly educated and skilled talent resource. Yet this resource is not being utilized.

Global gender gaps in employment and wages persist – even in countries where human capital differences between women and men are relatively small. Gaps in employment are especially sizeable in South Asia, the Middle East and North Africa, and include two well-documented patterns of gender stratification: disparities in the attainment of management positions, and gender segregation, the over- or under-employment of women relative to men in different occupations.

GENDER STRATIFICATION AND SEGREGATION

Gender stratification – the disproportionately high representation of men in managerial, power-wielding positions – continues to garner considerable attention around the world, especially in light of recent trends suggesting that progress in closing leadership gender gaps has slowed (Hausmann et al., 2012). The erosion of human capital differences between women and men led some to speculate that leadership gaps would resolve on their own, in time. Yet in most countries, including the most industrialized, women on average represent less than 30 percent of senior managers (Grant Thornton, 2011). For example, in 2012, men held 85.7 percent of all executive officer positions, 83.4 percent of board of director seats, and 95.7 percent of all CEO positions in US-based Fortune 500 companies. Of these, more than one-quarter did not employ any female executive officers at all (Catalyst, 2013). Recruitment is stagnating with only an 8 percent increase in female executive officers since 2009 (Catalyst, 2009, 2013).

Just as widespread as stratification are patterns of gender segregation: the over- or under-employment of men relative to women in certain occupations. According to a 2009 study published by the European Commission, there was absolutely no overlap between the top six occupations with the largest numbers of women and men respectively. Established measures of segregation suggest that, on average, more than 25 percent of employed populations in EU countries would have to change jobs to equalize the distribution of women and men across occupations (European Commission, 2009). Although Scandinavian countries have recorded faster rates of desegregation in recent years, Mediterranean countries and some Eastern European ones have become *more* segregated – keeping overall levels of segregation somewhat constant over the last 15 years. In North America, patterns of occupational segregation also remain.

Not surprisingly, there are not only inequalities in the nature and status of the work women and men do, but also gaps in how they are compensated (Blau and Kahn, 2007; Carter and Silva, 2010a, 2011; Galinsky et al., 2011; US Department of Labor and US Bureau of Labor Statistics, 2012). This wage gap is accounted for, in part, by differences in the kinds of work men and women do, as well as by differences in how much they work outside of the home (CONSAD Research Corp, 2009; National Equal Pay Task Force, 2013; US Bureau of Labor Statistics and US Department of Labor, 2013). But this does not entirely explain the wage gap. It's not just that men choose or have access to occupations that are more highly valued than those in which women find themselves. Even when men work in occupations that are dominated by women, they still out-earn them (Williams, 1992; Wingfield, 2009). This is hardly the case for women working in occupations dominated by men. In occupations with a mix of each gender, men still earn more than women. Further, even when women and men perform similar work – and human capital differences in qualifications and experience are controlled – men enjoy higher rates of compensation than women (Carter and Silva, 2010b; Corbett, 2013; Lips, 2013). There is unequivocal evidence that it pays to be a man.

These disparities in employment opportunities and outcomes come at a real cost (Esteve-Volart, 2009; Cuberes and Teignier-Baqué, 2011). If women and men are equally talented – and evidence suggests they are (Hyde, 2005) – then stratification and segregation results in a suboptimal allocation of talent. For example, a preference for hiring men into managerial positions means that ultimately lesser talented men will be employed over more highly qualified women. And the result of such preferences is that over time, the average quality of the managerial talent pool drops. In the end, women's exclusion from managerial positions reduces aggregate productivity. Cuberes and Teignier-Baqué (2011) estimate that in a labor market with gender inequality in managerial occupations the output per worker is 76.4 percent of that in a market with equality. Cuberes and Teignier-Baqué (2011) also found that gender gaps in workforce participation – attributable, in part, to wage inequality – can lower income per capita by a magnitude of 40 percent relative to labor markets where women and men participate equally in paid work.

Esteve-Volart (2009) theorizes that when women are excluded from managerial positions, equilibrium wages and human capital investment are negatively impacted. These accrued costs can have a profound impact on the global economy. The 'economic success of tomorrow will no longer be decided by capital but rather by the production factor "talent." So in a sense, we are moving from capitalism to "talentism"', wrote Klaus Schwab, founder and executive chairman of the World Economic Forum (Schwab, 2011). The power of female talent to drive economies is significant. Greater female labor force participation could increase America's GDP by 9 percent, boost the euro zone's GDP by 13 percent, and Japan's GDP by 16 percent. Eliminating gender gaps can spur a 14 percent rise in per capita income by the year 2020 in China, Indonesia, Korea, the Philippines, Russia, and Vietnam (Daly, 2007).

BARRIERS FOR WOMEN

How can businesses seize on the economic opportunities that can come from closing gender gaps? Among large, especially US-based companies, programs intended to develop and retain women employees and to close gender gaps in hiring and promotion are common (Olson and Becker, 1983; Glick et al., 1988; Russ and McNeilly, 1995; Marlowe et al., 1996). Yet on the whole, they have had limited success in closing gender gaps (Kalev et al., 2006; Hausmann et al., 2012). One reason seems to be the assumption guiding these programs, that to close gender gaps one must address women's deficits. Research from Catalyst researchers (Carter and Silva, 2010a, 2011) and other experts (Hyde, 2005; Martell et al., 2012) suggest that this predominant focus on women – and fixing their deficits – is misguided, and therefore interventions or programs driven by this premise will be largely unsuccessful in effecting lasting change.

Several studies suggest that gender gaps are not due to differences in women's and men's capabilities or attitudes towards leadership. While it is commonly believed that women lack the leadership acumen that men have, meta-analytic research shows that women's and men's leadership behavior is *not* markedly different (Eagly et al., 1995; Hyde, 2005; Ayman and Korabik, 2010). For example, Eagly et al. (1995) analyzed several leadership styles including transformational, transactional, and laissez faire leadership, and concluded that person's sex was 'not a reliable indicator of how she or he would lead' (p. 586).

Yet implicit in some interventions is the notion that women lack the drive or ambition to lead. Newspaper headlines like '"Lack of ambition" deters women' (Whitehead, 2013) or 'Girls "lack ambition" for good jobs' (BBC News, 2013) remain incredibly common, but data reveal that women aren't held back by an 'ambition gap' – they're just held back. Catalyst research of nearly 1000 senior-level employees who shared similar backgrounds and characteristics found that women aspired to be CEO in *equal proportions* to men (Catalyst, 2004). Looking further down into the talent pipeline, Catalyst also tracked the career paths of more than 4100 women and men 'high potential' MBA alumni from 26 leading business schools in the United States, Canada, Europe, and Asia and found that women start behind – and stay behind – equally skilled men from day one of their careers, and this gap cannot be explained by ambition. When comparing women and men with similar aspirations to be CEO, Catalyst found men still got promoted faster and compensated at higher rates than women (Carter and Silva, 2010a).

If women's ambition doesn't account for gender gaps, perhaps these disparities can be explained by women's behaviors or choices? Catalyst's longitudinal research on MBA grads busted this myth as well. Contrary to popular beliefs that women are held back by taking time off to have children and splitting their energies between work and child-rearing responsibilities, Catalyst found that gender gaps were not explained by women choosing to become mothers. Even when considering just the women and men *without* kids, gender gaps persisted from the first job post-MBA among women and men with similar qualifications and ambitions.

Another common deficit-based explanation of gender gaps holds that women aren't proactive enough in managing their careers – including negotiating for higher salaries. Yet Catalyst found that 'high potential' women and men negotiated at *equal rates* for a higher-level position or greater compensation during the hiring process for their current job. Once hired, women and men used proactive career advancement strategies at *equal rates* as well. These strategies included seeking access to powerful colleagues, self-promoting, and asking for a variety of work assignments to increase skills. Yet even when women do 'all the right things' to advance their careers, they're offered fewer of the 'hot jobs' and opportunities that can lead to promotion (Carter and Silva, 2011). Regardless of the career advancement strategies used, men were more likely than women to reach the senior executive/CEO ranks. And the pay gap between equally skilled women and men's salaries started from day one of their careers: in their first post-MBA jobs it was $4600 and increased to over $31 000 as their careers progressed (Carter and Silva, 2010a).

If it's not women's capabilities, attitudes, behaviors or choices – what is it? Research suggests that around the world a 'think leader, think man' tendency persists where qualities associated with leadership are the qualities associated with men (Heilman, 2001; Schein, 2001; Eagly and Karau, 2002). For example, ambition and dominance are two traits commonly associated with leadership and the stereotypical male (Schein, 2001). At the same time, traits like sensitivity and friendliness that fit feminine stereotypes are deemed less important leadership traits. Taken together, this results in women being evaluated less positively than men for leadership positions (Eagly and Karau, 2002). In fact, leadership experts have identified interpersonal power and position power as two important sources of power for leaders, yet women are often deemed lacking in interpersonal power – especially in men's eyes (Ragins and Sundstrom, 1989). Men see women as less effective problem-solvers and less capable at inspiring others – skills that are highly valued among leaders (Catalyst, 2005).

If men are the 'typical' leader, gender binaries hold that women who lead are then 'atypical' and less effective. To ostensibly be effective, women must alter their 'natural' qualities to be more agentic and male-like (Catalyst, 2007). According to Rudman and Glick, to succeed in business women must overcome 'the double hurdle of prejudice toward women as less agentic and prejudice toward agentic women as unfeminine and unattractive' (Rudman and Glick, 2010, p. 176). Women in business are often deemed 'too tough, too soft, but never just right' (Catalyst, 2007, p. 14) and the notion that women are less strong and less committed than men – that trusting their judgment is risky – remains entrenched (Warren, 2009).

Even when women 'adapt' and act similarly to men in organizations, women are unrewarded and even penalized for their actions (Catalyst, 2007). For example, women's compensation growth was *slower* when they had changed jobs post-MBA compared to the women who had stayed put, while changing jobs paid off for men. The same was true for high potentials who deviated from traditional job tracks – women were penalized for doing so, men were not (Carter and Silva, 2010a). And take self-promotion – a career advancement strategy necessary for influencing people's perceptions of competence (e.g., Stevens and Kristof, 1995;

Rudman, 1998; Kacmar and Carlson, 1999; Kristof-Brown et al., 2002; Proost et al., 2010, 2012). Women who engage in self-promotion are judged as less attractive and lacking social skills, which in turn, decreased their likelihood of being hired (Rudman, 1998; Rudman and Glick, 2010).

Research on diverse workgroups demonstrates that even small amounts of gender and racial variability in teams are evaluated as less effective (Baugh and Graen, 1997). As the gender composition of a workgroup becomes increasingly female, members of these teams evaluate each other and the team more negatively. Of particular note, even men who are on these teams are evaluated more negatively, indicating that gender stereotypes of women being less effective workers drags down members' perceptions of performance (West et al., 2012).

POWER STRUCTURES

Bias caused by stereotyping – even if quite small – can have a significant impact over time. Utilizing computer simulations, researchers have uncovered that even trivial amounts of gender discrimination can drastically affect the percentage of women that reach leadership roles (Martell et al., 1996; Robison-Cox et al., 2007). In one simulation where only 1 percent of variance was accounted for by sex bias, a company that began as having an equal number of women and men available for promotion resulted in a company where only 35 percent of women actually reached top leadership levels (Martell et al., 1996). Even though women hold these biases too, men are more likely than women to evaluate women leaders negatively (Catalyst, 2005).

What's more, stereotypic bias likely contributes to and compounds another problem that maintains gender gaps: homo-social reproduction (Elliott and Smith, 2004; Carter and Silva, 2010b). For example, Catalyst found that among MBA grads, although more women than men had mentors, men's mentors were more likely than women to have enough clout to offer sponsorship – access to the types of opportunities, information, and resources that can make careers take off (Carter and Silva, 2010b). While the career advice and guidance that mentors provide is useful, the benefit of sponsorship is what really helps men and women advance. Sponsors have the power to actively advocate on one's behalf at the decision-making table. Mentors can often provide sponsorship too, but only when they have enough influence to do so. Catalyst found that only when men and women had equal opportunities to receive sponsorship from mentors that were equally highly placed within their organizations did the gender gap in promotion rates disappear. But men were much more likely to have highly placed mentors to begin with (Carter and Silva, 2010b).

Men's greater access to sponsors is largely due to processes of homo-social reproduction. Men are more likely to develop networks where sponsorship is exchanged with other men, just as women are more likely to form networks with other women. This pattern would not be so problematic if men and women were equally represented in positions of power. But due to gender gaps in positions of power, men are better positioned to benefit from homo-social reproduction. Power tends to get shared amongst a largely male network – not due to malicious or willful intent to exclude women, but due to human nature. We form stronger networks with people like us, and in the workplace this can translate into a closed loop whereby managers select individuals who are socially similar to themselves for hiring and promotion (Kanter, 1977; Brewer and Brown, 1998; Bergmann, 2005). Ultimately, predominantly male networks preclude women's access to powerful sponsors.

To overcome stereotypic bias and the challenges that homo-social reproduction present in maintaining gender gaps, we need leaders who can create inclusive cultures – cultures where women and men have equal opportunities to make contributions and advance to leadership roles. Men are well-positioned to help drive this cultural evolution in workplaces because they hold most of the leadership positions, set the tone, and control power structures that can make a difference in women's careers. Inclusive male leaders can transcend the stereotypes and support people around them who only don't look and act like themselves. Therefore, fostering inclusive cultures where power is shared more equitably can ensure more employees have access to critical sponsorship opportunities.

As the most powerful stakeholders, men are in a strong position to influence change and build followership across cultural, demographic, functional, and organizational group borders. In fact, the role of dominant groups in minority-led social movements has long been studied by social theorists. 'The more oppressed the minority group, the more essential may be aid from members of the dominant group in initiating the liberation movement', write Gary T. Marx and Michael Useem (1971). A historical precedence exists of dominant groups leading societal change. Citing the work of Farmer (1966); Kellogg (1973); and Meier and Rudwick (1966), Marx and Useem explain:

> Caste Hindus initiated many of the early efforts aimed at ameliorating the condition of the Untouchables, and white abolitionists were primarily responsible for the formation of many of the early antislavery societies, and for hooking these into a national system. In the case of civil rights, whites played a crucial role in the founding of the NAACP, the Urban League, and CORE. . .

In the same way, men can lead greater inclusion by honing, fine-tuning, then employing inclusive leadership skills.

INCLUSIVE LEADERSHIP

So, how can organizations equip men with the leadership skills they need to create inclusive cultures and close gender gaps? First they need to shed pervasive, 'old hat' philosophies about leadership. Ironically, despite a plethora of self-help books and scholarly research on leadership, many myths persist about what makes leaders effective, and these myths continue to inform the leadership behaviors that are taught in business schools and practiced in corporations around the world. Regrettably, the brand of leadership that many in business see as effective, isn't effective at all and can create work cultures that reinforce gender gaps instead of closing them (Yukl, 1999; Grant et al., 2011; Cain, 2012).

For too many people, the image that epitomizes effective leadership is a charismatic, larger-than-life extravert who knows the answer to every problem, can swoop in and 'save the day,' give inspirational speeches, command respect, commitment and unwavering followership. While this image isn't an inherently negative one, it just doesn't accurately reflect how the most effective leaders typically function in reality (Yukl, 1999). What's more, this larger-than-life view of leadership obscures some of the most important behaviors needed to be an effective leader, namely, forming relationships with followers (Yukl, 1999; Avolio et al., 2009). At its best, leadership is not about the leader her- or himself but about relationships between leaders and followers. And within that relationship sometimes the leader becomes the follower, and the follower becomes the leader.

Leadership experts understand that the most effective leaders are those who can enable their followers to lead rather than being dependent on them for direction, and can learn from, develop and leverage the diverse talents and perspectives of their followers. Critical to achieving these outcomes is the ability to form high-quality relationships with followers. But this is exactly where a majority of leaders are likely falling short. Patterns of homo-social reproduction suggest that a majority of leaders are only effective at forming these high-quality exchange relationships – one outcome of which is sponsorship – with people who share their gender and other socio-demographic characteristics. Because career development outcomes are so dependent on these relationships and the resources and opportunities that they offer, teaching leaders how to be inclusive – that is, to form these high-quality relationships across socio-demographic lines – can be a powerful way to help close gender gaps and enable leaders to be more effective at leveraging the best available talent.

MALE BARRIERS

Why haven't more organizations been successful in teaching their leaders – mostly men – this skill of inclusive leadership? One reason may be that the relationship focus and power sharing associated with inclusive leadership are antithetical to the types of leadership behaviors expected from men. For example, egalitarian men in high-powered positions are seen as feminine, weaker, and more likely to be homosexual than other men (Rudman et al., in press). This research suggests that men might be penalized for power-sharing leadership styles and rewarded more for the larger-than-life, leader-centric styles that dominate popular culture. Failing to conform to masculine norms has severe consequences for men in the workplace (Moss-Racusin et al., 2010; Rudman et al., in press). One study found that when male leaders make a mistake they are viewed as less competent, less desirable to work for, and less effective than female leaders making the same mistake (Thoroughgood et al., 2013). Thus, the pressure to conform to masculine expectations for business leadership is arguably a significant barrier that keeps men from exhibiting more inclusive leadership styles.

If attempts to develop inclusive leadership are squarely framed as initiatives to address gender gaps, Catalyst identified three more barriers that come into play for men: a lack of awareness of gender issues, apathy, and fear. 'When you're from the dominant group you also don't have that history of struggle and analysis that comes from the nondominant group's perspective', noted one respondent in a study examining obstacles that keep men from leading efforts to address organizational gender gaps (Prime and Moss-Racusin, 2009, p. 16). In addition to this real lack of awareness, the study found that some men believed that by virtue of being male they were uninformed about issues of gender and, therefore, perceived that they lacked the knowledge they need to be effective champions of gender equality initiatives.

In addition to real and perceived ignorance, apathy ranked high among men's barriers – it was mentioned in 74 percent of reports about what keeps men from championing efforts to close gender gaps. According to experts Catalyst interviewed, men often hear the word 'gender' and think it has everything to do with women and nothing to do with men. Helping men understand how they can benefit from closing gaps, the research suggests, is critical to engaging men to take a leading role in fostering gender equality. Men remain indifferent and therefore unlikely to support gender equality unless they appreciate how they can gain personally from changing the status quo (ibid.).

Overcoming fear is a critical factor as well: 74 percent of men's comments pointed to fear as a major hurdle to championing gender initiatives. Thirty-four percent of comments referenced a 'zero-sum' attitude, namely fears about a loss of status or belief that although beneficial to women, equality could come at the expense of men. Other men reported fears about unwittingly committing an offensive act that may expose themselves to criticism from women – even in the context of working together with women to end bias (ibid.).

OVERCOMING BARRIERS WITH INCLUSIVE LEADERSHIP: ROCKWELL CASE STUDY

How can organizations overcome these barriers and engage men successfully in leading efforts to close costly gender gaps? Rather than engaging men, many organizations have unwittingly alienated men by exclusively focusing on women, inadvertently jeopardizing the success of their gender initiatives in the process (Goodstein and Burke, 1991; Burke and Black, 1997; Holladay et al., 2003; Kidder et al., 2004). Bringing men along is critical, and some companies are leading the way. Take the example of Rockwell Automation examined in a recent Catalyst study (Prime et al., 2012).

Rockwell Automation is a global engineering company headquartered in Milwaukee, USA. It began with what some might call a 'diversity and inclusion' challenge: making its North American sales division – historically white men-dominated – more inclusive to women and ethnic/racial minorities. Working with a US-based leadership development organization called White Men as Full Diversity Partners (WMFDP), Rockwell singled out white men for leadership development training – the group *least* likely to support diversity initiatives. They began with the critical premise that group identities matter and that being effective at leading both those like us and those different from us means understanding and managing perceptions of our own group affiliations.

How did Rockwell address the three chief barriers to male engagement in closing gender gaps: apathy, fear, and a lack of awareness? To generate momentum and avoid apathy, Rockwell framed the intervention around leadership and learning a business critical skill – not simply a run-of-the-mill 'diversity program'. To overcome ignorance and lack of awareness, programs focused on critical thinking about how colleagues' group memberships affect their own work experiences. Male managers were given the tools to spot inequality, rather than relying on women and ethnic minorities to do the work. And to address fear, programs focused on how to suspend one's beliefs to fully engage with perspectives that differ from one's own; address rather than avoiding difficult points of difference among colleagues; and, actively seek out perspectives of colleagues from different backgrounds. These three skills taught men at Rockwell how to better engage with women – see differences for learning rather than being afraid. Taken together, the programs focused on demonstrating a personal commitment to inclusion – that is, leading by focusing on the self first and being the change they wanted to see, rather than waiting or expecting others to change.

What was the impact? Co-workers of lab participants reported a decline in negative gossip, an increase in workplace civility, improved communication, and heightened respect between co-workers. Mindsets shifted too: managers became more aware that group-based inequities exist, and in turn, let go of their belief that top talent naturally rises to the top of organizations. Managers also became more committed and saw it as their role as leaders to play an integral role in creating a more inclusive work environment where all talents can be valued equally.

To build on early successes, more than 1500 Rockwell Automation employees throughout the organization were then offered participation in additional WMFDP learning labs. The labs included women and men from different ethnic and racial backgrounds, and created opportunities for employees to practice and learn in a safe space. By offering learning experiences that were both supportive and challenging, Rockwell created a cadre of employees that were more consistently:

- thinking critically about social groups;
- taking responsibility for being inclusive – that is, focusing on self rather than others as the locus of change;
- inquiring across differences;
- listening empathically; and
- addressing difficult or emotionally charged issues.

What did this mean in practical terms for the day-to-day lives of Rockwell employees? A follow-up study by Catalyst researchers looked at this very question. This qualitative study revealed that as a result of WMFDP learning labs, male leaders at Rockwell were connecting with women in ways they hadn't before, setting the stage for the high-quality relationships critical to career outcomes. The study revealed that the five skills Rockwell leaders learned in the labs had prepared them to engage in a critical dialogue – an activity that research suggests can be highly effective in developing relationships across difference (Nagda et al., 2009).

Critical dialogue is an open-ended, judgment-free type of conversation, where the goal is to learn and explore the different perspective of each person involved. Research suggests that closed-ended discussions and debates can hinder inclusivity within organizations, while open-ended and non-judgmental conversations can bridge the divides that keep men and women from talking about gender and developing partnerships to address gender disparities (Nagda, 2006; Nagda et al, 2009). One woman interviewed by Catalyst highlighted the newfound value of 'starting a conversation with an intention'. She said:

> My boss does it all the time – my intention is not that you speak for all women, or my intention is not to let me off the hook for this. . . . Before, there were implicit underlying expectations, and now, we can have conversations on anything.

As Rockwell employees revealed, critical dialogue has the power to connect colleagues across bridges of difference and foster fear-free, open environments of exchange where employees feel free to share diverse perspectives and to identify inequities and points of conflict.

As dramatic as these results were, the culture change at Rockwell didn't end there. Rockwell Automation sustained and amplified critical dialogue in their organization by equipping a critical mass of their employees with dialogic skills, including methods of demonstrating vulnerability, self-disclosing, suspending judgment, inquiring across difference, and exploring conflicts. One way managers built up and role-modeled these skills was via the 'fishbowl' technique – a strategy involving active listening and sharing to promote collaborative learning about potentially polarizing issues.[1] Armed with these skills, colleagues from various backgrounds were able to reach understandings about points of difference and commonality and to earn others' respect and empathy. For example, whites and people of color agreed that there needed to be greater power sharing, and that women and non-whites needed to have greater access to leadership positions.

Employees at Rockwell Automation also formed formal and informal communities of practice (CoPs) at all ranks devoted to fostering inclusion. A key strategy for the CoPs is continued emphasis on honing dialogue skills to ensure that alliances to bring about change remain strong, especially among white men. White men's focus groups later commented on the persistence of closed power structures and networks – something many white men were blind to beforehand. In this way, foundations for successful partnerships and alliances to create more inclusive work norms, practices, and policies were established.

ROCKWELL LESSONS LEARNED

Much can be learned from Rockwell Automation's approach to inclusive leadership. By focusing on building critical dialogue across gender and racial groups, an array of barriers fell at Rockwell. Apathy was countered by raising awareness about what men can gain from gender equality and the costs of doing nothing. Real and perceived ignorance of the challenges women faced at the organization were undercut by dialogue within and across gender groups. And fears were allayed among Rockwell managers by discouraging 'zero-sum' thinking, creating an open and constructive environment to dialogue about issues of gender, and the exposure of male role models who champion gender inclusion and challenged the status quo. Along the way, Rockwell Automation avoided common pitfalls to inclusion initiatives, including:

- lack of buy-in and understanding about what the inclusion challenges are;
- coercion or shaming techniques;
- creating an 'us' versus 'them' atmosphere;
- viewing white males as 'the problem';
- a didactic style unsuitable for adult learners; and,
- burdening people from under-represented or minority groups with having to teach trainees from dominant groups (Prime et al., 2009).

Rather than being made to feel responsible for group-based inequities that they themselves did not create in the workplace, Rockwell's white male managers felt empowered to lead the more inclusive workplaces. From seeking out and exploring varied perspectives to becoming more direct in addressing emotionally charged matters, managers improved on the skills needed for leading in today's diverse marketplace.

Three take-away lessons from Rockwell can thus be drawn. First, managers at Rockwell acquired critical, inter-group dialogue skills and connected across differences with their colleagues. By realizing common goals shared among white men and women and people of color, employees of all backgrounds were inspired to make change together, and in turn, a foundation for successful partnerships to foster more inclusive work norms and practices was established.

The next milestone in the change process was increased commitment to action (Nagda et al., 2009). Managers shared what they learned with their team and forged alliances to address the problems and points of conflict they'd been uncovering using their dialogic skills (ibid.). This ensured that employees of all backgrounds – not just women and people of color – were more engaged and motivated to make change.

Third, by forming formal and informal CoPs devoted to fostering inclusion, Rockwell did not let action eclipse dialogue. Through CoPs, Rockwell increased the likelihood of future buy-in and continued commitment to goals around inclusion.

BEYOND ROCKWELL: SPARKING CHANGE TO CLOSE GENDER GAPS

The results at Rockwell are a testament to the power of turning old ideas about leadership upside down and recognizing how important relationship building and 'identity work' – understanding and managing group identities – are to effective leadership. It's clear that in order to drive culture change, people first and foremost have to get talking – and do so using tangible tools and deliberate training.

Other organizations can learn from Rockwell, where an emphasis on inclusive leadership made the critical difference. Recognizing that followers were affected by their identities as white males was a breakthrough for Rockwell managers – one that made them more inclusive leaders and improved their all-round leader effectiveness. As one Rockwell employee later reported: 'We could now have these conversations, and it would not change the way you were treated in the workplace (in a negative way)'.

By encouraging white men to view identity and relationship work as essential leadership work – not just as something to help women and ethnic minorities succeed – companies can avoid pitfalls inherent in more narrowly defined 'diversity training' programs. By emphasizing inclusive leadership, organizations can engage men and build a lasting foundation for closing gender gaps and dismantling exclusive work cultures.

NOTE

1. For more information about the fishbowl technique, see Kacen (1998).

REFERENCES

Avolio, B.J., F.O. Walumbwa and T.J. Weber (2009), 'Leadership: Current theories, research, and future directions', *Annual Review of Psychology*, **60**(1), 421–49.

Ayman, R. and K. Korabik (2010), 'Leadership: Why gender and culture matter', *The American Psychologist*, **65**(3), 157–70.

Baugh, S.G. and G.B. Graen (1997), 'Effects of team gender and racial composition on perceptions of team performance in cross-functional teams', *Group and Organization Management*, **22**(3), 366–83.

BBC News (2013), 'Girls "lack ambition" for good jobs', BBC News, 4 June, accessed 11 September 2013 at http://www.bbc.co.uk/news/education-22764034.

Bergmann, B.R. (2005), *The Economic Emergence of Women*, 2nd edition, New York: Palgrave Macmillan.

Blau, F.D. and L.M. Kahn (2007), 'The gender pay gap: Have women gone as far as they can?' *Academy of Management Perspectives*, **21**(1), 7–23.

Brewer, M.B. and R.J. Brown (1998), 'Intergroup relations', in S.T. Fiske, D.T. Gilbert and G. Lindzey (eds), *Handbook of Social Psychology*, John Wiley and Sons, pp. 554–94.

Bureau of Labor Statistics (2011), *Women in the Labor Force in 2010*, Washington, DC: US Department of Labor, accessed 11 September 2013 at http://www.dol.gov/wb/factsheets/Qf-laborforce-10.htm.

Burke, R.J. and S. Black (1997), 'Save the males: Backlash in organizations', *Journal of Business Ethics*, **16**(9), 933–42.

Cain, S. (2012), *Quiet: The Power of Introverts in a World That Can't Stop Talking*, New York: Crown Publishing Group.

Carter, N.M. and C. Silva (2010a), *The Pipeline's Broken Promise*, New York: Catalyst.

Carter, N.M. and C. Silva (2010b), *Mentoring: Necessary But Insufficient for Advancement*, New York: Catalyst.

Carter, N.M. and C. Silva (2011), *The Myth of the Ideal Worker: Does Doing All the Right Things Really Get Women Ahead?*, New York: Catalyst.

Catalyst (2004), *Women and Men in US Corporate Leadership: Same Workplace, Different Realities?*, New York: Catalyst.

Catalyst (2005), *Women 'Take Care,' Men 'Take Charge': Stereotyping of US Business Leaders Exposed*, New York: Catalyst.

Catalyst (2007), *The Double-bind Dilemma for Women in Leadership: Damned if You Do, Doomed if You Don't*, New York: Catalyst.

Catalyst (2009), *Catalyst Census: Fortune 500 Women Executives*, New York: Catalyst.

Catalyst (2013), *Catalyst Pyramid: US Women in Business*, New York: Catalyst.

CONSAD Research Corp (2009), *An Analysis of Reasons for the Disparity in Wages Between Men and Women*, Pittsburgh: CONSAD Research Corp.

Corbett, C. (2013), *The Simple Truth about the Gender Pay Gap (2013)*, Washington, DC: AAUW, accessed 16 September at http://www.aauw.org/resource/the-simple-truth-about-the-gender-pay-gap/.

Cuberes, D. and M. Teignier-Baqué (2011), *Gender Inequality and Economic Growth*, Washington, DC: World Bank.

Daly, K. (2007), 'Gender inequality, growth, and global ageing', Global Economics

Paper No. 154, New York: Goldman Sachs, accessed 11 September 2013 at http://www.womenandtechnology.eu/digitalcity/servlet/PublishedFileServlet/A AAATKMI/Gender-inequality-Growth-and-Global-Aging.pdf.

Eagly, A.H. and S.J. Karau (2002), 'Role congruity theory of prejudice toward female leaders', *Psychological Review*, **109**(3), 573–98.

Eagly, A.H., S.J. Karau and M.G. Makhijani (1995), 'Gender and the effectiveness of leaders: A meta-analysis', *Psychological Bulletin*, **117**(1), 125–45.

Economist (2011), 'Closing the gap', 26 November, *The Economist*, accessed 11 September 2013 at http://www.economist.com/node/21539928.

Elliott, J.R. and R.A. Smith (2004), 'Race, gender, and workplace power', *American Sociological Review*, **69**(3), 365–86.

Esteve-Volart, B. (2009), 'Gender discrimination and growth: Theory and evidence from India', Working Paper.

European Commission (2009), *Gender Segregation in the Labour Market: Root Causes, Implications and Policy Responses in the EU*, Luxembourg: Publications Office of the European Union.

Farmer, J. (1966), *Freedom, When?*, New York: Random House.

Florida, R., C. Mellander and Y. Sun (2012), '*Talent vs. trade in regional economic development*', Working Paper, Toronto, ON: Prosperity Institute, accessed 11 September 2013 at http://martinprosperity.org/2012/08/27/ talent-vs-trade-in-regional-economic-development/.

Galinsky, E., K. Aumann and J.T. Bond (2011), *Times Are Changing: Gender and Generation at Work and at Home*, New York: Families and Work Institute.

Glick, P., C. Zion and C. Nelson (1988), 'What mediates sex discrimination in hiring decisions?' *Journal of Personality and Social Psychology*, **55**(2), 178–86.

Goodstein, L.D. and W.W. Burke (1991), 'Creating successful organization change', *Organizational Dynamics*, **19**(4), 5–17.

Graduate Management Admission Council (2012), *2012 Application Trends Survey*, Reston: GMAC, accessed 11 September 2013 at http://www.gmac. com/~/media/Files/gmac/Research/admissions-and-application-trends/2012-app lication-trends-survey-report.pdf.

Grant, A., F. Gino and D. Hofmann (2011), 'Reversing the extraverted leadership advantage: The role of employee proactivity', *Academy of Management Journal*, **54**(3), 528–50.

Grant Thornton (2011), *The Global Economy in 2012: A Rocky Road to Recovery*, Grant Thornton International Business Report, accessed 11 September 2013 at http://www.internationalbusinessreport.com/reports/2011/global_overview.asp.

Hausmann, R., L.D. Tyson and S. Zahidi (2012), *Global Gender Gap*, Geneva: World Economic Forum, accessed 11 September 2013 at http://www.weforum. org/issues/global-gender-gap.

Heilman, M.E. (2001), 'Description and prescription: How gender stereotypes prevent women's ascent up the organizational ladder', *Journal of Social Issues*, **57**(4), 657–74.

Holladay, C.L., J.L. Knight, D. Paige and M.A. Quinones (2003), 'The influence of framing on attitudes toward diversity training', *Human Resource Development Quarterly*, **14**(3), 245–63.

Hyde, J.S. (2005), 'The gender similarities hypothesis', *The American Psychologist*, **60**(6), 581–92.

International Labour Organization (2004), *Global Employment Trends for Women 2004*, Geneva: ILO, accessed 11 September 2013 at http://www.ilo.org/

wcmsp5/groups/public/---ed_emp/---emp_elm/---trends/documents/publication/wcms_114289.pdf.

International Labour Organization (2012), *Key Indicators of the Labour Market: 7th edition*, Geneva: ILO, accessed 11 September 2013 at http://www.ilo.org/empelm/pubs/WCMS_114060/lang--en/index.htm.

Kacen, L. (1998), 'Intergroup bridging using the dynamic circles exercise (DCE)', *Simulation and Gaming*, **29**(1), 88–100.

Kacmar, K.M. and D.S. Carlson (1999), 'Effectiveness of impression management tactics across human resource situations', *Journal of Applied Social Psychology*, **29**(6), 1293–311.

Kalev, A., F. Dobbin and E. Kelly (2006), 'Best practices or best guesses? Assessing the efficacy of corporate affirmative action and diversity policies', *American Sociological Review*, **71**(4), 589–617.

Kanter, R.M. (1977), *Men and Women of the Corporation*, New York: Basic Books.

Kellogg, C.F. (1973), *NAACP: A History of the National Association for the Advancement of Colored People*, Baltimore, MD: Johns Hopkins University Press.

Kidder, D.L., M.J. Lankau, D. Chrobot-Mason, K.A. Mollica and R.A. Friedman (2004), 'Backlash toward diversity initiatives: Examining the impact of diversity program justification, personal, and group outcomes', *International Journal of Conflict Management*, **15**(1), 77–102.

Kristof-Brown, A., M.R. Barrick and M. Franke (2002), 'Applicant impression management: Dispositional influences and consequences for recruiter perceptions of fit and similarity', *Journal of Management*, **28**(1), 27–46.

Lips, H.M. (2013), 'The gender pay gap: Challenging the rationalizations. Perceived equity, discrimination, and the limits of human capital models', *Sex Roles*, **68**(3–4), 169–85.

Marlowe, C.M., S.L. Schneider and C.E. Nelson (1996), 'Gender and attractiveness biases in hiring decisions: Are more experienced managers less biased?', *Journal of Applied Psychology February*, **81**(1), 11–21.

Martell, R.F., C.G. Emrich and J. Robison-Cox (2012), 'From bias to exclusion: A multilevel emergent theory of gender segregation in organizations', *Research in Organizational Behavior*, **32**, 137–62.

Martell, R.F., D.M. Lane and C. Emrich (1996), 'Male–female differences: A computer simulation', *American Psychologist*, **51**(2), 157–8.

Marx, G.T. and M. Useem (1971), 'Majority involvement in minority movements: Civil rights, abolition, untouchability', *Journal of Social Issues*, **27**(1), 81–104.

Meier, A. and E.M. Rudwick (1966), *From Plantation to Ghetto: An Interpretive History of American Negroes*, New York: Hill and Wang.

Moss-Racusin, C.A., J.E. Phelan and L.A. Rudman (2010), 'When men break the gender rules: Status incongruity and backlash against modest men', *Psychology of Men & Masculinity*, **11**(2), 140–51.

Nagda, B.A. (2006), 'Breaking barriers, crossing borders, building bridges: Communication processes in intergroup dialogues', *Journal of Social Issues*, **62**(3), 553–76.

Nagda, B.A., P. Gurin, N. Sorensen, C. Gurin-Sands and S.M. Osuna (2009), 'From separate corners to dialogue and action', *Race and Social Problems*, **1**(1), 45–55.

National Center for Education Statistics (2011), *Digest of Education Statistics,*

2011, Washington, DC: NCES, accessed 11 September 2013 at http://nces. ed.gov/programs/digest/d11/ch_3.asp.

National Equal Pay Task Force (2013), *Fifty Years After the Equal Pay Act: Assessing the Past, Taking Stock of the Future*, Washington, DC: The White House, accessed 11 September 2013 at http://www.whitehouse.gov/sites/default/ files/image/image_file/equal_pay-task_force_progress_report_june_10_2013. pdf.

Olson, C.A. and B.E. Becker (1983), 'Sex discrimination in the promotion process', *Industrial and Labor Relations Review*, **36**(4), 624–41.

Prime, J. and C.A. Moss-Racusin (2009), *Engaging Men in Gender Initiatives: What Change Agents Need to Know*, New York: Catalyst.

Prime, J., H. Foust-Cummings and E.R. Salib (2012), *Calling All White Men: Can Training Help Create Inclusive Workplaces?*, New York: Catalyst.

Prime, J., C.A. Moss-Racusin and H. Foust-Cummings (2009), *Engaging Men in Gender Initiatives: Stacking the Deck for Success*, New York: Catalyst.

Proost, K., F. Germeys and B. Schreurs (2012), 'When does self-promotion work?', *Journal of Personnel Psychology*, **11**(3), 109–17.

Proost, K., B. Schreurs, K. De Witte and E. Derous (2010), 'Ingratiation and self-promotion in the selection interview: The effects of using single tactics or a combination of tactics on interviewer judgments', *Journal of Applied Social Psychology*, **40**(9), 2155–69.

Ragins, B.R. and E. Sundstrom (1989), 'Gender and power in organizations: A longitudinal perspective', *Psychological Bulletin*, **105**(1), 51–88.

Robison-Cox, J.F., R.F. Martell and C. Emrich (2007), 'Stimulating gender stratification', *Journal of Artificial Societies and Social Simulation*, **10**(3), 8.

Rudman, L.A. (1998), 'Self promotion as a risk factor in women: The costs and benefits of counterstereotypical impression management', *Journal of Personality and Social Psychology*, **74**(3), 629–45.

Rudman, L.A. and P. Glick (2010), *The Social Psychology of Gender: How Power and Intimacy Shape Gender Relations*, New York: The Guilford Press.

Rudman, L.A., K. Mescher and C.A. Moss-Racusin (in press), 'Penalizing men who request a family leave: Is flexibility stigma a femininity stigma?' *Group Processes and Intergroup Relations*.

Russ, F.A. and K.M. McNeilly (1995), 'Links among satisfaction, commitment, and turnover intentions: The moderating effect of experience, gender, and performance', *Journal of Business Research*, **34**(1), 57–65.

Schein, V.E. (2001), 'A global look at psychological barriers to women's progress in management', *Journal of Social Issues*, **57**(4), 675–88.

Schwab, K. (2011), 'Times favor talent-driven economy', *The China Post*, 2 November, accessed 11 September 2013 at http://www.chinapost.com.tw/com mentary/the-china-post/special-to-the-china-post/2011/11/02/321716/Times-fav or.htm.

Stevens, C.K. and A.L. Kristof (1995), 'Making the right impression: A field study of applicant impression management during job interviews', *Journal of Applied Psychology*, **80**(5), 587–606.

Thoroughgood, C.N., K.B. Sawyer and S.T. Hunter (2013), 'Real men don't make mistakes: Investigating the effects of leader gender, error type, and the occupational context on leader error perceptions', *Journal of Business and Psychology*, **28**(1), 31–48.

US Bureau of Labor Statistics and US Department of Labor (2013), *Employed*

Persons by Occupations, Sex and Age, accessed 11 September 2013 at http://www.bls.gov/cps/cpsaat09.htm.

US Department of Labor and US Bureau of Labor Statistics (2012), *Highlights of Women's Earnings in 2011*, Washington, DC: US Bureau of Labor Statistics.

Warren, A.K. (2009), *Cascading Gender Biases, Compounding Effects: An Assessment of Talent Management Systems*, New York: Catalyst.

West, T.V., M.E. Heilman, L. Gullett, C.A. Moss-Racusin and J.C. Magee (2012), 'Building blocks of bias: Gender composition predicts male and female group members' evaluations of each other and the group', *Journal of Experimental Social Psychology*, **48**(5), 1209–12.

Whitehead, P. (2013), '"Lack of ambition" deters women', *Financial Times*, 20 February, accessed 11 September 2013 at http://www.ft.com/cms/s/0/f4c4dada-6af6-11e2-9670-00144feab49a.html.

Williams, C.L. (1992), 'The glass escalator: Hidden advantages for men in the "female" professions', *Social Problems*, **39**(3), 253–67.

Wingfield, A.H. (2009), 'Racializing the glass escalator: Reconsidering men's experiences with women's work', *Gender & Society*, **23**(1), 5–26.

Yukl, G. (1999), 'An evaluative essay on current conceptions of effective leadership', *European Journal of Work and Organizational Psychology*, **8**(1), 33–48.

17. Preventing violence against women and girls

Michael Flood

INTRODUCTION

Men's violence against women and girls is a blunt expression of the pervasive gender inequalities that characterize countries across the globe. Men's violence against women both expresses and maintains men's power over women. Indeed, rape, domestic violence and other forms of violence have been seen as paradigmatic expressions of the operation of male power over women (Miller and Biele 1993, p. 53). Whether in workplaces or elsewhere, efforts to build gender equality must reckon with men's violence against women.

The term 'men's violence against women' is used here to refer to the wide variety of forms of violence and abuse perpetrated by men against women, including physical and sexual assaults and other behaviours that result in physical, sexual, or psychological harm or suffering to women. Data from across the globe documents that substantial proportions of women experience violence. In Australia for example: (1) the *Personal Safety Survey Australia* finds that nearly one in six women (16 per cent) have experienced violence by a current or previous partner since the age of 15 (ABS, 2006); (2) the Australian component of the *International Violence Against Women Survey* finds that over a third of women (34 per cent) who have ever had a boyfriend or husband report experiencing at least one form of violence during their lifetime from an intimate male partner (Mouzos and Makkai, 2004, p. 44).

Most women who experience violence in their relationships and families are in paid employment. In turn, it is likely that many if not most of the men who perpetrate violence against women and girls are in paid employment. Thus, there are victims and perpetrators in every workplace. This violence has a direct impact on women's and men's participation at work, workplaces themselves may contribute to or tolerate violence against women and workplaces can play key roles in preventing and reducing violence. I return to these arguments below. In addition, women are subjected to violence in workplaces themselves. For example:

- Sixty-two per cent of women had experienced violence at work within the last five years, according to a representative survey in the state of Victoria, Australia. This violence included: being sworn at or shouted at; hostile behaviours; being intimidated or threatened; bullying; victimization; physical attacks; racial harassment, sexual harassment, robbery; wounding or battering; stalking; and rape (URCOT 2005, p. 7).
- One-quarter of women (25 per cent) and one in six men (16 per cent) aged 15 years and older have experienced sexual harassment in the workplace in the past five years (Australian Human Rights Commission 2012, p. 15).
- In a survey completed by over 3600 union members in Australia, with 81 per cent of respondents female, nearly one-third of respondents (30 per cent) had personally experienced domestic violence (McFerran 2011, p. 6). Among those individuals who had experienced domestic violence in the last 12 months, nearly one in five (19 per cent) reported that the violence continued at the workplace, for example through abusive phone calls and e-mails and the partner physically coming to work (ibid., p. 10).

Feminist concern with men's violence against women is based on the recognition that this violence both expresses and maintains gendered inequalities of power. Men's violence against women has an impact not just on individual women, but on women *as a group*. Men's violence is a threat to women's mobility, self-esteem and everyday safety. This violence imposes a curfew on women. Sexual violence and other forms of violence act as a form of social control on women, limiting their autonomy, freedom and safety and their access to paid work and political decision-making. Men's violence thus has the general social consequence of reproducing forms of men's authority over women.

Before exploring the significance of men's violence against women for workplaces, what do we know about the causes of this violence? I outline these below, focusing on the determinants of intimate partner violence in particular – of both domestic violence and sexual violence perpetrated by men against women in the context of relationships and families, although I also draw on scholarship on other forms of men's violence against women.

THE FOUNDATIONS OF MEN'S VIOLENCE AGAINST WOMEN

Three decades of research have identified key determinants of men's violence against women. We can group these into three broad clusters:

Gender Roles and Relations

The most well-documented determinants of men's violence against women can be found in gender norms and gender relations. Whether at individual, community, or societal levels, there are relationships between how gender is organized and violence against women.

Individual men's use of violence is enabled by wider gender inequalities. When a man hits an individual woman, or pressures her into sex, or sexually harasses her, his actions are only made possible because of a wider web of collective or structural conditions: the social relations of peer groups, collective ideologies and discourses of gender and sexuality, organizational cultures, institutional conditions and wider patterns of gender inequality (Flood, 2007).

First, men's gender-role attitudes and beliefs are critical. Men's agreement with sexist, patriarchal and sexually hostile attitudes is an important predictor of their use of violence against women. Putting this another way, some men are less likely to use violence than other men. Men who *do not* hold patriarchal and hostile gender norms are *less* likely than other men to use physical or sexual violence against an intimate partner (Schumacher et al., 2001; Murnen et al., 2002).

Violence-supportive attitudes are based in wider social norms regarding gender and sexuality. In fact, in many ways, violence is part of 'normal' sexual and intimate relations. For example, for many young people, sexual harassment is pervasive, male aggression is expected and normalized, there is constant pressure among boys to behave in sexually aggressive ways, girls are routinely objectified, there is a sexual double standard and girls are pressured to accommodate male 'needs' and desires. These social norms mean that sexual coercion actually becomes 'normal', working through common heterosexual norms and relations (Flood and Pease, 2006, p. 24).

There are important determinants of intimate partner violence in relationships and families. A key factor here is the power relations between partners – are they fair and just, or dominated by one partner? Men's domestic violence in families and homes is only understandable in the context of power inequalities. In fact, it can be seen as a development of dominant–submissive power relations that exist in 'normal' family life (Hearn, 1996, p. 31). Cross-culturally, male economic and decision-making dominance in the family is one of the strongest predictors of high levels of violence against women (Heise 1998).

Men's use of 'coercive control' against their female partners – of 'a range of tactics designed to isolate, intimidate, exploit, degrade and/or control a partner' (Stark, 2010, p. 203) – is enabled by persistent gender inequalities (Stark, 2006, p. 1022). A man is more able to control his wife or partner because he can exploit her roles as a housekeeper, wife and mother, because she does most of the unpaid work in the house while he is free to advance his career and because she has been socialized to feel responsible for his emotional well-being and his sexual interests.

Another factor at the level of intimate relationships and families is marital conflict. This conflict interacts with the power structure of the family. When conflict occurs in an asymmetrical power structure, there is a much higher risk of violence (Heise, 1998; Riggs et al., 2000).

Peer and friendship groups and organizational cultures are important influences too. Some men have 'rape-supporting social relationships', whether in sport, on campus, or in the military and this feeds into their use of violence against women. For example, there are higher rates of sexual violence against young women in contexts characterized by gender segregation, a belief in male sexual conquest, strong male bonding, high alcohol consumption, use of pornography and sexist social norms (Flood, 2007, pp. 5–6).

There is also international evidence that the gender roles and norms of entire cultures have an influence on intimate partner violence. Rates of men's violence against women are higher in cultures emphasizing traditional gender codes, male dominance in families, male honour and female chastity (Heise, 1998).

Social Norms and Practices Relating to Violence

The second cluster of causes of men's violence against women relate to other social norms and practices related to violence. Three in particular are worth discussing: domestic violence resources, violence in the community and childhood exposure to intimate partner violence.

First, there is US evidence that when domestic violence resources – refuges, legal advocacy programs, hotlines and so on – are available in a community, women are less vulnerable to intimate partner violence (Dugan et al., 2003). Second, violence in the community appears to be a risk factor for intimate partner violence. Members of disadvantaged communities may learn a greater tolerance of violence through exposure to violence by their parents, delinquent peers and others (Vezina and

Herbert, 2007). Third, childhood exposure to intimate partner violence contributes to the transmission of violence across generations. Children, especially boys, who witness violence or are subjected to violence themselves are more likely to grow up with violence-supportive attitudes and to use violence (Flood, 2007, pp. 8–9).

Access to Resources and Systems of Support

The third cluster of causes concern women's and men's access to resources and systems of support. Again, a range of determinants are significant: low socioeconomic status, poverty and unemployment; lack of social connections and social capital, social isolation; neighbourhood and community characteristics; personality characteristics (and antisocial behaviour and peers); alcohol and substance abuse; and situational factors such as separation.

Rates of reported domestic violence are higher in areas of economic and social disadvantage and there are moderate associations between male partners' perpetration of physical aggression and their socioeconomic status (Holtzworth-Munroe et al., 1997; Riggs et al., 2000; Schumacher et al., 2001; Riger and Staggs 2004; Stith et al., 2004). Disadvantage may increase the risk of abuse because of the other variables that accompany this, such as crowding, hopelessness, conflict, stress, or a sense of inadequacy in some men. Social isolation is another risk factor for intimate partner violence. Among young women, rates of domestic violence are higher for those who aren't involved in schools or don't experience positive parenting and supervision in their families. In adult couples, social isolation is both a cause and a consequence of wife abuse. Women with strong family and friendship networks experience lower rates of violence (Flood, 2007, p. 12).

Intimate partner violence is shaped also by neighbourhoods and communities: by levels of poverty and unemployment and collective efficacy, that is, neighbours' willingness to help other neighbours or to intervene in anti-social or violent behaviour (ibid., p. 14). In indigenous communities, interpersonal violence is shaped by histories of colonisation and the disintegration of family and community.

Another factor is personality characteristics. Spouse abusers on average tend to have more psychological problems than non-violent men, including borderline, mood disorders and depression (Abbey and McAuslan 2004; Riggs et al., 2000; Schumacher et al., 2001; Stith et al., 2004; Tolan et al., 2006). Adolescent delinquency – antisocial and aggressive behaviour committed during adolescence – is a predictor of men's later perpetration of sexual assault (Abbey and McAuslan, 2004).

Men's abuse of alcohol or drugs is a risk factor for intimate partner violence. Men may use being drunk or high to minimize their own responsibility for violent behaviour. Some men may see drunk women as more sexually available and may use alcohol as a strategy for overcoming women's resistance (Flood, 2007, pp. 9–11).

There are also situational factors that increase the risk of intimate partner violence. For example, there is evidence that women are at risk of increasingly severe violence when separating from violent partners (Brownridge 2006).

GENDER, VIOLENCE AND THE WORKPLACE

Men's violence against women is a workplace issue. First, this violence has a direct impact on women's and men's participation in and productivity at work. Second, workplaces contribute to the cultures and inequalities that allow violence against women to flourish. Third, workplaces can play vital roles in preventing and reducing men's violence against women. There is thus a powerful, threefold business case for workplaces and organizations to address men's violence against women.

Impacts on Workplaces

Domestic violence, sexual violence, sexual harassment and other forms of violence against women have a profound impact on workplaces. Key impacts of this violence include 'higher rates of absenteeism, loss of pro-ductivity, reduced employee morale and increased need for support in the workplace for victims' (Wells et al., 2013, p. 19). Domestic violence has a direct impact on the economy. In Australia for example, the economic cost of violence against women and their children was estimated to be $13.6 billion in 2009 (National Council to Reduce Violence Against Women and their Children, 2009). There is increasing recognition among employers that there are both ethical and economic reasons to address and prevent violence against women.

Men's violence against women has both direct and indirect impacts on work and employment. Domestic violence has significant negative conse-quences for women's physical and mental health, both short and long term and in turn these diminish their workforce productivity and participation (Murray and Powell, 2008, pp. 3–5; Women's Health Victoria, 2012, pp. 11–13). Economic costs associated with victimization include absen-teeism, lost productivity related to use of sick leave, distraction and lack of concentration, underperformance, poor workplace relationships, access to employment support services, and so on, and staff replacement. There are further, second generation costs to do with counselling, changing schools, child protection, increased use of government services and juvenile and adult crime (Access Economics, 2004). Domestic violence has wider impacts at work. Friends, family and colleagues may also take leave from work for various reasons and staff may try to protect or support victims (Women's Health Victoria, 2012, pp. 13–14). Domestic violence also impedes women's capacity to gain and maintain employment (Murray and Powell, 2008, p. 4). As McFerran (2011, p. 2) summarizes:

> The evidence is that women with a history of domestic violence have a more disrupted work history, are consequently on lower personal incomes, have had to change jobs more often and are employed at higher levels in casual and part time work than women with no experience of violence.

Domestic violence also may 'come' to work, with the workplace a site of domestic violence and associated behaviours itself. For example, victims may experience physical or verbal harassment by perpetrators during work hours and they may be stalked at or around their workplaces (Murray and Powell, 2008, pp. 4–5; Women's Health Victoria, 2012, p. 14). Men seeking to coerce and control their female partners or ex-partners may target them at work to increase their control and compromise their economic independence (McFerran, 2011, p. 3).

While domestic violence impacts on employment, employment in turn impacts on domestic violence. Participation in paid work allows some women to find assistance and support, to benefit from financial security and independence and to maintain social networks and support, which can be vital in gaining safety (Murray and Powell 2008, p. 6). Being in employment is a key pathway to women leaving a violent relationship (McFerran, 2011, p. 2). Women may seek assistance in the workplace for experiences of violence, whether these occur inside or outside the workplace setting, through workplace support mechanisms and collegial networks (Powell, 2011, p. 27).

Workplaces as Contributors to Violence Against Women

Workplaces themselves may contribute to the problem of men's violence against women. To the extent that workplace norms and relations are marked by gender inequality, they intensify the wider gender inequalities in which violence against women flourishes. Workforces are influential spaces in which gender-inequitable norms and behaviours may be enforced, or challenged. At work, gender inequalities are produced and sustained by a variety of processes, including men's and women's internalization of privilege and disadvantage; gendered constructions of particular occupations and of management and leadership; men's interactive performances or accomplishment of gender and dominance; men's collective social relations (including segregation, exclusion and male-focused networking) and men's use of women's presence to construct masculinities and men's privilege (Flood and Pease, 2005). To summarize: 'Unjust gender relations are maintained by individual men's sexist and gendered practices, masculine workplace cultures, men's monopolies over decision-making and leadership and powerful constructions of masculinity and male identity' (Flood and Pease, 2005, p. 121). Workforces also may contribute to violence against women through the ways in which they respond to employees who are victims of violence or its perpetrators.

There is now substantial evidence that violence-supportive attitudes are encouraged and institutionalized in the peer relations and cultures of particular organizations and workplaces. The institutional contexts for which most research has been done include male-dominated and homosocially focused male university colleges, sporting clubs, workplaces and military institutions (Flood and Pease, 2006, pp. 36–42). For example, in professional sports, there is evidence that risks of sexual violence against women by male athletes are higher in contexts and cultures involving intense male bonding, high male status and strong differentiation of gender roles, high alcohol and drug consumption, ideologies and practices of aggression and toughness and practices of group sex (ibid., p. 37). In military institutions, violence against women is promoted by norms of gender inequality and other bonds that foster and justify abuse in particular peer cultures (Schwartz and DeKeseredy 1997; Rosen et al., 2003). Interviews with female victims of violence in the Canadian military find that specific aspects of military culture contribute to and condone this violence (Harrison, 2002). A US study provides quantitative support for an association between patriarchal male bonding in peer cultures and violence against women. Using survey data among 713 married male soldiers at an Army post in Alaska, Rosen et al. (2003, pp. 1064–5) found an association between 'group disrespect' (the presence of rude and aggressive behaviour, pornography consumption, sexualized discussion and encouragement of group drinking) and the perpetration of intimate partner violence, at both individual and group levels.

Several mechanisms may produce the increased prevalence of violence-supportive attitudes and violent behaviour among men in such contexts. One is 'group socialization': in joining particular sporting teams or fraternities, men are actively inducted into the existing norms and values of these contexts. Another is 'identification'. Membership of a high-risk group may itself not be sufficient to increase one's adherence to violence-supportive beliefs or one's likelihood of assaultive behaviour and members may also have to identify with the group and see it as a reference group (Humphrey and Kahn, 2000, p. 1320). Another mechanism is 'self-selection': men with pre-existing violence-supportive attitudes and behaviours and an orientation towards other features of these contexts such as heavy drinking may join groups with similar norms.

Studies focused on or comparing particular occupational groups are rare, but they suggest that some workplace and professional cultures involve less violence-supportive norms than others and that occupational cultures and training can encourage positive shifts in violence-supportive attitudes. In a Hong Kong study, police officers and lawyers had narrower definitions of violence against women than psychologists, social workers and nurses, which may reflect the former groups' work in settings where legal and more restrictive definitions of criminal behaviour are dominant (Tang and Cheung, 1997). White and Kurpius (1999) conducted an American study among people working or studying in mental health and counselling. They found that, alongside a persistent gender gap, undergraduates had more negative attitudes towards rape victims than graduate counselling students, who in turn had more negative attitudes than the mental health professionals. One factor here may be self-selection, where those men who stay in mental health and counselling are more sensitive to issues of gender and violence such that the gap between their and women's views lessens (ibid., p. 993). Another factor may be the cultures of these fields themselves, with counsellor training and occupational norms also encouraging intolerance for violence.

However, occupational cultures and training also can intensify violence-supportive norms. A Queensland study found no gender differences in blaming attributed to victims or assailants by male and female police officers (although both drew on gender stereotypes in their decision-making) (Stewart and Maddren 1997, p. 930). The authors suggest that this may reflect police training producing uniformity in attitudes. However, a very different interpretation of this uniformity is possible. Referring to the findings in some studies that there are few gender differences in police attitudes and behaviours regarding domestic violence, Stalans and Finn (2000) note that this may reflect the fact that female officers have learned the norms and rules of these male-dominated occupations and thus conform to masculine norms. Their own study found that while female and male police officers did not differ in their arrest rates, *experienced* female officers were more likely to recommend battered shelters, less likely to recommend marriage counselling and gave greater emphasis to victims' own decision-making (ibid.). Male officers and rookie female officers approached domestic violence cases in similar ways, but experienced female officers were more empathetic to battered women and less likely to blame them. This may reflect such women having developed the confidence and security to challenge men's norms regarding domestic violence, or the result of experiences of discrimination or harassment on the job. Thus, it appears that actual gender differences in attitudes and behaviours in the police force were initially obscured by the male dominance of this profession, but more experienced female officers were able to express them. Further mechanisms producing uniformity in police officers' attitudes include self-selection out of the force by women with contrary attitudes or being weeded out by training and promotion (ibid.). This study does provide an example of occupational cultures reducing apparent gender differences in attitudes and behaviours regarding violence against women, but one in which such differences in fact were partially stifled or silenced by dominant masculine norms.

Any workplace involves informal social networks and peer relations and these too can contribute to men's violence against women. A series of studies document that a particular risk factor for men's perpetration of violence against women is their participation and investment in homosocial male peer groups. Beginning in the 1990s, DeKeseredy et al. in the USA documented that male peer support for sexual assault, including young men's attachment (close emotional ties) to abusive peers and peers' informational support for sexual assault (peer guidance and advice that influences men to assault their dating partners), were significantly correlated with sexual assault (DeKeseredy and Kelly, 1995; Schwartz and DeKeseredy, 1997). Among men, being more dependent on a male reference group for one's gender role self-concept is associated with attitudes conducive to the sexual harassment of women (Wade and Brittan-Powell, 2001), while having a homosocially focused social life can restrict men's acceptance of more progressive views of gender roles (Bryant, 2003). To the extent that individuals' peers share negative beliefs about gender and about violence and are involved in physically aggressive or coercive behaviours, those individuals are more likely to perpetrate relationship abuse (Reitzel-Jaffe and Wolfe 2001; Sellers et al., 2005, p. 389).

Among men in groups and contexts characterised by a hypermasculine subculture (whether in a workplace, a gang, or a sports team), higher violence-supportive attitudes and violent behaviours are shaped by several factors. The discussion earlier identified processes such as group socialization, identification and self-selection and this account can be extended by focusing on investment in and conformity to social norms and bonds as key processes. Godenzi et al. (2001, p. 11) argue that in such contexts, 'abuse is a by-product of the men's attempt to maintain a social bond with a conventional or traditional social order marked by gender inequality'. One process is 'attachment', in which having close emotional ties to significant others means that one is more likely to take their concerns, wishes and expectations into account. Another is 'commitment': men's investments in and loyalties to the dominant (patriarchal) social order and their interest in gaining the rewards of peer acceptance and status associated for example with sexually active and potentially abusive behaviour. Men's attitudes and behaviours also are shaped by 'involvement': their participation in activities associated with that sub-culture, including leisure activities involving time with patriarchal peers such as drinking or consuming and sharing pornography (ibid., p. 8). Finally, men's own 'belief' in the legitimacy of the dominant system of values plays a role, although this belief of course is influenced by multiple factors including childhood socialization and popular culture. Therefore, among men whose peer and social relations are characterized by norms and behaviours associated with violence against women, conformity with what is 'normal' in these contexts leads to violent attitudes and behaviours.

Workplaces as Sites for Prevention

Workplaces have been identified as key settings for the prevention of men's violence against women (VicHealth, 2007, p. 57). Organizations represent excellent sites for the introduction of prevention strategies to end violence against women, for several reasons. First, organizational efforts 'scale up' the impact of violence prevention, in that they have the potential to influence both their internal cultures and the communities that surround them. By changing its policies, practices and culture, an organization can not only change from within, but also have an impact in surrounding communities, serve as an example for other organizations, influence wider policy and inform community norms (Davis et al., 2006, p. 12). Organizations have the potential to reach large numbers of people and create conditions in which change can be promoted and sustained. Second, given the impacts of relationship and family violence documented earlier, employers are key stakeholders in prevention: 'they are responsible for setting policy, sharing information, promoting skills development and motivating employees, clients, consumers and partners to become engaged in efforts to end violence at the individual, family, community and societal levels' (Wells et al., 2013, p. 19). Third, given the violence-supportive cultures of some workplaces or organizations, intensive intervention is needed.

There are a range of benefits for workplaces in preventing and reducing men's violence against women, including direct and indirect economic and other benefits:

Direct benefits include increased productivity and decreased costs in relation to leave and staff replacement . . . Indirect benefits include supporting staff and being identified as an employer of choice who shows social responsibility and provides community leadership.. . . By being aware of domestic violence issues and having prevention strategies in place, employers can also better ensure that they are meeting equal opportunity and anti-discrimination requirements, as well as their duty of care in ensuring a safe work environment. (Murray and Powell, 2008, p. 3)

If workplaces are important sites for the prevention of violence against women, *what kind* of prevention activity is undertaken in workplaces?

PRIMARY, SECONDARY AND TERTIARY PREVENTION

One common way of classifying activities to prevent and respond to violence is a threefold classification in terms of *when* they occur in relation to violence:

- Before the problem starts: *primary* prevention – activities that take place *before* violence has occurred to prevent initial perpetration or victimization.
- Once the problem has begun: *secondary* prevention – immediate responses *after* violence has occurred to deal with the short-term consequences of violence, to respond to those at risk and to prevent the problem from occurring or progressing.
- Responding afterwards: *tertiary* prevention – long-term responses *after* violence has occurred to deal with the lasting consequences of violence, minimize its impact and prevent further perpetration and victimization.

Primary prevention strategies are implemented before the problem ever occurs. They are successful when the first instance of violence is prevented (Foshee et al., 1998, p. 45). Secondary prevention focuses on early identification and intervention, targeting those individuals at high risk for either perpetration or victimization and working to reduce the likelihood of their further or subsequent engagement in or subjection to violence. Secondary prevention is intended to reverse progress towards violence and to reduce its impact. For example, activities may focus on reducing opportunities for violence by supporting the men who are at risk of perpetrating violence. Secondary prevention efforts are successful 'when victims stop being victimized [e.g., by leaving violent relationships] or perpetrators stop being violent' (ibid.). Tertiary prevention is centred on responding after violence has occurred. Activities focus on minimizing the impact of violence, restoring health and safety and preventing further victimization and perpetration (Chamberlain, 2008, p. 3). Mostly, these activities include crisis care, counselling and advocacy and criminal justice and counselling responses to perpetrators.

These different forms of prevention contribute to each other. For example, rapid and coordinated responses to individuals perpetrating sexual violence can reduce their opportunities for and likelihood of further perpetration, while effective responses to victims and survivors can reduce the impact of victimization and prevent revictimization (ibid., p. 4). In short, the effective and systematic application of tertiary strategies complements and supports primary prevention.

WORKFORCE-BASED PREVENTION

In workforces, strategies for the *primary* prevention of intimate partner violence are scattered and underdeveloped. On the other hand, organizations and workforces are a common site for the development of improved responses to the occurrence of such violence. Most workplace-based efforts to reduce or prevent men's violence against women are centred on secondary or tertiary prevention (Wells et al., 2013, pp. 48–9). Strategies include training police, legal staff and other personnel in appropriate responses to and interventions into intimate partner violence; developing coordinated community responses to intimate partner violence; and sensitizing health care providers, encouraging routine screening for violence and developing protocols for the proper management of abuse (World Health Organization, 2002). There is evidence that such efforts do improve professional responses to the victims and perpetrators of intimate partner violence, increase women's safety and assist their processes of recovery.

Workplaces are increasingly prominent sites for domestic violence prevention and intervention. In the USA, UK and elsewhere, some larger companies now have domestic violence programs in their workplaces, it is mandatory in some jurisdictions for large organizations to have policies providing special leave related to domestic violence and violence prevention organizations and trade unions have developed training manuals and resources for workplace-based prevention (Murray and Powell, 2008, p. 7). Corporate alliances and public sector networks in the USA and elsewhere have developed workplace programs regarding intimate partner violence. While most strategies focus on responses to victimization (such as security measures, victim resources and education), many companies also engage in activities designed to raise awareness in general of intimate partner violence (Lindquist et al., 2006).

Strategies for workplace prevention vary according to the size, location and character of the workplace, who is initiating the activities and whom they target. Typical activities focused on employees include:

> the implementation of policies regarding workplace responses to incidents of domestic violence; statements from management to staff condemning domestic violence and supporting domestic violence prevention in forums such as messages on payslips, workplace newsletters and intranet sites; the training of key personnel who are likely to come into contact with domestic violence issues in the workplace, including managers, employee assistance program staff and human resources personnel; and the display of posters and information sheets that provide information about domestic violence and sources of assistance. (Murray and Powell 2008, p. 8)

Efforts may be employer-led, based on brokerage partnerships, union-based, or organized in other ways (ibid.). Employer-led efforts involve incorporating prevention strategies – such as flexible leave provisions, increased security, flexible shifts and the provision of referral information – into existing human resources structures or organisational processes (ibid., p. 9). In brokerage models, domestic violence prevention is done as part of philanthropic or corporate social responsibility activities. Businesses may support domestic violence services and promote awareness in their organization and the wider community and may receive awareness training and support in return (ibid., p. 10). Unfortunately, little data is available, based on robust impact evaluations, with which to assess the effectiveness of these efforts (ibid., p. 15).

ENGAGING MEN IN WORKFORCE-BASED VIOLENCE PREVENTION

In engaging men in the prevention of men's violence against women, there are important reasons to include strategies focused on workplaces. Workplaces are important gathering points for men, important spaces where men can be found. Paid work historically has been a central source of masculine identity and authority, the primary way in which many men define their value and being (Pease, 2002, p. 7). Research on men, class and work documents that whether on the factory shopfloor among working-class men or in boardrooms and offices among middle- and ruling-class men, there are powerful interrelationships between work, masculinities and gender inequalities (Flood and Pease, 2005). Workplaces are an important site of male leadership and influence and they can be influential spaces where masculine norms are formed and enforced (Wells et al., 2013, pp. 17–19).

What are some examples of workplace-based efforts to engage men in the prevention of men's violence against women? Given that men's violence against women is the outcome of a complex interplay of individual, relationship, social and cultural factors, violence prevention too must work at multiple levels. There is a spectrum of primary prevention strategies, addressing determinants of men's violence at different levels of the social order (Flood, 2011). I discuss examples of workplace-based efforts to engage men in primary prevention at different levels of the spectrum of prevention, beginning with those at the smallest levels involving individuals or face-to-face education and moving towards the largest levels involving organizations, communities and policies and legislation.

The most localized form of prevention is transferring information and skills to individuals and increasing their capacity to prevent or avoid violence against women. Individual men (and women) can contribute here in their professional roles. For example, teachers, carers and physicians may help boys and young men to increase their equitable attitudes, health care practitioners may engage patients and parents to promote healthy relationships and leaders and public figures may speak to boys and men to encourage non-violence (Davis et al., 2006). Doctors, teachers, police, child care workers and other professionals can play an important role in transmitting information, skills and motivation to clients, community members and colleagues and they can be effective advocates for prevention policies (ibid.). For example, the US Family Violence Prevention Fund encouraged coaches (and other adult men, including fathers, teachers, uncles, older brothers and mentors) to teach boys that there is no place for violence in a relationship.

The second level of strategy concerns community education. One important stream here is face-to-face educational groups and programs. Education programs that are intensive, lengthy and use a variety of teaching approaches have been shown to produce positive and lasting change in attitudes and behaviours (Flood 2005–06). The vast majority of face-to-face education addressing violence against women takes place in schools and universities and few programs are focused on men in workplaces. In relation to interpersonal violence, the most common primary prevention education that has occurred in workplaces in general concerns sexual harassment. Various studies have demonstrated that workplace training can improve attitudes towards sexual harassment, among employees in universities and in federal government workplaces (Antecol and Cobb-Clark 2003). In fact, such training has been shown to have an effect on organisational cultures over and above the impact of individual training, in that more widespread training in a workplace is associated with a greater recognition of sexual harassment, regardless of whether or not individual training has been undertaken (Antecol and Cobb-Clark, 2003). However, workplace training engaging men faces obvious barriers. There is evidence that men are not as receptive as women to organizational efforts to eliminate gender bias (Prime et al., 2009, p. 2). Men are less supportive of diversity programs for minorities and more likely than women to respond with backlash (Kidder et al., 2004, p. 93).

Another important stream of community education includes communication and social marketing strategies. Again, there is evidence that such campaigns can produce positive change in the attitudes and behaviours associated with men's perpetration of violence against women (Donovan and Vlais, 2005). And again, relatively few social marketing efforts have focused on men in particular workplaces or institutions.

Still at the level of community education, two strategies that are increasingly prominent are 'social norms' and 'bystander intervention' efforts. 'Social norms' campaigns highlight the gap, for example, between men's perceptions of other men's agreement with violence-supportive and sexist norms and the actual extent of this agreement. By gathering and publicizing data on men's attitudes and behaviour, they seek to undermine men's conformity to sexist peer norms and increase their willingness to intervene in violent behaviour (Flood 2005–06). 'Bystander intervention' approaches seek to place 'a sense of responsibility and empowerment for ending sexual violence on the shoulders of all community members'. They distinguish between 'passive' bystanders, who do not act or intervene and 'active' or 'pro-social' bystanders who take action – whether to stop the perpetration of a specific incident of violence, reduce the risk of violence escalating and prevent the physical, psychological and social harms that may result; or strengthen the conditions that work against violence occurring (Powell, 2011, pp. 8–10). Both these strategies are particularly relevant in workplaces.

A third level of prevention strategy involves educating providers and other professionals. There are a small number of initiatives that engage male professionals in workplaces in fostering gender equality or nonviolence. For example, in Pakistan, an NGO called Rozan has run gender violence sensitization workshops with police in order to transform the way that the institution thinks about and responds to violence against women (Lang, 2003, p. 11). In South and Central America, the Pan American Health Organization (PAHO) has trained soccer coaches to promote adolescent health and introduce gender equity in relationships to boys aged eight to 12 (Schueller et al., 2005, p. 3).

The three levels of prevention discussed thus far can include strategies that take place in workplaces or that involve particular groups of workers or employees. However, a further level of prevention – changing organizational practices – is *focused* on workplaces and other institutions (Davis et al., 2006, p. 12). As articulated above, this level of prevention embodies the recognition that workplaces and other organizations can play key roles in building non-violent internal cultures and in fostering wider social change.

In focusing on workplaces, one plausibly could stretch the concept of 'bystander' above such that it applied also to these institutional entities. This would have value in highlighting the roles of organisations in allowing and sustaining such behaviours as domestic violence or sexual harassment and their collective (and indeed legal) responsibilities to change. A workplace, through its policies, procedures and leadership, may be a passive or prosocial bystander to men's violence against women (Powell, 2011, p. 28). This assumes that such entities have agency or the capacity to act and this will be truer of specific organizations or workplaces rather than more diffuse or sprawling institutions (McDonald and Flood, 2012, p. 26).

There are very few primary prevention initiatives that engage men in workplaces in organizational change. However, if we count professional sports players as workplace 'professionals', then some of the most well-developed workplace initiatives aimed at men have taken place among athletes in sporting workplaces. In Australia, two of Australia's most popular sporting codes – Australian Rules football and rugby league – have developed violence prevention programs for their athletes and the wider communities associated with the sports. Both are team-based, contact sports played largely by males. The Australian Football League (AFL) was thrown into crisis in 2004 after a series of allegations of sexual and physical assaults against women by AFL players. In the wake of these alleged incidents and under considerable public pressure, the AFL announced their intention to address the issue of violence against women within the AFL and beyond. As a result, the organization announced the adoption of a 'Respect and Responsibility' program designed to 'create safe, supportive and inclusive environments for women and girls across the football industry as well as the broader commuity' (AFL, 2013). In the wake of similar crises, Rugby League has also taken steps to address violence against women through their player education program 'Playing by the Rules'. However, 'Respect and Responsibility' represents a more comprehensive and far reaching program to prevent violence against women, in that it addresses an entire organization, not only some members of that organization.

The AFL's 'Respect and Responsibility' initiative was formulated and managed in collaboration with violence prevention agencies and launched in November 2005. It incorporated model anti-sexual harassment and anti-sexual discrimination procedures across the AFL and its member clubs, changes to AFL rules relating to problematic or violent conduct, the education of players and other club officials, dissemination of model policies and procedures and a public education program. In 2005, a full-time 'Respect and Responsibility' manager was appointed by the AFL, in an ongoing position. In 2008, AFL Victoria extended the initiative with the program 'Fair Game – Respect Matters' (AFL Victoria, 2013). This is intended to foster cultural change throughout the sporting code, in encouraging community clubs to assess their own cultures and inviting players, coaches and supporters to improve their attitudes and behaviours towards women. The program is ongoing and currently undergoing scholarly evaluation.

A recent Australian violence prevention project that at least aspired to generate organizational change is called 'Stand Up: Domestic Violence is Everyone's Business'. Run by the Melbourne-based NGO Women's Health Victoria, this workplace program aimed to strengthen the organizational capacity of a male-dominated workplace to promote gender equality and non-violent norms (Durey, 2011, p. 6). The program took place over 2007–11 with the trucking company Linfox. It focused in particular on building the capacity of employees, particularly men, to challenge violence-supportive attitudes and behaviours. The project began with training for employees, focused on bystander intervention and was extended with engagement with the company at other levels including the development of domestic violence policies. However, the project faced significant institutional barriers and its impact was uneven. The training itself was limited in duration and there were limits to the whole-of-company engagement in and support for the project. The report on this project illustrates the wider truth that deliberate culture change in workplaces is complex, takes time, requires leadership and ultimately, can be difficult to achieve (ibid., p. 74). The project has since been followed by a guide to developing workplace programs for the primary prevention of violence against women (Women's Health Victoria, 2012).

While efforts to engage men in violence prevention in corporate workplaces are relatively rare, there are some significant initiatives engaging corporate men in the promotion of gender equality. One substantial Australian effort is 'Male Champions of Change'. As Wells et al. (2013, p. 24) describes:

Male Champions of Change (MCC) is a corporate initiative composed of business and institutional leaders convened by the Australian Human Rights Commission. MCC has a broad mandate of promoting and inspiring women's leadership in the workplace but includes a specific objective to address violence in the workplace. The initiative includes CEOs and board members from corporations who are leading efforts to address women's equality in the workplace. MCC highlights three incremental steps in achieving gender equality in the workplace: promote organizational interest and work to remove barriers and challenges; shift from policy to practice and implementation, ensuring commitment and buy-in across all levels of leadership and front line; and be a driving force for true culture change within an organization where a culture of inclusive leadership is emphasized . . . This initiative helps to advance the point that men and women can work together to promote greater equality and safety in the workplace and in society.

The largest-scale level of prevention focuses on influencing policies and legislation. Law and policy are valuable tools in fostering primary prevention strategies in the workplace. For example, they may be used to mandate workplace-based prevention efforts, support primary prevention initiatives and strengthen the legislated obligations of workplaces and other organizations.

CONCLUSION

In order to build gender-just workplaces, we must address those dimensions of gender inequality that constrain or influence women's and men's workplace participation and experience. Men's violence against women is a critical dimension of gender inequality with a profound impact on the workplace. In turn, workplaces themselves may contribute to the problem of men's violence against women through violence-supportive cultures and institutionalized patterns of male privilege. Efforts to address this violence thus far have focused largely on secondary and tertiary prevention, providing support for victims and survivors and, to a lesser degree, responding to perpetrators. These must be complemented by a systematic engagement in primary prevention. In particular, we must engage men in workplaces in the primary prevention of men's violence against women. There are some promising workplace-based initiatives focused on men and they are buttressed by a much more well-established body of experience and scholarship on involving men in violence prevention in other settings. However, much more must be done if workplaces are to become both places of and contributors to gender equality and non-violence.

REFERENCES

Abbey, A. and P. McAuslan (2004), 'A longitudinal examination of male college students' perpetration of sexual assault', *Journal of Consulting and Clinical Psychology*, **72**(5), 747–56.

ABS (Australian Bureau of Statistics) (2006), *Personal Safety Survey Australia*, Canberra: Australian Bureau of Statistics (Cat. 4906.0).

Access Economics (2004), *The Cost of Domestic Violence to the Australian Economy*, Canberra: Office of the Status of Women, Australian Government.

AFL (2013), 'Respect & responsibility', accessed 12 September 2013 at http://www.afl.com.au/news/game-development/respect-and-responsibility.

AFL Victoria (2013), 'Fair game respect matters program', accessed 12 September 2013 at http://aflvic.com.au/index.php?id=528.

Antecol, H. and D. Cobb-Clark (2003), 'Does sexual harassment training change attitudes? A view from the federal level', *Social Science Quarterly*, **84**(4), 826–42.

Australian Human Rights Commission (2012), *Working Without Fear: Results of the Sexual Harassment National Telephone Survey 2012*, Sydney: Australian Human Rights Commission.

Brownridge, D.A. (2006), 'Violence against women post-separation', *Aggression and Violent Behavior*, **11**(5), 514–30.

Bryant, A. (2003), 'Changes in attitudes toward women's roles: Predicting gender-role traditionalism among college students', *Sex Roles*, **48**(3/4), 131–42.

Chamberlain, L. (2008), *A Prevention Primer for Domestic Violence: Terminology, Tools and the Public Health Approach*, VAWnet: The National Online Resource Center on Violence Against Women (March).

Davis, R., L.F. Parks and L. Cohen (2006), *Sexual Violence and the Spectrum of Prevention: Towards a Community Solution*, Enola, PA: National Sexual Violence Resource Center.

DeKeseredy, W.S. and K. Kelly (1995), 'Sexual abuse in Canadian university and college dating relationships: The contribution of male peer support', *Journal of Family Violence*, **10**(1), 41–53.

Donovan, R.J. and R. Vlais (2005), *VicHealth Review of Communication Components of Social Marketing/Public Education Campaigns Focused on Violence Against Women*, Melbourne: Victorian Health Promotion Foundation.

Dugan, L., D.S. Nagin and R. Rosenfeld (2003), 'Exposure reduction or retaliation? The effects of domestic violence resources on intimate-partner homicide', *Law & Society Review*, **37**(1), 169–98.

Durey, R. (2011), *Working Together Against Violence: Final Project Report*, Melbourne: VicHealth & Women's Health Victoria.

Flood, M. (2005–06), 'Changing men: Best practice in sexual violence education', *Women Against Violence*, **18**, 26–36.

Flood, M. (2007), 'Background document for preventing violence before it occurs: A framework and background paper to guide the primary prevention of violence against women in Victoria', Melbourne: Victorian Health Promotion Foundation, unpublished.

Flood, M. (2011), 'Involving men in efforts to end violence against women', *Men and Masculinities*, **14**(3), 358–77.

Flood, M. and B. Pease (2005), 'Undoing men's privilege and advancing gender equality in public sector institutions', *Policy and Society*, **24**(4), 119–38.

Flood, M. and B. Pease (2006), *The Factors Influencing Community Attitudes in Relation to Violence Against Women: A Critical Review of the Literature*, Melbourne, Victorian Health Promotion Foundation.

Foshee, V., K.E. Bauman, X.B. Arriaga, R.W. Helms, G.G. Koch and G.F. Linder (1998), 'An evaluation of safe dates, an adolescent dating violence prevention program', *American Journal of Public Health*, 88(2), 45–50.

Godenzi, A., M.D. Schwartz and W.S. DeKeseredy (2001), 'Toward a social bond/male peer support theory of woman abuse in North American college dating', *Critical Criminology*, **10**, 10–16.

Harrison, D. (2002), *The First Casualty: Violence Against Women in the Canadian Military*, Toronto: James Lorimer & Company.

Hearn, J. (1996), 'Men's violence to known women: Historical, everyday and theoretical constructions by men', in B. Fawcett, B. Featherstone, J. Hearn and C. Toft (eds), *Violence and Gender Relations: Theories and Interventions*, London: Sage.

Heise, L.L. (1998), 'Violence against women: An integrated, ecological framework', *Violence Against Women*, **4**(3), 262–83.

Holtzworth-Munroe, A., N. Smutzler and L. Bates (1997), 'A brief review of the research on husband violence Part III: Sociodemographic factors, relationship factors and differing consequences of husband and wife violence', *Aggression and Violent Behavior*, **2**(3), 285–307.

Humphrey, S.E. and A.S. Kahn (2000), 'Fraternities, athletic teams and rape: Importance of identification with a risky group', *Journal of Interpersonal Violence*, **15**(12), 1313–22.

Kidder, D.L., M.J. Lankau, D. Chrobot-Mason, K.A. Mollica and R.A. Friedman (2004), 'Backlash toward diversity initiatives: Examining the impact of diversity program justification, personal and group outcomes', *The International Journal of Conflict Management*, **15**(1), 77–102.

Lang, J. (2003), *Elimination of Violence Against Women in Partnership with Men*, background document for UNESCAP's subregional training workshop on Elimination of Violence Against Women in Partnership with Men, 2–5 December, 2003, New Delhi, India.

Lindquist, C., M. Clinton-Sherrod, et al. (2006), *Inventory of Workplace Interventions Designed to Prevent Intimate Partner Violence*, Atlanta, GA, Centers for Disease Control and Prevention.

McDonald, P. and M. Flood (2012), *Encourage. Support. Act! Bystander Approaches to Sexual Harassment in the Workplace*, Sydney: Human Rights Commission.

McFerran, L. (2011), *Safe at Home, Safe at Work? National Domestic Violence and the Workplace Survey (2011)*, Sydney: Australian Domestic and Family Violence Clearinghouse and Centre for Gender Related Violence Studies, University of New South Wales.

Miller, P. and N. Biele (1993), 'Twenty years later: The unfinished revolution', in E. Buchwald, P. Fletcher and M. Roth (eds), *Transforming a Rape Culture*, Minneapolis: Milkweed Editions.

Mouzos, J. and T. Makkai (2004), *Women's Experiences of Male Violence: Findings from the Australian Component of the International Violence Against Women Survey (IVAWS)*, Canberra: Australian Institute of Criminology, Research and Public Policy Series, No. 56.

Murnen, S.K., C. Wright and G. Kaluzny (2002), 'If "boys will be boys," then girls will be victims? A meta-analytic review of the research that relates masculine ideology to sexual aggression', *Sex Roles*, **46**(11–12), 359–75.

Murray, S. and A. Powell (2008), 'Working it out: Domestic violence issues and the workplace', *Australian Domestic and Family Violence Clearinghouse*, Issues Paper No. 16, April.

National Council to Reduce Violence Against Women and their Children (2009), *Economic Cost of Violence Against Women and Their Children*, Canberra: Australian Department of Families, Housing, Community Services and Indigenous Affairs.

Pease, B. (2002), *Men and Gender Relations*, Melbourne: Tertiary Press.

Powell, A. (2011), *Review of Bystander Approaches in Support of Preventing Violence Against Women*, Melbourne: Victorian Health Promotion Foundation (VicHealth).

Prime, J., C.A. Moss-Racusin and H. Foust-Cummings (2009), *Engaging Men in Gender Initiatives: Stacking the Deck for Success*, New York: Catalyst.

Reitzel-Jaffe, D. and D.A. Wolfe (2001), 'Predictors of relationship abuse among young men', *Journal of Interpersonal Violence*, **16**(2), 99–115.

Riger, S. and S. Staggs (2004), 'Welfare reform, domestic violence and employment: What do we know and what do we need to know?' *Violence Against Women*, **10**(9), 961–90.

Riggs, D.S., M.B. Caulfield and A.B. Street (2000), 'Risk for domestic violence: Factors associated with perpetration and victimization', *Journal of Clinical Psychology*, **56**(10), 1289–316.

Rosen, L.N., R.J. Kaminski, A.M. Parmley, K.H. Knudson and P. Fancher (2003), 'The effects of peer group climate on intimate partner violence among married male U.S. army soldiers', *Violence Against Women*, **9**(9), 1045–71.

Schueller, J., W. Finger and G. Barker (2005), 'Boys and changing gender roles: Emerging programme approaches hold promise in changing gender norms and behaviours among boys and young men', *YouthNet*, 'YouthLens on Reproductive Health and HIV/AIDS', No. 16, August.

Schumacher, J., S. Feldbau-Kohn, A.M.S. Slep and R.E. Heyman (2001), 'Risk factors for male-to-female partner physical abuse', *Aggression and Violent Behavior*, **6**(2–3), 281–352.

Schwartz, M.D. and W.S. DeKeseredy (1997), *Sexual Assault on the College Campus: The Role of Male Peer Support*, Thousand Oaks, CA: Sage.

Stalans, L.J. and M.A. Finn (2000), 'Gender differences in officers' perceptions and decisions about domestic violence cases', *Women & Criminal Justice*, **11**(3), 1–24.

Stark, E. (2006), 'Commentary on Johnson's "Conflict and control: Gender symmetry and asymmetry in domestic violence"', *Violence Against Women*, **12**(1), 1019–25.

Stark, E. (2010), 'Do violent acts equal abuse? Resolving the gender parity/asymmetry dilemma', *Sex Roles*, 62(3–4), 201–11.

Stewart, A. and K. Maddren (1997), 'Police officers' judgements of blame in family violence: The impact of gender and alcohol', *Sex Roles*, **37**(11/12), 921–33.

Stith, S.M., D.B. Smith, C.E. Penn, D.B. Ward and D. Tritt (2004), 'Intimate partner physical abuse perpetration and victimization risk factors: A meta-analytic review', *Aggression and Violent Behavior*, **10**(1), 65–98.

Tang, C.S.-K. and F.M.-C. Cheung (1997), 'Effects of gender and profession type on definitions of violence against women in Hong Kong', *Sex Roles*, **36**(11/12),

837–49.

Tolan, P., D. Gorman-Smith and D. Henry (2006), 'Family violence', *Annual Review of Psychology*, **57**(1), 557–83.

URCOT (2005), *Safe at Work? Women's Experience of Violence in the Workplace*, Melbourne: Department for Victorian Communities.

Vezina, J. and M. Herbert (2007), 'Risk factors for victimization in romantic relationships of young women: A review of empirical studies and implications for prevention', *Trauma, Violence & Abuse*, **8**(1), 33–66.

VicHealth (2007), 'Preventing violence before it occurs: A framework and background paper to guide the primary prevention of violence against women in Victoria', Melbourne: Victorian Health Promotion Foundation (VicHealth).

Wade, J. and C. Brittan-Powell (2001), 'Men's attitudes toward race and gender equity: The importance of masculinity ideology, gender-related traits and reference group identity dependence', *Psychology of Men and Masculinity*, **2**(1), 42–50.

Wells, L., L. Lorenzetti, H. Carolo, T. Dinner, C. Jones, T. Minerson and E. Esina (2013), *Engaging Men and Boys in Domestic Violence Prevention: Opportunities and Promising Approaches*, Calgary, AB: The University of Calgary, Shift: The Project to End Domestic Violence.

White, B.H. and S.E.R. Kurpius (1999), 'Attitudes toward rape victims: Effects of gender and professional status', *Journal of Interpersonal Violence*, **14**(9), 989–95.

Women's Health Victoria (2012), *Everyone's Business: A Guide to Developing Workplace Programs for the Primary Prevention of Violence Against Women*, Melbourne: Women's Health Victoria.

World Health Organization (2002), *World Report on Violence and Health*, Geneva: World Health Organization.

Index

Gender in organizations